United in Diversity?

International Policy Exchange Series

Published in collaboration with the
Center for International Policy Exchanges
University of Maryland

Series Editors

Douglas J. Besharov
Neil Gilbert

United in Diversity?
Comparing Social Models in Europe and America
Edited by
Jens Alber and Neil Gilbert

SCHOOL *of*
PUBLIC POLICY

United in Diversity?

Comparing Social Models in Europe and America

Edited by

JENS ALBER

NEIL GILBERT

OXFORD
UNIVERSITY PRESS

2010

OXFORD
UNIVERSITY PRESS

Oxford University Press, Inc., publishes works that further
Oxford University's objective of excellence
in research, scholarship, and education.

Oxford New York
Auckland Cape Town Dar es Salaam Hong Kong Karachi
Kuala Lumpur Madrid Melbourne Mexico City Nairobi
New Delhi Shanghai Taipei Toronto

With offices in
Argentina Austria Brazil Chile Czech Republic France Greece
Guatemala Hungary Italy Japan Poland Portugal Singapore
South Korea Switzerland Thailand Turkey Ukraine Vietnam

Copyright © 2010 by Oxford University Press, Inc.

Published by Oxford University Press, Inc.
198 Madison Avenue, New York, New York 10016
www.oup.com

Oxford is a registered trademark of Oxford University Press.

Library of Congress Cataloging-in-Publication Data

United in diversity? : comparing social models in Europe and America /
edited by Jens Alber and Neil Gilbert.
p. cm. — (Center for the International Exchange of Policy Information
comparative policy series ; 1)
Includes bibliographical references and index.
ISBN 978-0-19-537663-0
1. Europe—Social policy.   2. United States—Social policy.
3. Public welfare—Europe.   4. Public welfare—United States.
I. Alber, Jens, 1947–   II. Gilbert, Neil, 1940–
HN373.5.U55 2010
320.6094—dc22
2009008635

9 8 7 6 5 4 3 2 1

Printed in the United States of America
on acid-free paper

PREFACE

The eastern expansion of the European Union (EU) to twelve new member states—ten of which had been under protracted communist rule—elicited mixed reactions in Western Europe. Many observers agreed with former EU Commissioner Sandra Kalniete that the enlargement hailed "Europe's triumph over the twentieth century" and finally restored European unity. Others feared that the EU institutions might become overstretched by the growing heterogeneity of interests and living conditions. There was also concern that rather than embracing the ideal of a European social model endorsed by the European Commission, the new member states might be more attracted to the social model of the United States.

When the EU presidency moved to Germany in 2007, a group of scholars organized a conference in Berlin to explore the extent to which the new member states of the European Union might be influenced by the European or American social model and to determine whether the juxtaposition of these two "models" actually made analytical sense. With generous support from the Social Science Research Center, Berlin, and the European Foundation for the Improvement of Living and Working Conditions, which we gratefully acknowledge, a conference cosponsored by these institutions was held in Berlin in May 2007. Scholars from both sides of the Atlantic were invited to present their empirical analyses of how the United States and Europe compare with respect to selected features of state and society. Participants also included discussants from the new member states, who were invited to comment upon the individual papers from their perspectives. The presentations were critically discussed in further detail by a group of invited general discussants from Europe and the United States.

This volume is based on the papers presented at the Berlin conference, which were revised in light of the lively wide-ranging conversation and critical observations generated by the participants. As editors, we are extremely grateful to our discussants whose thoughtful comments proved of invaluable help to our authors in the process of re-thinking and re-writing their contributions. In alphabetical order, our thanks extend to Jerzy Ciechański, Dušan Drbohlav, Martin Potúček, Péter Róbert, Andrzej Rychard, Zsolt Spéder, Tine Stanovnik, István Stumpf, and Iván Szelényi who served as our experts for the new member states; to Maria Helena André, Douglas J. Besharov, Heinrich Best, Tony Fahey, Ron Haskins, Mariá Ladó, Stephan Leibfried, Bernd Marin, Lawrence M. Mead, Jiří Musil, Claus Offe, Dieter Pougin, Richard Rose, and Sven Steinmo who served as general discussants; to Robert Anderson and Willy Buschak representing the European Foundation for the Improvement of Living and Working Conditions as our much-appreciated coorganizer and cofinancier, to Jutta Allmendinger as President of the Social Science Research Center, Berlin, which hosted and cofinanced us, and to State Secretary Franz Thönnes from the German Ministry of Employment Social Affairs who opened the conference representing the German government.

Finally, we wish to thank a group of staff members at the Social Science Research Center without whose administrative and technical help neither the conference nor the book would have been possible: above all we appreciate and thank Martina Sander-Blanck and Marion Obermaier for their superb work in managing the chores of manuscript preparation, and Christoph Albrecht, Florian Fliegner, Philipp Lenarz, and Bettina Mertel for an outstanding job in handling the administration and technical preparation. Our special gratitude is owed to the group of young musicians from the Julius Stern Institute of the University of Fine Arts, Berlin, who contributed to an unforgettable conference dinner with tunes from both sides of the Atlantic and from the old and new parts of the enlarged European Union.

CONTENTS

CONTRIBUTORS

JENS ALBER
Research Unit "Inequality and
    Social Integration"
Social Science Research Center
    Berlin (WZB)
Berlin, Germany

JUTTA ALLMENDINGER
Social Science Research Center
    Berlin (WZB)
Berlin, Germany

REBECCA M. BLANK
Department of Commerce
Economics and Statistics
    Administration
Washington, D.C.

RICHARD V. BURKHAUSER
College of Human Ecology
Cornell University
Ithaca, New York

FRANCIS G. CASTLES
University of Edinburgh, and
Department of Political Science
Australian National University
Canberra, Australia

KENNETH A. COUCH
Department of Economics
University of Connecticut
Storrs, Connecticut

CHRISTIAN EBNER
Social Science Research Center
    Berlin (WZB)
Berlin, Germany

WERNER EICHHORST
Institute for the Study of Labor
Bonn, Germany

RICHARD B. FREEMAN
Harvard University, and
National Bureau of Economic Research
Cambridge, Massachusetts

MARKUS GANGL
Department of Sociology
University of Wisconsin-Madison
Madison, Wisconsin

NEIL GILBERT
School of Social Welfare
University of California, Berkeley
Berkeley, California

NADIA GRANATO
Institute for Employment Research
Nuremberg, Germany

ANTON HEMERIJCK
Scientific Council for Government
    Policy (WRR)
The Hague, The Netherlands

CHARLES HIRSCHMAN
Department of Sociology
University of Washington
Seattle, Washington

FRANK KALTER
University of Mannheim
Faculty of Social Sciences
Mannheim, Germany

ULRICH KOHLER
Research Unit "Inequality and
    Social Integration"
Social Science Research Center
    Berlin (WZB)
Berlin, Germany

PATRICIA MALONEY
Department of Sociology
Yale University
New Haven, Connecticut

KARL ULRICH MAYER
Department of Sociology
Yale University
New Haven, Connecticut

MICHAEL P. MCDONALD
Department of Public and
    International Affairs
George Mason University
Fairfax, Virginia

RITA NIKOLAI
Social Science Research Center
    Berlin (WZB)
Berlin, Germany

ANTHONY DANIEL PEREZ
Department of Sociology
University of Washington
Seattle, Washington

STEIN RINGEN
Social Sciences Division
University of Oxford
Oxford, United Kingdom

JOHN SAMPLES
Center for Representative
    Government
CATO Institute
Washington, District of Columbia

CHIARA SARACENO
Social Science Research Center
    Berlin (WZB)
Berlin, Germany

United in Diversity?

INTRODUCTION

JENS ALBER AND NEIL GILBERT

PERCEPTIONS OF SIMILARITIES AND DIFFERENCES BETWEEN EUROPE AND THE UNITED STATES IN THE SOCIAL SCIENCES

The question of the relationship between the United States and Europe has occupied a prominent place in the social sciences ever since the works of the nineteenth century classics. One of the key issues dividing various schools of thought was whether similarities or differences are more noteworthy. A second key issue was which society would provide the role model that the other would follow, or if they might eventually converge.

The major differences justifying the notion of American exceptionalism were highlighted in the early works of the classics, among them most prominently Alexis de Tocqueville. After visiting the United States in 1831/32 for less than one year at the age of 26, he published his penetrating analysis of social, economic and political life in the new world (de Tocqueville, 1835–40 [1964]). America, he wrote, "exhibits in her social state an extraordinary phenomenon. Men are there seen on a greater equality in point of fortune and intellect, or, in other words more equal in their strength, than in any other country of the world, or in any age of which history has preserved the remembrance." He found that "wealth circulates with inconceivable rapidity, and experience shows that it is rare to find two succeeding generations in the full enjoyment of it" (p. 29). As for education he did "not believe that there was another country in the world where in proportion to the population there were so few ignorant, and at the same time so few learned individuals." (p. 30) But equality of circumstance, heightened mobility, and educational attainment were not the only conditions that marked the United States as qualitatively different from other countries. His observations suggested that American society was more rights-oriented, more religious, more engaged in civic life and political activity than other countries—essentially those of Western Europe (which he occasionally referred to as the Old World).

In a similar vein, the German sociologist and economist Werner Sombart drew attention to peculiar features of the American society which help to answer the question he posed in his famous book title *Why Is There No Socialism in the United States* (Sombart 1976 [1906]). Looking at the economic, social, and political position of workers, Sombart identified the absence of status distinctions rooted in a feudal past, the better chances for regional and social mobility, the higher wage levels leading to a much higher standard of living, and the interaction of better political and economic integration of workers as the key factors explaining why American workers adhere to the prevailing social order and are not susceptible to revolutionary ideas. In short, Sombart concluded: "All socialist utopias come to nothing on roast beef and apple pie" (Sombart 1976 [1906]: 106).

These classical concepts were later adopted and further developed in Seymour Martin Lipset's theory of American exceptionalism (Lipset 1997; Lipset and Marks 2000). According to Lipset, the fact that the United States neither had a feudal past nor state churches has led to a peculiar institutional order without conservative or socialist parties as well as to a particular "American creed," which is characterized by a unique mixture of liberty, egalitarianism, and laissez faire on the one side, as well as by egalitarianism and populism on the other. The latter characteristics Lipset saw rooted in the traditions of universal suffrage and of protestant sects, which are congregational rather than hierarchical so that a political ethos of equality and a religious ethos of self-responsibility and voluntarism mutually reinforce each other. As a result, the United States is described by Lipset as less statist, less welfare-oriented, more religious and moralistic and more laissez-faire than European nations (Lipset 1997: 27).

Recent scholarship has focussed on more fine-grained comparisons of specific differences in selected dimensions. Trying to understand variations in economic performance and concentrating on the question of how economic activities are coordinated, Peter Hall and David Soskice (2001) have made an attempt to classify "varieties of capitalism." Basically they distinguish between two types called "coordinated market economies" and "liberal market economies." In the former, collective actors like unions, employers, banks, and the government seek to coordinate their actions and to engage in long-term, trust-based relations and mutually beneficial cooperation. In the "liberal"-type economic activities are coordinated by markets, and competitive relations with more short-term orientations prevail. Whereas liberal market economies are characterized by corporate financing via the stock market, wage determination on the firm level, and loosely regulated labor relations, coordinated or social market economies tend to finance corporations via banks, have coordinated wage bargaining above the firm level, and provide for industrial citizenship with workers' councils and stricter employment protection (Pontusson 2005). The United States is counted as a liberal market economy, while European countries are predominantly ranked as coordinated or social market economies with the exception of Ireland and the United Kingdom, which are placed together with the United States, Australia, Canada, and New Zealand in the group of liberal market economies.

Fred Block has recently taken issue with the typology of the varieties of capitalism school on dual grounds (Block 2007, 2008). First, he finds the classification of the U.S. system as an uncoordinated liberal market economy misleading, because U.S. firms have recently created a rich fabric of interfirm collaborations and of collaboration with government agencies and universities, after legislation in 1984 had created an antitrust exemption for research consortia. According to Block, a "developmental network state" promoting technological innovations in the interest of commercializing scientific breakthroughs has risen in marked contrast to the continued lip service paid to the idea of unfettered free markets and to the slogan that government is the source rather than the solution of problems. A plethora of new government agencies now engages in providing "targeted resources" for projects, promising marketable innovations and in brokering connections between researchers, financiers, and government bureaucracies. Secondly, Block sees the United States and Europe on "diverging trajectories," because entire industries, such as meat packing, which had provided unionized jobs with social benefits shifted to employment of a low-wage labor force with fewer entitlements in the United States, because the government formed an alliance with the religious Right which Block sees as an example of a "Polanyian countermovement" against modernity, and because the new forms of technology policy and regulation are not embedded in a public or parliamentary discourse. In sum, Block sees the United States on a different trajectory from other developed market societies.

Another attempt to classify countries focuses on the characteristics of their social policies and yields various types of "welfare regimes." This typology supports the notion that relevant differences in the makeup of societies do not coincide with the U.S.–Europe divide. Building on earlier work of Richard Titmuss (1958), Gøsta Esping-Andersen classified Western countries into three types of welfare regimes which he called residual, corporatist, and social-democratic (Esping-Andersen 1990, 1999). The first group gives relatively great prominence to selective and means-tested benefits and consists of the United States, Australia, Canada, New Zealand, but also—although Esping-Andersen is not very explicit on this—of Ireland and the United Kingdom (Esping-Andersen 1990: 52, 74). The second group relies predominantly on earnings-related social transfers that reflect the recipients' position in the labor market and consists of continental European countries such as Austria, Belgium, France, and Germany. The third model gives predominance to universal benefits for all citizens and also to social services and is found in Scandinavia. Once again, we thus find a typology which cuts across the U.S.–Europe divide and accentuates differences between European countries as well as similarities between specific European nations and the United States.

In contrast to the writers who—in whatever differentiated form—highlight differences between societies on both sides of the Atlantic, there are other social scientists who are much more impressed by the similarities. Even though Werner Sombart's classical piece started by explaining a major difference—i.e. the absence of well-organized socialism in the United States—it also contained two contradictory ideas about future similarities. First, much in the sense that Karl Marx believed England to form a model for the development of other European nations, Sombart was convinced that the economic system of the United States as the country with the highest capitalist development exemplified the future economic organization of Europe (Sombart 1976 [1906]: 35). In a somewhat surprising and frequently overlooked twist of his argument at the end of his book, he also expressed his conviction, however, that in the future socialism would come to blossom in the United States so that Europe and America would converge in the direction of the European model (Sombart 1976 [1906]: 119).

The idea of convergence has been developed and refined by theorists of industrial society (Wilensky and Lebeaux 1965; Wilensky 2002) and of post-industrial society (Bell 1973). According to the former, industrial societies are subject to similar trends and become more alike as work shifts from the private household to the firm, as families and households become smaller, as women move into the workforce, as fertility shrinks and the proportion of older people grows, as educational opportunities expand, as employment structures shift in favor of higher proportions of skilled workers, as productivity grows, and as more economic resources and more democratic political structures combine to elicit the development of welfare state schemes, which compensate the loss of earnings from work especially in old age. According to the latter, human capital and theoretical knowledge will become the key resources in postindustrial societies, the university and the research institute will become key institutions, professional work will become the preeminent element in the occupational distribution, and the balance of the private and public sectors will become a key structural problem, while resistance to bureaucratization and adversary cultures will grow (Bell 1973, 1976).

Building on these traditions, recent scholarship has taken a closer empirical look at similarities and differences between the United States and European nations. Different answers have been given from various perspectives. Addressing the issue from the perspective of the United States, several analyses have reaffirmed American exceptionalism, highlighting characteristics such as religiosity, participation in civil society, individualism, flexible and competitive market economy, assimilation of immigrants, egalitarianism, and privatization of social welfare (e.g., Schuck and Wilson 2008). A study of the development of religious life in the United States by James Morone (2003) offers a nuanced view of American exceptionalism. On the one side he questions the assumption of a weak American state arguing that the U.S. government has always been strong in terms of moral intervention and that a weak state could neither have outlawed liquor sales from coast to coast nor put "3 percent of its population in jail or prison, on parole or under probation" (Morone 2003: 3). On the other hand, he describes a peculiar ambivalence of religiousness in America with an authoritarian tradition of Victorian puritanism as well as an emancipating social gospel tradition each of which came to prominence in different times over the course of U.S. history.

Departing from the notion of a big trade-off between growth and equality, and basically applying the varieties of capitalism typology, Jonas Pontusson (2005) has systematically compared indicators of economic performance in Europe and the United States. Four of his results are particularly noteworthy: (1) There is phase-specific variation in the performance of different models so that institutional effects are not constant and much depends on the concrete choices of policy makers. (2) The commonly drawn distinction between the United States and the EU hides the huge variation among EU member states. (3) Internally coherent economies perform better than incoherent economies, which should caution against importing certain isolated features of institutional design from one country to the next. (4) Among three highly correlated factors that characterize social market economies—wage compression, employment protection, and reliance on payroll taxes—the detrimental effect of payroll taxes on employment is largest.

Pontusson's key result—presented in very differentiated form—that there need not necessarily be a trade-off between equality and efficiency squares well with the insights of Blank and Freeman's (1994) earlier effort to study trade-offs between social protection and economic flexibility on the basis of comparisons between Europe and the United States. There the authors concluded, from the data presented in a collected volume, that "there is little empirical evidence for large trade-offs between labor market flexibility and social protection programs in general" (p. 36) and that "the research and policy community actually knows quite a bit less about the aggregate effect of social protection programs on individual behavior or on the aggregate economy than is typically claimed" (p. 39). Similar skepticism marked a more recent attempt to muster what we know about potentially harmful effects of labor market regulation in comparative perspective by Esping-Andersen and Regini (2000).

Comparing Europe and the United States along the dimensions of demographic and economic growth, the role of the state, and social inequality, Alber (2006) concludes that the range of variation among the EU countries is larger than the differences between Europe and the United States on most empirical indicators so that the United States is usually located well within the social space spanning the societies of Europe. In contrast to the dichotomous distinction between liberal and coordinated market economies in the varieties of capitalism school, he also finds vast variation within these models. In terms of population dynamics, macroeconomic performance and standard of living, the Scandinavian countries are as highly successful as the liberal English-speaking nations, even though their social policies are in many respects more similar to the less successful continental welfare states. Keune (2008) similarly asserts that in comparing wages, social protection, employment, and industrial relation policies, the results "do not add up to anything remotely approaching a coherent European Social Model." Recognizing diversity in structures and philosophies, Grahl and Teague (2000) still discern commonalities that underpin a (Western) European social model; however, they argue that this model is in crisis—being undermined by recent economic developments.

Analyzing the substance and direction of social welfare reforms since the mid-1990s, Gilbert (2004: 181) finds the United States and Europe converging as policies are repeatedly being reframed by common market-oriented principles that emphasize work, privatization, individual responsibility, and targeting of benefits. He notes that "Freud's axiom concerning the 'narcissism of minor differences' suggests that the closer nations come to resemble each other the more they magnify minute dissimilarities as a means to reinforce social cohesion." This axiom implies that as convergence increases European policy makers are likely to go to great lengths to try and differentiate their social welfare initiatives from those of the United States.

Similarly borrowing the title of his forthcoming book from Freud's expression, Baldwin (forthcoming) draws on a wide range of empirical indicators in several hundred graphs and statistics on everything from health care, sexual behavior, civil society activities, municipal waste, and conservation to per capita church income, and concludes that not only is there a wide spectrum of difference among the EU-15 countries, but that the United States fits well within the span of most quantifiable measures. This implies, as he puts it, that "whatever incoherence attaches to the concept of the West attaches equally to that of a unified Europe" (Baldwin, forthcoming, p. 102 [manuscript]).

While social scientists have been interested in mapping the similarities and differences between Europe and the United States in the pursuit of knowledge, there are other parties interested in these issues for political reasons.

SIMILARITIES AND DIFFERENCES IN NORMATIVE POLITICAL DISCOURSE

In the days of the system rivalry between democracies with market economies and the Communist bloc, the United States and the member states of the European Union were tightly coupled partners in what Karl Deutsch once called a "security community." They not only had common interests in preserving external security, but also considered each other to be part of a value based community, which shared the tradition of enlightenment, of freedom, democracy, and the rule of law.

When the Soviet empire collapsed and the common external threat ceased to exist, it was expected that different national interests would come stronger to the fore again. Scholars and policy pundits depicted different scenarios for the future, ranging from the notion "the west against the rest" (Huntington 1993) to the idea that, after the triumph of capitalism over communism, the old fundamental cleavage between two economic and political systems would cede to the new rivalry between two versions of the market economy: the Rhine model of socially bridled capitalism built on relations of trust and financed by patient capital from banks with long-term interests and the American model of more or less unfettered market rule financed by impatient capital from investors in the stock market who expect high short-term returns (Albert 1993).

The new scholarly interest in varieties of capitalism coincided with a renewed political interest in the nature and extent to which qualitative differences exist between the United States and the EU. Seeking to strengthen the social elements of the European unification process, the EC Commission presided by Jacques Delors in the mid-1980s launched the idea of a system of "corporatist concertation" or coordination on the European level. A conference held in 1985 in Val Duchesse near Brussels brought top European representatives from business, labor, and the Commission together in order to introduce the "social dialogue" between the "social partners" as a form of collective bargaining on the supranational level. The Single European Act passed in 1987 gave the social dialogue formal recognition making it a key element of decision making procedures in the EU. When the 1992 Maastricht Treaty transformed the Union from an essentially economic organization to a political entity with extended supranational sovereignty, European policy makers perceived a growing need to build a common European identity. As "defining oneself in opposition to others is a natural way to assert one's existence" (Cohen-Tanugi 2008: 217), differences with the United States were now increasingly stressed, and EU policy makers and public officials began to articulate the idea of what might well be considered European exceptionalism, based on a cluster of economic, social, and political values that unites the member states. This concept is identified as the "European Social Model," a formal definition of which was given in the Presidency Conclusions of the Nice European Council meeting of 2000:

The European social model, characterized in particular by systems that offer a high level of social protection, by the importance of the social

> dialogue and by services of general interest covering activities vital for
> social cohesion, is today based, beyond the diversity of the Member States'
> social systems, on a common core of values. (European Council, 2000b)

Beyond social protection, social dialogue, and services that promote social cohesion, the common core of values includes "pluralism, nondiscrimination, tolerance, justice, solidarity and equality between women and men" (*Official Journal of the European Union*, 2004). In addition, the Treaty establishing the European Community identifies five common elements: a high level of employment, sustainable and noninflationary growth, economic competitiveness, an elevated quality of life, and a high level of the quality of the environment (*Official Journal of the European Union*, 2003). These formulations convey the breadth of social, economic and political life embraced by the "European social model."

From its initial conception in the Delors commission, the notion of a European social model was offered as an alternative to the American form of market capitalism, which Delors saw as advancing economic growth without regard for solidarity and social progress (Jepsen and Serrano Pascal, 2006). Ever since, discussions and analyses of the European social model have emphasized a contrast to the American approach. As Grahl and Teague (2000: 209) explain, "the European social model is defined first by its scope—it covers *both* social welfare and employment relations—which is clearly wider than the U.S., for example." A competitive edge is implicitly voiced in the 2000 Lisbon European Council goal for the European Union 'to become the most dynamic knowledge-based economy in the world, capable of sustainable economic growth with more and better jobs and greater social cohesion' (European Council, 2000a). Although "most" signifies more than everywhere else in the world, the United States is the immediate reference against which the European model tends to be judged. In a 2001 speech in Paris, Commission President Romano Prodi made this explicit when he said that the EU's goal is to establish "a superpower on the European continent that stands equal to the United States" (here quoted following Rifkin 2004: 298)

The European Council's statements in Lisbon, along with other official pronouncements, reflect the objective to create a system that enjoys the thriving market economy of the United States enhanced by additional dimensions of societal well-being. More recently, Anthony Giddens (2005) explains that the European social model aims to combine economic dynamism with social justice—echoing Delors' initial formulation three decades ago. In a major attempt to review European achievements in comparison to the United States, Jeremy Rifkin (2004: 201) praised the EU as a successful model of "sacrificing a degree of national sovereignty in return for a greater measure of security and opportunity." While he perceives the United States as "reverting back to an earlier era where allegiance is to the nation-state and final authority rests with the sovereign government" (p. 295), he sees the EU not only as "a kaleidoscope of cultural diversity" (p. 247), which "is best positioned between the extreme individuation of America and the extreme collectivism of Asia" (p. 365), but also as a successful new institutional mix, "made up of universal human rights, networks, and multilevel governance" (p. 279).

The enthusiasm governing debates over the prospects of the "European dream" in the EU-15 was dampened somewhat when the two-stage eastern enlargements to first ten, then twelve new member states confronted the EU with new challenges due not only to the significant gap in economic standards of living but also to different ideas regarding policies. The widespread concern that the new members might pursue social or fiscal dumping policies in order to accelerate economic catching-up was explicitly voiced in a policy paper by a think tank in France. The authors of this paper identified "liberalisation presented as an ideology" as one of the key challenges facing the new member states. They also expressed a concern that the new member states might not yet share "the conviction of the Fifteen that seeking economic convergence alone will not be enough and must be accompanied by a gradual convergence in the social area," and made it clear "for certain new member states" "that they fully understand that joining the European social model does not only consist of applying the *acquis communautaire*—i.e. the entire body of European laws and regulations (J.A. and N.G.)—but also reviewing again, after their transition, the relationship between economic progress and social progress" (Jouen and Papant 2005: 14, 15, 19).

While conveying the tone of a schoolmaster, this paper is a rather concise representation of the concerns, which led citizens in France and the Netherlands to reject the proposed EU constitution in 2005, and a majority of the people of Ireland to reject the new Consolidated Version of the Treaty on European Union in 2008. There is widespread concern that after having lived for decades under the shadow of the Soviet Empire, the postcommunist countries might look more to the United States than to the EU as a social and political model. This is made likely for a number of reasons. First, their adoption of the market economy and the restructuring of their social security systems have been strongly shaped by the IMF and the World Bank under the impact of the so-called Washington consensus, with its emphasis on rapid privatization. Second, the United States welcomed these countries as members of NATO long before the European Union opened up its ranks. Third, the accession process left some of them with bad memories, because the accession criteria were perceived by some as an encroachment upon their national sovereignty which asked them to meet standards that not all the established members of the club fulfilled themselves. Donald Rumsfeld, then U.S. Secretary of Defense, fuelled the concerns nourished in some of the old member states when he drew a polemical distinction between old and new Europe. Originally coined to distinguish between proponents and opponents of the war against Iraq, the concept was soon extended to distinguish a group of supposedly dynamic countries actively facing the future from a passive and nostalgic group clinging to the past and supposedly coping only reluctantly with the new necessities in a globalized world (Alber et al. 2008).

The war against terrorism and against Iraq also deepened the rift between the EU and the United States. As Steinmo and Kopstein (2008: 20) put it, "Americans believed that 9/11 changed the world; Europeans believed that what it really changed was America." Ever since the invasion of Iraq there is concern expressed in various publication titles that America and Europe may be "Growing Apart?" (Kopstein and Steinmo 2008), that we may witness "The End of the West" (Kupchan 2002) or that we find the "Allies at War" (Gordon and Shapiro 2004).

More recent developments which led to more pragmatic policy approaches on both sides of the Atlantic shed doubt on the assumption that the EU and the United States represent different social models, and raise the question as to what extent such models exist outside the minds of diplomats and politicians seeking to stitch together a common identity. How much unity is there still within Europe after the Eastern enlargements have considerably increased economic and cultural diversity? And to whatever extent one might discern a distinct set of commonalities that represent the core of a European approach how different are the European characteristics of social, economic, and political life from those of America?

These are the questions that stood at the center of a conference which the Social Science Research Center Berlin organized together with the European Foundation for the Improvement of Living and Working Conditions on the occasion of the German EU Presidency in Berlin in 2007. Scholars from both sides of the Atlantic and from old and new member states of the EU were invited to discuss to what extent old and new member states are similar enough to warrant speaking of a "European social model" and to explore how much unity and diversity there is to be found when comparing EU member states to the United States. This book collects the revised versions of the contributions to this conference. Before we look at the results in detail, we need to clarify the conceptual dimensions of a social model in order to delineate more clearly the selected key elements with which we are dealing in this book.

THE ISSUES DEALT WITH IN THIS BOOK

The manifold attempts to define the substance of the European social model in official EU documents make two things rather clear: First, Jacques Delors' famous dictum that the EU is an unidentified political object applies equally well to the concept of the European social model, which is rarely defined with any precision. Second, the concept is obviously complex and multidimensional, referring to characteristics of the state, the economy, and the society. This multidimensional character of the meaning of EU membership is also underlined by the so-called Copenhagen criteria, which were developed to determine what it takes to be eligible for EU membership. The Copenhagen criteria require that there is a functioning market economy, that the state institutions guarantee democratic governance, the rule of law, and human rights, and that the candidate countries adhere to the obligations of membership as specified in the EU treaty and other official EU documents.

It follows then that the term European social model is to encompass more than a mere model of social policy. In the dimension of the economy, it means that Europe seeks to combine the growth dynamic of a market economy with the coordinating social dialogue of the collective bargaining partners. In the dimension of the state, it means that European countries are not only free democracies, but also welfare states that supplement the market with a second sphere of the distribution of life chances that is designed to smooth social inequalities. In the dimension of society, it means that in addition to providing freedom and opportunity, European societies should also promote bonds of solidarity between individuals which strengthen social cohesion.

These dimensions can then be used to develop a conceptual grid, which helps to develop a more systematic picture with respect to three crucial issues: (1) What do European societies have in common with the United States? (2) What distinguishes them from their transatlantic counterpart? (3) How much variation is there within Europe and how do intra-European differences compare to the difference between the EU-Average and the United States? (Table 1) Another issue—which the table does not reflect—is to what extent national-level comparisons between single European countries and the United States really make sense given that there is much heterogeneity within countries and that there are vast differences in size between some European countries with less than 5 million inhabitants and a country like the United States with a population of some 300 million. As Jeremy Rifkin (2004: 65) suggested (without actually following his own advice) "rather than thinking of Germany in comparison to the U.S., we should think of it in comparison to California—Germany being the largest state in the European economy and California the largest state in the U.S. economy."

Although we are very much aware of the internal variation within countries and of the problems related to choosing nation-states as the unit of analysis, we here stick to this conventional procedure—mostly because the institutions that shape the social and political conditions that we are dealing with in this book are frequently national in character.

The task set for this book then is to systematically elaborate how much European countries and the United States have in common and how much variation we find within the enlarged European Union in selected subdimensions in Table 1. Drawing on contributions by U.S. and European scholars who represent multidisciplinary backgrounds, the book does not comprehensively embrace all relevant aspects of a comparison of social models, but selectively focuses on some key aspects. A first block of eight chapters deals with selected characteristics of the state. Two companion papers first examine the different concepts of democracy in Europe and the United States, which are at the root of different courses of state action. Then the structure and degree of electoral participation is examined. Third, the different levels and structures of public expenditure are put under scrutiny. Fourth, variations in the conception of social citizenship are examined with respect to minimum income legislation. A second block of eight chapters then deals with selected policy outcomes in the sense of four aspects of socioeconomic conditions. First, we examine to what extent the goal of full employment is reached. Second, we look at the degree of income inequality and at patterns of social mobility. Third, we examine to what extent educational benchmarks are met. Fourth, we examine how countries on both sides of the Atlantic have coped with the rising tide of immigration.

Delving into these dimensions the authors address more specific questions such as:

- How do we measure the functioning/performance of democracy? By which indicators do some countries stand out as better-functioning democracies than others? Do Europeans and U.S.-Americans share identical democratic ideals?
- To what extent is political participation socially skewed or polarized? Do rates of political participation differ in Europe and the United States and what factors account for observable differences?
- How do U.S. and European national budgets vary in terms of social expenditure and of expenditure for internal and external security? To what extent are the dynamics of public expenditure different? What happens to measures of spending when the basis of comparisons shift?
- How do concepts of citizenship involve a right to a guaranteed minimum income in Europe and the United States? To what extent are social programs for the poor in Europe and the United States conditioned on work efforts? How have respective policies changed in recent times?
- Is there an employment gap between Europe and the United States? How is it measured? To what extent can mass unemployment be seen as the dark side of the European model? What explains national differences in employment performance?
- How widespread and embedded is income inequality in Europe and the United States? How frequent is social mobility and how far is the social distance travelled by people from deprived backgrounds?
- How are educational opportunity and cognitive inequality distributed in European countries and the United States? How are these impacted by educational policies? What is the comparative quality of high/tertiary education and of minimum education?
- To what extent are immigrants socially integrated in Europe and the United States? What accounts for the different economic success of various groups of immigrants in various countries?

Each of these dimensions is examined by senior researchers from both United States and Europe, who operationally define measures of these elements and empirically analyze data in order to identify points of convergence and divergence. By analyzing the social models in terms of the selected eight

Table 1: The European and American Social Models: Similarities and Differences

Dimensions	Similarities	Differences	Differences within Europe
State: Varieties of Democracy	— Democracies with basic human rights, free elections and free press — Public policies supplementing the market with a second sphere of distribution and creating educational opportunity through systems of public education	— Different state structures (fragmented system of decision making in United States with many veto points) — Different state traditions (no feudal past, little need for centralized power) — Historical sequence democratization bureaucratization; patronage tradition, welfare state skepticism — Different party systems	— Unitary and federal systems — Different electoral systems — Different party systems — Different systems of interest intermediation — Different welfare regimes with different financing structures and different structures of public expenditure
Economy: Varieties of Capitalism	— Capitalist market economies with mass consumption, high levels of economic activity with service sector predominance, shrinking demand for low-skill labor, highly developed technology	— Higher GDP per capita in United States — Different labor market structures — Different regulation and bargaining structures and different modes of corporate financing	— Widely discrepant standards of living (GDP per capita) — Different labor market structures with widely discrepant female and service sector employment
Society: Varieties of Secular Postindustrial Society	— Secular societies with religious freedom — Class societies with unequal distribution of income and property — Open societies with high mobility — Immigrant societies with ethnic cleavages — Aging societies with demographic imbalances	— No feudal past/no state churches in United States — More inequality/poverty in United States — Different degrees of ethnic fragmentation — Different fertility patterns — Different associational structures with different welfare mixes and different degrees of voluntarism	— Different degrees of inequality and poverty — Different levels and structures of immigration — Different fertility levels and family patterns — Different associational structures

subdimensions, this book represents what we would consider a middle-range approach to the comparative analysis of societal well-being in Europe and United States. (One can easily imagine a much wider range of comparisons, including for example, health care, crime, housing, consumption, religious observance, gender equality, family life and environmental quality.) In pairing European and U.S. contributions, this volume offers a view of how the selected dimensions of social, economic, and political life tend to be perceived from both sides of the Atlantic. The various academic disciplines represented in this volume bring a range of relevant expertise to bear on the different areas of interest. Finally, the empirical orientation seeks to abide by de Tocqueville's (1835–40: 16) objective standard of "have never knowingly moulded facts to ideas instead of ideas to facts."

REFERENCES

Alber, Jens (2006) The European Social Model and the United States, *European Union Politics* 7(3): 393–419.

Alber, Jens, Fahey, Tony, and Saraceno, Chiara (eds) (2008) *Handbook of Quality of Life in the Enlarged European Union*. London: Routledge.

Albert, Michel (1993) *Capitalism against Capitalism*. London: Whurr Publications.

Baldwin, Peter (forthcoming) *The Narcissism of Minor Differences. How Unlike Each Other are America and Europe?* Oxford: Oxford University Press.

Bell, Daniel (1973) *The Coming of Post-Industrial Society*. New York: Basic Books.

Bell, Daniel (1976) *The Cultural Contradictions of Capitalism*. New York: Basic Books.

Blank, Rebecca and Freeman, Richard B. (1994) Evaluating the Connection between Social Protection and Economic Flexibility, in Rebbeca M. Blank (ed.) *Social Protection versus Economic Flexibility. Is There a Trade-Off?* Chicago and London: The University of Chicago Press, pp. 21–41.

Block, Fred (2007) Understanding the Diverging Trajectories of the United States and Western Europe: A Neo-Polanyian Analysis. Politics and Society 35(1): 3–33.

Block, Fred (2008) Swimming Againts the Current: The Rise of a Hidden Developmental State in the United States. *Politics and Society* 36(2): 169–206.

Cohen-Tanugi, Laurent (2008) The Atlantic Divide in Historical Perspective: A View from Europe, in J. Kopstein and S. Steinmo (eds) *Growing Apart? America and Europe in the Twenty-First Century*. Cambridge: Cambridge University Press, pp. 211–224.

Esping-Andersen, Gøsta (1990) *The Three Worlds of Welfare Capitalism*. Cambridge: Polity Press.

Esping-Andersen, Gøsta (1999): *Social Foundations of Post-Industrial Economies*. Oxford: Oxford University Press.

Esping-Andersen and Regini, Marino (eds) (2000) *Why Deregulate Labour Markets?* New York: Oxford University Press.

European Council (2000a) 'Presidency Conclusions: Lisbon European Council, 23 and 24 March 2000' Available from: http://www.bolognaberlin2003 (accessed February 2006). http://www.europarl.europa.eu/summits/lis1_en.htm

European Council (2000b), Presidency Conclusions: Nice European Council Meeting 7, 8, and 9 December 2000. Available from: http://europa.eu.int/council/off/conclu/dec2000/dec2000_en.htm (accessed February 2006).

Giddens, Anthony (2005) The World Does Not Owe Us a Living: The Future of the European Social Model, Policy network paper, mimeo.

Gilbert, Neil (2004) *Transformation of the Welfare State: The Silent Surrender of Social Responsibility* New York: Oxford University Press.

Gilbert, Neil (2008) Recent Welfare Reforms and Future Directions: Political Issues, Paper presented at the Conference on Social Policies in Canada and the U.S., organized by the French Directorate of Research, Evaluation Studies, and Statistics of the Social Ministries, Paris, February pp. 7–88.

Gordon, Philip H. and Shapiro, Jeremy (2004) *Allies at War. America, Europe, and the Crisis over Iraq.* New York: McGraw-Hill.

Grahl, John and Teague, Paul (2000) Is the European Social Model Fragmenting? in Christopher Pierson and Francis Castles (eds) *The Welfare State Reader.* Cambridge: Polity Press.

Hall, Peter A. and Soskice, David (2001) An Introduction to Varieties of Capitalism in Peter A. Hall and David Soskice (eds) *Varieties of Capitalism. The Institutional Foundations of Comparative Advantage.* Oxford: Oxford University Press, pp. 1–68.

Huntington, Samuel P. (1993) The Clash of Civilizations? *Foreign Affairs* 72(3): 22–49.

Jepsen, Maria and Serrano Pascual, Amparo (2005) 'The European Social Model: An Exercise in Deconstruction', *Journal of European Social Policy* 15(3): 231–245.

Jouen, Marjorie and Papant, Catherine (2005) 'Social Europe in the throes of enlargement, Notre Europe', Policy papers No 15, Notre Europe. Online. Available from: http://www.notre-europe.eu/uploads/tx_publication/Policypaper15-en.pdf (accessed 10 July 2008).

Keune, Maarten (2008) EU Enlargement and Social Standards: Exporting the European Social Model? Working Paper 2008.01, European Trade Union Institute for Research, Education and Health and Safety, Brussels.

Kopstein, Jeffrey and Steinmo Sven (eds) (2008) *Growing Apart? America and Europe in the Twenty-First Century.* Cambridge: Cambridge University Press.

Kupchan, Charles (2002) The End of the West, Atlantic Monthly November 2002 (http://www.theatlantic.com/doc/print/200211/kupchan)

Lipset, Seymour Martin (1997) *American Exceptionalism: A Double Edged Sword.* New York: W.W. Norton

Lipset, Seymour Martin und Marks, Gary (2000) *It Didn't Happen Here. Why Socialism Failed in the United States.* New York, London: Norton.

Morone, James (2003) *Hellfire Nation. The Politics of Sin in American History.* New Haven, CT: Yale University Press.

Official Journal of the European Union (2003) Selected Instruments Taken from the Treaties: 2. Treaty Establishing the European Community, http://europa.eu.int/eur-lex/en/treaties/selected/livre202.html (accessed February 2006).

Official Journal of the European Union (2004) Treaty Establishing a Constitution for Europe, C310, Vol. 47, 16 December, http://europa.eu.int/eur-lex/lex/en/treaties/index.htm (accessed February 2006).

Pontusson, Jonas (2005) *Inequality and Prosperity. Social Europe vs. Liberal America.* Ithaca, NY: Cornell University Press.

Rifkin, Jeremy (2004) *The European Dream. How Europe's Vision of the Future is Quietly Eclipsing the American Dream.* New York: Tarcher.

Schuck, Peter and Wilson, James Q. (eds) (2008) *Understanding America: The Anatomy of an Exceptional Nation*, New York: Public Affairs.

Sombart, Werner (1976) *Why Is There No Socialism in the United States.* White Plains: International Arts and Sciences Press. [German original 196: Warum gibt es in den Vereinigten Staaten keinen Sozialismus? Tübingen: Mohr.]

Steinmo, Sven and Kopstein, Jeffrey (2008) Introduction: Growing Apart? America and Europe in the Twenty-First Century, in J. Kopstein and S. Steinmo (eds) *Growing Apart? America and Europe in the Twenty-First Century.* Cambridge: Cambridge University Press, pp. 1–23.

Titmuss, Richard (1958) *Essays on the Welfare State.* London: Allen and Unwin.

Tocqueville, Alexis de (1835–40 [1964]) *Democracy in America.*

Wilensky, Harold (2002) *Rich Democracies.* Berkeley, CA: University of California Press.

Wilensky, Harold and Lebeaux, Charles (1965) *Industrial Society and Social Welfare.* New York: The Free Press.

PART I

STATE: STRUCTURE AND POLICY

SECTION I

DEMOCRATIC FUNCTIONING

1

DEMOCRATIC QUALITY IN AMERICA AND EUROPE

STEIN RINGEN

There is next to no dispute today that democracy is better than nondemocracy. Democracy protects freedom, fosters development and well-being, and encourages good government—at least usually and better than any alternative system. There is ample evidence for democracy providing these benefits, as summarised recently in Human Development Report (UNDP 2002). That no doubt helps to explain why democracy is advancing strongly in the world. From 1985 to 2000, the number of authoritarian regimes in the world decreased from 67 to 26. More than two-thirds of the world's people live in countries with multi-party electoral systems (if China came around, it would be more than 90%) (UNDP 2002).

However, if we set aside the old dispute between democracy and autocracy, and instead look inside the democracies and ask how good they themselves really are, we are on less well-trodden ground. We are all aware of massive problems

21

in modern democracy: slowness and arbitrariness of decision-making, corruption, unfair competition distorted by money, declining voter participation and party membership, and much disenchantment among citizens.[1] What does a good democracy look like?

Those of us who live in countries that are governed democratically are fortunate and privileged, and we know it. But how good are our democracies? Are some better than others? How do America and Europe compare?

DEMOCRATICNESS

The instinctive way in political science to approach the question of democratic quality is to ask how democratic a country is. It seems intuitively obvious that the more democratic the better. As we will see, that intuition is not as obvious as it may appear, but let us nevertheless start there—and with the United States, one of the great model democracies of the world.

Robert A. Dahl, the doyen of democracy studies in political science, has in recent years crowned a long lifetime of research and reflection on the theory and practice of democracy with a series of three brief, beautifully simple yet penetrating books about democracy in general and American democracy in particular. In *On Democracy* (Dahl 1998), he makes the case for democracy as opposed to nondemocracy. Government by consent, he says, is something we should want and aspire to because it produces desirable consequences. He lists these in ten points: democracy prevents cruel and vicious rule, it guarantees citizens certain fundamental rights that undemocratic systems cannot grant, it ensures its citizens a range of personal freedoms, it enables them to protect their fundamental interests, it provides them the opportunity to exercise self-determination and to live under laws of their own choosing, it gives them the opportunity to exercise moral responsibility, it fosters human development, it fosters a relatively high degree of political equality, it discourages war and it encourages prosperity. Never perfectly, of course, and always with flaws. But compared to any known alternative, and as a general rule, democracy is desirable.

In this summary of the experience of democratic as compared to nondemocratic government he establishes two fundamentals. First, *why* democracy is desirable. It is desirable because of observable beneficial consequences and because these are consequences that take their goodness from being good for people. For example, it is not because it makes America great that democracy is desirable; it is because it helps Americans, and other citizens in other democracies, to live good, decent and moral lives. Secondly, he dismisses the conventional wisdom that democracy is good for fairness but bad for efficiency. Experience shows that democracy out-competes the opposition on both fairness and efficiency.

In *How Democratic Is the American Constitution?* Dahl (2001) moves on from that platform to look critically inside America's political system. He ends that scrutiny by questioning its very democratic credentials and thereby reminds us that, although democracy is far and away the desirable form of government, there are serious shortcomings in even the most respected democracies. The American Constitution, he finds, is outdated and has not been kept up to date with democracy as it has subsequently evolved. Judged by today's standards of democracy, Dahl finds at least four serious defects: The overwhelming power of the office of the president and the way presidents are elected; the inequality of representation, in particular in the Senate; the role of the Supreme Court, which takes it beyond judicial review to 'judicial legislation' and the historical dictatorship in the near to impossibility of changing and modernising the Constitution and moving Americans forward along with changing expectations.

In *On Political Equality* (Dahl 2006), he turns to the tug of war in capitalist democracy between political equality and economic inequality. While democracy in theory presupposes equality, in the real world, paradoxically, where democracy is most advanced, economic and social conditions are notoriously unequal. Democracy seems to live most comfortably with market capitalism and market capitalism thrives on inequality.

Although we live in societies of inequality, we do enjoy a range of political equalities. The first equality is in the vote—an institution we mostly take for granted when we have it but that is utterly magical. It enables citizens to appoint their leaders and to throw them out if they are no good, and it gives everyone an equal say in these matters so that no individuals or small groups are able to decide public business on their own. Elections are complicated and costly. Any economist can prove that this is an inefficient way of spending time, organisation, and money. The fact that we continue to hold elections is proof that citizens value democracy and understand its logic of equality.

The next equality is rights. Where there is democracy, human and political rights are universal. Everyone has the right to speak, read and discuss freely; to worship freely; to form families freely; and to be treated fairly by the police and in the courts. This too is cumbersome and costly, but no economic calculus is going to compel us to give away our basic rights. On the ground, these democratic virtues are always imperfect but no less real for that.

But beyond basic rights, in modern capitalism, it's all inequality, sometimes shocking inequality. In the United States, we must go back to the nineteenth century, to what we would now consider predemocratic times, to find economic inequality on today's level. The driving force in this revolution is a strong concentration of new wealth from economic growth in the hands of the 1% or so who are the very richest.

In the American system, and no doubt in other democracies as well, economic inequality is transgressing (probably increasingly so) into the machinery of democracy.[2] Political candidates, parties and campaigns are dependent on large donations from rich individuals or institutions. This disqualifies anyone from entering into politics who is unable to obtain the blessing of economic power. Elected politicians answer more to money and less to voters. Public policy distorts in favor of minority interests. In America in particular (as shown elsewhere in this volume, see the chapter by Alber and Kohler) this follows through to a sharp inequality of political participation whereby, to put it crudely, the well-off vote and control the power of the vote while the poor are absent from political participation and influence. It's starting to look like an elected dictatorship. 'Because of a decline of the direct influence of citizens over crucial governmental decisions, and also in the influence of their elected representatives, political inequality might reach levels at which the American political system dropped well below the threshold for democracy broadly accepted at the opening of the twenty-first century' (Dahl 2006: 94).

These findings in the American model democracy contain important conclusions about the state of democracy in the world, and disconcerting ones. Still, they do not tell us all that much of what we might want to know. We are told reliably that there are shortcomings, but how serious are they? Any real democracy will obviously fall short compared to ideal principles and it is therefore in the nature of things that any case study will identify imperfections. With its shortcomings, is American democracy still a good democracy? How are we to know?

The approach of assessing democracies by how democratic they are has been generalised into a now well-tried approach for the measurement of democracy.[3] The most authoritative source is the *Polity* project (presently *Polity IV*).[4] This project measures 'the degree of democracy' on a year-by-year basis, covering a period of roughly 200 years, for all independent states (with populations of more than 500,000). The indicators are as follows:

- Whether or not there is a functioning polity (i.e. functioning central political authority having been established and not interrupted)
- Openness (democracy) or closeness (autocracy) of political institutions
- The durability of the polity (number of years since last regime transformation)
- Institutionalised procedures for the transfer of executive power
- Competition in executive recruitment
- Independence of/constraints on the chief executive
- Institutional structures of political expression
- Competitiveness of participation

The regime classification, based mainly on expert assessment, is on a scale from +10 (most democratic) to –10 (least democratic).

The *Polity* comparisons show, not surprisingly, that there are vast differences between the countries of the world in how democratic they are but that there is little or no difference in the degree of democracy among the established democracies. The United States, for example, is at the top of the *Polity* scale. A more recent effort is the 2007 Democracy Index of the Economist's Intelligence Unit, which finds a good deal of difference between 'full democracies' and 'flawed democracies' but not much difference to mention between the 'full democracies'.[5] The state of the art in political science suggests that once countries are consolidated democracies, they are pretty similar in how good they are as democracies.

DEMOCRATIC QUALITY

My hypothesis is that the established view in political science on comparative democracy is mistaken and that there are in fact vast differences in quality between democratic countries, including those that are usually considered to be the most advanced and established ones. I have therefore been uncomfortable with the kind of research I have referred to above as evidence of democratic quality and have come to believe that there are good reasons to be distrustful of that evidence for this purpose (Ringen 2007). I underline *for this purpose.* The works I have referred to are the best in the business, but I don't think their approach is the appropriate one towards an authoritative answer to the question of how *good* a democracy is. To ask how good a democracy is, is not the same as to ask how democratic it is.

The purpose of democracy is not to be democratic. Democracy is *for* something. It would seem elementary that if we want to compare how good the democracies are, a beauty contest of how they do democracy will not take us far. We need to get deeper into the matter and establish how well they do what we should want and expect of them. To observe a democracy from the point of view of how good it is, we must follow through from observing how democracy is done and establish what it produces of democratic value.

In *What Democracy Is For* I have discussed in some length the definition and purpose of democracy. The definition I arrive at is basic and minimalist: a polity is democratic if its citizens in a securely institutionalised manner hold the ultimate control over collective decisions. That is democracy because this is what is required for citizens to have good reasons to trust that collective decisions are made and will continue to be made on the basis of respect for their interests. Power resides with citizens (collectively, of course). Either citizens exercise their power themselves in some form of direct democracy, or they delegate it to élites who then hold it in trust and use it under the knowledge that citizens retain the super-power to retract delegated power or to shift it to other élites of their choice.

As to democracy's purpose, there are of course many, but my conclusion is still that it can be summed up in a final purpose, which is to offer citizens security and protection. Citizens are exposed to various dangers that flow from the necessity of living together in community and then of some kind of governance and rule. In my view, democracy is finally for the purpose of promoting and protecting the *freedom* of women and men and families to live their lives according to their own understanding of what it is that constitutes a good and reasoned life. Therefore, when we ask how good a democracy is, the research task is to try to establish how well it protects and promotes freedom and security of freedom.

I should inject here a small parenthesis to explain that I think the concept of freedom is powerful but also exceedingly complex as a normative and analytic one. I devote a full chapter in *What Democracy Is For* to making some sense of this complexity. Here I can only say that I build on a tradition from Aristotle up to Isaiah Berlin, John Rawls, and Joseph Raz to arrive at an understanding of freedom as being the master of one's own life and that this again rests on a function of rights, resources, and reason.

MEASUREMENT

Until recently, the theory of social measurement took it to be more or less obvious that the site of social quality and change was in one way or other 'the system'. Development, for example, was seen to be something that happened in 'the economy'. The consequence of that view was that measurement approaches used 'the system' as the unit of observation. Development was observed for countries, usually with the GDP per capita indicator.

In the last couple of decades, however, there has occurred what amounts to a change of paradigm. That has come about through a better understanding of just what the site of quality is and from there a better understanding of 'the unit problem', of what is the appropriate unit of observation. We are now inclined to argue that social quality resides ultimately with the persons who belong to or live in a system and not exclusively in the system itself (at least so we will argue if we work within a framework of democratic values). Systems have *potential* but the *value* contained in that potential is manifested or not in the lives of persons. If development is for people, it needs to be measured in terms of how it manifests itself in the lives of persons (see, e.g., Sen 1999). If that is the case, we need to use the person as a relevant unit of observation. This has not made the system irrelevant as a unit of observation, but we would now see measurement approaches that observe only the system as insufficient. The measurement of development, to stay with that example, would observe first the system and its potential, using, for example, the GDP per capita indicator, but then in addition the value that flows from that potential into the lives people live, using, for example, poverty as an indicator.

Comparative democracy has not moved on to postparadigm-change methodology, but remains stuck in what Guillermo O'Donnell has called a 'narrow focus on the regime' (O'Donnell et al. 2004). When we ask how democratic a country is, we ask only what the system looks like without following through to considering what that system does for the people who inhabit it and whom it is supposed to serve. This is not up to date with developments in normative theory about what it is that makes democracy desirable or good. As Robert Dahl has shown, the reason we can now say authoritatively that democracy is better than nondemocracy, is that we have sorted out how to make that assessment. Democracy is preferable if and to the degree that beneficial consequences follow that take their goodness from being good for people. Having come to that conclusion theoretically, we must follow up methodologically. It is not enough to observe the regime, we must also observe people.

There is a very specific logic behind the change of paradigm according to which the measurement of social quality depends on a double book-keeping in which information both about the system and about the lives of those who live in it is recorded. Neither one nor the other is on its own enough. In the case of development, again, it is not enough to observe the living conditions of persons. These could theoretically be better than is ensured in the potential of the economy, for example, if poverty is held back by development aid rather than by the economic potential of the country itself. This well-being would be precarious and this country should therefore not be considered an economically developed one. Nor is it enough to observe the country's economic potential. Two countries with the same economic potential but that differ in their performance on poverty should not be considered equally developed. We need to observe *two* things—potential in the system and life quality for persons—and to measure quality by a combined use of both observations—by combined micro and macro measurement and applying an element of methodological individualism, the methodologist might say. The Human Development Index (by the United Nations Development Programme) is a case in point. Development is here measured in an index based on the economic potential of each country and the standard of health and education in its people. This change in approach makes a very considerable difference in measurement results.[6]

Above, I have concluded *theoretically* that to ask about democratic quality should be to ask about democracies' performance in terms of their final purpose of promoting and protecting freedom. Now I conclude *methodologically* that in order to measure and compare democratic quality with some robustness, we need to break away from the traditional regime bias in political science, pay much more attention to persons, and move on to double book-keeping.

I know that I am up against strong instincts in political science. It seems intuitive that the democracy that is the most democratic is the best one. Of course this may be true, but if so, it needs to be established empirically. The best democracy is the one that best does what we should want it to do for us. It also seems intuitive that the way to measure democracy is to measure how well the machinery of democracy works. For many purposes, this is no doubt the right approach, but not for the normative purpose of measuring quality. The way to measure quality is not to consider the beauty of the regime, or at least that is not sufficient. We need to follow through and observe what the regime does and what product comes out of it for those it is for. I think mainstream political science has been too content to stick with what seems to be obvious and not reflected sufficiently upon the fact that often 'obvious' is just another word for doing things the way they have always been done.[7]

COMPARING QUALITY

In Table 1-1, I show the position of eleven democracies on an index of democratic quality that ranges from 8 (high quality) to 0 (low quality) and on the eight indicators that are used to estimate the index. These democracies are the relevant ones for which I have data for the America–Europe comparison in the project reported in this book from a broader comparison of twenty-five democracies reported in *What Democracy Is For* (with some updating of the data). What these eleven democracies have in common is that they, by mainstream measurement, are on the top of the ladder of degree of democracy (all are on level 10 of the *Polity* index, except France and Poland, which are on level 9). These then are among the most democratic countries in the world and there is no measurable difference between them in democraticness. Since I consider only established democracies, various things are given and need no consideration, mainly that political, civil and human rights are more or less equally established in all.[8]

I use a small battery of indicators that I analyse with the simplest possible methodology. Each indicator is dichotomised and all are given equal weight, something that enables me to pull the data I use together into an elementary additive index.[9]

The way I think about this comparison is like this: Democracy is for citizens. I put myself in the shoes of the citizen and ask what his or her democracy looks like for his or her life. This methodological individualism is in my opinion the democratic way of measuring social quality; it is to observe what social conditions mean for people. I take it that citizens want freedom to live their lives as they themselves see best. They look to their system of governance and want to see institutions and decision-making that promote and protect their freedoms. They want to experience their lives to be under their own control and they want to see reasons that enable them to trust that their freedoms will persevere tomorrow and into the future.

I start by looking to the regime. In a good democracy, the regime will be so arranged that it displays to citizens good reasons for them to believe that their freedoms are protected and safe. This depends on two conditions. First, that citizens have reason to trust that their democracy is firmly established as a fair democracy that respects *their* interests and gives *them* protection. This I call the regime's *solidity*. Second, that the regime is capable of efficient and fair decision-making. This I call its *capacity*.

I then look to the life situation of citizens. In a good democracy, citizens are ensured, in addition to basic rights, a minimum of resources to live free lives. This I call *security*. Furthermore, they have reason to live with confidence about the future of freedom. This I call *trust*. These qualities are realised when citizens are free to shape their own lives by objective standards and when they subjectively feel that their lives are free and safe. The decisive democratic test is the degree to which freedom and the security of freedom extends to *everyone* in the citizenry.

Thus I have two units of observation, the regime and the person—my double book-keeping. For each kind of observation, I identify two dimensions, the solidity and capacity of the regime and the security and trust of persons. For each dimension, I use two indicators (which are explained below). That gives me in all eight indicators, four to display the quality of *potential* in the regime and four to display realised *value* in the lives of citizens. For each indicator, I define a single cut-off point between good and not good quality. To countries on the 'good' side of the dichotomy I allocate a score of 1, to the others a score of 0. From this, I estimate a final index of democratic quality on a range from 8 to 0. The portrait I draw with these indicators in Table 1-1 gives the state of democratic quality in these leading democracies at the beginning of the twenty-first century (as far as possible I have used data for 2002).

The first indicator captures democratic consolidation. Citizens know their democracy from its historical record. If in that record they see responsiveness to changing circumstances that are in tune with democratic ideals and principles, they have reason to trust that their political culture is safely democratic. If they see failures in responding democratically, in particular at critical historical junctures, they have reason to fear that their political culture is more shallowly democratic or less responsive to their interests and protection.

My proxy operational indicator here (since no empirical measure to my knowledge is available on consolidation directly) is the timing of finality in the establishment of universal suffrage. That is usually the timing of universal female suffrage, but in some cases the final extension of the vote to minorities. By around 1920, the intellectual case for universal suffrage had been won. Democracies that then or shortly thereafter introduced universal suffrage (in my index before 1940) have a proven history of being democratically responsive. Those that delayed have a historical record of being democratically resistant. In some southern states of the United States, for example, universal suffrage was not finally imposed until 1965 (in the Voting Rights Act). In France, the introduction of female suffrage was delayed until 1944, and in Belgium, Canada, and Italy, universal suffrage was not finally attained until 1948, 1950, and 1945, respectively. These are democracies in which at least some section of the citizenship has reason to see recent historical evidence of disregard for their rights and interests.[10]

The second indicator is of press freedom. In electoral democracies, democratic rule is exercised by élites but in principle under the oversight and control of citizens. Their most important instrument of control, in addition to the vote, is a free press. A free press informs élites about the wishes of citizens and citizens about the doings of governing élites, and holds élites to answer for how they exercise power. A democracy is hardly thinkable without a free press. A good democracy is one in which the press is not just free but robustly free (see Ringen 2003).

All the democracies in my comparison have a free press. In two of them, however, France and Italy, according to the measurement of press freedom by Freedom House, there are limitations in press freedom so that one would not say that these democracies enjoy the benefits of a robustly free press. [11]

The third indicator is of government effectiveness. For a democracy to be capable of protecting its citizens, its institutions of governance must be able to produce and implement necessary legislation and other decision-making. Following the World Bank's indicator of government effectiveness, which again is based on international survey data, all the democracies in my comparison are classified as effective in decision-making capacity, except for Italy. [12]

The fourth indicator is of nondistortion in government decision-making. Decision-making needs to be not only effective but also fair, which is to say that decisions of public policy should appropriately reflect the citizens' interests and demand for security. That depends on decision-making being free from distorting influences in the processes. The most important source of distortion is what the economist Arthur Okun called the transgression of economic power into the processes of democratic politics (Okun 1975). This indicator goes to the degree to which the processes of governance are protected against the political use of economic power. [13]

My classification of the countries on this indicator is informed by the Corruption Perception Index compiled by Transparency International and the Graft Index devised by the World Bank (as reproduced in UNDP 2002). However, since these data do not directly go to the important idea of transgression, it is also based on best judgement. The result is that all but three of these democracies—Belgium, Canada, and the Netherlands—are classified as not having an adequate capacity for decision-making without distorting transgression by economic power.

The fifth and sixth indicators are of security of resources. Freedom depends, once rights are given, on citizens having access to a modicum of resources to be able to make use of rights and practically shape their own lives according to their own goals and aspirations. Resources in this meaning are in the form of physical and human capital, which I here take practically to mean purchasing power and health. [14] We should therefore expect a system of democratic governance to perform adequately in translating available economic resources into a system of protection for citizens against poverty and avoidable deprivations in health. Two indicators follow: the level of income poverty and the security of health care.

My operational indicators are first relative child income poverty. I allocate the score of 1 to countries with a child poverty rate of less than 10% according to the 'league table of child poverty' compiled by UNICEF (2005). That, for example, just pushes postunification Germany to the 'wrong' side of the divide although Western Germany specifically has a lower than 10% child poverty rate. This, I think, can be seen as an appropriate sensitivity in the measurement to strains in German democracy after reunification. The second indicator is operationalised by public health expenditure as a percentage of GDP in 2002. The level of *public* expenditure on health care is an indicator of the effort in the country's public policy relative to economic capacity to make (quality) health care available to people irrespective of their own economic ability to purchase health care or health insurance, and hence of the availability of quality health care to *everyone* in the population. In estimating the indicator relative to GDP, it reflects public policy efforts relative to economic capacity, which is to say differences in political effort after controlling for differences in economic ability. Private health expenditure is outside of the indicator. Britain gets a score of 0 because of its low level of public spending on health in spite of the National Health Service, which appropriately reflects deep concerns in Britain itself over the quality of health care, and the United States gets a score of 0 because of a low level of public spending on health care in spite of a high level of private spending and reflecting known inadequacies in health care coverage in that country.[15]

The two last indicators are of citizens' perceptions. Democratic delivery is ultimately as experienced by citizens, and the way citizens experience delivery is in confidence, safety, and trust: confidence in government, trust in the security of rights and liberties, trust in an order that enables people to trust each other (see e.g. Gambetta 1988). Two indicators follow: the degree of confidence in the population in political institutions and the degree of general trust in the future of freedom.

Confidence and trust are not straightforward indicators to apply. In a vibrant democracy, we should expect citizens to be critical of those who rule and therefore to award them no more than optimal confidence (Rose 1994). In today's democratic world, however, confidence and trust is very thin and the problem is not too much of it but too little (see e.g. Norris 1999; Boudon 2002; O'Neill 2002, and Parr et al. 2003). Therefore, the view that is taken here is that, relative to the overall state of confidence and trust, more is better than less. Even in those democracies in which confidence and trust are on a relatively high level, it is nowhere on an uncritical level.

These indicators are operationalised with data from the World Value and the European Value Surveys 1990 and 2000. They are defined strictly so as to allocate quality scores to democracies in which the level of confidence and trust has been stable or increased in recent years (against a general trend of decline) *and* is on a higher level than the average for all the democracies included in the comparison. The indicator of confidence in government is based on two questions about 'confidence in parliament' and 'confidence in the civil service'. The score of 1 is allocated to countries in which the level of confidence increased on both questions from 1990 to 2000 *and* is above the average for the countries included in the comparison on both questions in the 2000 round of surveys. Confidence is measured as the percentage responding 'a great deal' or 'quite a lot'. The score hence depends on both *trends* and *levels* in confidence and relies on a pattern of response and not any single figure. The average 2000 confidence in Parliament is 40% and in the civil service 43%. The United States, for example, gets a 0 score on 'confidence in parliament' because of a 38% response in 2000, and a 0 score on confidence in the civil service in spite of a 55% response in 2000 because that was down from 59% in 1990. The indicator of trust in freedom is based again on two questions about 'freedom of choice and control in life' and 'trust in people'. The score of 1 is allocated to countries in which the reported experience of freedom increased on both questions from 1990 to 2000 *and* trust was above average on both questions in the 2000 round of surveys. Experience of freedom of choice and control in life is measured as the percentage responding 'a great deal' (7–10 on a 1–10 scale). Trust in people is measured as the percentage responding 'most people can be trusted'. The average 2000 response for freedom/control is 64% and for trust in people 36%.[16]

Before commenting on the results, let me just add methodologically that although technically I give all eight indicators the same weight in the index, I in reality give extra weight to the subjective indicators of confidence and trust by building them on four demanding value questions and by the strict operational definition I apply. In my framework, I think it is appropriate that citizens' judgements count heavily.

FINDINGS AND DISCUSSION

Table 1-1 gives relative quality scores on these indicators for 11 democracies. The general view in political science is that in the case of established democracies, although they differ greatly in constitutional arrangements and political conventions, there is little to distinguish between them in how good they are as democracies. This exercise disconfirms that view and shows that even among these leading democracies, the quality of democracy differs greatly. In the original comparison of twenty-five democracies, which also includes Nordic countries, the range of measured quality stretches from the lowest to the highest index score. Democracies, then, we can safely conclude, differ not only in how they do democracy but also in how good they are.

This result is entirely credible. The old conclusion was distorted by regime bias and a product of outdated methodology. The new conclusion is a product

Table 1-1: Relative Democratic Quality in Selected Democracies, ca. Beginning of the Twenty-First Century

	Solidity		Capacity		Security		Trust		
	(1)	(2)	(3)	(4)	(5)	(6)	(7)	(8)	INDEX
North America									
Canada	0	1	1	1	0	1	1	0	5
United States	0	1	1	0	0	0	0	0	2
Old EU members									
Belgium	0	1	1	1	1	0	0	0	4
France	0	0	1	0	1	1	0	0	3
Germany	1	1	1	0	0	1	0	0	4
Italy	0	0	0	0	0	0	0	0	0
Netherlands	1	1	1	1	1	0	0	1	6
Spain	0	1	1	0	0	0	0	0	2
United Kingdom	1	1	1	0	0	0	0	0	3
New EU members									
Czech Republic	1	1	0	0	1	0	0	0	3
Poland	0	1	0	0	0	0	0	0	1

(1) Consolidated democracy; (2) Freedom of the press; (3) Government effectiveness; (4) Economic transgression; (5) Child poverty; (6) Public health care; (7) Trust in state institutions; (8) Trust in future freedom pre-government.

of getting the methodology right and of bringing postparadigm-shift methodology into comparative democracy and the move to double book-keeping. The operational indicators I have been able to use are not all ideal, but the index results are persuasive. By and large, democracies that are known to be troubled or immature—in the original comparison, for example, Mexico, Chile, South Africa, India, and Italy—are in the bottom range of the index, while those that are known to be more solid—for example, New Zealand, Holland, and the Scandinavian countries—are in the top range. The surprising result, perhaps, is that the two great model democracies of the world, the United States and Britain, are both in the lower part of the quality ranking.

To read these results more carefully, consider the case of the United States, which is on index level 2. Indicator by indicator, the story told for that country is, firstly, that when Americans consider their political system and what it does for them, they see a democracy that they, or at least some of them, have reason to fear may not be there for their protection when they need it. To classify American democracy as poorly consolidated is no doubt unorthodox. However, in political science orthodoxy, the meaning of consolidation is not well developed theoretically. If we take it to mean 'not in danger of being overturned or constitutionally perverted' American democracy is probably safe enough. However, if we start from a notion of democracy's purpose and take that to be the provision of universal protection of freedom and ask how well that purpose is consolidated, American democracy simply is immature. Not even equality of formal political rights was established de jure until 1965 and to this day the political system continues to be fraught with extensive de facto inequalities of integration, participation, and influence by race, location, and class, which are otherwise characteristics usually associated with second rate democracies that don't work.

Americans can nevertheless take comfort from living in a political system that is blessed with a robustly free press and effective decision-making institutions. However, these same institutions, although adequately capable of getting decisions made, work in an environment that is wide open to the political use of economic resources with the danger of democratic distortions in decision-making that follows from the transgression of economic power into the domain of democratic politics. This is not primarily a problem of corruption, although possibly that too, but of allowing moneyed interests extra influence in the political culture, and thereby more or less eroding the one-person one-vote principle of influence.

Looking to their own lives, Americans, or some of them, see that their need for a modicum of resources to make effective use of rights and realise lives of freedom and autonomy, is poorly protected. The United States is abundantly affluent, but the basic conditions of full citizenship are not available to all sections of the population. This logic obviously rests on an understanding of political citizenship as depending not only on rights, although this is the first and basic condition, but also on a modicum of resources to make use of rights and live in autonomy. I underline *a modicum*; the logic is not equality of resources but the satisfaction of basic needs.

Finally, in their end assessment of confidence and trust, Americans seem to agree with the relatively despondent interpretation of the quality of their democracy that can be read out of the objective indicators. Their trust in political institutions is comparatively low, their trust in each other comparatively low and their trust in the future of democracy comparatively low. Taken together then, this is a story of consistency: weaknesses in the foundation of democracy, combine with inequality of treatment, and a deficit of trust.

I have included Canada in the present comparison to show that this is not a North American story, but a story of the United States specifically. The Canadian story is comparatively one of a stronger democratic foundation, more equality of treatment and more trust.

How, then, does Europe compare? The short answer is, not at all. Among the old European Union (EU) member countries included in the comparison, the quality of their democracies ranges from comparatively high in the Netherlands to very low in Italy and with the rest distributed equally between these extremes. The same lack of conformity is found for the two countries in my comparison that represent the Central European countries that have recently escaped from authoritarianism and very recently acceded to the EU. The difference between Poland with its very low score and the Czech Republic with its comparatively higher score is entirely believable in light of the difference in democratic traditions in these two countries. Hence, not only is there no North American model of democracy by quality, there is also no European model, not even any Western or Eastern European Model. Nor is there any trace of an American–European dimension in the diversity of democratic quality. Here there are no models at all, only national traditions and national narratives.

A final comment is in place on the two model democracies, the United States and Britain. These are often seen to be in the same family in international comparison and superficially this is confirmed here in that both end on a relatively low quality score. But they arrive there in different ways. While the United States story is consistent in that it is a democracy with weaknesses in the foundations that performs poorly, the British story is more paradoxical: a democracy that performs poorly in spite of relatively strong foundations. One overall conclusion to be drawn from this enquiry into democratic quality is that there is much that can and should be done to improve the performance of the world's democracies for their populations. The comparison between the United States and Britain suggests that this will have to be done in different ways in different countries. If American democracy might need to be repaired all the way from the foundations, British democracy has more to work on and can more easily improve itself by devising better procedures.

REFERENCES

Altman, Daniel and Perez-Liñán, Anibal (2002) Assessing the Quality of Democracy: Freedom, Competitiveness and Participation in Eighteen Latin-American Countries, *Democratization*, 9: 85–100.

Bollen, Kenneth and Jackman, Robert W. (1989) Democracy, Stability and Dichotomies, *American Sociological Review*, 54: 612–621.

Bollen, Kenneth and Paxton, Pamela (2000) Subjective Measures of Liberal Democracy, *Comparative Political Studies*, 33: 58–86.

Boudon, Raymond (2002) *Déclin de la morale? Déclin des valeurs?* Paris: Presses Universitaires de France.

Casper, Gretchen and Tufis, Claudiu (2002) Correlation versus Interchangeability: The Limited Robustness of Empirical Findings on Democracy Using Highly Correlated Datasets, *Political Analysis*, 11: 196–203.

Dahl, Robert A. (1998) *On Democracy*, New Haven: Yale University Press.

Dahl, Robert A (2001) *How Democratic Is the American Constitution?* New Haven, CT: Yale University Press.

Dahl, Robert A. (2006) *On Political Equality*, New Haven, CT: Yale University Press.

Diamond, Larry and Morlino, Leonardo (eds) (2005) *Assessing the Quality of Democracy*, Baltimore, MD: Johns Hopkins University Press.

Freedom House (annual) *Freedom in the World*, New York: Rowman & Littlefield.

Freedom House (annual) *Press Freedom*, New York: Rowman & Littlefield.

Gambetta, Diego (ed.) (1988) *Trust: Making and Breaking Cooperative Relations*, Oxford: Blackwell.

Inglehart, Ronald, Basañez, Miguel, Díez-Medrano, Jaime, Halman, Loek and Luijkx, Ruud (eds) (2004) *Human Beliefs and Values. A Cross-Cultural Sourcebook Based on the 1999–2002 Values Surveys,* Madrid: Siglo XXI Editores.

Inkeles, Alex (ed.) (1991) *On Measuring Democracy: Its Consequences and Concomitants,* New Brunswick: Transaction.

Klingemann, Hans-Dieter and Fuchs, Dieter (eds) (1995) *Citizens and the State,* Oxford: Oxford University Press.

Lagos, Marta (2003) 'A Road with No Return?' *Journal of Democracy,* 14: 163–172.

Munck, Gerardo L. and Verkuilen, Jay (2002) Conceptualising and Measuring Democracy: Evaluating Alternative Indices, *Comparative Political Studies,* 35: 5–34.

Norris, Pippa (ed.) (1999) *Critical Citizens: Global Support for Democratic Governance,* Oxford: Oxford University Press.

O'Donnell, Guillermo, Vargas Cullel, Jorge and Iazzetta, Osvaldo M. (2004) *The Quality of Democracy: Theory and Applications,* Notre Dame: University of Notre Dame Press.

Offe, Claus (ed.) (2003) *Demokratisierung der Demokratie: Diagnosen und Reformvorschläge,* Frankfurt: Campus.

Okun, Arthur M. (1975) *Equality and Efficiency: The Big Tradeoff,* Washington D.C.: Brookings Institution Press.

O'Neill, Onora (2002) *A Question of Trust,* Cambridge: Cambridge University Press.

Østerud, Øyvind, Engelstad, Fredrik and Selle, Per (2003) *Makten og demokratiet,* Oslo: Gyldendal Akademisk.

Parr, Susan J., Putnam, Robert D. and Dalton, Russel J. (2003) 'A Quarter Century of Declining Confidence', *Journal of Democracy,* 11: 5–25.

Ringen, Stein (2003) Why the British Press is Brilliant, *British Journalism Review,* 14: 31–9.

Ringen, Stein (2004) A Distributional Theory of Economic Democracy, *Democratization,* 11: 18–40.

Ringen, Stein (2007) *What Democracy Is For: On Freedom and Moral Government,* Princeton, PA: Princeton University Press.

Rose, Richard (1994) Postcommunism and the Problem of Trust, *Journal of Democracy,* 5: 18–30.

Sen, Amartya (1999) *Development as Freedom,* Oxford: Oxford University Press.

Siaroff, Alan and Merer, John W. A., (2000) Parliamentary Election Turnout in Europe Since 1990, *World Politics,* 50: 916–927.

UNDP (2002) *Human Development Report 2002,* New York: Oxford University Press.

UNDP (2005) *Human Development Report 2005,* New York.

UNICEF (2005) *League Table of Child Poverty,* Report Card No. 6, Florence: UNICEF International Child Development Centre.

2

LIBERALISM AND DEMOCRACY IN AMERICA TODAY

JOHN SAMPLES

In other times and other places, some have seen politics and democracy as an end to be valued for its own sake. Not participating in politics amounted to falling short of one's telos or purpose in the universe. In a world defined by this "liberty of the ancients," politics is central to life; life outside the polity is hardly a human life at all. Politics represented a realization of the higher self, implicit in human nature, a self far better than the self that has been revealed by choices outside of the political.

New Europeans take after Thomas Hobbes who saw politics and government as a creation of individuals to attain the end of civil peace, itself a means to all other ends desired by the citizens. The instrumental and limited character of politics defines modernity and its most characteristic political theory, liberalism. Politics and government have their uses, but they lie at the margins, not the center, of a life well lived.[1]

The older, more collective ideals have not been abandoned. Some thinkers have understood individual freedom as autonomy or being the master of one's life, a task that leads to demands for social resources equal to the undertaking (see Ringen 2007). Democracy has few critics and many admirers, not least among those people who believe politics remains essential to a life well lived.

Let us imagine that a representative person of the New Europe is called upon to choose a model of politics for his nation. A political model comprises the political institutions and organizations of a society. An institution has been defined as "the rules of a game in a society" or "the humanly devised constraints that shape human interaction" that include "norms and understandings" (see North

1990: 5; Eichengreen 2006: 4). An organization is a "group of individuals bound by some common purpose to achieve objectives"; like institutions, organizations provide a setting for human interaction, in this case, political interaction.[2]

This chapter examines two models of politics—the American and the European. In theory and practice, these models share some features. Both more or less protect private property and more or less rely on market prices to guide economic life. But the two models also differ. The American model developed historically as a strong exemplar of the modern idea of politics and liberty. Apart from the United Kingdom, Europeans value government and collective choice much more than the Americans.

What are the goals by which the New European should judge these models? Normative answers to that question compose much of the Western philosophical tradition. Instead of trying to add to that tradition, an unlikely task, I seek to explicate the primary goals governments actually pursue: liberty, equality, and welfare.

THE AMERICAN MODEL

The Constitution of the United States dates back to 1787. The Constitution both establishes the organization of the government and reflects the norms and understandings that constrain the American politics even today. The original designers of the political institutions of the United States (along with those who opposed ratification of the Constitution) were "sincerely devoted to liberty and a Republican Government."[3]

Liberty
The famous lines from the Declaration of Independence reveal the liberal goals of the first generation of Americans:

> We hold these truths to be self-evident, that *all men are created equal*, that *they are endowed by their Creator with certain unalienable Rights*, that among these are *Life, Liberty and the pursuit of Happiness*. (emphasis added)

The context of this statement indicates that both equality and rights exist before formation of a government. Such equality implies an equality of rights, which are in turn specified (but not limited to) as right to life, liberty, and the pursuit of happiness. All have the same rights, which exclude special power and privileges for individuals or groups. In particular, the equality claim means that neither nature nor God grants authority to some over the others (Zuckert 2002: 213). Even in this situation before formation of a government, the famous words of the Declaration foresee a world of contract, not of status.

At the same time, the rights of the humanity are negative rights. The right to life requires that others, including those who possess the means of political violence, do not take my life from me. The right to liberty requires the forbearance of others, including the public officials. It does not involve a claim against others so that I might be the master of my own life. We have a right to pursue happiness but not a right to be happy, at least not a publicly recognized right to happiness enforceable against the government and other citizens. More generally, we have no right to the salvation of our souls, the ultimate and enduring happiness sought until recently by most people at most times.

The phrase "pursuit of happiness" seems somewhat out of place. John Locke thought the purpose of creating a government was to protect "life, liberty and property." Happiness and property were not thought incompatible in the early United States. Thomas Jefferson, the primary author of the Declaration, subscribed to Locke's theory of property (Zuckert 2002: 221). Declarations of rights in Massachusetts and Virginia also tied together the possession and use of property with seeking and securing happiness (Zuckert 2002: 220). The right to property is also a negative right—other citizens and the government should abstain from making it their own or damaging it in any way. This right implies also the forbearance of others in the use of one's property.

These three rights "amount to the affirmation of a kind of personal sovereignty, rightful control over one's person, actions, and possessions in the service of one's intents and purposes" (Zuckert 2002: 224). Humans have these rights against other people but most importantly, against the government which appeared and appears to be the most credible threat to liberty and a life of one's own.

The Preamble to the U.S. Constitution states that the Constitution seeks "to form a more perfect Union, establish Justice, insure domestic Tranquility, provide for the common defence, promote the general Welfare, and secure the Blessings of Liberty to ourselves and our Posterity." The language is much more capacious than in the Declaration. The words seem to adumbrate larger goals for collective effort and to justify a larger and a more powerful government. The causal reader might think liberty was just one value among many affirmed in the preamble, and the problem of governing was maintaining the most fitting balance among the many ends enshrined in the preamble.

How should we understand the words of the preamble? James Madison proposed amending the preamble to include "a declaration, that all power is originally vested in, and consequently derived from, the people. That Government is instituted and ought to be exercised for the benefit of the people; which consists in the enjoyment of life and liberty, with the right of acquiring and using property, and generally of pursuing and obtaining happiness and safety. That the people have an indubitable, unalienable, and indefeasible right to reform or change their Government, whenever it be found adverse or inadequate to the purposes of its institution."[4] Given Madison's intimate knowledge of the writing of the Constitution, his proposal indicates that the Constitution sought the same goals as the Declaration of Independence or what might be called the liberal goals.

Other evidence indicates the importance of liberty in the American institutions. The Constitution sought to establish a government of "limited and enumerated" powers. The Constitution is a grant of power from the people to a government to protect and secure their rights. If a power is not clearly set out in the Constitution, the government may not legitimately exercise it. From the first, the power of the U.S. government was limited by what the creators of the document chose to leave out. The process, almost as much as the content, of the U.S. Constitution bespeaks its liberal character.

The Constitution was amended early on to include a Bill of Rights. These additions reflected demands from the states that had passed the original constitution. The Constitution eventually was amended to include a Bill of Rights because the original document "did not contain effectual provisions against encroachments on particular rights, and those safeguards which [citizens] have been long accustomed to have interposed between them and the magistrate who exercises the sovereign power."[5] The purpose of the Bill of Rights was "to limit and qualify the powers of Government, by excepting out of the grant of power those cases in which the Government ought not to act, or to act only in a particular mode." The Bill of Rights thus bespeaks a liberal intent to control government and expand liberty.

Republican

> That *to secure these rights*, Governments are instituted among Men, deriving their just powers from the *consent of the governed*,

What kind of government best serves liberty? The Declaration of Independence does not answer this question. Those who wrote (and ratified) the U.S. Constitution considered the new government a republic; indeed, they believed no other form of government "would be reconcileable with the genius of the people of America" (Madison 1961, "Federalist no. 39": 250). They understood a republic to be "a government which derives all its powers directly or indirectly from the great body of the people; and is administered by persons holding their offices during pleasure, for a limited period, or during good behaviour" (ibid., 250). Later, in a similar vein, James Madison would say that a dependence on the people is "the primary control on the government" (Madison, "Federalist no. 51": 349).

No doubt threats to the rights of individuals come from nobles and kings, the traditional opponents of republics. However, government itself also posed a powerful threat to the basic rights. But who or what is "the government?" In setting out the initial amendments to the Constitution, Madison remarked that the Bill of Rights would protect citizens "against the abuse of the Executive power, sometimes against the Legislative, and, in some cases, against the community itself; or, in other words, against the majority in favor of the minority" (ibid.) Indeed, Madison believed "that in a Government modified like this of the United States, the great danger lies rather in the abuse of the community than in the Legislative body. The prescriptions in favor of liberty ought to be levelled against that quarter where the greatest danger lies, namely, that which possesses the highest prerogative of power. But this is not found in either the Executive or Legislative departments of Government, but in the body of the people, operating by the majority against the minority." (Ibid. Similar views can be found in John Adams (1987), *The Founders' Constitution*: 59–60).

It is the people who create a government (including a declaration of rights) to protect their rights, and yet Madison argues that majorities in control of the government are an abiding and perhaps the most potent threat to those rights. Madison believed this paradox could be reconciled through a design of political institutions that would foster a government by the people but not by the majorities—a government that would respect both the rights of its citizens and the "permanent and aggregate interests of the community" (Madison 1961, "Federalist no. 10": 57). Of course, that meant the basic law should recognize the rights of the minorities. But Madison and his peers wanted more than paper protections for rights and the larger interests of the community.

The solution of Madison and his peers was to fragment the government. The society itself is "broken into so many parts, interests, and classes of citizens, that the rights of individuals or of the minority, will be in little danger from interested combinations of the majority" (Madison 1961, "Federalist no. 51": 351). On top of that favorable social fragmentation, the U.S. Constitution creates institutions that complicate forming a political will to act. Representation filters and refines the direct will of the people (or a majority). Moreover, the sheer size of the American republic combined against itself with its social fragmentation make it more difficult for the majorities and their demagogues to trample on the rights of the minorities (Madison 1961, "Federalist no. 10": 64).

The U.S. government is also divided from within. The legislative and executive branches are supposed to struggle with one another. The judiciary is designed to constrain both the competing branches of the U.S. government. Authority is divided yet again between the national government and the states, the latter being a check against a consolidated government. The U.S. government thus relies on a "policy of supplying by opposite and rival interests, the defect of better motives" (Madison 1961, "Federalist no. 51":349).

From the start, the rules of the game and the political organizations in the United States were liberal and republican. Over time, such a government may do less than one that concentrates and facilitates the exercise of power. That relative inactivity may forgo opportunities to benefit its citizens (or at least, some of its citizens). No doubt such losses do occur. But the rights at issue, in regard to the government, require an absence of action to be vindicated. To the extent the U.S. government has acted less than its European counterparts, it has fulfilled the intentions of its designers.

EQUALITY AND PROSPERITY

The liberal republic was procedural. Government protected rights, not least the right to property, and individuals made choices and produced social outcomes validated by individual consent. Government was not empowered to judge or to modify the outcomes so long as no one had violated the rights of others. Yet, as an empirical matter, American government does restrict and regulate the freedom of individuals and not just to prevent or redress the violations of rights. Instead, the government pursues two overarching goals: equality and prosperity. Each of these two goals has its justifications and its difficulties.

Equality
The Declaration of Independence said individuals are created equal and endowed equally with rights against the government and their fellow men. This formal equality now competes in American culture with egalitarianism. Many assume that departures from equality must be justified. In contemporary societies like the United States, the egalitarian argues, inequality comes from natural and social assets, both of which are distributed in a morally arbitrary fashion. The government should seek to improve outcomes for the least advantaged people in the society. The purpose of the political enterprise becomes improving the lot of the poor to meet the demands of justice (Rawls 1971).

This egalitarianism seems at odds with American political culture in many ways. It may demand coercive redistribution of wealth, thereby infringing on the Declaration's rights to liberty and property. I might suggest, however, that the difference between this egalitarianism and American liberalism goes deeper than the question of property rights. The Declaration implies that the relief of the poor lies with individuals and not with the collective power. In a liberal polity, individuals will have the responsibility for meeting whatever obligations to the poor exist.

The actual collective choices of American government indicate a measure of egalitarianism. Means-tested policies account for perhaps $500 billion annually in spending on the poor in the United States.[6] Much of that spending on the poor goes to social services. In recent years, the national legislature has steadily increased subsidies to the poor through a version of the negative income tax— the earned income tax credit. In 2000, this program spent $26 billion, which went out to 55 million individuals (Moffitt 2003: 133–4). The federal income tax rates for the two bottom quintiles are negative. For these income groups, the earned income tax credit and another credit (the refundable child credit) outweigh the income tax that they would otherwise pay (Congressional Budget Office, Historical Effective Tax Rates 1979–2004, December 2006: Summary Table 1).

Marginal income tax rates are also progressive in intent and outcome. In 2004, the effective tax rates for lowest to the highest household income quintiles are as follows:

Lowest quintile 4.5%
Second quintile 10.0%
Middle quintile 13.9%
Fourth quintile 14.2%
Highest quintile 25.1%
Top 1% 31.1%

Overall, tax rates are progressive. Individual income tax rates on the two lowest quintiles are negative. Social insurance taxes are structured the opposite way; the lowest quintile pays about an average effective tax rate for social insurance (ibid).

We turn now to the shares of federal tax liabilities by income group. The lowest quintile bears less than 1% of the federal tax burden. The next 20% pay less than 5% of all taxes. The next income groups pay more: the middle 20% bears 10% of the federal tax burden and the fourth quintile pays more than 17% of the whole federal tax. That means the top 20% pays 67.1% of the cost of the government; one-fifth of the population paid over two-thirds of the cost of the government in 2004. The breakdown within the top quintile is striking. The top 1% of the population pays just over 25% of the total federal tax burden in the United States (ibid., Summary Table 2).

Welfare

Originally Americans had the rights to life, liberty, and the pursuit of happiness. Individuals could define and pursue happiness as they wished, provided they did not infringe on the rights of others. They could pursue wealth through free exchange or a more leisurely life devoted perhaps to family or faith. Over a period of time, the pursuit of happiness has been transformed into the welfare of the individual. That welfare, in turn, has been defined mostly in terms of income and wealth, perhaps because these parameters can be reliably measured. The state has taken on the task of maximizing the welfare of the individual.

No advanced contemporary state assumes the entire responsibility for assuring the welfare of its citizens. Yet, after World War II, developed nations committed themselves to managing the economy in the name of prosperity. In the United States, this commitment became law in the Employment Act of 1946, which accorded Americans the right to have an opportunity to be employed (Santoni 1986: 11). This commitment to welfare continued under Ronald Reagan who saw his proposed budget and tax reforms as a means to national prosperity and not primarily to liberty.[7] This reconciliation of liberty and prosperity has been marked by a retreat from collective efforts to perfect economic life.

Liberalization has been largely accepted in the United States as the means to prosperity. Experience has shown that active intervention by the government has little appeal. Congress proved to be inept at countercyclical policy; budget deficits (most of the time) and surpluses (rarely) had little to do with the business cycle. Congress also had little effective control over much of the national budget. Spending on entitlement programs—pensions for the old and medical care for the elderly and the poor—could be increased but not cut back; total spending became a function of demographics and not a function of the legislative will, disciplined by elections. Only the defense budget and a small portion of overall spending—so-called discretionary spending—could be cut by the Congress. Taxes were both reduced and raised in the post-1980 era, but the revenues rarely matched the spending. Regulations, like much of the spending, have proven to be more a search for deadweight rents than a perfection of failing markets. The older faith in management of the economy by the government has fallen victim to a skepticism created by government failure.

American policymakers have struggled with these failures by reducing the ambit of democracy as a way to liberty and wealth. The management of the overall economy has been delegated to the monetary authority. The Federal Reserve Board neatly summarizes its independence from the elected branches of the U.S. government:

> The seven members of the [Federal Reserve] Board of Governors are nominated by the President of the United States and confirmed by the U.S. Senate...The full term of a Governor is fourteen years; appointments are staggered so that one term expires on January 31 of each even-numbered year...Once appointed, Governors may not be removed from office for their policy views. The lengthy terms and staggered appointments are intended to contribute to the insulation of the Board—and the Federal Reserve System as a whole—from day-to-day political pressures to which it might otherwise be subject.[8]

The president and Congress may appoint but not remove the Federal Reserve's members. In practice, the president and Congress have become guarded even in their criticism of Federal Reserve's policies. The reason for this forbearance is not difficult to discern. Most informed people, not excluding the president and members of Congress, believe that the Federal Reserve's policies and its independence have produced a strong U.S. economy that has largely been free of recessions since 1982. Management of the economy by the government has thus been reduced and depoliticized.

Congress has also delegated its limited powers over the budget to external entities on three occasions since 1980, all in pursuit of controlling government deficits (or government spending, depending on the sponsor) and thereby, achieving better economic outcomes. Two laws—Gramm Rudman Hollings I (1986) and Gramm Rudman II (1987)—established targets for reducing the deficit. If those targets were not met through the ordinary legislative process, officials external to the legislative branch were given the authority to mandate automatic cuts in spending.[9] Congress itself appears to have chosen to vitiate the democratic element in government to achieve better economic policy. In doing so, Congress may have marginally increased liberty by reducing government spending compared to a world without budgetary caps.

How has the pursuit of prosperity changed the liberal republican institutions and organizations of the United States? The legislature was designed to be part of a fragmented system of governance that limited the government by complicating its activities. Certainly those who hoped for a robust management of prosperity by the state saw that fragmentation as a problem. Since 1980, however, those who wished to restrain government spending have also concluded that fragmentation of power and logrolling have increased spending and fostered continual deficits. Moreover, members of Congress themselves thought that the national legislature was too responsive to the beneficiaries of the government programs to restrain spending or cut the deficit (Jacobson 1992: 208–211). The institutional solution has been to concentrate power in the Federal Reserve or in the presidency against a policy background where spending on the largest programs cannot be reduced, come what may.

Wealth and liberty have the greatest weight in the American model, in practice more than in theory. The two are now assumed to be compatible. Equality explicitly matters to few Americans outside the academy, but the practices of the government and the charitable choices of individuals in the United States indicates equality counts for something, though politically not as much as liberty or wealth.

None of this means that individuals are alone or that society is atomistic. It does mean that social life arises from consent and choice rather than an engulfing community that prefers to manage the individual. With that liberty come responsibilities for living a good life and proper conduct toward others. Such proper conduct will range from—at the least recognition of the rights of other individuals to at the most contributing to the success of others.

INTERNATIONAL COMPARISONS

The United States is, of course, not the only model of government on offer today. European nations are different in many respects and the nations of the continent and the Nordic region, are more different from the United States than the nations of the United Kingdom. However, we can usefully consider the European model as a proportional electoral system in which the entire electorate occupies a single district. The legislature elected by these electoral rules then has a wide ambit, especially regarding the regulation and redistribution of property. It is unified with the executive, marginally constrained by the judiciary, and dominant in a federal system (Alesina and Glaeser 2006: 82–83). Compared to the American model, the European model facilitates government activity, especially in doing things that a majority wants done. In the absence of constraints, that majority would generally transfer income from individuals wealthier than the median voter to the bottom half of the income distribution. The European model thus consists of larger governments that tax, regulate, and manage economic life more than in the United States. "The rules of the game" in Europe also include norms and understandings that favor equality of outcome and foster unhappiness with inequality (Alesina et al. 2001). In general, Europeans are more comfortable with the exercise of collective power and compared to the United States accord more weight to state interests than to individual liberty.

Liberty

The framers and ratifiers of the American constitution understood liberty largely as the absence of coercion. Government was needed to protect the rights to life, liberty, and property from others. In the absence of such a threat from the others, liberty existed where government did not act. Given those understandings, we might measure liberty by the actions of government—the larger the government actions, lesser the liberty.

Taxation is a good measure of negative liberty. Among the OECD nations, the United States has a substantially lowest tax burden compared to other countries (OECD 2006). The tax burden in the United States is half that of Sweden and about 60% of the average tax burden in the European Union (EU). The United States also has the lowest level of government spending as a percentage of GNP among developed nations (ibid). A broader index of the size of government tells a similar story. Taking into account government consumption, government enterprises, transfer and subsidies, as well as marginal rates, the United States still has the least intrusive government compared to many European nations (Gwartney and Lawson 2006: 15–17). The same conclusion arises from a measure of microeconomic regulation, in particular, an index of regulations on credit, labor markets, and business in the United States and some European nations although the United States is the second most liberal nation, behind Iceland and just ahead of Canada. The larger economies of Europe are all well above the median score in this regard.[10] The freedom to trade internationally offers an exception to our story of American liberalism since the United States performs relatively poorly compared to Europe. Americans remain somewhat less free on this dimension than Germans and do not compete at all against the likes of Ireland (Gwartney and Lawson 2006: 15–17).

Americans are free in another respect that would astound those who profess democracy as collective liberty. Politics itself is optional: no one is forced to vote, and no one is coercively prevented from voting, provided that they are eligible for the franchise. A skeptic might wonder if this liberty leads to differential rates of turnout along class lines, differences that ultimately lead to less demand for a larger welfare state.

Other measures of individual freedom provide a different assessment of the United States. Stein Ringen has created an index of the quality of democracy and applied it to twenty- five democracies (Ringen 2007: 42 [Chapter 1]). Sweden and Norway have the highest scores; the United States fares poorly. This is not surprising. Ringen believes that democracy requires a great deal of redistribution carried out by an activist government. Defined that way, Scandinavian nations will turn out to be better democracies than the United States. But why should we define democracy in that way (or only in one way)?

To his credit, Ringen offers normative arguments to support the conception of democracy constituting his index. He sees democracy as a means to individual freedom understood in part as negative liberty, the freedom to lead one's life free of coercion from the state and one's fellow citizens. Ringen is both attracted and appalled by negative liberty. He believes individuals are ultimately the best judges of their own well-being. He is appalled because he defines negative liberty as "the liberty to do as one wants without interference or coercion." Ringen then cites Berlin's view that this liberty implies "an idea that freedom comes from more of everything, from ever more rights and ever more abundance." Such freedom is insatiable and destroys the individual that pursues it while "parading an ideology of greed and selfishness to a world of mass poverty, environmental depletion, and cultural antagonism" (Ringen 2007: 204).

Ringen endorses an ideal of positive liberty that embraces the autonomy of the individual. Truly free individuals seek not to do what they want but rather to be the master of their lives. This ideal means everyone should have the resources and arenas they need to exercise their liberty. Ringen's index reflects this autonomy ethic. It could have been called an index of positive liberty especially given the instrumental nature of democracy.

Ringen has not given us an index of democracy based on "Stein Ringen's preferred conception of democracy" or on "a conception of democracy informed by positive liberty." Instead, it is a measure of the quality of democracy in general. Ringen believes that his conception of democracy and its measures have attained general acceptance, but this is not the case. Libertarian doctrines see redistribution as a continual violation of the individual right to property. Such ideas attract support from many, not least in the United States. Libertarian conception of democracy might include measures of redistribution as indicators of rights violations and thus as signs of democratic (or perhaps, liberal democratic) weakness. In the absence of agreement with his underlying normative commitments, Ringen's index cannot claim to be a measure of democracy per se but rather a measure of social democracy (democracy defined inter alia by positive liberty).

We might also wonder whether Ringen is measuring democracy or something else highly correlated with his conception of democracy. The nations that score highest on this index are small and culturally homogenous. In a recent comparison of the U.S. and European welfare states, Alberto Alesina and Edward Glaeser conclude that ethnic conflict reduces spending on social welfare (Alesina and Glaeser 2006: Chapter 6). We would expect culturally homogenous nations to spend more on social welfare than large, diverse nations. Conflating cultural homogeneity and democracy raises questions of construct validity for this index.

Equality

I have argued that the United States redistributes income presumably in pursuit of greater material equality than would exist just from individual choices. The government thus undertakes the enterprise of equality at a cost to liberty and property rights. But the question remains how the United States compares to Europe on this issue.

Personal income tax rates in the United States are de jure progressive, but they are less progressive than they were in the 1970s or in 1981 because the top rates have dropped from 70% (itself a decrease from 90% in the mid-1970s) to just over 39%. The question of how progressive the tax code might be depends on the incidence and progressivity of other taxes. A recent study concludes that the U.S. tax code has become less progressive over the last generation. This change may be accounted for by a decline in corporate taxes and in estate and gift taxes combined with a sharp change in the composition of top incomes away from capital income and toward labor income. The modification of the top statutory tax rates has contributed only modestly to this decline in progressivity. The authors conclude that the U.S. tax system is now less progressive than France's tax code.[11]

Alberto Alesina and Edward Glaeser recently argued that European nations redistribute more to the poor than does the government of the United States (Alesina and Glaeser 2006: 21–33). They conclude that "if one were to be born poor, one would choose to be born in Europe, especially if risk averse." (Alesina and Glaeser 2006: 49). I shall return to this claim. Alesina and Glaeser attribute these differences in part to the European preference for proportional representation in contrast to the American system of fragmented power with judicial review. The logic of this argument is clear: if majorities have plenary power to redistribute, and if the average income is higher than the median income, the median voter will prefer to redistribute from the upper half of the income distribution to the lower half. This preference reflects the greater wealth of the upper half of the income distribution; the median voter would have much less to show for his votes if he proposed taking income from the poor and giving it to the upper half of the income distribution.

This redistribution will continue to the point of optimal predation. In other words, the median voter will redistribute until the necessary taxation to support the redistribution reduces the incentives to work, save, and invest to the point that the recipients of the redistribution could be better off with a lower marginal tax rate on the upper half of the income distribution. Discovering this point of optimal predation would be the central problem in a majoritarian democracy. Indeed, Peter Lindert argues that high-spending welfare states in Europe have carefully considered the effects of taxation on the overall economic growth. These nations favor taxes that are both more progrowth and regressive (Lindert 2004: 31).

Alesina and Glaeser argue that ethnic conflict, primarily between African-Americans and the descendants of European immigrants account for much of the variation between the U.S. and Europe in the rents going to the poor. They note that European nations are ethnically homogenous, which builds support for redistribution; after all, the predatory majority is composed of people with the same ethnic background, and even in the larger society, both the predatory group and their targets are ethnically similar. In Europe, the wealth is transferred from "us" to "us" as it were. The United States is an ethnically heterogeneous society in which the dominant group of European descendents associates poverty with minority groups, primarily African-Americans. The dominant groups are, Alesina and Glaeser conclude, thus less willing to redistribute from "us" to "them" (Alesina and Glaeser: Chapter 6).

In the United States, assistance to the poor is not limited to compulsory redistribution through the government. In 2000, Americans contributed some $190 billion to charities; on a per capita basis, American contribution to charities is almost twelve times the comparable sum for Europe as a whole (Alesina and Glaeser 2006: 44). Five years later, estimated giving to charities equaled $260.28 billion, a real increase of 6.1% (Brown 2006). Moreover, the Independent Sector, a U.S. organization that studies charities, estimates that volunteers donated almost $240 billion in labor to charitable causes in 2000.[12] Together, these outlays are larger than means-tested spending on the poor in the United States. It appears that redistribution by the government may crowd out charitable contributions by private groups and individuals in Europe.

Many consider government redistribution of wealth to be morally praiseworthy or even essential. European nations give money to the poor because their voting rules accord relatively unrestricted power to majorities to redistribute wealth in their societies. The government thus compels the donor to give to the poor. If an act must be freely chosen to be truly moral,[13] it follows that redistribution to the poor in the United States is morally superior to the compulsory provision of income to the poor in Europe. Indeed, it is difficult to see how

European redistributions can be called moral at all. It is simply an expected outcome of majority voting without constitutional protection for property.

European policies favoring redistribution depend on ethnic homogeneity. As globalization goes forward, we would expect labor to become more mobile, leading to more ethnically heterogeneous populations. The nations of the New Europe could expect on average to become more heterogeneous. Selecting institutions that redistribute in pursuit of equality may work for a time, but all things being equal, we would expect such policies either to end or to increase ethnic conflict in the larger society. A society favoring the European model may be called upon in the future to forgo the benefits of globalization to attain social peace. Of course, public opinion may simply stop supporting the European model as a nation, explicitly or implicitly, choosing the benefits of globalization over the goal of equality.

We might address also the question of political equality. It has long been fashionable to claim that the United States is a plutocracy. The word means "government by the wealthy" or "the rule of the wealthy." Critics point to the number of millionaires in the U.S. Senate as evidence of plutocracy (Alber and Kohler in this volume). The authors of the American Constitution sought to protect the minorities from the tyranny of the majorities, not least the minority of property owners from the majorities led by the demagogues. They established such institutional barriers to the will of the majority to protect not the interests of the wealthy but rather the "rights of other citizens and…the permanent and aggregate interests of the community" (Madison 1961, "Federalist no. 10": 57). The Constitution was eventually amended to allow taxation of income at what became a marginal rate of 90%. The courts also refused to protect economic liberties against legislative majorities. The courts did, however, pledge to protect the political process from majoritarian abuses.[14] Even with little constitutional protection for property, the wealthy and business interests might dominate politics. The scholarly evidence we have, however, does not support this claim.

The United States generally allocates votes on the principle of "one person, one vote." Adult citizens with few exceptions have the franchise. How is the vote exercised? Voter turnout is lower in the United States than in most European nations largely because of the salience of elections, the use of compulsory voting and postal voting, and the presence of a highly competitive party system (Franklin 2001: Chapter 10). Americans also vote more often than Europeans (McDonald 2006). Within the United States, income, education, and age also appear to affect the likelihood of voting; in those respects, the sample self-selected on Election Day appears to be older, wealthier, and more educated than the population eligible to vote in the United States (Flanigan and Zingale 1998: 40).

Yet, if everyone voted, the results would not change much. The margin of winners would typically increase. Nonvoters do not differ much from voters in ideology, partisanship, or issue positions (Teixeira 1992: 94–97). In the United States, the richest group of voters has been from 30% to 50% more likely to identify themselves as liberals (that is, supporters of the welfare state). The same is true of education: the most educated Americans are the most likely to identify themselves as liberals.[15] We might also keep in mind that while income and education are correlated to voting, they cannot dominate the process for sheer lack of numbers. In 2000, we can estimate that almost two-thirds of voters were at the 68 percentile of income or below. Just over one-third of those were at the 33 percentile or below.[16]

Critics often say campaign finance in the United States allows the wealthy to dominate politics. In the United States, all of the funding for election campaigns to Congress and most of the funding for presidential campaigns comes from private individuals. Neither businesses nor labor unions are permitted to directly donate to national campaigns, but both may set up organizations to solicit campaign contributions from designated individuals. Such contributions are limited by law and need to be disclosed. Individuals and organizations may also fund as many of the speeches as they wish about political issues at any time including during an election campaign.

Who gives? Scholars recently found that 80% or more of "significant donors" reported an annual family income of over $100,000. The donors are also well-educated with more than one-half holding postgraduate degrees. Compared to the general population, they also tended to be older, male, and white (Wilcox et al. 2003: 65 [Table 4.1]). Because about 18% of all U.S. households earn over $100,000 annually and about 9% of Americans hold an advanced degree, it follows that contributors are not an accurate sample of the U.S. population as a whole.[17] Yet, wealthy people are not monolithically conservative in outlook and Republican in partisanship (Briffault 1999: 563, 575). In 2004, 29% of the wealthy professed liberalism, 19% identified themselves as moderates while 48% professed conservatism.[18] The rich have become much more liberal over the past decade. The median percentage of rich households identifying as liberal from 1972–88 was 16%; the corresponding number for 1990–2000 was 26%. Now the number is 29%. Second, the richest Americans are more liberal than the poorest citizens, a difference that has grown remarkably in recent years. In 2004, the rich were about 31% more likely than the poor to identify as a liberal. Over the longer run, about 17% of the poorest U.S. households have identified themselves as liberal over the past thirty years, while about 21% of the rich professed liberalism.[19] In 2000, 36% of the rich have identified themselves as Democrats, 54% said Republican, and another 10% said they were independents. In the past decade, as many as 41% of the rich have identified themselves as Democrats; the number of Democrats among the rich rose sharply from 1988–96 and declined modestly thereafter.[20] Another 10% in 2000 said they were independent of any party.[21]

Until Election Day 2002, the political parties could raise so-called soft money without limits on contributions. Taken together, those who gave $1 million or more donated just under $137 million. Of that sum, 63% went to the Democratic Party, the party of the left. In 2004, other groups were able to raise contributions not limited by law. Thirty-five of the top fifty of these groups as measured by contributions were affiliated with the Democratic Party. The Democratic affiliates raised about $390 million or 79% of all the fundraising by these groups.[22] In 2004, four individuals gave these Democratic affiliates just over $73 million or just under one-fifth of all the money raised by these groups.[23] During the 2004 presidential campaign, Democrats raised more money than Republicans.

Critics argue that campaign contributions distort the political process in two ways. Money is said to change the position of representatives from the positions they would take if the contribution were not given. It is also purported to change how hard a legislator works for a position he already shares with a contributor. These are the corruption and the access questions.

The corruption question has been extensively studied by scholars. Roll call voting by representatives shows little influence by contributions if a study controls for constituency, party, and ideology (Ansolabehere et al. 2003: 105–130). Critics argue that such studies miss the influence of money because roll call votes are a subset of all voting on bills in Congress. An exhaustive study found that campaign contributions by business had little influence on issues of interest to business as a group (Smith 2000: 126). We also have strong evidence that American politicians rapidly respond to changes in the public mood rather than to business interests (Stimson et al. 1995: 543–565). See also the review of the effective of public opinion on public policy outcomes in Burstein 2003: 29–40.)

The access question suggests contributors influence the priorities of legislators. Two decades ago, a study of four issues found that members did respond to contributions (Hall and Wayman 1990: 797–820). More recently, Gregory Wawro, a political scientist at Columbia University, has studied whether campaign contributions affect legislative entrepreneurship, a concept similar to access (Wawro 2000: 2). Do members provide services (introducing and managing bills, committee work, and voting) to interest groups in exchange for campaign contributions? Wawro collected data about donations and activities by members of Congress from 1984 to 1992. Using a sophisticated analysis that takes into account many factors that affect the work of members of Congress, Wawro concluded that members of Congress do not exchange access for contributions.[24]

Three political scientists devised an experiment to test whether Political Action Committees have better access than constituents to a member's time. Their result was striking: "Contrary to the perception that PACs buy access to legislators at the expense of constituents, these results suggest that constituency is a more important influence on scheduling requests than PAC status" (Chin et al. 2000: 543). Another study found that groups with a PAC do have more contacts with legislators than groups without a PAC because groups with PACs "have an organizational presence in a greater array of districts." For that reason, groups with PACs may have a lobbying advantage but "that advantage derives from their ability to organize effectively in many regions of the country" (Hojackni and Kimball 2001: 176). As one scholar of interest groups notes, "the constituency link remains particularly helpful when trying to gain access to a legislator's office. One can (say conclude) conclude that money may not be the most effective currency when seeking access or lobbying for legislators' votes" (Ainsworth 2002: 199–200).

If money rules in the United States, its face in politics would be the modern corporation. Firms and trade associations are the most frequently found interest groups in Washington (Hart 2004: 50). The concern has been that unity among business interests precludes influence by other parts of society thereby undermining democracy.

The leading study on this topic remains Mark A. Smith's *American Business and Political Power* (2000). Smith collected comprehensive data on the positions of business on public policy as measured by the activities of the U.S. Chamber of Commerce. On the question of business unity and democracy, Smith's conclusions are worth quoting at length:

> Issues marked by a common business position are precisely those for which government decisions are affected most strongly by election outcomes and the responsiveness of officeholders to their constituents. Policies match the collective desires of business only when citizens, through their policy preferences and voting choices, embrace ideas and candidates supportive of what business wants. To bolster its odds of winning in politics, business needs to seek back(ing) from the broader public. (Smith 2000: 8)

On issues where business is unified, policy decisions in the United States are "highly responsive to the preferences and participation of the citizenry." (Smith 2000: 114). Public opinion and elections remain the most potent influences on policies of interest to all businesses. It is vital to recognize that Smith's analysis includes business lobbying and campaign contributions as potential factors explaining policy outcomes.[25]

Smith also examines the hypothesis that business holds sway over democratic politics by withholding the capital needed to finance growth, thereby posing a threat to the incumbent officials. Smith's empirical examination of American lawmaking from 1953 to 1996 provides little support for this hypothesis (Smith 2000: 160–161).

If policymaking follows public opinion (or public opinion as expressed in elections), then business might mold public opinion to its ends, thereby undermining democracy indirectly. Smith finds some evidence that conservative think tanks have affected public opinion. He also notes that such influence is often diluted by think tanks hostile to business interests or other factors molding public opinion. Hence, the affect of business on public opinion is better described as influence rather than domination (Smith 2000: 212–213). Regarding the public sphere and the formation of public opinion, we should also keep in mind that American media lean left in their selection of news and that the university faculty who have considerable influence over opinion formation among elites are almost exclusively to the left politically.[26]

Business interests may influence particular issues. Recent studies suggest that business interests have more power to define the public agenda on environmental policy than the environmental groups do (see Kamieniecki and Kraft 2007: 333). Other studies argue that business groups have considerable influence over agency rulemaking (Webb Yackee and Webb Yackee 2006). But even when Republicans dominated Congress, environmental groups often successfully defended stringent environmental policies (Berry 1999: 110–114). Moreover, a recent, comprehensive study of the influence of business on environmental regulation found that corporations often do not take a position on such legislation and that when business is unified in opposition to environmental bills the public mood tends to be on the opposite side and to have influence on policymaking. The study also reported little influence by business over agency rulemaking (Kamieniecki 2006: 250–251).

The claim that the wealthy dominate American politics offers an example of the fallacy post hoc, ergo propter hoc. If a person believes democracy necessarily leads to a larger European-style state, the relatively small U.S. government demands an explanation. The domination of the American politics by the wealthy offers one. But making sense is not the same as stating the truth. However, a reader might object that the lessened progressivity of taxation in the United States over the past three decades surely proves the domination of the wealthy. Marginal tax rates dropped from 70% to 50% in 1981 and then again to 28% in 1986. The 1981 changes attracted a bipartisan majority. Sen. Bill Bradley, a prominent left-leaning member of Congress, noted: "The 1981 tax law demonstrated clearly that many Americans are concerned about the tax treatment of the wealthy—probably because they hope to be wealthy themselves someday" (Conlan et al. 1990: 38). The 1986 reductions depended on shifting $130 billion in taxes onto corporations, hardly evidence of the domination of the wealthy (White and Wildavsky 1989: 532). But business and the wealthy also lost the political game in the tax increases in 1982 and 1984 as well as with later increases in the marginal rate in 1990 and 1993. When their interests are in conflict, business has never been able to defeat organizations representing recipients of public pensions. The choice between cuts in programs for the poor and higher taxes for business went against the latter in 1982 and 1986 (White and Wildavksy 1989: 552). The wealthy and business interests, rather than dominating American politics, seem on the whole to be far less important to policy outcomes than public opinion and elections.

Prosperity

At the end of World War II, European per capita gross domestic product (GDP) was 42% of the comparable figure for the United States. This measure of

European well-being continuously improved, reaching 80% of the U.S. level by the end of the 1980s. Continued convergence might have been expected, but the opposite has happened: European per-capita GDP now equals 70% of the U.S. number (Alesina and Giavazzi 2006: 4–5). During much of this era, Europeans were working harder than Americans and were just as productive. From the mid-1970s onward, Europeans began to work less on average, but their productivity growth remained strong enough to keep pace with the United States, in part because U.S. productivity declined starting in 1973. In the last ten years, the years of relative decline for Europe, Americans have both worked more and enjoyed higher growth in labor productivity (Alesina and Giavazzi 2006: 55). On a per capita basis, Americans work in the taxed market sector 50% more than do the French (Prescott 2004: 2). In Western Europe, the average annual growth of per capita GNP fell by more than half during 1973–2000 as compared to the 1950–73 period (Eichengreen 2006: 7). We can speak of the earlier period (1950–73) in both Europe and the United States as the golden age of prosperity. In Europe, the later period (1973–2000) may be called a "silver age" of undoubted wealth and doubtful trends. The United States had its problems also during this silver age, but in the last decade, its economic performance became noticeably better than that of Europe.

The golden age of European economic life arose from extensive growth. At first, Europe could grow by simply rebuilding after the war, switching labor into productive uses, and restoring the capital stock. Thereafter growth could continue "by exploiting the backlog of new technologies developed between the two world wars but not yet put to commercial use." Europe responded remarkably to the challenges of the time—the term "miracle" did not seem out of place—in part because of its institutions. Trade unions, employers associations, and managerial governments mobilized savings, financed investments, and stabilized wages consistent with full employment. Various nonmarket institutions—government planning agencies, state holding companies, and industrial conglomerates—got interdependent industries up and running simultaneously. Banks having relationships with their industrial clients provided patient funding to efficiently operate intensive and large-scale technologies (Eichengreen: 2006: Chapter 1).

In time, Europe needed to switch to intensive growth "based on increases in efficiency and internally generated innovation." The institutions of the golden age were not adept at this new challenge, a task that will likely define the future for developed and emerging economies. Financial markets, not banks integrated with firms, proved better at allocating capital in a period of technological change and uncertainty. Trade unions limited the application of new technologies and adaptations to international competition, thereby constraining job creation and increase in productivity. Systems of codetermination hampered efforts to restructure failing industries. State holding companies increasingly became the vehicles of special interests and means to bailout declining industries. The costs of welfare-state benefits and labor market protections increasingly became an obstacle to growth and adaptation (Eichengreen 2006: 9).

Europeans may insist, however, that the recent economic record reflects that their institutions are working well. For example, the declining per capita output may reflect a European preference for leisure over work at some margin. Their political institutions empower them to enforce that preference, but the institutions have little in themselves to do with the outcome. Not only does this analysis suggest that European institutions are working well, it also agrees with a conventional European stereotype: Americans are materialistic and joyless drudges caught on a hedonistic treadmill of their own making. Europeans, in contrast, have made a superior tradeoff between work and leisure, one that leaves them just rich enough to live the good life.

The economist Edward Prescott offers an alternative explanation of labor-leisure choices made by the Europeans and the Americans. Prescott examines national output, labor supply, and productivity statistics relative to the United States for the years 1970–74 and again for 1993–96. He finds that labor supply in the latter period is much higher in the United States and Japan than it is in Germany, France, and Italy. In contrast, during the earlier period, Europeans worked more hours per person than Americans. Prescott concludes that higher tax rates in Europe account for the differences in labor supply. When U.S. and European tax rates were comparable, their labor supplies were also similar. Indeed, Prescott finds the effects of tax rates on labor to be roughly similar across countries. Reductions in tax rates can lead to increases in labor supply. In Spain, a flattening of the income tax schedule led to a 12% increase in labor supply. Indeed, Prescott finds that if France reduced its effective tax rate on labor income from 60% to 40% (the rate in the United States), "the welfare of the French people would increase by 19% in terms of lifetime consumption equivalents." This increase in welfare takes into account the decrease in leisure associated with this change in the tax system (Prescott 2004: 3, 8–9) This welfare gain is remarkably large. It is also not a tradeoff against leisure. French taxes impose a large deadweight welfare loss on the nation.

I do not claim that United States has an unblemished record of liberalism in economic policy. If you examine American policy before 1980, it is evident that the U.S. government was on track to converge with the European median on the relative share of national wealth devoted to the state. Had the earlier trend continued, the United States would now have a government that spends about 39% of GDP (Germany spends about 45% of GDP on government). In fact, in 2005, the U.S. government spent just over 31% of its wealth on the state (Figure 2-1).

Yet there is a difference. The nations of the European model responded to the challenges of economic change by staying as they were. This did not at least mean that people, industries, and nations were protected for a time from unhappy changes brought by the end of the golden age. Those expectations, along with

Figure 2-1 U.S. government spending as a percentage of GDP, actual and trend, 1980 to 2005

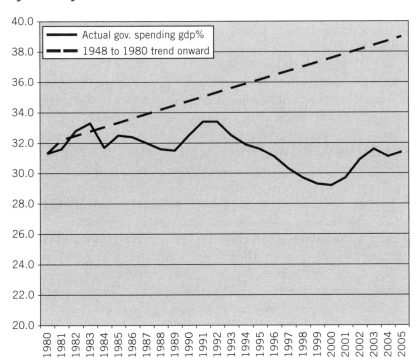

Source: Executive Office of the President, Office of Management and Budget, Budget of the U.S. Government, Historical Tables Fiscal Year 2007, Table 15.3, p. 312 (GPO 2006).

the customary rents created by the older institutions, now complicate or even prevent the liberalizing reforms that might renew European growth.[27]

The United States addressed this challenge by changing. History partially explains this feat. The United States had expanded its government less than Europe prior to 1980; consequently, fewer people benefited from the policy status quo and would fight to maintain it. The persistence of historically large public sector deficits seems also related to the new trend in the size of the American government. The deficits both constrained spending in the 1980s and fostered a budget deal in 1990 that placed caps on spending. Finally, the end of the Cold War permitted a decline in defense spending throughout most of the 1990s. Yet, surpluses arrived, the spending caps went, and the war on terrorism commenced, leading to increases in government spending but not a return to the pre-1980 trend. The political organization of the United States does not explain much about this new trend; Congress, the presidency, and the courts were similar to the organizations that moved the nation toward European levels of spending. The liberal political culture of the United States made a difference. When economic hard times come, a liberal nation tends to see government as the cause of the problems. Liberalizing reforms can garner public support despite efforts to conserve the status quo.

CONCLUSION

The American model began as liberal theory realized as political fact. Over time, American institutions have changed to take some notice of redistribution and to accord greater weight to welfare. But the American model remains notably liberal. This model will not satisfy everyone; no model can. Those who crave collective endeavors or deem politics essential to the good life will disdain the American model; they fail to see that coercion and violence, the means and for some, the appeal of the state, offer more danger than opportunity. Those who live in homogenous societies will be perplexed by the individualism of Americans; they will fail to see its advantages in a nation where the meaning of "we" is not given by ethnic affiliation. The American model at its best is a civil association that provides a rule of law in which people can pursue their gods and their happiness at peace with others. Such aspirations seem compatible with liberty and wealth and even a measure of redistribution for the least advantaged. The American model seems most apt for our globalizing times and for societies that are less a people and more a collection of individuals and groups. It is a model especially apt for the future of the New Europe.

REFERENCES

Adams, John. (1987) *The Founders' Constitution,* Volume 1, Chapter 2, Document 12.

Ainsworth, Scott H. (2002) *Analyzing Interest Groups: Group Influence on People and Policies*, New York: Norton.

Alesina, Alberto and Giavazzi, Francesco (2006) *The Future of Europe: Reform or Decline,* Cambridge, MA: The MIT Press.

Alesina, Alberto and Glaeser, Edward (2006) *Fighting Poverty in the US and Europe: a World of Difference,* New York: Oxford University Press.

Alesina, Alberto., di Tella, Rafael and MacCulloch, Robert (2001) Inequality and Happiness: Are Europeans and Americans Different? NBER Working Paper no. 8198.

Anderson, Martin (1990) *Revolution, the Reagan Legacy,* Stanford: Hoover Institution Press.

Ansolabehere, Stephen., de Figueiredo, John M. and Snyder Jr., James M. (2003) Why is There so Little Money in U.S. Politics?, *Journal of Economic Perspectives*, 17, Winter: 105–130.

Berry, Jeffrey (1999) *The New Liberalism: the Rising Power of Citizen Groups*, Washington, DC: Brookings Institution.

Briffault, Richard (1999) Public Funding and Democratic Elections, *University of Pennsylvania Law Review,* 148: 563–590.

Brown, Melissa S. (ed.) (2006) *Giving USA 2006: The Annual Report on Philanthropy for the Year 2005,* 51st edition, Giving USA Foundation.

Burstein, Paul (2003) The Impact of Public Opinion on Public Policy: A Review and an Agenda, *Political Research Quarterly,* 56: 29–40.

Chin, Michelle L., Bond, Jon R. and Geva, Nehemia (2000) A Foot in the Door: An Experimental Study of PAC and Constituency Influence on Access, *Journal of Politics,* 62: 534–549.

Congressional Budget Office (December 2006) Historical Effective Federal Tax Rates 1979–2004. Online. Available HTTP: <http://www.cbo.gov/doc.cfm?index=7718> (accessed 27 June 2008).

Conlan, Timothy J., Wrightson, Margaret T. and Beam, David R. (1990) *Taxing Choices: The Politics of Tax Reform,* Washington, DC: Congressional Quarterly Press.

Eichengreen, Barry (2006) *The European Economy since 1945: Coordinated Capitalism and Beyond,* Princeton: Princeton University Press.

Farrier, Jasmine (2004) *Passing the Buck,* Lexington, KY: University Press of Kentucky.

Flanigan, William H. and Zingale, Nancy H. (1998) *Political Behavior of the American Electorate,* Washington, DC: Congressional Quarterly Press.

Franklin, Mark N. (2001) The Dynamics of Electoral Participation, in Laurence Leduc, Richard Niemi, and Pippa Norris (eds), *Comparing Democracies 2: Elections and Voting in Global Perspective,* Thousand Oaks CA: Sage, pp. 148–168.

Gregor, Mary (ed.) (1997) *Immanuel Kant: Groundwork of the Metaphysics of Morals.* Trans., Cambridge: Cambridge University Press.

Groseclose Timothy and Milyo, Jeffrey (2005) A Measure of Media Bias, *Quarterly Journal of Economics,* 70: 1191–1237.

Gwartney, James and Lawson, Robert (2006) *Economic Freedom of the World: 2006 Annual Report,* Vancouver: The Fraser Institute.

Hall, Richard L. and Wayman, Frank W. (1990) Buying Time: Moneyed Interests and the Mobilization of Bias in Congressional Committees, *American Political Science Review,* 84: 797–820.

Hart, David M. (2004) "Business" is not an Interest Group: On the Study of Companies in American National Politics, *Annual Review of Political Science,* 7: 47–69.

Hibbing, John and Theiss-Morse, Elizabeth (2002) *Stealth Democracy,* Cambridge: Cambridge University Press.

Hojackni, Marie and Kimball, David (2001) PAC Contributions and Lobbying Contacts in Congressional Committees, *Political Research Quarterly,* 54: 161–180.

Jacobson, Gary C. (1992) *The Politics of Congressional Elections,* 3rd ed., New York: Harper Collins.

Kamieniecki, Sheldon (2006) *Corporate America and Environmental Policy: How Often Does Business Get Its Way?* Stanford, CA: Stanford Law and Politics.

Kamieniecki, Sheldon and Kraft, Michael E. (2007) Conclusions: The Influence of Business on Environmental Politics and Policy, in Sheldon Kamieniecki and Michael E. Kraft (eds), *Business and Environmental Policy: Corporate Interests in the American Political System*, Cambridge, MA: The MIT Press.

Klein, Daniel B. and Stern, Charlotta (2005) Professors and their Politics: The Policy Views of Social Scientists, *Critical Review* 17, 3–4: 257–303.

Kurland, Philip and Lerner, Ralph (2000) *The Founders' Constitution*, Indianapolis: Liberty Fund, Volume 5, Document 11.

Levy, Leonard (2001) *Origins of the Bill of Rights*, New Haven: Yale Nota Bene.

Library of Congress, Congressional Research Service (2001) "Cash and Noncash Benefits for Persons with Limited Income: Eligibility Rules, Recipient and Expenditure Data. FY1998–FY2000"CRS Report RL 31228; November 19.

Lindert, Peter H. (2004) *Growing Public: Social Spending and Economic Growth since the Eighteenth Century*, New York: Cambridge University Press.

Madison, James. *The Founders' Constitution*, Volume 5, Bill of Rights, Document 11.

Madison, James (1961) Federalist no. 10, in Jacob Cooke (ed.) *The Federalist*, Middletown, CT: Wesleyan University Press.

Madison, James (1961) Federalist no. 39, in Jacob Cooke (ed.) *The Federalist*, Middletown, CT: Wesleyan University Press.

Madison, James (1961) Federalist no. 51, in Jacob Cooke (ed.) *The Federalist*, Middletown, CT: Wesleyan University Press.

McDonald, Michael P. (2006) 5 Myths About Turning Out the Vote, *The Washington Post*, Oct. 29.

Moffitt, Robert A. (2003) The Negative Income Tax and the Evolution of U.S. Welfare Policy, *The Journal of Economic Perspectives*, 17(3): 119–140.

North, Douglass (1990) *Institutional Change, and Economic Performance*, Cambridge: Cambridge University Press.

OECD (2006) *OECD in Figures 2006–7 edition*, Paris: OECD Publications.

Piketty, Thomas and Saez, Emmanuel (2007) How Progressive is the U.S. Federal Tax System? A Historical and International Perspective, *The Journal of Economic Perspectives*, 21, Winter: 3–24 (22).

Prescott, Edward C. (2004) Why Do Americans Work So Much More than Europeans? *Federal Reserve Bank of Minneapolis Quarterly Review*, 28, 1: 2–13.

Rawls, John (1971) *A Theory of Justice*, Cambridge: Harvard University Press.

Ringen, Stein (2007) *What Democracy is For: On Freedom and Moral Government*, Princeton NJ: Princeton University Press.

Santoni, Gary J. (November 1986) *The Employment Act of 1946: Some History Notes*, Federal Reserve Bank of St. Louis.

Smith, Mark A. (2000) *American Business and Political Power: Public Opinion, Elections, and Democracy*, Chicago, IL: University of Chicago Press.

Smith, Mark A. (2007) *The Right Talk: How Conservatives Transformed the Great Society into the Economic Society*, Princeton, NJ: Princeton University Press.

Stimson, James A., Mackuen, Michael B and Erikson, Robert S. (1995) 'Dynamic Representation', *The American Political Science Review*, 89, 3: 543–565.

Teixeira, Ruy (1992) *The Disappearing American Voter,* Washington, DC: Brookings Institution.

U.S. Census Bureau (2005) *Statistical Abstract of the United States 2004–05: The National Data Book,* 124th ed., Baton Rouge, LA: Claitor's Law Books and Publishing Division.

Wawro, Gregory (2000) *Legislative Entrepreneurship in the U.S. House of Representatives,* Ann Arbor, MI.: University of Michigan Press.

Webb Yackee, Jason and Webb Yackee, Susan (2006) A Bias toward Business? Assessing Interest Group Influence on the U.S. Bureaucracy, *The Journal of Politics,* 68: 128–139.

White, Joseph and Wildavsky, Aaron (1989) *The Deficit and the Public Interest: The Search for Responsible Budgeting in the 1980s*, Berkeley, CA: University of California Press.

Wilcox, Clyde., Cooper, Alexandra., Francia, Peter, Green, John C., Herrnson, Paul S., Powell, Lynda., Reifler, Jason and Webster, Benjamin A. (2003) With Limits Raised, Who Will Give More? The Impact of BCRA on Individual Donors, in Michael J. Malbin (ed.) *Life After Reform: When the Bipartisan Campaign Reform Act Meets Politics*, Lanham, MD: Rowman and Littlefield.

Zuckert, Michael (2002) *Launching Liberalism,* Lawrence, KS: University Press of Kansas.

SECTION II

POLITICAL INTEGRATION

3

THE INEQUALITY OF ELECTORAL PARTICIPATION IN EUROPE AND AMERICA AND THE POLITICALLY INTEGRATIVE FUNCTIONS OF THE WELFARE STATE

JENS ALBER AND ULRICH KOHLER

CONTRASTING IMAGES OF POLITICAL PARTICIPATION IN EUROPE AND AMERICA: THE IDEAS OF A EUROPEAN SOCIAL MODEL AND OF AMERICAN EXCEPTIONALISM

The Eastern enlargement of the European Union (EU) raised the issue as to what extent the new member states would follow in the policy footsteps of the old member states rather than taking the United States as their role model. Drawing a polemical distinction between "old" and "new Europe", a former U.S.

secretary of defense suggested that the Central and Eastern European countries might adhere more closely to the United States as the superpower that helped end their dependence upon the Soviet Empire. This chapter will examine to what extent patterns of political participation differ between the United States and Europe and where exactly the new member states fit in this comparison.

In a comparative perspective, voter turnout in the United States is notoriously low. Why so many citizens of the oldest democracy in the modern world choose to disenfranchise themselves voluntarily is a question that has puzzled sociologists and political scientists for decades. From a rational choice perspective, going to the polls may appear as irrational behavior, because a single vote counts very little and may not be worth the effort of casting a ballot. But why then do the citizens of European democracies participate so much more frequently—and, as we shall see, so much more equally—in elections? Such questions have occupied a central place in comparative political science research upon which we build here with some new comparative data that focus on the degree of inequality of political participation in old and new member states of the EU as well as in the United States.

Basically, there are two interpretations of the discrepant voting behavior in Europe and America, both of which have normative connotations. From one perspective, which we might call the theory of "American exceptionalism" as first developed by Seymour Martin Lipset (Lipset 1969, 1997; Lipset and Marks 2000), nonvoting is interpreted as not only rational, but also reasonable behavior, which is rooted in certain peculiar features of the American political system, and of the American society, which distinguish the United States from Europe.[1] The other perspective, which we might label as the idea of a "European social model" sees the higher voter turnout in Europe as a result of a higher degree of political integration of the masses which is linked to a more inclusive character of the European state. The "American exceptionalism" school of thought stresses above all the peculiar characteristics of the American political institutions but also points out specific features of American society which promote nonvoting.[2] From this perspective, nonvoting is typical in a *social setting*, which is marked by the following features:

- A high level of well-being and basic satisfaction with the way things are going so that people have more interesting things to do than indulge in politics (Lipset 1969: 217)
- Many cross-pressures—which are typical for an open society with low class barriers, intersecting group affiliations and high rates of social mobility—complicating choice and dampening political emotions (Lipset 1969: 203, 206, 209)
- An active civil society with ample chances for voluntary action, which provide alternative forms of political participation to voting, thus diversifying the channels and chances of political action (Lipset 1969: 67; 1997: 26)

Primarily, however, the "American exceptionalism" perspective links the low voter turnout to specific features of the American *political system*, above all to the peculiarities of the American electoral system, which result in a number of disincentives for voting. From this perspective, the most important institutional impediments to voting are as follows:

- Voting is burdensome requiring a specific act of previous registration (Lipset 1997: 45).
- Elections are held on weekdays so that people must take off from work in order to vote (Lipset 1997: 45).
- There is a plethora of political offices to be filled by elections, which means that there are many diverse channels of political participation that diminish the desire to participate in any one particular way and voters get tired of the recurrent acts of voting (Lipset 1997: 43).
- The federal system of decision-making and the divided form of American government disperse political responsibilities, thus making each single act of voting much less relevant than in more centralized political systems (Lipset 1997: 39–40).
- Politics are less relevant to citizens because the scope of state action is limited, so that crucial decisions structuring people's life chance are basically made in the market sphere (or at least outside the scope of state responsibilities), thus rendering the results of elections comparatively irrelevant (Lipset 1969: 186; 1997: 27).[3]

There is little reason to assume that the American impediments to voting—which all increase the cost of voting relative to the expected benefits—impinge very differently on specific social classes. As Lipset himself observed, "The more cohesive and stable a democratic system is, the more likely it becomes that all segments of the population will react in the same direction to major stimuli" (Lipset 1969: 33).

Lipset refers to two features fostering political integration, which are also highlighted by proponents of the "European social model."[4] First, he notes that electoral turnout reflects the scope of state action or, as he calls it, the degree of "statism," which influences the relevance of government policies (Lipset 1969: 186; 1996: 27). Secondly, he notes that "the combination of a low vote and a relative lack of organization among the lower-status groups means that they will suffer from neglect by the politicians who will be receptive to the wishes of the more privileged, participating, and organized strata" (Lipset 1969: 216–17). This idea very much resembles the notion of a vicious circle, which Piven and Cloward (1988) developed to denote the American political process: The more socially skewed the political participation is, and the less lower-income groups participate in elections, the less incentive there is for politicians to design policies that consider the concerns of lower classes; and the more policies are geared to the articulated interests of the better-off, the more the lower classes become politically alienated and turn away from the political process.[5]

The positive mirror image of this negative scenario is what a political system should look like from the perspective of the European social model: On the input side, all citizens participate (more or less) equally, and political office is not only for the rich who can afford the cost of electoral campaigns, but open for everyone, because the costs of elections are borne to a large extent by the public purse, which distributes public subsidies among the competing parties according to the number of votes they could mobilize. This results in a more representative structure of parliament that reflects the social structure of society without very strong distortions.[6] On the output side, universal welfare state programs incorporate the entire population into schemes, which provide social rights to all citizens at a level generous enough to deter the middle and upper classes from exiting to private solutions. Hence, public welfare is neither fragmented into many categorical schemes—which segment political loyalties—nor bifurcated into specially targeted schemes for a stigmatized poor part of the population on the one side and more generous schemes for the middle classes on the other. In the European social model, public welfare schemes have a dual politically inclusive effect: (1) The welfare schemes foster the political integration of all citizens regardless of income or status, because all citizens have not only the same voting rights but also universal social rights attached to citizenship. (2) Supplementing the market with a second arena for the distribution of life chances, the state not only ameliorates social inequalities in the market sphere, but also gives all citizens—rather than only the rich who are affected by tax cuts or by public investment decisions—an important stake in political decisions thus increasing the salience of politics for everyone. This makes not only for higher levels of political participation, but also for a fairly equal distribution of voter turnout across all social strata.

It is impossible here to subject all these propositions similarly to an empirical test. Based on some new comparative data, we can, however, pursue a set of relevant descriptive and analytical issues. On *descriptive grounds* we can investigate the following aspects:

- How high is the voter turnout in Europe and America, and where do the new member states stand in this respect?
- Is the voter turnout less socially skewed in Europe and how do the old and new member states compare to America?

On *analytical grounds* we will probe the following questions:

- To what extent can cross-national differences in voter turnout be explained by the institutional rules of the electoral game?

- To what extent do we find social inequalities of political participation, which contradict the idea that institutional impediments impinge similarly on all social groups?
- To what extent can cross-national differences in patterns of voter turnout be related to the inclusiveness of the state, and do differences vanish once the impact of welfare state programs is held constant?
- Is nonvoting an indication of political satisfaction and to what extent are its effects counteracted by other forms of political participation?

LEVELS OF ELECTORAL PARTICIPATION IN EUROPE AND AMERICA

Following U.S. official statistics, only one in two Americans bothers to vote in the U.S. presidential elections. Even though representing the highest level since 1968, the official voter turnout in the 2004 presidential election stood at just 56.7% (Federal Election Commission 2005a: 5). A proper understanding of these figures, however, requires a certain familiarity with the intricacies of American electoral statistics.[7] Generally, one expects the voter turnout rate to equal the number of votes cast divided by the eligible electorate. However, the size of the eligible electorate in the United States is difficult to estimate. Using the size of the population at voting age as denominator, the voter turnout rates officially reported by the Federal Election Commission considerably underreport the voter turnout, because the voting age population includes resident aliens who do not have the right to vote.

For a proper comparison of American and European voter turnout rates, it is necessary to use the voter turnout rates that are similarly defined. The United States Election project (http://elections.gmu.edu/; McDonald and Popkin 2001) provides an accurate estimate of the voter turnout rates based on the voting eligible population (VEP), which is defined as the population at voting age that actually holds the rights of citizenship. In Figure 3-1, we compare the average voter turnout during the last three American presidential elections (before 2008) according to this rectified procedure—56%—with the average voter turnout rates in the last three national elections of the European countries. The European data are provided by the International Institute for Democracy and Electoral Assistance (IDEA; http://www.idea.int/index.cfm).[8] The comparison of the American and European figures is based on the assumption that the electoral registers of European countries provide complete lists of the VEP.[9] This seems justified for electoral systems where administrations are responsible for maintaining continuously updated lists of voters, or where the registration for voting is compulsory. To the best of our knowledge, this is the case in all European countries except Ireland and Malta.

Figure 3-1: Voter turnout in the last three national elections (averages)

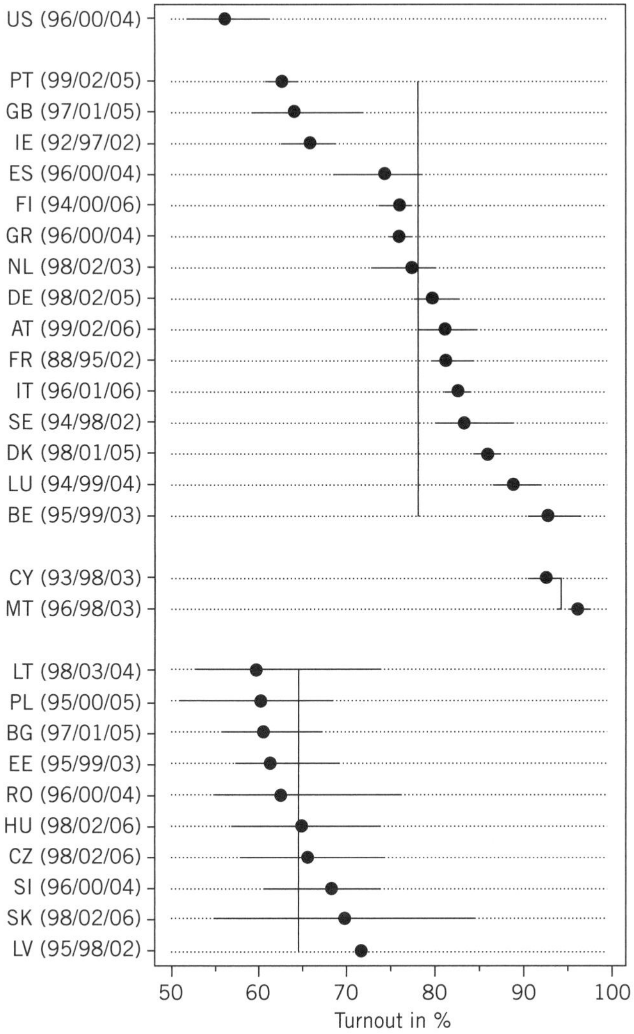

Data Sources: http://www.idea.int/vt/; USA: McDonald/Popkin 2001; and http://elections.gmu.edu/
Country abbreviations according to International Standardization Organization (ISO 3166).

In Figure 3-1, we have divided the European countries into three groups. The first group consists of the fifteen traditional EU member states, which we here refer to as EU-15, "Western Europe," or "old member states." A second group is formed by the new member states of the EU, which had come under communist rule after World War II but joined the EU in 2003 or 2007. These countries will be called "postcommunist new member states" or "transformation countries." Finally there is a group of two further countries—Malta and Cyprus—which belong neither to the old EU nor to the transformation countries and which we grouped together as "Mediterranean periphery countries." To facilitate comparisons between the three European country groups and the United States, we have calculated group averages,[10] which are plotted as vertical lines in the graphs.

The overriding finding illustrated in Figure 3-1 is that the American voter turnout is low by Western European standards, and that the postcommunist new member states are more similar to the United States than to Western Europe. The American voter turnout of 56% compares to an average voter turnout of 78% in Western European countries, and 64% in the transformation countries. Not a single Western European country has voter turnout rates below the American level, and the United Kingdom,[11] Portugal, and Ireland are the only countries to approximate the low American figure. In the case of the postcommunist new member states, the averages based on the three last elections conceal the fact that the voter turnout has recently been shrinking. Averaging 71% in the first election after the transformation, which we covered here, voter turnout has declined to 59% in the most recent one, thus being only slightly above the American voter turnout level.

The question then is how can we explain these differences? Do they reflect differences in the inclusiveness of the state, as proponents of the European social model would suggest, or are they merely the result of different election procedures resulting in voter fatigue, as theorists of "American exceptionalism" would have it? In order to capture the impact of different election systems, we have compiled some key characteristics of the institutional setting in which elections are embedded (Table 3-1). The table lists for each election for which we present comparative voter turnout data: the timing of the event—weekend or workday; the branch of government which was elected—legislative (parliamentary) or executive (presidential); whether voting was compulsory or not; whether registration for voting was an administrative act or required a special individual effort; the type of electoral system that prevailed in each country; the degree of competitiveness of the election; and how many parties held more than 5 % of the seats in the national parliament.[12] What follows is a brief discussion of the likely impact which each of these factors exerts on voter turnout.

Holding elections on a weekend rather than on a workday is frequently assumed to reduce the costs of participation, thus leading to higher turnout rates in countries with weekend elections (Oppenhuis 1995; Lijphart 1997; Franklin 2004).[13] Table 3-1 shows that only four European countries follow the example of the United States in scheduling elections on workdays (United Kingdom, Ireland, the Netherlands, and Denmark).[14] Average voter turnout in these four countries amounted to 73%, which is 17 percentage points higher than the American turnout rate. This suggests that the scheduling of elections alone cannot account for the American turnout gap.

National elections also differ according to the branch of government for which the voters cast their ballot. We here aimed at elections for the legislative branch of the democracy, that is, at elections to the national parliament. Some countries, however, also elect the executive branch (i.e. the president) directly, and we consider presidential elections as a "first-order election" where the president has not merely representative functions but also plays an important role in forming the government or in exercising executive power. This is the case not only in the United States, but also in Finland, France, Lithuania, Poland, and Romania.[15] The three transformation countries with executive elections have lower voter turnout rates than the other postcommunist countries (61% vs. 66%), whereas the two Western European countries with presidential elections do not differ sizably from other EU-15 countries (79% vs. 78%). Hence, the American voter turnout remains low from a European perspective, even if we compare the United States only to the Western European countries with executive elections.

Compulsory voting effectively boosts electoral participation even in countries where noncompliance does not result in specific punishments. Greece, Italy, Luxembourg, Belgium, and Cyprus all have compulsory voting.[16] Average turnout in the four Western European countries with compulsory voting amounted to 85%, compared to 76% in the other old member states. Even if we abstract from countries with compulsory voting, the remaining Western European countries thus have much higher voter turnout than the United States.

The methods of voter registration have an impact on turnout because countries differ with respect to the institutional hurdles they put in front of the citizens. Whereas some countries hold individual citizens responsible to register for elections, so that the initiative rests with the individual, others make public administrations responsible for maintaining lists of eligible voters and for contacting them prior to the election. The more individual initiative is required for registration, the higher is the hurdle or the effort it takes to participate. Comparative data on this crucial difference are rather difficult to obtain. The best source to our knowledge is the expert survey of the "ACE Electoral Knowledge Network" (http://aceproject.org/). Even this source cannot give a clear indication of the cost it takes the voter to get registered in practice. It does, however, provide information as to whether registration lists are obligatory or not. Assuming that countries which do not have obligatory registration put higher responsibilities on individual voters, we take this as a rough proxy for the individual effort required to register. Ireland is the only EU-15 country that resembles the United States in not having compulsory registration and it also stands out for its low electoral turnout.[17] This suggests that differences in registration procedures may indeed account for some of the observed national differences in electoral participation.

With respect to electoral procedures, it is often argued that due to the "winner take all" principle many votes are wasted in countries with majority vote. From this perspective, voter turnout should be higher in proportional systems than in majority systems (Powell 1986; Oppenhuis 1995). Table 3-1 lists which of the

Table 3-1: Institutional Characteristics of Elections

	Average Turnout	Election on Weekend	Electoral Branch	Compulsory Voting	Bureaucratic Registration	Electoral System	Competitiveness	No. of Parties
US (96/00/04)	56	No	Exec.	No	No	FPTP	3	2
PT (99/02/05)	63	Yes	Leg.	No	Yes	List PR	10	4
GB (97/01/05)	64	No	Leg.	No	Yes	FPTP	8	3
IE (92/97/02)	66	No	Leg.	No	No	STV	15	3
ES (96/00/04)	74	Yes	Leg.	No	Yes	List PR	6	2
FI (94/00/06)	76	Yes	Exec.	No	Yes	List PR	5	5
GR (96/00/04)	76	Yes	Leg.	Yes	Yes	List PR	3	2
NL (98/02/03)	77	No	Leg.	No	Yes	List PR	6	6
DE (98/02/05)	80	Yes	Leg.	No	Yes	MMP	3	4
AT (99/02/06)	81	Yes	Leg.	No	Yes	List PR	4	4
FR (88/95/02)	81	Yes	Exec.	No	Yes	TRS	26	3
IT (96/01/06)	83	Yes	Leg.	Yes	Yes	List PR	2	5
SE (94/98/02)	83	Yes	Leg.	No	Yes	List PR	20	6
DK (98/01/05)	86	No	Leg.	No	Yes	List PR	6	6
LU (94/99/04)	89	Yes	Leg.	Yes	Yes	List PR	11	5
BE (95/99/03)	93	Yes	Leg.	Yes	Yes	List PR	2	10

EU-15	78						8	5
CY (93/98/03)	92	Yes	Exec.	Yes	Yes	List PR	5	4
MT (96/98/03)	96	Yes	Leg.	No	No	STV	4	2
Med. Periph	94						5	3
LT (98/03/04)	60	Yes	Exec.	No	Yes	Parallel	5	4
PL (95/00/05)	60	Yes	Exec.	No	Yes	List PR	16	6
BG (97/01/05)	60	Yes	Leg.	No	Yes	List PR	22	4
EE (95/99/03)	61	Yes	Leg.	No	Yes	List PR	8	6
RO (96/00/04)	62	Yes	Exec.	No	Yes	List PR	15	5
HU (98/02/06)	65	Yes	Leg.	No	Yes	MMP	2	2
CZ (98/02/06)	65	Yes	Leg.	No	Yes	List PR	4	4
SI (96/00/04)	68	Yes	Leg.	No	Yes	List PR	15	5
SK (98/02/06)	70	Yes	Leg.	No	Yes	List PR	5	7
LV (95/98/02)	72	Yes	Leg.	No	—	List PR	3	6
NMS-10	64						10	5

two basic types prevails in each country and also gives a more fine-grained differentiation in brackets based on a classification proposed by the International
IDEA. First Past The Post (FPTP) and Two-Round Systems (TRS) are two variants of majority systems. List Proportional Representation (LPR) and Single-
Transferable Vote (STV) are variants of proportional election systems. Finally,
Mixed Member Proportional Systems (MMP) and parallel systems combine
majority and proportional systems, but are counted here as proportional systems.[18] Based on the crude dichotomous distinction, the table provides two central results: (1) In Europe, proportional systems are much more widespread than
majority systems. (2) These systems also tend to have higher rates of voter turnout (79% vs. 73%).[19] A closer analysis of the two Western European countries
with majority systems, that is, France and the United Kingdom, shows that this
cannot fully explain the European–American turnout gap. Despite their similar electoral systems, France and Britain have widely discrepant voter turnout
levels, and participation in France is much higher than in the United States.

The competitiveness of the election is another potential determinant of voter
turnout. If the election result is believed to be narrow, the expected weight of the
individual vote is presumably perceived to be higher. To the extent that rational voters compare the costs and benefits of voting, the expectation of a narrow
election result should thus increase voter turnout (Powell 1986; Jackman 1987;
Kirchgässner 1990; Gray and Caul 2000; for a discrepant assessment see also
Ferejohn and Fiorina 1975). In Table 3-1, the competitiveness of the election is
measured by the absolute difference between the two strongest parties or candidates. The smaller this difference, the closer should be the political battle.
By this yardstick, the results were very narrow in the three recent American
presidential elections as well as in some European elections. A simple bivariate
linear regression analysis of the data shows that the degree of competitiveness
increases voter turnout within each country group. For the Western European
countries, every percentage point of increasing closeness boosts voter turnout by 0.07 percentage points. For Eastern Europe, the respective coefficient
is 0.17 percentage points, and for the two Mediterranean countries it is even at
0.76 percentage points. The predicted voter turnout for a hypothetical Western
European country with the competitiveness level of the United States would be
78%,[20] which is much higher than the observed American level of 56%. Hence,
taking the competitiveness of elections into account would even increase the
gap in voter turnout between Western Europe and the United States.

The last column in Table 3-1 shows how many parties obtained more than 5% of
the vote in the national election. In a multiparty system, small parties are able to tailor their policies to suit the demands of specific groups. Consequently, voter turnout should be higher than in systems with only few parties, which are less able to
appeal to specific voter interests. Table 3-1 shows that the American political system
is essentially a two-party system, while Greece, Spain, Hungary, and Malta are the
only European countries with two-party systems. The United Kingdom, Ireland,

and France are similar in also having only a limited number of parties. Analyzing the relationship between voter turnout and the number of parties by means of bivariate regression shows that multiparty systems tend to have higher turnout. In Western Europe, each additional party increases turnout by 2.8 percentage points, in the postcommunist countries the respective increase amounts to 0.88 percentage points. The predicted value for a Western European country with only two parties is 71%. Even though this is lower than the average voter turnout we actually observe, it is still 15 percentage points higher than the observed American level.

We conclude that none of the institutional factors regarded here can explain the European–American voter turnout gap alone. The question then is if the ensemble of institutional characteristics related to electoral procedures helps to understand differences in turnout. There are two ways to analyze this problem. The first one is to compare the U.S. voter turnout figure only to Western European countries that are institutionally very similar. A simple way to find most similar countries is to count the number of election arrangements in the Western European countries that are different from the United States.[21] Judged by this yardstick, the Western European countries that are most similar to the United States are the United Kingdom, Ireland, and France. All three countries have distinctly higher voter turnout than the United States, although Britain and Ireland stand out for their comparative low levels of voter turnout within the old EU-15. Hence the result is ambiguous, as some but not all of the observed turnout gap between Europe and America can be related to differences in the institutional rules of the game.

A second way to trace the combined impact of institutional regulations is to use a linear regression of voter turnout on all institutional characteristics to predict what turnout level a Western European country would have if it had all the properties of the electoral system of the United States. A hypothetical Western European country with the properties of the American electoral system would have a voter turnout of 63%. Even though this is much lower than the observed Western European average of 78%, it is still several percentage points higher than the actually observed American level of 56%.

To a certain extent, then, our analysis provides empirical support for Lipset's assertion that the low electoral turnout in America must be interpreted as a result of peculiar features of the American electoral system, which lower the incentive to go to the polls. However, these institutional factors cannot account for the entire participation gap. In addition, Lipset assumed that institutional incentives impinge similarly upon all social groups. If all voters are rational actors who similarly weigh the costs and benefits of electoral participation as impinged by institutional impediments for registration on the one side or by the likely impact of one's vote given the closeness of the political competition on the other, we should expect voter turnout to be roughly similar across all social strata. If, on the other hand, voter turnout reflects the inclusiveness of the political system, we should expect American and European voter turnout to be perhaps similar among the higher strata, but different among the lower strata whom we expect to be more politically integrated in Europe due to the more representative shape of the input side of the political process, and the more encompassing and universal welfare state arrangements on the output side. From this perspective, we would also expect a rather low degree of inequality in political participation in Europe, but a high degree of polarization in America where welfare state schemes are less encompassing and more bifurcated with more generous entitlements for the middle classes on the one side and more stingy categorical entitlements for specific lower-class groups on the other (Klass 1985; Glazer 1988), while political representation on the input side is more skewed in favor of the higher-income strata. In short, we expect voter turnout among the higher strata to be similar in Europe and America, while we expect the turnout of lower strata to be higher in the more inclusive European welfare states. The following analysis of the social distribution of voting and nonvoting examine to what extent the data bear out these expectations.

THE SOCIAL INEQUALITY OF ELECTORAL PARTICIPATION

Voter turnout rates may be low because all groups of a society abstain similarly from voting, or because specific groups fail to participate. Our first empirical question thus is if the European–American turnout gap is the same throughout all social groups or if it systematically varies by social class. In other words, we ask which of the groups produce the observed gap—those at the bottom, at the top, or at the middle of the income and skill distribution.

Voter Turnout in Different Social Groups

A comparison of the social stratification of voter turnout has to rely on surveys. These surveys should fulfill a number of conditions. First, and most obviously, they must contain reliable measures of electoral participation and of socio-economic position. Second, the samples should cover at least the entire eligible population of each country; or, if more than the eligible population is covered, there must be information that allows us to restrict the analysis to potentially eligible voters. Finally, all data should be measured in comparable ways throughout all countries under observation. Unfortunately, there is not a single survey that meets all these conditions. The two international comparative survey programs that come close to meeting all standards—the International Social Survey Programme (ISSP) and the Comparative Study of Elections Systems (CSES)—both have only incomplete coverage of European countries. The only survey program with a complete coverage of all EU member states is the "European Quality of Life Survey" (EQLS), which does not include the United States. The European Social Survey (ESS) offers high-quality data for a broad, yet incomplete, set of European countries, and also fails to include the

Table 3-2: Turnout by Social Class (Numbers Represent Average Results of Different Surveys)

	No. of Surveys	Income			Education		
		1st Quint.	2nd–4th Quint.	5th Quint.	Low	Inter-mediate	High
US	4	55	72	83	46	69	86
AT	5	78	85	91	78	85	91
BE	5	89	91	94	88	90	93
DE	7	81	89	93	77	90	95
DK	5	91	94	95	89	94	96
ES	7	82	83	84	83	79	85
FI	5	72	80	89	77	77	88
FR	5	73	79	84	80	76	80
GB	5	67	72	74	74	69	75
GR	3	91	91	91	92	88	91
IE	5	77	82	82	80	79	84
IT	2	86	93	92	88	94	95
LU	3	62	79	84	70	79	77
NL	7	84	90	91	84	90	94
PT	7	74	74	80	74	72	80
SE	7	83	89	94	86	85	93
EU-15		79	85	88	81	83	88
CY	3	95	93	98	98	88	95
MT	1	99	97	92	100	96	98
Med.Periph		97	95	95	99	92	97
BG	3	72	78	77	77	73	82
CZ	7	58	68	71	57	67	82
EE	2	56	68	78	54	63	78
HU	7	73	81	87	74	86	94
LT	1	84	87	84	85	84	92
LV	3	73	77	83	64	75	89
PL	7	57	66	71	57	70	78
RO	1	91	89	88	92	89	89
SI	5	75	81	84	75	78	85
SK	4	74	84	83	74	83	88
NMS-10		71	78	81	71	77	86

United States. In all these survey programs, nonvoters are underrepresented, either because of a systematic undercoverage of nonvoters, or because social desirability considerations affect the answering behavior.

Using averages of all available suitable surveys, Table 3-2 shows how voter turnout varies by income and education. The data columns 2–4 give the percentage of voters in the lowest, middle, and highest income quintiles (based on equivalent disposable household income), and the columns 5–7 show the respective figures for people at three different levels of education.

The overall result is that the higher social strata tend to participate very similarly in all countries. The participation of the lower social strata varies widely, however, being much higher in Europe than in America. With respect to income, turnout of those in the top income quintile is 83% in the United States, compared to 88% in Western Europe and 81% in the postcommunist countries. In the lowest income quintile, only 55% go to the polls in America, while turnout in Europe stands at 79% in the EU-15 and at 71% in the new member states of Eastern Europe. The Czech Republic, Estonia, and Poland are the only countries where the lower strata abstain from voting to a degree similar to the United States. The same pattern results with respect to education. Among those with the highest educational degree, the American voter turnout rate of 86% is very similar to the average voter turnout rate of highly educated people in Western Europe (88%) or in the ten Eastern European new member states (86%). Vast differences in voter turnout rates appear among those with little schooling. Whereas only 46% of poorly educated Americans go to the polls, the respective figures for their European peers are 81% in Western Europe and 71% in the transformation countries. The United States thus stands out for its remarkably high inequality of electoral participation.

It is beyond the scope of this chapter to examine what policy consequences result from the differences in political participation in Europe and America. We must assume, however, that the actual voters form—together with the masters of investment decisions who can resort to the *exit* rather than the *voice* mechanism of political influence—the relevant reference group for politicians who seek office or reelection. The fact that voting is so much more socially skewed in America than in Europe means that the median voter in European countries resides at a much lower point in the social structure than the median voter in the United States. In order to rally half of the electorate behind them, European politicians must thus dig much further down in the structure of social inequality than the political elites in America. As Figure 3-2 shows, the average income position of American voters is higher than in any European country. If they want to win elections, European politicians must thus tailor their policies more to the concerns of lower strata than their American counterparts who can afford to be more receptive to "the wishes of the more privileged, participating, and organized strata," as Lipset (1969: 216) put it.

The question then is why the political participation is so much less skewed in Europe. In the next two sections we investigate to what extent the more equal distribution of electoral participation in Europe may be related to the higher inclusiveness of the European state(s).

The Inequality of Electoral Participation and the Inclusiveness of the State

Based on Table 3-2 in the previous section, the dots in Figure 3-3 show the voter turnout gap, which separates higher and lower social strata (calculated as the simple difference in turnout). In order to capture the variability of survey results, the figure also displays horizontal lines showing how far the results of

Figure 3-2: The average position of voters in the national income distribution

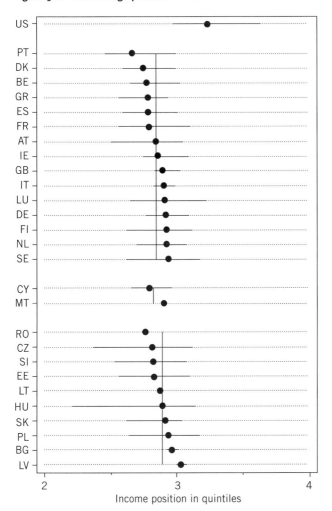

Income position in quintiles

Data Sources: CSES I, CSES II, ISSP '04, ISSP '02, ESS '02, ESS '04, EQLS '03.

different surveys are apart. The longer these lines are, the more insecurity there is in our knowledge of the degree of polarization in a given country. However, the major finding of the previous section is clearly reiterated—turnout inequality is higher in the United States than in any other country under observation. Judged from data of four different surveys (ISSP 2002, ISSP 2004, CSES I, CSES II), electoral participation in the highest American income quintile is between 22 and 35 percentage points higher than in the lowest income quintile. For Western Europe, the gap is less than 10 percentage points on average, and Finland is the only country for which we find at least one survey that produces a gap of a magnitude similar to the United States.[22] Even the Eastern European

Figure 3-3: The inequality of electoral participation in the dimensions of income and education

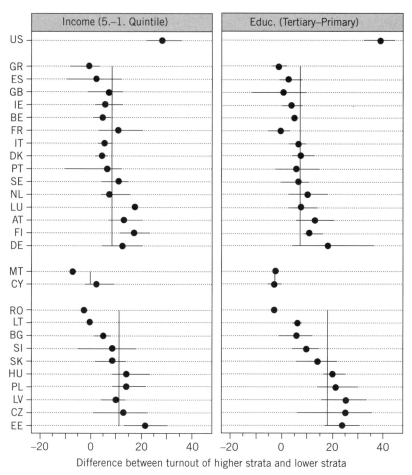

Difference between turnout of higher strata and lower strata

Data Sources: CSES I, CSES II, ISSP '04, ISSP '02, ESS '02, ESS '04, EQLS '03.

countries, which stood out for their comparatively low overall turnout, do not reach the American level of inequality in electoral participation.

If Lipset's assumption that all segments of the population will react similarly to major stimuli in cohesive and stable democratic systems is right (Lipset 1969: 33), the remarkable social inequality in voting cannot be attributed to the impact of institutional settings. Conceptually, there is little reason to assume that institutional hurdles impinge very differently on specific social groups; empirically, there is no statistical association. As the example of the Eastern European countries shows, low overall voter turnout need not necessarily translate into high inequality of electoral behavior. Moreover, those Western European countries which are institutionally most similar to the United States—France, Ireland, and the United

Kingdom—do not show a comparable level of turnout polarization. In fact, these countries even show relatively small inequality of electoral participation. A more formal statistical comparison of the degree of polarization in America and Western Europe also reveals the extraordinarily high degree of inequality in America. If we insert a hypothetical country with the same institutional characteristics as the United States into the regression for Western European nations, we statistically predict a gap of 9.5 percentage points, whereas the actually observed difference in the United States is 33 percentage points.[23] Hence, institutional features of the election system may travel a certain distance in explaining cross-national differences in overall turnout, but they cannot explain why turnout is so much more unequal in the United States than in Europe.

Proponents of the European social model would relate the differences to the greater inclusiveness of the state in Europe. In order to test this hypothesis, we have compiled some indicators that tap state characteristics on the output side of the political process. These indicators are presented in Table 3-3, together with a summary measure of the degree of inequality expressed as the average of the two results for income and education differentials. For the input side, for which there are few comparable data, we can only trace if political parties get direct or indirect state support for the funding of election campaigns.[24] For the output side, we have used two indicators which capture the scope of the tax and welfare state, (a) total tax revenues expressed as a percentage of gross domestic product (GDP), and (b) the social expenditure ratio, expressed in gross and net terms (Adema and Ladaique 2005).[25] The more public funding there is for elections, the less effective campaigning is confined to candidates or parties who can mobilize huge sums of private money, and the more widespread appeal there probably is to voters from all social strata. On the output side, we would expect more universal welfare states—which have more encompassing social programs that provide benefits to all citizens free of stigma—to appeal to all social strata similarly. Even though it is only a very crude measure, the gross social expenditure ratio is used here as a proxy for more inclusive welfare states. The effect of the net social expenditure ratio, which also includes voluntary welfare programs and taxation, should be less straightforward, because the benefits thus defined are distributed less equally or come as employment-related entitlements and thus incorporate the lower classes less effectively into the political order.

With respect to campaign financing, the United States stands out as a country that limits its scarce public funding to presidential elections.[26] It is also the country with the highest degree of electoral inequality. Further, cross-national analysis is impeded by the fact that all European countries have varieties of more or less generous public funding, but more precise comparative information on the quantity of public funding is lacking.

Statistical comparisons with respect to the output side of state action are possible, because social expenditure ratios do show considerable cross-national variation. The American gross social expenditure ratio of 15% compares to an

Table 3-3: Overall Polarization and Indicators for Inclusiveness

	Electoral Polarization	Social Expenditure (Gross) as % of GDP	Social Expenditure (Net) as % of GDP	Total Tax Revenue as % of GDP
US	34	15	23	26
GR	−1	25		35
ES	3	20	17	35
GB	4	24	23	36
FR	5	30	27	43
BE	5	27	23	45
IE	5	15	12	30
PT	6	23		34
IT	6	25	22	41
DK	6	30	22	49
SE	9	31	26	50
NL	9	25	22	38
LU	12	22		38
AT	13	28	22	43
FI	14	26	20	44
DE	15	28	28	35
EU-15	7.4	25	22	40
MT	−4	19		
CY	0	18		
Med. Periph.	−2	19		
RO	−3			
LT	3	13		
BG	5			
SI	9	24		
SK	11	18	17	30
HU	17	20		38
PL	18	22		34
LV	18	13		
CZ	19	20	18	38
EE	23	13		
NMS-10	12	18	18	35

average of 25% in Western Europe and to a mean slightly below 20% in the transformation countries. In this sense, the higher degree of polarization may be related to different scopes of welfare arrangements. However, there is also considerable variation within Europe. Figure 3-4 presents an analysis of the association between social expenditure ratios and the inequality in voter turn-out. Country groups are plotted with different marker symbols in the scatter plots of the figure, and a nonparametric regression line[27] illustrates the relation-ship between the two variables for each group. The result is that there is hardly any statistical association. In Western Europe, electoral inequality stays more or less the same regardless of the level of gross social expenditure. In Eastern Europe, there is some indication for a higher polarization in countries with less

Figure 3-4: The inequality of electoral participation in countries with different scopes of state action

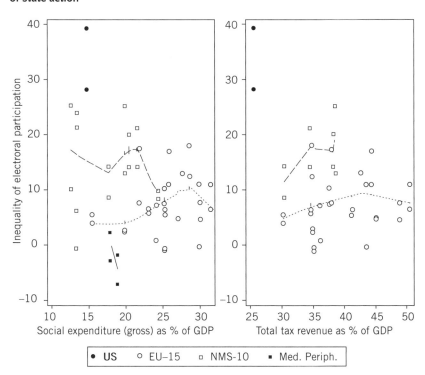

Data Sources: CSES, ISSP, ESS, EQLS (inequality of electoral participation); OECD, Eurostat (Indicators of scope of state action).

developed welfare states. However, the degree of electoral inequality is much lower in these countries than in the United States despite the fact that some of them have similarly low levels of social spending.

Practically the same finding results if we measure the scope of state action by the revenue share in the GDP. While the United States does have a lower revenue ratio than any European country for which we have data, there is considerable variation within Europe, which is not associated with the degree of inequality in electoral participation. Neither of the other two indicators for inclusiveness— the net social expenditure ratio and the pension expenditure ratio—show the United States to have exceptional values, nor do these measures correlate with the inequality of electoral participation within the country groups.

With respect to the majority of the indicators shown in Table 3-3, the United States appears as having a less encompassing state than the European countries. However, as long as we lack a European country with a similarly low scope of state action, we cannot really test whether it is the inclusiveness of the state that produces the patterns in electoral participation, or rather some other factor. If we put both indicators of the scope of state activities—that is, the gross social expenditure ratio and the revenue share—together into a multiple regression, the American pattern of electoral behavior is not explained by the data. A hypothetical Western European country with as limited a welfare state as the United States would have a statistically predicted voter turnout inequality of 3.7 percentage points, while the observed American gap is actually 34 percentage points.

The macrocomparisons based on crude indicators of state action thus fail to provide convincing evidence for the hypothesis that universal welfare state programs and a more inclusive state foster the political integration of all citizens. However, there is also a possibility to test the hypothesis with reference to microcomparisons of various groups of respondents within countries. If encompassing welfare states are more politically inclusive, thus leading to a lower degree of turnout inequality, we would expect the European–American differences to vanish among population groups for which the welfare state arrangements on both sides of the Atlantic are rather similar.

The Inequality of Electoral Participation among Pensioners

The United States has an encompassing social security scheme providing similarly universal and fairly generous benefits as European pension schemes in old age, as well as a Medicare scheme providing public health to the pensioner generation. Hence we should expect the population above retirement age in America to display a much less socially skewed pattern of electoral participation and to become more similar to their European peers than the younger generation.[28] In Europe, in contrast, we would not expect the degree of electoral polarization to vary sizably between age groups as all age-cohorts are similarly incorporated into welfare state schemes.

Figure 3-5 compares the turnout inequality within the pensioner generation—that is, respondents who are 65 years of age and older—to the turnout of people at prime working age of 30–64 years (excluding the group of youngest voters who generally stand out for their low voter turnout). The dots show the level of inequality for the younger age group, while the arrows point to the electoral polarization among the elderly.

Results in Figure 3-5 show that the degree of electoral inequality is much smaller for pensioners in the United States, whereas older and younger cohorts in Europe do not differ much in their degrees of polarization. Concerning the inequality with respect to education, there are only three European countries—Austria, Germany, and Latvia—that approximate the American pattern. Concerning the polarization with respect to income, only four other countries—France, Luxembourg, Slovakia, and Czech Republic—display a tendency similar to the United States. Hence, the United States is the only country for which we consistently find lower voter turnout inequality in the pensioner generation than in the working-age generation, regardless of which dimension of social inequality is examined. This also implies that the degree of electoral

Figure 3-5: Turnout inequality in the pensioner generation and the younger generation

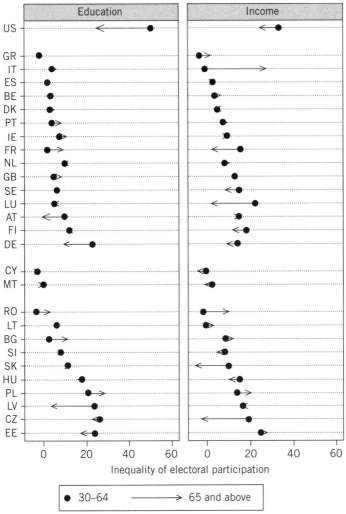

Data Sources: CSES I, CSES II, ISSP '04, ISSP '02, ESS '02, ESS '04, EQLS '03.

inequality among old Americans is more similar to Western European standards than among the young who are not similarly attached to universal welfare programs in America. The differences between Europe and America do not vanish completely among the elderly population. Yet a difference of 42 percentage points among the younger age groups is reduced to a gap of merely 25 points in the pensioner generation who are similarly incorporated into welfare state schemes as their peers on the other side of the Atlantic. This sustains our impression that more inclusive state institutions foster political integration with more widespread and less socially skewed electoral participation.

THE MEANING OF NONVOTING

Voting can only be interpreted as an indication of successful political integration if it can be demonstrated that nonvoters are politically more alienated than
voters, and that nonvoters also resort less frequently to other forms of political
participation so that abstention from the act of voting is not compensated by
other and perhaps even more engaging forms of political action. Hence, we will
examine: (a) if voting is associated with political satisfaction or rather coupled
with dissatisfaction, and (b) to what degree voting goes together with or is an
alternative to other forms of political engagement.

To what extent can nonvoting be interpreted as a sign of satisfaction with the
political status quo, which induces people to indulge in more interesting things
than voting? On the macro level, we find that low rates of electoral turnout
are not a typical characteristic of more affluent nations. In Europe, turnout is
high in rich countries like Denmark, Sweden, or the Netherlands, but relatively
low in the poorer countries of Central Eastern Europe and of Southern Europe.
On the individual level, we can examine more directly if political satisfaction
breeds voting or abstention from the polls. Based on data from the two CSES
modules, the ESS of the years 2002 and 2004, and the ISSP of 2004, Figure 3-6
shows the difference in the electoral participation of people who are politically
satisfied with the way democracy works in their country and those who are
not,[29] controlling for gender, age, household income, and employment status.
The result of this analysis is that politically satisfied citizens are more likely to
go to the polls than those who are dissatisfied. Hence it is not true that satisfied
people have more interesting things to do than indulge in politics. By participating in elections, politically satisfied people apparently express their loyalty
to the prevailing political order, while more alienated people abstain from voting. This sustains our notion that high voter turnout may be interpreted as a
sign of successful political integration.

The question then is to what extent nonvoting is compensated by other forms
of lawful political action. Figure 3-7 shows the proportion of respondents who
had contacted a politician in the last year, who worked together with other
people in an activity group, or who participated in a protest march or demonstration in the previous year. Two results stand out. First, Americans contact
politicians more frequently than Europeans and while shying away from participation in a protest march they are also more likely to work together with other
people in activity groups.[30] A closer look reveals, however, that these alternative forms of participation are distributed just as unequally as the act of voting.
Rich and better-educated citizens contact politicians more frequently, they also
engage in activity groups more often, and they are also more likely to take part
in demonstrations than poor or lower-educated people. Analyses not shown
here for reasons of space reveal that the inequality of these alternative forms
of political participation is higher in the United States than in the European

Figure 3-6: The difference in turnout of politically satisfied and dissatisfied groups

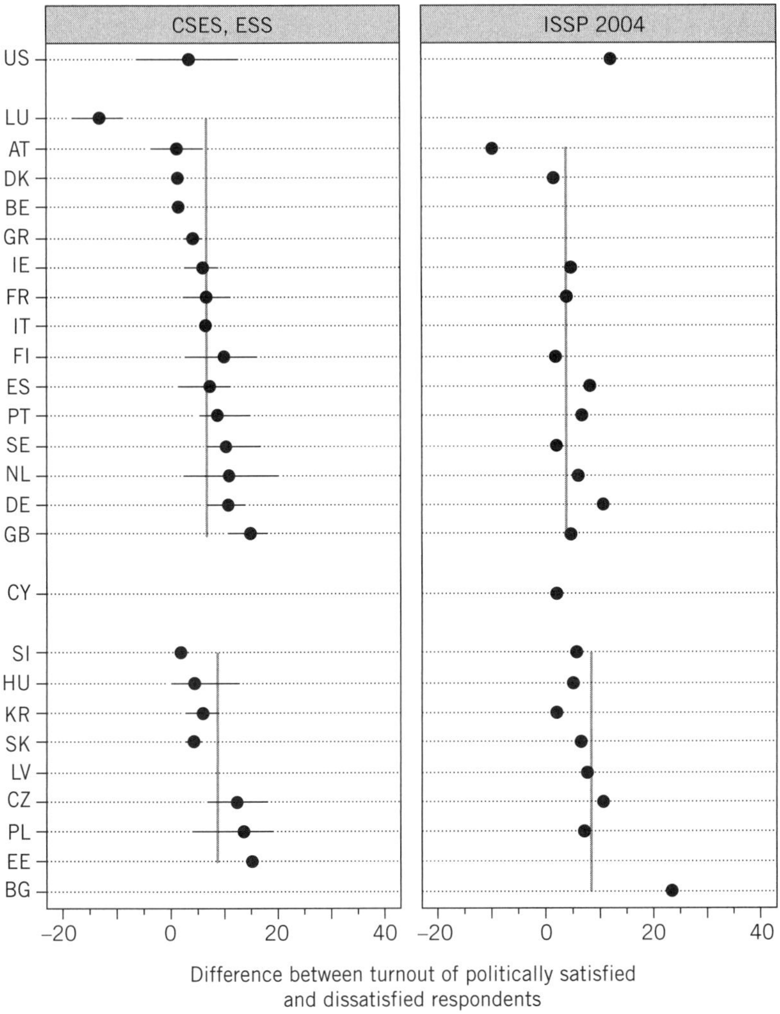

Difference between turnout of politically satisfied
and dissatisfied respondents

Data Sources: CSES I, CSES II, ESS '02, ESS '04, ISSP '04.

countries. However, the crucial finding from our perspective is that nonvoters use alternative forms of political behavior less frequently than voters.

Figure 3-8 shows to what extent the fraction of political activists among voters differs from the fraction of political participants among nonvoters. It reveals that in practically all countries voters engage more frequently in other forms of political action than nonvoters. Obviously, different forms of political participation feed on each other rather than serving as substitutes. However, the other forms of political participation are also more socially skewed in America than in Europe. Hence the high inequality in political involvement in America is not

Figure 3-7: Participation rates in alternative forms of political action

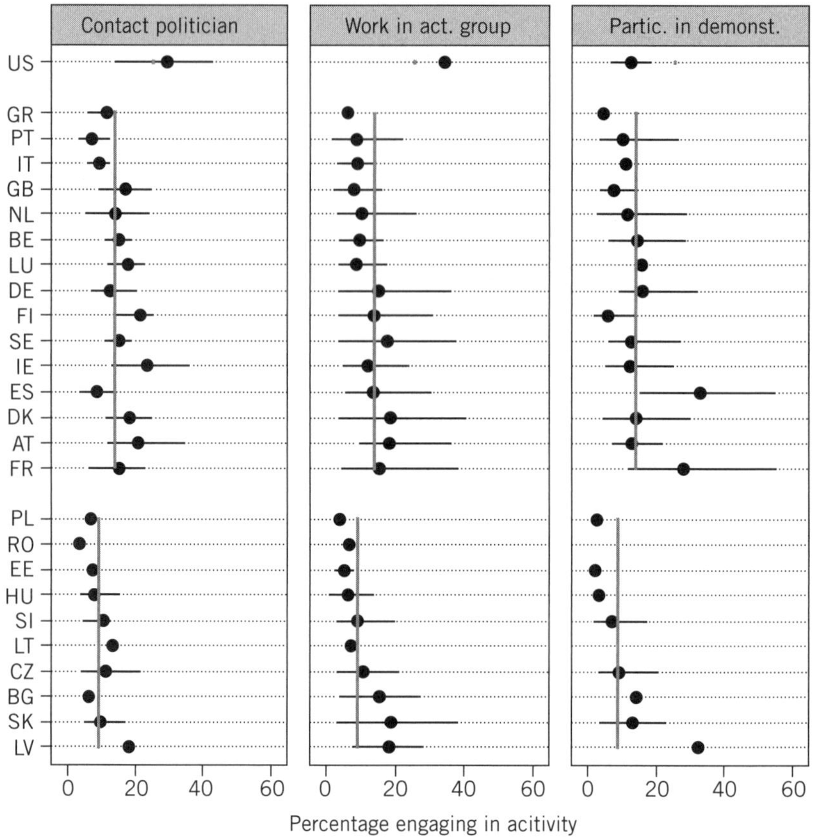

Percentage engaging in acitivity

Data Sources: CSES I, CSES II, ESS '02, ESS '04, EQLS '03, ISSP '04.

confined to the act of voting but extends to other forms of political engagement as well. In this sense, inequalities of political participation reinforce rather than compensate each other in the United States.

CONCLUSIONS

We have shown that electoral turnout is higher and less socially skewed in Western Europe than in the United States. The differences in the levels of turnout can partly be related to differences in election procedures, but since election procedures provide similar incentives or disincentives to all social groups they cannot explain the much higher inequality of electoral participation in America. There is some evidence to sustain the notion that the higher inclusiveness of the (Western) European State(s) fosters political integration and the

Figure 3-8: Participation in alternative forms of political action among voters and nonvoters

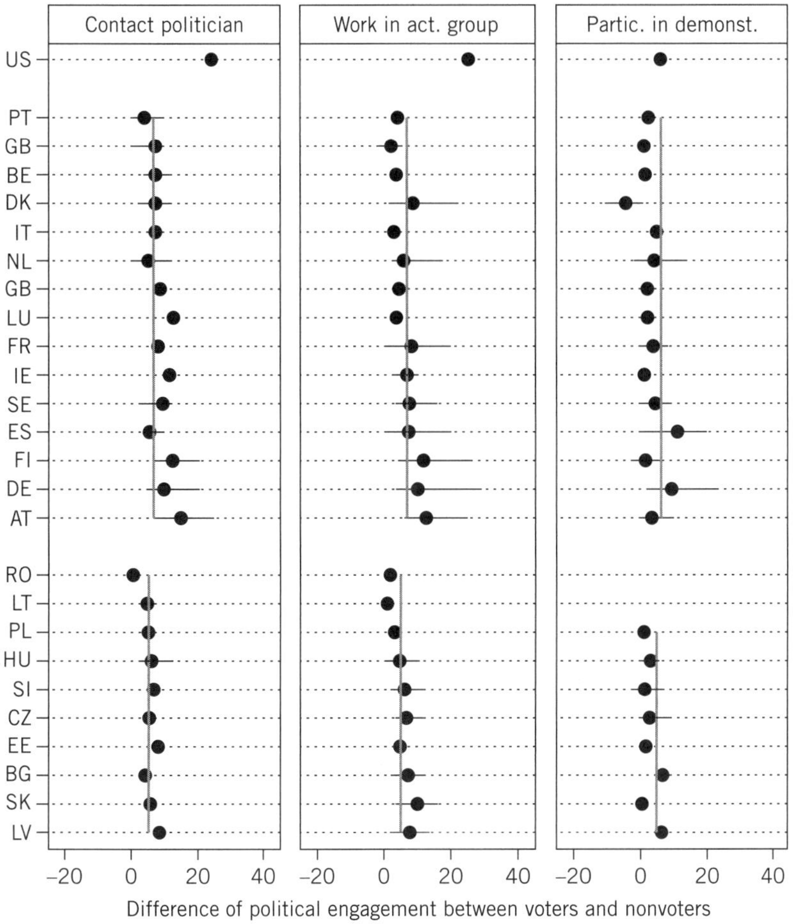

Difference of political engagement between voters and nonvoters

Data Sources: CSES I, CSES II, ESS '02, ESS '04, EQLS '03, ISSP '04.

equality of electoral participation. In line with this notion, differences between Europe and America diminish considerably when the analysis is confined to the pensioner generation whose integration into welfare state schemes is largely similar on both sides of the Atlantic.

In many respects, the new member states of the EU stand at the crossroads between the two poles represented by the United States and Western Europe. While the level of voter turnout is rather low and has been shrinking in recent years in the new member states, the inequality of electoral participation is still much lower than in the United States. It is up to national policy makers of the new member states to decide which of the two rather distinct models of political participation in democracies they find more appealing for their countries.

However, they should be aware of the political implications of their choices. If the aim is to foster widespread political participation and to give citizens across all social strata similar weight in the political process, then there are reasons to follow the Western European rather than the American variety of democracy.

REFERENCES

Alber, Jens (2000) Warum die meisten amerikaner nicht wählen, einige aber doch, *Leviathan*, 28, 3: 319–342.

Adema, Willem and Ladaique, Maxime (2005) *Net Social Expenditure, 2005 Edition—More Comprehensive Measures of Social Support*, Paris: OECD. Available online at: <http://www.oecd.org/dataoecd/56/2/35632106.pdf> (accessed 13 July 2008).

Bennet, Stephen E. and Resnick, David (1990) The Implications of Nonvoting for Democracy in the United States, *American Journal of Political Science*, 34, 3: 771–802.

Best, Heinrich (2007) New Challenges, New Elites? Changes in the Recruitment and Career Patterns of European Representative Elites, *Comparative Sociology*, 6, 1–2: 85–113.

Best, Heinrich and Cotta, Maurizio (eds) (2000) *Parliamentary Representatives in Europe 1848–2000. Legislative Recruitment and Careers in Eleven European Countries*, Oxford, UK: Oxford University Press.

Campbell, Andrea Louise (2002) Self-Interest, Social Security, and the Distinctive Participation Patterns of Senior Citizens, *The American Political Science Review*, 96, 3: 565–574.

Campbell, Andrea Louise (2003) Participatory Reactions to Policy Threats: Senior Citizens and the Defense of Social Security and Medicare, *Political Behavior*, 25, 1: 29–49.

Cleveland, William S. (1979) Robust Locally Weighted Regression and Smoothing Scatterplots, *Journal of the American Statistical Association*, 74, 368: 829–836.

Corrado, Anthony (2005a) Money and Politics: A History of Federal Campaign Finance Law, in Anthony Corrado, Thomas E. Mann, Daniel R. Ortiz, Trevor Potter, and Frank J. Sorauf (eds) *The New Campaign Finance Sourcebook*, Washington, DC: Brookings Institution Press, pp. 7–47.

Corrado, Anthony (2005b) Public Funding of Presidential Campaigns, in Anthony Corrado, Thomas E. Mann, Daniel R. Ortiz, Trevor Potter, and Frank J. Sorauf (eds) *The New Campaign Finance Sourcebook*, Washington, DC: Brookings Institution Press, pp. 180–204.

Davidson, Roger H. and Oleszek, Walter J. (1998) *Congress and Its Members*, 6th ed., Washington, DC: Congressional Quarterly Inc.

Davidson, Roger H. and Oleszek, Walter J. (2006) *Congress and Its Members*, 10th ed., Washington, D.C.: Congressional Quarterly Inc.

Federal Election Commission (2005a) *Federal Elections 2004, Election Results for the U.S. President, the U.S. Senate and the U.S. House of Representatives,*

Washington: Federal Election Commission. Available online at: <http://www.
fec.gov/pubrec/fe2004/federalelections2004.pdf> (accessed 13 July 2008).

Federal Election Commission (2005b) Federal Election Commission, Annual
Report 2004. Available online at: <http://www.fec.gov/pdf/ar04.pdf>
(accessed 30 June 2008).

Ferejohn, John A. and Fiorina, Morris P. (1975) Closeness Counts Only in
Horseshoes and in Dancing, *American Political Science Review*, 69, 3:
920–925.

Franklin, Mark (2004) *Voter Turnout and the Dynamics of Electoral Competition
in Established Democracies since 1945*, Cambridge, UK: Cambridge University
Press.

Glazer, Nathan (1988) The American Welfare State: Incomplete or Different?,
in Nathan Glazer (ed.) *The Limits of Social Policy*, Cambridge, MA : Harvard
University Press, pp. 168–194

Gray, Mark and Caul, Miki (2000) Declining Voter Turnout in Advanced
Industrial Democracies, 1950 to 1997—the Effects of Declining Group
Mobilization, *Comparative Political Studies*, 33, 9: 1091–1122.

Jackman, Robert W. (1987) 'Political Institutions and Voter Turnout in the
Industrial Democracies', *American Political Science Review*, 81, 2: 405–423.

Kirchgässner, Gebhart (1990) 'Hebt ein „knapper" Wahlausgang die
Wahlbeteiligung? Eine Überprüfung der ökonomischen Theorie der
Wahlbeteiligung anhand der Bundestagswahl 1987', in Max Kaase, Hans-
Dieter Klingemann (eds) *Wahlen und Wähler. Analysen aus Anlass der
Bundestagswahl 1987*, Opladen, Germany: Westdeutscher Verlag, pp. 445–447.

Klass, Gary M. (1985) Explaining America and the Welfare State: an Alternative
Theory, *British Journal of Political Science*, 15, 4: 427–450.

Leighly, Jan and Nagler, Jonathan (2007) Unions, Voter Turnout, and Class Bias
in the U.S. Electorate, 1964–2004, *The Journal of Politics*, 69, 2: 430–441.

Lijphart, Arend (1997) Unequal Participation: Democracy's Unresolved
Dilemma—Presidential Address, *American Political Science Review*, 91,
1: 1–14.

Lipset, Seymour Martin (1969) *Political Man*, London, UK: Heineman
Educational Books.

Lipset, Seymour Martin (1997) *American Exceptionalism. A Double-Edged
Sword*, New York, NY; London, UK: Norton.

Lipset, Seymour Martin and Marks, Gary (2000) *It Didn't Happen Here. Why
Socialism Failed in the United States*, New York, London: Norton.

McDonald, Michael and Popkin, Samuel L. (2001) The Myth of the Vanishing
Voter, *American Political Science Review*, 95, 4: 963–974.

Oppenhuis, Erik V. (1995) *Voting Behavior in Europe: a Comparative Analysis
of Electoral Participation and Party Choice*, Amsterdam, Netherlands: Het
Spinhuis.

Piven, Frances Fox and Cloward, Richard A. (1988) *Why Americans Don't Vote*,
New York: Pantheon Books.

Piven, Frances Fox and Cloward, Richard A. (2000) *Why Americans Still Don't
Vote*, Boston, MA: Beacon Press.

Powell, G. Bingham (1986) American Voter Turnout in Comparative Perspective, *American Political Science Review*, 80, 1: 17–43.

Rifkin, Jeremy (2004) *The European Dream. How Europe's Vision of the Future is Quietly Eclipsing the American Dream*, New York: Tarcher/Penguin.

Shaffer, Stephen D. (1982) Policy Differences Between Voters and Non-Voters in American Elections, *The Western Political Quarterly*, 35, 4: 496–510.

Shipler, David K. (2004) *The Working Poor*, New York, NY: Vintage Books.

Sombart, Werner (1906) *Warum gibt es in den Vereinigten Staaten keinen Sozialismus?* Tübingen, Germany: Mohr.

U.S. Census Bureau (2007) Statistical Abstract of the United States 2007. Available online at: <http://www.census.gov/prod/www/abs/statab2006_2009.html> (accessed 07 May 2008).

Verba, Sidney (2003) Would the Dream of Political Equality Turn out to Be a Nightmare? *Perspectives on Politics*, 1, 4: 663–679.

Wells, Herbert George (1906) *The Future in America*, New York: Harper & Brothers.

Wilensky, Harold L. (2002) *Rich Democracies. Political Economy, Public Policy, and Performance*, Berkeley, CA; Los Angeles, CA; London, UK: University of California Press.

4

INCOME INEQUALITY AND PARTICIPATION IN ELECTIONS IN THE UNITED STATES

MICHAEL P. McDONALD

Democratic legitimacy flows from citizens to representatives through elections. If the representatives derive their policy goals exclusively from being elected to office, they will structure their campaigning and legislating to develop and maintain a reelection constituency of supportive voters (Mayhew 1974; Fenno 1977). Yet, a critical ingredient is missing from American democracy: voters. Voting in the United States is a costly process that individuals may opt out of. As a result, American election participation is among the lowest of the industrialized democracies (Hill 2006). Since 1972, turnout rates among eligible voters average 55.3% in presidential elections and a lower 39.6% in midterm congressional elections. Even in the 2008 presidential election, the most stimulating election since 1964, turnout was only 61.7%, leaving millions of potential American voters on the sidelines.

There would not be much cause for alarm if those shirking their citizen duties were much like those who are actively engaged. Similar to a representative survey sample, voter preferences would be similar to those in the overall population and the will of the people would be accurately expressed, even though all the eligible voters did not bother to vote. Alas, this is not the case. American election scholars (e.g., Lazarsfeld 1944; Campbell et al. 1960; Burnham 1967; Wolfinger and Resonstone 1980; Leighley and Nagler 1992) consistently find civic engagement is skewed toward those of higher "socioeconomic status," well-educated persons of higher income who are posited to be better equipped to overcome voting costs. When candidates craft policy positions to persuade voters, the needs of nonvoters go unaddressed (Verba et al. 1995).

Here, I examine income inequality among American voters in the 2000, 2002, 2004, and 2006 elections. Analysis of meaningful variation between the American states provides clues as to the institutional structures that cause a participation gap between the poor and wealthy in the United States, and may be instructive of contributory factors toward inequality elsewhere. Still, even under the best of circumstances, a wide participation gap between the poor and the wealthy remains. The gap appears to be endemic of voluntary elections that generally provoke little interest among all American citizens, regardless of their income.

THE UNITED STATES ELECTORAL SYSTEM

The United States election administration is, like much of America's strongly federal system, decentralized. Under the United States constitution, states administer elections, voter qualifications are the same as those for the various state legislatures, and Congress has authority to override state laws.[1] Today, election administration is largely a state matter performed within relatively loose, although increasingly tightening, federal guidelines. State demographic characteristics, such as education, income, and race vary greatly across the large, heterogeneous country. There is no national election even for the president, which because of an institution known as the "electoral college" is effectively decided by a series of contests among the various states rather than a direct popular vote. Variation in state contexts and election rules thus shapes who votes.

America's curious decentralized election administration is the product of sharp disagreements among the country's Founding Fathers' concerning voter eligibility. As Keyssar (2000) relates, Benjamin Franklin and others viewed voting as a natural right and sought to expand suffrage, while Madison and others feared that once the Pandora's box was opened, then there would be in Adams' words "no end of it" and the franchise would be expanded to all beyond white men, including African-Americans and women.

Even over 200 years ago, these debates concerned income inequality with respect to owning property. Those favoring limiting suffrage to property owners argued, similar to later democratic elite theorists (e.g., Lipset 1960; Milbrath 1965), that only competent and independent elites have the capacity to be good democratic citizens. Those opposed to widespread suffrage feared that propertyless persons would be too easily swayed by those with property or be willing to destroy liberty by using government to transfer wealth from the rich to the poor. Those favoring expanding suffrage argued that property was not an indicator of competence and that expanding suffrage would increase support for the newly established democratic government whose constitution opened with the phrase, "We the people ..." and not, "We the people with property..." In a refrain that would be echoed throughout expansion of voting rights to African-Americans following World War II and young people following the Vietnam War, they argued that landless miltiamen who were willing to fight and die for American independence deserved all the privileges of citizenship.

Unable to agree upon uniform national voting qualifications, the Founding Fathers entrusted election administration where it currently resided, with the states. The compromise among the Founding Fathers profoundly affected American elections, resulting in an evolving patchwork of state election laws that have at times served state political interests to expand or to constrict the electorate. In the course of American political development, the federal government has increasingly encroached upon the states' prerogatives, for example, extending the franchise to nearly all American citizens and forbidding the use of discriminatory electoral procedures such as poll taxes and literacy tests. Yet, despite increased uniformity in American election administration, there remain substantial differences in election procedures among the states.

Perhaps one of the most exceptional differences within the United States and with other industrialized democracies is its system of voter registration. Voting in the United States is a costly two-step process that requires prospective voters to first register to vote and then to cast a ballot (Erikson 1981; Timpone 1998). In most states, eligible citizens must submit properly completed registration forms to their local election administrators prior to the election. If a registered voter moves, a voter typically must update their voter registration or, if they move between states, register anew with their new state of residence. Some states require that a voter registration form must be received by local election administrators a month (28 to 30 days) prior to an election, in other states voters can register and vote on the election day, with many state deadlines falling between these extremes.

Registration laws affect the electorate's composition. As an election nears, peripheral citizens become interested in politics and may seek to become politically active. The number of new registrants increase as a deadline nears (Gimpel et al. 2007) and voter turnout increases commensurately with shorter deadlines (Wolfinger and Rosenstone 1980; Leighley and Nagler 1992). One institution known as election day registration, where prospective voters can register and vote at a polling place on election day, further lowers voting costs by tying together the act of registering and voting (Timpone 1998) and scholars have consistently found a statistically strong positive increase in voter turnout rate of 7 percentage points or more in election day registration states (Knack 1995; Mitchell and Wlezien 1995; Rhine 1996; Highton 1997).

Voter registration is just one cost that American voters bear. Prospective voters must also seek out information to learn about candidates' policy positions, which in America's weak party system is often at variance from their party's platforms. Voting benefits are small if a voter does not perceive meaningful differences among candidates (Downs 1957). The expected voting benefit is even smaller, given the almost infinitesimal probability that a single person will cast a decisive vote between two candidates (Riker and Ordeshook 1968).

Given this framework, it is remarkable that anyone votes at all since by any rational calculation voting costs greatly outweigh benefits. While this economic approach to modeling, voting is deficient to explain observed voter turnout rates (Green and Shapiro 1996), the cost and benefit framework helps explain why we observe an American electorate biased toward those of higher socioeconomic status (Downs 1957). Individuals of higher socioeconomic status are better equipped with cognitive skills to navigate voting procedures and process campaign messages, and have more leisure time to devote to these activities. Conversely, those of lower socioeconomic status do not have sufficient levels of education to easily navigate voting procedures and learn the significance of candidate policy proposals, and often must work longer hours for lower wages and prefer spending their scarce leisure time available on other activities. Whatever the causal mechanism, studies consistently find an electorate biased toward those of higher socioeconomic status (e.g., Lazarsfeld 1944; Campbell et al. 1960; Burnham 1967; Wolfinger and Rosenstone 1980; Leighley and Nagler 1992).

Complicating a simple picture of the U.S. elections is that the states are not perfect demographic reflections of the nation as a whole and are indeed quite heterogeneous. For example, according to the 2000 U.S. census, the Gini income inequality index ranged from 0.40 in Alaska to 0.50 in New York (the District of Columbia was 0.55).[2] The states vary, too, with respect to education levels, racial composition, and many other demographic characteristics that are often associated with voter turnout rates.

Taking place against the backdrop of varied state election laws and demographic contexts are the elections themselves. Elections for various representative offices occur within the United State's dense federal government structure. Americans do not lack chances to participate in elections. At the national level, presidential elections take place every four years and elections for the House of Representatives and one-third of the Senate occur every two years. Within states, gubernatorial elections and elections of other statewide officials (which may include elections to the post of state Attorney Generals, judges, and even such esoteric offices as state Insurance Commissioner along with voting on questions relating to state constitutional revision and bond issuance), and elections for state legislatures and local governments typically occur in nonpresidential election years, though even here there is considerable timing variation. Elections are generally a two-stage process, where voters first select candidates in primary elections to run as political party nominees in general elections.[3] High-profile presidential general elections tend to have the highest turnout since they pique the interest of peripheral voters, but can also be affected by the presence of an interesting election for a lower ballot office (Cox and Munger 1989) or a controversial state constitutional amendment question (Tolbert et al. 2001).

Like many other countries influenced by the United Kingdom, the United States generally selects candidates by single-member plurality-win elections, particularly for federal offices (Lijphart 1999). Election outcomes are generally unknown only when two strong candidates vie in a competitive election. To return to the cost and benefit voting framework (Downs 1957), an individual's expected benefit of voting is a function of the differential policy positions of candidates multiplied by the probability that they will be the decisive voter. Voter turnout goes down when elections are forecast to be lopsided victories for one candidate, such as in the 1996 presidential election when President Clinton leapt to an early commanding lead in all preelection polls, and goes up when a close election pits two different candidates against each other, as happened in the 2004 presidential election between President Bush and Senator Kerry. In contrast to other countries, voters are less likely to "waste" a vote for a candidate with small levels of support—and thus calculate their probability of being pivotal differently—in countries that use other electoral systems, such as the many variants of proportional representation.

The peculiar manner of electing American presidents adds another layer of complexity. In a compromise between the large and small states, the American Founding Fathers decided to elect the president through an institution known as the electoral college, whereby voters in each state select delegates (equal in number to a state's representation in Congress) that, in turn, elect the president. Nearly all states award all of their electoral college delegates to the presidential candidate that receives a vote plurality within the state. Thus, it is possible for votes to be arranged in such a manner that the candidate who wins the national popular vote does not win the electoral college, as happened in 2000. Because voters in some states overwhelmingly support Democrats or Republicans, it is known with a high degree of certainty before the presidential election which candidate will win the electoral college delegates of these states. In order to win a majority of the electoral college, presidential campaigns thus concentrate their efforts in so-called "battleground states" where the election outcome is uncertain. Voters in battleground states are doubly stimulated by the increased chance that they will be pivotal and by campaign voter mobilization efforts. Voter turnout is thus depressed elsewhere.

The complexity of the U.S. election may seem daunting for those who might wish to reduce the nation to a single case for comparative purposes. Yet, scholars who study American electoral participation leverage state variation in election laws, demographic context, and levels of electoral competition to test causal hypotheses of what affects their voter turnout. Compared to cross-national comparisons that sometimes have difficulty controlling for nongeneralizable nation-specific factors, the validity of studies of state turnout in American presidential elections is enhanced by the relatively uniform culture that American elections occur in. Decentralized election administration is a boon for scholars of American politics, and is also a boon for those who seek electoral reform in the United States, since the little laboratories of the states can be utilized to observe reform effects, such as adopting public financing of state elections in Arizona and Maine or first enacting women suffrage in Wyoming, before they are adopted elsewhere.

INEQUALITY AMONG STATE ELECTORATES

The previous section makes clear that there are substantive differences in state election administration, demography, and election characteristics. To properly understand inequality among the American electorate, then, one must examine inequality among individual states' electorates. The primary data sources that include citizens' income information for such an analysis, election surveys, are often inadequate because they are conducted on national samples that are not of sufficient size to provide reliable state level estimates. Fortunately, the Current Population Survey (CPS), a publicly available survey conducted by the United States Census Bureau to calculate important statistics such as state unemployment rates, has sufficiently large state sample sizes.[4] In November of a federal election year, the CPS includes a limited number of voting and registration questions, which makes it well suited to explore inequality among state electorates. A drawback of the CPS is that attitudinal questions known to affect participation, such as trust in government, and questions about other forms of participation, such as volunteering for a campaign, are not asked.

On a typical survey, a greater proportion of survey respondents report voting than aggregate statistics indicate (for a review, see McDonald 2005), and the CPS is no exception. In 2004, 63.8% of CPS respondents who reported to be U.S. citizens of voting age (age eighteen and older) reported voting, compared with aggregate statistics that indicate 60.3 % of voting-eligible citizens voted. Scholars of so-called survey "overreport" bias offer many explanations for the phenomenon, from lying by survey respondents to survey nonresponse by persons who participate neither in the surveys nor in the voting. Evidence from vote validation studies, where survey responses are verified by examination of government records of voting (used to validate an individual's voter registration), suggests that respondents of higher socioeconomic status are more likely to report voting when they did not, which scholars attribute to those people who fit the profile of a voter desiring to present themselves as a good citizen to an interviewer. Any bias, then, manifests most likely as higher reporting of voter turnout rates among those of the higher socioeconomic status than has actually occurred and thus contributes to an underestimation of the participation gap between persons of low and high socioeconomic status.

I am interested in examining participation rates among the poor and the wealthy. The CPS reports total family income by income ranges rather than quintiles, as presented by Alber and Kohler in their comparative analysis of inequality and participation across countries (see their chapter in this volume). To construct analogous income ranges, while at the same time attempting to avoid issues with small state income-category subsample sizes, I reduce the CPS income ranges into four categories that are roughly analogous to national quartiles.[5] A limitation of this approach is that these data cannot account for cost-of-living adjustments in different regions of the country. Persons living in the lowest family income category, $25,000 and below, are comparatively better off in rural areas such as Mississippi and Louisiana where their money can stretch further than in dense urban areas such as Los Angeles and New York City, where housing and food are less affordable.

The United States 2000, 2002, 2004, and 2006 CPS citizen voting-age population (CVAP) turnout rates are plotted in Figures 4-1 through 4-4, with the national voter turnout rate at the top and state voter turnout rates (including the District of Columbia) plotted in descending order of a state's overall voter turnout rate. Three rates are plotted on each row, the overall voter turnout rate (represented by a dot) bracketed by the voter turnout rate for those reporting family income less than $25,000 and those with family income over $75,000 (represented by hashes). In all cases, the voter turnout rates are lower for the lower level of family income and thus are represented by the left hand hash mark. Along the right-hand column is the difference in voter turnout between the highest and lowest family income categories. Keep in mind that these statistics are drawn from a survey and have a statistical sampling error, which for the income categories is on the order or ±4% for the income categories and ±2% for the overall voter turnout rate (depending on the sample size), so small observed differences are not statistically meaningful.

Overall Participation Rates

The 2000 and 2004 presidential elections were similar in nature: they were both closely contested in relatively the same field of battleground states. The 2002 and 2006 midterm congressional elections were less so: the country was closely divided in 2002 but saw a significant swing to the Democrats in the 2006 election, which helped make elections in heavily Republicans states like Montana unusually competitive. Furthermore, because one-third of the Senate is up for election on a rotating basis across the states, a different set of U.S. Senator elections were held in 2002 and 2006 (and 2000 and 2004, but the presidential election is the primary draw for voters in these elections). As a consequence, state voter turnout rates between the two closely contested and similar presidential elections are more correlated with one another (r = .85) than the more variable midterm elections (r = .78). Despite this difference, these voter turnout rates are highly correlated, suggesting that systemic factors explain voter turnout variation among the states. While registration rates vary across elections, voter registration is more permanent than voter turnout since the act of registration will persist if a registrant does not move.[6] As a consequence, state registration rates

Figure 4-1: Turnout and income inequality in the 2000 U.S. presidential election

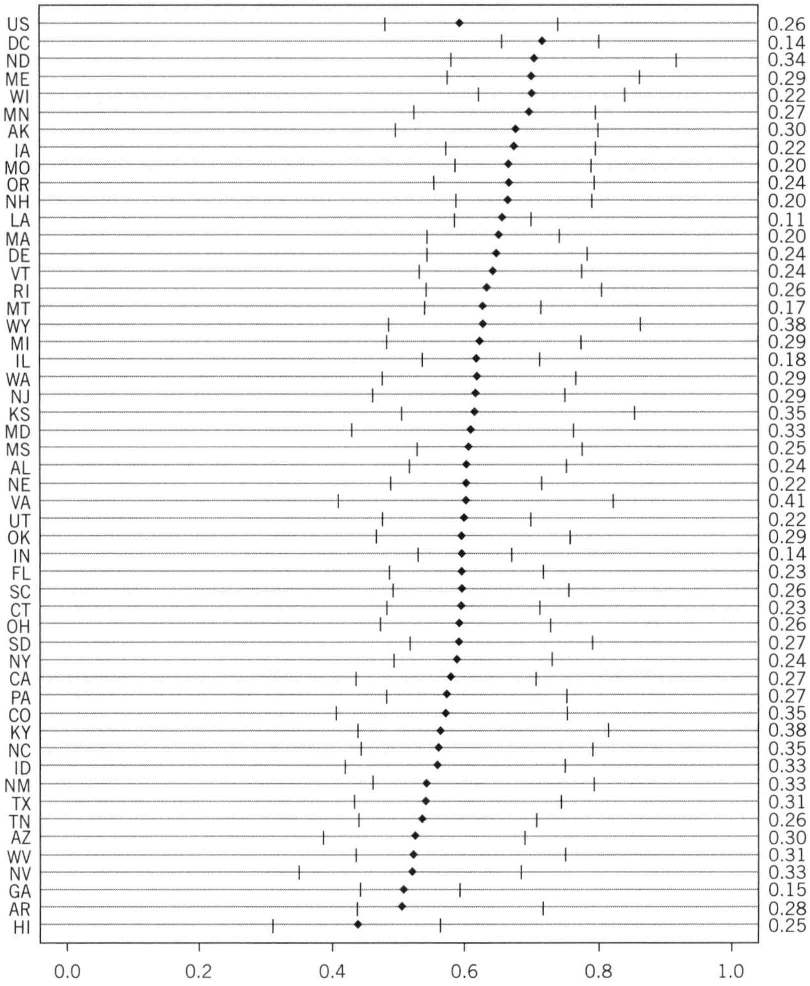

Source: 2000 Current Population Survey. States are sorted in decreasing order by CVAP turnout rate, represented by a dot. Left and right hash marks represent CVAP turnout rates for persons making less than $25,000 and more than $75,000, respectively. Differential voter turnout rates between these income categories are presented in the right hand column.

are highly correlated with one another, even across the most dissimilar 2000 and 2006 elections (the correlation for voter registration rates is 0.76 between these two elections and the turnout rate correlation is 0.54).

Correlation coefficients presented in Table 4-1 show that voter turnout rates among the poor and the wealthy are generally highly correlated with a state's overall voter turnout rates, albeit with some variability. In all four elections, columns 1 and 2 show that state voter turnout rates among the poor correlate

Figure 4-2: Voter turnout and Income Inequality in the 2002 U.S. Congressional Election

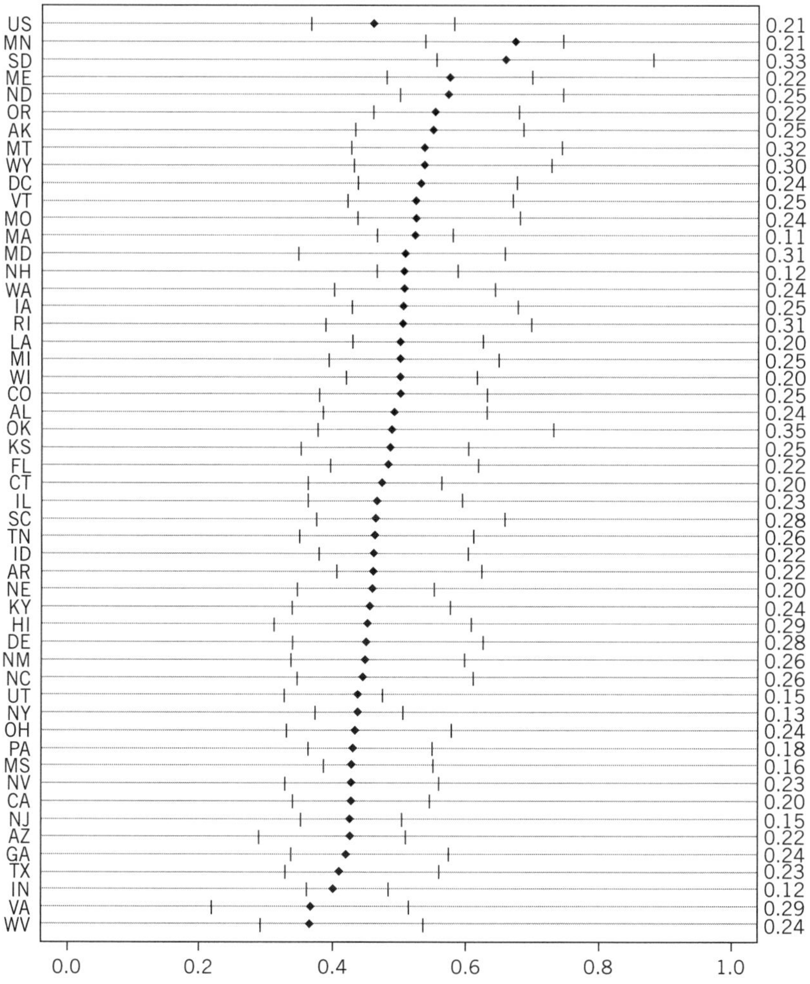

State	Differential
US	0.21
MN	0.21
SD	0.33
ME	0.22
ND	0.25
OR	0.22
AK	0.25
MT	0.32
WY	0.30
DC	0.24
VT	0.25
MO	0.24
MA	0.11
MD	0.31
NH	0.12
WA	0.24
IA	0.25
RI	0.31
LA	0.20
MI	0.25
WI	0.20
CO	0.25
AL	0.24
OK	0.35
KS	0.25
FL	0.22
CT	0.20
IL	0.23
SC	0.28
TN	0.26
ID	0.22
AR	0.22
NE	0.20
KY	0.24
HI	0.29
DE	0.28
NM	0.26
NC	0.26
UT	0.15
NY	0.13
OH	0.24
PA	0.18
MS	0.16
NV	0.23
CA	0.20
NJ	0.15
AZ	0.22
GA	0.24
TX	0.23
IN	0.12
VA	0.29
WV	0.24

Axis: 0.0   0.2   0.4   0.6   0.8   1.0

Source: 2002 Current Population Survey. States are sorted in decreasing order by CVAP turnout rate, represented by a dot. Left and right hash marks represent CVAP turnout rates for persons making less than $25,000 and more than $75,000, respectively. Differential turnout rates between these income categories are presented in the right hand column.

more highly with a state's overall voter turnout rate than among the wealthy. Voter turnout rates among the poor and the wealthy are more highly correlated with overall state voter turnout rates in midterm rather than presidential elections. Column 3 shows that voter turnout rates between the two income categories are correlated with one another, though less than either category's correlation with a state's overall voter turnout rate, and are also more highly correlated with each other in the lower voter turnout midterm congressional

Figure 4-3: Voter turnout and income inequality in the 2004 U.S. presidential election

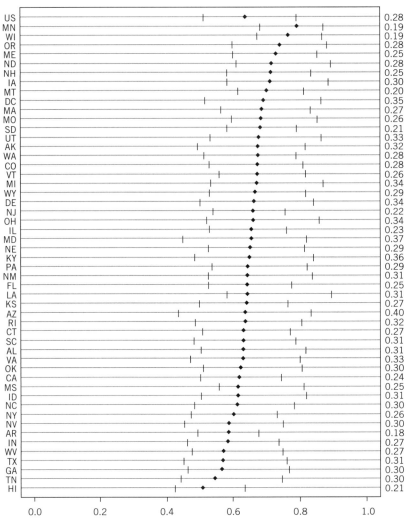

Source: 2004 Current Population Survey. States are sorted in decreasing order by CVAP turnout rate, represented by a dot. Left and right hash marks represent CVAP turnout rates for persons making less than $25,000 and more than $75,000, respectively. Differential turnout rates between these income categories are presented in the right hand column.

elections. These statistics point toward a theme revisited below that there is less variation among voter turnout rates when the electorate is reduced to core voters, be it for habitual voters among the otherwise low participatory poor or in low voter turnout midterm elections.

Table 4-1 suggests that participation among America's underclass is influenced by some of the same factors that prompt other Americans to vote.

Figure 4-4: Voter Turnout and Income Inequality in the 2006 U.S. Congressional Election

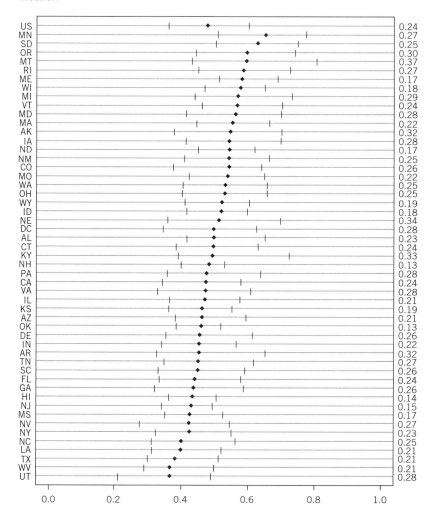

Source: 2006 Current Population Survey. States are sorted in decreasing order by CVAP turnout rate, represented by a dot. Left and right hash marks represent CVAP turnout rates for persons making less than $25,000 and more than $75,000, respectively. Differential turnout rates between these income categories are presented in the right hand column.

Looming large among these factors is the competitive nature of the elections. Emblematic of the influence of electoral competition is Hawaii, a strongly Democratic state far from the U.S. mainland. Because a Democrat is almost assured to win Hawaii's electoral college votes in a typical presidential election, the presidential campaigns spend very little resources on the state and do not use the candidate's precious campaigning time to fly to Hawaii, unless it happens to be the candidate's home state, as it is for Barack Obama. The result is

Table 4-1: State Current Population Survey Turnout Rate Correlation Coefficients

	State Turnout Rate Correlations Between Overall and Persons in Family Income Categories		State Turnout Rate Correlations Between Persons in High and Low Family Income Categories
Year	<$25,000	>$75,000	
2006	0.92	0.88	0.74
2004	0.85	0.77	0.62
2002	0.91	0.86	0.74
2000	0.87	0.67	0.51

that Hawaii had the lowest voter turnout rate in 2000 and 2004. Yet, Hawaii does not rank at the bottom in midterm election years because recent Hawaiian gubernatorial elections have been closely contested. At the extreme is the consistently high voter turnout rate state of Minnesota, a battleground state that experienced close gubernatorial and U.S. Senate races in midterm elections. Voter turnout rates for the states in-between can be largely explained by other electoral competitive contexts.[7] For example, the self-reported voter turnout rate for the seven most heavily targeted presidential battleground states in the 2004 election was 3.9 percentage points higher than in other states.[8]

Another factor affecting voter turnout is the voter registration process. States with election day registration (Idaho, Maine, Minnesota, New Hampshire, Wisconsin, and Wyoming; and Montana in 2006 and Iowa in 2008) or no registration (North Dakota) tend to have voter turnout rates above the median, if not near the top, averaging a voter turnout rate of 62.2% over the four elections. States with voter turnout rates consistently near the bottom tend to require their voters to register 1 month prior to the election, such as Arkansas, Georgia, Nevada, Tennessee, Texas, and West Virginia, among others.[9] These states averaged a voter turnout rate of 53.8% over the four elections. Registration rates reflect the differential voter turnout rates, with election day registration states averaging an overall 75.4% voter registration rate compared to 68.3% for those states that require registration 1 month prior to the election.

Participation Inequality

Easy access to the polling booth in an interesting election worth voting for seems to pull voters, both poor and wealthy, to the polls. Yet, are there systemic patterns to the participation gap between the poor and the wealthy? Along the right hand side of Figures 4-1 through 4-4 are the voter turnout rate "gap" or differential between those with family income of more than $75,000 and those making less than $25,000. To the eye, the numbers may appear to be random, but closer inspection reveals patterns with voter turnout levels, suggesting the participation gap narrows under certain circumstances.

The first clue of a pattern is the overall national participation gap, which for the high-stimulus presidential elections is higher than in the low-stimulus midterm elections. These midterm elections appear to be of such low interest that only the truly hardcore politicos are interested in voting, regardless of their income level. Closer inspection of the lowest state level voter turnout in midterm elections shows that those states below the median voter turnout rate in 2002 averaged a participation gap of 22.1% and compared with a gap of 24.4% for those above and in 2006 averaged 22.5% versus 25.6%, respectively.

The converse also appears to be true that elections can be so stimulating that the poor close their participation gap with the maximally stimulated wealthy. For presidential elections, in 2000 the gap averaged 25.0% for states above the median voter turnout rate and 27.8% for states below the median voter turnout rate. In 2004 the gap averaged 27.6% and 28.0%, respectively. In the most competitive presidential state level contests, the participation gap between the rich and poor narrows because all voters become more interested in voting. In midterm elections, narrowing is observed in the least contested elections because all voters are less interested in voting. It is in these intermediate elections, the closely fought midterm contests among the states and the states that the presidential candidates fail to contest, that the participation gap is the largest.

Evidence suggests greater access to the vote narrows the participation gap between the poor and the rich. Easy registration processes increases registration rates among the poor more than among the wealthy and thus reduce the income registration gap. Election day registration states averaged a registration rate of 66.1% among the poor and 85.7% among the wealthy, compared to 57.5% among the poor and 81.1% among the wealthy in states with a registration deadline of a month. The differences appear to be systemic as the pattern holds for all four elections. A similar pattern holds for voter turnout rates. Election day registration states averaged a voter turnout rate of 51.4% among the poor and 75.5% among the wealthy, compared to 42.8%t among the poor and 68.7% among the wealthy in states with a registration deadline of 1 month. In every election except 2000, the voter turnout rate gap between the poor and wealthy was lower in the election day registration states than in states with registration deadlines of a month. The 2000 exception appears to be caused by a lower voter turnout rate among the poor in the election day registration states in 2000 versus 2004, particularly in the nonbattleground states of Idaho and Wyoming which had voter turnout rates among the poor below 50% in 2000, and above 50% in 2004.

If America's voluntary elections explain why those of lower status participate at lower rates, is it possible to lure the poor to the polls with policies that directly affect their income? In 2006, the Democratic Party attempted to increase voter turnout among the poor, and hopefully increase their support for Democratic candidates, by appealing directly to their pocketbooks.[10] Democrats placed ballot questions that would amend state constitutions to raise the minimum wage in Arizona, Colorado, Missouri, Montana, Nevada, and Ohio. The Democratic efforts to increase voter turnout among the lower class does not appear to have been successful. Voter turnout rates among the poor in these states increased between 2002 and 2006 from an average of 37.6% to 38.7%. Whatever stimulating effect these ballot questions had on the poor was more than offset by voter turnout increases among the wealthy, which increased an even greater amount from an average of 62.3% to 64.1%.

Recall that these CPS statistics are drawn from income category ranges that are consistent across all states, but cannot be adjusted for the overall wealth or poverty of an individual state. As a consequence, overall state voter turnout rates are a weighted average of the proportion of persons in the highest and lowest income categories, and are not a simple average like the quintiles as presented by Alber and Kohler in this volume. The effect on the analysis is most apparent in the figures for the two poorest states, Mississippi and Louisiana.[12] In all four elections, the hash mark for the voter turnout rate among the poor is, on an average, pressed closer to Mississippi and Louisiana's overall voter turnout rate than in other states (these states are most easily identified in the 2004 presidential election in Figure 4-3). Voter turnout rates in these states would be almost 1 percentage point higher if they had the same income distribution as other states. The effect is opposite for the two wealthiest states, Alaska and Connecticut.

DISCUSSION

America has a volunteer electorate that is required to actively verify their voting eligibility through a costly registration process before they are permitted to vote. Participation is a choice, and voting by America's lower classes, and their relative participation gap with the wealthy, is largely driven by citizen's interest in choosing to participate in the elections. America's dense federal structure and single-member district electoral system—and exceptional presidential electoral college—attribute high importance to specific conditions in states and localities. Thus, even a "national" presidential election does not have the same stimulating effect across the entire United States. Where elections are interesting, people participate, where they are not, voter turnout is weak.

While participation among all income classes is strongly correlated with a state's overall turnout rate, there appears to be a sweet spot, or perhaps more accurately termed a rotten spot, where the participation gap between the poor and wealthy widens when elections are only moderately stimulating. When elections are highly stimulating, the wealthy reach a point where further voter turnout increases are difficult to achieve and the poor begin to close the participation gap. When elections are uninteresting—particularly when one candidate is heavily favored to win—the electorate is stripped down to core voters who habitually participate. There seems to be less of a socioeconomic bias among these core voters, which manifests itself in a lower participation gap when the wealthy occasional voters are washed out of the electorate. Still, even in states that are highly stimulating or generally uninteresting, there remains a substantial participation gap between the poor and the wealthy.

America's system of voter registration can be reformed to provide more access to the poor, and thus reduce the inequality among America's electorate. Reducing the costs of access by making the registration process less burdensome reduces a registration gap between the poor and the wealthy. However, it is unclear if this directly translates into lowering the voter turnout gap directly by reducing the registration costs or by raising everyone's participation to a level where the poor begin to catch up with the overstimulated wealthy since the Election Day registration states have higher voter turnout rates.

Making elections more interesting for the disadvantaged by appealing directly to their pocketbook through targeted policies offered to them on the ballot does not seem to work. States that allowed voters to vote on policies to increase the minimum wage in 2006 did have marginally higher voter turnout rates for the poor, but so, too, the rates among the wealthy increased. Perhaps this was a result of increased class conflict battled in the public sphere, thereby raising participation among all the social classes (Schattschneider 1960).

A solution to increase electoral participation by America's poor is thus to increase the voter turnout for everyone to the point where the poor begin to catch up with the wealthy (dispensing with a tongue-in-cheek solution to lower voter turnout where everyone becomes uninterested to participate). There are many reforms on the table. Election day registration was adopted in Montana in 2006 and is scheduled to take effect in 2008 in Iowa, with variations adopted in North Carolina and Nevada. Minnesota has proposed to join North Dakota to essentially implement universal voter registration conducted by the state. Proposals aimed to increase electoral competition (see McDonald and Samples 2006 for a review) include scrapping the electoral college for a direct election of the president, which will dramatically increase presidential election competition in nonbattleground states; changing the way in which congressional and state legislative districts are drawn to reduce the role of incumbents who use the process to increase their electoral safety; and experimentations with full public financing of state elections in Arizona, Maine, and Connecticut to level the playing field between incumbents and challengers.

What can other countries learn from the American experience? The decentralized U.S. electoral system can really work only in a large, populous country with a highly federal government, and thus America's overarching institutional structure would be difficult to import into any European country. The varied implementation of election administration among the numerous states, however, permits me to make two recommendations to reduce the participation gap between the poor and wealthy—and to increase turnout for everyone—based on "best practices" among the states.

1. *Make Voting Accessible.* Place the burden of determining eligibility to participate in elections on the government, rather than the individual citizen. America's costly two-step process of voter registration first and voting second works to limit access to voting and thus depresses turnout among persons of all income levels.
2. *Make Elections Meaningful.* If voting is not mandatory, then voters must have a reason to participate in the elections. Like a sporting event, more people watch a game when the stakes are high and the contestants are equally matched. Sadly, in too many of American elections that take place in single-member plurality-win districts, and even in the oddly structured presidential electoral college, the election outcome is well known in advance and citizens do not bother to waste their time by voting. When elections are competitive, people are stimulated to participate and voter turnout goes up.

I have written these two recommendations as broad guidelines rather than specific policies since even in the United States, electoral rules are a product of political development and cultural variation among the many states. American history has shown that electoral reform is not neutral to the fortunes of the political parties: almost always, one party has perceived an advantage or disadvantage. Thus, reform has rarely been adopted without impassioned debate. Adoption of reform will be generally successful in three settings: when one political party controls the mechanisms to implement policy without obstruction, when all parties see no overt advantage to reform, and when compromises can be brokered whereby two or more counterbalancing reforms are adopted simultaneously. Any attempt to improve the performance of an electoral system should thus be taken wisely with anticipation of obstacles, both visible and hidden, on the pathway to reform.

REFERENCES

Burnham, Walter Dean (1967) "Party Systems and the Political Process." In *The American Party Systems*, William N. Chambers & Walter Dean Burnham, Eds. New York, NY: Oxford University Press.

Campbell, Angus, Converse, Philip E., Miller, Warren E. and Stokes, Donald E. (1960) *The American Voter*, New York: Wiley and Sons.

Cox, Gary W. and Munger, Michael C. (1989) Closeness, Expenditures, and Turnout in the 1982 U.S. House Elections, *The American Political Science Review*, 83, 1: 217–231.

Downs, Anthony (1957) *An Economic Theory of Democracy*, New York, NY: Harper and Brothers Publishing.

Erikson, Robert S. (1981) Why Do People Vote? Because They Are Registered, *American Politics Quarterly*, 9, 3: 259–276.

Erikson, Robert S. and Tedin, Kent L. (2005) *American Public Opinion: Its Origins, Content and Impact*, 7th ed. New York: Pearson Longman.

Fenno, Richard F. (1977) U.S. House Members and Their Constituencies: An Exploration, *American Political Science Review*, 71, 3: 883–917.

Gimpel, James, Dyck, Joshua J. and Shaw, Daron R. (2007) Election Year Stimuli and the Timing of Voter Registration, *Party Politics*, 13(3): 351–374.

Gini, Corrado (1912) 'Variabilità e Mutabilità', reprinted in, E. Pizetti and T. Salvemini (eds) *Memorie di Metodologica Statistica*, Rome, Italy: Libreria Eredi Virgilio Veschi.

Green, Donald and Shapiro, Ian (1996) *Pathologies of Rational Choice*, New Haven, CT: Yale University Press.

Highton, Benjamin (1997) Easy Registration and Voter Turnout, *The Journal of Politics*, 59, 2: 565–575.

Hill, David (2006) *American Voter Turnout*, Boulder, CO: Westview Press.

Keyssar, Alexander (2000) *The Right to Vote: the Contested History of Democracy in the United States*, New York: Basic Books.

Knack, Stephen (1995) Does "Motor Voter" Work? Evidence from State-Level Data, *The Journal of Politics*, 57, 3: 796–811.

Lazarsfeld, Paul (1944) *The People's Choice*, New York: Columbia University Press.

Leighley, Jan E. and Nagler, Jonathan (1992) Socioeconomic Class Bias in Turnout, 1964–1988: the Voters Remain the Same, *The American Political Science Review*, 86(3): 725–736.

Lijphart, Arend (1999) *Patterns of Democracy: Government Forms and Performance in Thirty-Six Countries*. New Haven, CT: Yale University Press.

Lipset, Seymour Martin (1960) *Political Man*, New York: Doubleday Company, Inc.

Mayhew, David R. (1974) *Congress: the Electoral Connection*, New Haven, CT: Yale University Press.

Mitchell, Glenn E. and Wlezien, Christopher (1995) The Impact of Legal Constraints on Voter Registration, Turnout, and the Composition of the American Electorate, *Political Behavior*, 17, 2: 179–202.

Milbrath, Lester W. (1965) *Political Participation*, Chicago, IL: Rand McNally.

McDonald, Michael P. (2005) Reporting Bias, in Benjamin Radcliff and Samuel Best (eds) *Polling in America: An Encyclopedia of Public Opinion*, Westport, CT: Greenwood Press.

McDonald, Michael P. and Samples, John (eds) (2006) *The Marketplace of Democracy: Electoral Competition and American Politics*, Washington DC: Brookings Press.

Rhine, Staci L. (1996) An Analysis of the Impact of Registration Factors on Turnout in 1992, *Political Behavior*, 18, 2: 171–185.

Riker, William H. and Ordeshook, Peter C. (1968) A Theory of the Calculus of Voting, *The American Political Science Review*, 62, 1: 25–42.

Schattschneider, E. E. (1960) *The Semi-Sovereign People: A Realist's View of Democracy in America*, New York, NY: Holt, Rinehart, and Winston.

Shaw, Daron R. (2006) *The Race to 270: the Electoral College and the Campaign Strategies of 2000 and 2004*, Chicago, IL: University of Chicago Press.

Timpone, Richard J. (1998) Structure, Behavior, and Voter Turnout in the United States, *The American Political Science Review*, 92, 1: 145–158.

Tolbert, Caroline J., Grummel, John A. and Smith, Daniel A. (2001) The Effects of Ballot Initiatives on Voter Turnout in the American States, *American Politics Research*, 29, 6: 625–648.

Verba, Sydney, Kay L. Schlozman, and Henry Brady. (1995) *Voice and Equality: Civic Voluntarism in American Politics*. Cambridge, MA: Harvard University Press.

Wolfinger, Raymond E. and Rosenstone, Stephen (1980) *Who Votes?* New Haven, CT: Yale University Press.

PATTERNS OF PUBLIC EXPENDITURE

5

PATTERNS OF STATE EXPENDITURE IN EUROPE AND AMERICA

FRANCIS G. CASTLES

INTRODUCTION

The notion that the concepts and realities of stateness are radically different in Europe and America is hardly a new one. The idea of an American exceptionalism defined by a unique combination of liberty and equality of opportunity dates back to De Tocqueville's *Democracy in America* (1835) and to the perennial sociological debate stimulated by Werner Sombart's (1906) questioning of *Why There is No Socialism in the United States*. Today, the idea of transatlantic difference still flourishes, with its latest variant in the concept of a distinctive "European social model" frequently—implicitly or explicitly—counterposed to an American counterfactual in which the socially protective role of the state is far weaker.

This chapter is empirical and descriptive rather than theoretical and causal. I seek to map similarities and differences rather than explain them. Using cross-national data on various aspects of public expenditure development largely from Organization for Economic Cooperation and Development (OECD) and Eurostat sources, the chapter explores whether the character of public intervention in the United States is distinctively different from that of the countries constituting the European Union (EU) and whether patterns of public intervention in the United States and Europe are becoming more or less alike over recent decades. Like earlier work on the reality of a European social model by Castles (2002) and Alber (2006), the chapter's method of determining these questions is to seek to identify the extent of homogeneity or heterogeneity in European public expenditure outcomes by comparing and contrasting the public policy characteristics of the EU countries with patterns typical of the families of nations making up the wider European polity and in countries outside Europe.

The essential logic of inquiry here is also very similar to that of the earlier studies by Castles (2002) and Alber (2006). However, the strategy of comparison I employ and the conclusions I reach differ in some respects from those of Alber's study. Differences in conclusions must wait until the end. The differences in strategy are fourfold:

1. Alber's analysis of the scope of state activities looks only at the quanta of total public expenditure and total social expenditure in EU countries and the United States. I focus on a much wider range of spending dimensions. I look at the big aggregates of spending, including total public expenditure, total social expenditure, and total "core" or nonsocial expenditure. I look at the salience of these different types of spending, as well as examining the relative priorities governments accord to social security, defense, and public order spending (i.e., social security vis-à-vis the external and internal security of the state). Finally, I look at some key parameters of social provision including the balance between in-kind services and cash benefits, the relative generosity and distributional slant of income maintenance cash benefits (using decommodification scores as a proxy measure), and differences in the balance of public and private spending on social provision. I do not for a moment claim that these measures capture all aspects of stateness, but do suggest that they provide the basis for a quite comprehensive picture of cross-national differences in patterns of state activity.

2. Alber's conclusions concerning differences between Europe and the United States are based on differences between the United States and the mean values for the EU countries and family of nations' subgroups within Europe. Where differences within Europe exceed those between Europe and America, he argues that the case for both a separate European model and for American exceptionalism is substantially weakened. I agree with

Alber's logic, but, in addition to mean values, employ two rather more formal measures of dispersion among country groupings: the coefficient of variation (CV) and the standard deviation (SD). The use of these statistics makes it possible to offer more precise comparisons of the extent of the similarity or dissimilarity of different country groupings as well as to ascertain the extent of expenditure convergence over time.

3. Alber uses both OECD and Eurostat data in determining differences in total public expenditure and social expenditure patterns, but it would appear that Eurostat is his predominant source for data on the European countries, with OECD data only used for information concerning the United States. The problem with this approach is that Eurostat and OECD measures of given public expenditure variables are not identical. For instance, the OECD figure for total social expenditure as a percentage of GDP (gross domestic product) derived from the OECD Social Expenditure Database is on average around 3 percentage points lower than the corresponding Eurostat figure for total spending on social protection because Eurostat includes some expenditure items, which the OECD classifies as private expenditure. Thus, the use of Eurostat figures for European countries and OECD figures for the United States distorts the comparison between them, with the effect, in the case of the social expenditure example, of almost certainly exaggerating the differences between European and American levels of spending. Hence, in what follows, we rely primarily on the OECD figures using Eurostat data only to allow very tentative and cautious comparisons with the postcommunist and the former Soviet countries that were part of the 2005 enlargement of the EU and which are not currently member states of the OECD.

4. Finally, Alber's paper frequently draws attention to comparisons and contrasts between state activities in the United States and in other, what he calls, "Anglo-Saxon" nations, which in his usage is a term used to denote Ireland (sic) and the United Kingdom. Apart from the United States, he does not consider the expenditure profiles of other non-European English-speaking nations. However, in the context of a strategy of inquiry premised on the potentiality for policy divergences between different families of nations, there is an obvious possibility that the true dividing line is not between a European model and American exceptionalism, but between a European model excluding Ireland and the United Kingdom and an American experience possibly typical of that of other English-speaking countries, with, arguably, the similarities running even deeper between the United States and other settler societies such as Australia, Canada, and New Zealand. By examining spending patterns in both an EU of 14 (the preenlargement countries minus Luxembourg) and an EU of 12 (EU-14 minus the UK and Ireland) and in various subgroupings of English-speaking countries, we seek to test out these possibilities.

The purpose in this chapter is to map similarities and differences in the degree of stateness of countries and groupings of countries and maps are at their most useful where they provide an accurate scale of measurement. For this reason, I seek to be as precise as possible in the use of terminology. In my subsequent presentation, I describe a grouping as exhibiting a *coherent* policy stance only where it has a reported coefficient of variation of less than 10.0 (i.e., where all the cases have extremely similar values). Relaxing the criterion of similarity somewhat, but insisting also on a strong criterion of difference, I only denote groupings as being *distinct* from one another where they are relatively coherent (with coefficients of variation of less than 13.0) and exhibit a difference in means exceeding 1 S.D. of the entire OECD distribution. For a grouping to serve as a *model* for other nations, it must be both coherent and distinct (i.e., exhibiting values with a coefficient of variation of 10.0 or under and with a mean at least 1 S.D. greater or smaller than one or more other groupings). For an individual country to serve as a model for others, it must be in some sense exceptional. The definition of *exceptionalism* as employed in this analysis denotes circumstances where a country's value on a given dimension of state activity is simultaneously at one or other extreme of the OECD distribution and also at least 1 S.D. greater or smaller than the adjacent case in the distribution. The terminological benchmarks elaborated here are necessarily arbitrary and make coherence, distinctiveness, model status, and exceptionalism in varying degrees relatively uncommon phenomena. Because the terms are unambiguously defined, they make it possible to apply these descriptions transitively across different dimensions of state activity. Because they denote uncommon phenomena, they make these terms ("coherent, distinct, model and exceptionalism") signifiers of interesting and sometimes dramatic features of the policy landscape of modern Europe and the wider OECD world.

In what follows, I examine distributions relating to levels and changes in the size and salience of major public expenditure categories and in the key parameters of social spending. I also address the question of whether OECD countries are becoming more or less Americanized in the sense that their patterns of public spending have been becoming more similar to those of the United States over recent decades. Each topic covered in the analysis is discussed in relation to a table presenting information for the widest range of OECD and Eurostat countries for which data are available. A conclusion reflects briefly on whether the analysis presented in the chapter as a whole justifies notions of a European social model and American exceptionalism.

THE SIZE AND SALIENCE OF SPENDING CATEGORIES

The two main aggregate spending measures, which have featured as indicators of the reach of the modern state in comparative research, are the total outlays of general government and total public social expenditure both measured as percentages of GDP. The first of these indicators is an inclusive measure of the sum of government activities insofar as they involve public spending. The second has been particularly prominent in the postwar literature on the postwar sources of increased state interventionism, precisely because it has been in the social arena that public spending has increased most dramatically. Indeed, the focus on social spending has often served to distract attention from trends in other—nonsocial—categories of public spending, including spending on general public services, defense, public order, education, and economic affairs. These categories of spending are included as components of a third aggregate measure here described as "core expenditure" and also measured as a percentage of GDP. Aggregate spending measures are necessarily imprecise indicators of the scope of government. They miss out what is accomplished by regulation, what is accomplished by focusing spending in particular directions, and what can be accomplished by providing incentives for private activity. Nevertheless, as Hofferbert and Budge (1996) point out, while "money is certainly not all there is to policy…most policy implementation will languish without it.…Expenditures are clearly a major as well as the most visible and accessible measure of government activities."

Total Outlays

Research on trends and the determinants of growth in total public expenditure has been largely the province of economists (see Peacock and Wiseman 1961; Tanzi and Schuknecht 2000; Sanz and Velázquez 2004) and political scientists (see Huber and Stephens 2001; Castles 2006). Main concerns have been with the sources of the vast expenditure growth of the early postwar decades and, more controversially and recently, whether that growth has now peaked and is shifting into reverse as a consequence of economic globalization and the turn to neoliberal ideology in the 1980s and 1990s.

Table 5-1 shows values of the means of total outlays of general government in 1980, 1990, and 2003 for various country groupings in Western European nations that had become members of the EU before or as a consequence of the enlargement of 1995, in postcommunist countries that joined the EU in 2005, and in English-speaking countries outside Europe that are member states of the OECD. In addition, the table shows measures of dispersion for each country grouping (CV) and for the wider OECD grouping as a whole (both the CV and SD).

The figures for most country groupings and for the OECD as a whole demonstrate a marked increase in total spending between 1980 and 1990 and a much smaller contraction between 1990 and 2003. Schuknecht and Tanzi (2005) and Alber (2006), effectively measuring contraction from peak points reached in most countries in the early 1990s, suggest that the recent trend is markedly downward. Castles (2006), using 1980 as the notional high-water mark of the

Table 5-1: Average Values and Coefficients of Variation for Total Outlays of General Government as a Percentage of GDP in Various Groupings of OECD and Eurostat Countries, 1980, 1990, and 2003

	1980	1990	2003
Preenlargement EU:			
Continental	51.2 [10.6]	51.1 [7.8]	50.8 [4.5]
Southern Europe	34.7 [14.6]	47.5 [12.2]	46.6 [10.3]
Scandinavian	51.5 [22.8]	55.9 [11.8]	55.3 [7.2]
EU-12	45.8 [22.9]	51.1 [11.4]	50.5 [9.5]
EU-14	45.8 [21.2]	49.9 [12.3]	48.9 [13.0]
Postcommunist EU:			
Eastern Europe	n/a	n/a	50.4 [5.1]*
Former Soviet	n/a	n/a	*34.4 [3.1]*
All	n/a	n/a	*41.4 [16.1]*
English-speaking:			
United States	31.4	37.1	36.5
European	46.2 [9.6]	42.7 [1.7]	38.9 [16.4]
Non-European	33.7 [12.6]	40.7 [17.3]	37.7 [6.5]
All	38.8 [19.9]	41.5 [12.3]	38.2 [9.6]
OECD	43.7 [23.0]	48.3 [14.7]	47.4 [14.4]
Standard Deviation	10.1	7.1	6.8

Source and notes: With the exception of figures for the former Soviet grouping and the grouping containing all eight postcommunist nations joining the EU in 2005, which are calculated from data in the *Europa Yearbook Database*, figures for the remaining groupings are calculated from the OECD, *Economic Outlook Database*. Country groupings in this and later tables as follows: EU-14 = all pre-1995 enlargement EU countries minus Luxembourg; EU-12 = EU-14 minus UK and Ireland; Continental = Austria, Belgium, France, Germany, and the Netherlands; Southern Europe = Greece, Italy, Portugal, and Spain; Scandinavian = Denmark, Finland, and Sweden; Postcommunist EU = Czech Republic, Estonia, Hungary, Latvia, Lithuania, Poland, the Slovak Republic, and Slovenia; Eastern Europe = the Czech Republic, Hungary, Poland, and the Slovak Republic; Former Soviet = Estonia, Latvia, and Lithuania; English-speaking = US, Australia, Canada, Ireland, and UK; European = Ireland and the United Kingdom; Non-European = English-speaking minus UK and Ireland; OECD = EU-14 + Eastern Europe + Non-European. Figures in parentheses are coefficients of variation. Figures in italics not strictly comparable with other figures in the table. *Missing data for the Slovak Republic.

golden age of postwar public expenditure development, sees an essentially flat trend, with the peaks in the early 1990s attributable to the costs of unemployment and debt financing (i.e., not representing real increases in service provision and, so, after the early 1990s, when these costs began to decline, not representing real contractions in spending either).

Irrespective of which interpretation is correct, it is difficult to regard trends in total outlays since 1980 as indicative of major globalization or neoliberal ascendancy effects across the OECD as a whole. A decline in average spending of less than 1 percentage point of GDP by OECD countries between 1990 and 2003 simply does not warrant such a conclusion. In terms of trajectories of expenditure development, the major contrast between country groupings is between the strong growth of spending in Southern Europe and its decline in the Ireland–UK pairing, a decline entirely caused by the very substantial decline in Irish spending levels measured in terms of a massively growing level of per capita GDP. A declining CV in the OECD grouping as a whole is strongly suggestive of overall convergence effects, but no less rapidly declining CVs within most country groupings are indicative of the simultaneous emergence of increasingly coherent family of nations' profiles.

At the beginning of the period, Ireland and the UK constituted the only coherent subgrouping within the OECD and there was no sign of distinctiveness in the sense that this term is used here. However, by 2003, most groupings, including EU-12, but not EU-14, are coherent and all the preenlargement EU groupings other than EU-14 are distinct from both the non-European and overall English-speaking groupings in manifesting average values more than 1 S.D. apart. In terms of overall spending, it is, therefore, possible to argue that the countries of the EU-12 constitute a model to the low expenditure countries after 1990. It is not, however, possible to argue that the U.S. case is exceptional within the English-speaking world. In 1980, the United States shared with Australia the position of lowest public spender amongst the OECD countries covered by this comparison. However, in both 1990 and 2003, Australia spent less than the United States and, in 2003, Ireland, the major country of public expenditure contraction in the 1990s, had the lowest expenditure level of all. This is an instance where the true dividing line in terms of degrees of stateness seems to lie not between Europe and America, but between the EU countries excluding Ireland and the UK and the English-speaking countries in general.

With the exception of the countries of Eastern Europe, the figures for the postcommunist EU are not strictly comparable with those discussed above. Nevertheless, these figures are interesting and appear to tell a story of another marked family of nations divide within the newly enlarged European polity. OECD data for Eastern Europe (the Czech Republic, Hungary, and Poland) suggest a coherent grouping very akin to EU-12 in terms of the size of the state. Eurostat data for the former Soviet countries of Estonia, Latvia, and Lithuania point to a no less coherent grouping of small state nations. Thus, what the really small states with spending below 40% of GDP in 2003 (the English-speaking grouping other than the UK + Spain + the former Soviet grouping) have in common is that they are either outside Europe or on its farthest peripheries.

Total Social Expenditure

Cross-national data for total social expenditure have been the main test bed for theories of public expenditure development in the postwar era. Sociological accounts have focused on the extent to which expenditure growth has reflected needs, whether deriving from stages of economic development and the changing age structure of the population (see Wilensky 1975) or from the changing risk structure of contemporary societies (see Taylor-Gooby 2004). Political science accounts were initially concerned with the impact of partisan control of government (see Castles 1982) and more recently with the impact of diverse institutional design (see Immergut 1992; Schmidt 1996). Since the early 1990s, the focus of research has changed to establishing whether welfare state retrenchment has been occurring and how far any such trends are attributable to globalization (see Huber and Stephens 2001; Swank 2002; Castles 2004).

Table 5-2 presents figures analogous to those in Table 5-1 showing average values and measures of dispersion for total social expenditure in OECD and postcommunist Eurostat countries between 1980 and 2003. Table 5-2 shows that social expenditure trends did not mirror those for total outlays, with social spending increasing continuously throughout the period. Figures for the period after 1990, in particular, are very difficult to square with the notion of a globalization-driven process of retrenchment. In these years, total social spending increased in every single grouping as well as in the United States. At the same time, with the exception of the Continental grouping and the Irish–UK pairing, convergence was taking place across the board, although not quite to the same degree as in respect of total outlays. Viewing the trajectory of change from the perspective of 1980 suggests a continued gradual expansion of welfare state spending, with a pronounced catch-up by the countries of Southern Europe in the 1980s and, with lesser certainty because of missing data, by the countries of Eastern Europe in the 1990s.

Table 5-2: Average Values and Coefficients of Variation for Total Social Expenditure as a Percentage of GDP in Various Groupings of OECD and Eurostat Countries, 1980, 1990, and 2003

	1980	1990	2003
Preenlargement EU:			
Continental	22.8 [5.5]	24.2 [4.6]	25.9 [11.8]
Southern Europe	14.0 [24.4]	18.1 [16.5]	22.3 [8.2]
Scandinavian	24.1 [21.6]	26.8 [12.0]	27.1 [11.3]
EU-12	20.2 [27.1]	22.8 [18.7]	25.0 [13.9]
EU-14	19.7 [26.4]	21.9 [21.0]	24.0 [17.3]
Postcommunist EU:			
Eastern Europe	n/a	15.6 [4.1]*	21.0 [12.4]
Former Soviet	n/a	n/a	13.3 [2.7]
All	n/a	n/a	18.1 [24.1]
English-speaking:			
United States	13.3	13.4	16.2
European	16.7 [0.8]	16.4 [7.3]	18.0 [16.5]
Non-European	12.8 [13.0]	15.3 [17.7]	17.1 [5.0]
All	14.3 [17.1]	15.7 [13.3]	17.5 [9.5]
OECD	18.5 [29.5]	20.2 [24.6]	22.4 [19.3]
Standard Deviation	5.4	5.0	4.3

Source and notes: With the exception of the figures for the former Soviet grouping and the grouping containing all the postcommunist EU nations, which are calculated from data in the *Europa Yearbook Database*, figures for the remaining groupings are calculated from the OECD, *Social Expenditure Database* (2007). Country groupings as in Table 5–1. Figures in italics not strictly comparable with other figures in the table. *Missing data for Hungary and Slovak Republic. Figures in parentheses are coefficients of variation.

Because within-grouping convergence in social expenditure was not taking place to the same degree as in the case of total outlays, family of nations characteristics in 2003 are less pronounced than in the case of outlays, with the non-European and overall English-speaking groupings again showing strong similarities, but only the Southern European grouping among the preenlargement EU countries manifesting a coherent profile. This means that, despite the fact that the gaps between the English-speaking countries and EU-12 and EU-14 easily exceed 1 S.D., these groupings are not distinctive from one another in the sense used here. That is precisely because, as Alber (2006) points out in his earlier analysis, variation within the EU (even without the British and Irish cases) is too great for a wider European grouping to be meaningfully identified or, to put it another way, in respect of overall social spending levels, the EU is not sufficiently coherent to provide a model for others. In respect of spending levels, at least, there is no common "European social model." On the other hand, and very interestingly in terms of the debate on a possible Americanization of European social policy, the English-speaking countries do qualify according to our criteria as a model of parsimony for the high-spending countries of Western Europe.

Again, it should be noted that the United States was not an exceptional case. In 1990, the United States was by a small margin the lowest spender of this sample of OECD countries, but not so in 1980 or in 2003. Here, once more, the real contrast is between the low-spending English-speaking world, of which the United States is a typical example, and EU countries, which, for the most part, spend a great deal more. Moreover, the divide between the English-speaking world and Western Europe is seemingly replicated by a divide within the postcommunist EU between Eastern European countries typically spending at and around the average for the Southern European family of nations, and a former Soviet grouping spending even less than the non-European English-speaking countries. In this sense, the 2005 enlargement represented a further step away from a coherent European social model.

Core Expenditure

Core expenditure as calculated here is a residual category obtained by deducting total social expenditure from total outlays. Its subcategories include the most basic functions of the state including public administration, defense, and the maintenance of public order as well as more modern functions including education, economic services (including subsidies and state aid), and environmental services. It also includes expenditure on debt servicing, the costs of which in certain OECD countries, particularly in Continental and Southern Europe, increased very markedly throughout the course of the 1980s and declined again almost as rapidly from the early 1990s onwards.

Superficially, Table 5-3 provides a picture of core spending trends resembling that for total outlays in Table 5-1. In the OECD as a whole, spending goes up in

Table 5-3: Average Values and Coefficients of Variation for Core Expenditure of General Government as a Percentage of GDP in Various Groupings of OECD and Eurostat Countries, 1980, 1990, and 2003

	1980	1990	2003
Preenlargement EU:			
Continental	28.4 [15.9]	26.9 [12.2]	25.0 [9.8]
Southern Europe	20.8 [17.1]	29.5 [16.1]	24.3 [16.1]
Scandinavian	27.4 [24.4]	29.0 [14.4]	28.2 [2.8]
EU-12	25.6 [22.1]	28.3 [13.6]	25.5 [11.8]
EU-14	26.2 [21.1]	28.0 [13.0]	24.9 [13.6]
Postcommunist EU:			
Eastern Europe	n/a	n/a	28.2 [12.5]*
Former Soviet	n/a	n/a	*21.1 [6.7]*
All	n/a	n/a	*23.3 [12.6]*
English-speaking:			
United States	18.1	23.7	20.3
European	29.5 [14.6]	26.4 [7.2]	20.9 [16.2]
Non-European	21.1 [15.8]	25.4 [17.3]	20.6 [12.2]
All	24.4 [22.8]	25.8 [12.8]	20.7 [12.9]
OECD	25.3 [21.7]	27.6 [13.7]	24.7 [15.3]
Standard Deviation	5.5	3.8	3.8

Sources and notes: Core Expenditure = Total Outlays of General Government minus Total Social Expenditure. All figures calculated from the databases referred to in Tables 5–1 and 5–2. Country groupings as in Table 5–1. Figures in italics not strictly comparable with other figures in the table. *Missing data for the Slovak Republic. Figures in parentheses are coefficients of variation.

the 1980s and declines again in the 1990s, leading to a moderate degree of convergence. Country groupings including Scandinavia, the two wider EU aggregations, the overseas English-speaking countries, and the English-speaking countries in general follow the same pattern. An important difference, however, is that the growth of core spending in the 1980s is shallower than that of outlays and, in the 1990s, the pattern of decline is more pronounced, particularly in the English-speaking world. In fact, what expenditure retrenchment there was in these years occurred in the realm of core spending, with cuts particularly concentrated in the areas of defense, education, and economic affairs (see the contributions to Castles 2007). A point to note, however, although not shown in the table, concerns the timing of cuts in real service provision (public servants, teachers, policemen on the beat). In the 1980s, debt servicing increased, so that, in some instances, increased spending in these years disguised declining levels of service provision. In the 1990s, debt servicing declined, so that the apparent decline in service provision occurring in these years was, in some instances, more apparent than real.

For both 1980 and 1990, the figures in Table 5-3 suggest a series of negatives. With the minor exception of the Ireland–UK pairing in 1990, there were no coherent groupings, no distinctiveness, and no models. By 2003, however, a more pronounced decline in spending in the English-speaking countries had produced a marked distinctiveness between them and the countries making up EU-12 not to mention between them and the now coherent Continental and Scandinavian groupings. According to our criterion, neither EU-12 nor the English-speaking groupings constitute models in 2003, although a strong case might be made for assigning that status to the Scandinavian grouping (on the defining characteristics of the Nordic model, see Kautto et al. 2001).

Given that the U.S. spending figure is the lowest in each column of Table 5-3 and, in all three columns, is more than 1 S.D. lower than the figure for the English-speaking grouping as a whole, it might appear that here, in respect of core expenditure, we might encounter an instance of American exceptionalism. In fact, the United States is never an extreme case in the core spending distribution, with Spain and Finland spending less in 1980, Germany and Australia in 1990, and Ireland, Spain, and Australia in 2003. Given that defense spending is an important component of core spending and that the United States was throughout one of the foremost spenders in this area, this is scarcely a surprising finding. Nor is the finding of a continued bifurcation of the postcommunist grouping into a big state (bigger even than Scandinavia) Eastern Europe and a coherent small state former Soviet grouping, a pattern quite consistent across all the dimensions of state activity for which I present data in this chapter.

The Salience of Social Security

Having examined the size of the main aggregates of public spending, and discovering only limited support (in respect of total outlays) for the notion of a European social model and none for American exceptionalism, I now move on to examine the salience of different types of spending and, in particular, the degree to which they privilege social security over external and internal security. The data I use is only very recently available and derives from recent efforts by the OECD and Eurostat to encourage member nations to report public spending according to the internationally standardized Classification of the Functions of Government (hereinafter COFOG data—for an introduction to the availability of this data, see Fraser and Norris 2007).

Table 5-4 presents COFOG data for spending on defense, public order, social protection, and health as percentages of GDP in 2002 for most of the countries featured in earlier tables, although data are missing for the former Soviet grouping and for Australia and Canada. Because I wish to test out the supposition that a major difference between the United States and Europe is the priority given in the former to the functions of military defense and the maintenance of public order, I calculate the ratio of spending on external plus internal security vis-à-vis social security (i.e., social protection + health) and these figures are shown in the final column of Table 5-4. Defense and public order are the two "Night Watchman" functions of the state, which until the late nineteenth century were the paramount objects of public spending and government revenues. How far the world of public policy has been transformed over the course of the

Table 5-4: Average Values and Coefficients of Variation for COFOG Functional Expenditure Categories as Percentages of GDP and the Ratio of External Plus Internal Security Spending to Social Security Spending in Various Groupings of OECD Countries, 2002

	1 Defense Spending	2 Public Order Spending	3 Social Protection Spending	4 Health Spending	Ratio of 1 + 2 to 3 + 4
Preenlargement EU:					
Continental	1.4 [37.7]	1.5 [20.5]	20.0 [12.7]	6.1 [18.2]	0.11 [21.9]
Southern Europe	2.0 [77.1]	1.6 [38.1]	15.9 [18.7]	5.5 [26.9]	0.17 [26.2]
Scandinavian	1.7 [18.6]	1.3 [18.2]	22.4 [5.6]	6.8 [6.1]	0.10 [12.3]
EU-12	1.7 [55.4]	1.5 [27.7]	19.2 [18.2]	6.1 [19.0]	0.13 [32.7]
EU-14	1.7 [56.4]	1.5 [29.3]	18.2 [23.6]	6.1 [17.5]	0.14 [34.1]
Eastern Europe	1.6 [22.7]	2.0 [10.4]	16.3 [12.4]	4.7 [38.8]	0.17 [25.1]
English-speaking:					
United States	3.7	2.1	7.3	7.1	0.40
European	1.6 [88.4]	1.9 [37.2]	12.3 [40.2]	6.5 [4.3]	0.18 [38.7]
All	2.3 [68.5]	2.0 [26.1]	10.6 [42.7]	6.7 [5.9]	0.25 [54.9]
OECD	1.8 [53.7]	1.7 [26.7]	17.2 [26.3]	5.9 [23.2]	0.16 [47.1]
Standard Deviation	.94	.39	4.5	1.3	0.07

Source and notes: Figures for preenlargement EU and Anglo-American groupings calculated from Appendix 3B of Fraser and Norris (2007) reporting general government expenditure by COFOG function (1993 SNA) as a percentage of GDP. Data for Eastern Europe supplied by Paul Norris from Eurostat sources for 2003. No data available for Australia or Canada, so that non-European category cannot be calculated. No data available for the former Soviet grouping or Slovenia. Figures in parentheses are coefficients of variation.

twentieth century is indicated by the OECD average ratio between these forms of spending and spending on health and social protection, which shows that, at the turn of the millennium, the resources devoted to the external plus internal security of the state amounted to just 16% of spending on social security.

Figures for the separate categories of spending defy easy summary and, in some cases, defy standard expectations. Readers would probably not be surprised that social protection expenditure is higher in the EU countries and that spending on defense and public order is higher in the English-speaking world or that differences between these groupings in public order and social protection spending exceed 1 S.D. of the OECD distribution. They may be more surprised to learn that public expenditure on health is at least marginally higher in the English-speaking nations and the United States than in EU-12. Arguably, however, the most important generalization concerning these spending categories relates to the very high degree of variation manifested by most country groupings in respect of most expenditure components, with health and social protection spending in Scandinavia and health spending in the groupings making up the English-speaking world the only exceptions. There is little family of nations' coherence here, few if any signs of distinctive groupings and absolutely no sign of a European social model. These findings strongly confirm Alber's

(2006) conclusion that, in a great many respects, variation amongst the EU countries is as great as or greater than the difference between these countries and the United States.

However, Table 5-4 shows that in at least one respect this conclusion does not hold. Looking at the ratio between external and internal security vis-à-vis social security also reveals a degree of variation that rules out ideas of coherence, distinctive groupings, and exemplary models; although it is clear that night-watchman functions are somewhat more salient in Southern and Eastern Europe and the English-speaking world than in Scandinavia or Continental Europe. It does not, however, rule out American exceptionalism, with the United States exhibiting a ratio of external plus internal security spending equivalent to 40% of social security spending, a figure more than 2 S.D.s greater than the next highest countries: Greece, with a ratio of 0.24, and the United Kingdom, with a ratio of 0.23. What this says about the American case is open to interpretation. It is not just a matter of the United States being a superpower with exceptionally high defense spending needs and of having a preference for imprisoning its citizens, since Greece actually spends a slightly greater proportion of its GDP on defense and public order combined than the United States. What makes the real difference is the conjunction of high spending in these areas combined with the lowest level of spending on social protection in the OECD. Why the United States' level of public commitment in this area is so low will become clearer in the next section on the key parameters of social spending (see, in particular, the discussion of Table 5-7).

KEY PARAMETERS OF SOCIAL SPENDING

So far, I have examined differences in the size of various public expenditure aggregates and the salience of welfare spending vis-à-vis other expenditure categories. In this section, I focus on key features of the system of social provision insofar as these can be revealed through patterns of spending. Contrary to the view that measures based on spending data are blunt instruments for differentiating types of social policy, we show that spending-related indicators can provide us with important information concerning the structure, distributional outcomes, and the balance of public and private inputs in modern welfare states.

Welfare State Structure

Recent editions of the OECD Social Expenditure Database have made it possible for researchers not only to disaggregate expenditure by function (i.e., pensions, disability, sickness, unemployment, family, etc.), but also by whether social provision is made through cash payments (i.e., income maintenance benefits) or through in-kind benefits (i.e., services). This latter structural distinction is important for a variety of reasons. First, social care services have been identified as a characteristic aspect of the Scandinavian or Nordic model of welfare provision (see Anttonen and Sipilä 1996). Second, recent theorizing on the responsiveness of social policy systems to the "new social risks" inherent in postindustrial development (see Esping-Andersen 1999; Taylor-Gooby 2004) suggests that, in many instances, service provision is likely to grow at the expense of cash provision. Finally, those who see the guiding force of recent social policy development as being the progressive implementation of neoliberal ideas appear to be suggesting that the trend of recent development has, on the contrary, been toward a greater emphasis on means-tested cash benefits (see Gilbert 2002). In what follows, therefore, I use the level of the ratio of in-kind to cash social provision as an indicator of the commitment by different country groupings to diverse modes of provision and changes in the ratio as an indicator of whether recent policy reform initiatives are moving such groupings in a post-industrial service state or a more traditional transfer state direction.

Table 5-5 provides the requisite information. An initial point to note is that, with the exception of the overseas English-speaking grouping in 2003, services (which here include spending on health) remain subordinate to cash benefits as objects of state welfare largesse. That said, Table 5-5 also demonstrates a very clear trend toward greater service salience. Between 1980 and 2003 and with no exceptions at all, the salience of service spending has been increasing across the universe of advanced welfare states, although with a minor dip in some groupings in 1990, presumably as a consequence of increased cash spending on

Table 5-5: Average Values and Coefficients of Variation for the Ratio of In-kind Social Benefits to Cash Social Benefits in Various Groupings of OECD Countries in 1980, 1990, and 2003

	1980	1990	2003
Preenlargement EU:			
Continental	.41 [22.1]	.45 [22.1]	.58 [14.6]
Southern Europe	.47 [9.8]	.44 [12.4]	.48 [11.4]
Scandinavian	.79 [19.6]	.71 [9.4]	.85 [9.8]
EU-12	.52 [34.8]	.51 [27.6]	.61 [26.5]
EU-14	.56 [35.7]	.54 [28.3]	.66 [28.9]
Eastern Europe	n/a	.47 [18.6]*	.56 [33.0]
English-speaking:			
United States	.54	.69	.92
European	.77 [27.9]	.69 [22.4]	.91 [17.1]
Non-European	.90 [48.9]	.94 [29.4]	1.06 [18.3]
All	.85 [39.9]	.84 [29.6]	1.00 [17.9]
OECD	.62 [44.3]	.59 [37.3]	.70 [34.4]
Standard Deviation	.27	.22	.24

Source and notes: All figures calculated from OECD, *Social Expenditure Database* (2007). No data available for the former Soviet grouping or Slovenia. * Missing data for Hungary and the Slovak Republic. Figures in parentheses are coefficients of variation.

unemployment at around that time. Clearly, an important part of this trend is attributable to increased real spending on health, which has been an electoral priority in most countries. However, even after removing health from the equation, as in Table 5-8, the trend toward greater service provision remains clear. It should be noted, moreover, that this trend is not a consequence of declining cash spending. Between 1980 and 2003, cash spending in seventeen OECD states increased from 11.6% to 13.2% of GDP, while in-kind benefits increased from 6.6% to 8.9% of GDP. Thus, the evidence provided here seems to favor a postindustrial rather than a neoliberal interpretation of recent structural trends in social spending.

Finally, I return to the main theme of whether there are major differences in this dimension of state spending as between Europe and America and the answer is that major differences are not there. Certainly, Table 5-5 confirms the suspicion that there is an emergent family of nations' coherence in Scandinavia. However, the Scandinavian bias toward service provision is not shared with most of the other EU countries, but primarily with English-speaking nations both inside and outside Europe. Initially, the United States was not among them, with a pattern of spending much closer to the strong cash benefit preference of the Continental and Southern European groupings. That has changed over the past quarter century as American public health spending on Medicare and Medicaid has increased and now the United States is a reasonably typical member of the English-speaking grouping (although obviously not in terms of the coverage of public health provision). Scandinavia is distinct from Southern Europe in both 1990 and 2003 and, arguably, may be seen as a model to other EU countries of the way forward in the "new risk" society. It is clear, however, that the balance between cash benefit and in-kind provision does not represent a fracture line between European and American models of social policy.

Welfare State Decommodification

Gøsta Esping-Andersen (1990) has famously argued against the use of expenditure measures of welfare state effort, devising an alternative decommodification measure designed to capture the redistributional effects of high coverage rates, high replacement rates, long contribution periods, and other such variables influencing the generosity of old-age pension, sickness, and unemployment benefits. In reality, however, the decommodification index only amounts to an expenditure index focussed on state spending on particular categories of individuals rather than in aggregate. Esping-Andersen's index, which has been widely accepted as a strong predictor of income inequality and poverty levels, was initially elaborated for a single year—1980—but recent research by Scruggs (2004) has provided decommodification scores for the same eighteen countries featuring in the original study from early in the 1970s through to 2002. It is the latter data, which I used to construct Table 5-6.

Table 5-6: Average Values and Coefficients of Variation for Decommodification Index Scores in Various Groupings of OECD Countries, 1980, 1990, and 2002

	1980	1990	2002
Preenlargement EU:			
Continental	29.5 [5.9]	30.2 [7.5]	30.3 [9.3]
Southern Europe	20.6	24.2	26.7
Scandinavian	32.4 [13.2]	33.5 [9.8]	32.5 [7.4]
EU-12	29.5 [14.9]	30.6 [12.1]	30.7 [9.6]
EU-14	28.2 [17.3]	29.3 [15.5]	30.0 [10.9]
English-speaking:			
United States	18.6	19.0	18.1
European	22.4 [3.4]	23.0 [4.9]	26.8 [11.1]
Non-European	21.2 [15.8]	20.6 [16.2]	20.4 [20.1]
All	21.7 [11.4]	21.5 [12.9]	22.9 [20.9]
OECD	26.7 [20.0]	27.4 [20.4]	27.9 [18.7]
Standard Deviation	5.4	5.6	5.2

Source and notes: All figures calculated from *Comparative Welfare Entitlements Data Set* (Scruggs, 2004). No data for the postcommunist grouping or most countries of Southern Europe. The figure reported for the latter grouping is for Italy alone. Figures in parentheses are coefficients of variation.

Table 5-6 shows emerging coherence and convergence in decommodification scores over time within the preenlargement EU, but not in the English-speaking world, where a preexisting commonality in pattern of the Irish–United Kingdom pairing had disappeared by the end of the period. In contrast to the expenditure measures discussed earlier in the chapter, there has been no clear trend to convergence across the OECD as a whole. In 1980, the Continental countries displayed a coherent pattern and, by 1990, the Scandinavian countries had joined them. By 2002, the EU-12 countries also manifested sufficiently similar decommodification scores to meet the coherence criterion used in this chapter. However, by that year, none of the groupings qualify as being distinct from one another. The various families of nations within the EU, including here the Irish–United Kingdom pairing, were not far enough apart in values to qualify by the 1 S.D. criterion, while the overseas and overall English-speaking groupings, which easily met that criterion, were much too disparate to qualify.

The EU-12 does, however, qualify as a model for the low decommodification countries of the English-speaking world and, on the basis of inference from earlier aggregate expenditure figures, also for the countries in the former Soviet grouping, with the status of the countries of Southern and Eastern Europe for which data are also missing much more difficult to predict. This brings the candidate dimensions for a European social model excluding Britain and Ireland to two, with EU-12 distinguished by high levels of total outlays and by high levels of welfare state decommodification. The gap between the decommodification scores of EU-12 and the United States is vast in 2002 (more than two SDs), but the United States does not qualify as exceptional at any time since 1980, since its scores are very similar (sometimes higher and sometimes lower) than those of Australia. It is worth noting, however, that these two countries are both increasingly being left behind by the rest of the pack (see also the figures in Table 5-8), with the difference between them and the remainder of the English-speaking world itself exceeding 1 S.D. by 2002. Exceptionalism or no, there is evidence here that the American welfare state is very different in character from that in most other advanced nations and in a manner with potentially major implications for distributional outcomes.

The Welfare State Mix

The final set of dimensions of state activity addressed here brings into sharp focus cross-national differences in preferences for public over private action. It has always been widely recognized by welfare state scholars that unadorned comparisons of the gross size of public spending miss out on two key factors that influence the quantum of economic resources devoted for social purposes: one is the extent of taxation on public welfare state benefits and contributions and the other is the extent of private expenditure for social purposes paid for by individuals and enterprises. Until recently, we have not been in a position to identify these dimensions of expenditure in a systematic manner, but now thanks to pioneering work by Adema and Ladaique (2005), this is possible for most of the OECD countries featuring in this analysis.

The categories of spending featuring in Table 5-7 require some explanation. *Gross public social expenditure* is essentially the same category of spending as total social expenditure analyzed in Table 5-2, although the data are for different years. *Tax incidence* is the sum of taxes on benefits and contributions including tax credits equivalent to cash benefits. It is this latter item that accounts for the fact that in some countries tax incidence is negative (i.e. adds to the sum of gross public social expenditure). Deducting tax incidence from gross spending provides a figure for *net public social expenditure*, which may be seen as the sum of economic resources devoted by the state to social purposes. The fourth column of Table 5-7 reports the sum of *net private social expenditure*, which, added to net public expenditure, gives us a figure for *net total social expenditure*, which is the sum total of spending for social purposes in a given country. A recent paper by Castles and Obinger (2007) argues that tax incidence is a key instrument of redistribution, allowing countries with higher taxation of benefits to pay substantially higher benefits to those in need, thereby mitigating poverty and inequality.

Table 5-7 is difficult to summarize. One key point to note is that, as we move across the table from left to that right, European and English-speaking spending totals become much more similar, with a difference between EU-12 and English-speaking countries of 8.4% of GDP in respect of gross public spending becoming a mere 2.8% of GDP in respect of net total spending. This

Table 5-7: Average Values and Coefficients of Variation for the Major Dimensions of the Public/Private Social Expenditure Mix in Various Groupings of OECD Countries, 2001

	Gross Public Social Expenditure	Tax Incidence	Net Public Social Expenditure	Net Private Social Expenditure	Net Total Social Expenditure
Preenlargement EU:					
Continental	25.6 [10.7]	3.5 [34.5]	22.1 [14.4]	2.4 [52.3]	24.3 [11.3]
Southern Europe	22.0 [15.4]	3.2 [13.3]	18.8 [15.8]	.8 [84.8]	19.5 [17.8]
Scandinavian	27.9 [9.8]	6.4 [14.6]	21.6 [10.5]	1.2 [72.2]	22.8 [13.2]
EU-12	25.6 [12.9]	4.3 [39.5]	21.3 [13.6]	1.7 [71.1]	22.9 [14.6]
EU-14	24.3 [18.9]	4.2 [42.8]	20.1 [19.5]	1.8 [73.8]	22.1 [19.1]
Eastern Europe*	19.0 [8.2]	1.5 [4.8]	17.6 [9.3]	.2 [141.4]	17.6 [7.2]
English-speaking:					
United States	14.7	−3.2	17.9	8.5	23.1
European	17.8 [31.8]	3.8 [81.1]	14.1 [18.6]	2.0 [113.1]	17.9 [42.7]
Non-European	16.8 [11.0]	−.5 [433.7]	17.4 [2.7]	5.4 [50.1]	21.5 [6.7]
All	17.2 [18.4]	1.2 [278.3]	16.0 [14.1]	4.0 [71.8]	20.1 [22.0]
OECD	22.3 [22.4]	3.1 [84.5]	19.3 [18.2]	2.2 [97.0]	21.4 [17.9]
Standard Deviation	5.0	2.6	3.5	2.2	3.8

Source and notes: All figures calculated from Adema and Ladaique (2005). Country groupings as in Table 5–1. Figure for Southern Europe is for Italy and Spain only. No data available for former Soviet grouping or for Slovenia. *Figure for Eastern Europe is for the Czech and Slovak Republics only. Figures in parentheses are coefficients of variation.

transformation is, in turn, brought about by the fact that tax incidence is much lower and the mix between public and private expenditure is quite different in the English-speaking world than in the EU. These are findings based on group means and not on measures of dispersion, which, with the exception of the tight clustering of the overseas English-speaking countries in respect of net public and net total spending provide little evidence of coherent grouping in respect of the new dimensions of spending elaborated here. Moreover, the only groupings that are distinct from one another are the Continental and non-European groupings both of which exhibit levels of net total social expenditure more than 1 S.D. greater than in the, here, only two-country, Eastern European grouping. Although somewhat far-fetched in real world terms, Eastern Europe qualifies as a model of low net total spending for the bigger spending countries of Europe and the English-speaking world.

Table 5-7 tells us relatively little about country groupings, but it speaks volumes concerning the nature of American social policy exceptionalism. In the first column of the table, the United States, spending just 14.7% of GDP, starts out as almost the lowest spender in the OECD, but in the last column, spending 23.1% of GDP, it finishes as the fourth biggest spender, behind only Germany,

France, and Sweden. And what makes for this transformation are two features in respect of which the United States is, indeed, quite exceptional: it has a much lower (in fact, markedly negative) tax incidence on welfare spending and a hugely greater level of private spending than any other country in the OECD. Moreover, if we regard private and public welfare spending as to some degree substitutes or functional alternatives, it seems reasonable to reverse the apparent logic of Table 5-7 and argue that America's exceptionally low public spending and its preference for providing income maintenance supplements through tax credits can be explained by a prior preference for private over public spending. That in turn also explains American exceptionalism in respect of the balance between external plus internal security and social security, for, counting in private spending into the American social security total in Table 5-4, gives that country a ratio very similar to those of Greece and the United Kingdom: at the high end of the distribution, but not qualitatively different from those of other nations.

The Americanization of Social Policy

We have now discovered at least some features of American social policy development that makes it quite distinctively different from other OECD countries. Before trying to sum up the findings, I seek to investigate one final issue suggested by the topic of this volume: whether changes in the character of European and other OECD states over the past quarter century have made them more like the United States.

Table 5-8 seeks to do this by providing evidence of the extent to which various dimensions of social policy have changed relative to the values manifested by the United States over recent decades. This table differs from earlier ones in presenting individual country figures rather than averages and dispersion measures for groupings of countries. The table contains figures for three sets of variables, each measured in 1980 and at a date early in the new millennium. The three variables are total social expenditure (as earlier in Table 5-2), spending on social services other than health as a percentage of GDP (an alternative measure of the shift to service provision to that appearing in Table 5-5), and decommodification scores (as in Table 5-6). Figures in the table represent the extent to which these countries exceed or fall short of values recorded by the United States and comparisons between 1980 and the early years of the new century show whether values have become more or less like those of the United States with the passing of time. Values that have become less like those of the United States are highlighted in the text. Since values could become more like those of the United States because American values have been trending downwards, it is worth noting that total social expenditure in the United States increased by 2.9% of GDP between 1980 and 2003 and social services by 0.1 of a percent of GDP, but that the United States' decommodification score declined by 0.5 between 1980 and 2002. None of the highlighted figures in the final column

Table 5-8: Country-Specific Distances Relative to the United States in Respect for Total Social Expenditure as a Percentage of GDP, Social Services Spending as a Percentage of GDP, and Decommodification Index Scores, 1980 and Early 2000s

	(1) SOCX 1980	(2) SOCX 2003	(3) Social Services 1980	(4) Social Services 2003	(5) DECOM 1980	(6) DECOM 2002
Austria	9.3	9.9	.1	2.6	9.2	10.7
Belgium	10.2	10.3	−.6	.6	11.9	12.5
France	7.5	12.5	.4	1.7	9.1	8.9
Germany	9.7	11.1	.1	.9	11.0	12.6
Netherlands	10.8	4.5	.4	1.2	13.2	16.5
Greece	−1.8	5.1	−.8	.6	n/a	n/a
Italy	4.7	8.0	−.6	−.2	2.0	8.6
Portugal	−2.5	7.3	−.9	.4	n/a	n/a
Spain	2.2	4.1	−.7	.3	n/a	n/a
Denmark	11.9	11.4	3.9	5.2	14.4	16.8
Finland	5.1	6.3	1.1	2.7	9.3	12.0
Sweden	15.3	15.1	4.2	6.4	17.8	14.4
Ireland	3.5	−.3	−.3	.2	3.2	10.8
United Kingdom	3.3	3.9	−.3	2.2	4.3	6.6
Australia	−2.4	1.7	−.4	1.5	1.5	−.2
Canada	.8	1.1	2.0	1.7	6.4	7.0
Mean	5.5	7.0	.6	1.8	8.7	10.6
Standard Deviation	5.4	4.4	1.6	1.8	5.0	4.6

Source and notes: Columns 1 and 2 = total social expenditure as a percentage of GDP minus the value for the United States in the year in question, calculated from the OECD, *Social Expenditure Database* (2007). Columns 3 and 4 = spending on social services other than health as a percentage of GDP minus the value for the United States in the year in question, also calculated from OECD (2007). Columns 5 and 6 = decommodification index scores minus the value for the United States in the year in question, calculated from the *Comparative Welfare Entitlements Data Set* (Scruggs 2004). Negative signs indicate a value lower than that for the United States. Highlighted figures indicate cases where country-specific distances relative to the United States were greater in the early 2000s than in 1980. No data available for the postcommunist countries of the EU. No decommodification index scores for most of the countries of Southern Europe.

of Table 5-8 would cease to count as instances of lessened similarity with the United States if an adjustment were made to take into account this marginal decline in the American decommodification level.

The basic story told by Table 5-8 is that, despite trends toward globalization and shifts towards neoliberal ideology, countries have, in general, been becoming less rather than more similar to the United States. This is true of eleven countries out of sixteen in respect of total social expenditure, nine countries out of sixteen in respect of social services, and ten countries out of fifteen in respect of decommodification scores. It should also be noted that the apparently rather lower figure for social services is somewhat deceptive. All four Southern European countries manifest values more similar to those of the United States at the end of the period than at the beginning, but that is because these countries' values started out lower than those of the United States and the growth trend all have experienced in recent decades has not yet succeeded in giving them positive values as high as their earlier negative ones. If existing trends continue, that is likely to occur in coming decades.

American social provision may be exceptional in certain respects, but across the dimensions measured here, the United States has not conspicuously served as a model for other advanced nations in recent decades. That is most certainly true of the nations making up EU-12, but there is equally no evidence of the kind of polarization sometimes suggested by which European countries move farther away from the American model, while the other English-speaking countries become more similar. In respect of social spending, Britain and Canada have moved away from American levels of provision, while Australia, which started out as a much lower spender than the United States is now a higher spender. Ireland's markedly declining social spending as a percentage of GDP is the one instance clearly conforming to the polarization hypothesis. In the area of social service provision, Australia and the United Kingdom have moved decisively away from the American level of spending, while Canada (an original big spender in this area) and Ireland have taken tiny steps back. Finally three out of four English-speaking countries have shifted away from the rather distinctive low decommodification profile common to both the United States and Australia (see the discussion of Table 5-6 above). There is, therefore, no more evidence that the English-speaking countries are likely to enjoy an Americanized future in respect of the dimensions of social provision covered here than there is that the EU as a whole is moving in such a direction.

CONCLUSIONS

This chapter began by presenting a strategy of comparison somewhat different from that employed in Alber's study of "The European Social Model and the United States." The chapter concludes by contrasting the findings of the two inquiries. Alber's summing up suggests that "for most indicators the range of variation within the European Union is bigger than the gap between Europe and the United States" and that "counter to the idea of policy convergence, differences in the developmental trajectories of countries with different institutional arrangements persist" (Alber 2006: 393). The findings reported here demonstrate that, in respect to many dimensions of state activity, Alber is absolutely right in arguing that differences within the EU absolutely overwhelm the difference between Europe and the United States. However, that conclusion does not hold in respect to all the dimensions of spending covered by this study and there are instances where elements of a European social model appear to be emerging and where a strong case can be made for American exceptionalism.

The difference in conclusions concerning the emergence of a European social model could be seen as a matter of splitting hairs. The European model identified here in respect to high levels of total spending and high levels of benefit decommodification is a model pointing to the similarities within EU-12 rather than EU-14. This originally Continental (and to a lesser extent Scandinavian) model has been assimilated in Southern Europe over the last two decades and now stands as a beacon for those who wish to improve levels of social protection in the new member states. Alber can properly defend his view by arguing that Britain and Ireland are indeed long-term members of the European Community that have not assimilated EU standards. The proposition offered here can be defended by arguing that, in an analysis premised, as both of these are, on putative family of nations differences and on possible differences between Europe and the United States, it makes sense to consider the possibility that, at least, some of the differences in question are attributable to the fact that some members of the EU share characteristics with the United States in virtue of their membership of the English-speaking family of nations.

However, not all the differences between Europe and America are of this kind: in some respects, including the balance between social and external plus internal security spending, the tax incidence on public social spending and the extent of private social expenditure, America is quite exceptional. Although not technically displaying exceptionalism in respect of low levels of decommodification, a case can also be made that the United States along with Australia are set apart from other OECD countries. A possible interpretation of these differences is that they all stem from a very marked American preference for private over public interventions, which limits and transforms the role of the state in many different ways. The cultural antecedents of that difference in preferences are outside the scope of this chapter. So too are consequences, but postulated linkages between low levels of decommodification and low tax incidence on the one hand and high levels of poverty and inequality on the other go a long way to explaining the extremely high American values that Alber's earlier study identifies in these latter respects. It is good news, therefore, that the evidence presented here does not suggest that the majority of OECD countries have favored policies that make them more like the American exemplar.

Finally, it should be pointed out that policy convergence and differences in the trajectory of family of nations' developmental patterns are not necessarily in conflict. In many instances, greater overall similarities amongst wider groupings of nations such as the EU or the OECD can go along with greater emergent similarities within the subgroupings making up such collectivities. In technical terms, all that is required is for the degree of dispersion (measured by the CV) of the subgroups and wider grouping to decrease simultaneously, but for the dispersion of some or all of the subgroups to decline to a greater degree. This is essentially what was happening to the three categories of state spending analyzed in Tables 5-1–5-3. As a recent study shows (Castles and Obinger 2008), this has been a very general phenomenon in the recent political economy of the advanced democratic states, applying not only to policy inputs and outcomes, but also to their political and economic antecedents. Fortunately, we do not always have to choose between greater similarity and persisting difference.

REFERENCES

Adema, Willem and Ladaique, Maxime (2005) Net Social Expenditure, 2005 Edition. More Comprehensive Measures of Social Support, OECD Social, Employment and Migration Working Papers No. 29, Paris.

Alber, Jens (2006) The European Social Model and the United States, *European Union Politics*, 7, 3: 393–419.

Anttonen, Anttonen and Sipilä, Jorma (1996) European Social Care Services: Is it Possible to Identify Models, *Journal of European Social Policy*, 6, 2: 87–100.

Castles, Francis G. (ed.) (1982) *The Impact of Parties*, London: Sage Publications.

Castles, Francis G. (2002) The European Social Model: Progress Since the Early 1980s, *European Journal of Social Security*, 4, 1: 7–21.

Castles, Francis G. (2004) *The Future of the Welfare State*, Oxford: Oxford University Press.

Castles, Francis G. (2006) The Growth of the Post-war Public Expenditure State: Long-term Trajectories and Recent Trends, TranState Working Papers, No. 35, University of Bremen.

Castles, Francis G. (ed.) (2007) *The Disappearing State?* Cheltenham, UK: Edward Elgar.

Castles, Francis G. and Obinger, Herbert (2007) Social Expenditure and the Politics of Redistribution, *Journal of European Social Policy*, 17, 3: 206–222.

Castles, Francis and Herbert Obinger (2008) Worlds, Families, Regimes: Country Clusters in European and OECD Area Public Policy, *West European Politics*, 31, 1 & 2: 321–344.

Esping-Andersen, Gøsta (1990) *The Three Worlds of Welfare Capitalism*, Cambridge, UK: Polity.

Esping-Andersen, Gøsta (1999) *Social Foundations of Postindustrial Economies*, Oxford: Oxford University Press.

Fraser, Neil and Norris, Paul (2007) Data on the Functions of Government: Where are We Now? In Castles, Francis (ed.) *The Disappearing State?* Cheltenham, UK: Edward Elgar.

Gilbert, Neil (2002) *Transformation of the Welfare State: The Silent Surrender of Public Responsibility*, Oxford, UK: Oxford University Press.

Hofferbert, Rick and Budge, Ian (1996) Patterns of Postwar Expenditure Priorities in Ten Democracies, in Louis Imbeau and Robert McKinley (eds) *Comparing Government Activity*, London: Macmillan.

Huber, Evelyne and Stephens, John (2001) *Development and the Crisis of the Welfare State*, Chicago, IL: University of Chicago Press.

Immergut, Ellen (1992) *The Political Construction of Interests: National Health Insurance Politics in Switzerland, France and Sweden, 1930–1970*, New York, NY: Cambridge University Press.

Kautto, Mikko; Fritzell, Johan; Hvinden, Bjørn; Kvist, Jon and Uusitalo, Hannu (eds.) (2001) *Nordic Welfare States in the European Context*, London: Routledge.

OECD (2007) Social Expenditure Database, Paris.

Peacock, Alan and Wiseman, Jack (1961) *The Growth of Public Expenditures in the United Kingdom*, Princeton, NJ: Princeton University Press.

Sanz, Ismael and Velázquez, Francisco (2004) The Evolution and Convergence of the Government Expenditure Composition in the OECD Countries, *Public Choice*, 119, 1–2: 61–72.

Schmidt, Manfred (1996) When Parties Matter: a Review of the Possibilities and Limits of Partisan Influence on Public Policy, *European Journal of Political Research*, 30, 2: 155–183.

Schuknecht, Ludger and Tanzi, Vito (2005) *Reforming Public Expenditure in Industrialized Countries: Are There Trade-offs?* European Central Bank: Working Paper, No. 435.

Scruggs, Lyle (2004) *Comparative Welfare Entitlement Data Set*, University of Connecticut.

Swank, Duane (2002) *Global Capital, Political Institutions, and Policy Change in Developed Welfare States*, Cambridge, UK: Cambridge University Press.

Tanzi, Vito and Schuknecht, Ludger (2000) *Public Spending in the 20th Century: A Global Perspective*, Cambridge, UK: Cambridge University Press.

Taylor-Gooby, Peter (ed.) (2004) *New Risks, New Welfare: The Transformation of the European Welfare State*, Oxford, UK: Oxford University Press.

Wilensky, Harold (1975) *The Welfare State and Equality*, Berkeley, CA: University of California Press.

6

COMPARATIVE ANALYSES OF STATENESS AND STATE ACTION: WHAT CAN WE LEARN FROM PATTERNS OF EXPENDITURE?

NEIL GILBERT

What types of public expenditure can be computed to assess "stateness" and state action? And once these measures of expenditure are agreed upon, what meaning can be drawn from simple rank-order comparisons (or more sophisticated statistical clusters) of where the United States and the European nations stand according to the computations employed. Conventional measures of state action often focus on two major realms of activity—defense and social welfare—and involve some metric of public expenditure, typically calculated as a percentage of gross domestic product (GDP). In examining what meanings can be drawn for comparative measures of similarities and differences in United States and European activity in these realms, I will comment on defense, but concentrate mainly on the realm of social welfare.

There are fundamental differences between public spending on defense and social welfare not only in what such spending buys, but in how it impacts the behavior of other countries. It is widely recognized that the United States spends considerably more than Western Europe on defense, whether computed in absolute dollars, spending per capita, or as a percentage of the gross national product (GNP). In 1999, U.S. military expenditures were almost 50% higher than Western European expenditures measured as a proportion of the GNP, three times higher measured as a percentage of central government spending and two and a half times higher calculated on dollars per capita. Among the nineteen members of NATO (North Atlantic Treaty Organization), only Greece and Turkey spend a higher percentage of their GDP on defense than the United States—in 2002 the U.S. defense expenditures amounted to 64% of the total NATO defense expenditures (see for example Chamberlin 2003; U.S. Department of State 2004).

The empirical measures are fairly clear-cut. But what does this sharp empirical difference in defense spending between the United States and Western Europe signify? Does it reflect distinct social models of state activity regarding the degree of concern around issues of homeland protection and external security? Does the large difference indicate divergent models of peacefulness? (This is suggested by the Economist Intelligence Unit's Global Peace Index, which places the United States among the least peaceful countries in the world, ranking 96th just below Iran and almost 50 levels above the highest ranked Western European country.)[1] Otherwise, do the different levels of military expenditure in this case reflect the degree to which European allies benefit from what economists call externalities or neighborhood effects of United States spending on defense? If a friendly neighbor paid to have a fire hydrant installed in front of his house, it would increase your sense of security and reduce any necessity you might otherwise have felt to submit to the same expense of having a hydrant installed in front of your house. Even if the neighbor were not all that friendly, it would be in his interest to help put out a fire next door before it spreads to his home.

Defense spending generates direct interaction effects among countries, which are bolstered by formal alliances and historical friendships that cannot be discounted (nor exactly quantified). One might ask what would the levels of military spending in Western Europe look like if the United States declared itself neutral, as do several European countries, and reduced its military spending and presence accordingly? Interaction effects distort any interpretation of how and to what extent differences in defense spending might represent alternative social models. The external security provided by their U.S. allies reduces the level of public spending required by European countries to achieve an acceptable level of military protection, resulting in more public funds being potentially available for investment in welfare state benefits and programs.

In contrast to public spending in the realm of defense, U.S. social welfare spending has relatively limited impact on social expenditures in other advanced industrial nations. Increased spending on old-age pensions or disability by the United States, for example, would have little immediate bearing on pension expenditures in Western European countries. And Castles finds no evidence of decreases in social welfare expenditures that might have interaction effects leading to the proverbial race to the bottom (see Castles 2004: 21–47). Thus, social welfare expenditures allow for straightforward comparisons between United States and the European countries, which are not contaminated by interaction effects. But even here the interpretation of comparative measures is far from self-evident.

Direct social expenditure defined by spending on social welfare as a percentage of GDP is a measure widely employed by policy analysts, researchers, and journalists to represent an important element of state action—and I should say that I must count myself among this group of users (Gilbert 2002; Guo and Gilbert 2007). Specifically, this conventional metric of social expenditure generated by the Organization for Economic Cooperation and Development (OECD) has been used to depict the generosity of welfare states and to compare "welfare efforts" made by different countries.[2] Despite its pervasive use, however, over the last decade it has become increasingly evident that for comparative purposes the direct expenditure standard of social accounting is deeply flawed; it conveys only part of the picture and in so doing presents a distorted view of state action. Although the index of social spending has gained some degree of normative credibility by repetition, the fact that it is widely employed does not strengthen its utility or meaningful interpretation as a comparative measure of the magnitude of social welfare effort or generosity.[3]

SOCIAL ACCOUNTING: DIFFERENT LEDGERS

It has long been recognized that in addition to the checks written directly by the government, comprehensive measures of a state's "generosity" and "welfare effort" should include other sources of social expenditure that promote individual and family welfare. As early as the 1930s, special tax deductions and exemptions were identified as a form of government transfer in Arthur Pigou's classic text "Economics of Welfare," an idea later elaborated on by Richard Titmuss (see his analysis of social, occupational, and fiscal welfare in Titmuss 1958: 34–55). Although the idea was bandied about for several decades, it was not until the mid-1970s that data on tax expenditures became available and were introduced as a regular component of the president's budget in the United States, which was among the first countries to collect this information (for a discussion of this development in the United States, see Surrey 1974 and Goode 1977).

But tax expenditures are not the only measures that need to be weighed into a comprehensive calculation of welfare effort. Taxes on social benefits also count. When social benefits in cash are considered part of the recipients' income, they may be subject to direct income tax as well as sales and value- added taxes, which reduce the amount of cash subsidies that the beneficiaries actually consume on goods and services; thus, many governments "claw back" a significant portion of cash benefit by taxing them. This is increasingly recognized. When the value-added tax was extended to cover domestic fuel in the United Kingdom, for example, policymakers adjusted cash payments to low-income recipients to compensate for the loss in real value of these benefits.[4]

Beyond spending and taxing, governments can also create and manage social expenditures through their powers of regulation. One state can require private employers to finance various forms of social protection that another state might provide through taxing and spending. These off-the-ledger arrangements for social protection usually include employer payments for absence from work due to sickness and maternity leave as well as required pension contributions to employer-based or individual pension plans.

Finally, according to the OECD, a full accounting of social expenditures should include all transfers, cash and in-kind, by public and private institutions that provide people support and protection against the risks of modern life (OECD 1999a). (This definition excludes transfers between households.) Under the OECD definition of social expenditures, voluntary private social benefits form another component in the comprehensive measure of welfare effort. From an individual recipient's point of view, it does not much matter whether, for example, their employer is statutorily required to provide child care, health insurance, and pensions or whether such benefits are granted voluntarily. Voluntary social expenditures include a range of employer-provided benefits as well as many in-kind social supports that are delivered by private nonprofit organizations funded through charitable contributions. But voluntary private benefits are rarely entirely a private matter. Although these benefits are not legally mandated, government still affects the behavior of private institutions and individuals by offering tax incentives that encourage them to provide additional social expenditures. (Part of the voluntary financing is counted as public spending under the category of tax expenditures.) Through this tax mechanism offering public support for private responsibility the state enables voluntary spending on social benefits. Thus, in addition to public and publicly mandated private benefits, a comprehensive ledger of the ways state action generates social expenditure needs to include the value of voluntary private social benefits.

In 2007, voluntary private benefits on health and work-related pensions in the United States were partially subsidized by approximately $260 billion in federal tax expenditures (Bureau of the Census 2007). Charitable contributions provided $241 billion for community purposes in 2002—three-quarters of this amount came from individual contributions (American Association of Fund-Raising Counsels 2003). "Tax deductions are a monetary ointment to salve the strains of charity," which provide an indispensable incentive for individuals to support services of their choice (Vickery 1962). On the relationship between voluntary giving and tax exemptions research suggests that a huge proportion of large-sum donors would substantially reduce their contributions if the deductions were removed (Manser 1971: 10; and Voluntary Giving and Tax Policy 1972).

As it became increasingly clear that the conventional measure of social expenditure as a percentage of GDP failed to account for all channels of social spending and as additional data on these channels became available, by the mid-1990s, researchers at the OECD developed a new ledger for social accounting (Adema et al. 1996). This ledger of Net Total Social Expenditure (NSE) introduces the most rigorous and comprehensive index of social spending to date. Specifically, it incorporates the cumulative value of benefits distributed through direct public expenditures, tax expenditures, publicly mandated private expenditures, and voluntary private social expenditures, reduced by the cost of direct and indirect taxes on these benefits.

How do countries measure up on the new index of NSE compared with the conventional yardstick of social spending as a percentage of GDP—the "gross public social expenditure" index? Analysis of twenty-three of the OECD countries for which data are available shows (see Table 6-1) that in 87% of the cases their ranks on social spending change as the operational definition becomes more inclusive. In many cases, these changes are not trivial. For example, measured by gross public social expenditure as a percentage of GDP, Denmark stands second in welfare effort, Germany as fourth, and the United States as twentieth comes in close to the bottom of the list.

In contrast, when ranked on the most comprehensive measure—net social expenditure—Germany jumps to number one, and the order of standing between the United States and Denmark is reversed as the United States moves up to the sixth place and Denmark drops into the seventh place. (Denmark's

Table 6-1: Rank of Twenty-Three OECD Countries Compared by Gross Public Social Expenditure and Net Total Social Expenditure as % of GDP

Country	Gross Public Social Expenditure Rank	Net Total Social Expenditure Rank
Sweden	1	3
Denmark	2	7
France	3	2
Germany	4	*1*
Austria	5	10
Finland	6	15
Belgium	7	5
Italy	8	9
Norway	9	12
United Kingdom	10	4
Netherlands	11	8
Czech Republic	12	16
Iceland	13	17
Spain	14	18
New Zealand	15	20
Australia	16	11
Slovak Republic	17	19
Canada	18	13
Japan	19	14
United States	*20*	*6*
Ireland	21	21
Korea	22	22
Mexico	23	23

Source and calculation: see Appendix A.

decline is due in part to taxes, which claw back a relatively high proportion of their social expenditures—a process under which it is difficult to distinguish social expenditures from "social churning" of public funds.)

On this comprehensive ledger of social accounting, the range of social expenditure among the United States and most Western European countries has narrowed. There is much greater correspondence in the overall proportion of the GDP transferred as social benefits through public interventions—via direct spending, indirect measures, regulatory measures, and incentives—in advanced industrialized societies than appears when judged by the conventional measure of gross public spending. According to this comprehensive measure, most Western European countries and the United States have allocated roughly equivalent proportions of their resources to social welfare transfers, but in somewhat different ways.

COMPARING AND INTERPRETING EXPENDITURES: FOUR ISSUES

However, even with the more rigorous measure of NSE, at least four issues remain which confound reasonable interpretation of what meaning can be drawn from ranking countries on their social spending in relation to their GDP. These issues involve the assumption of proportionality, indifference to need, incomplete coverage, and the discounted activities of the "other hand."

Proportionality

In comparing the levels at which states seek to provide for social welfare, social expenditure as a percentage of the GDP is based on a scale of measurement, which favors proportionality over absolute spending. This metric ignores population size and wealth, which makes the substantive meaning of comparative state efforts difficult to interpret. Consider, for example, country X, which has the same size population but three times the GDP of country Y. If country X spends twice as much on social welfare as country Y, each of its citizens is on an average receiving twice the amount of social benefits as in country Y—yet country X will be ranked lower in social expenditures as a percentage of GDP. What does this mean? Is country X making less of a social welfare effort than country Y? Is it less active in promoting social expenditure than country Y? That interpretation can be made only if one assumes that state action in the realm of social welfare should be proportionately equivalent regardless of population size and wealth. Is it unlikely that citizens in country X seeking to maximize their social benefits will flock to country Y because it has a higher social welfare expenditure ranking based on the conventional measure?

The assumption of proportionality is made in the absence of any knowledge about the need for social spending. It is an assumption that bears critical scrutiny. Various analysts have suggested that among the wealthy nations at a certain point of affluence growth of social expenditure might be expected to slacken as citizens possess greater resources to make private arrangements for security.[5]

Taking these considerations into account, another way of comparing social expenditure is in terms of per capita state spending controlled for purchasing power of different currencies. Here, as seen in Table 6-2, the countries' ranks are quite different from where they were placed when measured according to expenditures as a percentage of GDP. They also vary according to whether we are considering per capita gross public social expenditure or per capita net total social expenditure.

What can we learn from comparative measures of social expenditure? As shown in Table 6-3, both the position and distance in comparative rankings of social expenditures of Denmark, Germany, and the United States vary according to which measures are employed. Thus, for example, Denmark, which ranked

Table 6-2: Rank of Twenty-Three OECD Countries Compared by Gross Public Social Expenditure and Net Total Social Expenditure in Per Capita Spending Adjusted for Purchasing Power Parity (PPP)

Country	Gross Public Social Expenditure Per Capita in PPP Order	Net Total Social Expenditure Per Capita in PPP Order
Norway	1	2
Denmark	2	8
Sweden	3	3
Austria	4	10
France	5	4
Belgium	6	7
Germany	7	5
Finland	8	13
Netherlands	9	9
United Kingdom	10	6
Italy	11	15
United States	12	1
Canada	13	11
Australia	14	12
Ireland	15	16
Spain	16	17
Japan	17	14
New Zealand	18	18
Czech Republic	19	19
Slovak Republic	20	20
Korea	21	21
Mexico	22	22
Iceland	N.A	N.A.

Source and calculations: see Appendix A.

Table 6-3: Social Expenditure Rank of Denmark, Germany, and the U.S. Among Twenty-Three OECD Countries by Alternative Measures

Country	Gross Public Social Expenditure as % of GDP	Net Total Social Expenditure as % of GDP	Gross Public Social Expendture Per Capita PPP	Net Total Social Expenditure Per Capita PPP
Denmark	2	7	2	8
Germany	4	1	7	5
United States	20	6	12	1

second according to gross public social expenditure drops to eighth when the comparison is on per capita NSE; Germany moves from the fourth to the fifth place when the metric shifts to per capita gross social expenditure; and the United States climbs from the twentieth in gross public social expenditure to the first place when the comparison is made according to per capita net social expenditure.

Even if there were firm agreement on which of these indices provides the best or most meaningful measure for comparative judgments, what they are actually comparing remains extremely cloudy. Whatever measure one might choose, they all embody assumptions and limitations that constrain meaningful conclusions that might be drawn from position and distance of rankings and the monetary sums on which they are based. Any interpretation of these measures must contend with the three other issues: What are the standards of need for judging the value of different levels of public spending? (Is more spending always better?) Do these measures of spending capture the full range of government action? What is the other hand up to?

Need

Whether social expenditures are compared on the bases of gross public social expenditure or NSE as a percentage of GDP or per capita social spending, such comparisons are based on a normative assumption regarding "stateness" or state action—simply stated, where social spending is concerned, the more, the better. States that spend a higher proportion of their GDP or more dollars per capita on social welfare measures are leaders and those that do not are laggards. It is assumed that they provide more social protection than those that spend less. In the absence of any criteria of need, this implicit judgment provides no basis for empirical evaluation. If social spending by the state is made to achieve a desirable condition of social well-being (or security) then to compare these social expenditures without reference to social and material needs that must be met conveys the impression that needs are either irrelevant to the social conditions being sought or are equal among all the countries being compared. Empirically we know the material conditions are not equal.[6] (If the levels of material need among countries are different to begin with, can we meaningfully compare levels of social expenditure without somehow adjusting for this difference?)

The absence of any controls for standards of well-being or need makes it extremely difficult to determine what different levels of social expenditure actually represent. For example, consider two countries of roughly equivalent population size and wealth—one which has an unemployment rate that is 4% higher than in the other country. Country X with the higher rate of unemployment has a higher rate of social expenditure than country Y (with low unemployment) whether measured as a percentage of GDP or per capita social expenditure. For purposes of comparative analysis, what does the higher level of social expenditure represent—more "stateness" or state action? Or is it just a surrogate for higher unemployment? (If state X offer its citizens greater social protection or social well-being than state Y, then one way for state Y to achieve the same level of "well-being" is to increase unemployment.)

In 1990, with 20% of the Dutch labor force out on disability or sick leave, spending on these social benefits amounted to 7% of the GDP. Comparative studies indicate that the incidence of sickness and disability claims in the Netherlands were considerably higher than in neighboring Western European countries.[7] To what extent did the high level of social expenditure at that time signify the state's generosity, an authentically higher incidence of disability, a more permissive climate, or a disincentive to work created by a high replacement rate (up to 70% of the last gross wage)?[8]

Various attempts have been made to reformulate the operational measure of social expenditure by including a standardized measure of need. The Need, Expenditure, and Taxes (NET) Index of Welfare Effort constructed in 1988 was one of the earliest systematic efforts to design a comprehensive measure of social expenditure, which calculated direct public expenditures plus tax expenditures as a percentage of GDP controlling for standardized tax burden and a standardized measure of need. (See Gilbert and Moon 1988: 326–340; and the expanded version in Gilbert and Gilbert 1989. For similar efforts see Clayton and Pontusson 1998; and Castles 2004.) In this study, the standardized index of need was constructed based on the unemployment rate, the dependency ratio, and the percentage of single-parent families.

Yet the issue remains that there are many ways to conceptualize "need," which could yield different results. The authors of the NET Index of Welfare Effort recognized "there are a number of variables that might plausibly be used to estimate the magnitudes of need among countries." They suggested that rates of pretransfer poverty might offer one of the best estimates, though variations in the definition of poverty would again yield vastly different results. For example, according to the oft-used relative measure of poverty as those with less than 50% of the median income, the poverty rate in the United States is twice as high as that in the Czech Republic—at the same time 50% of the median net household income in the United States adjusted for purchasing power parity is almost four times as high as that of the Czech Republic. Even the operational definitions of unemployment rates vary among countries.[9]

Coverage

Although, to date, the OECD's definition of NSE provides the most comprehensive measure of social spending and in theory covers different levels of government spending, it best captures government activity at the national level and fails to capture a considerable amount of direct and indirect social spending by regional, state, and local governments—where the data are often difficult to come by.[10] This is likely to introduce a systematic bias in what gets included in the final calculations. That is, the NSE would tend to offer a more comprehensive account of the full range of government social spending for relatively small countries in which social spending is highly centralized at the national level of government than in larger more decentralized countries.

In the United States, for example, state, county, and city governments fund a wide range of social programs, particularly in the areas of mental health, child welfare, education, health, and, to a lesser degree, income maintenance. In addition to federal income tax, state income taxes are collected in forty-two of the fifty states, among which there is considerable variation. There is also significant variation among tax expenditures for social purposes at the state level. In 2006, eighteen states in the United States had state earned income tax credit programs.[11] Several states provide other tax credits for child care, property tax, and health insurance (Karger and Stoesz 2006: 244). More than thirty states provide general assistance benefits, which are financed and administered by state, county, or local units of government. State and locally mandated private social expenditures range from state mandated health insurance coverage to city mandated rent control programs.[12] (The total private subsidy generated by rent control programs in cities throughout the United States is immensely difficult to calculate.) And there are many other local variations of mandated social expenditures. In San Francisco, for instance, developers constructing large downtown offices are required to include a child care facility in the building or to pay $1 per square of the total property into a city child care fund. Finally, although the NSE index includes government rent subsidies and other benefits that help with housing costs, it does not include public subsidies for housing generated via tax expenditures for home mortgage deductions, which amounted to roughly $80 billion in the United States in 2007 (Bureau of the Census 2007); nor does it capture the cash value of government credit-subsidies for home mortgages. In the United States where there is a relatively high proportion of residential home ownership, about 25% of the entire nonfarm residential mortgage debt was publicly guaranteed.[13]

There is likely to be an interaction effect between social expenditures at the national and local levels of government—with local expenditures reducing the pressure on national spending. The failure to capture the full range of social spending would tend to distort comparative analyses by magnifying the percentage of GDP that goes to social expenditures in those countries where taxing and spending is more highly centralized.

The Other Hand

Voltaire observed long ago that "in general, the art of government is taking as much money as possible from one class of citizens to give to the other." In making public expenditures for social purposes the state must use two hands—one to collect the money and the other to distribute it. The OECD's NSE index focuses our attention on the total sum that is being directly or indirectly dispensed by government (expressed as a percentage of GDP)—the hand that is giving out the money, so to speak. The NSE index shows that this hand employs several processes and policy instruments to promote social spending. That is, the state may engage in direct spending for social purposes or it may employ indirect methods to channel funds for social purposes through special tax deductions and credits (tax expenditures), through regulatory measures that mandate private spending, and through tax incentives that stimulate voluntary private contributions for social purposes.

Among these various approaches the largest proportion of funds tallied by the NSE index comes from direct public social expenditures. The NSE index, however, tends to ignore what the government is doing with the other hand to raise these funds. This conveys an implicit assumption that among the countries being compared the public funds spent on social purposes come from the same source—current tax revenues. The issue of the "other hand" arises when current tax revenues are not enough to cover government expenditures and require a high level of deficit spending. How then does one compare and interpret the relative "stateness" or welfare generosity of two countries one which has financed its NSE partially by creating debt that shifts the tax burden to another generation and the other country, which has financed a lower level of NSE entirely from the current tax revenues? The NSE index sheds little light on those countries that are spending more now by mortgaging future social spending.

The assumption of proportionality, indifference to need, incomplete coverage, and the discounted activities of the "other hand" seriously undermine scientific confidence in what we might learn of a substantive nature about "stateness" or state action from comparative analyses based on the standard (OECD) measures of social expenditure. Still, I have no doubt that this measure will continue to be employed. To do comparative analysis, one needs something to compare and the NSE index represents the main body of quantitative data readily available. Knowledgeable researchers will qualify use of these data by statements such as "despite all these well-taken objections, though there remains something of importance which is captured by crude public expenditure statistics, particularly when the differences are as dramatic as [a table in the study] shows them to be between the three countries here under study" (Goodin et al. 1999: 82). But the authors' explanation of the "something of importance" here does not go beyond the fact that the gross social expenditure figures showed differences among countries. These differences, of course, will vary depending upon the measure of spending and even then their meaning remains clouded by all of the issues raised above.

DYNAMICS OF SOCIAL SPENDING: CONVERGENCE TOWARD INDIRECT METHODS

There is another way of looking at the measure of social expenditures, which allows us to compare stateness or state action while avoiding most of the issues noted above.[14] This perspective involves shifting the analytical lens from comparing the relative magnitude of social welfare spending (ranking states from highest to lowest levels of social expenditure) to comparing how they do it —the dynamics of social spending. A comparative analysis of the dynamics of social spending focuses our attention on state action framed by two closely related questions: To what extent do states generate social expenditures through different policy instruments? To what extent are social expenditures channeled through public and private sources? These questions are related because empirically, alternative policy instruments promote different degrees of public and private activity. As noted earlier, the policy instruments typically employed involve the spending, taxing, and regulatory powers of the state, which can be seen as actions that favor either direct or indirect methods of generating and encouraging social expenditure.

The direct method of social expenditures takes place when government writes a check to fund social programs and benefits. The sum of this direct spending minus the money clawed back through taxes collected on these benefits represents the net direct social expenditure. States also generate and encourage spending on social benefits through indirect methods that include legislative mandates, which require private spending for social purposes and tax measures for social purposes, which provide both cash benefits to families and children, and incentives for the voluntary provision of private social benefits, such as employer sponsored health insurance and pensions, and charitable contributions. (As OECD explains, the measures here are incomplete since they do not include tax breaks for pensions due to the lack of comparable data sets; (OECD, 2007 The Social Expenditure Database.) The sum of social spending linked to these indirect methods minus taxes collected on these benefits represents the net "indirect" social expenditure.

These alternative methods have various political implications. Direct methods of state-generated social spending are more transparent, simpler to calculate accurately, and, hence, the connection between direct spending and taxing is easier to grasp than the indirect methods. Measures to increase direct social spending tend to be accompanied by a clear understanding that taxpayers (current or future) will have to cover the costs. Indirect methods, such as tax expenditures have an immediate effect of reducing taxes on those who benefit. The loss of tax revenues eventually may have to be compensated for through other tax increases, but the connection is blurred. Also tax expenditures that provide favorable treatment of employer benefits, for example, compensate for a relatively small proportion of these benefits, the rest of which are shouldered by the employer. Similarly, mandated benefits, avoid the political hazard of imposing a conspicuous tax burden by shifting the visible costs to a third party, sometimes even to another level of government. In the United States, for example, the Individuals with Disabilities Education Act is a federally mandated program that requires subnational units of government to spend around $30 billion a year to serve pupils with disabilities—to which the federal government contributes only 8% of the expense.[15]

As shown in Table 6-4, the majority of social expenditures in all the countries involve the instrument of direct public spending, with considerable variation among the sample of twenty-three OECD countries on the extent to which they employ indirect methods. Korea, the United States, the Netherlands, and Australia generate the highest percentage of social expenditure through indirect methods while Spain, the Czech Republic, Denmark, and New Zealand are at the bottom. The United States and Korea are distinct outliers with around

Table 6-4: Countries Ranked by Use of Direct and Indirect Methods of State Activity

Country	Net Direct Social Expenditure %	Net Indirect Social Expenditure %	Rank of Net Indirect Social Expenditure
>10%			
Korea	58.0	42.0	1
United States	60.2	39.8	2
Netherlands	77.8	22.2	3
Australia	79.6	20.4	4
Japan	79.7	20.3	5
Mexico	80.6	19.4	6
Canada	80.8	19.2	7
United Kingdom	84.1	15.9	8
Germany	87.0	13.0	9
5%–10%			
Belgium	89.7	10.3	10
France	90.0	10.0	11
Sweden	91.2	8.8	12
Norway	93.8	6.2	13
Italy	94.1	5.9	14
Austria	94.5	5.5	15
<5%			
Ireland	95.2	4.8	16
Iceland	95.7	4.3	17
Slovak Republic	95.8	4.2	18
Finland	96.0	4.0	19
New Zealand	96.9	3.1	20
Denmark	96.9	3.1	20
Czech Republic	97.8	2.2	21
Spain	98.2	1.8	22

Table 6-5: Countries Ranked By Use of Public and Private Channels of Expenditure

Country	Net Public Social Expenditure %	Net Private Social Expenditure%	Rank of Net Private Social Expenditure
Korea	61.00	39.00	1
United States	63.64	36.36	2
Netherlands	79.19	20.81	3
Australia	80.09	19.91	4
Canada	82.76	17.24	5
Japan	84.16	15.84	6
United Kingdom	84.55	15.45	7
Germany	90.22	9.78	8
Sweden	91.15	8.85	9
Belgium	91.81	8.19	10
France	92.96	7.04	11
Norway	93.78	6.22	12
Austria	94.50	5.50	13
Italy	94.52	5.48	14
Iceland	95.65	4.35	15
Finland	96.00	4.00	16
Ireland	96.00	4.00	16
New Zealand	96.86	3.14	17
Denmark	96.89	3.11	18
Slovak Republic	97.60	2.40	19
Spain	98.24	1.76	20
Mexico	98.39	1.61	21
Czech Republic	100.00	0.00	22

40% of their NSE (and at 13% Germany is well above the mean) generated and encouraged through the use of taxing and regulatory powers.

By adjusting the analytical lens a bit further, we can calculate the proportion of the NSE that is publicly generated and encouraged but comes through private channels—the sum of mandated and voluntary private social expenditures—in comparison to the proportion that comes straight from public sources—the sum of direct public spending and the cost of tax expenditures that are similar to direct public cash benefits to households, (but not tax expenditures that are aimed at stimulating voluntary private social benefits, such as employer health insurance). In this calculation of public and private spending, the voluntary private social expenditures include the value of that portion of tax expenditures which support private social benefits. It comes as no surprise that comparing the proportion of funds that travel through public and private channels of social expenditure (as shown in Table 6-5) results in a rank order, which closely mirrors the extent to which states employ direct and indirect methods.

What does comparative analysis from this perspective tells us? Rather than trying to formulate distinct regime types or social models based on the countries' ranks and distributions, I would locate the dynamics of social expenditure along a continuum. At one end of the continuum are countries that emphasize public responsibility for social welfare through direct government spending at the other end are countries that (while still assuming a high degree of public responsibility) place more emphasis on public support for private responsibility through the use of regulatory and taxing instruments—the exceptional cases at this end being Korea and the United States.

This cross-sectional analysis of state action shows how things currently stand, but not where they are going. Is the relationship of public and private responsibility changing, and if so in what direction? There are several reasons to think that mean scores on the indices of indirect methods and private social expenditure are going to rise. Data from the OECD indicate that between 1990 and 2003 on average gross private social spending showed a slight increased as a percentage of GDP in a sample of twenty-eight countries. This may mark the beginning of a steeper long-term trend. Since 1992 thirty countries have incorporated private individual accounts into their mandatory pension systems, including Denmark, United Kingdom, Italy, Poland, Slovakia, and Hungary (Kritzer 2005: 32, 36). As these private pension programs mature, it is likely that the proportions of private social expenditure will accelerate.

The use of indirect methods is also likely to increase—as the direct method of taxing and spending seems to have reached a limit. With regard to direct spending, although measures of gross social expenditure as a percentage of GDP are seriously limited for making meaningful comparisons of the magnitude of spending among countries, they can be used to detect trends.[16] Since the calculations are conducted the same way on the same categories every year, their biases are likely to be constant so that the data generated can provide a reliable guide to the overall trend in social spending over time (even as they under-, or overestimate the magnitude of expenditures for the specific countries). As Alber notes according to the Eurostat measure the aggregate spending as a percentage of GDP for the EU-15 peaked in the mid-1990s, dropped about 1% and has remained fairly stagnant through 2004 (Alber 2006). As for the taxes, the average tax rates in OECD countries climbed by more than a quarter from 25.8% to 32.8% of the GDP over the fifteen years, between 1965 and 1980. From 1980 to 1997, however, the rate of increase slowed down considerably (and was even reversed in a few countries) creeping up from 32.8% to 36.9% of the GDP over seventeen years (OECD 1999b: 65–67). With tax rates at an average of 36.9% of the GDP in 1997, there may still be wiggle room for governments to maneuver, but the plateauing of taxes after 1980 lends weight to Douglas Besharov's observation that many governments are approaching a tax ceiling, which will be difficult to raise for political and economic reasons (Besharov et al. 1998). However, for various reasons, not the least of which involves population aging, the states will experience continued pressure to increase social spending.

Under the circumstances, one might imagine that the dynamics of social expenditure will increasingly come to rely on policy instruments that encourage or mandate private provisions. If this scenario is correct, we might anticipate a gradual shift in state action away from the long-standing emphasis on taxing and direct spending for social welfare toward measures designed to generate public support for private responsibility.

REFERENCES

Adema, Willem (1999) *Net Social Expenditures*, Labour Market and Social Policy Occasional Papers, No. 39, Paris: OECD.

Adema, Willem; Einerhand, Marcel; Eklind, Bengt; Lotz, Jorgen and Pearson, Mark (1996) Net Public Social Expenditure, Labour Market and Social Policy Occasional Papers, No. 19, Paris: OECD.

Alber, Jens (2006) The European Social Model and the United States, *European Union Politics*, 7, 3: 393–419.

American Association of Fund-Raising Counsels (2003) *Giving USA 2003*, New York: AAFRC.

Besharov, Douglas with Ehrle, Jennifer and Gardiner, Karen (1998) Social Welfare's Twin Dilemmas: "Universalism vs. Targeting" and "Support vs. Dependency", Paper presented at the International Social Security Association Research Conference, Jerusalem, Israel (January 25–28, 1998).

Bureau of the Census (2007) *Statistical Abstract of the United States, 2007*, Washington D.C.: U.S. Government Printing Office.

Castles, Francis G. (2004) *The Future of the Welfare State: Crisis Myths and Crisis Realities*, Oxford, UK: Oxford University Press.

Chamberlin, Jeffrey (2004) Comparisons of U.S. and Foreign Military Spending: Data from Selected Public Sources, Congressional Research Service Report for Congress, January 28.

Clayton, Richard and Pontusson, Jonas (1998) Welfare State Retrenchment Revisited: Entitlement Cuts, Public Sector Restructuring and Inegalitarian Trends in Advanced Capitalist Societies, *World Politics*, 51: 67–98

Gilbert, Neil (1995) *Welfare Justice: Restoring Social Equity*, New Haven, CT: Yale University Press.

Gilbert, Neil (2002) *Transformation of the Welfare State: The Silent Surrender of Public Responsibility*, New York: Oxford University Press.

Gilbert, Neil and Gilbert, Barbara (1989) *The Enabling State: Modern Welfare Capitalism in America*, New York: Oxford University Press.

Gilbert, Neil and Moon, Ailee (1988) Analyzing Welfare Effort: An Appraisal of Comparative Methods, *Journal of Policy Analysis and Management*, 7, 2: 326–340.

Goode, Richard (1977) The Economic Definition of Income, in Joseph Pechman (ed.) *Comprehensive Income Taxation*, Washington D.C.: Brookings Institution, pp. 1–30.

Goodin, Robert; Headey, Bruce; Muffels, Ruud and Dirven, Henk-Jan (1999) *The Real Worlds of Welfare Capitalism*, Cambridge, UK: Cambridge University Press.

Guo, Jing and Gilbert, Neil (2007) Welfare Regimes and Family Policy: A Longitudinal Analysis, *International Journal of Social Welfare*.

Hicks, Alexander and Swank, Duane (1992) Politics, Institutions, and Welfare Spending in Industrialized Countries, *American Political Science Review*, 86, 3: 658–674.

Johnson, Nicholas and Lazere, Ed (1999) State Earned Income Tax Credits, *Poverty Research News*, Joint Center for Poverty Research, Northwestern University.

Karger, Howard and Stoesz, David (2006) *American Social Welfare Policy*, New York: Pearson Education.

Kritzer, Barbara (2005) Individual Accounts in Other Countries, *Social Security Bulletin*, 66, 1: 31–37.

Manser, Gordon (1971) *The Voluntary Agency—Contribution or Survival?*, Washington Bulletin, 22 (20), October.

McGranahan, Donald (1970) Social Planning and Social Security, Bulletin No. 7, Geneva: International Institute for Labour Studies.

Moroney, Robert (1991) *Social Policy and Social Work: Critical Essays on the Welfare State*, New York: Aldine de Gruyter.

OECD (1991) *Economic Surveys: The Netherlands*, Paris: OECD.

OECD (1999a) *OECD Social Expenditure Database, 1980–1996*, Paris: OECD.

OECD (1999b) *Revenue Statistics: 1965–1998*, Paris: OECD.

OECD (2007) The Social Expenditure Database: An Interpretative Guide Soc X 1980–2003, Paris: OECD.

Nivola, Pietro (1998) The New Pork Barrel, The Public Interest, 131, Spring: 92–104.

Rich, Spencer (1989) Social Welfare Spending, *Washington Post*, April 11.

Rys, Vladimir (1946) The Sociology of Social Security, *Bulletin of the International Social Security Association*, 1–2: 3–34.

Surrey, Stanley (1974) *Pathways to Tax Reform*, Cambridge, MA: Harvard University Press.

Swank, Duane (2001) Political Institutions and Welfare State Restructuring: the Impact of Institutions on Social Policy Changes in Developed Countries, in Paul Pierson (ed.) *The New Politics of the Welfare State*, New York: Oxford University Press, pp. 197–237.

Tax Credit Resources. Org. (2002–2008) State EIC Programs: An Overview. Available online at : <http://www.taxcreditresources.org/pages.cfm?content ID=39&pageID=12&Subpages=yes> (accessed 4 October 2007).

Titmuss, Richard (1958) *Essays on the Welfare State*, 2nd ed. London: Unwin University Books.

U.S. Department of State (2003) World Military Expenditures and Arms Transfers, February 6. Available online at: <http://www.globalsecurity.org/military/library/report2003/wmeat9900/index.html> (accessed 22 September 2007).

Vickery, William S. (1962) One Economist's View of Philanthropy, in Frank Dickinson (ed.) *Philanthropy and Public Policy*, New York: National Bureau of Economic Research, pp. 31–56.

Voluntary Giving and Tax Policy (1972) New York: National Assembly for Social Policy and Development.

Wilensky, Harold (1975) *The Welfare State and Equality*, Berkeley, CA: University of California Press.

GDP per capita PPP ☆ gross public social expenditure as % of GDP= per capita spending PPP on gross public social expenditure
GDP per capita PPP ☆ net current private social expenditure as % of GSP= per capita spending PPP on net current private social expenditure
GDP per capita PPP ☆ net total social expenditure as % of GSP= per capital spending PPP on net total social expenditure

Country	Gross Public Social Expenditure as % of GDP	Net Current Private Social Expenditure as % of GDP	Net Total Social Expenditure as % of GDP	GDP Per Capita in PPP	Gross Public Social Expenditure Per Capita in PPP	Net Current Private Social Expenditure Per Capita in PPP	Net Total Social Expenditure Per Capita in PPP
Australia	18.0	4.2	21.1	35870	6456.6	1506.54	7568.57
Austria	26.0	1.2	21.8	37800	9828	453.6	8240.4
Belgium	24.7	2.0	23.2	36080	8911.76	721.6	8370.56
Canada	17.8	3.5	20.3	37420	6660.76	1309.7	7596.26
Czech Republic	20.1	0.0	18.5	21740	4369.74	0	4021.9
Denmark	29.2	0.7	22.5	36960	10792.32	258.72	8316
Finland	24.8	0.7	20.0	34500	8556	241.5	6900
France	28.5	1.8	27.0	33540	9558.9	603.72	9055.8
Germany	27.4	2.6	27.6	31870	8732.38	828.62	8796.12
Iceland	19.8	0.7	18.4				
Ireland	13.8	0.4	12.5	43700	6030.6	174.8	5462.5
Italy	24.2	1.2	21.9	31030	7571.32	372.36	6795.57
Japan	16.9	3.2	20.2	34150	5771.35	1092.8	6898.3
Korea	6.1	3.9	10.0	23890	1457.29	931.71	2389
Mexico	5.1	0.2	6.2	11160	569.16	22.32	691.92
Netherlands	21.4	4.5	22.1	37390	8001.46	1682.55	8263.19
New Zealand	18.5	0.5	15.9	27770	5137.45	138.85	4415.43
Norway	23.9	1.2	20.9	48190	11517.41	578.28	10071.71
Slovak Republic	17.9	0.4	16.7	18720	3350.88	74.88	3126.24
Spain	19.6	0.3	17.0	29610	5803.56	88.83	5033.7
Sweden	29.8	2.2	26.0	35480	10573.04	780.56	9224.8
United Kingdom	21.8	3.6	23.3	35940	7834.92	1293.84	8374.02
United States	14.7	8.5	23.1	46280	6803.16	3933.8	10690.68

Data source:
Data on social expenditure as % of GDP are from DELSA/ELSA/WD/SEM (2005) 8, table Annex 3. From gross pubic to total net social spending, 2001.
GDP per head in PPP are from "The world in 2007", *The Economist*, pp85.
Data on social expenditure per capital in PPP are calculated by GDP per head in PPP multiplying by corresponding social expenditure as % of GDP.
GDP per head in PPP is missing for Iceland; therefore Iceland was excluded in tables.

SECTION IV

CITIZENSHIP AND WELFARE

7

CONCEPTS AND PRACTICES OF SOCIAL CITIZENSHIP IN EUROPE: THE CASE OF POVERTY AND INCOME SUPPORT FOR THE POOR

CHIARA SARACENO

The idea that there is a social dimension to citizenship, and that social rights are as integral to citizenship rights as civil and political rights, dates, of course, back to T.H. Marshall (1950). According to his approach, in order to enable individuals to act as full and knowledgeable citizens, it was necessary to decommodify the satisfaction of some basic human needs. Thus, to use contemporary policy language, Marshall's concept embodied a vision of active as opposed to passive social citizenship; although this concept, based largely on an idea of citizens as paid workers, applied mainly to men, while women were expected to achieve it in a mediated way, as wives. The concept also proposed a view of social justice whereby inequality would not disappear, but at the same time would not seriously undermine the life chances of the less privileged.

The state would have a crucial, and positive, role in granting this social justice through various forms of income support (mainly old-age pensions, sickness and unemployment benefits) access to education, and health care.

This concept of social citizenship is not very different from that envisaged in the "European Social Model" (ESM) developed, first, by each individual Western European country (with all their diversities) and, more recently (particularly from the Lisbon Agenda onward), in the form of a definition by the European Union (EU) itself. Notwithstanding the country-specific differences and the diverse definitions of the ESM found in public documents and debates, there still seems to be a shared consensus that such a model has the following features (see, e.g., Alber 2006; Giddens 2006: 2):

- A developed and interventionist state, funded, therefore, by relatively high levels of taxation
- A robust welfare system, mainly based on work, but which provides effective social protection to all
- The limitation, or containment, of economic and other forms of inequality

A compulsory old-age pension for workers (funded through either social insurance or the public budget), and either a citizenship pension or a "last resort" pension for the elderly poor, unemployment benefits, sickness benefits, maternity, and, more recently, parental benefits (at least for the employed), are part of the income-support/income-protection package provided by all EU countries. These income-support/income-protection packages are being provided, albeit with varying degrees of generosity, different funding strategies, and different degrees of universalism in the different member states of the EU. Most, but not all, of the EU countries also have a "last resort" minimum income provision in their welfare packages. The presence and the specific characteristics of these provisions are usually not taken into consideration in comparative welfare-state analysis and welfare-state typologizing. Yet, as Leibfried (1993) argues, the way a welfare state addresses poverty is a testing ground for evaluating the contents and limits of social citizenship. Moreover, concern over and protection from poverty is often identified as a specific feature that differentiates the European from the U.S. understanding of social justice and social citizenship. Since the European Council's agreement of 1992 (Council Recommendation 92/441/EEC of 24 June 1992), the provision of "a minimum of resources" (not only income, but also health services, education, and housing) has also been part of the values and goals promoted by the EU. However, this is being done in a less stringent way than with regard to the goals of curtailing budget deficits and promoting employment growth.

In the Lisbon Agenda, the EU and each individual country stressed the role of the state—and of the supranational EU state—in developing this social model within the context of the changing world environment and global competition. In fact, in Lisbon, the EU set itself the goal of becoming "the most competitive and dynamic knowledge-based economy in the world, capable of sustainable economic growth with more and better jobs and greater social cohesion and respect for the environment." The importance of social cohesion—with all its conceptual ambiguity—was placed on par with that of growth, and growth was not to occur at the cost of increasing inequality. This goal implicitly contrasted "social Europe" with the U.S. model, which was seen as more successful in competing at the economic level, but less concerned with issues of social cohesion, inequality, and the environment.

Is this assumption empirically verified? Does the ESM deliver on its promises to combat inequality and promote social inclusion? To what degree can national policies within the EU be seen as variants of a common model as opposed to quite different and even contrasting models of social citizenship? This question is particularly relevant—and the answer is far from self-evident—for two dimensions of the ESM package, gender equality and social inclusion/exclusion. I will address the latter dimension here, with a specific focus on poverty and deprivation. I will focus on three points, in particular. First, I will examine whether, midway through the period set for the Lisbon agenda, substantial improvements regarding the incidence of poverty and social exclusion have been made within the EU. Second, through an analysis of national minimum income support measures, I will asses whether there is a common understanding across the EU regarding the right to a minimum of resources. Third, I will analyze the degree to which EU-level policies and interventions serve to promote the development of a common approach in this area.

POVERTY, SOCIAL EXCLUSION, AND DEPRIVATION IN THE EU: STILL SHORT OF THE LISBON TARGETS

The terms poverty, social exclusion, and deprivation, although often used interchangeably, actually indicate the different levels and aspects of individual and social disadvantage. When the EU introduced the term social exclusion in its official policy language, it had the laudable intention of focusing on the multidimensional nature of poverty, as well as on the societal mechanisms that cause exclusion. However, the term continues to be used with different meanings, and its indicators remain simplistic and confused—particularly so in the policy discourse (for an overview of the debate see, e.g., Saraceno 2002). Within the scientific debate, a great deal of work has been done in recent years in an effort to analytically distinguish these different dimensions and to develop adequate indicators for them (see, e.g., Nolan and Whelan 1996; Leisering and Leibfried 1999; Whelan and Maitre 2007). But these suggestions have not yet been translated into more sophisticated indicators at the policy level, except in Ireland and the UK, where a measure combining income poverty and deprivation indicators is now in use (Heikkilä et al. 2006). In order, however, to assess the EU and single countries' performance with regard to the Lisbon goals, one can start from the indicators—however debatable and debated (for an overview, see Marlier et al. 2007)—the EU uses to assess their own performance. In the short list of the so-called Laeken indicators, four are identified as relevant for the field of social inclusion/social cohesion: (1) at-risk-of-poverty rate after social transfers (percentage of persons with equivalent disposable income below 60% of the national median); (2) long-term unemployment rate (those unemployed twelve months or more as percentage of the total active population who have remained unemployed for 12 months or longer); (3) low education among the young (percentage of the 20- to 24-year-old young not having completed at least upper secondary education); (4) regional cohesion (coefficient of variation of employment rates across regions within countries). I will focus on the first two, since they concern specifically the issue of poverty. The third, which overcomes a purely economic definition of poverty and deprivation, is the object of Allmendinger's et al. chapter in this book.

The definition of income poverty as the basis of the first indicator is doubly relative. First, it refers to the average standard of living and not to some notion of basic goods (as is the case for the U.S. poverty line). Second, the society of reference consists of the single countries, not a European average. These two characteristics may be problematic at the policy discourse level for two, somewhat opposite, reasons. First, no European country uses the relative poverty line when defining entitlement to income support for the poor. They may refer to the unemployment indemnity, as in Denmark and the United Kingdom, or to the minimum wage, as in France and the Czech Republic, or to a more or less generous basket of goods, as in Germany, or some other criteria. But they never use the 60% below the median income as a criterion. All countries, therefore, irrespective of their generosity and universality, are likely to appear as bad performers with regard to their ability to provide the poor with an income above the 60% threshold. Of course, the containment of poverty does not depend primarily upon minimum income provisions. Yet, it is a bit strange that an indicator is adopted to monitor progress at the EU level that is not used by the member countries in shaping their specific income-support policies for the poor. In order to overcome this possible contradiction, the Commission and the Social Protection Committee have agreed to define the 60% threshold as indicating not the poor, but those "at risk" of being so—a sort of linguistic diplomacy. Second, reference to national standard of living generates another paradox. As seen in Figure 7-1, both in 1999 and in 2004 many Eastern European countries presented lower at-risk-of-poverty rates than many richer Western countries. However, these percentages refer to quite different levels, that is, median incomes. The Estonian median in 2000 was 18% of the Luxembourg median (Brandolini 2007).[1] Brandolini has calculated that if a common European standard were used, based not simplistically on the European median, but, following Atkinson's (1998) compromise proposal, on the weighted geometric average of national and EU poverty lines, the at-risk-of-poverty rate in 2000 would have been 61% in the Czech Republic, 23% in Italy, and 7% in Germany. In Eastern European countries, 80% of incomes were below, or at best comparable to, the incomes of the poorest living in Central and Northern Europe (see also Fahey 2007, for a similar approach). If this approach were followed, the incidence of poverty in Enlarged Europe in 2000 would have gone up from 15% to 23%. A similar calculation might be made for the more recent years. Brandolini has also calculated that the head-count poverty ratio is more or less the same on both sides of the Atlantic, around 23%, when area-wide lines are adopted, whereas it is 50% higher in the United States than in the EU-25 when country- or state-specific poverty lines are used as a basis. The internal disparities within the EU-25, are, however, lower than the ones in the United States.

Whelan and Maitre (2007) have addressed the issue of taking intra-European differences in levels of living into account in a different way. By using a deprivation index, they are able to show that economic vulnerability rates vary substantially between three groups of countries. The three groups are: (1) twelve nations with a per capita gross national product (GNP) above the EU average (Finland, Sweden, Denmark, Germany, Luxembourg, Austria, Belgium, the Netherlands, France, Ireland, the United Kingdom, and Italy). (2) The seven countries with a per capita GNP between 60% and 100% of the EU average (Spain, Greece, Portugal, Malta, Cyprus, Slovenia, and the Czech Republic), and (3) the six countries with a per capita GNP is below 60% of the average for EU. In the first group, the deprivation rate was never higher than 23% in 2003, rising to 31% in the second group, and to 41% in the third group. Also the two most recent EU members, Bulgaria and Romania (as well as Turkey) had a 41% deprivation rate with a per capita GNP at 35% of the EU-25 average. Yet, in the richer countries the poor are more sharply differentiated from the rich than in the poorer ones.

The data shown in Figure 7-1, based on the EU/Eurostat definition of "at-risk-of-poverty," must be, therefore, read with caution as the data underrepresent the incidence of this risk in Europe.

The data for 1999 and 2005 are not fully comparable, since Eurostat no longer uses the European Community Household Panel as the basis for these statistics but has changed to the EU-SILC (Community Statistics on Income and Living Conditions). Based on national data from the five largest countries, which account for over 50% of the EU-25 population, however, Atkinson (2007) suggests that the Eurostat estimate of no substantial change may be well-founded. There is some change in the ranking, which we cannot interpret given the changes in the database; but the overall picture is about the same. Again, the distribution of the risk of poverty across countries according to these criteria conceals substantial differences in the standard of living, ranging

Figure 7-1: At risk of poverty rate (EUROSTAT definition) in Europe before and after transfers, 1999–2005

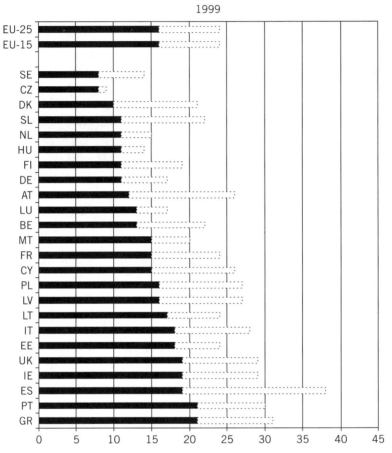

Percentage of people living in households with equivalized disposible income less than 60% of median national income

■ After transfers   ⁝⁝ Before social transfers (pensions excluded)

Figure 7-1: Continued

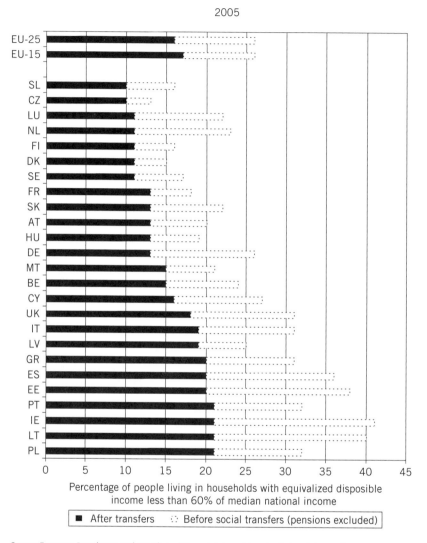

2005

Percentage of people living in households with equivalized disposible income less than 60% of median national income

■ After transfers   ⠴ Before social transfers (pensions excluded)

Source: Eurostat: Population and social conditions database (downloaded 20 July 2007).

from Latvia, where the poverty threshold is 27% of the European median (€7,716 in 2005) to Luxembourg, where the threshold is set at 201% of the same median (Eurostat 2007). Moreover, the efficacy of transfers (excluding pensions) in reducing the incidence of poverty seems to vary substantially across Europe. It is minimal in most Southern European countries excluding Spain, as opposed to quite significant in Lithuania, Estonia, Ireland, Spain, the United Kingdom, and Germany. Of course, the specific social transfer package may be made up quite differently: generosity varies not only with regard to minimum provisions, as we will see later, but also with regard to benefits that touch a larger portion of the population than the officially poor, for example, unemployment benefits and particularly child and other family related benefits. Interestingly, there is no clear relationship between the incidence of pretransfer poverty and the impact of transfers. Some countries, such as the Czech Republic, Slovenia, and the Scandinavian nations, have both low levels of at-risk-of-poverty and a low impact of transfers. Others, like Spain, Estonia, and Lithuania, have high levels in both. Still others, like Latvia and Portugal, have high levels of at-risk-of-poverty and a low redistributive impact of transfers.

Not only has the incidence of poverty not substantially decreased, but there is also a persistently higher risk of poverty among children compared to the rest of the population, except in the three Scandinavian countries and in Cyprus, as shown in Figure 7-2. The UNICEF/IRC (2007) report also shows that some European countries belong to the group of OECD countries with the highest incidence of child poverty, particularly when a more complex indicator than the simple household income is used.

Among the explanations of the lack of improvement in risk of poverty rates is the only slight improvement in the incidence of the long-term unemployment rate: from 3.9% to 3.3% for the EU-25, since the launch of the Lisbon Agenda. Another partial explanation is the fact that most of the increase in employment rates is the result of temporary employment. Substantial cross-country differences remain, however, although they do not overlap with either difference as regards the risk of poverty or the overall unemployment rates (Figure 7-3). For instance, Sweden, Italy, and Portugal have about the same overall unemployment rate; but long-term unemployment is minimal in Sweden, while in Italy and Portugal, it accounts for about half of all unemployed. Different labor market dynamics are at play here, also different active labor market policies. The long-term unemployed receive different levels of income support in the two countries: the benefit is more generous in Sweden than in Italy. Thus, the higher incidence of long-term unemployment in the latter country cannot be viewed as a consequence of excessively generous unemployment benefits causing some kind of welfare dependency.

The quota of the so-called working poor, that is, those who, although working, live in households having incomes below the national threshold, is substantial, indicating that having a job does not always protect from poverty. In the EU, 8% of all workers live in households below the national median threshold, ranging from 3% in the Czech Republic, 4% in Belgium and Finland to 13% in Greece, and 14% in Poland and Portugal (European Commission 2007; see also Bardone and Guio 2005; Marlier et al. 2007).

Why has Europe, as a whole, not achieved the goals it set for itself? The answer is at least twofold. First, there has probably been an under evaluation of cross-country differences not only with respect to "objective" starting points,

Figure 7-2: At risk of poverty rate for children, compared to that of the population as a whole, 2005

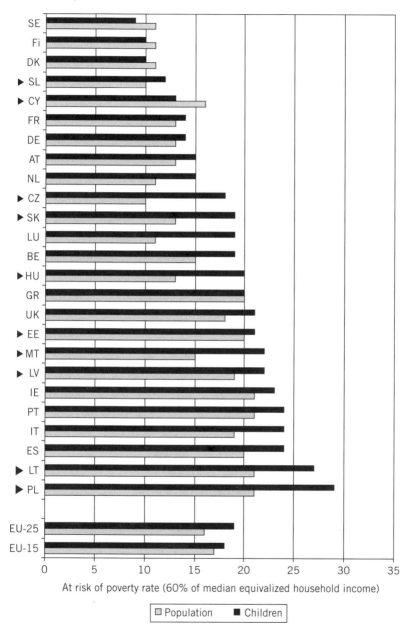

At risk of poverty rate (60% of median equivalized household income)

□ Population   ■ Children

Source: Eurostat: Population and social conditions database (downloaded 20 July 2007). ▶indicates new member countries.

Figure 7-3: Unemployment and long-term unemployment rates, 1999 and 2005

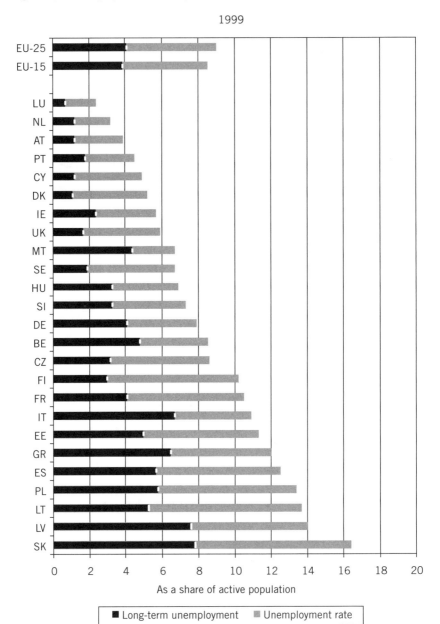

Figure 7-3: Continued

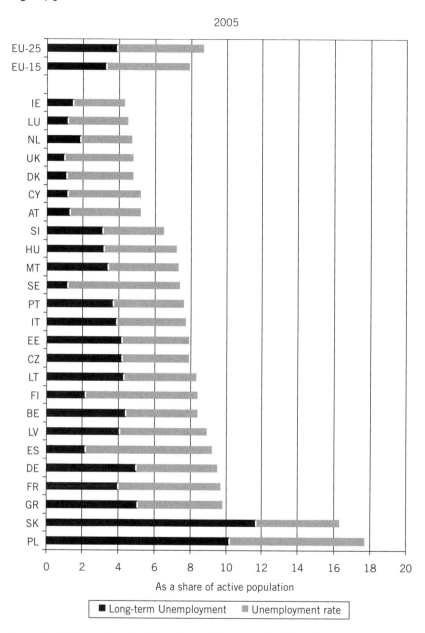

2005

As a share of active population

■ Long-term Unemployment   ■ Unemployment rate

Source: Eurostat: Population and social conditions database (downloaded 20 July 2007).

but also in regard to the priority assigned to combating poverty and social exclusion, political consensus, and administrative and governance capabilities. Second, notwithstanding a great deal of EU initiative in this field since at least the 1980s, the introduction of a minimum common standard in outcomes, if not in policies, and in rights, if not in instruments, has proven more difficult than the launch of the common currency. In the next two sections, I will look at diversity in national policies and at EU initiatives.

INCOME-SUPPORT MEASURES FOR THE POOR IN THE EU COUNTRIES

Income-support measures for the poor—although rooted in modern-day poor laws and in charity—is a comparatively recent addition to welfare-state packages (Loedemel and Trickey 2000; Saraceno 2002). The income-support measures existed in only a handful of European countries in the 1950s and 1960s, but they expanded rapidly and were subject to internal reforms in the 1980s and 1990s due to the weakening of two of the main pillars of postwar social citizenship: full and stable employment for men, and stable marriages as a means of redistributing both income and care. In the former communist countries, such income-support measures were introduced only following the fall of the communist regimes and during the transition period (Cantillon et al. 2007). These measures are only one component of social assistance, however, and social assistance is only one component of the overall welfare-state package. The income-support measures for the poor can be fully understood only by looking at the entire package, including the internal boundaries between social security and social assistance. The different impact of income transfers on the incidence of poverty evidenced in Figure 7-1 is, in fact, only in limited part the consequence of the greater or lesser generosity and universality of minimum income provisions for the poor. Other transfers, such as family or unemployment benefits, are also important. Bradshaw (2006), for instance, argues that child allowances have an important role in reducing the proportion of children who live in poor households (see also World Bank 2007). Furthermore, income-support measures targeted at the poor are a complex package themselves. They may be linked to other benefits (housing, free social services, and so forth), the value of which should be taken into account when assessing and comparing policies.

Understanding the complexities of income-support systems would require detailed, in-depth case studies. Comparative studies, however, either involve only a limited number of countries or they focus on a limited number of dimensions: the institutional framework, the level of generosity, and the target definition. Gough et al.'s (1997) observation that the growing importance of means-tested schemes in Europe and the mounting debate on welfare dependency are not matched in academic studies is still true. With few exceptions (Leibfried 1993; Gough et al. 1997; Ferrera 2005), antipoverty policies and, specifically, minimum-income provisions remain at the fringe of mainstream comparative welfare-state analysis and typologizing. This knowledge deficit is not compensated for, at least at the descriptive level, by the European bodies in charge of monitoring social policies within the EU. The data produced by MISSOC are quite deficient, for instance: they are often imprecise and inconsistent across countries—sometimes simply incomprehensible. The much richer national reports on social inclusion are full of interesting information, however not always comparable, since countries have developed and pursued this reporting exercise in a highly self-referential way and/or based on their own traditions (or lack of them) in social reporting. Sound and fully comparable data on all countries is lacking on essential issues such as eligibility rules, income thresholds, qualifying age, duration of entitlement, links to other benefits, whether the benefits are right-based or discretionary, associated requirements, efficiency in targeting, and so forth.[2] These conditions are important for assessing the boundaries within which income support for the poor is defined as part of social citizenship: to whom it is provided, for how long, under which conditions, and so forth. Further, this policy field in recent years has witnessed many changes and seems to be in a constant process of restructuring. Rules concerning particularly duration, entitlement, generosity, and patterns of enforcement regarding the requirement to be available for work are in a constant flux and information may quickly become outdated.

The following description of the main features is based on MISSOC 2006 data, integrated with the overview by Heikkilä et al. (2006) and other, less comprehensive but more detailed sources. Attention will be given in particular to the institutional framework, eligibility rules, generosity, and work requirements for the beneficiaries.

In most EU countries, income support for the poor is part of the social citizenship package in the sense that a noncategorical safety net exists for all persons below a given income threshold. This safety net may be the last addition to a number of more categorical social minima, such as in France, where the RMI (*revenu minimum d'insertion*) is an addition to a complex system of *minimaux sociaux* that include means-tested income-support measures targeted at the elderly, lone mothers, widows, and the disabled. Ireland, Portugal, Spain, and Malta have similar systems. In the United Kingdom and Ireland, there are three distinct measures: one for the nonable-bodied and lone mothers with a very young child, one for the able-bodied without a job, and one for the working poor. In the Scandinavian countries, Austria, Germany, the Netherlands, and most of the Eastern European countries, there is only one minimum income provision for all categories (but in the Eastern European countries, child allowances may be means tested). Exclusively categorical measures exist only in Greece and Italy (Matsaganis et al. 2003; Matsaganis 2005; Sacchi and Bastagli 2005; Saraceno 2006). In Italy, there may also be more universal measures at the local level, but with considerable variation across municipalities. There are also strong cross-regional differences in Spain (Arriba and Moreno 2005). Here, in fact, a national framework law formally mandates the regions to set such a measure in place, but without setting common standards. Hungary appears to have no general minimum income provision in the MISSOC data basis and in Heikkilä et al.'s (2006) overview, but is included in the countries having one in the cited supporting document to the Joint Report on Social inclusion (2007).

Available data on institutional frameworks, with all their shortfalls, indicate that differences are significant along most dimensions of this measure.[3] It is not only an issue of administrative and organizational frameworks, with some countries having a fully centralized and others a fully decentralized system. Decentralization often implies some degree of differentiation in the way entitlement is defined and resources are provided. Thus, the most decentralized systems—such as the Spanish, the Austrian, the Latvian, the Slovakian, and the Polish—provide benefits of quite varying levels depending on the region and even the municipality, with the risk that benefit recipients in the poorer regions get much less than recipients in the richer regions (World Bank 2007).[4] In other systems, such as in Germany, Sweden, and Portugal, eligibility rules, income thresholds, and basic income are nationally regulated, but additional benefits (for rent, heating, or other expenses) are at the discretion of the local governments. These within-country differences based on regional disparities suggest that income support for the poor is less strongly rooted in a social citizenship framework based on residence in the same country than pensions, unemployment, maternity, parental, and child benefits. Local welfare-state arrangements may have a substantial impact in shaping this particular item of the social citizenship package, adding to cross-national diversities.

Eligibility rules may also differ. In a few countries—France, Luxembourg, and Spain—adults under 25 are not eligible for general income support in their own right, unless they have children of their own. In France, the young can benefit from specifically targeted measures that are less automatic than the RMI and more strictly linked to work and training. In the Netherlands, individuals aged 21 or 22 may receive a lower benefit if the municipality deems that a full benefit would be a disincentive to work. Nonnationals are in principle eligible in all countries, as long as they have a legal residence in the country where they claim the benefit. But in most countries, this entitlement includes a time requirement (length of legal stay in the country). In the most decentralized countries, such as Spain, there may also be a similar requirement for nationals coming from other regions. Illegal resident nonnationals are excluded everywhere, although they might receive occasional lump sum payments.

Eligibility rules are also linked to income thresholds: the lower the income threshold, the narrower the definition of poverty used and the smaller the eligible population, but also the narrower the definition of the level of unacceptable deprivation. Level of generosity, in fact, operates together with eligibility rules in shaping the actual size and personal characteristics of income support recipients. In countries with a very low-income threshold, only the poorest with the lowest human capital have access to this form of support. Generosity involves the degree to which the minimum-income benefit permits an adequate standard of living. This depends on income thresholds and basic amounts, but also on the equivalence scales used to equivalize the income needs of different-sized households. Thresholds may be defined in reference to some absolute poverty line (basket of goods), in reference to some other existing social minimum (e.g., the minimum wage, or the noncontributory old-age pension), or again in reference to an average standard of living (e.g., the average wage). Equivalence scales may presume higher or lower economies of scale and patterns of intrahousehold solidarity. Furthermore, Cantillon et al. (2007) observe that the comparative level of generosity of the various countries may be assessed differently depending on whether one considers the purchasing power of benefits, their relationship to average wages, or to relative poverty levels. In particular, these authors point out that in the former communist countries the purchasing power of social assistance recipients is lower than that found in Spain and Portugal, which have the lowest levels within the "old" EU. Yet, compared to average wages or relative levels of poverty, minimum-income protection seems substantial. In Poland, in particular, lone parents on social assistance receive 60% of the average wage, which is higher than either Sweden or Finland's rates. The EU Commission's Supporting Document to the 2007 Joint Report on Social Protection and Social Inclusion points out that only a few countries provide workless households with a minimum income and related benefits (e.g. for housing), which are sufficient to lift them close to, or above the 60% of median income threshold. This happens, moreover, only with respect to specific family types, which may differ across countries (see also the analyses in Standing 2004, on a smaller number of countries). Figure 7-4, taken from the same document, illustrates these differences.

With regard to duration of entitlement, in most EU countries benefits are paid as long as need persists, and even where there is a time limit, it concerns the duration of each social assistance period, not that over the life time. Revisions, however, may be more or less frequent and tight. This approach differs from that in the United States, where, particularly after the Temporary Assistance for Needy Families (TANF) reform there is a time limit on entitlement to benefits. Time limits seem to be enforced particularly in the Eastern European countries, although data are imprecise (in addition to MISSOC 2007, see also Heikkilä et al. 2006, World Bank 2007). In Latvia, benefits can be taken for a maximum of nine months per year. In Estonia, the case is reviewed every month, in Lithuania and Slovenia every three to six months; but apparently it can be renewed if the need persists. The same occurs in France. In Portugal, a revision is compulsory after twelve months, but with the possibility of a renewal. In Slovakia, after twenty-four months of benefit receipt, the case passes on from the state to the municipality.

In all countries, able-bodied beneficiaries of working age are in principle expected to be available for work. In all European countries, "activation" and welfare-to-work goals have entered not only the debate, but also the policy domain since the 1990s (Loedemel and Trickey 2000). They have been formally implemented in all systems that have been put in place since the late 1980s,

Figure 7-4: Net income of social assistance recipients, for three jobless family types, 2003, as percentage of the at-risk-of-poverty threshold, including housing benefits. Only countries where noncategorical social assistance benefits are in place are considered

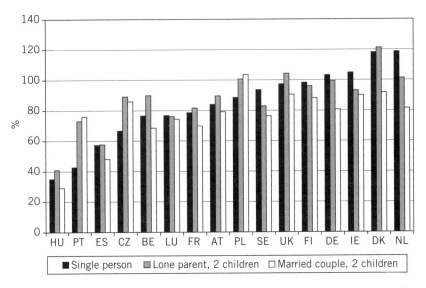

Source: Commission of the European Communities 2007. Joint EC-OECD project using OECD tax-benefit models and Eurostat.

starting with the French RMI. Policy practices are still very diverse, however. While in some countries (e.g., Denmark and Sweden), social assistance beneficiaries are activated after three months (the under-30s) or twelve months (those aged 30 and over) through a wide range of activation measures (individual job training, rehabilitation programs, prerehabilitation programs, flex jobs, light jobs, and so forth), in other countries, the work test merely requires applicants to register as unemployed and to confirm that they are actively looking for work. In some countries, as in France, Belgium, Slovenia, and some Spanish regions, beneficiaries must sign an actual contract, in which they engage themselves in some activity, be it in rehabilitation or training. In the United Kingdom, the requirement to be available for work has been made even organizationally visible, by unifying unemployment indemnity and income support for the able-bodied in the job seeker allowance now administered by the job centers. A similar move has been made with the German Hartz reform in 2005, which has unified unemployment assistance (not the unemployment indemnity as such) with social assistance. In particular, this reform, which is still experimental, has reduced the duration of entitlement for the former, while unifying the basic amount of the two benefits and linking both to activation measures (Leschke et al. 2006; Eichhorst et al. 2006). In order to create an incentive for participation in paid work, a few countries disregard a portion of earnings, so that beneficiaries are better-off working than not working. This is the case, for instance, in Cyprus, the Netherlands, Germany, and Belgium. In Latvia, the benefit continues to be paid, on a sliding scale, for three months after a person has started to work. The United Kingdom has introduced a specific scheme targeted to low income workers, the work tax credit, which follows the same logic as the U.S. earned income tax credit (topping up low income and "making work pay"). However, the U.K. credit is paid weekly or monthly, not on an ex-post yearly basis, thus offering a more efficacious support when it is needed. Moreover, there is a complex system taking account of expenses incurred in working, up to a certain point. Also France has introduced a similar scheme, the *prime pour l'emploi*, in 2001. Both in the United Kingdom and in France, a condition to receive this subsidy is that at least one person in the household works a minimum number of hours.

Activation goals, although shared across Europe, may differ in motivation and content, depending not only on the situation in national labor markets, but also on the type of national welfare state and the prevailing social citizenship culture (Taylor-Gooby 2004; Castles 2004; Barbier 2005). In some countries, the focus is mainly on welfare dependency risks, although research has not offered clear evidence of such risks. In other countries, the focus is rather on the social exclusion risks linked to a too long exclusion from the labor market and to an underdevelopment of personal capabilities. Barbier, for example, distinguishes between two ideal types. The first emphasizes incentives, sanctions, and in-work benefits, and is mainly found in Anglo-Saxon countries. The second ideal type is universalistic, providing relatively generous and unconditional income support for the poor. Availability for paid work is requested, but not strictly enforced. This type also provides a variety of services for the unemployed, including training and placement in protected, more or less temporary, jobs. Thus, in this case, too, paid work is perceived and proposed as the main road to social integration and fully active citizenship. However, this goal is in principle achieved by providing opportunities and skills rather than through financial incentives and sanctions. According to Barbier, the continental welfare states do not have a model of their own; rather they combine elements of these two ideal types. In recent years, they seem to be moving more towards the Anglo-Saxon, than the Scandinavian one, insofar as they are more strictly enforcing working requirements. Yet, if no work is available, individuals maintain their entitlement to support. Notwithstanding these differences, it is fair to say that all European countries have increasingly moved from a focus on support to a focus on activation, strongly emphasizing both the duty and integrative virtues of (paid) work and participation in the labor market. From this point of view, one might say that they have become more similar to the United States.

In the United Kingdom, Ireland, and the Netherlands, concern over activation has particularly modified the way lone mothers asking for social assistance are perceived and dealt with. In these countries, lone mothers asking for income support were traditionally exempted from the requirement to be available for work, insofar as their primary duty was child care. In recent years, however, they have been increasingly and explicitly framed as potential breadwinners whose primary duty is to provide income to their children—similar to what has happened in the United States (see, e.g., Lewis 2006; Orloff 2006). This is a major cultural as well as policy shift, which stresses the role of paid work as the main route to social integration, while underplaying the value of, and need for, unpaid work, as well as the risk of transposing lone mothers from the rank of social assistance recipients to that of the working poor. Particularly in the case of lone mothers, child-care costs, in fact, may greatly reduce the gains obtained from leaving social assistance for gainful employment. The best example is Ireland, where a marginal effective tax rate of 54% for lone parents (with two children, but with no child-care costs) shoots up to 131% when child-care costs are included (Commission of the European Communities 2007: 23, and, for a more general discussion, OECD 2005; Marlier et al. 2007: 91–93).

Analyses of the impact of these activation policies offer a mixed picture. Together with an enlargement of options for low-income and jobless people, and a focus on the provision of employment and other services, observers point to risks of stigmatization, of creating revolving door mechanisms, and of "creaming" (aiding only the better qualified beneficiaries) (e.g. Larsen 2005). The low-qualified and the older unemployed receive few advantages (see, for instance, Leschke et al. 2006 and Eichhorst et al. 2006 on the German case).

Together with the activation of social assistance recipients, an emerging problem in Europe is that of "making work pay." Interestingly, as they started to implement their welfare-to-work policies, reforming their minimum income and their unemployment benefits, some countries (e.g., the United Kingdom and France) have also developed new income-support instruments focused on poor workers and on poor workers' households, thus indirectly acknowledging that being in paid work does not always protect people from poverty.

DISCOURSES AND PRACTICES: THE EU LEVEL

The EU's internal redistributive policies have been guided by the principles of cross-country and interregional social justice. The structural funds have the official aim of redressing both inter- and intracountry economic imbalances. From this perspective, therefore, the idea that the EU should play an active role in promoting social justice across its member countries and in developing a common social citizenship is a constituent part of the construction of the EU itself. This has, however, been more successful at the macro than at the micro level, and possibly more within the EU-15 than within the EU-25 and EU-27, since enlargement has greatly increased the need for cross-country redistribution while not proportionally increasing the resources to be redistributed.

A recent critical overview of EU policies aimed at combating poverty and social exclusion argues that the fight against poverty and exclusion could never be solidly linked to the social rights of all citizens within the EU framework (Marlier et al. 2007). The 1992 recommendation regarding the "guarantee of minimum resources" aimed at encouraging countries that still did not have a "last resort" safety net to provide one. Thus, we might say that the guarantee of minimum resources has become part of a developing "ESM." But the recommendation is a weak instrument. Some countries—such as Portugal and Spain—did take it up to develop their antipoverty policies, but others, such as Greece and Italy, still do not have such a last resort instrument. EU policies themselves contributed to fragmentation and policy opacity. The structural funds have existed alongside the various experimental programs and the fight against poverty and exclusion—very few bridges have been built between them. No meaningful evaluation has been made of the Funds' impact on poverty and exclusion. There was no continuity in the experimental programs, which went through phases of stagnation and incertitude and other phases of acceleration. Under such conditions, the experimental advances that were made have had little influence on large-scale social policies. Furthermore, the growing strength and legitimacy of the subsidiarity principle has limited the functional weight of the Commission in terms of coordination, exchange, and stimulation. Few governments have taken on the battle against poverty and exclusion. They prefer to decentralize to lower levels of the administration, which does not always entail the transfer of adequate resources and in many cases actually means delegating responsibilities to the private sector. This in turn has restricted the local administrations' capacity to act.

The two summits held in the year 2000 (in Lisbon and Nice) marked a change in approach and the assumption of a more active role on the part of the Commission, albeit within the framework of the subsidiarity principle. The new orientations adopted at these summits were modeled on the Open Method of Coordination (OMC), which defines the roles of the Commission and of the member states.[5] The OMC puts responsibility for stimulation, coordination, and the promotion of exchanges into the Council's hands and confers the full accountability for the fight against poverty and exclusion on the member states. As in other areas, the OMC was based on three institutional instruments. They are: (1) The establishment of a high-level committee (Social Protection Committee) made up of those who are responsible for this area in the Council and in the respective governments; (2) The design of a Community Action Programme to combat social exclusion; (3) The creation and deployment of the National Action Plans for Inclusion (NAPs/inc), their periodical revision by means of a Joint Report, and the application of a shared system of indicators conceived at the Laeken Summit in 2001 (under the Belgian presidency) for evaluation of the evolution of the situation, as well as progress and setbacks with regard to the measures that have been implemented. The OMC is based on "moral suasion" rather than enforcement. There are no penalties for not fulfilling the requirements, not even in the sense of "naming and shaming." As such, it is a very fragile policy instrument (Daly 2006), particularly compared not only to the Economic and Monetary Union (EMU), but also to employment policies.

Since the Nice Summit in 2000, three Joint Reports on Social Inclusion have been published by the Commission. The first was published in 2002, the second in 2004, and the third in 2006. These reports describe the main trends regarding poverty and exclusion in the EU and assess the impact of national policies. The quality of the national reports on which they are based, however, varies quite substantially as regards the kinds of data they provide and the degree to which they indicate specific targets and objectives to be monitored and assessed over time through specific indicators. Often, they are more or less coherent lists of measures, experiences, and (mainly output) data.

In the second round of NAPs/inc, the presidency conclusions of the March 2002 Barcelona European Council stated that "the European Council stresses the importance of the fight against poverty and social exclusion. Member states are invited to set targets, in their National Action Plans, for significantly reducing the number of people at risk of poverty and social exclusion by 2010" (see Social Protection Committee 2003). To the (limited) extent to which member states have taken up this invitation (see Marlier et al. 2007), the resulting targets are specific to each country. They are not necessarily coherent, in that different criteria for defining poverty thresholds are used, and different dimensions of social exclusion are highlighted in the various member states. Since 2002, the ten new countries have also been involved in this process. They elaborated their own diagnoses and a number of guidelines for action under the Joint Inclusion Memoranda, which were both approved in December 2002. Later, the ten new members designed and applied their own respective NAPs/inc.

The OMC process in the area of social exclusion slowly gained some kind of visibility and legitimacy at least in individual member countries. A debate started to develop on the use of indicators and target setting, as well as on the opportunity and means to strengthen the impact of "moral suasion" within the OMC. But the Commission redefined the whole mechanism. Following the 2004 Kok Report, which evinced the lack of progress towards Lisbon's objectives and recommended that overriding priority be given to economic and employment growth policies, the 2005 Midterm Review of the Lisbon Agenda stressed that priorities should be refocused on employment and competition. It thus confirmed the secondary importance given to social policies, and particularly policies against poverty and social exclusion, in the European political agenda. Of course, one could argue—as did the Kok Report—that the reduction of poverty and social integration would be the natural consequence of more employment and a more competitive economy. But this argument is far from being empirically grounded, as shown above. In any case, following this reorientation of priorities, in the spring of 2005, a new approach was adopted—the Revised

Lisbon Strategy—in which the weakest point of the triangle, social cohesion, was dropped and the focus was switched to the primacy of economic development and employment. Countries are now requested to prepare a National Action Plan for overall social protection and social inclusion. Social inclusion policies to combat poverty and social exclusion have become just a subsection of national plans where employment policies and pensions play the major role. Although the official rationale for this change was "mainstreaming" and developing an integrated approach, the risk that the issue will be sidelined is very real, particularly in countries that have not taken the exercise seriously.

The question of the right to be protected from poverty and social exclusion as based on European citizenship was also indirectly raised within the framework of the process that led to the elaboration of a European Charter of citizens' rights in the 1990s.[6] However, this process created more expectations than results. In the meantime, the proposal for a European Constitution has come to a halt.

Against this background of fragmented policies and ambivalent and changing discourses and priorities, the year 2010 was proclaimed as the European Year against Poverty and Social Exclusion, following the European Council's conclusion in March 2006 that every effort should be made in order to make "a decisive impact on the eradication of poverty and social exclusion by 2010." But, contrary to what occurred in the area of employment, no specific target was set, once again leaving it up to each individual country to set its own targets. These targets may be quite dissimilar, however, because of not only different national choices and goals concerning the actual reduction of poverty, but also because different poverty thresholds are used and different dimensions of social exclusion are highlighted in the various member states.

INCOME SUPPORT WHEN POOR: AN INCOMPLETE SOCIAL RIGHT IN EUROPE?

Throughout Europe, the notion that there should be some kind of safety net for the poor is widely shared, and most countries have some kind of income-support provision not only for those who are excluded from the labor force because of age or invalidity, but also for the able-bodied. This is certainly a distinct feature of the European concept of social citizenship, compared to that prevalent in the United States. Provisions in this field, however, are more varied across Europe than the more "standard" items of the welfare-state package such as pensions or unemployment benefits. They are also more subject to intracountry variation as well as to more or less radical reforms. Furthermore, entitlement is not firmly rooted in law in all countries and there is often a degree of discretion in granting it. The right to receive income support when poor, therefore, appears to be both a weak and an incomplete social right: not all countries have it, and those that do, grant it on the basis of quite different conditions and for quite different durations.

The EU has certainly promoted a common framework for debate on how to protect European citizens from poverty, thereby including protection from poverty in the framework of European citizenship. But it has been successful neither in promoting the economic and employment conditions necessary to combat and diminish the incidence of poverty, nor in persuading the countries that still lack them to provide adequate safety nets. This failure is particularly evident in the "old" EU-15, where fourteen years after the 1992 Recommendation, Greece and Italy still lack a noncategorical, universal minimum-income provision. The success appears to have been greater in the new member states, particularly the former communist countries. The introduction of such a measure has been, although at the very last minute, part of the negotiations leading to enlargement and more generally to the reform of social security systems in the face of the new experience of mass poverty during the process of transition. Nonetheless, the recently changed focus of EU discourse may slow down the process through which these measures are established. The shift in focus from the provision of a minimum of resources to the risks of welfare dependency subtly undermines the legitimization of income support, while depicting social assistance recipients as morally vulnerable individuals. Notwithstanding the rhetoric on "more and better jobs," any job seems to be more socially acceptable than no job, irrespective of qualifications and compensation. At the same time, the risks of remaining poor while working are undervalued. The shifting boundaries between provisions for the workless poor and the working poor mirror a parallel blurring of distinctions between the living conditions of the former and the most disadvantaged of the latter. In this perspective, one might say that Europe has become more similar to the United States. Yet, unlike the United States, most countries do keep a universal last resort safety net and do not terminate entitlement to income support after a maximum period, irrespective of the persistence of need. Furthermore, notwithstanding the broad differences in policy measures and policy aims that exists across Europe in this field, as well as the changing discourses and shifting focuses, the persistence of poverty remains in the policy and political agenda of most national countries and of the EU as an item of concern. This concern should mobilize collective resources and not only private responsibilities. From this perspective, in most European countries, income support for the poor continues to be framed as a social right, although weak and incomplete.

REFERENCES

Alber, Jens (2006) The European Social Model and the United States, *European Union Politics*, 7(3): 393–419.

Arriba, Ana and Moreno, Louis (2005) Spain—Poverty, Social Exclusion and "Safety Nets", in Maurizio Ferrera (ed.) *Welfare State Reform in Southern Europe. Fighting poverty and Social Exclusion in Italy, Spain, Portugal and Greece,* London: Routledge, pp. 141–203.

Atkinson, Anthony (1998) *Poverty in Europe,* Oxford: Basil Blackwell.

Atkinson, Anthony (2007) La Politica Sociale Dell'Unione Europea, l'Agenda di Lisbona e il Monitoraggio Delle Dinamiche Nazionali, in Andrea Brandolini and Chiara Saraceno (eds) *Povertà e Benessere. Una Geografia Delle Disuguaglianze Economiche in Italia,* Bologna: il Mulino, pp. 541–562.

Barbier, Jean-Claude (2005) Citizenship and the Activation of Social Protection: A Comparative Approach, in Jørgen Goul Andersen, Anne-Marie Guillemard, Per H. Jensen and Birgit Pfau-Effinger (eds) *The Changing Face of Welfare. Consequences and Outcomes from a Citizenship Perspective,* Bristol, UK: The Policy Press, pp. 113–134.

Bardone, Laura and Guio, Anne-Catherine (2005) In-Work Poverty , *Statistics in Focus,* Population and Social Conditions 5/2005, Luxembourg: Eurostat.

Bonny, Ives and Bosco, Nicoletta (2002) Income Support Measures for the Poor in European Cities , in Chiara Saraceno (ed.) *Social Assistance Dynamics in Europe,* Bristol, UK: The Policy Press, pp. 81–126.

Brandolini, Andrea (2007) Measurement of Income Distribution in Supranational Entities: The Case of the European Union , in Stephen P. Jenkins and John Micklewright (eds.) *Inequality and Poverty Re-examined,* Oxford: Oxford University Press, pp. 62–83.

Bradshaw, Jonathan (2006) *A Review of the Comparative Evidence on Child Poverty,* York, UK: Joseph Rowntree Foundation.

Cantillon, Bea; van Mechelen, Natascha and Schulte, Bernd (2007) Minimum Income Policies in Old and New Member States , in Jens Alber, Tony Fahey and Chiara Saraceno (eds) *Handbook of Quality of Life in the Enlarged European Union,* London: Routledge, pp. 218–234.

Castles, Francis G. (2004) *The Future of the Welfare State: Crisis Myths and Crisis Realities,* Oxford: Oxford University Press.

Commission of the European Communities (2007) Joint Report on Social Protection and Social Inclusion, Supporting Document, Commission Staff Working Document, Brussels, 6.03.2007, SEC (2007) 329.

Daly, Mary (2006) EU Social Policy after Lisbon, *Journal of Common Market Studies,* 44(3): 461–481.

Eichhorst, Werner; Grienberger-Zingerle, Maria and Konle-Seid, Regina (2006) Activation Policies in Germany: From Status Protection to Basic Income Support, Discussion Paper No. 2514, Bonn, Germany: IZA.

Eurostat (2007) Living Conditions in Europe, 2002–2005, Luxembourg: Office for Official Publications of the European Communities.

Fahey, Tony (2007) The Case for an EU-wide Measure of Poverty, *European Sociological Review,* 23(1): 35–48.

Ferrera, Maurizio (ed.) (2005) *Welfare State Reform in Southern Europe. Fighting Poverty and Social Exclusion in Italy, Spain, Portugal and Greece,* London: Routledge.

Giddens, Anthony (2006) *Europe in the Global Age*, Cambridge, UK: Polity Press.

Gough, Ian, Bradshaw, Jonathan, Ditch, John, Eardley, Tony and Whiteford, Peter (1997) Social Assistance in OECD Countries, *Journal of European Social Policy*, 7(1): 17–43.

Heikkilä, Matti; Moisio, Pasi; Ritakallio, Veli-Matti; Bradshaw, Jonathan; Kuivalainen, Susan; Hellsten, Katri and Kajanoja, Jouko (2006) Poverty Policies, Structures and Outcomes in the EU-25, Report for the Fifth European Round Table on Poverty and Social Exclusion 16–17 October 2006, Tampere, Finland; Helsinki: Stakes.

Larsen, Jørgen E. (2005) The Active Society and Activation Policy: Ideologies, Contexts and Effects, in Jørgen Goul Andersen, Anne-Marie Guillemard, Per H. Jensen and Birgit Pfau-Effinger (eds) *The Changing Face of Welfare. Consequences and Outcomes from a Citizenship Perspective*, Bristol, UK: The Policy Press, pp. 135–150.

Leibfried, Stephan (1993) Towards a European Welfare State?, in Catherine Jones (ed.) *New Perspectives on the Welfare State in Europe*, London: Routledge, pp. 135–156.

Leisering, Lutz and Leibfried, Stephan (1999) *Time and Poverty in Western Welfare States*, Cambridge: Cambridge University Press.

Leschke, Janine, Schmid, Günther and Griga, Dorit (2006) On the Marriage of Flexibility and Security: Lessons from the Hartz-reforms in Germany, Discussion Paper SP I 2006–108, Berlin, Germany: WZB.

Lewis, Jane (2006) Work/Family Reconciliation, Equal Opportunities and Social Policies: the Interpretation of Policy Trajectories at the EU Level and the Meaning of Gender Equality , *Journal of European Public Policy*, 13, 3: 420–437.

Loedemel, Ivar and Trickey, Heather (eds.) (2000) *An Offer You Can't Refuse: Workfare in International Perspective*, Bristol, UK: The Policy Press.

Marlier, Eric, Atkinson, Anthony, Cantillon, Bea, and Nolan, Brian (2007) *The EU and Social Inclusion: Facing the Challenges*, Bristol, UK: The Policy Press.

Marshall, Thomas. H. (1950) *Citizenship and Social Class*, Cambridge: Cambridge University Press.

Matsaganis, Manos (2005) Greece—Fighting with Hands Tied behind the Back: Anti-poverty Policy without a Minimum Income, in Maurizio Ferrera (ed.) *Welfare State Reform in Southern Europe. Fighting Poverty and Social Exclusion in Italy, Spain, Portugal and Greece,* London: Routledge, pp. 33–83.

Matsaganis, Manos; Ferrera, Maurizio; Capucha, Louis, and Moreno, Louis (2003) Mending Nets in the South: Anti-poverty Policies in Greece, Italy, Portugal and Spain, *Social Policy & Administration*, 37: 639–655.

Nolan, Brian and Whelan, Christopher T. (1996) *Resources, Deprivation, and Poverty*, Oxford: Clarendon Press.

OECD (2005) *Extending Opportunities: How Active Social Policy Can Benefit Us All*, Paris: OECD.

Orloff, Ann S. (2006) 'Farewell to Maternalism? State Policies and Mothers' Employment, in Jonah Levy (ed.) *The State After Statism*, Cambridge, MA: Harvard University Press, pp. 230–268.

Sacchi, Stefano and Bastagli, Franca (2005) Italy—Striving Uphill but not Stopping Halfway: the Troubled Journey of the Experimental Minimum Insertion Income , in Maurizio Ferrera (ed.) *Welfare State Reform in Southern Europe. Fighting Poverty and Social Exclusion in Italy, Spain, Portugal and Greece,* London: Routledge, pp. 84–140.

Saraceno, Chiara (ed.) (2002) *Social Assistance Dynamics in Europe*, Bristol, UK: The Policy Press.

Saraceno, Chiara (2006) Social Assistance Policies and Decentralization in the Countries of Southern Europe, *Revue Française des Affaires Sociales* 1 (January–March): 97–118.

Social Protection Committee (2003) Fight Against Poverty and Social Exclusion: Common Objectives for the Second Round of National Action Plans—Endorsement, Brussels, 25 November. Available online at: http://ec.europa.eu/employment_social/social_inclusion/docs/counciltext_en.pdf (accessed 16 June 2008).

Standing, Guy (ed.) (2004) *Minimum Income Schemes in Europe*, Geneva: ILO publications.

Taylor-Gooby, Peter (ed.) (2004) *New Risks, New Welfare. The Transformation of the European Welfare State*, Oxford: Oxford University Press.

UNICEF (2007) Child Poverty in Perspective: an Overview of Child Well-Being in Rich Countries, Report Card No. 7, Florence: International Child Development Centre.

Whelan, Christopher T. and Maitre, Bertrand (2007) Poverty, Deprivation and Economic Vulnerability in an Enlarged Europe, in Jens Alber, Tony Fahey and Chiara Saraceno (eds) *Handbook of Quality of Life in the Enlarged European Union*, London: Routledge, pp. 201–217.

World Bank (2007) *Social Assistance in Central Europe and the Baltic States*, Washington DC: World Bank.

8

THE NEW AMERICAN MODEL OF WORK-CONDITIONED PUBLIC SUPPORT

REBECCA M. BLANK

O bservers have long discussed American "exceptionalism" in social policy. Throughout the twentieth century, the United States had a more limited welfare state than most Western European nations.* Over the last 15 years, the United States has made substantial changes in its social assistance programs. These changes place the United States on the forefront of developing a new model for the provision of social assistance, under which more dollars are delivered to able-bodied recipients through work-conditioned transfers rather than through cash assistance programs to nonworkers. This chapter describes these changes and discusses the strengths and weaknesses of this new American system.

A HISTORY OF AMERICAN EXCEPTIONALISM

Historically, the configuration of social assistance programs in the United States has looked different from the programs available in many Western European nations. The U.S. social safety net was more limited. There were virtually no public assistance programs that provided universal coverage; most programs were targeted on specific populations. There were limited entitlements to public support; even those few programs that did have an entitlement had very limited benefits, and benefit levels often varied across states.

*Thanks are due to Emily Beam for excellent research assistance.

For instance, in 1990, the primary cash assistance program for families with children was Aid to Families with Dependent Children (AFDC). While all states were required to run this program, benefit levels were set at the state level and varied widely across the states, from $118 per month in Alabama for a single-parent family of three to $846 per month in Alaska. The only national benefit entitlement program was the Food Stamp Program, which provided in-kind benefits through "coupons" that could be used to purchase food. In the median state in 1990, a nonworking single mother with two children would receive $364 per month from AFDC and $237 in food stamps. This would provide annual income of $7,212 (counting food stamps as cash income), which was only 73% of the official poverty line for a family of three in 1990.[1]

It is worth noting that the official poverty line in the United States is used to measure the problem of poverty but is not a parameter for program benefits; that is, programs are not designed to raise people to the poverty line. Hence, 13.3% of all persons in the United States in 2005 lived in families whose income was below the official poverty line; many of these families received assistance from some government programs.

Other U.S. social assistance programs also were characterized by limited eligibility and low benefits. The absence of a national health insurance system in the United States limited public benefits to families. The public health insurance program for low-income individuals that was available in the United States, Medicaid, only covered certain low-income persons, typically those on public assistance who were disabled, elderly, or single parents and their children. Many programs, such as housing subsidies or cash subsidies, provided in-kind rather than cash support. The extensive use of in-kind rather than cash benefits was a way of supporting only publicly approved expenditures, such as housing or food. General cash support ran the risk of being used to buy things (alcohol, durables) that the public did not deem necessary and was not willing to pay for. The only group able to receive somewhat more generous (and inflation-indexed) cash support payments was low-income disabled or elderly persons who were eligible for the Supplemental Security Income (SSI) program.

In addition to these public assistance programs, the United States has long had a number of very large social insurance programs that provide more universal benefits. Social Security, aimed at providing retirement and survivors' pensions as well as support to disabled workers, is financed by having current workers pay into the system to support current retirees. Benefits are based on past earnings, but those with lower earnings receive a higher benefit relative to their contribution. Hence, the program is somewhat redistributive, but all workers have a claim on Social Security benefits. While Social Security is not primarily an antipoverty program but an elderly pension program, it has had very substantial antipoverty effects. Engelhardt and Gruber (2006) suggest that rising Social Security benefits can explain the entire decline in elderly poverty among those who turned 65 between 1950 and 1995. The elderly also have access to a universal public health insurance program, Medicare. The social safety net for the elderly in the United States is stronger than among other age groups, and elderly poverty is lower.

Unemployment insurance (UI) is also universally available to workers who lose their jobs, regardless of earnings. All employers pay into the system. Like Social Security, lower-income workers receive a higher share of benefits relative to earnings, but all qualifying workers who lose their jobs can collect UI. There are, however, sharp restrictions on eligibility; workers who quit voluntarily or who are fired for cause are typically not eligible for UI payments. Furthermore, UI is available for only 26 weeks in the United States, a much shorter time period than in many Western European nations. Finally, the United States also has a large Workers' Compensation Program, which provides assistance to those disabled or injured while on the job.

Why is it that the United States is less willing to provide generous social assistance to lower-income families and is more concerned about "misuse" of public funds? Observers have given a variety of answers to this question over the years. One important factor has been the heterogeneity of the U.S. population. On the one hand, the large immigrant populations that regularly arrived in the United States were always the target of suspicion by those who had been in the United States longer. On the other hand, the unique history of race (and racism) in America created long-term problems with universalist programs. Prior to the 1960s, for instance, southern states largely excluded black women from public assistance programs (Piven and Cloward 1971). Alesina et al. (2001) provide evidence to suggest that racial heterogeneity was the primary reason for less redistributive policies within the United States.

The United States also has a long political tradition of antistatism and wariness toward large federal government programs. Lipset (1990) suggests that this is at least partially due to the founding history of the United States. Founded through revolution and the overthrow of the existing British Colonial government, in part because of the imposition of high taxes, U.S. citizens were suspicious of any future government efforts to recreate high tax systems. Furthermore, the U.S. Constitution created a federalist structure for the country. State governments rather than the national government were invested with residual government powers. There is a strong presumption in U.S. political thought that local and state governments are closer to the people and more responsive to democratic decision-making by citizens. This political culture is hostile toward federal mandates and entitlements, and far more willing to accept a dispersed and (nationally) inequitable system of public assistance for destitute citizens.[2]

Third, the history of economic expansion (closely linked with increases in literal size of the country as the frontier moved west) and the history of immigration created a strong belief in the power of economic opportunity within the United States. The myth that "everyone who works hard will be successful in the United States" was grounded in an economic experience in which large numbers of people did arrive destitute but were able to create economically stable lives. In many cases, their children and grandchildren experienced substantial upward economic mobility, in part due to hard work but also due to overall national economic growth that increased earnings and job opportunities for all citizens. One result of this was a deep belief in the power of the market to create jobs and to create economic opportunities.[3] This is the flip side of suspicion of government: Americans look to the market economy, not to government programs, for economic support. In fact, it is not an accident that the creation of nationally legislated public assistance programs in the United States did not occur until the Great Depression of the 1930s—the deepest and longest period of economic stagnation in U.S. history. Only in the face of sustained high unemployment and a sharp reduction in incomes was it politically possible for programs such as Social Security, UI, and AFDC to emerge at the federal level.

U.S. WELFARE REFORM IN THE 1990S

The 1990s were a period of substantial reform in the social assistance system for low-income families in the United States. A variety of legislative changes fundamentally altered the ways in which the United States provided public support. While the United States had always had a limited cash support system for nonworking adults who were caring for children (primarily women who were single parents), the 1990s reforms shrank this system even further. Replacing it were a new set of programs designed to support low-wage workers in the economy. In short, the United States moved from a (limited) cash support system to a system of work-conditioned public transfers. Both of these were supplemented with various in-kind programs.

Note that I do not use the term "workfare," but instead use the term "work-conditioned transfers." In the United States, workfare has a very particular meaning. It is a public assistance system that places adult parents (usually single mothers) into public sector jobs and requires that they work in these jobs for a specified period each month in order to receive their monthly public assistance benefits. This is actually quite uncommon in the United States. The most prominent example of a workfare system was established in New York City in the late 1990s. Almost no other states or localities link benefits with required placement in public sector jobs.

The reforms of the 1990s grew out of a variety of political and economic pressures.[4] Most notably, they grew out of a concern with the disincentives imbedded in cash assistance programs. By providing maximal dollars for those who worked zero hours, and then taxing away benefits as a woman went to work, these programs have an imbedded disincentive against work. A voluminous research literature, largely by U.S. economists, documents the existence of such disincentives, although there is more disagreement about the magnitude of such effects.[5]

The dual goals of encouraging work as well as providing support to non-workers create inherently contradictory pressures within a cash public assistance system. On the one hand, if one wishes to provide substantial support to those who cannot work at all, this is best done by providing cash support to nonworkers. This costs money, however, and creates an incentive for recipients to claim themselves unable to work. On the other hand, if one wishes to provide incentives to work among those who are able, this typically means providing limited benefits for those who choose not to work, and making sure that benefits do not decline rapidly as work increases. But the more slowly that benefits decrease with income (the so-called "benefit reduction rate") the more workers who are eligible for some public assistance benefits. This too costs money and pulls more people into the public assistance system.

Of course, if a program can clearly distinguish between those who cannot work and those who choose not to work, these conflicts go away. When AFDC was first established, single mothers were assumed to be nonworkers by definition, so the concern about work incentives in welfare was not a strong one. But expectations about women in the labor market changed dramatically in the 1960s and later decades. By the 1990s, the great majority of U.S. adult women, even women with small children, were in the labor force working at least part-time. It was no longer acceptable to assume that single mothers should not work; indeed, there was growing criticism of the welfare system because it allowed poor women to stay home. This was considered unfair to lower-income married women whose income was too high to qualify for welfare but who had to work for economic survival. Over time, critics began to argue that it was also unfair to poor women, who were not getting the labor market experience that would allow them to support their families and escape poverty. The expectation that women can and should work eroded political support for the AFDC program and for cash welfare for single mothers.

Work disincentives were only one problematic incentive in welfare programs. The second issue that became quite politically important in the United States was the incentives that welfare programs created for women to become single mothers.[6] Initially, most participants in AFDC programs were widows, but by the 1960s and 1970s more AFDC participants were divorced women. By the late 1970s and 1980s, a rapidly increasingly share of AFDC participants were never-married women. While increasing divorce and declining marriage rates were surely caused by a wide variety of factors, growth in never-married single mothers was fastest among lower-income women. Marriage among black women fell particularly rapidly; by 1990, 28% of all births and 66% of African American births were to unmarried women. Concern about these demographic changes became an increasingly important political issue. Research was mixed on the extent to which the welfare system was a cause of rising numbers of non-marital births. While one or two papers suggested the impacts were large, quite a few papers indicated the effects were small or even nonexistent.[7] Research conclusions, however, had little effect on the public debate, which linked welfare and nonmarital childbearing.

These concerns and others came together by the early 1990s to create a demand for welfare reform. President Clinton was particularly supportive of these efforts and made them a centerpiece of his 1992 presidential campaign, calling for an end to welfare "as we know it." When the Republicans took over control of Congress in the midterm elections of 1994, they quickly presented their own welfare reform bill, which significantly modified some of the changes proposed by the Clinton Administration.[8]

Despite intense debates over the details of the legislation, however, the motivation behind welfare reform was widely agreed upon. The desire was to create a system that encouraged women to enter the labor market. This would, it was argued, move women into a better long-term economic situation by allowing them to acquire labor market experience and to serve as working role models for their children, while also discouraging out-of-wedlock childbearing. It was also hoped that these changes would reduce government costs.

A number of states experimented with welfare-to-work programs in the late 1980s and early 1990s. These demonstration programs were evaluated with a randomized design evaluation of participants versus nonparticipants, which was viewed as highly credible. The results from these evaluations indicated that welfare-to-work programs would increase earnings and reduce government spending on welfare.[9] This evidence further fueled the call for national welfare reform.

The reforms of the 1990s consisted of two parts. First, changes in cash support systems greatly reduced the availability of support to nonworkers and increased incentives to work. Second, a variety of legislative changes increased the support available to low-wage workers through other programs. Both of these were important, and I describe them each in turn.

Changes in the Cash Welfare System

Legislation passed in 1996 fundamentally reformed the cash welfare system in the United States. The old AFDC program was abolished and replaced with a federal block grant to the states, the Temporary Assistance to Needy Families (TANF) block grant. Most federal program requirements were abolished, and states were given greater discretion over the design of cash assistance programs. In return, states were required to implement stronger efforts to move welfare recipients off welfare and into work. As a result of this legislation, every state in the United States made major changes to its programs. Among these were the following:[10]

- A growing share of women on welfare was required to participate in mandatory welfare-to-work programs in order to remain eligible for cash support. In most cases, this was not job-training but short-term assistance in preparing and searching for work.
- Women who were assigned to these programs but failed to meet the participation requirements (this often meant failing to show up for required training sessions) were subject to sanctions and could have their welfare payments reduced or eliminated. In some states, these reductions were temporary; after multiple infractions they became permanent in some states.
- The federal support for any recipient was time-limited. States could not provide assistance to any adult recipient for more than 60 months from a TANF-funded program. At their discretion, states could exempt 20% of their caseload from these time limits, and they could continue to support recipients with state dollars. In almost all states, welfare offices began to warn women that "the clock is ticking" on their time limit, and they had to find employment and leave welfare.
- As a further incentive to work, many states lowered the benefit reduction rate, so that welfare benefits did not fall as rapidly as earnings rose. Doing so increased incentives for women to move into work (they got to keep more of their earnings) and provided greater subsidies to lower-wage and part-time workers. In these states, women were often able to continue to collect some welfare payments as they worked in low-wage jobs, providing them with more income while working. There is, of course, a conflict between take-up of these subsidies and the time limit.
- As women went to work, all states put more dollars into work-support payments rather than into cash assistance to nonworkers. For instance, states greatly increased their child care assistance. In many states, even after a woman left welfare, she was often eligible for some ongoing childcare support or transportation subsidies designed to help subsidize her earnings and keep her employed.

Changes in Other Policies that Increased Support for Low-Wage Workers

Also in the early to mid-1990s, a variety of other legislative changes were designed to help support low-wage workers. Many of these were part of an explicit strategy on the part of the Clinton Administration to help "make work pay," as a way to support the effort to move women off welfare and into work.

At the center of these changes were substantial expansions in the Earned Income Tax Credit (EITC). The EITC operates through the federal income tax system and offsets taxes for low-wage workers in low-income families. It is refundable, so workers eligible for an EITC offset that is greater than their tax liability can receive a check back from the government. For families with children, the EITC expansions were very large. By 2000, a woman with two children working in a low-wage job could receive almost $4,000 from the federal government as an EITC payment. The EITC was particularly well-targeted, helping only low-income families, not just low-wage earners (many of whom live in higher-income families). Furthermore, this expansion created substantial incentives for entering employment since it provided large subsidies to low-wage work.[11] The expansion of the federal EITC also spurred a number of states to create their own state EITCs, most of them designed to add onto and increase the federal credit amount. In 2006, eighteen states had a state EITC.

At the same time that it expanded the EITC in the mid-1990s, Congress also enacted expansions in the minimum wage. The higher minimum wage reinforced the EITC expansions and further increased the value of work. By 1997, any women working full time at the minimum wage was above the poverty line for a family of three when her earnings and EITC subsidy were both counted. Unfortunately, inflation eroded the value of the minimum wage between 1997 and 2007; during this period, there were no increases at the federal level, although many states raised state minimum wages. In July 2007, the federal minimum wage went from $5.15 to $5.85; it will continue to rise over the next few years, going to $6.55 in 2008 and $7.25 in 2009. In contrast, the EITC subsidy is inflation-indexed. As a result, the EITC has become increasingly important over time.

While the United States does not have a national health insurance system, it has steadily expanded the availability of public health insurance since the late 1980s, particularly for children in lower-income families. By 2000, all children in poor and near-poor families had access to Medicaid, the U.S. public health insurance program. While parents working at low-wage jobs might not be covered by health insurance, their children continued to have Medicaid access. (And many women who left welfare had ongoing Medicaid eligibility for some period of time.) A large push by states also occurred in the late 1990s to increase the number of eligible children actually using Medicaid and regularly accessing health care.[12]

Other policies also supplemented the income available from low-wage work. Increased efforts at child support enforcement have slowly increased the dollars received by single mothers from absent fathers. Food stamps, which are theoretically available to virtually all low-income families, were often hard to access by workers who had less discretionary time than nonworking welfare recipients. Following welfare reform in the mid-1990s, the Food Stamp Program redesigned eligibility and access so that working parents could more easily receive benefits. For instance, offices that certify food stamp eligibility are now much more likely to be open on weekends or later in the evening. As a result, food stamp receipt among working low-income families has grown over the past several years.

These multiple policy changes all increased the incentives to work. The returns to employment increased through expansions in the EITC, the minimum wage, and lower benefit reduction rates. The incentives to leave welfare also increased through time limits, welfare-to-work efforts, and sanctions. Expanded access to public health insurance or food stamps among working low-income families also made work more attractive. These policy changes were further enhanced by a period of very strong economic growth in the late 1990s. The United States experienced its longest and strongest economic expansion over this decade. The economy was labor-short, and employers actively recruited women leaving welfare into jobs. Unemployment was low, and very few women who were able to search for work failed to find it. Jobs were not always stable and many women experienced quite a bit of job turnover, but another job was almost always available for someone who actively looked for it.

CHANGING BEHAVIOR AMONG SINGLE MOTHER FAMILIES AFTER THE MID-1990S

While these policy and economic changes could be expected to reduce welfare participation and to increase work, even those who had strongly supported these reforms were surprised by the magnitude of response. In a five-year period from 1996 to 2001, welfare caseloads fell by 50%. In the early 2000s, there were fewer women receiving welfare than at any time since the late 1960s, even though the population of single mothers was much larger.

Figure 8-1 shows these changes between 1979 and 2006, plotting the number of families receiving AFDC (prior to 1996) and TANF (after 1996). Caseloads fell dramatically in the late 1990s, and they continued to decline throughout the 2000s, despite a slower economy. This decline started prior to the implementation of welfare reform (shown in Figure 8-1 with the vertical line), consistent with the idea that other policy and economic changes were also driving welfare caseloads down, but the decline accelerated after the passage of welfare reform. In 1995, the average single mother received 24% of her income from public assistance programs. By 2004, she received only 5% of her income from these programs.[13]

As welfare usage fell, work and earnings increased. Labor force participation rose rapidly among single mothers in the late 1990s, which resulted in significant increases in earnings. Between 1995 and 2004, average earnings increased from 54% to 66% of women's total income. Furthermore, overall incomes rose as well. Between 1995 and 2004, average income among single mother families rose from $20,000 to $23,500 in inflation-adjusted 2000 dollars. In short, the average expansion in earnings more than exceeded the average decline in welfare

Figure 8-1: Total AFDC/TANF caseloads

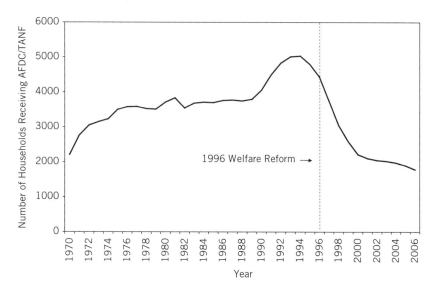

Source: Website for Agency for Children and Families, Department of Health and Human Services (http://www.acf.dhhs.gov)

benefits among these families. This is consistent with official U.S. poverty data, which shows steady declines in poverty among single-mother households over the late 1990s. Furthermore, these gains were not lost in the 2000s when the economy slowed down and unemployment rose somewhat. On average, single mothers appeared to keep their jobs and to maintain greater earnings and higher overall incomes.

A large number of research efforts in the United States have attempted to measure the relative effectiveness of welfare policy reforms, EITC expansions, economic growth, and other policy changes on caseload declines and increases in employment and income. There are a number of reviews of this literature,[14] which suggest that all of these factors were important in producing the behavioral changes in work and welfare usage that occurred. Indeed, it is almost surely the confluence of so many changes, all pushing in the same direction, which interacted with each other and resulted in much more rapid change than any program by itself could have created.

These changes in the United States have been watched with great interest. The EITC in particular has generated policy interest from other countries. For instance, the United Kingdom's Working Families Tax Credit was partially modeled on the EITC and appears to have had similar effects in increasing employment.

Any overall evaluation of welfare reform, to date, must conclude that the majority of single mothers appear to be working substantially more and have higher overall incomes. A few caveats on these results are important, however. First, if increased work means expanded work expenses for clothing or transportation, this increase in income may not have produced a substantial increase in overall family well-being. There is clear evidence that consumption among single-mother families increased (consistent with income increases), but much of the increase in consumption appears to have gone into items such as adult clothing or increased transportation expenses (Kaushal et al. 2006). This is in sharp contrast to the effect of policies designed to increase income among families with children in the United Kingdom over the past decade, where increased consumption appears to have raised expenditures on children (Gregg et al. 2006).

Second, at least some women at the very bottom of the income distribution appear to be doing worse following welfare reform. Particularly over the 2000s, there is a growing group of single mothers who report themselves as neither working nor on welfare. At least half of these women report they are not living with other adults, and their income levels are extremely low. A growing body of literature documents the problems faced by these "disconnected" women who have left welfare but not found stable employment. A high proportion of these women have significant barriers to work, including adults or children in their household with health problems that require personal care; personal health problems, particularly problems relating to depression and mental health; very low skill or cognitive levels; past or current problems with domestic violence and abuse; or problems with substance abuse.[15] The recent growth in the share of disconnected women is particularly worrisome. This group may have a limited ability to fully support themselves through employment, but many of them have hit time limits or sanctions and lost their access to public benefits. This group appears to have been made worse off by these policy changes.

The new and expanded programs that were put in place in the mid-1990s are still being closely watched in the United States. Both government agencies and private researchers continue to monitor the size and composition of welfare caseloads, as well as income and employment among those who leave welfare. Overall, these policy changes have achieved much of what their supporters wanted, moving large numbers of single mothers into work and leaving them with at least somewhat higher incomes than when they were on welfare. It will remain an ongoing challenge to maintain these gains through future economic cycles and to bring more women into steady employment and economic self-sufficiency.

THE CHANGING STRUCTURE OF SOCIAL ASSISTANCE IN THE UNITED STATES

This section discusses the size and scope of the current set of social assistance policies in the United States in the mid-2000s, providing a sense of how the social safety net fits together following the recent changes. Table 8-1 lists the major U.S. social assistance programs and shows their relative size and magnitude in 1990 and 2004. The top part of Table 8-1 describes means-tested public assistance programs while the bottom part describes the more universal social insurance programs.

Among the public assistance programs, the Medicaid program (public health insurance for eligible low-income families) dominates all others in size. Its costs have risen rapidly in step with overall increases in health insurance costs. The largest share of Medicaid expenditures go for care of the elderly and disabled, particularly for those in long-term care facilities. While approximately two-thirds of Medicaid recipients are low-income nonelderly and nondisabled adults or children, they receive only about one-third of the Medicaid dollars.

The most rapidly growing program has been the EITC, which has almost quadrupled in terms of dollars spent over this period. All of these dollars go to working low-income families.

Cash assistance to low-income families, provided through state and federal funds to the TANF block grant in 2004, has become a relatively small program, serving relatively few people. Furthermore, over the past decade, the dollars spent through TANF are increasingly spent on subsidies for working recipients (child care subsidies, benefits for workers) and an increasingly small share of these dollars go to nonworking recipients.

In contrast, cash assistance to low-income disabled and elderly individuals, provided by the SSI program, has grown, partly through increases in number of participants and partly through somewhat higher benefits per participant. The elderly and disabled are the only two groups in the United States who can count on receiving means-tested monthly cash benefits without work requirements, although there is growing interest in helping younger disabled individuals enter the workforce.

In-kind programs have always been an important part of the U.S. safety net. The Food Stamp Program has expanded over the past decade, with efforts to reach out to more working, low-income families who are no longer receiving cash welfare support but who may be eligible for food stamps. Housing programs have also grown in size over time. These programs receive funding from the federal government, but require matching funds and action by local governments. Hence, their availability is quite varied; some communities are more active in utilizing these programs and providing housing subsidies to eligible residents. As a result, a relatively small share of low-income families receives housing subsidies in the United States. Job training programs in the United States (outside of those funded through the TANF block grant for women receiving welfare) have always been very small and have declined in size.

It is worth noting that U.S. public assistance programs are deeply affected by the country's federalist structure. Most programs share funding between state and national governments. In many cases, states have substantial control over

Table 8-1: U.S. Social Assistance Programs

A. Public Assistance Programs	Program Cost (millions of 2004 dollars)		# Families Participating (thousands)		Average Benefit in 2004	Level of Government	
	1990	2004	1990	2004		Financing	Delivery
Medicaid[a]	98,766	277,658	25,255[c]	51,971[c]	$4,614	Federal/State	State
Earned Income Tax Credit	10,112	40,024	12,542	22,270	$1,797	Federal	Federal
Supplemental Security Income	20,770	39,767	4,817[c]	6,988[c]	$428[j]	Primarily Federal	Federal
Food Stamp Program[b,d]	23,698	31,037	20,049[c]	26,672[c]	$202[j]	Primarily Federal	State/Local
Housing Subsidies[b,d]	21,519	32,111	4,710	5,190	$6,187[h]	Federal	Local
Temporary Assistance to Needy Families[a]	30,172	13,497	4,057[i]	1,979[i]	$360[i]	Federal/State	State/Local
Job Training[a]	2,417	2,168	630[c,e]	814[c,e]	$2,663[h]	Federal/State	State/Local

B. Social Insurance Programs	Program Cost (millions of 2004 dollars)		# Individuals Participating (thousands)		Average Benefit in 2004	Level of Government	
	1990	2004	1990	2004		Financing	Delivery
Social Security[b] *Retirement and Survivors*	305,060	434,621	35,559	40,503	$925[j]	Federal	Federal
Disability	34,346	89,058	4,266	8,619	$785[j]		
Total	339,406	523,678	39,825	49,123	—		
Medicare[f]	148,809	326,509	34,203	42,395	$7,702[h]	Federal	Federal
Unemployment Insurance[b]	26,293	33,292	8,100	7,400	$1,006[j]	Federal/State	Federal/State
Workers' Compensation[f,g]	23,313	32,501	—	—	—	Federal/State	State

Notes: Except where noted, all data as of 2004. Other years are inflation adjusted to 2004 dollars. There are a large number of smaller programs (WIC, emergency shelter grants, etc.) not included.

a 2003 data.

b 2006 data. Social Security beneficiaries as of 31 December 2006.

c Individual recipients. Medicaid, SSI, the Food Stamp Program, and TANF include adults and children.

d Does not include state funding for a small number of programs.

e Does not include programs for displaced workers.

f 2005 calendar year data. Medicare enrollment as of July.

g Excludes private insurers and self-insured companies.

h Average benefit is calculated by dividing total benefits by number of recipients.

i Calendar year data.

j Average monthly benefit.

Sources:

AFDC/TANF: U.S. Department of Health and Human Services, Administration for Children and Families. Caseloads: http://www.acf.hhs.gov/programs/ofa/caseload/caseloadindex. htm. Cost: 7th Annual Report to Congress, 2006.

Food Stamps: Food and Nutrition Service, U.S. Department of Agriculture, http://www.fns.usda.gov/pd/fssummar.htm.

Medicaid: Medicare & Medicaid Statistical Supplement, 2006, Tables 14.4 and 14.12; National Health Expenditures, Office of the Actuary, Center for Medicare and Medicaid Services.

Housing Subsidies: 2000 and 2004 Green Book, U.S. House Ways and Means Committee; HUD Accountability Reports (households, 1999–2004) http://www.hud.gov/offices/cfo/ reports/2006/2006par.pdf.

Job Training: 1979–1999: Green Book, U.S. House Ways and Means Committee; Employment and Training Administration, 2000–2003: Department of Labor (http://www.doleta.gov/ performance/charts/).

EITC: Internal Revenue Service (1975–2001 taken from Green Book, Tables 13 and 14, 2002–2004 from http://www.irs.gov/taxstats/indtaxstats/article/0,id=134951,00.html)

SSI: Social Security Administration, SSI Annual Statistical Report, 2004 and 2005. "Indicators of Welfare Dependence," HHS 2006 Report to Congress, Appendix A, http://aspe.hhs. gov/hsp/indicators06/apa.pdf.

Social Security: Cost: Social Security Administration, http://www.ssa.gov/OACT/STATS. Average monthly benefit and participants: http://www.ssa.gov/OACT/ProgData/icp.html.

Medicare: Cost and Benefits paid: 2006 Annual Report of the Boards of Trustees of the Federal Hospital Insurance and Federal Supplementary Medical Insurance Trust Funds, Table III.B4 and III.C1, and analogous tables from earlier annual reports. (Pulled from the 2005 SSA Annual Statistical Supplement.) Enrollment: Center for Medicare and Medicaid Services, Medicare Enrollment Reports, http://www.cms.hhs.gov/MedicareEnRpts/Downloads/HISMI05.pdf.

UI: 1983–2004: Unemployment Insurance Outlook and Green Book, U.S. House Ways and Means Committee. 1979–1982: Congressional Budget Office, http://www.cbo.gov/ ftpdocs/50xx/doc5026/doc06-Part3.pdf.

Workers' Comp: Office of the Actuary, Center for Medicare and Medicaid Services, http://www.cms.hhs.gov/NationalHealthExpendData/02_NationalHealthAccountsHistorical.asp.

the determination of benefit eligibility and the provision of services. Hence, the geographic location of a poor family has substantial influence on the level and type of benefits that a family might receive.

Not surprisingly, the social insurance programs in the United States dwarf the means-tested programs, in part because they serve many more people. The bottom part of Table 8-1 shows the primary social insurance programs. Social Security provides pensions through its "retirement and survivors" payments, and provides assistance to disabled workers and their families as well. Disability payments and participation have been increasing particularly rapidly in recent years. Overall, Social Security accounted for almost 5% of GDP by 2004.

Medicare, which provides public health insurance to elderly workers, is growing even faster than Social Security, again reflecting the steep rise in health insurance prices in the United States over this time period. Both Social Security and Medicare are predicted to grow in the years ahead as the post–World War II baby boom generation moves toward retirement age. Like many other countries, the United States is facing a serious long-term funding crisis for these programs. These funding problems are likely to be particularly acute for the Medicare program, given the growth in health care expenses in the United States.

In comparison to Social Security and Medicare, UI and Workers' Compensation programs are relatively small, although they are at least as large as most of the public assistance programs. Both UI and Workers' Compensation have shrunk somewhat over the past 15 years. Participation in UI among eligible unemployed appears to have fallen over this time period, and benefits became somewhat more restricted.

Figures 8-2a and b show how spending on these programs has changed over the past 25 years. Figure 8-2a plots spending on public assistance programs while Figure 8-2b plots spending on social insurance programs. Everything is shown in inflation-adjusted 2004 dollars. Figure 8-2a shows the dramatic decline in AFDC/TANF spending over time, while the EITC rises quickly to become one of the largest programs. The costs of the Medicaid program rise rapidly and soon become too large to graph on the same scale. Other programs generally increase over this time period. The Food Stamp Program initially declines along with TANF, but increases again in the 2000s as the program was redesigned to better serve the growing number of working single-mother families.

Figure 8-2b shows changes in social insurance programs over this same 25-year period. Social Security and Medicare spending rise almost linearly, while the unemployment and workers' compensation programs are reasonably steady in size. UI shows a clear cyclical pattern, as expected.

Figures 8-3a and b show the number of households that participate in public assistance programs (Figure 8-3a) and in social insurance programs (Figure 8-3b) over the past 25 years. In general, participation trends mirror spending trends, but there are a few notable exceptions. Comparing Figures 8-2a and 8-3a,

Figure 8-2: (a) Spending on Public Assistance Programs, 1979–2004; (b) Spending on Social Insurance Programs, 1979–2004

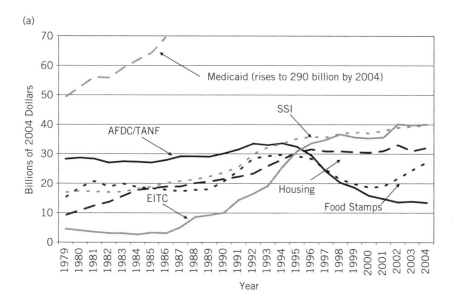

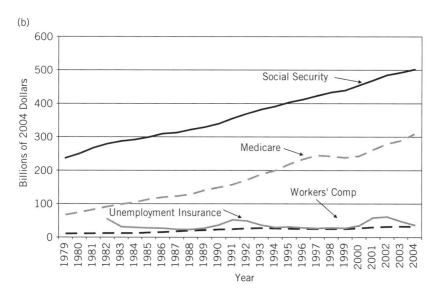

it is clear that the increase in Medicaid spending is being driven much more by a rise in costs per participant than by a rise in the number of participants. While numbers of participants have risen, spending has grown much more rapidly. The EITC shows strong growth in participation as well as spending.

Figure 8-3: (a) Number of Households Participating in Public Assistance Programs, 1979–2004. (b) Number of Individuals Participating in Social Insurance Programs, 1979–2004

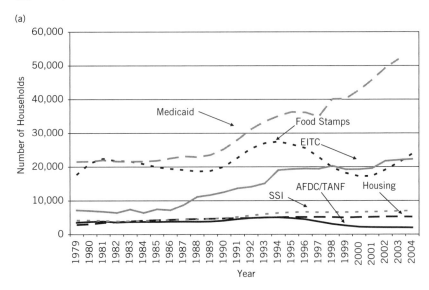

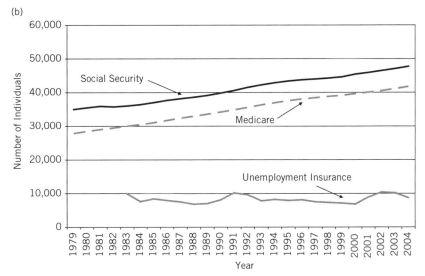

Note: Medicaid, Food Stamps, and SSI measured in number of individual recipients.

The number of participants in the Food Stamp Program makes it one of the largest public assistance programs by the mid-2000s, although not one of the most expensive. This reflects its universal nature, available to virtually all low-income families. Many people receive food stamps, although the amount received may be quite small.

Figure 8-4: (a) Public Assistance Spending as a Share of GDP, 1979–2004. (b) Social Insurance Program Spending as a Share of GDP, 1979–2004

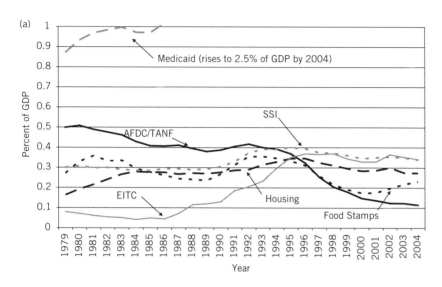

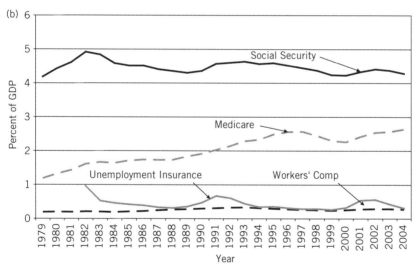

As Figure 8-3b shows, participation in the big social insurance programs is rising as steadily as spending. The rising costs in these programs are driven by both growing participation and growing dollars spent per participant.

Finally, Figures 8-4a and b show changes in these programs as a share of overall GDP. These graphs indicate whether these programs have grown relative to the size of the U.S. economy. As Figure 8-4a indicates, Medicaid has grown rapidly by any measure. The declines in AFDC/TANF and the growth in the EITC as a share of U.S. GDP are expected. Figure 8-4b indicates that Social Security, although rising in expenditures, has remained a relatively constant share of GDP. Medicare, however, is growing rapidly.

Interestingly, the size of the welfare state in the United States has risen markedly over the past 25 years. The share of GDP going into public assistance programs has grown from 2.3% to 3.8%, and the share in social insurance programs has risen from 6.3% to 7.7%. Much (but not all) of this growth has been driven by rising health care costs in Medicaid and Medicare.

Among public assistance programs, even if we ignore Medicaid, there has been no decline in overall spending between 1990 and 2004. As a share of GDP, the non-Medicaid public assistance programs have stayed at 1.3%, at a time when GDP has grown sharply. In short, welfare reform has not meant a decline in the U.S. spending on public assistance. The increase in work-conditioned transfers has been as large as the decline in support for nonworking families.

LESSONS FROM THE U.S. EXPERIENCE

It is always somewhat dangerous to apply lessons from one country to any other country. Differences in history, demographics, political institutions, and in social norms make cross-country comparisons difficult. Nonetheless, let me point out several aspects of U.S. welfare reform history that might be of interest to outside observers.

The United States is increasingly modeling a very different type of welfare state than seen elsewhere, with work-conditioned transfers as the central means of providing assistance to nonelderly, nondisabled citizens. The key elements of this new policy configuration are wage subsidies for low-wage workers, combined with other family subsidies to help increase income and cover work-related expenses. This includes such things as food stamp assistance, health insurance coverage, and child care subsidies. Expanded child support collections from absent fathers are also growing in importance. These policies make low-wage work a more viable option for families with children headed by low-skilled adults.

Furthermore, the U.S. experience over the past 10 years indicates that work can increase significantly among a population that has not worked at historically high levels. After 1995, single mothers have multiple and growing incentives to leave cash assistance and to enter employment. The level at which this occurred exceeded anyone's expectations. Job availability was an important component of this movement into work. This underscores the extent to which job-holding is possible, even among populations with limited past labor market experience and with multiple time demands from children and other family members.

There remain a substantial number of problems with the work-conditioned transfer system in the United States. The lack of universal health coverage means that many families still face barriers to receiving healthcare, particularly among adults. The availability of child subsidies to working low-wage women has grown enormously, yet there are still many women who do not receive these subsidies. The lack of inflation indexing for the minimum wage means that erosion in low wage levels occurs over time. Yet, despite these problems, the degree of public support for low wage workers in the United States is very substantial and far superior to what it was 15 years ago.

The cost of this system, of course, is that it provides support only to workers. Strong work incentives require limited payments to those who do not hold a job. Persons who are seriously disabled or elderly have support through other programs. But individuals who do not qualify as disabled, yet who face significant barriers to work and are unable to work steadily, may find themselves without public resources and experience destitution. The evidence suggests that the women who have left welfare, not found steady work, and who are most economically disadvantaged following welfare reform, are those with health, personal, and family problems that limit their ability to find and hold full-time steady employment.

A key question for this system of work-conditioned support is whether or not it can maintain a high level of long-term political support in the United States. The previous cash support system was the target of constant attacks, as recipients were portrayed as "lazy" and misusing public tax dollars. Such public attacks have been less frequent in the past 10 years. So far, the system has achieved reasonably wide-spread political support. States did not cut their work-oriented welfare programs in the early 2000s, although a number of states experienced much tighter state budgets for several years. The federal government reauthorized the TANF block grant in 2006 without cutting dollars available to states from this block grant, despite a growing federal budget deficit. The EITC receives bipartisan support from a wide range of politically officials. If this work-conditioned support system turns out to be more political stable and supportable in the long run, the policy changes of mid-1990s may be viewed as good long-term policy, despite the flaws inherent in any work-conditioned public assistance system.

The U.S. system makes the most sense, of course, in a country in which low-wage jobs are available and abundant. In general, less-skilled workers can find low-wage work in the United States. In fact, many observers have written extensively about the ways in which the U.S. economy is more flexible and market-driven, creating a larger number of lower-wage jobs than occurs in many European nations where employers face larger costs to employment with a more regulated labor market. While the flexible labor market in the United States has obvious problems, particularly apparent in the rising inequality in incomes that are visible in that country (Freeman 2007), it has maintained relatively low unemployment rates and high job growth rates over the past two decades.

Given that the U.S. economy is structured in a way that creates low-wage jobs, the work-conditioned transfer system that has emerged over the past decade may be a good policy response to cushion the problems that arise when significant numbers of less-skilled workers find themselves in jobs with limited earnings opportunities. Of course, in a country where work is less available, work requirements as a precondition to receiving public support are a much less attractive policy, and leaves more people without public assistance.

The U.S. social assistance system remains a work in progress. Less discussed in this chapter, a major challenge for the system is the funding problems facing the more universalist social insurance pension and health care programs for the elderly. Substantial changes in the funding for and benefits from these programs are likely to be enacted in the decade ahead.

The means-tested programs within the U.S. social assistance system have recently undergone substantial change. The long-run viability and sustainability of these newly expanded work-conditioned transfers remains to be seen. It is possible that growing attention to the problems of those who are not working steadily (such as the growing number of single mothers who are disconnected from work but who have lost access to welfare benefits) may lead to some retrenchment, particularly if the United States experiences a period of sustained higher unemployment when jobs are less available. I suspect, however, that the work-conditioned system of support for low-income families will be a prominent and perhaps even growing part of the U.S. social welfare state. In a country with a large number of low-wage jobs, and with a long-term historical emphasis on the market and on market work as the key to long-run economic opportunity, this configuration of programs may be more attractive than the more traditional cash welfare programs of the past.

REFERENCES

Alesina, Alberto, Glaeser, Edward, and Sacerdote, Bruce (2001) Why Doesn't the U.S. Have a European-Style Welfare System, *Brookings Papers on Economic Affairs*, 2: 187–254.

Blank, Rebecca M. (1997) *It Takes A Nation: A New Agenda for Fighting Poverty*, Princeton, NJ: Princeton University Press.

Blank, Rebecca M. (2002) Evaluating Welfare Reform in the United States, *Journal of Economic Literature*, 40, 4: 1105–1166.

Blank, Rebecca M. (2007) Improving the Safety Net for Single Mothers Who Face Serious Barrier to Work, *Future of Children*, 17, 2: 183–197.

Blank, Rebecca M. (forthcoming 2009) What We Know, What We Don't Know, and What We Need to Know about Welfare Reform, in James Ziliak (ed.) *Welfare Reform and Its Long-term Consequences for America's Poor*, Cambridge: Cambridge University Press.

Blank, Rebecca M. and Haskins, Ron (2001) *The New World of Welfare.* Washington, DC: Brookings Institution Press.

Blank, Rebecca M. and Kovak, Brian (2009) The Growing Problem of Disconnected Single Mothers in Carolyn J. Heinrich and John Karl Scholz (eds.) *Making the Work-Based Safety Net Work Better,* New York: Russell Sage Press.

Bloom, Dan and Michalopoulos, Charles (2001) *How Welfare and Work Policies Affect Employment and Income: A Synthesis of Research,* New York: MDRC.

Committee on Ways and Means, U.S. House of Representatives (1990) *Green Book: Background Material and Data on Programs within the Jurisdiction of the Committee on Ways and Means,* Washington, DC: U.S. Government Printing Office.

Engelhardt, Gary V. and Gruber, Jonathan (2006) Social Security and the Evolution of Elderly Poverty, in Alan J. Auerbach, David Card and John M. Quigley (eds) *Public Policy and the Income Distribution,* New York: Russell Sage Foundation, pp. 259–287.

Esping-Andersen, Gøsta (1990) *The Three Worlds of Welfare Capitalism,* Princeton, NJ: Princeton University Press.

Freeman, Richard B. (2007) *America Works: Critical Thoughts on the Exceptional U.S. Labor Market,* New York: Russell Sage.

Gregg, Paul, Waldfogel, Jane and Washbrook, Elizabeth (2006) Expenditures Patterns Post-Welfare Reform in the UK: Are Low-Income Families Starting to Catch Up?, *Labour Economics,* 13 , 6: 721–746.

Grogger, Jeffrey and Karoly, Lynn A. (2005) *Welfare Reform: Effects of a Decade of Change,* Cambridge, MA: Harvard University Press.

Gruber, Jonathan (2003) Medicaid, in Robert Moffitt (ed.) *Means-Tested Transfer Programs in the United States,* Chicago, IL: University of Chicago Press, pp. 15–77.

Haskins, Ron (2006) *Work over Welfare: The Inside Story of the 1996 Welfare Reform Law,* Washington, DC: Brookings Institution Press.

Hoffman, Saul D. and Seidman, Laurence S. (2003) *Helping Working Families: The Earned Income Tax Credit,* Kalamazoo, MI: W.E. Upjohn Institute for Employment Research.

Kaushal, Neeraj, Gao, Qin, and Waldfogel, Jane (2006) Welfare Reform and Family Expenditures: How Are Single Mothers Adapting to the New Welfare and Work Regime? National Bureau of Economic Research Working Paper 12624, Cambridge, MA: NBER.

Lipset, Seymour Martin (1990) *Continental Divide: The Values and Institutions of the U.S. and Canada,* New York: Routledge.

Lipset, Seymour Martin (1996) *American Exceptionalism: A Double-Edged Sword,* New York: W.W. Norton and Company.

Moffitt, Robert (1992) Incentive Effects of the U.S. Welfare System: A Review, *Journal of Economic Literature* 30, 1: 1–61.

Moffitt, Robert (ed.) (1998) *Welfare, the Family, and Reproductive Behavior: Research Perspectives,* Washington, DC: National Academy Press.

Murray, Charles (1984) *Losing Ground: American Social Policy 1950–1980*, New York: Basic Books.

Piven, Frances Fox and Cloward, Richard A. (1971) *Regulating the Poor: The Functions of Public Welfare*, New York: Random House.

Weaver, R. Kent (2000) *Ending Welfare as We Know It*. Washington, DC: Brookings Institution Press.

PART II

SOCIETY: CONDITIONS AND OUTCOMES

SECTION V

THE GOAL OF FULL EMPLOYMENT

9

WELFARE AND EMPLOYMENT: A EUROPEAN DILEMMA?

WERNER EICHHORST AND ANTON HEMERIJCK

THE REFORM CAPACITY OF THE SEMISOVEREIGN EUROPEAN WELFARE STATE

Is the European welfare state fit for globalization? This question has haunted European policymakers for over a decade. Sluggish growth and elusive job creation round the turn of the new millennium have given way to a fierce ideological battle between different socioeconomic "models," triggering political strife and antagonistic advocacy coalitions. A casual glance at the 2005 French referendum campaign over the Constitutional Treaty reveals the contest between two polarized positions. The French version of the European social model was pitted against a false stereotype of the "Anglo-Saxon" model of capitalism, allegedly a "free market without a safety net," producing high levels of poverty and inequality. Politicians across the Channel, like Tony Blair in his address to the

European Parliament on June 23, in turn posed the rhetorical question: "What type of social model is it that has 20 million unemployed?"

In the early 1990s, the Organisation for Economic Cooperation and Development (OECD) received a mandate to examine the labor market performance of its member countries. The OECD Jobs Strategy, published in 1994, launched a critical attack on the "dark side" of double-digit unemployment of many of its European OECD members. Hovering around 10% with little signs of improvement (OECD 1994), unemployment rates in the large economies of France, Germany, and Italy were twice as high as in the United States. The employment rate was about twelve points below the United States. The OECD economists argued that Europe's generous welfare states, with their overprotective job security, high minimum wages, and generous unemployment insurance, heavy taxation, and their overriding emphasis on coordinated wage bargaining and social dialogue, had raised the costs of labor above market clearing levels. Moreover, strong "insider–outsider" cleavages with unfavorable employment chances for the young, women, the old and the unskilled, prevented the rigid European labor markets from producing employment rates, on a par with the United States, the United Kingdom, or New Zealand. The OECD thus portrayed the fundamental dilemma of Europe's mature welfare states in terms of a trade-off between welfare equity and employment efficiency. The policy recommendations that naturally followed from this analysis included retrenchment of unemployment compensation, deregulation of job protection legislation, reduction of minimum wages, decentralization of wage bargaining, and lower taxation.

The OECD Jobs Strategy shocked the welfare-friendly mainland European policy elites, social-democratic and Christian democratic parties and trade unions of different political colors. In the course of the 1990s, the slow, fragmentary and half-hearted implementation of the recommendations of the OECD Jobs Strategy came to be attributed to political deadlock, opposition and trade union protest. It was argued that serious reform in mature welfare states proved politically unrewarding because losses are concentrated and resisted by vested interests, while the gains are spread out only thinly. As a result, deadlock prevailed in spite of unsatisfactory employment performance and mounting social and political discontent. The European welfare state, as Paul Pierson put it, proved to be an "unmovable object" (Pierson 1998).

But is this image of a "frozen welfare status quo" in the face of a severe employment crisis truly correct? Are European political economies only fit for globalization if and when they give up their postwar commitment to generous and encompassing welfare provision? Are mainland European welfare states really that ossified and resilient, unable to improve their employment record? We believe not. The majority of the member states of the European Union (EU) have undertaken remarkably comprehensive welfare and labor market reforms in the years since the 1990s. Many of these reforms, however, have not followed the conventional retrenchment and deregulation recipes of the OECD, but rather took a liking to social pacts, activation, active aging/avoidance of early retirement, part-time work, lifelong learning, parental leave, gender mainstreaming, flexicurity (balancing flexibility with security), and reconciling work and family life. At first sight, these reforms seem to have resulted in relatively robust employment growth, especially for women and more recently older workers. While in 1997 the EU-15 employment rate trailed 12.8 percentage points behind the United States, by 2005 the gap was more than halved to 6.3 percentage points. Mirroring the improvement in employment performance, standardized unemployment rates fell to 7.1% in the Eurozone economies, but as the chapter by Saraceno shows long-term unemployment remained a serious problem.

To say that European welfare states are far from sclerotic is not to say that they are all in good shape. But rather than extrapolating policy recipes from recent economic performance, urging European OECD members to recast their social market economies along the lines of American capitalism, a more illuminating way to understand recent reform dynamics is to contextualize existing social policy repertoires and reform dynamics in the face of the changing economic and technological challenges and evolving social and demographic structures. Today, four sets of challenges confront policy makers with the imperative to redirect the welfare effort, to redesign institutions and to elaborate on new principles of social justice. First, *from outside*, international competition is challenging the redistributive scope and decommodifying power of the national welfare state. Many academic observers believe that the increase in cross-border competition in the markets for money, goods, and services has substantially reduced the maneuverability of national welfare states (Scharpf and Schmidt 2000). Economic internationalization constrains countercyclical macroeconomic management, while increased openness exposes generous welfare states to trade competition and permits capital to move to the lowest-cost producer countries. Second, *from within*, aging populations, declining birth rates, changing gender roles in households due to the mass entry of women into the labor market, the shift from an industrial to a service economy, and new technologies in the organization of work present new challenges. According to Esping-Andersen (1999), the most important reason why the existing systems of social care have become overstretched stems from the weakening of labor markets and traditional family units as the default providers of welfare. Third, while policy makers must find new ways to manage the adverse consequences of economic internationalization and postindustrial differentiation, their endeavor to recast the welfare state is severely constrained, *from the past*, by long-standing social policy commitments in the areas of unemployment and pensions. In a period of permanent austerity and lower economic growth, the maturation of welfare commitments (the policies put in place to cater to the social risks associated with the postwar industrial era) now seem to crowd out the available space for new social policy initiatives, especially in social services

(Pierson 2001). Finally, as an intervening variable in the process, issues of work and welfare have become ever more intertwined with processes of European political and economic integration since the 1980s. It is fair to say that in the EU we have entered an era of semisovereign welfare states (Leibfried and Pierson 2000). European economic integration has fundamentally recast the boundaries of national systems of employment regulation and social protection, both by constraining the autonomy for domestic policy options but also by opening opportunities for EU-led social and employment coordination and agenda setting (Ferrera 2005; Zeitlin 2005).

WELFARE REGIMES AND EMPLOYMENT PERFORMANCE

Employment is the most important measure for judging the sustainability of the welfare state and the success of social and economic policy. The reason for this is simple: benefits and social services have to be paid by the taxes and social security contributions from those in work. The more working people there are, the broader this funding base is. In the event of long-term unemployment, incapacity to work and early retirement, spending on social security goes up while at the same time revenues fall. From a sociological perspective, having a job also benefits people by giving them enhanced opportunities for self-actualization and self-esteem. Participating in the labor market is today the most important form of social interaction and, as such, is an indispensable element in achieving social cohesion.

Employment performance is conditioned not only by the economic and social policy challenges facing each welfare state, but more critically by variations in substantive policy design and institutional capabilities, including systems of political decision-making and interest mediation (Scharpf and Schmidt 2000; Ferrera et al. 2000). Hence, it would be a mistake to overgeneralize the nature of welfare state change and to overlook these national distinctions and diverse trajectories. If Europe does have models, they are definitely plural rather than singular (Alber 2006; Hemerijck et al. 2006). There is a rich literature on "worlds" or "families" of welfare, which dates back to the 1980s and shows how key variables are systematically related to one another, producing distinctive clusters of nations in four "social Europes"—Scandinavian, Conservative Continental, Southern European, and "Anglo-Irish" (Esping-Andersen 1990; Ferrera et al. 2000).

While the Continental welfare states rely on relatively high income replacement benefits, linked to the claimant's employment history and family situation, the Nordic welfare states not only offer generous income guarantees, but also a wide range of public social services and an active labor market policy aimed at maximizing employment for both men and women. The Anglo-Saxon welfare states rely on relatively modest individualized income-dependent unemployment, sickness, and old age benefit, with strict rules to social assistance. In the Mediterranean welfare states, the family makes up for the underdevelopment of formal social assistance and services, while social insurance transfers cover core workers, especially in the area of pensions.

The eight new Central and Eastern European member states (NMS), which joined the EU in May 2004, occupy a special place. They have gone through two radical changes in the past 65 years—the shift from capitalism to state-socialism in the 1940s and from state-socialism back to capitalism after 1989. Before World War II, CEE welfare provisions mainly had a Bismarckian character, that is, welfare arrangements were linked to and based on employment and occupation. The state-socialist era saw a universalization of the employment-based welfare system through full (and largely obligatory) employment. The state-socialist welfare state (Kornai 1992) suffered from low-quality services, queues, underemployment, limited choice, and a generally low standard of living, even if it was also able to abolish deep poverty, create more equality, offer universal and free health and education services, and facilitate female employment by providing child care, extended maternity leave, and child benefits. After 1989, radically new ideas emerged concerning solidarity, equality, and redistribution and the role and responsibilities of the state, the market, and the individual. Profound welfare state reforms were the result. It is difficult to place the NMS welfare state in a particular group. By and large, they are minimal welfare states: the percentage of GDP dedicated to social expenditure is low compared to the rest of the EU. Cumulative reforms since 1989, however, have made these systems more "hybrid" rather than coherent regimes. While social benefits seem to be focused more and more on income replacement and linked to individual labor market histories in a Continental "Bismarckian" style, health care, family policy, and social assistance display important universalistic as well as "Anglo" market-based trends (Keune 2006).

With respect to employment, there has been a significant increase in virtually all mature European welfare states over the last decade whereas the new member states experienced a transformation crisis. Figure 9-1 shows the employment/population ratios among people in the working age population. What is striking is, first, the long-term increase in employment in most countries and, second, some persistent differences in the overall share of people in gainful employment across countries and families of welfare states.

Figure 9-2 shows the long-term development of employment rates for selected European countries and the United States. Unfortunately, there are no similar time series for the new member states. The convergence over time within the EU is striking. Now, both the Anglo-Saxon and the Scandinavian countries have about 75% to 80% of the working-age population in employment. The same level is also achieved by the Netherlands after an impressive increase in employment over the last two decades. The other Continental and Southern European countries are still behind with employment rates of 60% to 70%. But even there

Figure 9-1: Employment/population ratios 1997 and 2006

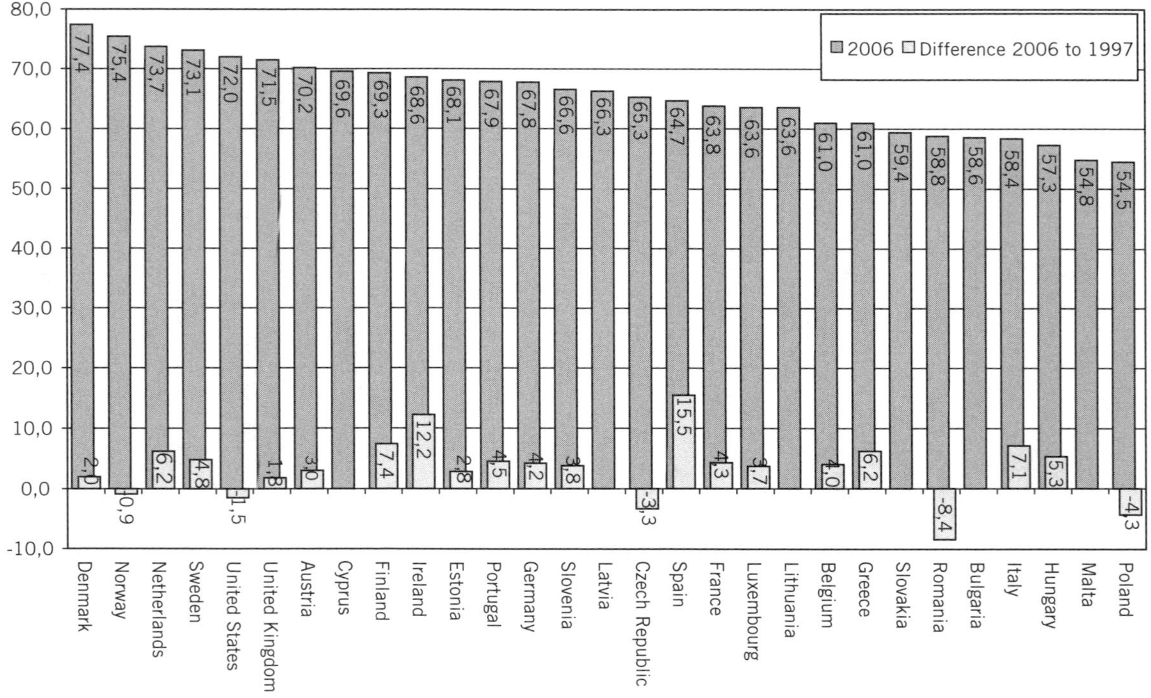

Country	2006	Difference 2006 to 1997
Poland	54,5	-4,3
Malta	54,8	
Hungary	57,3	5,3
Italy	58,4	7,1
Bulgaria	58,6	
Romania	58,8	-8,4
Slovakia	59,4	
Greece	61,0	6,2
Belgium	61,0	4,0
Lithuania	63,6	
Luxembourg	63,6	3,7
France	63,8	4,3
Spain	64,7	15,5
Czech Republic	65,3	-3,3
Latvia	66,3	
Slovenia	66,6	3,8
Germany	67,8	4,2
Portugal	67,9	4,5
Estonia	68,1	2,8
Ireland	68,6	12,2
Finland	69,3	7,4
Cyprus	69,6	
Austria	70,2	3,0
United Kingdom	71,5	1,8
United States	72,0	1,5
Sweden	73,1	4,8
Netherlands	73,7	6,2
Norway	75,4	0,9
Denmark	77,4	2,0

Source: European Labor Force Survey.

Figure 9-2: Employment/population ratios, 1980–2006

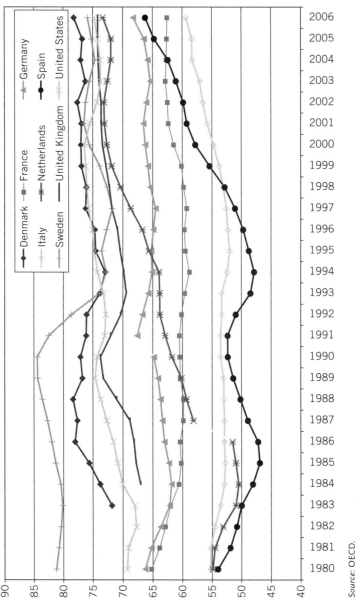

Source: OECD.

we can see some progress, in particular in Spain and Italy while France and Germany have been more stagnant.

Mirroring the improvement in employment performance, standardized unemployment rates declined in most European countries over the last decade as Figure 9-3 shows. What is most remarkable is the strong decline in unemployment in some Southern and Continental European countries such as Spain, France, Italy as well as in Sweden and Finland, which could overcome the deep crisis of the 1990s. Even the low-unemployment countries Denmark and the Netherlands achieved further progress so that there is now virtually full employment with lower unemployment and higher employment rates than in the United States, even though, as the chapter by Saraceno (in this volume) shows, the incidence of long-term unemployment is still high.

High employment is not only found in market-oriented arrangements. The government plays an important role in the Scandinavian welfare state model as an employer in the labor-intensive social services sector. As a result, the Scandinavian welfare states create wide opportunities for men and women with lower education levels to work in the public sector, as well as creating employment for highly trained professionals. About a quarter of the labor force in Denmark and Sweden (mainly women) are employed in the public services sector. The expansion of the number of jobs in social services, child care, and care for the elderly from the 1970s onward gave rise to a self-reinforcing mechanism: more women entered the labor market, leading to a marked reduction in the amount of care provided within (working) families, which in turn led to an increase in demand for professional care services.

The response of the Continental and Mediterranean welfare states to the process of economic restructuring in the 1970s and 1980s was aimed at keeping open unemployment low by limiting labor supply with the help of a host of early retirement options. Growing demands on social security led to burgeoning costs to be borne by the labor market. From the middle of the 1980s onward, employers in Continental welfare states increasingly began using labor-saving technology and shedding less productive employees via the social security system. This turned the Continental productivity squeeze into an inactivity trap. A vicious cycle arose of high gross wage costs, low net wages, the exit of less productive workers, and rising social costs, creating a spiral of falling employment and rising economic inactivity. This also undermined the financial basis of the social security system. It was not until the second half of the 1990s that there was a limited increase in the employment rate in the Mediterranean welfare states, which, in fact, have seen some of the biggest employment gains in the EU over the last decade. The Netherlands occupies a special place comparatively, because it was the first Continental welfare state with a historically low female employment rate to improve its performance, trending toward Scandinavian levels.

Figure 9-3: Standardized unemployment rates

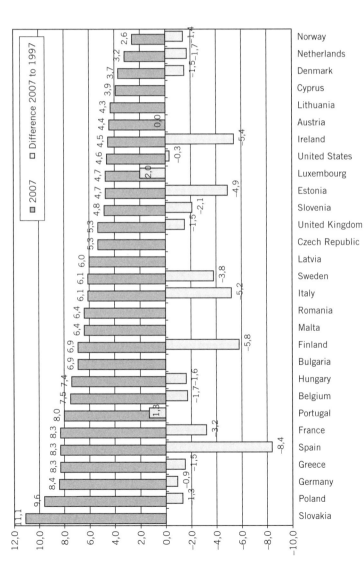

Source: European Labor Force Survey.

In the "prime age" age group, aged 25–54 years, a strong convergence can be observed since the middle of the 1990s (Figure 9-4). Over the last decade, we can observe substantial recovery in the Scandinavian countries after the crisis in the early 1990s, but also considerable improvement in the Continental and Southern European countries. The Anglo-Saxon welfare states also showed a trend of upward consolidation so that most welfare states now have prime age employment rates of 75% to 85% except for some of the Central and Eastern countries.

There is much more regime-specific variation regarding the employment rates of older workers, women and the low-skilled. Differences in the extent to which these three groups are integrated into the labor market basically determine differences in the overall employment rate. With respect to the 55–64 age cohort (see Figure 9-5), Belgium has the lowest employment rate of the EU-15 (32%) while Sweden has the highest (almost 70%). In the EU-27, Poland and Malta still have particular problems regarding the labor market position of older cohorts. The Continental and Mediterranean welfare states and most of the new EU member states saw a dramatic fall of more than 30% in the employment rate of older workers from the 1980s due to early retirement, particularly among men. Since the end of the 1990s, the employment rate among older workers has been increasing strongly in Finland, but also in some Continental welfare states, with the Netherlands taking the lead.

Looking at gender, we see some cross-country convergence in the employment rate of men between 70% and 80% (Figure 9-6). Male employment declined slightly in Denmark and Norway, but grew in most other EU-15 countries. Again, there is a structural gap in male employment in most CEE countries compared to the EU-15.

The labor market entry of women is the most striking recent development in European welfare states (see Figure 9-7). In the early 1970s, the Netherlands had the lowest female employment rate in the OECD, at 29.2 per cent. This was lower than the figure in Ireland, Greece, Spain, and Italy, where the rate was just above 30%. Since then the employment rate of women has grown strongly. In net terms, the rate in the Netherlands has increased to 67%, the sharpest rise of any OECD member state. The female employment rate in the Netherlands is currently still lower than in the Scandinavian welfare states, but here as elsewhere younger cohorts are undergoing a notable convergence in the direction of stronger labor force participation.

The low—and only marginally increasing—employment rate among women in the Mediterranean welfare states, in particular, points to a number of key barriers on the Southern European labor market. In the Continental and Anglo-Saxon welfare states, the ability to work part-time has created an important means of entry to the labor market for women, in particular in the Netherlands. In countries with a long-standing tradition of female employment, such as the Scandinavian countries, part-time employment is less common. For younger

Figure 9-4: Prime age employment rates (25–54 years), 1997 and 2006

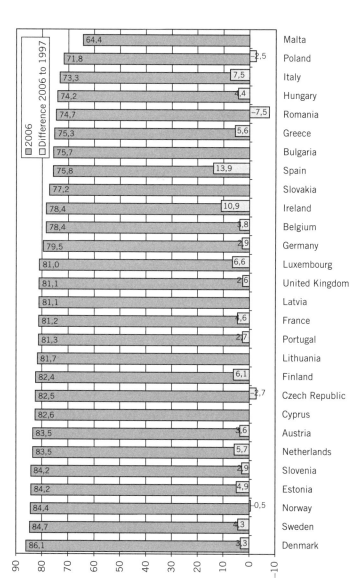

Legend: ■ 2006, □ Difference 2006 to 1997

Country	2006	Difference 2006 to 1997
Malta	64,4	
Poland	71,8	−2,5
Italy	73,3	7,5
Hungary	74,2	4,4
Romania	74,7	−7,5
Greece	75,3	5,6
Bulgaria	75,7	
Spain	75,8	13,9
Slovakia	77,2	
Ireland	78,4	10,9
Belgium	78,4	3,8
Germany	79,5	2,9
Luxembourg	81,0	6,6
United Kingdom	81,1	2,6
Latvia	81,1	
France	81,2	1,6
Portugal	81,3	2,7
Lithuania	81,7	
Finland	82,4	6,1
Czech Republic	82,5	−2,7
Cyprus	82,6	
Austria	83,5	3,6
Netherlands	83,5	5,7
Slovenia	84,2	4,9
Estonia	84,2	4,9
Norway	84,4	−0,5
Sweden	84,7	4,3
Denmark	86,1	3,3

Source: European Labor Force Survey.

Figure 9-5: Employment rates of older workers (55–64 years), 1997 and 2006

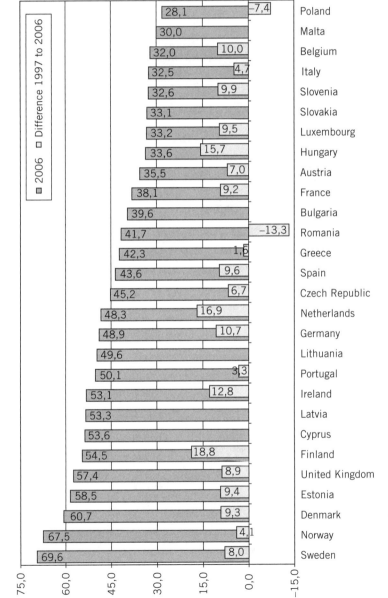

Source: European Labor Force Survey.

Figure 9-6: Employment rates of men, 1997 and 2006

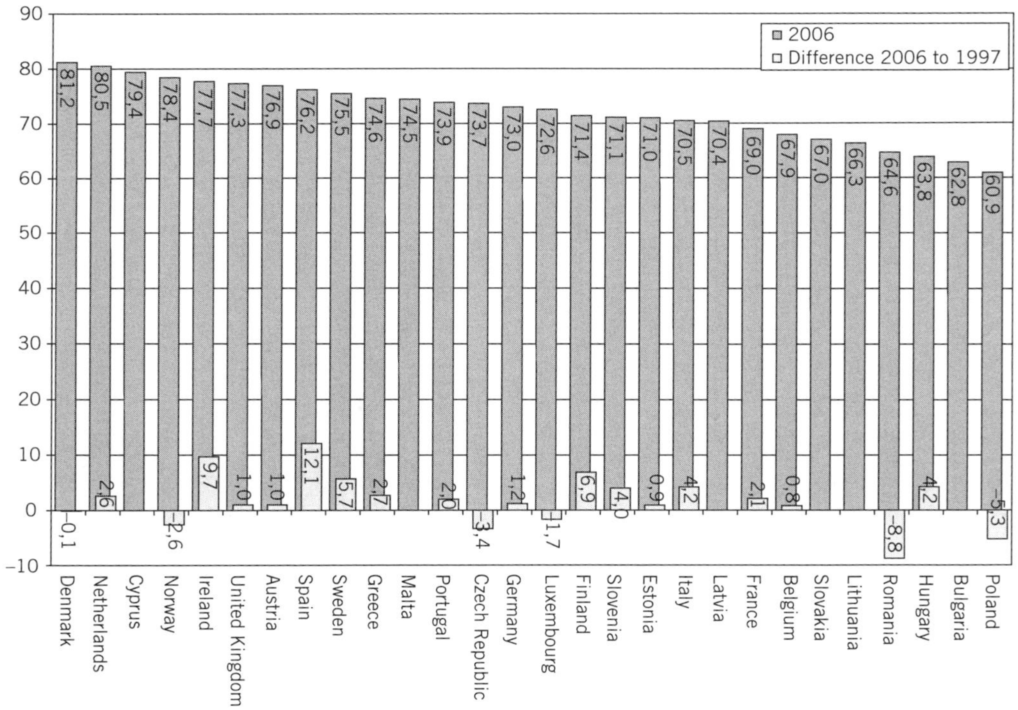

Legend:
- 2006
- Difference 2006 to 1997

Country	2006	Difference 2006 to 1997
Poland	60,9	−5,3
Bulgaria	62,8	
Hungary	63,8	4,2
Romania	64,6	−8,8
Lithuania	66,3	
Slovakia	67,0	
Belgium	67,9	0,8
France	69,0	2,1
Latvia	70,4	
Italy	70,5	4,2
Estonia	71,0	0,9
Slovenia	71,1	4,0
Finland	71,4	6,9
Luxembourg	72,6	1,7
Germany	73,0	1,2
Czech Republic	73,7	−3,4
Portugal	73,9	2,0
Malta	74,5	
Greece	74,6	2,7
Sweden	75,5	5,7
Spain	76,2	12,1
Austria	76,9	1,0
United Kingdom	77,3	1,0
Ireland	77,7	9,7
Norway	78,4	−2,6
Cyprus	79,4	
Netherlands	80,5	2,6
Denmark	81,2	−0,1

Source: European Labor Force Survey.

Figure 9-7: Female employment and share of women's part-time work, 2006

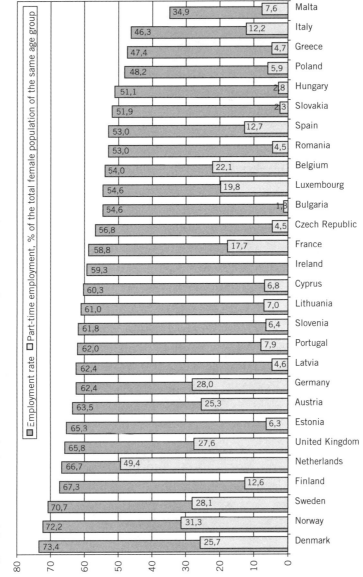

Legend: ■ Employment rate □ Part-time employment, % of the total female population of the same age group

Country	Employment rate	Part-time employment
Malta	34,9	7,6
Italy	46,3	12,2
Greece	47,4	4,7
Poland	48,2	5,9
Hungary	51,1	2,8
Slovakia	51,9	2,3
Spain	53,0	12,7
Romania	53,0	4,5
Belgium	54,0	22,1
Luxembourg	54,6	19,8
Bulgaria	54,6	1,5
Czech Republic	56,8	4,5
France	58,8	17,7
Ireland	59,3	
Cyprus	60,3	6,8
Lithuania	61,0	7,0
Slovenia	61,8	6,4
Portugal	62,0	7,9
Latvia	62,4	4,6
Germany	62,4	28,0
Austria	63,5	25,3
Estonia	65,3	6,3
United Kingdom	65,8	27,6
Netherlands	66,7	49,4
Finland	67,3	12,6
Sweden	70,7	28,1
Norway	72,2	31,3
Denmark	73,4	25,7

Source: European Labor Force Survey.

cohorts, female employment in Southern and Continental Europe is rapidly catching up to Northern European averages.

Employment rates by skill levels differ mostly for the labor force with less than upper secondary schooling or vocational training, less so for the high skilled. Figure 9-8 shows marked differences in low skill employment across countries and families of welfare states. Particular deficits are found in the CEE countries, but also in some Continental European countries such as Belgium, Italy, or Germany where only about half of the low-skilled are integrated into the labor market. Given the strong pressures of technological progress and globalization, it is interesting to see that there is no general decline in the employment rates of the low skilled.

Today the highly skilled groups surpass, by about 15 percentage points, the Lisbon benchmark of 70% participation in gainful employment, independently of welfare regime characteristics. Hence, there is considerable convergence of employment at a high level.

Regarding the role of the state, there are core policy areas with direct impact on the labor market, in particular (a) regulatory policies such as employment protection or statutory minimum wages, and (b) the provision of monetary benefits and services. Regarding the latter element of government activity, we can basically differentiate between social spending for benefits and expenditure for services, especially active labor market policies, public child care and education. Despite changes in the overall economic environment and sequences of policy reforms, expenditure levels on social protection expressed as a percentage of GDP have remained relatively stable or even increased over the last two decades (see also the chapters by Castles and Gilbert in this volume).

Turning to services, the variation across countries and families of welfare states is more pronounced. The provision of public child care and preschooling shows marked differences across countries, with the Scandinavian countries, Belgium and France, offering the best infrastructure, and most Continental, the Mediterranean and the Central European, countries lagging behind (Table 9-1, OECD 2007b). This is a major factor driving or restricting female employment.

Public child care provision is no longer seen merely as a facilitator of female employment or as a means to reconcile family and work. It is increasingly perceived as the first pillar of life-long learning (Figure 9-9). As investments at early stages of the lifecycle provide the basis for further success in education and training, they are seen as an effective and efficient tool to ensure skills acquisition also at later stages of general education or vocational training (see also Allmendinger in this volume). As a consequence, there are also marked differences in terms of participation and intensity of lifelong learning activities (OECD 2005). In general, participation in continuous education and training is more pronounced in the Scandinavian countries and the United Kingdom where on-the-job training is also a functional equivalent to more formal vocational training. However, despite some increases in most countries, the adjustment of

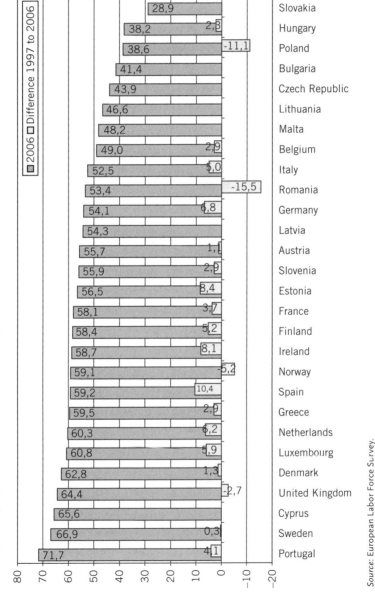

Figure 9-8: Employment rates of the low skilled, 1997 and 2006

■ 2006 □ Difference 1997 to 2006

Country	2006	Difference 1997 to 2006
Slovakia	28,9	
Hungary	38,2	2,3
Poland	38,6	-11,1
Bulgaria	41,4	
Czech Republic	43,9	
Lithuania	46,6	
Malta	48,2	
Belgium	49,0	2,9
Italy	52,5	5,0
Romania	53,4	-15,5
Germany	54,1	6,8
Latvia	54,3	
Austria	55,7	1,1
Slovenia	55,9	2,5
Estonia	56,5	8,4
France	58,1	3,7
Finland	58,4	5,2
Ireland	58,7	8,1
Norway	59,1	5,2
Spain	59,2	10,4
Greece	59,5	2,5
Netherlands	60,3	6,2
Luxembourg	60,8	5,9
Denmark	62,8	1,3
United Kingdom	64,4	2,7
Cyprus	65,6	
Sweden	66,9	0,3
Portugal	71,7	4,1

Source: European Labor Force Survey.

Table 9-1: Child Care and Preschool Enrollment, ca. 2004

	Enrollment in Daycare for the Under-3s and Preschool from 3 to 6 years (%)				Expected Years in Education for 3- to 5-Year Olds
	Under 3 Years	3 Years	4 Years	5 Years	3 to 5 Years
Denmark	61.7	81.8	93.4	93.9	2.7
Norway	43.7	79.4	86.9	89.0	2.6
Sweden	39.5	82.5	87.7	89.7	2.6
Belgium	38.5	99.3	99.9	99.7	3.1
Netherlands	29.5	32.3	74.0	98.4	1.7
United States	29.5	41.8	64.1	77.0	1.8
France	26.0	100.0	100.0	100.0	3.2
United Kingdom	25.8	50.2	92.0	98.2	2.4
Portugal	23.5	63.9	79.9	90.2	2.3
Finland	22.4	37.7	46.1	54.6	1.4
Spain	20.7	95.9	100.0	100.0	3.1
Slovak Republic	17.7	60.3	71.7	84.7	2.2
Ireland	15.0	48.0	46.6	100.0	1.5
Germany	9.0	69.5	84.3	86.7	2.4
Hungary	6.9	71.0	92.3	97.8	2.6
Greece	7.0	..	57.2	84.1	1.4
Italy	6.3	98.7	100.0	100.0	3.0
Austria	4.1	45.9	82.1	93.1	2.2
Poland	2.0	26.1	35.7	46.2	1.1
Czech Republic	3.0	68.0	91.2	96.7	2.6

Source: OECD Family Database.

skills over the lifecycle is still far from perfect. Particular deficits are found in the Continental and Southern European countries as well as in most NMS.

The differences in the allocation of public resources to either investment policies (such as education and training) or to compensating policies such as social benefits and passive and active labor market policies are most evident in Figure 9-10, which shows how public spending on education and social expenditure as a percentage of GPD combined in 2004. While the overall association between both areas of public spending is positive, some countries, in particular the Scandinavian ones, as well as Belgium and France, combine above-average spending on social policies with above-average spending on education. Germany and Italy, in contrast, spend greatly on social schemes but spend relatively less on education. Many new EU member states devote few resources to social policies, but some achieve the European average in terms of educational spending such as Poland, Hungary, and the Baltic states.

Data on the earnings dispersion of full-time workers and the incidence of low pay, i.e., earning lower than two-thirds of the median, show a proliferation of inequality in most countries (Table 9-2). Yet, there are marked differences between country clusters. Some CEE countries such as Hungary and Poland

Figure 9-9: Participation in lifelong learning, 1997 and 2006

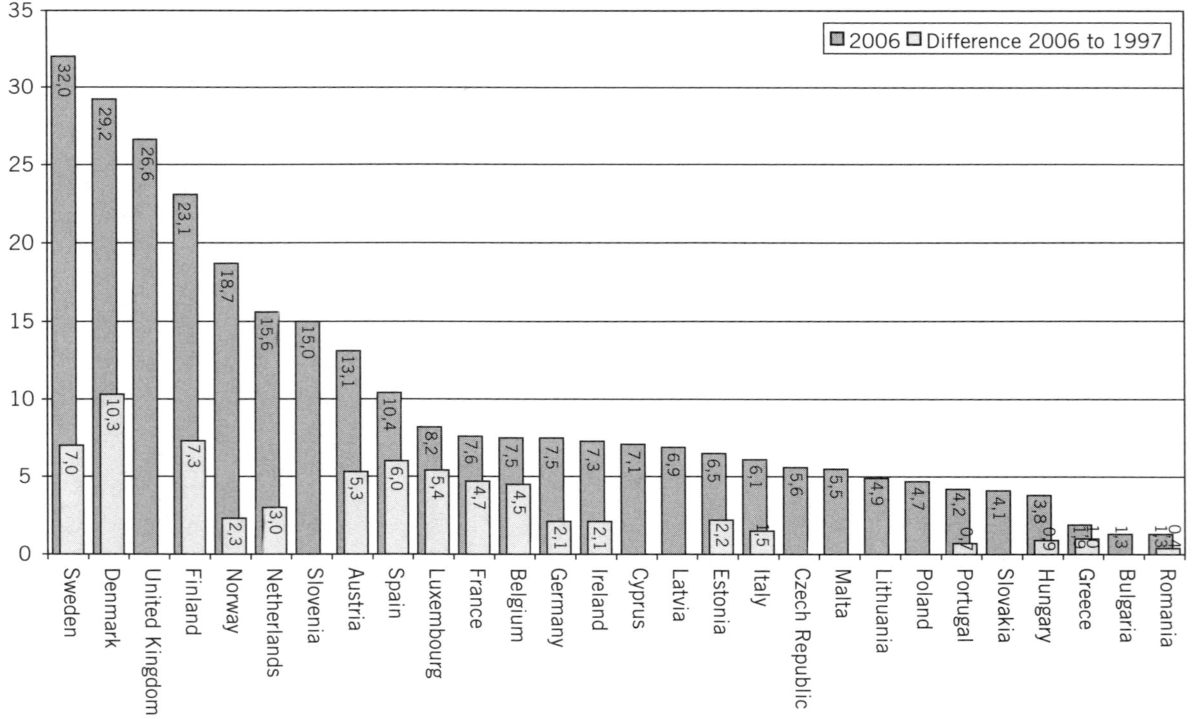

Legend: ■ 2006 □ Difference 2006 to 1997

Country	2006	Difference 2006 to 1997
Romania	0,4	1,3
Bulgaria	1,3	
Greece	1,8	
Hungary	0,9	3,8
Slovakia	4,1	
Portugal	4,2	0,7
Poland	4,7	
Lithuania	4,9	
Malta	5,5	
Czech Republic	5,6	
Italy	6,1	1,5
Estonia	6,5	2,2
Latvia	6,9	
Cyprus	7,1	
Ireland	7,3	2,1
Germany	7,5	2,1
Belgium	7,5	4,5
France	7,6	4,7
Luxembourg	8,2	5,4
Spain	10,4	6,0
Austria	13,1	5,3
Slovenia	15,0	
Netherlands	15,6	3,0
Norway	18,7	2,3
Finland	23,1	7,3
United Kingdom	26,6	
Denmark	29,2	10,3
Sweden	32,0	7,0

Source: Eurostat.

Figure 9-10: **Public social expenditure and spending on education in percent of GDP, 2004**

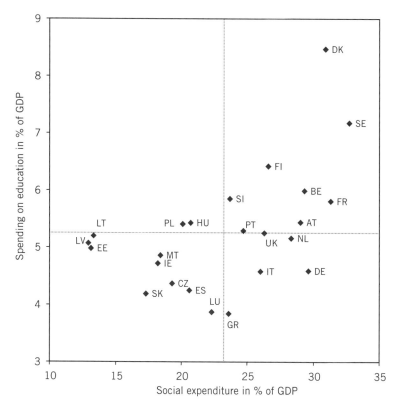

Source: Eurostat.

and the Anglo-Saxon labor markets have a large wage dispersion, while the Scandinavian countries continue to have relatively egalitarian wage structures.

Summarizing the data presented on employment performance, we can see first and foremost, an overall improvement in employment and a significant decline in unemployment across most European welfare systems over the last 10 years.

- The average employment rate of the EU-15 countries increased considerably from 61% in 1997 to 66%, the EU-27 moved from 61% to 65%.
- The employment rate for women rose from 52% to 59% in the EU-15 (57% for the EU-27), bringing it within reach of the Lisbon objective of 60% in 2010.
- For older workers, aged 55–64 years, the employment rate has risen from 36% to 45% in the EU-15 and to 44% in the EU-27. Here, the distance to the Lisbon target of 50% is a bit larger.

Table 9-2: Earnings Dispersion and Incidence of Low Pay

| | Ratio of | | | | | | | |
| | 9th to 1st Earnings Deciles | | 9th to 5th Earnings Deciles | | 5th to 1st Earnings Deciles | | Incidence of Low Pay | |
	1995	2005	1995	2005	1995	2005	1995	2005
Hungary	3.96	5.63	2.09	2.46	1.89	2.33	21.9	..
United States	4.59	4.86	2.17	2.31	2.11	2.10	25.2	24.0
Poland	3.40	4.31	1.97	2.18	1.72	1.98	17.3	23.5
Ireland	4.01	3.57	1.98	2.07	2.02	1.72	20.4	17.6
Spain	4.22	3.53	2.10	2.14	2.01	1.65	15.2	16.2
United Kingdom	3.48	3.51	1.88	1.96	1.85	1.79	20.0	20.7
Germany	2.79	3.13	1.79	1.84	1.56	1.70	11.1	15.8
France	3.08	3.10	1.93	2.01	1.59	1.54	..	..
Czech Republic	2.78	3.01	1.71	1.77	1.63	1.70	..	..
Netherlands	2.77	2.91	1.71	1.76	1.62	1.65	13.8	..
Denmark	2.47	2.64	1.69	1.73	1.46	1.53	..	..
Finland	2.34	2.42	1.66	1.70	1.41	1.43	..	7.0
Sweden	2.20	2.33	1.59	1.68	1.39	1.39	5.7	6.4
Norway	1.89	2.21	1.40	1.50	1.35	1.48	..	..

Source: OECD (2007a).

There is not only "contingent convergence" in performance—but also in terms of policies as we will show below. As there are still structural and long-lasting differences between different national welfare states or families of welfare states, it would certainly be wrong to say that Europe as a whole suffers from severe employment deficits—this is only true for some countries, but not for others.

The overall picture across the European countries shows that quite different economic and welfare state models can achieve high and probably sustainable employment levels. This suggests that there is no necessary trade-off between employment performance and the size of the welfare state, that a large public sector does not necessarily hurt employment mobility and competitiveness, that there can be a positive relationship between fertility and high levels of female employment and that labor market flexibility and low poverty more often than not go together with high levels of employment. Hence, high employment is not necessarily associated with higher inequality (see also Aiginger and Guger 2006; Esping-Andersen et al. 2002; Ferrera et al. 2000; Kenworthy 2004; Lindert 2004; OECD 2006a).

REGIME-SPECIFIC REFORM AGENDAS

The overall improvement in employment performance is related to ground-breaking social policy changes, which were enacted in the majority of European welfare states. Since the late 1970s, consecutive changes in the world economy, European politics (most spectacularly the demise of communism in Eastern Europe), labor markets, and family structures have disturbed the once sovereign and stable social and economic policy repertoires. As a consequence, all developed welfare states of the EU have been recasting the basic policy mix upon which their national systems of social protection were built after 1945. Below we render a stylized sketch of the reform agendas since the 1990s across the different regimes so as to bring out both the similarities and differences within regime clusters.

Nordic "Dual-Earner" Postindustrialism

Thanks to their overall institutional coherence, together with their strong full employment and active labor market policy legacy, the Nordic welfare systems have proven to be relatively well equipped for the challenges of economic internationalization, aging societies, gender equality, and transition to the postindustrial economy. In response to the oil shocks of the 1970s and 1980s, the Nordic countries expanded employment by increasing public sector employment. The lasting effect of the expansion of public services to families, together with the rise in female labor supply, has resulted in a high level of employment for both men and women, with women working largely in public social services, like education, child care, and elder care. This policy of "de-familialization" of caring responsibilities subsequently catalyzed the dual-earner norm throughout the Nordic countries (Kuhnle 2000).

This is not to say, that economic internationalization has not generated problems of costs competitiveness. The Swedish public employment growth strategy, based on fiscal demand stimulus and monetary devaluation in the 1980s, led to a severe macroeconomic imbalance in the early 1990s. Throughout the 1990s, Nordic countries grappled with pressures to contain high and increasing costs and to reorganize labor markets so as to generate more demand for private employment. Sweden and Denmark have begun to reduce public-sector employment but the tradition of universalism remains largely unquestioned even if cuts in replacement rates (e.g., sickness benefits) or basic guarantees (e.g., family allowances) have occurred. Eligibility for cash benefits, especially duration, has been tightened in Sweden and Finland. A core dimension in the Nordic reform agenda consisted of "activation," i.e., the modification of programs to encourage actual and potential beneficiaries to find and maintain gainful employment. Denmark has gone furthest in changing the institutional profile and logic of labor market policies. Denmark has deployed a wide array of "activating" instruments including information and counseling, subsidized employment in public and private sectors, training and educational initiatives, and job rotation combined with a (temporary) expansion of leave possibilities for employed workers (Andersen and Svarer 2007). The Danish model of "flexicurity" adheres to the principles of a "golden triangle" of a flexible labor market, generous social protection, and an active labor market policy (Erhel and Gazier 2007). The Nordic countries, and especially Finland, have pursued a deliberate human capital response, so as to secure a productive workforce, to the challenges of economic internationalization and postindustrial social change. The Finnish success can be traced back to a public education system, which generates highly skilled people and a culture of innovation. Coordinating public and private efforts, the Finnish government has deliberately invested in research and development. The idea that sustaining the welfare of an aging population requires a highly productive labor force is much more widespread in Scandinavia than in any of the other welfare clusters. Cognitive inequalities are substantially lower in Scandinavia and the diminishing impact of social origin on educational performance coincides with the expansion of universal day care. Important pension reforms have also been undertaken to strengthen the links between contributions and benefits in Sweden and Finland. In order to keep older workers in the workforce, Finland has developed policy approaches to improve the occupational health, work ability, and well-being of aging workers.

The Scandinavian tradition of universal coverage provided an effective safeguard against poverty and exclusion, spells out of work and broken or changing career trajectories, with low transaction costs. Moreover, the incentive structure of nationwide social insurance and active labor market policies implied portability, which promotes labor mobility, while avoiding poverty traps. A wide array of services has allowed the Nordic welfare state to respond more effectively to the needs of dual-earner families and to socialize the costs of care for children. As a consequence, high rates of labor market participation for both men and women and older workers have reduced the financial strains on pension systems. Spurred by the recession in the early 1990s, most reforms were based on a strong consensus among the social democratic governments and bourgeois parties as well as employers and trade unions, which all agreed on the need for modernization (Schludi 2005). The Nordic experience clearly shows that (high) expenditure levels are not the critical factor for effective policy responses to new challenges, but that system design and reform approaches are what really matter.

Reversing the Continental Syndrome of "Welfare without Work"

From the 1970s onwards, most Continental welfare states began using disability pensions, early retirement, and long-term unemployment schemes to remove older and less productive workers from the labor market. Both center-left and right governments preferred increasing social contributions over cutting social benefits. Luring people out of the labor market by facilitating early retirement, increasing benefits for the long-term unemployed, lifting the obligation of job search for older workers, discouraging mothers from job search, favoring long periods of leave, easing the access to disability pensions and reducing working hours made up the characteristic of the Continental welfare without work policy strategy that became popular in the 1980s and for most of the 1990s. Backed by the unions and employers, this strategy produced short-term gains, but eventually engendered a severe employment crisis in most Continental welfare states.

The continental employment problem is directly related to payroll-based social insurance financing and relatively strict labor market regulation. The strategy of boosting international competitiveness by early retirement and high-quality training and education may have placed a premium on high productivity, but its indirect effect was a substantial increase in the tax burden on labor, as ever fewer workers had to support ever more people outside the active labor market. Productivity growth thus led to a vicious cycle of rising wage costs and the exit of less productive workers, requiring further productivity increases and eliciting another round of workforce reductions through subsidized early exit (Hemerijck and Manow 2001). In addition, strict employment regulation, including minimum wages and hiring and firing restrictions, protected the insiders in key industries, while harming the participation of outsiders, youngsters, women, older workers, low skill groups, and ethnic minorities. From the 1990s onward, the policy of labor supply reduction came to be brandished as a policy failure and, if continued uncorrected, as a threat to the survival of the Continental welfare state and the Rhineland model more generally. But the Continental syndrome of welfare without work proved extremely difficult to reverse.

The severe recession in the early 1990s following the German unification produced a sharp rise in unemployment and public debt, constraining the scope for further labor supply reduction. From the early 1990s on, high taxes and the EMU entrance examination served to shift policy attention to employment creation, generating a multidimensional reform agenda to curtail passive welfare and pension commitments, to improve family policy, reform labor markets, and reduce social charges. The Dutch were the first who managed to escape the Continental employment crisis through a long-term strategy combining wage moderation, the activation of social insurance, active labor market policy, and more labor market flexibility, all developed largely in agreement and with the support of the social partners (Visser and Hemerijck 1997). In contrast to the Dutch success at "activation," the Belgian social insurance scheme has been transformed from a traditional Bismarckian system into one with an overriding emphasis on minimum income protection and universal coverage. Over time, this has resulted in a de facto targeting of benefits on the basis of individual, household, and family need. In France, minimum income protection has likewise shifted from payroll contributions to general taxation so as to reduce nonwage costs and encourage job creation. Germany has been much slower in embracing reform. Only the highly unpopular Hartz reforms pursued under the Social-Democratic/Green coalition government since 2002 sought to reduce benefit dependency and to activate the long-term unemployed into work via a combination of cuts in benefits, together with a shift towards a means-tested income support scheme for the long-term unemployed and more coherent activation measures (Clasen and Clegg 2006; Eichhorst et al. forthcoming). Both France and Germany now have a repertoire of: (a) less regulated work contracts such as fixed-term employment or temporary agency work, and (b) areas with low social contributions or employer subsidies, for example, low-wage jobs exempt from employers, contributions and a multitude of "contrats aidés" in France and "Minijobs" and different subsidization schemes in Germany. In combination with further steps in favor of more jobs, time flexibility, including part-time work, or wage moderation for standard jobs in the core of the labor market, these reforms contributed to making Continental welfare states more employment-friendly.

Pension reform in Continental welfare states has been especially difficult, but not impossible to implement (Immergut et al. 2007). Pension contribution rates have risen in Germany and the Netherlands, while Austria extended the reference period as part of a larger package of reforms. Germany has moved from gross to net wage indexation and France has shifted from wage to price indexation. The Netherlands, France, and Belgium have started building reserve funds to sustain pension provision when the baby-boom generation retires (Esping-Andersen et al. 2002). Germany took first steps in establishing a multipillar system of pension provision, including a partial privatization of pensions with a greater emphasis on occupational pensions. The age-limit for retirement will gradually be raised to 67 years. France represented a critical case of policy blockage until Sarkozy's entry into office in 2007, due to an absence of consensus among mainstream parties and between unions and employers.

From the mid-1990s onward, the new goal of reconciling work and family life gained prominence in Continental countries. While the Netherlands developed the "combination scenario" of child care through the workplace for mothers working part-time, the Schröder governments in Germany visibly put child care at the core of an increasingly employment-oriented policy. The Grand Coalition of CDU/CSU and the SPD expanded tax reimbursements to cover child care costs and introduced a new parental leave benefit, while expanding (public) child care facilities.

It is no exaggeration to say that the allegedly most change-resistant and veto-prone Continental welfare states have transformed the most over the past decade. Continental welfare states are in the midst of a general paradigmatic shift away from systems geared to income and status maintenance, toward activating and employment-friendly as well as gender-neutral welfare systems. This suggests an element of policy convergence with the Nordic model. The method of financing saw shifts from contributions levied on earnings from work to more general taxation. In the governance structure, we observe a weakening of the social partners in favor of privatization and/or more state control. We also observe a stronger role of the state regarding the provision of child care and of female friendly leave policies, albeit with a strong emphasis on "free choice" on the part of dual earner families. The state is not to interfere directly in family life.

Modernization Pains across Southern Welfare States under Fiscal Austerity

The modernization of southern welfare states proved particularly difficult, as external pressures from the entry into EMU and intensified economic internationalization combined with the rapid aging of the population and fierce social opposition against reform from a range of vested interests. Yet southern European states pursued an ambitious agenda of reform, including the attenuation of overly generous guarantees for privileged occupational groups, improved minimum benefits, the introduction and consolidation of safety nets, especially through means-tested minimum income schemes, increased family benefits and social services, measures against tax evasion, the reform of labor markets, and the modification of unemployment insurance benefits.

Italy saw a rapid growth of expenditures on public pensions after generous social security reforms in the 1970s. Deficits soared and by the early 1980s, escalating inflation made a reorientation of macroeconomic policy inevitable. By the late 1980s, Italy was becoming a "pension state." But proposals to rationalize the pension system and restore financial balance led only to incremental cuts and little progress. The Maastricht criteria for EMU membership subsequently made fiscal restraint indispensable, and also helped spur policy reforms in industrial relations, social security, and labor market regulation (Ferrera and Gualmini 1999). Within the pension system, the privileges enjoyed by civil servants to retire after only 20 years of service regardless of age (the so-called "baby pensions") was phased out. Pension rights were accorded to atypical workers, and lower pensions were repeatedly upgraded. Some traditional gaps in social coverage were also filled. The introduction of means-tested maternity benefits for uninsured mothers was accompanied by a reform of parental leave, and a means-tested allowance for families with three or more children was introduced. But little progress has been made in improving the functioning of the Italian labor market: rigid norms protecting the employed have only been relaxed marginally, and Italy's system of wage guarantees and unemployment compensation schemes has not been reformed. As the combination of labor-shedding policies, low female participation, and low birth rates were exacerbating the pension crisis similarly as in other Mediterranean countries, the Prodi government did recognize that caring services and leave arrangements—especially for families with small children and for the aged—are an urgent matter, but reform on these issues has been blocked by political contestation.

With respect to care, leave, and social services, Spain is much more of a front runner today (Guillén et al. 2003). When Spain joined the EC in 1986, it had a highly regulated labor market, but only a rudimentary system of social provision. In the recession of the early 1990s, unemployment rose to almost 25%, producing a sharp increase in unemployment compensation payments and a severe deterioration in public finances. In 1995, with an eye on early EMU entry, the government, unions, and employers agreed to the Toledo Pact that sanctioned pensions and labor market reform. With trade union consent, cuts in pension benefits for the "better off" were traded for improving the positions of lower-income earners. Spain also engineered a thoroughgoing decentralization in social services from central government to the regions. Regarding unemployment, reforms included new flexible contracts (which led to an explosion of temporary employment), a rationalization of unemployment benefits, activation measures, and broad changes in employment services (Moreno 2000). Unlike Italy, Spain has also progressed toward reducing inequalities in the labor market: in 1997, 2001, and 2005, labor laws relaxed the protection for core employees and improved the social security rights of irregular and temporary workers. Unemployment fell from 24% in 1994 to 8.5% in 2006 and was recently lower than in Germany or France. Like Spain, Portugal improved its minimum benefits in pensions, increased family allowances, as well as the basic safety net and experimented with minimum income schemes. Unemployment insurance was broadly reformed, occupational training and insertion programs were expanded, and specific incentives were introduced to promote a "social market for employment" based on local initiatives that targeted the most vulnerable workers.

Anglo-Irish Diverging "Third Ways"

The picture of the "Anglo-Saxon model" producing high levels of inequality is certainly true from the mid-1970s to the mid-1990s, when income inequality rose dramatically, further and faster than in almost any country in the world. In the United Kingdom, Westminster-style government (giving the governing party with a significant majority untrammeled decision-making powers) allowed Conservative governments in the 1980s and 1990s to speed up social security reform. Benefits eroded in real value and the middle classes were encouraged to opt out into nonpublic forms of insurance in pensions and health care. As the costs of targeted, means-tested benefits started to soar despite a tightening of eligibility rules inspired by the new "workfare" philosophy, a stricter benefit regime contained costs by reducing the number of claimants. These developments have had significant consequences. The erosion of universal provision has helped restore public finances, radical labor market deregulation has fostered an expansion of private employment, and inequality and poverty have markedly increased, partly because of the perverse effects of means-testing (Rhodes 2000).

After 1997, the Blair government embarked on a broad strategy of "third way" reform, fine-tuning benefit rules to neutralize the "traps" created by welfare-to-work schemes, and launching a fight against poverty and social exclusion by increasing minimum wage and income guarantees, reforming the tax code, and introducing new targeted programs. Much like the Conservatives before them, New Labour's approach has been to minimize regulatory burdens on the labor market, but its "welfare-to-work" strategy differs substantially from its predecessor's workfare policies. The New Labour approach has been built around a "rights and responsibilities" agenda that attaches conditions to benefits, requiring the unemployed to actively seek work and training. That has been matched, however, by more generous in-work benefits for those who take low-paid jobs, a policy now underpinned by a minimum wage. The most distinctive feature in New Labour's strategy of welfare reform is reliance on work and employability to address poverty, disadvantage, and social exclusion. In part, reforms were inspired by the active labor market policy tradition of the Nordic countries. In 1997, the Blair government introduced the New Deal for skills and compulsory job search, aimed at moving especially young workers from public benefits into employment (Clasen 2005). New Deal activation programs rely heavily on tax credits, which have gained in importance, particularly since the introduction of the Working Families Tax Credit (WFTC) in 1998, aimed at guaranteeing any family with a full-time worker a relatively generous minimum income (Glyn and Wood 2001). A national minimum wage was introduced from 1999, set at different levels for different age groups, and has been regularly raised since. However, in contrast to "third way" rhetoric about "learning and education as the key to prosperity," vocational training, skill enhancement, and upward mobility are rather limited. Since the mid-1990s, the trend toward higher inequality and poverty, although still high, has been halted, in part due to the introduction of a wide range of new tax credits.

In the late 1970s and early 1980s, the Irish mimicked British decentralization of wage bargaining and radical labor market deregulation. The United Kingdom and Ireland have parted company over the last twenty years. Instead of following the U.K.'s path of restricting union power, Irish governments have adopted a more coordinated strategy based on successive "social pacts," also to qualify for EMU. Beginning with the National Recovery accord of 1987–1991, cooperation with business and unions helped reform the economy and attract high levels of foreign direct investment, boosting Ireland's rates of output and employment growth. The revitalization of the Irish economy is also based on increased investments in education, preventing early departure from formal education and training, and facilitating the transition from school to work, in particular school leavers with low qualifications (NESC 2005). Poverty levels, however, did not initially decrease, principally because transfers per recipient, although rising significantly in real terms, lagged behind the exceptionally large increases in average income. Therefore, while there are fewer people relying on transfers as unemployment has declined, more of those reliant on them are relatively poorer. However, research does reveal a marked decline in poverty from 1994 (Nolan et al. 2000).

Recalibrating Welfare in Europe's New Member States

Since the fall of the Berlin wall, Central and Eastern European welfare states have been a laboratory of social policy experimentation, and as a result, they have remained underdefined. Characteristic of the transformation of the welfare state in Central and Eastern Europe has been the extended role for international organizations, like the World Bank and the IMF, especially in the area of old-age pensions. For most of the 1990s, the role of the EU in shaping social policy in the region was comparatively weak. Only since the new millennium has the EU started to push social policy issues on the political agenda of CEE countries. In May 2004, the Czech Republic, Estonia, Hungary, Latvia, Lithuania, Poland, Slovakia, and Slovenia became the first eight postcommunist Central and Eastern European economies to become full-fledged members of the EU. While participating in the Lisbon Strategy, there has been a growing interest in the NMS in the institutional structure and quality of social policies and services.

The collapse of state-socialism and the (re-)establishment of capitalism in 1989–1991 were accompanied by a deep economic crisis. In 1990–1994, economic growth and wages declined rapidly and inflation spiraled, bringing an end to full employment, with job losses ranging from 10% in the Czech Republic to 30% in Hungary. Unemployment rose from virtually zero to two-digit levels in countries like Poland, Slovakia, and Lithuania. Since 1995, the CEE economies have been growing again, as have real wages, but employment rates remained extremely low in Hungary, Slovakia, and Poland (Hemerijck et al. 2006).

The first decade of welfare transformation in Central and Eastern Europe saw the withdrawal of the state from the economy. In the early post-1989 period, the welfare state was used as a buffer to cushion the most dramatic effects of economic crisis and reform, especially the loss of income through unemployment. Early retirement provisions and disability pensions were widely used for redundant workers (Fultz and Ruck 2001; Müller 2002). Most CEE countries introduced a minimum wage and income-related social assistance schemes to combat poverty. However, inflation often depleted the real value of social benefits, leading to increasing poverty, not only among the old, but also among children, except for Slovenia and the Czech Republic. As an ethnic group, the Roma suffered the most from the social and economic hardship (Potucek 2007).

As the number of people on pension, unemployment or social assistance benefits increased dramatically, this led to a near fiscal crisis by the mid-1990s in most CEE countries. A new wave of reform took shape—with a view to containing costs and reducing welfare (Keune 2006). As elsewhere, welfare reform was heavily contested. Cost containment was achieved by tightening unemployment benefits, and the duration of benefits and replacement rates were reduced. Pension reform—particularly privatization and the individualization of savings—was also strongly advocated by the World Bank. State-socialist old-age pension systems were largely financed on a pay-as-you-go (PAYG) basis through transfers from state firms to the state budget; direct contributions by workers themselves were rare (Fultz and Ruck 2001). The introduction of the mandatory second tier of old age pension schemes run by private funds, in Hungary in 1998, Poland in 1999, Latvia in 2001, Estonia in 2002, and Slovakia in 2003, represents a clear indicator of the success of the World Bank's advocacy for pension privatization. The Czech Republic has thus far resisted the shift to compulsory private coinsurance, because the Czech economy was not in as deep a fiscal crisis as many of the other CEE countries and therefore less dependent on loans provided by the IMF and the World Bank, but also due to strong domestic political opposition from the ruling social democratic party and the trade unions. In 1995, the Czech government did agree to raise the statutory retirement age incrementally for women to 57–61 (the actual limit depending on the number of children) and for men to 62 up until 2007 (Potucek 2007).

Passive labor market policies still account for over half of all labor market spending in the CEE countries. Active labor market policies are relatively well developed in Hungary and Slovenia, while in the Czech Republic the attention paid to active and passive employment policy has fluctuated over the years according to the political colors of government, with social democrats more in favor of active policies and neoliberal parties more supportive of passive programs. Family and child care policies and maternity benefits constituted a prominent example of state-socialist welfare provision in most CEE countries. Traditional forms of public support for families with children weakened considerably during the transformation period. In Hungary, earnings-related maternity benefits were entirely abolished to be replaced by flat-rate benefits, which were linked to the level of the minimum pension. The provision of child care and kindergartens was at least partially recommodified in the Czech Republic. Family cash support dropped as well, with the important exception of Slovenia. Targeted, means-tested residual schemes were introduced in child allowances in the Czech Republic.

All postcommunist welfare states have evolved toward a hybrid mixture of conservative and liberal regime types, with a flavor of limited universalist elements. In many of the NMS, the new social policy repertoire seems to be crystallizing around three tiers, containing a compulsory Bismarckian social insurance, financed out of contributions, active labor market policies and public social assistance financed from general taxation, but run by local authorities. While the Visegrad countries have in important measures returned to their roots of Bismarckian social insurance from the late nineteenth century, the Baltic nations have seen a greater emphasis on means-testing and targeting.

THE RELATIVE SUCCESS OF THE EUROPEAN EMPLOYMENT STRATEGY

Neither the doomsday scenario of the demise of the European welfare state, predicted by OECD economists, nor the prevailing image of a "frozen welfare status quo" can be corroborated by the European welfare reform experience highlighted above. Over the past two decades, as the above inventory of reform shows, many European welfare states have—with varying degrees of success—taken measures in order to redirect economic and social restructuring by pushing through adjustments in macroeconomic policy, industrial relations, taxation, social security, labor market policy, employment protection legislation, pensions and social services, and welfare financing. The result has been a highly dynamic process of "self-transformation of the European social model(s)" (Hemerijck 2002), marked not by half-hearted retrenchment efforts but by more comprehensive trajectories of "recalibration," ranging from redesigning welfare programs to the elaboration of new principles of social justice (Ferrera et al. 2000; Ferrera and Hemerijck 2003). Many reforms were unpopular, but a fair amount occurred with the consent of opposition parties, trade unions, and employer organizations. In the process, we have seen the rise and fall, respectively, of the Swedish 1970s model of macroeconomic management and the German model of diversified quality production of the 1980s. In the 1990s, the Dutch employment miracle played a prominent role in discussions about the possibilities for a new "capitalism with a social face" in an age of global competition, industrial restructuring, and aging populations. The Celtic Tiger, the Danish "flexicurity" golden triangle, and the Finnish knowledge economy figured as model countries to emulate.

While we observe significant policy change in most welfare states in the EU, we have not seen brutal departures, except for the U.K. in the 1980s, from regime-specific historical origins. Rather we note more incremental transformative processes of sequential and cumulative policy adjustment across adjacent policy areas, with one reform building on the success and shortcomings of previous policy changes (Bonoli and Palier 2007; Hemerijck and Schludi 2000; Streeck and Thelen 2005).

Underneath these dynamic sequences of reforms, we do, however, observe a remarkable "convergence" of employment and social policy objectives and outcomes, the adoption of increasingly similar policy initiatives, encouraged also by the deepening of the EU social agenda. In the changed endogenous policy environment of the 1990s, it became clear that the active service-oriented welfare states were in a stronger position than the passive, transfer-oriented systems to make adaptations to the challenge of the feminization of the labor market. In labor market policy, the new objective became maximizing employment rather than inducing labor market exit, and this implied new links between employment policy and social security, triggering a change from passive policy priorities aimed at income maintenance toward active policy priorities aimed at activation and reintegration of vulnerable groups together with a strengthening of minimum income provisions. In the area of old-age pensions, the most important trend is the growth of compulsory occupational and private pensions and the development of multipillar systems with a tighter actuarial link between benefits and contributions.

Spending on child care, education, health, and elder care, next to training and employment services, has increased practically everywhere over the past decade. Throughout the EU, leave arrangements have also been expanded, both in terms of time and in the scope of coverage, to include care for the frail elderly and for children. All European welfare states are in the process of moving away from the breadwinner/caregiver model, under which mothers are expected to stay home with children, to a dual-earner model, under which mothers are expected to enter the labor force. This transition is not merely the product of changing gender values; it is also part of a more deliberate strategy of policymakers to confront population aging by attracting mothers into the workforce through activation programs, tax subsidies, part-time employment regulation, and the expansion of family services, and also to reverse falling levels of fertility (Orloff 2006).

With respect to financing, we observe an increase in user financing in the areas of child care, old age care, and medical care. At the same time, fiscal incentives have been introduced to encourage people to take out private services and insurance, especially in the areas of health and pensions. In many Continental welfare states, targeted benefits are increasingly financed through taxation and general revenues rather than social charges, whereas in Scandinavian countries contribution financing has been growing, especially in the area of pensions. As a result of intensified competition across the EU, many EU member states have started to pursue a hybrid strategy of lower statutory tax rates and a broadening of the tax base. Some of the NMS have gone as far as to introduce flat taxes. This implies a shift away from a focus on vertical redistribution between rich and poor citizens, but not necessarily a shift away from prevailing welfare commitments.

Since the mid-1980s, domestic issues of work and welfare have become ever more intertwined with processes of European political and economic integration. The introduction of the internal market and the introduction of the EMU, and Stability and Growth Pact, have added a new economic supranational layer to domestic social and economic policy repertoires of individual member states. Since the mid-1990s, the EU has taken on a far more proactive role as a central social policy agenda setter. The European Employment Strategy, based on the new Employment Title of the Amsterdam Treaty, launched in 1997, is exemplary of the EU's new role of agenda setting policy coordination, designed to catalyze rather than steer domestic social policy reform. Under the EES, respecting the principles of subsidiarity and proportionality, member states conduct their own policies but they are required to expose their policy experiences to common analyses and peer-group evaluation. In the absence of binding sanctions, social learning, discursive diffusion, comparing best practices, monitoring progress with specific timetables and reporting mechanisms, together with peer pressure, in light of common goals and objectives, serve to expose national policymakers to a new definition of the employment problems social policies are meant to address.

A comparison between the European Employment Strategy and the original OECD Jobs Strategy, with which we started our contribution to this volume, reveals one similarity and a number of important differences. Both reform campaigns abide by a supply-side diagnosis of the labor market. While in 1994, the OECD Jobs Strategy was met with lukewarm support and fierce opposition, we believe that the EES, being more cautious and less confrontational, has proven to be more effective in helping national policy makers to translate new labor market and social policy ideas into action.

Whereas the OECD Job Strategy focused on fighting unemployment, applying the concept of NAIRU (nonaccelerating inflation rate of unemployment) as a benchmark, the EES is more bent on raising the share of employed persons within the population as the key to comparative employment performance. The Lisbon summit of 2000 set target employment rates: By 2010, 70% of the EU population aged 15–64 should be in paid employment, with 60% of women. The Stockholm summit of 2001 complemented these with intermediary targets for 2005 and added a target for older workers (aged 55–64), namely 50% in 2010.

A second important difference between the two strategies is that the original OECD Jobs Strategy was based on a rather deductive and distinctly efficiency-oriented form of policy analysis, drawn up by the leading economists of the OECD. The EES, by contrast, followed a more inductive approach. But what is more critical is that policy analysis within the context of the EES is not a product of academic expertise, but rather a joint endeavor of domestic policymakers, civil servants, the European Commission, and other interested parties. The result is a more inclusive, albeit fuzzy, process of EU member state commitment, with a better chance of amplifying or intensifying reform. Due to the more "contextualized" (Hemerijck and Visser 2003) quality of the open method of coordination (OMC) to come to recommendations, the EES is particularly emphatic to processes of contingent convergence.

We maintain that the key contribution of the EES to improved labor market performance is mainly cognitive, but not as an afterthought, but as its major feat. The EES helped to redefine the European employment problem away from managing unemployment toward the promotion of employment, fostering the diffusion and acceptance of a new mental framework for employment policy redirection rather than concrete policy recommendations. We believe that the reorientation from managing unemployment to promoting employment, on the basis of activation, active aging/avoidance of early retirement, part-time work, lifelong learning, parental leave, gender mainstreaming, flexicurity, balancing flexibility with security, reconciling work and family life, is of a similar magnitude as the macroeconomic paradigm shift from Keynesianism to monetarism of the early 1980s. This surely was also the stronghold of the OECD Jobs Strategy. But while the OECD "one-size-fits-all" recommendations ran the risk of intensifying rather than narrowing the ideological rift between policy makers from Anglo-Saxon and the Rhineland and Nordic member countries of the

OECD, the EES's more consensual approach plausibly seems to have been far more effective in stimulating changes in policy thinking, also by deliberately shying away from single-minded policy recommendations. This, ironically, has resulted in narrowing rather than widening the real divergence across EU welfare states in policy and outcomes. The OECD itself, in turn, adopted a more subtle approach reflecting much of the policy interactions and balancing flexibility and security in the restated Job Strategy from 2006 (OECD 2006a).

Practically parallel to, and stimulated by, the development of a new labor market policy paradigm, the EU, through a series of agenda-setting EU presidencies, has in the past half a decade come to conceptualize a fairly coherent new narrative about how vital a role social policy has to play in the new era of economic internationalization and postindustrial social change. While the architects of the postwar welfare state, John Maynard Keynes and William Beveridge, could assume stable male-breadwinner families and expanding industrial labor markets, this picture of economy and society no longer holds. In order to connect social policy more fully with a more dynamic economy and society, EU citizens have to be endowed with capabilities, through active policies that intervene early in the life cycle rather than later with more expensive passive and reactive policies (Esping-Andersen et al. 2002). At the heart of the new narrative lies a reorientation in social citizenship, away from *freedom from want* toward *freedom to act*, prioritizing high levels of employment for both men and women as the key policy objective, while combining elements of flexibility and security, under the proviso of accommodating work and family life and a guaranteed *rich social minimum* serving citizens to pursue fuller and more satisfying lives.

REFERENCES

Aiginger, Karl and Guger, Alois (2006) The European Socioeconomic Model, in: Anthony Giddens, Patrick Diamond and Roger Liddle (eds) *Global Europe, Social Europe*, Cambridge, MA: Polity Press, pp. 124–150.

Alber, Jens (2006) The European Social Model and the United States, *European Union Politics*, 7(3): 393–419.

Alber, Jens (2008) Employment Patterns in the Enlarged EU, in: Jens Alber, Chiara Saraceno and Tony Fahey (eds) *Handbook of Quality of Life in the Enlarged European Union*, London, New York: Routledge, pp. 129–161.

Allmendinger, Jutta, Ebner, Christian, Nikolai, Rita (forthcoming) Education in Europe and the Lisbon Benchmarks, in Jens Alber and Neil Gilbert (eds) *United in Diversity? Comparing Social Models in Europe and America,* Oxford: Oxford University Press.

Andersen, Torben M. and Svarer, Michael (2007) Flexicurity—Labor Market Performance in Denmark, CESifo Working Paper 2108.

Bonoli, Giuliano and Palier, Bruno (2007) When Past Reforms Open New Opportunities, *Social Policy and Administration*, 41(6): 555–573.

Castles, Francis G. (forthcoming) Patterns of State Expenditure in Europe and America, in Jens Alber and Neil Gilbert (eds) *United in Diversity? Comparing Social Models in Europe and America*, Oxford: Oxford University Press.

Clasen, Jochen (2005) *Reforming European Welfare States: Germany and the United Kingdom Compared*, Oxford: Oxford University Press.

Clasen, Jochen and Clegg, Daniel (2006) Beyond Activation: Reforming European Unemployment Protection Systems in Post-Industrial Labour Markets, *European Societies*, 8(4): 527–553.

Eichhorst, Werner, Grienberger-Zingerle, Marina, and Konle-Seidl, Regina (forthcoming) *Activation Policies in Germany: From Status Protection to Basic Income Support*, German Policy Studies.

Erhel, Christine and Gazier, Berhard (2007) Flexicurity and beyond: micro-macro aspects of transitions management in the European employment strategy, Preparatory Workshop on the employment guidelines, 25 May (revised version, June), Lisbon.

Esping-Andersen, Gøsta. (1990) *The Three Worlds of Welfare Capitalism*, Cambridge, MA: Polity Press.

Esping-Andersen, Gøsta (1999) *Social Foundations of Post-industrial Economies*, Oxford: Oxford University Press.

Esping-Andersen, Gøsta, Gallie, Duncan, Hemerijck, Anton, and Myers, Jonathan (2002) *Why We Need a New Welfare State*, Oxford: Oxford University Press.

Ferrera, Maurizio (1996) The Southern Model of Welfare in Social Europe', *Journal of European Social Policy*, 6(1): 17–37.

Ferrera, Maurizio (2005) *The Boundaries of Welfare: European Integration and the New Spatial Politics of Solidarity*, Oxford: Oxford University Press.

Ferrera, Maurizio and Gualmini, Elisabetta (1999) *Salvati dall'Europa*, Milan: Il Mulino.

Ferrera, Maurizio and Hemerijck, Anton (2003) Recalibrating Europe's Welfare Regimes, in Jonathan Zeitlin and David M. Trubek (eds) *Governing Work and Welfare in the New Economy. European and American Experiments*, Oxford: Oxford University Press.

Ferrera, Maurizio, Hemerijck, Anton, and Rhodes, Martin (2000) *The Future of Social Europe: Recasting Work and Welfare in the New Economy*, Oeiras: Celta Editora.

Fultz, Elaine and Ruck, Marcus (2001) Pension Reform in Central and Eastern Europe: Emerging Issues and Patterns, *International Labour Review*, 140(1): 19–43.

Gilbert, Neil (2009, forthcoming) Comparative Analyses of Stateness and State Action: What Can We Learn From Patterns of Expenditure? In Jens Alber and Neil Gilbert (eds) *United in Diversity? Comparing Social Models in Europe and America*, Oxford: Oxford University Press.

Glyn, Andrew and Wood, Stewart (2001) New Labour's Economic Policy, in Andrew Glyn (ed.) *Social Democracy in Neoliberal Times. The Left and Economic Policy Since 1980*, Oxford: Oxford University Press, pp. 200–222.

Guillén, Ana, Álvarez, Santiago, and Silva, Pedro Adão E. (2003) Redesigning the Spanish and Portuguese Welfare States: The Impact of Accession into the European Union, *South European Society and Politics*, 8(1–2): 231–268.

Hemerijck, Anton (2002) The Self-Transformation of the European Social Model(s)', in Gøsta Esping-Andersen, Duncan Gallie, Anton Hemerijck, and John Myers (eds) *Why We Need a New Welfare State*, Oxford: Oxford University Press, pp. 173–244(72).

Hemerijck, Anton (2006) Social Change and Welfare Reform, in: Anthony Giddens, Patrick Diamond and Roger Liddle (eds) *Global Europe, Social Europe*, Cambridge, MA: Polity Press.

Hemerijck, Anton and Manow, Philip (2001) The Experience of Negotiated Reforms in the Dutch and German Welfare States, in Bernhard Ebbinghaus and Philip Manow (eds) *Comparing Welfare Capitalism. Social Policy and Political Economy in Europe, Japan and the USA*, London: Routledge, pp. 217–238.

Hemerijck, Anton and Schludi, M. (2000) Sequences of Policy Failures and Effective Policy Responses, in Fritz W. Scharpf and Vivien A. Schmidt (eds) *Welfare and Work in the Open Economy—From Vulnerability to Competitiveness*, Oxford: Oxford University Press, pp. 125–229(105).

Hemerijck, Anton and Visser, Jelle (2003) Policy Learning in European Welfare States, Manuscript, University of Amsterdam.

Hemerijck, Anton, Keune, Maarten, and Rhodes, Martin (2006) European Welfare States: Diversity, Challenges and Reform, in: Paul Heywood, Erik Jones, Martin Rhodes, and Ulrich Sedelmeier (eds) *Developments in European Politics*, Houndmills: Palgrave.

Immergut, Ellen M., Anderson, Karen, and Schulze, Isabelle (eds) (2007) *The Handbook of West European Pension Politics*, Oxford: Oxford University Press.

Kenworthy, Lane (2004) *Egalitarian Capitalism. Jobs, Incomes, and Growth in Affluent Countries*, New York: Russell Sage Foundation.

Keune, Maarten (2006) The European Social Model and Enlargement, in Maria Jepsen and Ampar Serrano (eds) *Unwrapping the European Social Model*, Bristol: Policy Press.

Kornai, Janos (1992) *The Socialist System: The Political Economy of Communism*, Oxford: Oxford University Press.

Kuhnle, Stein (2000) The Scandinavian Welfare State in the 1990s: Challenged but Viable, *West European Politics*, 23(2): 209–228.

Leibfried, Stefan and Pierson, Paul (2000) Social Policy, in: Helen Wallace, William Wallace, and Mark A. Pollack (eds) *Policy Making in the European Union*, 4th ed., Oxford: Oxford University Press, pp. 267–291.

Lindert, Peter H. (2004) *Growing Public: Social Spending and Economic Growth Since the Eighteenth Century*, Cambridge: Cambridge University Press.

Moreno, Luis (2000) The Spanish Developments of the Southern Welfare State, in Stein Kuhnle (ed.) *Survival of the European Welfare State*, London: Routledge, pp. 146–165.

Müller, Katharina (2002) Pension Reform Paths in Central-Eastern Europe and the Former Soviet Union, *Social Policy and Administration*, 36(2): 725–748.

NESC (2005) The Developmental Welfare State, The National Economic Social Council, Dublin, No. 113, May 2005.

Nolan, Brian, O'Connell, Philip J., and Whelan, Christopher T. (2000) *Bust to Boom: The Irish Experience of Growth and Inequality*, Dublin: Institute of Public Administration.

OECD (1994) *The OECD Jobs Study*, Paris: Organisation for Economic Co-operation and Development.

OECD (2005) *Promoting Adult Learning*, Paris: OECD.

OECD (2006a) *OECD Employment Outlook*, Paris: OECD.

OECD (2006b) *PISA 2006 Science Competencies for Tomorrow's World*, Paris: OECD.

OECD (2007a) *OECD Employment Outlook*, Paris: OECD.

OECD (2007b) *Babies and Bosses. Reconciling Work and Family Life*, Paris: OECD.

Orloff, Ann S. (2006) Farewell to Maternalism, in: Jonah D. Levy (ed.) *The State After Statism*, Cambridge, MA: Harvard University Press.

Pierson, Paul (1998) Irresistible Forces, Immovable Objects: Post-Industrial Welfare States Confront Permanent Austerity, *Journal of European Public Policy*, 5(4): 539–560.

Pierson, Paul (ed.) (2001) *The New Politics of the Welfare State*, Oxford: Oxford University Press.

Potucek, Martin (2007) Welfare State Transformations in Central and Eastern Europe, Prague Social Science Studies, Faculty of Social Sciences/Faculty of Arts, Charles University, Public Policy and Forecasting PPF-023.

Rhodes, Martin (2000) Restructuring the British Welfare State: Between Domestic Constraints and Global Imperatives, in Fritz W. Scharpf and Vivien Schmidt (eds) *Welfare and Work in the Open Economy: Diverse Responses to Economic Challenges*, Oxford: Oxford University Press, pp. 19–68.

Rhodes, Martin and Keune, Maarten (2006) EMU and Welfare States in East Central Europe, in: Kenneth Dyson (ed.) *Enlarging the Euro-Zone: The Euro and the Transformation of East Central Europe*, Oxford: Oxford University Press.

Scharpf, Fritz W. and Schmidt, Vivien A. (eds) (2000) *Welfare and Work in the Open Economy*, 2 volumes, Oxford: Oxford University Press.

Schludi, Martin (2005) *The Reform of Bismarckian Pension Systems: a Comparison of Pension politics in Austria, France, Germany, Italy and Sweden*, Amsterdam: Amsterdam University Press.

Streeck, Wolfgang and Thelen, Kathleen (2005) Introduction: Institutional Change in Advanced Political Economies, in: Wolfgang Streeck and Kathleen Thelen (eds) *Beyond Continuity. Institutional Change in Advanced Political Economies*, Oxford: Oxford University Press, pp. 1–39.

Visser, Jelle, Hemerijck, Anton (1997) *'A Dutch Miracle': Job Growth, Welfare Reform and Corporatism in the Netherlands*, Amsterdam: Amsterdam University Press.

Zeitlin, Jonathan (2005) The Open Method of Coordination in Action: Theoretical Promise, Empirical Realities, Reform Strategy, in: Jonathan Zeitlin and Philippe Pochet (eds) *The Open Method of Co-ordination in Action. The European Employment and Social Inclusion Strategies*, Bruxelles: SALTSA, P.I.E.-Peter Lang, pp. 447–503.

10

FULFILLING THE BALLYHOO OF A PEAK ECONOMY? THE U.S. ECONOMIC MODEL

RICHARD B. FREEMAN

From the 1990s into the first decade of the 2000s, many economic analysts viewed the United States as the peak economy in the advanced world. Economic freedom indices and indicators of competitiveness invariably placed the United States at or near the top of country rankings (along with the city-states of Hong Kong and Singapore). The success of small European economies such as Denmark, Austria, Ireland, or the Netherlands attracted some accolades, but the combination of full employment and rapid economic growth after the mid-1990s compared to the sluggish performance of other large economies made the United States the poster child of capitalism for this period. The Japanese economy that had frightened the Americans in the 1980s (recall Ezra Vogel's *Japan as Number One* [1979]) was mired in decade-long stagnation, and its population was stagnant and aging. Germany (Rhineland model) suffered high unemployment as it struggled to absorb East Germany with policies that made little economic sense. The Nordic neocorporatist economies that fared well in the aftermath of the 1970s oil shock and stagflation (Bruno and Sachs 1985) had a more checkered performance in the 1990s. Sweden's welfare state ran into a major recession and fiscal crisis (Freeman et al. 1997), and failed to reestablish its historically low unemployment rate in the ensuing recovery. Many analysts, particularly those associated with the major international financial and economic institutions, attributed the exceptional performance of the U.S. economy to its great reliance on the invisible hand of market forces and limited use of institutions and collective action to determine pay and outcomes. The message from the OECD (OECD 1994a, b), IMF (IMF 2003), and World Bank was that economic success required deregulation, weaker unions and labor laws, greater dispersion of wages, and flexibility for management in making key economic decisions.

This chapter offers a different interpretation of U.S. experience. Building on my "critical thoughts on the exceptional US labor market" in *America Works* (Freeman 2007), I argue that the standard reading of the U.S. experience ignores important aspects of the American model beyond flexibility and inequality. The section "U.S. Economic Performance" reviews the main areas of American economic success and failure. The following section "Rethinking the 'Very Good' of the U.S. System" argues that analyses of stress flexibility, deregulation of markets, and greater dispersion or inequality of pay as the hallmark of the U.S. economy miss the "shared capitalist" arrangements and private/public links that contribute to efficiency. The next section "Toward Broader Comparisons and Counterfactuals" notes that both English-speaking countries whose economic systems resemble those of the United States and continental EU economies that rely on social dialogue institutions have had sufficiently variegated outcomes to gainsay any simple generalization about national economic models. Looking to the future, I consider the strengths and weaknesses of the U.S. and other economic models to surmount the problems likely to pose the greatest challenge in the next decade: those associated with global warming, energy, and the environment, and increased globalization of labor markets.

U.S. ECONOMIC PERFORMANCE

There was a little girl,
Who had a little curl,
Right in the middle of her forehead.
When she was good,
She was very good indeed,
But when she was bad she was horrid.

Henry Wadsworth Longfellow

Figure 10-1 shows one of the key areas in which the economic performance of the United States was "very good indeed" from the mid-1990s through the late 2000s: generating high employment/population rates, extensive hours worked, low unemployment, and short spells of unemployment. Some other advanced EU countries also had high employment rates and low unemployment but their employment has been associated with fewer hours worked among the employed than in the United States. Proportionately more women are part-time workers in Europe than in the United States. In addition, there are relatively more

Figure 10-1: Performance differences, 2005

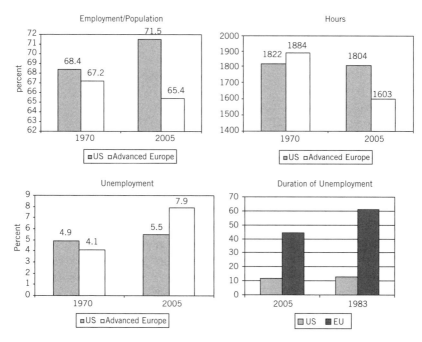

Source: Freeman 2007, America Works.

self-employed persons in Europe, many with a precarious economic position. In some countries, the measures of unemployment exclude persons on government training programs, who are in fact more like the unemployed than, say, students in secondary school or university. In the United States, the vast majority of workers, including women, are fully employed. That U.S. women, who bear and raise more children than European or Japanese women, work more hours, is striking. The United States managed to combine high female work time and fertility in part by marketizing household work (Freeman and Schettkat 2005). Americans cook less at home and buy more meals in the market. They spend less time watching children and make more use of daycare facilities than the citizens of other countries. Purchasing traditional household goods and services in the market "frees" the time of women for market work, with the result that employed American women work approximately eight hours more per week than employed European women. In addition, the United States has reduced career barriers to women (though equality in outcomes remains a distant goal). This is particularly important for college-educated workers, where women make up the majority of new university graduates in the United States and in most other advanced countries. Taking hours worked and the employment-population rate together, total annual work per adult in the United States exceeds that in advanced EU countries by about 30%, which in turn accounts for most of the United States–EU difference in GDP per capita.

The duration of joblessness figures in Figure 10.1 show that the U.S. labor market has avoided creating the class of long-term unemployed found in virtually all EU labor markets. Transitions between unemployment and employment and from job to job are faster in the United States than in EU countries, so that most of the unemployed move quickly into employment. In the United States, workers are more at risk of losing their job than Europeans with permanent jobs protected by legislation. The dynamics of transition among labor market states can be most readily seen in a Markov model of transitions among work and jobless states. In a two-state model, the rate of unemployment depends on the rate at which employed workers lose their job (Peu) and the rate at which unemployed workers gain jobs (Pue). The equilibrium unemployment rate is Peu/(Peu + Pue). This shows that proportionate changes in the levels of Peu and Pue can produce the same unemployment rate (double Peu and Pue and the equilibrium rate is the same). But because the average duration of unemployment is the inverse of the stay rate of unemployment, $1/Puu$ (= $1/(1-Pue)$) long-term joblessness can differ between countries with different transition probabilities even if those probabilities generate the same rate of unemployment. Commensurately, since the average duration of employment is just the inverse of the stay rate of employment, $1/Pee$ (= $1/(1-Peu)$), high transition probabilities also imply short average durations of job holding.

Both transition probabilities are much larger in the United States than in European economies. For instance, one estimate for the 1990s is that the probability that an unemployed person in one month finds a job in the next month (Pue) was 33% in the United States compared to 5% in Germany, while the probability that an employed person would lose their job was 1.6% in the United States compared to 0.4% in Germany—differences of over 6 to 1 and of 4 to 1. Another measure that shows the high degree of mobility in the United States is the annual rate of job-to-job mobility, which averaged 38% per year compared to 8.2% per year in EU. The rate of geographic mobility is also higher among American workers than among Europeans.

Levels of employment aside, the U.S. economy performed well in the 1990s and 2000s in the growth of productivity. With initially higher productivity than EU countries (in per worker terms more than in per hour terms) and a more rapidly growing work force, the United States might have been expected to have slower productivity growth as the EU kept on the path of catching up with the United States that it had been on since the 1950s. Instead, productivity increased more rapidly in the United States in both the service sector and manufacturing. Productivity rose in services due to innovative business practices, many associated with the application of information technology, and to flexible use of staff. Productivity rose in manufacturing with computerization and also with the offshoring of lower value-added activities to developing countries (Houseman 2007). The mid-1990s to 2000 growth of productivity resolved Solow's famous lament about seeing computers everywhere but in the productivity statistics. Firms figured out how to exploit the opportunities created by computerization, with the result that productivity grew especially rapidly in sectors that invested heavily in computers. American firms invested more heavily in R&D than European firms. In 2004, the ratio of business-funded expenditures on R&D to value added in industry was 2.40% for U.S. firms compared to 1.43% for firms in the EU-15. This also may have contributed to the more rapid and successful application of modern technologies in the United States.[1]

Overall, the employment and productivity performance of the U.S. economy in the 1990s and 2000s brought to an end the seemingly inexorable convergence of GDP per capita in advanced Europe and Japan toward the U.S. level. With population growing in the United States relative to the EU and Japan, the U.S. share of employment and output among advanced countries increased so that the United States maintained its dominant role in the world economy. But, my analysis suggests that even during this successful full employment run, there were sufficient "skeletons in the closet" to rule out any claims that the United States was *the* peak economy to which all other economies should aspire.

Skeletons in the Closet

The largest skeleton is in the distribution of national output. By virtually all metrics, inequality of incomes in the United States exceeds inequality in other advanced countries by a substantial amount. Using standard measures of earnings and income, the United States has the highest 90/10 earnings ratio and the largest Gini coefficient among advanced countries (see Figure 10.2). If we were to adjust the income statistics to take account of the fact that most advanced countries provide health insurance to all citizens while some 40 to 45 million Americans lack insurance, the inequality gap would be even greater. In addition, the income statistics leave out the 2 to 3 million Americans, largely men, in jail or prison at any point in time, who disproportionately fall in the lower end of income distribution. More surprising, perhaps, inequality in the United States exceeds the level of inequality in many developing countries that typically have much greater inequality than advanced countries. In 2005, Central Intelligence Agency data on the Gini coefficient measure of inequality placed the United States below the middle of developing country inequality, tied with China.

High inequality does not imply that economic growth bypasses low income workers. Regardless of the level of inequality, growth will improve the income of all workers if inequality is stable, and even when inequality increases, growth may be rapid enough to raise the earnings of lower income workers. This was the story of China from the 1980s to the 2000s: growth overwhelmed the huge rise of inequality to reduce poverty in the country. Historically, economic

Figure 10-2: Skeletons in closet: (a) The highest inequality in advanced economies in 2000; (b) The divergence between productivity and real earnings

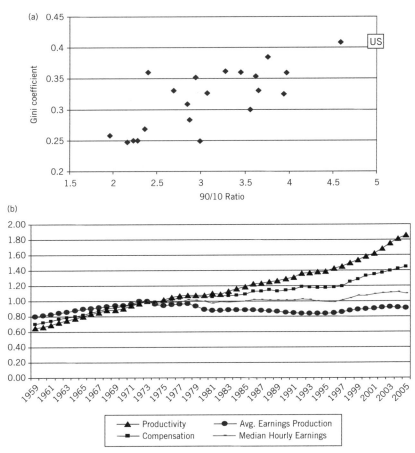

Source: Freeman in *America Works* (2007).

growth in the United States brought with it rising earnings for virtually all workers, as real earnings rose more or less at the same rate as productivity. By contrast, from 1990 to 2005, rapid productivity growth did not translate into commensurate increases in earnings. Real earnings stagnated for most U.S. workers. The vast bulk of increased GDP turned up in the pockets of persons at the top of the income distribution, in salaries, bonuses, returns on stock options or toward the end of the period, in capital income as capital's share of GDP increased.

Under some circumstances, rising inequality can be in the best interest of most citizens. If large increases in income for high earners are *necessary* for the economy to grow and if growth generates modest increases in the income of average or low earners, average or low earners gain from rising inequality.

When trickle-down is the only way to gain higher incomes, better trickle-down than income stagnation. It is hard, however, to justify trickle-down economics when little or nothing trickles down, or when business scandals per Enron, Global Crossing, and the like raise doubts that the high earnings going to persons at the top reflects their hard work in improving corporate performance. At first, the scandals seemed to be rare events—the proverbial few rotten apples in the barrel. But as the evidence about the extent of immoral if not illegal behavior at the top of corporations mounted, I began to wonder whether this was instead just the tip of an iceberg. When stock prices would rise, some firms grant backdated options to the lower prices, which contravened the purpose of options in motivating executives to take actions that would raise share prices. When stock prices would fall, firms would revalue options at the new lower price, which they would justify in terms of maintaining incentives. When disingenuous or dishonest reporting of corporate earnings could enrich insiders, some firms would report their books in ways that distorted economic reality. As the following quotes from the conservative business press make clear, one need not be some latent leftist to view these activities as a cancer at the core of the U.S. economic model:

> The Perfect Payday. Some CEOs reap millions by landing stock options when they are most valuable. Luck—or something else? (*Wall Street Journal*, March 18, 2006)

> The Great CEO Pay Heist Executive compensation has become highway robbery—we all know that. But how did it happen? And why can't we stop it? The answers lie in the perverse interaction of CEOs, boards, consultants, even the feds. (*Fortune* 2001)

> In late September, 2001, while the world and the market reeled from the attacks on the World Trade Center and the Pentagon, scores of American companies ladled out options to hundreds of executives, options now worth millions of dollars. Sleaze balls and profiteering ghouls: is that what business is about? (Editor, *Harvard Business Review*, PBS August 3, 2006)

> There is a certain class of political dictator who...justifies clinging to power by saying any possible successor would be worse. *Après moi, le déluge*, in the words of Louis XV. Some chief executives seem to be like that. They rule long after their best days are past, and collect huge sums while they're at it. (*Forbes*, April 25, 2002)

Sleaze balls and profiteering ghouls? Louis XV? Highway robbery? Not the kind of words one traditionally finds in principal–agent discussions of stock options and executive compensation. Rejecting the moralistic tone of the journalists, the economist in me quickly offered a scientific interpretation. The illegal or immoral behavior of these business leaders was readily explicable. It was normal human response to huge incentives—exactly what economics predicts and economists should have predicted had we thought properly about the ways huge incentives could distort judgment and moral behavior. If boards of directors made it easy for management to obtain extreme wealth by cutting larger and larger shares of the economic pie for itself or by lying about the size of the pie, why be surprised when many top managers cut larger slices or lied about the size of the pie. With corporate boards filled with friends of management, corporations contributing massively to political campaigns, and with the auditors and accountants, stockbrokers and financial advisors, and investment bankers dependent on management for contracts with the firm, no one seemed to have the incentive to step forward and ask if management deserved the money it was claiming, much less to ask if a different division of the pie might improve company performance.

There was one seemingly redeeming aspect on the distribution front during the 1990s and 2000s. This is in family incomes. Even as earnings stagnated for much of the workforce and the distribution of family incomes grew more unequal, the level of family incomes rose across most of the income distribution. The reason was that the number of earners in families and hours worked per family increased. These increases, while real, cannot persist into the future. Gains in family income due to additional time worked are invariably limited by the time available. With so many persons working full time, families cannot possibly keep incomes rising by adding more hours worked. In the long run, changes in family incomes will resemble changes in earnings. The failure of the U.S. job market to transform healthy growth of income per capita into commensurate increases in earnings for the majority of citizens is, arguably, the most disturbing aspect of the country's economic performance in the period of U.S. preeminence.

Why did income distribution become such a problem? Many economists attribute the rise in inequality to technological forces working through the market to benefit highly educated workers. Some attribute the increased inequality to globalization, which brought millions of workers from low-wage developing countries into competition with American workers. Some attribute the gains to management as reflecting management's greater span of control as firm size grows. Since almost all economic studies find that unionism reduces inequality, the decline in trade unionism in the United States (from 35% in the mid-1950s to 22% in 1980 to 12% in 2006) must have contributed to the rise in inequality. My estimates and those of others (Freeman (1996); Card, Lemieux and Riddell (2003)) suggest that the decline in unionism was directly responsible for a modest but nonnegligible part of the rise in inequality. It may have contributed more to inequality indirectly by marginalizing the major social group that favored a more even distribution of incomes within firms and in society broadly.

Inequality aside, the drop in union density is itself a skeleton in the closet. The disconnect between workers' desire for workplace representation and participation and what they obtain from firms is a major failure in the market for labor institutions. In the mid-2000s, over one half of U.S. workers without unions reported on national surveys that they wanted a trade union at their workplace. The failure of U.S. labor law and economic institutions to provide workers with the collective voice they seek at their workplace is emblematic of the shift in power within the U.S. economic system from labor to capital. Managements committed to a union-free workplace can generally prevent unionization regardless of the desires of their workers.

Looking beyond the labor market, there are other problems that keep the United States from fulfilling the ballyhoo of a peak economy: the American health care system, which costs 16% of GDP compared to 9% of GDP in other advanced countries without producing greater health or longer life spans, and which (as noted earlier) leaves millions without health insurance; a decaying infrastructure; perpetual trade deficits; inadequate regulation of financial institutions (exemplified in the subprime mortgage crisis); falling federal government investment in basic R&D; sluggish response to climate change; and rising cost of energy.

To be sure, all countries have problems that they have not fully addressed, much less resolved. Whether the list of skeletons is longer or shorter for the United States than for other advanced countries is unclear to me. The point of delineating the skeletons is not to disparage U.S. economic performance during its 1990s and 2000 full employment run, but to point out that the U.S. market-driven system, like the little girl in Longfellow's poem, did very well in some areas but not in others. Collectively, even if we judge the good aspects of U.S. performance as dominating the bad, the skeletons in the closest seem serious enough to reject the view that the United States was *the* peak capitalist economy.

RETHINKING THE "VERY GOOD" OF THE U.S. SYSTEM

Growth and Inequality, growth and inequality,
Go together like a horse and carriage
This I tell you brother
You can't have one without the other

The standard story is that U.S. economic success is based on relatively unregulated markets that react rapidly to changing economic circumstances and do so by offering large incentives to those at the top of the economic ladder to make appropriate economic decisions. The result is a dynamic, growing, full employment economy with massive inequality. As in the love and marriage song, the claim is that you cannot have the one without the other: high inequality is necessary for full employment and rapid productivity growth. It is necessary to motivate people to choose the highest-payoff economic activities and to work hard in providing what the market wants.

Almost all economists would agree that *some* inequality is necessary to give workers and firms the incentives to operate an efficient economy. "From each according to his ability, to each according to his need" may sound virtuous but if there is one thing economists know it is that an economy based on such a principle will not work well. Imagine a workforce where everyone is paid the same regardless of performance or a university class where everyone is given the same grade regardless of performance. Would employees work hard or even show up at work if their income was independent of their activity? Would students study to learn the material in the course with the guaranteed grade or would they devote their time to other activities? In experiments that I conducted with Alex Gelber on the number of mazes persons solve in a given period under different incentive schemes, participants solved the smallest number when we paid them the same lump sum regardless of their performance (Freeman and Gelber 2006). For those who distrust experimental evidence, after decades of paying equal wages for all, in June 2008 with Fidel Castro no longer running the country, Cuba abandoned its equal wages for all policy in favor of differentiated pay based on performance as a spur to the island's low productivity.

The question raised by U.S. experience is whether the observed level of inequality is necessary for economic efficiency, is more than necessary for efficiency—or, perish the heresy—is so high as to reduce efficiency. Does economic efficiency require that persons in the top income brackets be paid 10 times as much as the median worker...100 times...1000 times? How many billionaires are necessary for economic success, and how much of national output must they earn? Would the U.S. economy have had a less robust boom during the late 1990s if the Clinton Administration had not given firms tax advantages to pay top earning executives stock options instead of salaries? Would the economy have done better in the 2000s if the Bush Administration had tilted its tax cuts toward lower income citizens instead of toward the wealthiest Americans?

Some economists believe that unfettered markets invariably generate the inequality that maximizes economic performance and that we should accept that level even if we morally favor a different distribution. Interventions to redistribute income will, they argue, cost more than they are worth due to either the excess burden of taxes that reduces productive effort, the misdirection of resources, or to the outflow of capitalists and capital to lower tax environments, such as the Caribbean island tax havens.

Americans have more sympathy with these views than citizens in other advanced countries. Americans are more likely to regard inequality as an incentive than to view it as an unfair distributional outcome, and are less favorable to government intervention to reduce inequality. The evidence for these assertions is in Table 10-1, which records responses to questions relating to attitudes

Table 10-1: Attitudes of Swedes, Americans, and Persons in other Advanced
Countries toward the Incentive and Inequity Components of Inequality, 1999

	People Get Rewarded for Effort		Differences in Income Necessary for Prosperity		People get Rewarded for Skill	
	United States	Others	United States	Others	United States	Others
Strongly agree	11	5	4	4	15	6
Agree	50	35	20	16	55	43
Neither	22	25	27	22	16	23
Disagree	9	25	31	35	7	20
Strongly disagree	2	7	8	17	1	5
Don't know	6	3	9	6	6	3
Agree–Disagree	50	8	−15	−32	62	24

	Inequality Benefits Rich		Differences in Income Are Too Large		To Get On Top One Must Be Corrupt	
	United States	Others	United States	Others	United States	Others
Strongly agree	12	24	23	36	4	8
Agree	32	44	38	41	12	20
Neither	24	14	20	12	22	20
Disagree	16	11	9	7	35	30
Strongly disagree	4	3	3	1	21	18
Don't know	11	4	7	3	6	5
Agree– Disagree	24	54	49	69	−40	−20

	Govt Must Reduce Differences		Rich Should Pay More Taxes	
	United States	Others	United States	Others
Strongly agree	10	25	20	25
Agree	22	35	39	50
Neither	24	16	30	19
Disagree	23	14	1	1
Strongly disagree	14	6	1	1
Don't know	7	5	8	4
Agree– Disagree	−5	40	57	73

Source: Tabulated from ISSP, 1999 Social Inequality III.

toward inequality in the United States and in other advanced economies[2] from
the 1999 International Social Science Programme (ISSP) Social Inequality III
survey.[3] The line agree–disagree summarizes the responses in terms of the difference between the percentage that strongly agrees or agrees and the percentage

that strongly disagrees or disagrees. The top panel shows more Americans than persons in other countries are inclined to believe that "people get rewarded for effort"... or "for skill" and that differences in income are necessary for prosperity. The middle panel shows that Americans are less likely than the citizens of other countries to view inequality as benefiting the rich, that income differences are too large, or that to get to the top one must be corrupt. The bottom panels show that Americans are less likely to believe that government must reduce income differences and that rich people should pay more taxes. To some extent, at least, Americans appear to endorse the love and marriage view that inequality and prosperity go together, and to be leery of government redistributionist interventions.

Still, as the U.S. economy stumbled in the late 2000s and market forces failed to improve the incomes of regular workers, attitudes toward inequality hardened. The Syracuse University Maxwell Poll reported increased belief that income inequality is a serious problem, and that government should do more to try to reduce it.[4] A 2007 Pew Research Center study found that a rising proportion of Americans saw the country as dividing up between haves and have-nots and that twice as many saw themselves in the have-nots than a decade ago (34% vs. 17% in 1998). With approximately 4 in 5 Americans believing the country was going "in the wrong direction," about 2 in 3 reporting that wages were not keeping pace with inflation, and virtually everyone but Dick Cheney blaming the Bush Administration for the country's problems, the stage seemed set for reforms in the economic institutions and policies governing business, work lives, and the distribution of national income.[5]

Shared Capitalism: Incentives for All

Huge inequalities aside, there are other distinctive features of the U.S. economy that have contributed to economic success in a more egalitarian and collective way.

Table 10-2 documents one aspect of the U.S. economic system that has escaped the attention of many analysts. This is the extent to which U.S. firms have embraced shared capitalist forms of compensation and ways of organizing work. By shared capitalist compensation, I refer to modes of remuneration in which the pay and wealth of workers are directly tied to workplace or firm performance. These modes include profit sharing or gain-sharing, majority or minority employee ownership of the firm, and individual ownership of stocks and stock options that cover all or most employees. Nearly half of the American workforce is covered by at least one of these modes of compensation. The proportion of personal remuneration in the form of shared capitalist payments differs among workers, with executives getting much larger shares than regular workers but it is substantial even for the latter. Among workers with profit-sharing, the median worker reports about 8% of yearly income as a bonus for group/company performance. Among workers with ownership, the median owner's asset in the

Table 10-2: Percentage of U.S. Workers Covered By Shared Capitalist Pay, 2006

	All, 2006 (%)	For-Profit Companies (%)	Companies with Stock (%)
Profit sharing			
In profit-sharing plan	38.4	39.6	47.8
Received profit share last year	30.2	31.2	38.3
Gain sharing			
In gain sharing plan	26.8	27.8	34.6
Received gainsharing bonus last year	21.3	22.2	28.6
Own company stock	17.5	19.0	34.9
Stock options			
Hold stock options	9.3	10.0	18.6
Granted options last year	5.3	5.7	10.7
All of above	46.7	48.6	62.6

Source: Tabulated from NORC, General Social Survey, 2006.

firm amounts to 6 months annual pay. Firms that have shared capitalist modes of pay are also likely to create employee involvement committees, teams, or other groups to make economic decisions, presumably because the shared compensation has aligned their interests with the firm. Studies show that shared capitalist enterprises distribute assets and profits more evenly than other firms, and outperform them in productivity and growth. The lesson from this part of the U.S. model is to spread incentives to a large share of the workforce.

The United States offers huge potential rewards for successful innovation, and makes it relatively easy for individuals to set up firms to try out their ideas. Many of the high-tech Silicon Valley and dot.com start-ups attracted highly educated workers by offering shares in the firm that could pay off massively if the firm succeeded but would be worthless if it failed. The United States also has lenient bankruptcy laws for firms, so that an entrepreneur can set up a firm, fail, and then start again. In some lines of business, these features may suffice to produce economic dynamism but in other sectors, there also needs to be a tight link between business and research. To a greater extent than most countries, research universities in the United States have close ties with industry, with academic scientists and engineers consulting with firms, conducting research for firms, and with some academics setting up their own firms. The United States encourages university researchers who are supported by federal funds to patent the inventions they make and go commercial.

The country's success in research reflects both the use of market principles to organize scientific and academic activity and reliance on public and nonprofit financial support. There are a large number of research-granting organizations in the United States, from government agencies like National Institutes of Health (NIH) and National Science Foundation (NSF) to private foundations. Scientists compete for research grants through a collective peer review system and make their findings public knowledge, some of which findings government agencies insist be made freely available on the Internet. While the research system has problems (Freeman and Van Reenen 2008), overall it is a highly efficient mechanism for linking public and private activity in creating useful knowledge. In the eyes of many, it is a major source of U.S. economic success. Innovative government research has furthermore spurred commerce in many areas, of which the development of the Internet is most prominent. It is hard to imagine that without substantive federal investment in basic science and research, the United States would lead in so many high-tech areas and have comparative advantage in those sectors.

Open and Generous Capitalism

In the labor market, what is impressive about the United States is the openness of the society to new groups of workers, ranging from women who had traditionally been largely secondary earners to skilled and unskilled immigrants from countries that had not been traditional sources of immigration.

From 1992 to 2006, women constituted 51% of the growth of the civilian labor force in the United States. Among college graduates, they constituted 56% of the growth of labor supply.[6] In part, the influx of educated women into the work force was eased by the growing supply of low-wage immigrants, who help produce household services at low cost. Restaurant work, child care, gardening, and house-cleaning jobs are disproportionately held by immigrants, whose activities enable highly educated women to work full-time. To be sure, when highly educated women work more and gain higher earnings and less educated immigrants undertake household tasks at low wages, measured inequality is likely to rise, but this is a bit of a statistical illusion since the low-wage immigrants earn more than they would if they had stayed in their native country.

High-skilled immigrants make up over half of the country's science and engineering PhDs (less than 45 years old) and nearly 60% of postdocs. They have played a disproportionate role as entrepreneurs. To some extent, the United States draws "the best and brightest" immigrants because it has a wide earnings distribution that offers great opportunity for economic advancement, but I doubt that the opportunity to reach the upper 1% or 0.1% of the earnings distribution is a major driving force in the decision to immigrate. The link between high-skilled immigration and measured inequality in the United States is complicated. On the one hand, adding a high-wage person to the income distribution will mechanically raise measured inequality. On the other hand, the increased supply of highly skilled workers will reduce salaries of the high paid and thus lower inequality. The importance of high-skilled immigration rests not on its impact on inequality but on its seemingly positive contribution to economic growth and productivity.

Finally, U.S. capitalism differs from European or Japanese capitalism in the extent to which individuals and firms contribute to charitable causes and in the role of nonprofit nongovernment organizations in economic activity. There is nothing more emblematic of U.S. capitalism than Bill Gates making billions through innovation and sometimes monopolistic business practices and then giving away billions for good causes through the Gates Foundation. Ford, Rockefeller, Carnegie, and Hughes set up foundations years ago that today have huge impacts on the world.

But charitable donations and volunteering are not limited to the super-wealthy. Persons throughout the U.S. income distribution donate time and money for good causes. Alumni contribute hundreds of millions of dollars to their universities. On the order of 40% of Americans do some volunteer activity annually. And, while Milton Friedman famously denounced corporations for philanthropic behavior, firms continue to set up company foundations and donate to favored charities, perhaps motivated by the possible economic benefits they may gain from good will. Ronald Reagan set up a special unit in his White House to encourage companies to give more. Overall, charitable giving is approximately 2% of the U.S. national income. Volunteering is about the same proportion of working time. The nonprofit sector in the U.S. economy accounts for 5.2% of GDP and over 8% of wage and salaries.[7]

In sum, there are two sides to the U.S. economic model. There is the *greedy capitalism* side with huge monetary incentives to top persons who operate in relatively unfettered markets. But there is also the *shared/generous side*, with cooperative sharing arrangements and charitable behavior. The representation of the U.S. model as dependent exclusively on self-interest working in unfettered markets in response to huge inequalities is incomplete.

TOWARD BROADER COMPARISONS AND COUNTERFACTUALS

Motivated by the belief that the United States's superior performance in employment and unemployment is due to weaker labor market institutions and regulations than those in the EU, many researchers have estimated the adverse effects of employment regulation laws, unemployment insurance, and collective bargaining institutions on employment and unemployment. The primary evidence for these investigations is time series cross-country data, often developed by the OECD, which has produced over time increasingly better measures of regulations and institutions.

The first wave of studies made strong claims that the evidence showed conclusively that labor institutions were the main causal factor for Europe's weak employment performance and supported recommendations that countries deregulate labor markets and reduce social welfare protections to restore full employment. The most famous set of recommendations were the "ten commandments" of the OECD's 1994 Job Report (OECD 1994a, b), which called for (among other things): increased flexibility of working time; making wage and labor costs more flexible by removing restrictions; reforming employment security provisions; active labor market policies; and reforming unemployment and related benefit systems.

In succeeding years, this work has undergone critical review. A second wave of studies found that the regressions linking national economic problems to labor institutions were nonrobust to changes in the years and countries covered and to econometric specification and measurement of the key variables. Reviewing the OECD and other studies critically, Baker et al. (2004) and Howell et al. (2006) concluded that the empirics "provide little support for those who advocate comprehensive deregulation of OECD labor markets." They noted a "yawning gap between the confidence with which the case for labor market deregulation has been asserted and the evidence that the regulating institutions are the culprits." Baccaro and Rei (2005) reached similar results. Blanchard and Wolfers (2000) attributed the nonrobust results to "economic Darwinism (in which)...measures (were) constructed *ex post facto* by researchers who were not unaware of unemployment developments." My assessment (Freeman 2005, 2007) is that the early studies applied strong priors to weak data—a sure recipe for supporting the priors while learning little about how the economic world operates.

Updating and improving its estimates, the OECD now recognizes the limitations of its analyses: "the evidence of the role played by EPL (employment protection legislation) on aggregate employment and unemployment rates remains mixed"; evidence supports "the plausibility of the Jobs Strategy diagnosis that excessively high aggregate wages and/or wage compression have been impediments" to jobs, but "this evidence is somewhat fragile"; the effect of collective bargaining is "contingent upon other institutional and policy factors that need to be clarified to provide robust policy advice" (OECD 2004). In 2006, the OECD (OECD 2006a, b) stressed that the institutions of low unemployment European countries differ greatly from those in the United States and United Kingdom, which suggests that full employment can come from very different institution and policy regimes. However, Bassanini and Duval (2006)'s study, which took great care to deal with many of the robustness issues, found some empirical regularities consistent with the orthodox claims (along with some anomalous results—see Freeman 2007. Their analysis attributed about half of the 1982–2003 changes in unemployment among countries to taxes and labor regulations, with tax policies playing the larger role.

There is a fundamental problem in any effort to explain U.S.–EU differences in aggregate employment outcomes in terms of differences in labor institutions. The problem is that while employment outcome differences changed between the United States and the EU over time, institutional differences were relatively stable (Blanchard and Wolfers 2000; Lundquist and Sargent). From the 1960s through the 1980s, the United States had higher unemployment than EU countries. From the mid-1990s to the 2000s, it had lower unemployment. But in both periods the United States relied more on unfettered markets. By some measures, moreover, the differences in institutions diminished over time as EU countries moved to more market determination of outcomes. If we look at the mid-1990s economic boom that convinced many that the U.S. model was superior to the EU model, we find a similar problem: no Thatcher-style change in labor policies before the boom. Indeed, the major policy initiative preceding the mid-1990s boom was expansion of the Earned Income Tax Credit, the United States's major income redistribution program after Social Security.

So, how can analysts square essentially unchanged EU–U.S. differences in institutions or U.S. policies before/after the mid-1990s boom with changed differences in outcomes?

One possible explanation posits that the same institutions produce different outcomes in different economic environments and that the economic environment changed greatly over time. Perhaps the institutions that worked well in rebuilding Europe post–World War II did not fit the new economy of globalization and high tech of the 1990s/2000s. This hypothesis has prima facie plausibility—the economic problems of adjusting to the Internet and the rise of China and India differ from the problems of postwar reconstruction and catching up with the United States in technology and capital/labor ratios. But an interpretation based upon institutions differentially affecting outcomes in two periods is hard to test with time series cross-country data. If an institution had different impacts in the most recent period than it had earlier, the earlier observations cannot be used to estimate or test its effect in the recent period. From a policy perspective, if the changed environments hypothesis is valid, knowing that an institution or policy works in today's environment may provide no insight into whether it will work in the presumably different economic environment of the future.

There is another difficulty in using extant theories and data to determine the institutional reasons, if any, behind the differing performance of the U.S. and EU economies. This is that the United States is not *sui generis* but rather represents the institutions of a broader group of economies that Boxall, Haynes, and I (Freeman et al. 2007) have termed the "Anglo-American" economies—the United Kingdom, Canada, Australia, Ireland, New Zealand, as well as the United States. Our analysis demonstrates that the Anglo-American economies have well-defined institutional features that differentiate them from other advanced countries. Table 10-3 illustrates this with selected indicators of how labor markets operate from the World Economic Forum's Global Competitiveness Report. It gives the mean value of the indicators in the Anglo-American economies and in other advanced countries and uses a *t*-test to assess differences between the values. The *t*-statistics show that the AA economies are more business-friendly;

Table 10-3: Average Ratings of Anglo-American Compared to Other Advanced Economies (Low Ratings Imply More Reliance on Competitive Markets)

Panel A: Reported by Executives in The World Economic Forum, Global Competitiveness Report 2003

Mean, t-test	Wage Flexibility	Pay Link to Productivity	Hiring and Firing	Delegation of Authority	Cooperative Labor–Management Relations
Mean, AA	26	11	27	11	25
Mean, Other	60	39	53	18	25
t-Test	2.6	5.09	2.72	1.4	0.08
	AA firms have more control over wages	AA firms link pay to productivity more than others	AA firms have greater power to hire and fire	AA firms slightly more likely to delegate authority	No difference perceived in labor-mgt cooperation

Panel B: Reported by Labor Relations Practitioners and Academics in Global Labor Survey (Chor and Freeman 2005)

Mean, t-test	Labor Market Conditions	Freedom of Association/ Collective Bargaining	Labor Disputes	Regulations and Working Conditions	Employee Benefits
Mean, AA	16	15	12	13	13
Mean, Other	26	26	22	25	26
t-Test	4.13	5.03	3.34	3.29	5.67
	Labor market is more business-friendly in AA countries	AA countries make freedom of association and collective bargaining more difficult	AA countries have a more pro-business stance in disputes	Labor regulations are more pro-business in AA countries	Workers in AA countries have fewer benefits than in other advanced countries

Source: Freeman et al. (2007).

that they make it more difficult for workers to unionize and use collective bargaining to set pay; and that they give firms greater power in determining hiring and firing policies, paying fringe benefits, and setting pay than in other advanced economies. In short, the AA economies are a distinct cluster in "institution space," presumably in part because of their common language and historic development from the British economic and legal system.

Consistent with the orthodox interpretation of U.S.–EU differences, the AA countries as a group had higher employment–population ratios and greater inequality in the 2000s than most other advanced OECD countries. But they also have had a variegated set of economic experiences. In the 1990s, as the

United States was moving to the top of the measures of employment performance, Canada, the United States's closest neighbor in terms of economic institutions as well as geography, had its worst economic performance since the great depression. Ireland, which alone among the AA countries adopted a national wage-setting agreement that resembled the more institutional wage setting in continental Europe, outperformed the United Kingdom, in which the Conservatives had undertaken their Thatcherite deregulatory reforms. Australia maintained stronger labor institutions and regulations than New Zealand, and voted John Howard out of office when he sought to weaken labor protections and unions, while performing better than New Zealand, which had "out-Thatchered" Thatcher in deregulating its labor and product markets.

On the other side, the advanced European Union countries that rely extensively on labor institutions to determine outcomes also show a wide range of aggregate economic performance. As noted, Sweden suffered an economic meltdown in the early 1990s. By contrast, Norway did quite well (not solely because of oil as many oil rich countries have done poorly in transforming their natural resource into economic well-being); and later in the decade Denmark's economic success led many to hail its flexi-security policies as the best example of how an EU economy can keep unemployment low and labor mobility high while maintaining low inequality and strong unions. Differences in performance are also found among other close EU neighbors. In the 1990s, Germany struggled with joblessness while Austria and Switzerland maintained full employment. The Dutch revived one of Europe's sick economies through part-time work and an industry-based collective bargaining system that a decade earlier Calmfors and Driffill, et al (1988) had judged as the least efficient mode of collective bargaining. Italy proved that one of the most productive and prosperous parts of Europe could coexist with one of the highest unemployment areas under the same nominal institutional and legal system.

In short, variation in outcomes among countries with similar institutions and even within countries makes it difficult to reach any broad generalization about institutions and outcomes. The truth is that we do not know enough about how configurations of economic institutions fit together into economic systems to force the diverse experiences into a single theoretical framework nor do we have sufficiently good pseudoexperimental variation in data to derive strong empirical relations. Perhaps the most we can hope for from cross-country comparisons are good historical descriptions of which economy performed better on which dimensions in particular periods. If the U.S. economy worsens in the near future relative to EU economies (as the dollar has depreciated relative to the euro), then the view that we are closer to historians than rocket scientists in assaying variants of capitalist economies will gain greater adherence. If, contrarily, the United States maintains its employment and unemployment edge over EU economies, but continues to distribute most of the gains of economic growth to the wealthiest, the U.S. model will look as it does today—Longfellow's little girl with a curl, doing very good in some areas and horrid in others. If, however, by some sleight of the invisible hand or by some visible economic reforms, the United States buries its economic skeletons while avoiding major job loss or reduced growth then the U.S. model would indeed live up to its ballyhoo.

So, which is it for the new millennium? Return to normal economy status? Continued growth with inegalitarian distribution? Or improved peak economy performance?

ALTERNATIVE CAPITALIST MODELS IN THE NEW MILLENNIUM

I'm a Yankee Doodle Dandy, A Yankee Doodle, do or die, A real live nephew of my Uncle Sam, Born on the Fourth of July

The economic challenges of the next decade will almost certainly differ from those of the 1990s–2000s just as the problems of the 1990s–2000s differed from those of the 1970s and 1980s. To the extent that the new challenges will involve global warming, environmental, and energy issues, they would seem to have a more collectivist dimension than those in the past decade. This in turn could disadvantage the U.S. market-driven economy relative to economies with more centralized institutions and traditions of operating through social dialogue. If responses to natural resource shortages/price rises require a sharing of costs among different social groups under government or social partner agreements, the more institution-driven EU economies would seem to be better adept at making the necessary adjustments. The Nordic economies did better during the first oil price shock.

But the U.S. economic system has two features that could still give it a leg up in dealing with the new problems.

The first is that the country is the world's leader in research and development. It has the most successful academic research system, the world's top graduate universities, and a postdoctoral system that attracts new PhDs from around the world—all linked to the most R&D intensive and innovative businesses. To the extent that solutions to climate, environment, and energy problems require scientific and technological advance, the United States should be well-suited to develop and implement the new science and technologies. Imagine a U.S. administration that declared a "Manhattan Project/Man on the Moon" style project to seek new ways to deal with these global problems and spent say, $30 to $40 billion per year (roughly 2 to 3 months of Iraq war spending) on the basic science and technology that could produce the necessary breakthroughs.

The U.S. advantage in science and technology and higher education has diminished in recent years as other advanced countries and developing countries have invested heavily in university education and in research as well. In the 2000, the EU will graduate more doctorate scientists and engineers than the United States does; and in sheer numbers of newly trained scientists and engineers, China and to a lesser extent India and other developing countries are catching up with the advanced countries. But the United States holds a first-mover advantage in research that gives it close links with many of the best scientists in foreign countries, who were either trained in the United States or involved in collaborative projects with U.S. researchers. Rather than seeing these experts as competitors whose work endangers the well-being of the American economy, I view them as potentially part of a U.S.-led global effort to deal with the new challenges. No other country can be the hub of a global attack on the resource problems that endanger economic growth and well-being worldwide.

The second feature of the U.S. model that seems well-suited to dealing with the new challenges is the United States's openness to changes in who is in the work force and what they do. As noted, growth in the U.S. workforce has been partly spurred by women and partly by immigration—new groups to many high skill occupations. The transition probabilities from one labor market activity to another reflect the high-supply responsiveness of American workers to incentives, be it to move across employers, occupations, areas, or industries. When the demand for computer analysts increased in the 1990s, the supply increased much faster than the Bureau of Labor Statistics projected, as Americans with noncomputer backgrounds quickly trained themselves for the jobs. Since young persons are more mobile than older persons, demographic factors will give the United States an edge over other advanced countries in adjusting to change. If the market signals shift to new occupations or sectors, Americans will respond rapidly.

But natural resource—related problems are not the only challenge that will test advanced economies in the next decade. There will also be a huge problem in absorbing the Chinese, Indian, and workforces from other developing and transition countries into a single global labor market without causing major dislocation of workers in advanced countries. The initial U.S. notion that the developing countries would specialize in low-skill, low-wage activities while the United States, Japan, and the EU would compete among themselves for high-tech valued-added industries and occupations has proven false. The spread of higher education and the transfer of modern technology to highly populous low-wage countries has arguably made them competitive in skilled as well as unskilled work and made it increasingly difficult for market forces to raise the earnings of workers in advanced countries. It has shifted the balance of bargaining power in the labor market toward capital. Without the labor institutions to assure that workers obtain some of the gains from globalization, the United States would seem to be at greater risk of creating more have-nots with protectionist sentiments than other advanced countries. American unions are struggling to find new ways to organize and connect with workers. If they succeed, it could strengthen the U.S. model by reducing income differentials and providing workers with a greater voice in adjusting to change. But while I think that unions have a chance at gaining ground in the United States, most experts believe that they have little chance of regaining strength in the economy.

What are the odds that the U.S. model will meet these and other challenges as well or better than the competing variants of capitalism?

The national economic model that is likely to do best in the next decade or so will be the one with the greatest learning capacity and ability to implement new technologies and ideas in order to surmount the more collectivist problems that seem to lie ahead. This is flexibility of a broader and deeper kind than that which usually dominates discussions of labor market institutions. It is not an aspect of national economic models that researchers have explored in any depth, if at all. If the U.S. model rested exclusively on self-interest operating in unfettered economic markets, I would be dubious that it could adjust to the challenges. But this essay has argued that the U.S. economic model has complementary strengths that make me more sanguine about its prospects.

Of course, the scientific way to assess the likelihood that the American model (or any other model) will prove more effective in the future is not to engage in introspection but rather to run a prediction market in which people trade shares in possible outcomes. How much would you pay for a share that offered $1 if unemployment in the United States will be above that in the EU-15 in 2 years?... that the EU–U.S. gap in GDP per capita will be smaller than today... that income inequality in the United States will fall? More broadly, if the share price on the U.S. economic model living up to its ballyhoo in the next decade was 10 cents, would you buy or sell? What if the price was 20 cents? 50 cents? 80 cents?

REFERENCES

Baccaro, Lucio and Rei, Diego (2005) Institutional Determinants of Unemployment in OECD Countries: a Time Series Cross-Section Analysis (1960–98), International Institute for Labor Studies Discussion Paper DP/160/2005, Geneva: International Institute for Labor Studies.

Baker, Dean, Glyn, Andrew, Howell, David, and Schmitt, John (2004) Labor Market Institutions and Unemployment: A Critical Assessment of the Cross-Country Evidence, in David Howell (ed.) *Fighting Unemployment: The Limits of Free Market Orthodoxy*, Oxford: Oxford University Press, pp. 72–118.

Bassanini, Andrea and Duval, Romain (2006) Employment Patterns in OECD Countries: Reassessing the Role Policies and Institutions, OECD Economic Department Working Paper 486, June.

Blanchard, Olivier and Wolfers, Justin (2000) The Role of Shocks and Institutions in the Rise of European Unemployment: The Aggregate Evidence. *Economic Journal*, 110, 462: 1–33.

Bruno, Michael and Sachs, Jeffrey (1985) *Economics of Worldwide Stagflation*, Cambridge, MA: Harvard University Press.

Calmfors, Lars, Driffill, John, Honkapohja, Seppo, and Giavazzi, Francesco (1988) Bargaining Structure, Corporatism and Macroeconomic Performance, *Economic Policy*, 3(6): 14–61.

Card, David E., Lemieux, Thomas, and Riddell, W. Craig (2003) Unionization and Wage Inequality: A Comparative Study of the U.S, the U.K., and Canada, NBER Working Paper No. W9473. Online. Available from <http://ssrn.com/abstract=375325> (accessed 25 June 2008).

Chor, Davin and Richard B. Freeman. The 2004 Global Labor Survey: Workplace Institutions and Practices Around the World. NBER Working Paper No. 11598. Issued in September 2005.

Colvin, Geoffrey. (2001) *Fortune Magazine*, June 25.

Freeman, Richard B. (1996) Labour Market Institutions and Earnings Inequality, *New England Economic Review*, May/June, Special Issue Proceedings of a symposium on Spatial and Labor Market Contributions to Earnings Inequality: pp 157–168.

Freeman, Richard B. (2005) Labour Market Institutions Without Blinders: The Debate over Flexibility and Labour Market Performance, NBER Working Paper 11246.

Freeman, Richard B. (2007) *America Works*, New York: Russell Sage.

Freeman, Richard B. (2007) How Well Do the Clothes Fit? Priors and Evidence in the Debate over Flexibility and Labour Market Performance, Chapter 9 in Barry Eichengreen, Dieter Steifel, and Michael Landesmann (eds) *The European Economy in an American Mirror: Volume 1: Growth, Competitiveness and Employment,* Routledge.

Freeman, Richard B. and Gelber, Alexander M. (2006) Optimal Inequality/Optimal Incentives: Evidence from a Tournament, NBER Working Paper No. 12774.

Freeman, Richard B. and Schettkat, Ronald (2005) Marketization of household production and the EU-US gap in work, *Economic Policy Issue*, 41, 1: 6–50.

Freeman, Richard B. and Van Reenen, John (2008) What if Congress Doubled R&D Spending on the Physical Sciences? NBER, Innovation Policy and the Economy.

Freeman, Richard B., Boxall, Peter, and Haynes, Peter (eds) (2007) *What Workers Say: Employee Voice in the Anglo-American Workplace*, Ithaca, NY: Cornell University Press.

Freeman, Richard B., Swedenborg, Birgitta, and Topel, Robert (1997) *The Welfare State in Transition*, SNS-NBER Conference Volume, University of Chicago Press.

Houseman, Susan (2007) Outsourcing, Offshoring, and Productivity Measurement in US Manufacturing, *International Labour Review*, 146(1–2): 61–82.

Howell, David, Baker, Dean, Glyn, Andrew, and Schmitt, John (2006) Are Protective Labor Market Institutions Really at the Root of Unemployment? A Critical Perspective on the Statistical Evidence, CEPR Working Paper, July 14.

International Monetary Fund (IMF) (2003) 'Unemployment and Labor Market Institutions: Why Reforms Pay Off', Chapter 4 in *World Economic Outlook* (April), Washington, DC: IMF.

Lundquist, Lars and Sargent, Thomas J. (1998) The European Unemployment Dilemma, *Journal of Political Economy*, 106(3): 514–50.

Organization for Economic Cooperation and Development (OECD) (1994a) *OECD Jobs Study, Evidence and Explanations, Part I: Labor Market Trends and Underlying Forces of Change*, Paris: OECD.

Organization for Economic Cooperation and Development (OECD) (1994b) *OECD Jobs Study, Evidence and Explanations, Part II: The Adjustment Potential of the Labor Market,* Paris: OECD.

Organization for Economic Cooperation and Development (OECD) (2004) *OECD Employment Outlook,* Paris: OECD.

Organization for Economic Cooperation and Development (OECD) (2006a) *OECD Employment Outlook,* Paris: OECD.

Organization for Economic Cooperation and Development (OECD) (2006b), *OECD in Figures 2006–2007,* Paris OECD.

Vogel, Ezra (1979) *Japan as Number One*, Cambridge, MA: Harvard University Press.

SECTION VI

INEQUALITY AND MOBILITY

11

EGALITARIANISM VERSUS ECONOMIC DYNAMICS? AN EMPIRICAL ASSESSMENT OF THE FRIEDMAN CONJECTURE

MARKUS GANGL

INTRODUCTION

Institutions of modern welfare states necessarily and significantly interfere with citizens' private lives. This fact lies at the core of all public and academic discourse about whether, when, and how to appropriately intervene with respect to specific social problems, or about the fates and fortunes of those institutions of social support that were established throughout the industrial world in the twentieth century. On the one hand, interference with private lives is of course the very essence of all intervention, through social policies or otherwise, since intervention by definition presumes that individual behavior is alterable and that private circumstances may be changed for the better. On the other hand, any intervention, let alone one of the kind presented by mature welfare state arrangements that provide extensive safety nets through social insurance, public transfers, and a host of other targeted support measures, and that fund these activities through elaborate tax systems, is bound to raise important philosophical questions about the legitimacy as well as economic concerns about the overall efficiency and potentially harmful side effects of intervention.

Setting legitimacy issues aside for the moment, this chapter is concerned with assessing the case for negative behavioral consequences of elaborate welfare regimes. The economic critique of the welfare state comes in many hues and shapes, yet a genuine concern for potential disincentives to citizens' private economic action is the common theme underlying each and every serious contribution. In general, the economist's suspicion about extensive welfare programs is based on the insight that rational economic actors will take institutional features of their environment into account when making their private economic decisions on, for example, labor supply, human capital investment, or workplace effort. If so, guaranteed sources of nonearned income—like those provided through welfare states' safety nets—may reduce citizens' incentives to exploit available economic opportunities, which may ultimately have negative feedback effects on the economy and society as a whole.

One particularly important implication of the neoclassical model is its tenet of a negative association between the generosity of welfare states' safety nets and the level of economic dynamics, that is, that the economic egalitarianism and redistribution embedded in generous welfare state institutions might stifle competition, economic mobility, and innovation in the longer run. Or, as Milton Friedman (1962: 171–172) has famously put it in his *Capitalism and Freedom* nearly half a century ago:

> A major problem in interpreting evidence on the distribution of income is the need to distinguish two basically different kinds of inequality: temporary, short-run differences in income, and differences in long-run income status. Consider two societies that have the same distribution of annual income. In one there is great mobility and change so that the position of particular families in the income hierarchy varies widely from year to year. In the other, there is great rigidity so that each family stays in the same position year after year. Clearly, in any meaningful sense, the second would be the more unequal society. The one kind of inequality is a sign of dynamic change, social mobility, equality of opportunity; the other of a status society. The confusion behind these two kinds of inequality is particularly important, precisely because competitive free-enterprise capitalism tends to substitute the one for

the other.... in addition, inequality in [noncapitalist societies] tends to be permanent, whereas capitalism undermines status and introduces social mobility.

If so, as Friedman's famous treatise at length asserts, any society relying on the unfettered operation of markets would resemble the first type of society where substantial cross-sectional inequality between economic actors tends to get evened out over time through competition and changing fortunes, whereas a society that exhibits more egalitarian institutions may be more successful in bringing down cross-sectional inequality in the short run, but will inevitably pay a price in terms of subduing economic mobility and social dynamics. In the economic perspective, then, there is a trade-off between egalitarian redistribution and economic opportunity as redistribution undermines the very processes that generate economic mobility in the first place (cf. also Okun 1975). That is, redistributive egalitarian institutions are presumed to become a substitute for individual economic initiative in generating social stratification in modern economies.

Clearly, Friedman's core insight stems from what was originally framed as a pointed comparison between free-market capitalist and planned socialist economies published in the heydays of the cold war. Yet, leaving the specific historical context aside, the concern for whether or not redistributive institutions negatively affect economic mobility seems real enough—and relevant within the context of this transatlantic comparison of inequality in advanced capitalist economies that nevertheless differ significantly with respect to the generosity of their redistributive institutions. If strongly redistributive welfare institutions should indeed crowd out individual economic mobility and opportunity, then we should expect to find a significant transatlantic divide in terms of economic mobility—with the strong welfare states of Scandinavia and Continental Europe achieving significant reductions of cross-sectional inequality, if only at the cost of more limited economic mobility, whereas economies that exhibit weaker safety net systems like the United States or the Mediterranean countries would allow for a stronger role for economic opportunity and mobility in the determination of individual fortunes.

To assess the issue empirically, the remainder of this chapter will present a cross-national comparison of income inequality and economic mobility in the United States and eleven (Western) European Union (EU) member states. As this country sample provides significant variation in the generosity of welfare state institutions both from contrasting the United States to European economies, but also from differences between European economies themselves, this analysis will shed some light on the extent to which the more strongly redistributive Scandinavian and Continental European welfare states are in fact interfering critically with the workings of a modern market economy, at least as far as individual economic mobility is concerned.

Using panel data on income dynamics among prime-age workers in the mid-1990s, we will see, however, that standard inequality indices show surprisingly little cross-country variation in the degree to income mobility, the market, does erode inequality over time. That is, the neoclassical assertion about the redistributive element inherent in market competition is clearly correct insofar as markets generate mobility over time as economic opportunity gets reshuffled across individuals. Applied to the specific sample of advanced Western economies, however, the assertion that more generous welfare states would stifle economic dynamics seems largely unsupported by the data. By implication then, the redistributive effort exerted by European welfare states seems relatively well-directed in genuinely addressing market failures and ameliorating permanent economic inequality without evidence of major distortions of economic dynamics. Before jumping to this conclusion, however, the chapter will present and discuss its empirical evidence in greater detail in the following sections. In addition, the next section will provide a brief overview of the conceptual, theoretical, and methodological background of the analysis.

ECONOMIC MOBILITY OVER TIME AND ACROSS WELFARE REGIMES

Although the modern welfare state is widely associated with remedying social inequalities that exist at any point in time (e.g. Atkinson et al. 1995; Gottschalk and Smeeding 1997, 2000; Korpi and Palme 1998; Bradley et al. 2003), there is no implication that modern welfare states' policy goals were entirely static in nature. Quite to the contrary, economic change and dynamics have figured prominently in the economic philosophy of the welfare state since its inception. To be sure, welfare state institutions, and social insurance in particular, in their very core incorporate the notion of sheltering citizens from the consequences of economic misfortunes. Nevertheless, it has long been recognized that social protection through welfare state institutions entails elements of both vertical redistribution between permanently well-off and permanently disadvantaged citizens as well as life-cycle redistribution between good and bad periods in citizens' lives (cf. the classical study of Rowntree 1901; Falkingham and Hills 1995 for a more recent analysis). In addition, any exclusive focus on redistributive goals would surely negate the fact that considerations for economic efficiency or for promoting individual autonomy and self-sufficiency also figure prominently in the normative justification of welfare state intervention (cf. Esping-Andersen 1990; Goodin et al. 1999).

Nevertheless, the distinction between static and dynamic redistribution provides a conceptually important distinction as much as a truly critical test for the interaction between welfare state institutions and the market economy.

At the conceptual level, considering the dynamics of individual fortunes over time draws attention to an alternative mechanism of economic redistribution, namely the intertemporal redistribution of incomes that naturally occurs in market economies as individuals' bad fortunes reverse or economic rents are eroded in the process of economic competition. In consequence, there is a—potentially significant—egalitarian element inherent in the market process insofar as and to the extent that economic positions in market economies are not fixed over time. If so, market dynamics alone will tend to erode inequality of incomes over time so that income inequality at any point in time will overstate the true extent of economic inequality in society. In addition, the Friedman conjecture clearly implies the egalitarian impact of the market to be stronger in less regulated economies, so that, empirically, cross-country differences on standard inequality indicators should diminish whenever individual incomes are traced over some longer period of time, that is, incorporate the impact of economic mobility.

At the same time, alleviating sharp economic inequalities observed at any particular point in time remains much of the sine qua non of any welfare state institution. Naturally, then, a second line of welfare state critique might be to ask whether and to what extent interindividual redistribution achieved through public policies and intertemporal redistribution through means of market dynamics form complementary or even substitute mechanisms of redistribution in modern economies. Evidently, if both mechanisms acted much like substitutes this might undermine the justification for embedding current market economies in elaborate welfare state institutions on both efficiency and equity grounds: if the welfare state should achieve no more than free markets do over time, then much of the normative debate about the welfare state boils down to a preference for either institutionally assuring compression of inequality at each and every point in time or potential positive psychological or economic feedback to individual economic action and mobility. However, it may also be the case that markets and states act as complementary elements in shaping social stratification if and whenever welfare programs can be designed in ways to leave basic economic incentives intact, that is, whenever welfare state institutions actually manage to address market failures and lack of competitive resources in individuals rather than subdue economic initiative and motivation that might, over time, change individual fortunes for the better.

The redistributive impact of the welfare state vis-à-vis the market is ultimately an empirical question, depending as much on historic economic circumstance as on the historically specific design of the relevant programs and institutions. In consequence, advancing the public and academic debate about the viability of the welfare state first of all requires sound empirical evidence on the relationship between state and market sources of redistribution, as this chapter intends to provide. Nevertheless, it should be equally evident that no piece of empirical evidence will ever be able to settle the debate, due to both the necessarily limited nature—historically and institutionally—of just any piece of empirical data as well as the contingent nature of the relationship between markets and states that will be affected by changes in the quality of welfare state institutions.

That said, the remainder of this chapter presents results from a cross-national comparison of state and market sources of redistribution in the United States and eleven EU countries for the, roughly, mid-1990s. As a test of Friedman's above conjecture, we will present data on the level of income inequality and the extent of income mobility among individuals aged 25–54, presuming that, against the background of established social security systems in all these advanced economies, market dynamics will have the most relevant bearing on economic well-being in the prime working-age population. Using longitudinal data on individual incomes from the 1992–97 Cross-National Equivalent File (CNEF) of the U.S. Panel Study of Income Dynamics (PSID) (Hill 1992; Burkhauser et al. 2001 for the CNEF dataset) and the 1994–99 European Community Household Panel (ECHP, Eurostat 2002) for Belgium (BE), Denmark (DK), France (FR), Germany (GE), Greece (GR), Ireland (IRE), Italy (IT), the Netherlands (NL), Portugal (PT), Spain (ES), and the United Kingdom (UK), we will then be able to address both the inequality of market and disposable annual incomes in any given survey year as well as the extent of inequality on both measures that is eroded over a six-year observation window for each of these twelve advanced economies. Most importantly, the availability of longitudinal income data allows us to complement the standard measure of government redistribution, the comparison of inequality in the cross-sectional distribution of primary (market) incomes and inequality in the distribution of disposable (posttax, posttransfer) incomes, with a comparison between inequality in cross-sectional and longitudinal income data that assesses the egalitarian impact of economic mobility over time. In consequence, the data provide us with empirical information on the relative strength of either redistributive mechanism in countries that differ significantly in the generosity of their welfare institutions, and hence permit us to assess the extent to which market dynamics become subdued by extensive economic redistribution in the cross-section.

TAKING STOCK: WELFARE REGIMES, INEQUALITY, AND REDISTRIBUTION

As a first step of the analysis, Table 11-1 addresses the extent of inequality of market incomes in our twelve advanced economies, using the Gini coefficient and various percentile ratios as conventional inequality measures. Equally conventional, the empirical data suggest that wide disparities of equivalent

Table 11-1: Inequality of Equivalent Annual Market Income (Pregovernment)

	Gini	P90/P10	P90/P50	P75/P50	P50/P25	P50/P10
Denmark	0.30	3.86	1.74	1.33	1.41	2.22
Netherlands	0.35	4.66	2.02	1.47	1.41	2.31
Germany	0.37	4.69	2.22	1.47	1.40	2.12
Belgium	0.37	4.76	1.94	1.38	1.46	2.46
Italy	0.39	6.13	2.24	1.54	1.45	2.74
France	0.39	6.31	2.16	1.51	1.66	2.93
Greece	0.41	6.32	2.21	1.49	1.53	2.86
United States	0.41	7.88	2.29	1.59	1.68	3.44
United Kingdom	0.44	9.83	2.37	1.55	1.65	4.15
Ireland	0.47	39.05	2.58	1.63	1.82	15.12
Spain	0.47	11.22	2.74	1.61	1.55	4.09
Portugal	0.47	6.85	2.83	1.52	1.46	2.42

Notes: Population aged 25–54. Average of annual figures in the observation period. Equivalence
scale assumes $w_1=1$, $w_2=0.5$, and $w_{3..k}=0.3$.
Sources: ECHP 1994–99; PSID-CNEF 1992–97, balanced panel data.

annual earnings exist in all twelve economies under study: except for Denmark
on the low end, and the high-growth economies of Ireland, Spain and Portugal
on the high end, the Gini coefficient for earnings inequality clusters between
the high 30s to the low 40s for most of the countries. Expressed in terms of percentiles of the income distribution, this implies that the earnings ratio between
the ninth and the first decile is slightly below 5 in Germany, the Netherlands
and Belgium, around 6 in France, Italy and Greece, but almost 8 in the United
States and close to a factor of 10 in the United Kingdom. Again, Denmark is
the outlier on the low end, whereas ratios clearly soar for Spain and, particularly, Ireland.

Leaving aside the historically exceptional high-growth cases of the mid-1990s
Ireland, Spain, and Portugal for the moment, this corroborates the conventional
wisdom that, relative to Continental Europe, inequality of market incomes is
consistently higher in the United States, whereas the United States seems far
less special if compared to Britain or the Mediterranean countries. Also, while
the results clearly suggest lower market inequality in Continental Europe, the
difference to the U.S. data appears less pronounced overall than in some other
analyses of earnings inequality because the analyses reported in this chapter
include individuals with zero market incomes in any given year, that is, include
employment inequality (which tends to be stronger in Continental Europe) in
addition to earnings inequality more conventionally considered (and more pronounced in the United States).

Furthermore, Table 11-1 also provides evidence that practically all of the
cross-national variation in income inequality occurs in the tails of the income
distribution: on the top end, the income ratio between the ninth and fifth decile
ranges from a low of 1.74 for Denmark to 2.3 for the United States and up to

almost 3 for Portugal, at otherwise near constant income ratios between the upper quartile and the median income. Cross-national variation at the lower rungs of the income distribution is even more significant, with income ratios between the median and the first decile of market incomes being only slightly above 2 in Denmark and Germany, close to a factor of 3 in France, Italy, and Greece, but more like between 3.5 and 4 for the United States, the United Kingdom, or Spain.

To a considerable extent, these disparities in market incomes are of course mitigated by welfare policies, social insurance, and other programs of modern welfare states. For this particular sample of advanced economies and analogous to Table 11-1 above, Table 11-2 compiles the empirical evidence on inequality of disposable incomes from the PSID and ECHP source data. From this, a considerable reduction of inequality is evident from both the Gini coefficients and the percentile ratios. After taxes and transfers, Gini coefficients range between 0.20 for Denmark and 0.35 for the United States, that is, are down by about 10 percentage points on average relative to those found for pretax and pretransfer incomes. Welfare state redistribution in other words ameliorates around 30% of inequality in the distribution of primary incomes even among the prime working-age population. Also, percentile ratio measures are similarly reduced: the 90/10 percentile ratio is seen to fall from a 4–10 range down to between 2.3

Table 11-2: Inequality of Equivalent Annual Disposable Income (Postgovernment) and Redistribution

		Redistribution				Shrinkage	
	Gini	ΔGini (Absolute)	%Gini (Relative)	P90/P10	P50/P10	%P90/ P10	%P50/ P10
Denmark	0.20	0.10	0.33	2.32	1.50	0.40	0.32
Germany	0.25	0.11	0.31	2.98	1.65	0.36	0.22
Belgium	0.26	0.11	0.29	2.94	1.75	0.38	0.29
Netherlands	0.26	0.09	0.24	2.95	1.63	0.37	0.29
France	0.29	0.10	0.27	3.35	1.86	0.47	0.36
United Kingdom	0.31	0.13	0.30	4.11	2.15	0.58	0.48
Italy	0.32	0.07	0.18	4.50	2.29	0.26	0.17
Ireland	0.32	0.15	0.31	4.13	1.99	0.96	0.94
Greece	0.34	0.07	0.17	4.76	2.28	0.25	0.21
Spain	0.34	0.13	0.28	4.97	2.28	0.56	0.45
Portugal	0.34	0.13	0.27	5.03	2.24	0.27	0.07
United States	0.35	0.06	0.14	5.01	2.45	0.37	0.29

Notes: Population aged 25–54. Average of annual figures in the observation period. Redistribution assessed relative to cross-sectional market income (cf. Table 11-1, data columns 1, 2, and 6). Equivalence scale assumes $w_1=1$, $w_2=0.5$, and $w_{3,k}=0.3$.
Sources: ECHP 1994–99; PSID-CNEF 1992–97, balanced panel data.

for Denmark and 5 for United States, and the 50/10 percentile ratio comes down from its earlier 2–4 range to a low of merely 1.5 in Denmark and up to 2.5 in the United States.

At the same time, even among this set of advanced economies, there is considerable heterogeneity as to how strongly welfare state institutions interfere with the primary distribution of market incomes. Whereas most European welfare states achieve a reduction of income inequality of some 30% relative to income inequality of market incomes Italy, Greece, and the United States in particular stand out as the countries where redistribution is well below the average. That is, and despite working on relatively large disparities of market incomes to begin with, income inequality is either shrunk in a well below average fashion (in the Mediterranean welfare states, including Italy) or, in the case of the United States, at about average, which is clearly insufficient to bring wide inequalities in the primary distribution of incomes down to anything close to the likes of Continental European patterns in terms of inequality of standards of living.

IT'S ABOUT TIME: INEQUALITY AND REDISTRIBUTION IN DYNAMIC PERSPECTIVE

While much of the above is well known, there has been very little research on comparative income dynamics that would permit an assessment of (cross-national variation in) redistribution across the life course that occurs as a consequence of market dynamics. As a partial remedy to this, Table 11-3 below presents our estimates of inequality of market incomes across the six-year observation window available from our PSID and ECHP data sources. While a far cry from the ideal observation window spanning complete life courses or at least individuals' complete job histories, the results compiled in Table 11-3 certainly suggest that market dynamics comprise a significant redistributive element in themselves.

Over the course of six years, we see that market dynamics clearly erode income inequality observed at any point in time. On both the Gini coefficient and the percentile ratio measures, the distribution of individuals' average market incomes in the observation window is markedly more egalitarian than the distribution of point-in-time incomes: whereas, for example, Gini coefficients for point-in-time incomes were found to range between 0.30 (Denmark) and 0.47 (Ireland, Spain and Portugal) in our data, the Gini coefficients for average market incomes are as low as 0.26 for Denmark, around one-third in Continental Europe, slightly below or above 0.40 in the United States and the United Kingdom, and at 0.43–0.44 in Ireland, Spain, and Portugal. That is, market forces alone do considerably reshuffle individuals' economic fortunes over time, and this effect clearly contributes to equalize status disparities in the longer-term perspective.

Table 11-3: Inequality of Equivalent Six-Year Market Income (Pregovernment) and Mobility

	Gini	Mobility		P90/P10	P50/P10	Shrinkage	
		ΔGini (Absolute)	%Gini (Relative)			%P90/ P10	%P50/ P10
Denmark	0.26	0.04	0.13	3.31	2.01	0.14	0.09
Netherlands	0.32	0.03	0.09	4.15	2.08	0.11	0.10
Belgium	0.33	0.04	0.11	4.01	2.19	0.16	0.11
Germany	0.34	0.03	0.08	4.01	1.95	0.14	0.08
Italy	0.35	0.04	0.11	4.85	2.27	0.21	0.17
Greece	0.36	0.05	0.12	5.33	2.38	0.16	0.17
France	0.36	0.03	0.07	5.55	2.65	0.12	0.10
United States	0.37	0.04	0.09	5.89	2.72	0.25	0.21
United Kingdom	0.41	0.03	0.08	7.63	3.28	0.23	0.21
Spain	0.43	0.04	0.09	6.68	2.53	0.42	0.39
Ireland	0.44	0.03	0.07	10.16	4.08	0.89	0.89
Portugal	0.44	0.03	0.06	5.79	2.14	0.16	0.12

Notes: Population aged 25–54. Economic mobility assessed relative to cross-sectional market income (cf. Table 11-1, data columns 1, 2, and 6). Equivalence scale assumes $w_1=1$, $w_2=0.5$, and $w_{3..k}=0.3$.
Sources: ECHP 1994–99; PSID-CNEF 1992–97, balanced panel data.

Over and above the recognition of an egalitarian element inherent in market competition, the empirical evidence of Table 11-3, further suggests two important observations. First of all, and while undoubtedly significant, the redistributive power of the market pales against the cross-sectional redistribution achieved by taxes and transfers, which at least for this analysis using an arguably short observation window of six years, easily doubles the relative reduction of income disparities that occurs through market dynamics over time. More importantly, however, there is apparently little cross-national variation in the level of market dynamics over time. In all of the advanced economies for which we have data, we find that, over the course of just six years, the Gini coefficient drops by 3–4 percentage points and percentile ratios shrink between 10% and 20% relative to the single-year estimates. Interestingly, and in stark contrast to what mainstream neoclassical models would predict, there are no large differences in the absolute reduction of inequality effected by market forces across this range of advanced Western economies that differ so significantly in terms of welfare institutions. Even more so, a similar absolute magnitude of market-driven redistribution in these societies implies that, in relative terms, market dynamics in low-inequality countries—Denmark being the prototypical example—actually achieve an even greater reduction of inequality than what is evident for Anglo-Saxon countries usually considered as the hallmark of unfettered and efficient market economies.

COMPRESSING INEQUALITY: WELFARE STATES VERSUS MARKETS?

The above evidence of widespread empirical similarity in the level of economic mobility across advanced economies is certainly sufficient to invalidate more extreme claims about negative economic side effects of strong welfare state institutions. Against the background of the above results, there can be little doubt that fundamental economic dynamics remain intact in all of the twelve countries contrasted in this study—even in those countries where welfare state institutions empirically unleash far stronger redistributive efforts than those inherent in the dynamics of the market.

Acknowledging this negative empirical result, the efficiency of welfare state redistribution might still be questioned (let alone, of course, its moral desirability disputed on other principal grounds). The demonstrably powerful redistributive machinery of strong European welfare states might nevertheless be considered inefficient if such redistribution tends to merely substitute market dynamics, that is, whenever public policies would basically mimic and reproduce economic outcomes that could similarly be achieved through market processes alone. To check for this possibility, Table 11-4 repeats the above analysis

Table 11-4: Inequality of Equivalent Six-Year Disposable Income (Postgovernment) and Mobility

	Gini	Posttax/Transfer Mobility (Relative to Cross-Sectional Distribution of Disposable Income)		Redistribution (Relative To Distribution of Average Market Income)		Total Redistribution (Relative to Cross-Sectional Distribution of Market Income)	
		ΔGini (Absolute)	%Gini (Relative)	ΔGini (Absolute)	%Gini (Relative)	ΔGini (Absolute)	%Gini (Relative)
Denmark	0.17	0.03	0.15	0.09	0.35	0.13	0.43
Belgium	0.23	0.04	0.13	0.10	0.30	0.14	0.38
Germany	0.23	0.02	0.10	0.11	0.32	0.14	0.37
Netherlands	0.24	0.03	0.11	0.08	0.26	0.11	0.33
France	0.26	0.03	0.09	0.10	0.28	0.13	0.33
United Kingdom	0.28	0.03	0.10	0.13	0.32	0.16	0.37
Italy	0.28	0.04	0.12	0.06	0.18	0.11	0.27
Greece	0.29	0.04	0.13	0.06	0.18	0.11	0.28
Ireland	0.30	0.02	0.07	0.14	0.32	0.17	0.36
Spain	0.31	0.03	0.10	0.12	0.29	0.17	0.35
United States	0.32	0.04	0.10	0.06	0.16	0.10	0.23
Portugal	0.32	0.03	0.08	0.13	0.29	0.16	0.33

Notes: Population aged 25–54. Economic mobility assessed relative to cross-sectional income inequality and inequality of six-year market incomes, respectively (cf. column 1 in Tables 11-1–11-3). Equivalence scale assumes $w_1=1$, $w_2=0.5$, and $w_{3..k}=0.3$.
Sources: ECHP 1994–99; PSID-CNEF 1992–97, balanced panel data.

for individuals' six-year disposable incomes, that is, assesses inequality of post-government income after taking economic mobility over time into account. If redistribution and market dynamics were indeed close substitutes, one would expect that Gini coefficients for average disposable incomes over the six-year period would tend to be close to those established from cross-sectional data because government programs would already have largely smoothed out actual change in economic circumstances. On the other hand, if Gini coefficients for average disposable incomes over the six-year window are found to be significantly below those for cross-sectional disposable incomes, this clearly leaves an important role for economic mobility that is independent of government redistribution (and vice versa).

And very much as before, the empirical data tend not to support any strong version of the Friedman conjecture on this indicator. As evident from Table 11-4, the Gini coefficients for six-year average disposable incomes are in fact well below both those established for annual disposable incomes as well as below the Gini of average market incomes. As captured by this measure, inequality of long-term standards of living ends up being as low as below 0.20 in Denmark, around 0.25 or slightly below in Continental European welfare states, and around 0.30 in Southern Europe and the Anglo-Saxon world, including the United States.

Clearly, these figures are below those reported for disposable incomes in the cross-section (cf. Table 11-2), so that there is a significant degree of economic mobility over time in each country in the sample even after government redistribution is taken into account. More importantly, and as reported in our analysis above, the extent of cross-national variation in mobility levels is surprisingly modest. In all twelve advanced economies, market dynamics over a six-year observation window erode inequality by between two and four percentage points, with Germany and Ireland being at the lower end and Southern Europe, Belgium, and the United States at the upper end of the spectrum (cf. Table 11-4: column 2). Put differently, market forces everywhere diminish inequality of disposable incomes by some 10% over six years, with little indication that this proportion would vary systematically by either cross-sectional inequality in the primary distribution of market incomes or the level of public redistribution (cf. Table 11-4: column 3).

In fact, it is also readily evident from the data presented in Table 11-4 that public redistribution remains a powerful factor in itself despite the extended longitudinal perspective adopted here. Relative to observed inequality of market incomes averaged over six years (cf. Table 11-3), tax and transfer systems achieve a further reduction of inequality of a full 10 percentage points on the Gini in the majority of countries (cf. Table 11-4: column 4), which, like in the standard cross-sectional perspective, amounts to cutting longer-run market inequalities by about a third (cf. Table 11-4: column 5). Also, and again as in the cross-sectional data, the United States, Italy, and Greece stand out as achieving the least reduction of market inequality through government intervention.

What is more, since inequality of average disposable incomes is consistently below either inequality of average market incomes or inequality of cross-sectional disposable incomes, there is little in the data to suggest any strongly substitutive empirical relationship between market dynamics on the one hand, and the redistributive effort of the welfare state on the other. Summing up both components, we observe a consistent reduction of overall market inequality in the order of around 15 percentage points on the Gini in most European countries (cf. Table 11-4: column 6), which is equivalent to a combined redistributive impact of markets and welfare states of about a third or slightly higher (cf. Table 11-4: column 7). Redistribution, again, is evidently weaker in the United States, Italy, and Greece, but that seems to follow entirely from political choices rather than any differences in market competition and mobility. In fact, the strongest evidence against any claim that welfare state redistribution might merely substitute market dynamics in fact comes from noting that the overall amount of redistribution we observe in the longitudinal data (the last column of Table 11-4) is, for each and every country in this study, practically equivalent to the sum of cross-sectional redistribution through taxes and transfers (cf. Table 11-2 above) and the erosion of inequality that stems from market dynamics (as reported in Table 11-3 above). In other words, this very much implies that welfare state redistribution is clearly effective over and above what redistribution is achieved through economic dynamics and market dynamics achieve a reshuffling of economic fortunes that is largely independent of the redistributive impact of government policies.

This important point becomes even more evident if we plot the level of income dynamics observed in the twelve economies against the extent of cross-sectional redistribution. Figure 11-1 provides this plot for both the dynamics of pregovernment market incomes as well as for postgovernment disposable incomes and also includes the fitted bivariate regression line as an indicator of a statistical relationship between mobility and redistribution in the data (in addition, the latter is provided both for the full country sample and for a restricted sample excluding Ireland, Spain, and Portugal, that is, the three countries that exhibited extremely fast economic growth over the period).

From this, it is readily evident that there is virtually no relationship between the extent of cross-sectional redistribution through taxes and transfer programs on the one hand, and the level of market dynamics on the other. What is more, the finding of no relationship actually holds for mobility being assessed from both pregovernment and postgovernment incomes, and is not affected very much by the inclusion or exclusion of Ireland, Spain, and Portugal, although the relationship between mobility and redistribution does become slightly more negative once these countries are considered. In fact, Figure 11-1 forcefully brings home the message that redistribution by welfare state institutions and economic mobility through market dynamics are two starkly different mechanisms affecting social stratification in advanced economies. From

Figure 11-1: Redistribution and market dynamics

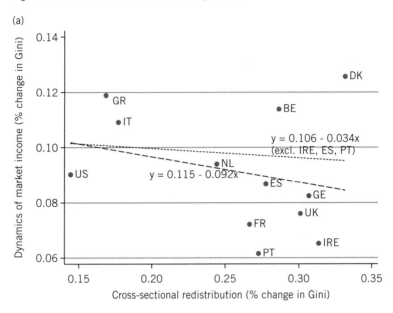

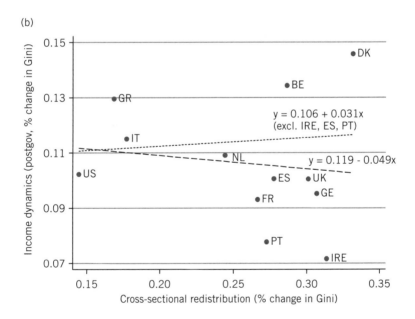

Note: Population aged 25–54. Equivalence scale assumes $w_1=1$, $w_2=0.5$, and $w_{3..k}=0.3$. Source data from Table 11-2, column 3 (x-axes, government redistribution), Table 11-3, column 3 (income dynamics, pre-government), and Table 11-4, column 3 (income dynamics, postgovernment).

this particular analysis, we in fact obtain no evidence that markets and welfare states would act as meaningful substitutes for each other and hence conclude that, empirically and for the particular observation window of the mid-1990s, there is little evidence that, at least as far as individual mobility is concerned, economic incentives were fundamentally marred by strong welfare state intervention in Denmark or Continental Europe.

To end this chapter on a slightly more critical note, however, one may in fact note one further piece of evidence that might be considered more indicative of potential inefficiencies associated with redistributive activity and government intervention. What Figure 11-1 above has pointed out is the fact that, in terms of the Gini coefficient at least, market dynamics are an equally important social force in all the twelve economies under study here—that is, economic mobility is of roughly similar importance relative to the degree of economic inequality in the primary distribution of income everywhere. However, this does not necessarily imply that welfare state institutions would be perfectly neutral with respect to economic dynamics over time; rather, to restate the above result once more, government intervention seems to leave incentives and opportunities for mobility by and large intact, though market dynamics do clearly not go fully unfiltered either.

To see this point more clearly, Figure 11-2 plots the ratio of income dynamics in the posttax/posttransfer distribution of income (from Table 11-4: column 2)

Figure 11-2: Redistribution and realized economic mobility

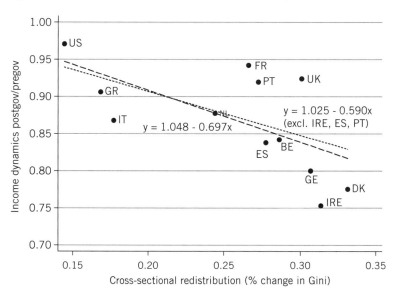

Notes: Population aged 25–54. Equivalence scale assumes $w_1=1$, $w_2=0.5$, and $w_{3..k}=0.3$. Post/pregovernment income dynamics ratio calculated from dividing the data in Table 11-4, column 2 (income dynamics, postgovernment) by the data from Table 11-3, column 2 (income dynamics, pregovernment); Table 11-2, column 3 (government redistribution).

and income dynamics in the pretax/pretransfer distribution of income (from Table 11-3: column 2) against the extent of redistribution in the cross-section (from Table 11-2: column 2). This ratio thus captures the degree to which dynamics of market incomes, that is, mobility along the primary distribution of income, translate into dynamics of disposable income, that is, mobility in the final distribution of income. In other words, the ratio of posttax/posttransfer income mobility to pretax/pretransfer income mobility expresses the extent to which changes in individual market income imply changes in disposable incomes, that is, individuals' actual standards of living. Clearly, the lower this ratio, the more strongly individuals are buffered from—positive or negative—economic shocks in the market, and social stratification more closely resembles a Friedmanite status society in consequence.

   In this regard, two important empirical results are immediately evident from Figure 11-2: first of all and quite as expected from the other results in this chapter, the degree to which changes in market incomes translate into real changes in standards of living is quite high in this sample of advanced capitalist economies. On average, slightly below 90% of all income mobility observed for market incomes actually translates into mobility along the final income distribution. However, there is also more evidence of a relationship between this mobility ratio and the strength of welfare state institutions in this case. Quite clearly, the United States is the outlier at the top end of this measure, whereas strong welfare states like Germany or Denmark come in at the low end. In fact, this measure quite sharply indicates the degree to which the U.S. economy actually represents an unfettered market economy in the true sense of the term: at a mobility ratio of some 97%, practically each and every change of market incomes does imply a change of disposable income here, so that changing economic fortunes literally directly impinge on individual economic status. This is clearly not true to the same extent in, for example, Germany or Denmark where welfare states apparently buffer around 20% of the total mobility observed in the primary distribution of income. That still leaves a very significant role for market dynamics in shaping social stratification, yet it is equally evident that the degree of buffering from economic change is considerably more significant in these two and other European countries.

DISCUSSION AND CONCLUSIONS

The empirical evidence presented in this chapter is easily summarized: the data from our transatlantic comparison of mobility patterns in twelve advanced economies clearly refute any notion that modern welfare state institutions would severely impact on incentives for economic mobility. As far as economic mobility is concerned, conjectures that social insurance and other cash transfer programs would stifle economic dynamics are just not at all borne out empirically for this particular sample of advanced economies—quite to the contrary, the quantitative estimates provided in this chapter suggest that market dynamics in fact play a veritable role in social stratification in all of the twelve countries, and that there is in fact surprisingly little variation across countries in the extent to which the distribution of income is affected by economic mobility over time. In that sense, this chapter wholeheartedly confirms earlier observations for a more limited set of countries that have similarly pointed to the fact that levels of economic mobility in strong European welfare states tend to resemble or even exceed those found in the United States (e.g., Aaberge et al. 2002; Burkhauser and Poupore 1997; Goodin et al. 1999).

As is always true with any piece of empirical research, important and legitimate concerns about the factual validity of the data remain. To begin with, the positive image painted for most European economies might be a methodological artifact related to differences in survey quality. For example, if measurement error was in fact larger in those European countries that had little experience with conducting panel surveys before the ECHP, volatility of incomes would likely be overestimated in the data and erroneously be attributed to strong economic dynamics in this chapter. On the other hand, a mechanism that might counteract any such tendency is the fact that attrition problems would also likely be correlated with panel survey experience in any particular country— yet attrition is likely to reduce observed dynamics because economic mobility and attrition are likely to be fundamentally correlated everywhere. Similarly, the analyses reported in this chapter are subject to the principal concern that the primary distribution of income observed in the data is not a valid estimate of the counterfactual income distribution that would result in the absence of welfare state intervention (e.g., Bergh 2005). As the welfare state potentially affects the distribution of market incomes through, for example, labor supply disincentives the extent of redistribution might be overstated in the quantitative estimates of this and other research. On the other hand, it seems evident that if the welfare state affects economic incentives then this should unequivocally reduce observed mobility over time that is, observed mobility in the data would represent a smaller fraction of potential economic mobility with stronger government intervention. Yet Denmark and Continental Europe show evidence of significant income mobility on par with the United States even in the observed data.

Eventually, while all of these concerns seem relevant, it seems unlikely that they would be sufficiently powerful to question the overall conclusions of this chapter and other research. If the evidence presented here is then provisionally accepted as factual, we are left with two possible conclusions. At one level, those supportive of government intervention could indeed comfort themselves by concluding that strong welfare state institutions of Scandinavia and Continental Europe empirically seem fairly well-aligned to the functioning of modern market economies, thus reconciling economic opportunity and social solidarity. Since mobility and redistribution are nothing like close substitutes in shaping social stratification in our empirical data, it may safely be inferred that European welfare states to an overwhelming degree manage to address true market failure in the sense of effectively redistributing economic resources and relieving permanent economic constraints in a way that would not have occurred from market dynamics alone, while leaving fundamental economic incentives largely intact. In fact, this would seem all the more true once some degree of income smoothing—that is, some degree of substitution of market-generated dynamics of income through social insurance—is actually considered as a legitimate and desirable goal of government intervention in itself. The only possible alternative reading to the above would be one that maintains an actual erosion of economic incentives through welfare state activity, yet that would have to rely on some additional and yet unspecified processes that disproportionately depress mobility chances in unfettered market societies. Whether that alternative reading would actually change the normative conclusions about the welfare state significantly is of course quite another issue.

One final caveat is perhaps in order. Clearly, though longitudinal in nature, the present inquiry has provided no more than a snapshot picture in historical terms. This chapter has safely concluded that there were few systematic differences in the extent of income mobility in this sample of twelve advanced economies during the mid-1990s. There is no implication that we could extrapolate this empirical picture to the present or the past in any straightforward fashion, or that the findings in themselves would contribute much to our understanding of the specific economic mechanisms that underlie the global similarities documented in this chapter (e.g., DiPrete 2002). To get ahead in either direction, we will have to revisit the empirical data repeatedly, very much in the same way as the institutional adaptation of welfare state institutions to changing economic circumstances remains a constant task for administrators and the wider public.

REFERENCES

Aaberge, Rolf; Björklund, Anders; Jäntti, Markus; Palme, Mårten; Pedersen, Peder J.; Smith, Nina and Wennemo, Tom (2002) Income Inequality and Income Mobility in the Scandinavian Countries Compared to the United States, *Review of Income and Wealth*, 48(4): 443–469.

Atkinson, Anthony B., Rainwater, Lee, and Smeeding, Timothy M. (1995) *Income Distribution in OECD Countries. Evidence from the Luxembourg Income Study*, Paris: Organisation for Economic Cooperation and Development.

Bergh, Andreas (2005) On the Counterfactual Problem of Welfare State Research: How Can We Measure Redistribution? *European Sociological Review*, 21(4): 345–357.

Bradley, David; Huber, Evelyne; Moller, Stephanie; Nielsen, François and Stephens, John D. (2003) Distribution and Redistribution in Postindustrial Democracies, *World Politics,* 55(1): 193–228.

Burkhauser, Richard V. and Poupore, John G. (1997) A Cross-National Comparison of Permanent Inequality in the United States and Germany, *Review of Economics and Statistics,* 79(1): 10–17.

Burkhauser, Richard V., Butrica, Barbara A., Daly, Mary C. and Lillard, Dean R. (2001) The Cross-National Equivalent File: a Product of Cross-National Research, Ithaca, NY: mimeo. Available online at: http://www.human.cornell.edu/pam/gsoep/equivfil.cfm (accessed 3 July 2008).

DiPrete, Thomas A. (2002) Life Course Risks, Mobility Regimes, and Mobility Consequences: a Comparison of Sweden, Germany, and the United States, *American Journal of Sociology,* 108: 267–309.

Esping-Andersen, Gøsta (1990) *The Three Worlds of Welfare Capitalism,* Cambridge, UK: Polity Press.

Eurostat (2002) *ECHP UDB Manual. European Community Household Panel Longitudinal Users' Database. Waves 1 to 6. Survey Years 1994 to 1999,* DOC. PAN 168/2002–12, Luxembourg: Eurostat.

Falkingham, Jane and Hills, John (eds) (1995) *The Dynamic of Welfare: The Welfare State and the Life Cycle,* New York: Prentice Hall.

Friedman, Milton (1962) *Capitalism and Freedom,* Chicago, IL: University of Chicago Press.

Goodin, Robert E.; Headey, Bruce; Muffels, Ruud and Dirven, Henk-Jan (1999) *The Real Worlds of Welfare Capitalism,* Cambridge, UK: Cambridge University Press.

Gottschalk, Peter and Smeeding, Timothy M. (1997) Cross-National Comparisons of Earnings and Income Inequality, *Journal of Economic Literature,* 35(2): 633–687.

Gottschalk, Peter and Smeeding, Timothy M. (2000) Empirical Evidence on Income Inequality in Industrialized Countries, in Anthony B. Atkinson and François Bourguignon (eds) *Handbook of Income Distribution, Volume 1,* Amsterdam: Elsevier, pp. 261–307

Hill, Martha S. (1992) *The Panel Study of Income Dynamics. A User's Guide,* Newbury Park, CA: Sage.

Korpi, Walter and Palme, Joakim (1998) The Paradox of Redistribution and Strategies of Equality: Welfare State Institutions, Inequality, and Poverty in the Western Countries, *American Sociological Review,* 63(5): 661–687.

Okun, Arthur M. (1975) *Equality and Efficiency: the Big Tradeoff,* Washington, DC: Brookings Institution.

Rowntree, Seebohm (1901) *Poverty: A Study of Town Life,* 2nd ed., London: Macmillan.

12

ARE THE INEQUALITY AND MOBILITY TRENDS OF THE UNITED STATES IN THE EUROPEAN UNION'S FUTURE?

RICHARD V. BURKHAUSER AND KENNETH A. COUCH

There are clear differences in how the United States and the various European Union (EU) countries weigh personal liberty and collective protection in establishing limits for their internal economic market arrangements and in forming public policies aimed at reducing individuals' economic risks. However, as Alber (2006), primarily using equivalized cross-national data from the Luxembourg Income Study (LIS) shows, heterogeneity of social institutions among EU countries and in the economic well-being of their populations are broad enough that along most dimensions, economic outcomes in the United States lie well within the extremes.

In contributing to this discussion, we show how economic growth over the last two business cycles has been distributed in the United States and compare those changes with changes in two EU countries with quite different social institutions—Great Britain and Germany. While income inequality is consistently highest in the United States over the past two decades, followed by Great Britain and Germany, income inequality in the United States changed little in the 1990s, fell in Great Britain, and rose in Germany. We show that outcomes in Great Britain over the 1990s business cycle are much closer to those in the United States than they are to Germany.

However, these results are somewhat controversial since the equivalence of data across countries and over time has emerged as a major methodological issue in the inequality literature, particularly with respect to the March Current Population Survey (CPS). The public use CPS is the principal data set used to capture levels of income and income inequality and their trends in the United States and is included in the LIS collection of cross-national equivalent data sets. We show however that both levels and trends in income and income inequality are affected by inconsistencies in the public use CPS data. Researchers who do not control for these inconsistencies will confuse improvements in the amount of income captured in the public use CPS data with real increases in income and income inequality and thus overstate the increase in income inequality in the United States, especially since 1994.

In addition, we show that measurement of levels and trends in inequality are sensitive to the years in which comparisons are made and to the concepts used to capture it. Changes in the distribution of individual labor earnings, which is only one source of private income (income from nongovernment sources) of one member of a household, may vary in different ways over time from trends in the total private household income of those individuals. Furthermore, private household income, which is also called pretax pretransfer household income, can vary from pretax posttransfer or before tax household income, which includes income from both private and government sources (e.g., social security benefits, welfare benefits). And, before tax household income can vary from posttax posttransfer or after tax household income, a measure commonly used in EU countries to capture the amount of a household's disposable income.

We then move from these various cross-sectional perspectives on inequality and look at intragenerational income mobility over this period. Once again, we find that there is more in common than there is different in the relationship between transitory and permanent inequality in our comparisons of the United States and Germany and in their long-term mobility outcomes.

Based on these specific country findings, which reinforce Alber (2006)'s findings of major heterogeneity within EU countries, we then focus on differences in the United States income distribution and that of the EU as a whole and speculate on how these differences will change as the EU attempts to becomes a more fully integrated economic and social land of opportunity.

TRENDS IN MEDIAN INCOME IN THE UNITED STATES

The economic well-being of a country can be measured in various ways. While we will focus on the distribution of income as a major social indicator of a country's success, a fundamental indicator of a country's growth in material well-being is the level of income (average or median) of its citizens. Figure 12-1, adapted from the U.S. Census Bureau's CPS series (DeNavas-Walt et al. 2007: Figure 12-1), shows that real (2006 U.S. dollars) median before tax (pretax posttransfer) household income has increased in the United States from $36,847 in 1967 to $48,201 in 2006.[1] However, those gains have clearly not been continuous. In particular, the growth in median income is sensitive to the influence of the business cycle. Since we are primarily interested in long-term trends, it is important to control for these cyclical fluctuations. A simple method for doing this is to compare outcomes at similar points in the business cycle. In Figure 12-1, peaks and troughs of the series on median before tax household income are identified. We focus on comparisons across the years 1979–1989 and 1989–2000, which roughly capture the peaks of the business cycles of the 1980s and 1990s in the United States.

From this perspective, Figure 12-1 shows that real median household income increased over both these periods. While income fell as the economy slipped into recession following the peak years of 1979 and 1989, the period of recovery that followed more than made up for this decline. After 2000, median before tax household income fell until 2004 but then rose in 2005 and 2006. While we have explained the pattern of rising incomes in terms of peak-to-peak comparisons, our story will not change using trough years 1983, 1993, and 2004 instead.

Just as it is important to control for the state of the economy to obtain secular trends in median income within a country, it is equally important to control for business cycle conditions within individual countries in cross national

Figure 12-1: Median household income, 1967–2006

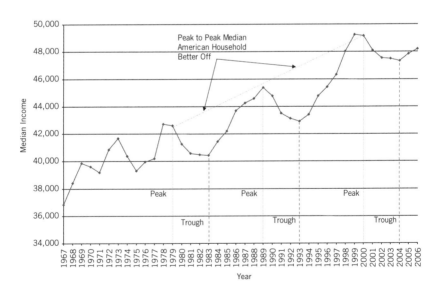

Note: March CPS Series. Income in 2006 CPI-U-RS adjusted dollars. Households as of March of the following year.
Source: DeNavas-Walt et al. (2007, Figure 1).

research, which we will do in our comparisons of the United States, Germany, and Great Britain over the 1990s.[2]

INCOME AND INCOME INEQUALITY TRENDS IN THE UNITED STATES, GREAT BRITAIN, AND GERMANY

Because this book focuses on economic opportunity in the United States relative to the EU countries, the information reported in Figure 12-1 must be adjusted so that it can be compared to similar information for EU countries. To do so, we switch from the before tax income of households reported in Figure 12-1 to after tax (posttax posttransfer) income. We also switch from the household as the unit of observation to the person by looking at the household size-adjusted after tax income of individuals. The measure of income we use in these international comparisons represents disposable income available to individuals and is most common in the literature that compares inequality and mobility in the United States with that of other countries. This is the case both because it better controls for the very different tax policies across countries, and second, because it can be calculated using cross-sectional data.[3]

Table 12-1 contains mean and median (after tax household size-adjusted) income as well as 90/10 ratios and Gini coefficients for individuals living in Germany, Great Britain, and the United States over the peak years of their respective business cycles.[4] Table 12-1 is drawn from Burkhauser et al. (2008a: Tables 4.1 and 4.1A), an analysis that makes extended comparisons across these countries using data from the Socio-Economic Panel (Germany), the British Household Panel Survey (Great Britain), and the CPS (United States). More information on technical details of the analysis, in particular the treatment of outliers, can be found there.[5]

The median after tax income values in Table 12-1 for individuals differ from those for households in Figure 12-1. However, their pattern of peaks and troughs are the same. Disposable individual household size-adjusted income (mean and median) increased over both the 1980s and 1990s business cycles in the United States. But the gains from economic growth were much more equally shared in the 1990s than in the 1980s, whether measured by the 90/10 ratio or the Gini coefficient.[6] While both mean and median after tax income increased over the 1980s in the United States, inequality measured by the 90/10 ratio and the Gini coefficient, rose. In contrast, in the 1990s, the United States mean and median after tax income increased and after tax income inequality decreased. While overall after tax income inequality rose over the entire period, all of this increase occurred in the 1980s.

Appropriate peak year comparisons of income are also reported for Great Britain and Germany over their 1990s business cycles in Table 12-1. After tax individual household size-adjusted income increased more in Great Britain

Table 12-1: After Tax and Before Tax Household Size-Adjusted Income and Income Inequality, in the United States, Great Britain, and Germany

	United States					Great Britain			Germany		
	1979 (1)	1989 (2)	2000 (3)	Percent Change 1979–1989 (4)	Percent Change 1989–2000 (5)	1990 (6)	2000 (7)	Percent Change (8)	1991 (9)	2001 (10)	Percent Change (11)
After Tax											
Mean	22,494	24,954	26,767	10.93	7.27	11,539	13,917	20.61	17,377	18,605	7.07
Median	20,892	22,135	23,707	5.95	7.10	10,583	12,788	20.84	16,146	17,054	5.62
90/10	4.71	5.82	5.42	23.67	−6.82	3.89	3.63	−6.78	3.10	3.39	9.59
Gini	0.301	0.344	0.336	14.17	−2.24	0.274	0.264	−3.59	0.231	0.250	8.18
Before Tax											
Mean	28,697	31,708	34,334	10.49	8.28	14,160	16,818	18.77	23,015	25,178	9.40
Median	25,195	26,597	28,500	5.56	7.15	12,602	15,008	19.09	20,894	22,366	7.05
90/10	6.351	7.719	7.656	21.54	−0.82	5.027	4.574	−9.01	3.895	4.584	17.69
Gini	0.352	0.387	0.387	9.94	0.00	0.316	0.304	−3.80	0.271	0.302	11.44

Notes:
a Income values are in 2000 United States dollars.
b Income values are in 2000 British pounds.
c Income values are in 2000 euros.
d Income values are in 2000 yens.
Source: Burkhauser et al. (2008a, Tables 1 and 1A).

than in the United States over the 1990s and inequality fell. In contrast, while after tax income increases in Germany were about the same as in the United States, inequality as measured by both the 90/10 ratio and Gini coefficient grew dramatically in Germany over the 1990s. Thus measured inequality in Germany, which had been substantially below levels observed for Great Britain at the beginning of the 1990s business cycle, was approximately equal to it by the end. Despite an improving trend for the United States in the 1990s, after tax income inequality in both Germany and Great Britain remained considerably lower.

The second panel in Table 12-1 reports the same inequality measures but does so for before tax individual household size-adjusted income.[7] Before tax income is typically used in inequality studies for the United States and was used in the series shown in Figure 12-1. Using this concept in cross-national comparative studies ignores the importance of tax policies in reducing inequality but can reveal their relative importance across countries. We provide this information here to show that the underlying results are similar to those of others who have used the public use CPS data to look at income inequality trends in the United States alone and that the tax systems in all three countries are progressive. Income in each of the countries is more equally distributed after taxes than before taxes in all years. Further, over the 1990s, business cycle the percentage increases in before tax inequality measured by both the 90/10 ratio and the Gini are much greater in Germany than are the percentage increases for those same values using after tax income. Likewise, in Great Britain and the United States, the percentage declines in before tax income inequality over this period are less for these values than for a 90/10 ratio or Gini value using after tax income.[8] Consistent with other research, this confirms the equalizing nature of taxes in the countries examined.

MEASURING CHANGES IN THE INCOME DISTRIBUTION USING KERNEL DENSITY ESTIMATION

In studying the distribution of economic well-being, dispersion and related measures of inequality are informative about the relative circumstances of individuals. But the location of the distribution and how it changes over time are also important to consider, since they inform us about the overall level of well-being. For example, a society as a whole unambiguously gains during periods when growth increases all incomes while inequality remains constant or declines. At the end of such a period, a given person at any point in the distribution will be absolutely better off than was the case initially and income inequality will not have increased. On the other hand, growth that raises everyone's income while increasing inequality is less desirable from a social perspective, other things being equal. But this type of growth where everyone is unequally better off is still preferable to growth that raises the incomes of the rich while reducing the income of the poor.

Table 12-1 shows that the United States in the 1980s and Germany in the 1990s each experienced growth that was accompanied by widening inequality. But summary measures of income inequality like a Gini coefficient cannot simultaneously characterize the average (or median) effect on incomes and the dispersion of experiences. A simple way to get a sense of how the distribution has changed over time is to examine it directly. We do this using a technique for calculating the distribution of income referred to as kernel density estimation.

Kernel density estimation provides an elegant alternative to the summary measures of inequality reported in Table 12-1 since it allows us to depict the entire income distribution in terms of its density function. Simply looking at the probability distribution of income, we can observe its location, spread, and modality simultaneously. A density function is the percentage of persons whose household size-adjusted income is at a specific level in the population. The sum of this distribution of probabilities is 1, representing all persons being examined. For a technical discussion of the kernel density method employed here in the context of measuring economic well-being, see Burkhauser et al. (1999).

Comparing the United States, Great Britain, and Germany

In Figure 12-2, from Burkhauser et al. (2008a: Figures 1, 2, and 3), we show how the distribution changed in each of the countries by estimating the probability density functions of individual disposable income in the peak years of their respective business cycles. The first panel of Figure 12-2 shows that in 1979 the distribution of after tax (disposable) income in the United States had the traditional inverted U-shape with the great mass of the population bunched around the mode of the distribution. By the end of the 1980s business cycle in 1989, the distribution had become much flatter. The middle mass of the distribution around the mode fell (fewer people were in the middle of the distribution) with the vast majority spilling toward the higher income tail of the distribution and a much smaller but still important group spilling toward the lower tail of the income distribution.

In contrast, the entire U.S. after tax income distribution moved to the right between 1989 and 2000, the two peak years bracketing the 1990s business cycle. More formally, the income distribution in 2000 attained first-order stochastic dominance over the 1989 distribution.[9] At every percentile of the 2000 distribution, the level of after tax income is higher than in 1989. While not every percentile gained at the same rate, all percentiles of the distribution moved to a higher level of income.

The second panel of Figure 12-2 captures the change in the after tax income distribution for Great Britain over their 1990s business cycle. As in the United States, the 2000 after tax income distribution attained first-order stochastic dominance over the 1990 distribution. Furthermore, the noticeable second

Figure 12-2: Distributions of after tax household size-adjusted income in peak business cycle years for the United States, Great Britain, and Germany

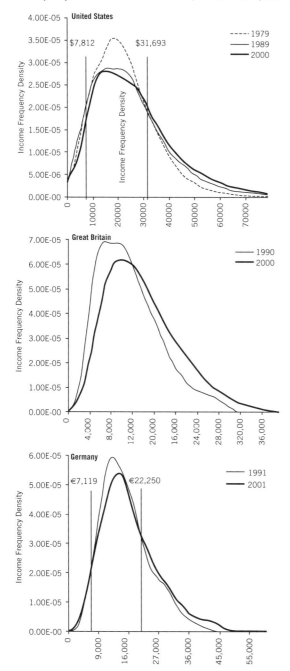

Notes: Estimations based on data from the March CPS Annual Demographic Files, 1980, 1990, and 2001; the British Household Panel Survey, 1991 and 2001; the German Socio-Economic Panel, 1992 and 2002, are in 2000 real values of each country's currency.
Source: Burkhauser et al. (2008a, Figures 1, 2, and 3).

hill in the 1990 distribution is considerably smoother in the 2000 distribution. While the modal value declined in Great Britain, a far larger proportion of the distribution remained bunched near the middle of the distribution than was the case in the United States. Nonetheless, the after tax income distribution movements in Great Britain and the United States were very similar over their 1990s business cycles.

This stands in sharp contrast to the movement in the after tax income distribution in Germany over their 1990s business cycle. In 1991, the distribution in Germany (Panel 3 of Figure 12-2) also had the traditional inverted U-shape with the great mass of the population near the mode of the distribution. In 2001, rather like the United States in the 1980s, the mass of the population near the mode of the distribution fell with the vast majority of people spilling to the right and becoming unequally richer and a smaller but important share becoming poorer.[10]

Burkhauser et al. (2008a) examine how the reduction in the middle of the income distribution in the United States over the 1980s business cycle and in Germany over the 1990s business cycle was distributed between the two tails of the distribution. In the United States for the 1979 and 1989 income densities, they define the left intersection, and the start of that tail, as the point where the income density in 1989 drops below the one for 1979. As can be seen in Panel 1 of Figure 12-2, this occurs at $7,812. The right intersection point, which defines the start of that tail, is the point where the income density in 1989 rises above its counterpart for 1979—$31,693. The left and right intersections and tails for Germany are defined in a similar manner.

Using these concepts for the United States, 7.18% of the entire distribution slid out of the middle of the distribution over the 1980s business cycle. But the vast majority of that 7.18% (82.46%) became richer. Over the German business cycle of the 1990s, an even greater percentage of the middle mass around the mode of the distribution (8.23%) slid into the two tails. But once again the vast majority (88.58%) became richer. Nonetheless, in the United States (17.54%) and in Germany (11.42%), a sizeable minority became poorer as income inequality rose.

How Vulnerable Populations Fared in the United States

Burkhauser et al. (2004b), using consistently top-coded before tax household size-adjusted income for individuals calculated from public use CPS data, also compare income distribution changes over the 1980s and 1990s business cycles but disaggregate by vulnerable populations to see if the dramatic changes in the distribution of income in the 1990s in the United States also affected the economic well-being of traditionally vulnerable groups—females, African Americans, single mothers, welfare recipients, and the less highly educated (less than high school and high school). Table 12-2, adapted from Burkhauser et al. (2004a: Tables 2, 3, 5, 6, and 7), shows the ratio of the mean before tax individual

Table 12-2: Trends in the Mean Income of Vulnerable U.S. Populations and Their Within Group Gini Values, 1979–2000

	Females/ Males (1)	African Americans/ Nonblacks (2)	Single Mothers/ Two-Parent Households (3)	Welfare/ Nonwelfare (4)	Less Than High School/ More Than High School (5)	High School/ More Than High School (6)
Year						
1979	0.917	0.618	0.485	0.410	0.524	0.778
1989	0.920	0.619	0.468	0.352	0.445	0.687
2000	0.935	0.689	0.482	0.414	0.444	0.677

Within Vulnerable Group Gini Values

	Females (1)	African Americans (2)	Single mothers (3)	Welfare (4)	Less Than High School (5)	High School (6)
1979	0.360	0.404	0.402	0.405	0.368	0.308
1989	0.393	0.437	0.458	0.455	0.394	0.343
2000	0.394	0.417	0.422	0.439	0.389	0.352

Source: Burkhauser et al. (2004b, Tables 2, 3, 5, 6 and 7).

income of each of these groups to the mean before tax individual income of their less vulnerable counterparts—males, nonblacks, mothers in two-parent households, nonwelfare recipients, and those with more than a high school education, respectively.

In 1979, at the start of the 1980s business cycle, each of these economically vulnerable groups had lower mean before tax income relative to their counterparts (the ratios in row 1 of Table 12-2 are all less than 1) and this was the case in 1989 (row 2) and 2000 (row 3) as well. Over the 1980s business cycle, this ratio remanded about the same for females and African Americans but fell substantially for all the other vulnerable groups. In contrast, over the 1990s business cycle, all the economically vulnerable groups except those with a high school education or less saw substantial increases in their mean income relative to the mean income of their less vulnerable counterparts. This is further evidence that the growth in the 1990s was much more evenly spread over the entire distribution than was the case in the 1980s.

Table 12-2 also reports that inequality (measured by a Gini value) within all of these traditionally vulnerable groups increased over the entire period. But that most of this occurred over the 1980s and that inequality actually fell over the 1990s for African Americans, single mothers, those on welfare, and those with less than a high school education.

Using the same kernel density estimation technique, Burkhauser et al. (2004a) also examine changes in the distribution of size-adjusted household before tax income of individuals within these vulnerable populations over the 1980s and 1990s business cycles. Except for those with low education levels, their distributions shifted significantly to the right over the 1990s, just as the distribution of the entire population did as shown in Figure 12-2. Hence in the 1990s for women, African Americans, single mothers, and those on welfare, not only did their entire distribution move to the right but their within-group before tax income inequality fell.

WHAT IS GOING ON IN THE UPPER TAILS OF THE DISTRIBUTION?

Thus far we have looked both at the domestic U.S. literature that focuses on before tax U.S. income inequality and the cross-national literature that compares after tax income inequality in the United States and other countries. Each of these literatures greatly depends on the public use CPS for its U.S. income data. But total income in the CPS is composed of many components and each of these sources of income is top-coded. This top-coding understates each source of income's highest values, reducing measured total income and its dispersion. Further complicating this issue is that the top-code values are raised periodically so that a greater range of the values reported can be observed by analysts. This results in measured trends in income inequality that may confuse real increases in income inequality with more accurate measures of real income at the top of the distribution over time. As Levy and Murnane (1992: 1376) state, "an increase in the top code can cause a spurious jump in inequality in measures that are sensitive to the upper tail of the distribution. A related problem is that, during a period in which the nominal top code is fixed, the data cannot reveal increases in inequality that may have taken place."

Figure 12-3, drawn from Burkhauser et al. (2008b: Figure 3), demonstrates the problems of using unadjusted public use CPS data to capture levels and trends in individual household size-adjusted before tax income inequality over time. It plots calculations of Gini coefficients using public use CPS data unadjusted for top-coding as well as a series adjusted to consistently topcode before tax individual income. (See endnote 5.) Using the unadjusted public use data, they find a large rise in inequality comparing Gini values over the 1990s business cycle (1989–2000). This finding has been reported by those who ignore top coding problems in the public use CPS. (See Larrimore et al. 2008 for a greater discussion of this issue and Feng et al. 2006 for a discussion of the problem of top coding in the context of long-term trends in labor earnings inequality.) The Gini values produced with consistently top-coded public use

Figure 12-3: Consistently top-coded and unadjusted Gini values of before tax household size-adjusted income based on public use and internal CPS data comparing Gini-trends using four different topcode methods

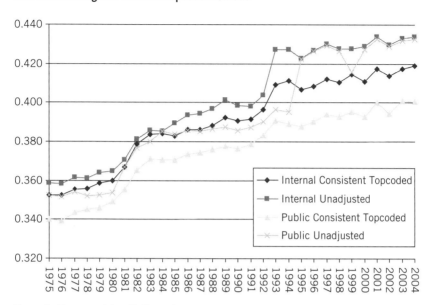

Source: Burkhauser et al. (2008b, Figure 3).

CPS data, not surprisingly, are lower than those in the unadjusted public use CPS data. But more importantly what Burkhauser et al. (2008b) show is that most of the increase in inequality over this period in the unadjusted CPS data occurs in 1994–1995. They argue that this jump in income inequality is caused by improvements in the amount of total income captured in the public use CPS data at the upper end of the income distribution rather than by a real increase in income for this part of the distribution. Hence, researchers who fail to correct for this improvement in measured income in the public use CPS will substantially overstate the real increase in income inequality in the United States from any period before 1994 to 1995 or later.

Given these trend differences reported in Figure 12-3, it is worth describing in a bit more detail why they occur.[11] To capture income inequality trends using consistent top-coding, each component of income for the years between 1975 and 2004 is examined to determine the greatest impact top-coding has on that income component in any individual year. Then, for each component, all other years are top-coded at the same percentile of the values reported for that income component. Thus, the portion of the distribution of responses recoded at a top value in the distribution is uniform over time. Burkhauser et al. (2004a) show that while this method systematically understates levels of labor earnings inequality, it captures trends in both the unadjusted U.S. Census Bureau internal and public use CPS based Gini values. In examining Figure 12-3, it can also be seen that consistently top-coding removes the cliff in measured inequality found in the unadjusted public use CPS data beginning in 1995. This cliff occurs in the unadjusted public use CPS data because the top codes were increased substantially in 1995 and because for the first time cell means (the mean value of all values topcoded for that income source) were used as the income values for top-coded values rather than the top-code values themselves. These trend results in the consistently top-coded data are similar to those obtained by researchers who simply removed the top 2% of the public-use data. Hence the results using consistent top-coding or the trimming procedures commonly employed by other researchers are both limited to what has been happening to household size-adjusted before-tax income and its distribution for the bottom 97% or 98% of the distribution.

Because of the large jump in inequality after 1994 measured using public-use CPS data and some dissatisfaction with adjustments to the data whether they be via consistent top coding or trimming of the tails of the distribution, Burkhauser's research team applied for and received permission from the Census Bureau to access the restricted use internal CPS data. The U.S. Census Bureau uses these internal CPS data to estimate the household income Gini values often referenced by those who consider these census-generated Gini values to be the most accurate available measure of inequality for the entire U.S. before tax income distribution. The Burkhauser et al. (2008b) calculations of Gini coefficients using these internal CPS data are also shown in Figure 12-3. These uncorrected internal CPS based Census Gini values also show substantial increases in the household size-adjusted income inequality of individuals over the period 1989–2000. But now the cliff begins in 1993. One would think that those calculations would be definitive. But Burkhauser et al. (2009) systematically document that there is inconsistent censoring at the top of the distribution in the internal CPS data as well.

Burkhauser et al. (2009) demonstrate that over the period 1975–2004, the unadjusted internal CPS data, like the public-use data, do not systematically capture the upper end of the before tax income distribution. Like the public use CPS, internal censoring, including top-coding, occurs on each individual source of income rather than on overall income, and they find that the share of persons living in households with one or more income sources top-coded varies from 0.1% to 0.8% over this period. While this is not a serious concern if one is only interested in the bottom 98% or even 99% of the income distribution, many feel that changes in patterns of compensation particularly for those at the top of the distribution in the past decade are important. To the extent this would influence trends in inequality, this impact cannot be directly measured even with the internal CPS data.

As can be seen in Figure 12-3, when the internal household size-adjusted income data is passed through the same consistent top-coding procedure discussed above, a more modest increase in Gini values appears to have occurred in the United States since 1989 than is found using the uncorrected internal data. For 1989–2000, the measured increase in inequality after correcting for changing top codes is 4.67% rather than 6.82%. However, even the smaller change measured using the consistently top-coded internal series is likely to be overstated. While consistent top-coding lowers the cliff beginning in 1993 in the internal data, it is still implausibly high and is more likely to be caused by the general change in CPS collection methods beginning in 1993 rather than any real change in the underlying income distribution (see Jones and Weinberg 2000). As can be seen in Figure 12-3, if you follow Gini trends from 1993–2004, all the years of internal data available since the start of the 1993 cliff, income inequality only increases by 1.45% and 2.43%, respectively, in these two internal series. Hence the rise in household size-adjusted before tax income inequality captured by internal Census files, once it is adjusted for censoring, tells much the same story for the bottom 99% of the income distribution as the adjusted public use CPS data. Income inequality has risen very little and much less than in the previous decade.

More formally, Burkhauser et al. (2008b) find that while there is a significant difference in the levels of Gini measured income inequality using the consistently top-coded public use data, the consistently top-coded internal data and the unadjusted internal data, there is no significant difference in their trends between 1975 and 1992 or in their trends between 1993 and 2004. But the annual rise in income inequality after 1993 is significantly smaller than before 1993.

Unfortunately, there is much greater uncertainty over how much the before tax income of the top 1% has changed since 1989 and how inclusion of those values would influence observed trends. A serious discussion if not a major debate is occurring in the United States over this issue.[12] If dramatic increases in the top 1% or 2% of the income distribution are significantly altering overall inequality in the United States or in EU countries, neither the CPS nor the other country data sets in LIS are likely to be able to capture it. Thus, for the present, all estimates of income inequality that depend on capturing this upper tail of the distribution are unlikely to be able to do so.

Researchers using components of the LIS data to capture trends in either before or after tax income inequality in the United States will find that the LIS method of trimming yields trends in the 1990s that are closer to those found in the uncorrected public use CPS data discussed above than in the consistently top coded CPS data we report.[13] Other things being equal, this is likely to raise the level of measured inequality in the United States relative to European countries. Moreover, the original country data supplied to LIS from other countries may have similar or even worse censoring problems. Across countries, the lack of data on the very top of the income distribution that CPS or other original country data sets miss may lead to substantial misstatements of inequality levels and trends as it appears to have done for the United States.

Problems of top coding have led some researchers to use 90/10 ratios as an alternative way of capturing trends in the income distribution. These researchers commonly believe that top-coding issues are not a problem for 90/10 measures since they do not affect those below the 90th percentile of the income distribution. However, Burkhauser et al. (2009) show that 90/10 trends measured using public use CPS data are affected by top-coding. The reason is that top-coding occurs for each source of income in the CPS. Any person who lives in a household whose measured income is below the 90th percentile but with one source of income top coded could impact the true 90th percentile value. Because Burkhauser et al. (2009) have access to the internal CPS values, they are able to show that such people exist and that top-coding is a problem that affects 90/10 income ratios in the public use CPS. Once individual income components are consistently top-coded, the adjusted 90/10 ratios are found to rise more moderately than when using the uncorrected public use CPS data. Even more importantly, once Burkhauser et al. (2009) correct for this problem, they show that the upward trends in their corrected 90/10 before tax income ratios from 1975 to 2004 are much higher than trends in their Gini values of before tax income inequality that are also controlled for censoring over this period. Thus, researchers who depend on 90/10 ratios to characterize changes in overall inequality over time will overstate the increases captured by measures that consider the broader distribution like the Gini index.

INCOME AND LABOR EARNINGS MOBILITY

Social policy in every country aims at providing a more equal set of opportunities to its citizens, if not a more equal set of outcomes. These social policies are intended to increase both current opportunities and broaden the path to future ones. Hence we now turn to cross-national comparisons of mobility.

One of the basic measures used to assess the degree of mobility of individuals is the transition from one position to another in the distribution over time. Often these types of transitions are computed by simply calculating the quartile or quintile of the income distribution for a person at one time and seeing where they are later. The transition probabilities associated with the probability a person starts at one location and remains there many years later are collectively seen as an indicator of the degree of permanent inequality as it is a measure of social immobility.

One concern in conducting studies of movement of individuals through the income distribution over time is the number of years used in the estimations. If two years of adjoining data are used in the estimations, then the transitions observed might be influenced by temporary, random economic shocks to individual earnings or income that may dissipate over time. Macroeconomic events often influence individual labor earnings and household incomes but they dissipate over time. But by following individuals for many years, the influence of these shocks is reduced. In other words, measures of the extent of permanent inequality in the sense of a person being stuck at one point in the distribution are likely to be both smaller and potentially quite different depending on the time frame one uses in the analysis.

Few countries have the long panels necessary to track the movement of individuals across the labor earnings or income distribution. The earliest and best known studies of such movements focus on Germany and the United States. Panel data sets for other countries are beginning to reach a point of maturity as well, and this literature is rapidly expanding.

As we have seen, Germany has a much lower level of inequality than the United States based on cross-sectional measures. A related question is whether that inequality is permanent or if people in the two countries have equal chances of mobility through the distribution. This concept of mobility is referred to as intragenerational mobility.

The first three studies to consider this issue were: Burkhauser and Poupore (1997) and Burkhauser et al. (1997a, b). Each of these studies finds that although cross-sectional inequality of labor earnings is lower in Germany, rates of intragenerational mobility are similar.

Labor Earnings Mobility

Table 12-3 contains transition probabilities for the labor earnings of men and women aged 25 to 55 years calculated using Panel Study of Income Dynamics (PSID) data for the United States and the Socio-Economic Panel (SOEP) for Germany for the years from 1983 to 1988 (Burkhauser et al. 1997a: Table 6). All sources of labor earnings—wages and salaries as well as self-employment—and all transitions within the period examined are included in the analysis. The columns show the different number of years used to calculate the transitions across labor earnings quintiles, and the rows contain probabilities that individuals with labor earnings in that quintile remain there. Results of tests for differences in the probability of remaining in the same quintile in each country are indicated by asterisks.

In the first column, where comparisons are made across adjacent years, one can see that in both countries, there are higher chances of remaining in either the top or bottom quintile than in one of the middle three categories. There is also a somewhat higher probability of remaining in the highest or 5th quintile from one period to the next in both countries.

As the transitions are calculated across increasingly large spans of time, the probability of remaining in a specific quintile drops markedly. The probability of remaining in a specific quintile if the transition is calculated over two adjacent years versus five yields very different results regarding the degree to which individuals have static labor earnings. For example, the probability of an individual remaining in the lowest or 1st quintile of the distribution of labor

Table 12-3: Quintile-Specific Yearly Labor Earnings Immobility in the United States and Germany[a,b]

Initial Quintile	Transition Period				
	$t + 1$	$t + 2$	$t + 3$	$t + 4$	$t + 5$
Quintile 1					
United States	75.0[c]	66.4[c]	61.0[d]	58.2	55.4
Germany	78.8	70.2	64.6	59.2	52.6
Quintile 2					
United States	60.9	52.5[d]	47.9	45.4	41.4
Germany	62.9	56.1	50.2	46.9	44.2
Quintile 3					
United States	61.1	53.0[d]	46.6	43.3	39.4
Germany	62.0	56.0	49.1	45.0	41.0
Quintile 4					
United States	65.6	60.2	54.6	51.2	49.0
Germany	67.2	62.2	56.8	53.6	49.8
Quintile 5					
United States	83.9	81.6	79.6	78.2	75.6[d]
Germany	84.7	82.8	81.5	80.6	81.7

Notes:
[a] Each entry shows the number of individuals not making a transition as a fraction of those in the quintile for that row.
[b] Data are from the 1989 Response–Nonresponse File of the Panel Study of Income Dynamics and the 1993 Syracuse University English Language Public-Use file of the German Socio-Economic Panel.
[c] Indicates that the U.S. and German rates are significantly different at the 1% level.
[d] Indicates that the U.S. and German rates are significantly different at the 5% level.
[e] Indicates that the U.S. and German rates are significantly different at the 10% level.
Source: Burkhauser et al. (1997a, Table 6).

earnings is 78.8% in Germany over a two-year span versus 52.6% over five years. This is a decrease in the chance of remaining at one position in the distribution of approximately one-third. Results with this pattern and the same order of magnitude are found for both the United States and Germany throughout the table. These decreases in the probability of remaining in the same quintile of the earnings distribution as time passes are associated with the idea that long-term measures of the extent of permanent inequality are likely to be different, at least in magnitude, once the influence of temporary events has passed.

The most important result from Table 12-3 is the remarkable degree of similarity in the persistence of labor earnings across the two countries. There are 25 paired estimates of probabilities of remaining in the same state from one point in time to another contained in the table. Only five of the paired probabilities can be said to be significantly different from each other using formal tests.

The information in Table 12-3 only considers the probability of remaining in the same quintile of the labor earnings distribution over time. While this information

Table 12-4: Average Quintile-to-Quintile Yearly Labor Earnings Mobility: United States and Germany[a,b]

Change in Quintile (Percent)	Transition Period				
	$t + 1$	$t + 2$	$t + 3$	$t + 4$	$t + 5$
Down 4					
United States	1.5	1.5	1.3	2.2	2.8
Germany	1.4	2.8	2.8	3.2	3.9
Down 3					
United States	1.2[c]	2.4	3.3	4.2	4.5
Germany	2.0	3.0	2.8	5.5	5.8
Down 2					
United States	3.7	5.5	6.5	7.4	8.1
Germany	4.3	5.4	6.6	5.8	7.6
Down 1					
United States	16.4[d]	18.3[d]	20.1	21.9	23.8
Germany	14.3	16.3	18.8	19.3	19.1
No Mobility					
United States	67.6[e]	61.4[e]	56.9[c]	52.4[d]	50.4
Germany	69.3	64.1	59.6	57.2	53.4
Up 1					
United States	16.7[e]	18.8[d]	19.9[e]	20.2[c]	18.2
Germany	15.1	16.0	17.1	16.9	20.6
Up 2					
United States	3.8	5.4	7.0	9.2	9.3
Germany	4.2	4.9	6.3	8.3	7.8
Up 3					
United States	1.4	2.1[d]	2.7	3.7	6.5[c]
Germany	2.1	4.0	3.9	5.1	3.8
Up 4					
United States	0.7	1.6	1.9[c]	2.0	3.4
Germany	0.7	2.4	3.8	2.7	4.8

Notes:
[a] Each entry shows the number of individuals not making a transition as a fraction of those in the quintile for that row.
[b] Data are from the 1989 Response–Nonresponse File of the Panel Study of Income Dynamics and the 1993 Syracuse University English Language Public-Use file of the German Socio-Economic Panel.
[c] Indicates that the U.S. and German rates are significantly different at the 10% level.
[d] Indicates that the U.S. and German rates are significantly different at the 1% level.
[e] Indicates that the U.S. and German rates are significantly different at the 5% level.
Source: Burkhauser et al. (1997a, Table 5).

on the extent of permanent inequality is interesting, it does not show the transitions of individuals to other quintiles. Table 12-4 contains summary information on transition probabilities for the United States and Germany in the same time period. These results are drawn from Burkhauser et al. (1997a: Table 5).

In Table 12-4, transitions of moving across states are summed in order to present the information in a consolidated form. For example, the entries in the row of Table 12-4 labeled "no mobility" are the averaged transition rates from each of the columns of Table 12-3. Again, the columns refer to the gap in the years used to calculate the transitions and formal tests are conducted of the differences in these aggregated probabilities.

The same pattern observed in Table 12-3 with respect to lack of mobility is observed in Table 12-4 although it is less pronounced due to the averaging across categories. Now, the probability of being in the same quintile in 1 year relative to the next is 69.3% in Germany and 67.6% in the United States. When the transitions are calculated using a gap of five years, the respective rates of immobility are 50.4% and 53.4%. Thus, as more years are used to make the calculations, the rates fall by 15% to 20%.

Looking at transitions either up or down in quintile, the patterns are fairly symmetric. For example, if a person were in a particular quintile of labor earnings in 1 year in the United States, they would have a 16.7% chance of moving up and a 16.4% chance of moving down by one quintile. In Germany, the comparable rates of transition are 15.1 and 14.3. In both countries, as transitions of more than one quintile are considered, the chances of experiencing that large a change in labor earnings declines and the pattern of reductions in the probability for larger changes appears symmetric whether a move up or down is being considered.

It should also be pointed out that the rates of transition to other states are complements to the probability of remaining in the state. So, as the chance of remaining in one earnings quintile decreases over time, this implies the chance of moving should increase as time passes. This pattern can also be seen in Table 12-4. For example, the chance of moving up four quintiles in labor earnings from 1 year to the next is 0.7 in both Germany and the United States. The chance of moving up four quintiles in five years is 3.4% in the United States and 4.8% in Germany. Thus, the odds of making any transition increase over time.

Again, one of the primary purposes in constructing a table containing respective transition probabilities is to see if mobility differs across the countries. Table 12-4 contains 45 pairs of transition rates, either to remain in the same quintile or to move. Of these, 14 are significantly different. If one examines the significantly different probabilities in relation to each other, it appears that there is a greater likelihood for individuals to move either up or down by one quintile in the earnings distribution in the United States and that this is associated with slightly less permanent immobility throughout the distribution of labor earnings in the United States.

Individual After Tax Income Mobility

The literature, which uses summary measures of income inequality, has shown that government transfers generally reduce the level of after tax household-size adjusted income inequality. We can also calculate transition probabilities for this measure as well. Table 12-5 contains calculations for the same years

Table 12-5: After-Tax Income Mobility, United States and Germany, Individuals Aged 25 to 55[a] (percent)

Change in quintile	Transition period				
	t+1	t+2	t+3	t+4	t+5
Down 4					
United States	0.8[b]	1.2[b]	1.4[b]	1.8[b]	1.4[b]
Germany	1.7	3.0	3.5	5.1	7.1
Down 3					
United States	2.1	3.9[c]	5.1	6.6[d]	7.0[c]
Germany	2.5	3.2	4.7	5.3	5.4
Down 2					
United States	4.2[c]	5.8[d]	7.3[c]	8.2	9.6[c]
Germany	4.7	7.4	8.1	8.8	8.0
Down 1					
United States	13.6[b]	15.0[b]	15.9[b]	15.7[b]	15.5[b]
Germany	18.7	19.3	19.7	19.5	21.4
No Mobility					
United States	68.1[b]	60.0[b]	53.7[b]	49.0[b]	44.7[b]
Germany	59.8	52.9	48.3	45.3	41.4
Up 1					
United States	17.3[b]	20.8[b]	23.2[b]	25.1	26.5[d]
Germany	21.3	23.2	25.3	25.6	29.0
Up 2					
United States	4.3[b]	7.2[b]	9.5[c]	11.9[d]	14.5
Germany	5.0	8.7	10.4	13.5	13.1
Up 3					
United States	2.3	3.4[c]	4.7[c]	5.9[b]	6.7[d]
Germany	2.0	2.8	3.9	4.2	4.5
Up 4					
United States	0.5[b]	1.0[d]	1.3	1.4	1.5
Germany	1.1	1.8	1.6	2.1	2.7

Notes:
[a] Each entry shows the number of individuals making the transition as a fraction of those eligible to make the transition (see: Burkhauser et al., 1997b, p. 128). Column totals will not sum to 1 as a result.
[b] Indicates that the U.S. and German rates are significantly different at the 1% level.
[c] Indicates that the U.S. and German rates are significantly different at the 10% level.
[d] Indicates that the U.S. and German rates are significantly different at the 5% level.
Source: Reprinted with permission from Cambridge University Press from Burkhauser, Holtz-Eakin and Rhody (1997b, Table 6.5).

for individuals aged 25–55 (taken from Burkhauser et al. 1997b: Table 6-5). Considering the impact of taxation, transfers, and household composition alters the basic perception of similarity across Germany and the United States one obtains in looking at labor earnings.

The rate of immobility is now significantly higher in the United States than Germany regardless of the number of time periods used in the calculations.

The probability of being in the same quintile of the distribution from 1 year to the next is 68.1% in the United States versus 59.8% in Germany. If five years are allowed to elapse before calculating the rate of immobility, an individual in the United States has a 44.7% chance of remaining in the same quintile versus 41.4% in Germany. In this table, we again observe the reduction in the rates of immobility over time in each country.

Corresponding to its higher rate of immobility, an individual has significantly less of a chance of moving up or down through the household size-adjusted after tax income distribution in the United States than in Germany. Again, there are 45 pairs of transitions examined in Table 12-5. The transition probabilities are significantly different from each other in 36 of the cases examined.

The results presented here are drawn from research published in the 1990s. Other researchers have subsequently updated and extended the analyses we have described. Gottschalk and Spolaore (2002) reconsider the comparison between Germany and the United States and draw similar conclusions. Ayala and Sastre (2002) use the European Community Household Panel (ECHP) along with the PSID to make similar comparisons between the United States, the United Kingdom, Germany, France, Italy, and Spain. In their work, the United States is within the bounds of the variation observed in the European countries. France is consistently found to have the least intragenerational mobility and Italy the most.

In studies of intragenerational after tax income mobility, it does not appear that cross-sectional inequality is strictly related to intragenerational mobility. Also, the extent of measured mobility depends in an important way on the time period considered. Government tax and transfers not only reduce cross-sectional inequality, they also significantly influence rates of intragenerational mobility.

AFTER TAX INCOME INEQUALITY WITHIN THE EUROPEAN UNION AS A WHOLE

While we have not provided a complete accounting of all the possible dimensions of inequality between the United States and EU countries, our findings are consistent with Alber (2006)'s view that the United States lies within the bounds of social outcomes found among EU countries.

However, from a U.S. perspective, a striking dissimilarity between individual EU countries and the United States is the very large differences in their geographic sizes and populations. Without even examining the data, one would think that it should be easier in a country like Sweden, with a population approximately 1% that of the United States, to achieve more uniform outcomes. One might also make the same observation about Portugal. Yet we know that average incomes are much lower in Southern Europe than in the Continental and Scandinavian countries. Any measure of inequality calculated using data from both Portugal and Sweden would clearly be higher than for either country considered alone. Hence it is likely that measured after tax income inequality in the EU as a whole would rise significantly if all the EU countries were treated as one unified collective that was much more similar to the United States in both size and heterogeneity of geography and population. Cross-country differences among EU members would have to be included in the calculations rather than comparisons simply being made between the larger and more heterogeneous population in the United States and these smaller and more homogeneous individual country populations.

While we have not examined this issue directly, others have. Table 12-6 is based on the work of Beblo and Knaus (2001, Table 1). They used the 1995 wave of the European Community Household Panel to tabulate the household size-adjusted after tax income distribution for the entire combined populations of the ten founding EU countries and the percentage of each decile of the distribution originating from each member country.

The bottom row of Table 12-6 shows the percentage distribution of the total population from each country. The population of Germany is 28.9% of the total while Portugal and Belgium contribute 3.5% and 3.6%, respectively. Across the other rows, one can see the proportion of individuals in each decile that come from each country. For example, although the population of Spain is only 13.9% of the total, 26% of all individuals in the lowest decile of income live there. Likewise, 10.6% of those in the lowest decile come from Portugal (with 3.5% of total population). In the highest decile of income, 42% live in Germany (population 28.9%) and 9.3% live in Italy (population 20.1%). Accounting for such cross-country differences would presumably increase measured inequality in the entire EU.

Beblo and Knaus (2001) then show that this is the case by calculating an inequality measure for each of the originating EU countries as well as for the group as a whole. They report the share of inequality originating from each country, from the additional component of cross-country inequality, and for the composite group. They find that there is a wide range of inequality across countries, with Portugal (highest inequality) having measured inequality 75% larger than the Netherlands (least inequality). The contribution of each country to the total, however, depends on the weight assigned to it in the calculation. So, although Portugal's internal level of inequality is quite high, its contribution to the whole is small because of its relatively small share of population and income. Similarly, although inequality within Germany is relatively small, it contributes a large share to total European inequality due to its large share of population and total income. The variation across countries contributes an additional 9.3% to total inequality. While an additional 9.3% contribution to total inequality probably does not fundamentally alter what we already know about comparative inequality in these originating countries, it is likely that the

Table 12-6: Distribution in Euroland in 1995 by Income Decile

Income Decile	Germany	Netherlands	Belgium	Luxembourg	France	Ireland	Italy	Spain	Portugal	Austria	EURO LAND
	Population Share (%)										
1	20.1	3.2	2.4	0.04	8.6	1.2	26.2	26.0	10.6	1.7	100
2	13.2	2.2	2.3	0.02	14.6	2.6	31.7	25.4	6.6	1.6	100
3	20.7	5.1	2.5	0.02	18.2	1.6	25.6	19.4	5.0	2.0	100
4	21.8	7.5	3.3	0.04	20.8	1.1	24.4	15.2	3.6	2.5	100
5	27.9	7.4	3.3	0.05	23.0	1.1	19.4	13.0	2.5	2.4	100
6	33.6	6.4	3.5	0.09	21.8	0.9	18.7	10.3	1.7	3.1	100
7	33.8	6.1	4.3	0.10	22.2	1.1	18.2	9.3	1.4	3.7	100
8	37.5	6.0	4.7	0.20	22.9	0.9	15.2	7.9	1.4	3.4	100
9	38.0	5.7	5.4	0.25	25.5	1.2	12.8	6.0	1.2	4.1	100
10	42.0	4.9	4.7	0.60	26.2	1.2	9.3	6.2	1.4	3.7	100
Mean	28.9	5.4	3.6	0.14	20.4	1.3	20.1	13.9	3.5	2.8	100

Note: Percentages may not sum up to 100 due to rounding.
Source: Beblo and Knaus (2001, Table 1).

importance of across-country variation in total inequality is much greater once the entire membership of the EU is taken into account.

Most recently, Brandolini (2007) has looked at this issue using data from the ECHP and LIS. The study compares EU-wide after tax income distribution and poverty rates in 2000 for the EU-15 and the EU-25 with after tax income distribution and poverty rates in the United States. Brandolini (2007) shows, not surprisingly, that after tax income inequality (Gini values of household size-adjusted after tax income estimated in Euros) within the EU-25, with its greater heterogeneity of populations, is substantially greater (0.378) than is the case for the EU-15 (0.294). When these Gini values are compared with similarly constructed U.S. Gini values estimated in dollars, he finds inequality in the United States (0.369) is within these two values. However, when purchasing parity across the EU countries is considered in the calculations, after tax income inequality in the EU-15 (0.313) falls as does EU-25 inequality (0.328). Adjustments for the cost of living in different regions of the United States have a minor impact on the estimates and adjusting for this, its inequality values remain approximately the same (0.368).

DISCUSSION

Our findings are consistent with Alber's (2006) contention that heterogeneity of social institutions among EU countries and in the economic well-being of their populations are broad enough that along most dimensions, economic outcomes in the United States lie well within the extremes.

We primarily focus on events in three countries—the United States, Great Britain, and Germany. The western states of Germany, since the aftermath of World War II, have had lower levels of after tax income inequality than either the United States or Great Britain. That was especially the case in the 1980s when its social policies generated substantial economic growth with no increase in after tax income inequality at a time when it increased substantially in both the United States and Great Britain. However, in the last decade of the twentieth Century, while economic growth continued in all three countries, after tax inequality fell in both Great Britain and in the United States while it increased in reunited Germany. This occurred despite massive redistribution from the western to the eastern states of Germany during this period. Like the United States and Great Britain in the 1980s, while the great majority of Germany's declining middle mass became unequally richer, a small share became poorer. Furthermore, even in the 1980s, when cross-sectional measures of inequality were substantially higher in the United States than in Germany, there was surprisingly little difference in their mobility rates across the income distribution.

Our comparisons suggest that rather than the experience of EU countries being fundamentally different from those of the United States, it may be that all our countries are struggling to adapt our social policies to changes caused by the evolving nature of our ethnic and cultural populations and by our attempts to increase economic growth in an ever-more competitive world economy. In setting its social policies for a confederation of thirteen states that first decided to formally unite in 1789 and in adapting those social policies over the subsequent centuries as it both expanded its geographical borders to fifty states and opened each of them to more ethnically and culturally diverse populations, the United States has struggled to establish a set of principles that would ensure social cohesion. Today, the United States continues to be much larger and more heterogeneous geographically, ethnically, and culturally than any single country in the EU. But it is much closer in size, geography, ethnicity and culture to the entire population of the EU-25. Today the citizens of the EU-25, considered as a part of a single supranational entity, are nearly as unequally distributed across the after tax income distribution as are citizens of the United States, but their mean real after tax income is substantially less.

This is the reality that confronts EU policymakers as they seek a set of social policies, which will move a still relatively loose confederation of nation states toward a united Europe. In doing so, member states of the EU will be forced to confront the broader regional, ethnic, and cultural differences that have shaped U.S. social policies in our efforts to both reduce inequality and raise living standards for our entire population.

Because cultures vary so significantly in the United States across states and regions, our collective national policies have tolerated greater differences than is the case in the more homogeneous societies of specific European countries. Our national policy is one that specifically allows for deviations at the state and local level. Moreover, national policies that redistribute resources across regions and states required collective approval. No doubt, this has also limited the extent of that redistribution. Nonetheless, to accommodate the broad regional and national differences that exist across the EU, it appears likely that policy formation will evolve in a manner that is bounded by similar considerations. In the context of income inequality, one challenge to a united EU is convincing citizens of its member states that reduction of inequality in the united EU that requires redistribution across national boundaries is in their collective interest. Similarly, it is also likely that the extent of generosity in the approval of redistributions across borders will be tempered to some degree by the interests of the member states just as it has been in the United States.

It remains to be seen just how much social policies created within the various countries of Europe will be collectively adopted in the future by the EU-25. But given the more heterogeneous EU-25 population over which they will govern, we expect these social policies to evolve more toward those of the United States than to the current policies of the more homogeneous individual EU countries.

That is, if the EU is ever going to be a more uniform "land of opportunity" for the citizens of all of its member states, where terms like social cohesion and solidarity do not stop at each country's border but encompass all EU citizens, we expect the common denominator of EU-wide social institutions will become more like those in the United States.

REFERENCES

Alber, Jens (2006) The European Social Model and the United States, *European Union Politics*, 7(3): 393–419.

Ayala, Luis and Sastre, Mercedes (2002) Europe vs. The United States: Is There a Trade-off between Mobility and Inequality? European Economy Group, Working Paper 19.

Bach, Stefan, Corneo, Giacomo, and Steiner, Victor (2007) From Top to Bottom: The Entire Distribution of Market Income in Germany, 1991–2001, DIW Discussion Paper No. 683, Berlin.

Beblo, Miriam and Knaus, Thomas (2001) Measuring Income Inequality in Euroland, *The Review of Income and Wealth*, 47(3): 301–320.

Brandolini, Andrea (2007) Measurement of Income Distribution in Supranational Entities: The Case of the European Union, in Stephen Jenkins and John Micklewright (eds) *Inequality and Poverty Re-Examined*, Oxford: Oxford University Press, pp. 62–83.

Brandolini, Andrea and Smeeding, Timothy M. (2008) Inequality (International Evidence) in Steven N. Durlauf and Lawrence E. Blume (eds.) *The New Palgrave Dictionary of Economics. Second Edition*, Palgrave Macmillan. The New Palgrave Dictionary of Economics Online. Palgrave Macmillan. Retrievd April 29, 2009, from http://www.dictionaryofeconomics.com/article?id=pde2008_I000273

Burkhauser, Richard V. and Poupore, John G. (1997) A Cross-National Comparison of Permanent Inequality in the United States and Germany, *Review of Economics and Statistics*, 79(1): 10–17.

Burkhauser, Richard V., Holtz-Eakin, Douglas and Rhody, Stephen (1997a) Labor Earnings Mobility and Inequality in the United States and Germany during the 1980s, *International Economic Review*, 38(4): 775–794.

Burkhauser, Richard V., Holtz-Eakin, Douglas, and Rhody, Stephen (1997b) Mobility and Inequality in the 1980s: A Cross-National Comparison of the United States and Germany, in Stephen Jenkins, Arie Kapteyn and Bernard van Praag (eds) *The Distribution of Welfare and Household Production: International Perspectives*, Cambridge, MA: Cambridge University Press, pp. 111–175.

Burkhauser, Richard V., Crews, Amy D., Daly, Mary C. and Jenkins, Stephen P. (1999) Testing the Significance of Income Distribution Changes Over the 1980s Business Cycle: A Cross-National Comparison, *Journal of Applied Econometrics*, 14(3): 253–272.

Burkhauser, Richard V., Butler, J.S., Feng, Shuaizhang and Houtenville, Andrew J. (2004a) Long Term Trends in Earnings Inequality: What CPS Can Tell Us, *Economic Letters*, 82(2): 295–299.

Burkhauser, Richard V., Couch, Kenneth, Houtenville, Andrew J. and Rovba, Ludmila (2004b) Income Inequality in the 1990s: Re-Forging a Lost Relationship? *Journal of Income Distribution*, 12(3–4): 8–35.

Burkhauser, Richard V., Feng, Shuaizhang and Jenkins, Stephen P. (2009) Using the P90/P10 Ratio to Measure Inequality Trends with the Current Population Survey: A View from Inside the Census Bureau Vaults, *The Review of Income and Wealth*, 55 (1): 166–185.

Burkhauser, Richard V., Oshio, Takashi and Rovba, Ludmila (2008a) How the Distribution of After-Tax Income Changed Over the 1990s Business Cycle: A Comparison of the United States, Great Britain, Germany and Japan, *Journal of Income Distribution*, 17(1): 82–87.

Burkhauser, Richard V., Feng, Shuaizhang, Jenkins, Stephen P., and Larrimore, Jeff (2008b) Trends in United States Income Inequality Using the International March Current Population Survey: The Importance of Controlling for Censoring, NBER Working Paper w14247.

Cato Unbounded (February 2007). Online. Available from http://www.cato-unbound.org/archives/february-2007/ (accessed 17 June 2008).

Danziger, Sheldon and Gottschalk, Peter (1993) *Uneven Tides: Rising Inequality in America*, New York: Russell Sage Foundation.

Danziger, Sheldon and Gottschalk, Peter (1995) *America Unequal*, Cambridge MA: Harvard University Press and New York: Russell Sage Foundation.

DeNavas-Walt, Carmen, Proctor, Bernadette D., and Lee, Cheryl Hill (2007) *Income, Poverty, and Health Insurance Coverage in the United States: 2006*, Series P-60, No. 231, Washington, DC: U.S. GPO.

Feng, Shuaizhang, Burkhauser, Richard V., and Butler, J.S. (2006) Levels and Long-Term Trends in Earnings Inequality: Overcoming Current Population Survey Censoring Problems Using the GB2 Distribution, *Journal of Business and Economic Statistics*, 24(1): 57–62.

Goodin, Robert E., Headey, Bruce, Muffels, Rudd, and Dirven, Henk-Jan (1999) *The Real World of Welfare Capitalism*, Cambridge: Cambridge University Press.

Gottschalk, Peter and Danziger, Sheldon (2005) Inequality of Wage Rates, Earnings, and Family Income in the United States, 1975–2002, *Review of Income and Wealth*, 51(2): 231–254.

Gottschalk, Peter and Smeeding, Timothy M. (1997) Cross-National Comparisons of Earnings and Income Inequality, *Journal of Economic Literature*, 35(2): 633–687.

Gottschalk, Peter and Spolaore, Enricco (2002) On the Evaluation of Economic Mobility, *Review of Economic Studies*, 69(1): 191–208.

Hauser, Richard and Becker, Irene (1993) The Development of the Income Distribution in the Federal Republic or Germany During the Seventies and Eighties, Cross-National Studies in Aging Program Project Paper No. 26,

All-University Gerontology Center, The Maxwell School, Syracuse University (December).

Jones, Arthur F. Jr. and Weinberg, Daniel (2000) The Changing Shape of the Nation's Income Distribution, Current Population Reports, U.S. Census Bureau (June).

Larrimore, Jeff, Burkhauser, Richard V., Feng, Shuaizhang, and Zayatz, Laura (2008) Consistent Cell Means for Topcoded Incomes in the Public Use March CPS (1976–2007), *Journal of Economic and Social Measurement*, 33 (2-): 89–128.

Levy, Frank and Murnane, Richard J. (1992) U.S. Earning Levels and Earnings Inequality: A Review of Recent Trends and Proposed Explanations, *Journal of Economic Literature*, 30, 3: 1333–1381.

Pen, Jan (1971) *Income Distribution,* New York: Praeger Publications.

Piketty, Thomas and Suez, Emmanuel (2003) Income Inequality in the United States, 1913–1998, *Quarterly Journal of Economics*, 118(1): 1–39.

Reynolds, Alan (2006) *Income and Wealth*, Westport, CN: Greenwood Press.

Saposnik, Rubin (1983) On Evaluating Income Distributions: Rank Dominance, the Suppes-Sen Grading Principle of Justice and Pareto Optimality, *Public Choice*, 40: 329–336.

SECTION VII

EDUCATIONAL OPPORTUNITY

13

EDUCATION IN EUROPE AND THE LISBON BENCHMARKS

JUTTA ALLMENDINGER, CHRISTIAN EBNER, AND RITA NIKOLAI

In recent years, the Organization for Economic Cooperation and Development (OECD) has moved educational policies to the top of its agenda. One reason for this intensifying commitment lies in the fact that education is increasingly perceived as key to full employment in the knowledge economy. Without the OECD's active stance, many recent developments would not have been achievable. Who would have thought a decade ago that there could be an international large-scale study on the measurement of students' cognitive competencies? After all, such comparative research easily translates into naming and shaming practices that national policy makers usually seek to avoid. Based on hard indicators, it discloses the potential of their young people, reveals the efficiency of their educational systems, ascertains the scope of equal opportunity they provide, and outlines the sustainability of the educational systems, thus putting pressure on national policy makers to reflect upon the virtues of their policies.

Traditional comparisons of the percentages of young people who obtain various grade levels used to be countered by the assertion that educational systems differ so profoundly that such percentages say virtually nothing about the actual quality of education obtained at a certain level. Thanks to the OECD initiatives, this argument has become much more difficult to defend today. And if it was once possible to insinuate that children from a low educational background simply lack the ability to attend upper-secondary schools, it has now become evident that other factors account for the social inequality of educational success: lack of support and lack of appropriate educational concepts and structures.

In its efforts to move education to the top of the policy agenda, the OECD has not been alone. The European Union (EU) has pursued similar objectives since the 1990s (Martens and Balzer 2007; Martens et al. 2007; Martens and Wolf 2006). In the course of the so-called Lisbon process following the 2000 European Council meeting in the Portuguese capital, the EU became the prime actor in the process of developing a European educational space. Given the EU's lack of legal jurisdiction in the field, the success of its agenda setting in educational policy came rather unexpected.[1] Unlike economic, monetary, or competition policy, educational policy is not a sphere in which the EU has the power to issue directives. The only means at its disposal are those of soft law fostering European-level cooperation. The relevant instruments include the European Social Fund, educational exchange programs such as *Socrates* and *Leonardo da Vinci*, legal instruments such as recommendations and communications, and organs such as the European Center for the Development of Vocational Education (CEDEFOP) and the Information Network on Education in Europe (EURYDICE). The EU also has the Open Method of Coordination (OMC),[2] a legal tool with which it can affect the policies of the member states. In the course of the Lisbon process, the European Commission issued quantified policy objectives for its member states, but left the specific ways in which these would be achieved in the national competence of its members.

This chapter discusses how important the EU's involvement in education has been. We outline Europe's demographic development, the change in labor markets and human resources. The interaction of these three areas of society points to an enormous need for action. We then discuss how to gauge the level of education in a population and what absolute and relative measures of educational achievement could look like. Then we examine the educational policy objectives formulated by the EU and describe to what extent the European countries have already accomplished them. Are there countries that already meet all of the objectives, and are there some which still fail to meet any of them? Are results for European countries similar, suggesting a joint social model in terms of educational policy? The chapter ends discussing two fundamental questions: First, how coherent are the individual goal dimensions of the Lisbon strategy and what can we learn from the degree of their correlation for future empirical research on education? Second, what do the indicators allow us to say about issues of equal opportunity and social exclusion in European countries and how much diversity is there within Europe in this respect? We conclude with a summary illustrating the analytical potential of the indicators and showing that purportedly simple measures have more to them than first meets the eye.

DEMOGRAPHY, CHANGING LABOR MARKETS, AND EDUCATIONAL PERFORMANCE

The world is currently inhabited by more than 6 billion people: 4 billion in Asia, 1 billion in Africa, 700 million in Europe, 600 million in Latin America, and 300 million in North America. World population will reach 9 billion in 2050 (United Nations 2007). This high population growth is not evenly distributed across the individual continents. It is disproportionately great in Asia and Africa, whereas a population decrease is in store for many European countries. This trend is associated with differences between the continents in terms of the population's median age. Europe currently has the population with the world's highest median age, and in several European countries this median age is expected to climb above 50 years by 2050. All available projections indicate that a smaller and older Europe is going to have severe problems supplying the labor force that its markets require.

Two strands of action come to mind. An obvious one is to open European borders, the consequence being a clear rise in the percentages of non-Europeans in the labor force. Europe is not preparing itself for that option. Since integration policy is deficient in almost all European countries, a new kind of educational policy is necessary, an active one that enlarges the number of persons with high-quality education, basic training, and continuous training. The Europe of tomorrow can no longer afford to turn its back on 20% of the upcoming generation and leave it underskilled and underqualified (OECD 2007). In a population that is shrinking in absolute terms, the small percentage of highly skilled Europeans will encompass so few people that they will not be able to function as the employment engine that the continent needs. This implies that Europe cannot continue to do without women, or with senior citizens who go on early retirement, but must pursue activation policies. In Germany, for instance, the age-limit for pensions has recently been lifted to 67 years, but in 2004 just 5% of the 64-year-old men were still gainfully employed. The corresponding figure for women in western Germany was 3%; in eastern Germany, only 1% (Hirschenauer 2007).

Population levels and developments differ widely within Europe (see Figure 13-1). Germany, France, the United Kingdom, Italy, Spain, and Poland are the most populous European countries. Hence their demographic development and educational structures have a particularly heavy impact on the future of Europe. But Germany, Italy, and Poland are also the countries experiencing particularly sharp population declines, which are not being offset by more positive developments in France and the United Kingdom.

Figure 13-1: Population of the European Union member states, 2005 and 2050

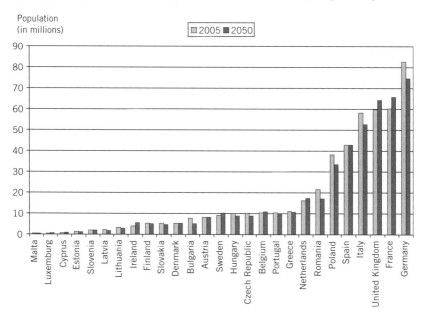

Source: Retrieved February 14, 2008, from EUROSTAT Online Database.

In addition to demographic changes, there are changing demands on jobs in tomorrow's labor markets. Recent developments were marked by a twofold structural change. First, unlike the burgeoning service (tertiary) sector, the industrial sector has lost many jobs since the early 1990s. Second, knowledge- and research-intensive economic activities have been spreading in both sectors at the expense of branches that are less dependent on the use of high-skilled labor and modern production techniques. The knowledge-intensive spheres of the economy have recently been the only ones with an increasing demand for labor (see Figure 13-2). The greatest losses have occurred in industry, especially where it is not research-intensive (Belitz et al. 2008).

For the less qualified working population, technological progress comes at the expense of employment opportunities. Expansion of the service sector also feeds the need for relatively qualified personnel. Corporate services—research and development, market and opinion research, and hardware consulting—will gain a great deal in importance (Belitz et al. 2008). There are no indications that this trend will reverse. In other words, while demographic change leads to an absolute scarcity of higher qualified personnel, changes in the economy entail a growing demand for highly skilled labor, and the European economy is likely to meet its limits of growth.

The educational policies of European countries have responded differently to these new challenges. First, there has been a general pattern of expansion.

Figure 13-2: Labor deployment (hours worked), by economic area in selected countries and regions, 1995–2005 (index 1995 = 100)

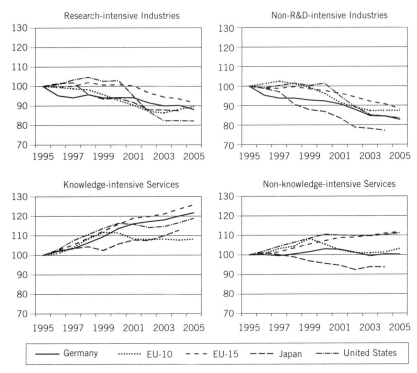

Source: EUKLEMS data base, calculations and estimates in Wirtschaftsstrukturen und Produktivität im internationalen Vergleich. Studien zum deutschen Innovationssystem [International comparison of economic structures and productivity: Studies on the German system of innovation] (p. 9), by H. Belitz et al. 2008 (No. 6–2008), Berlin and Hanover: NIW and DIW.

We see "a universal development in Western Europe since the Second World War: more years in education, the opening of the upper secondary educational institutions for larger parts of the population and, as tertiary education has lost its exclusive property, the change of elite universities into mass universities" (Müller et al. 1997: 178; our translation).[3] Second, however, the development illustrated in Figure 13-3 also reveals major differences in the starting levels and the degree of change within Europe. For example, Sweden and Ireland's 1991 levels of tertiary education among 25- to 34-year-olds exceed those achieved by Germany and Italy in 2005. Germany has achieved little recognizable progress since 1991. Whereas most other European countries continued investing heavily in educational policy and significantly lowered the percentage of persons who do not complete upper secondary school, this percentage has been rising in Germany up to 2005. Particularly high proportions of people without upper secondary schooling live in the southern European countries of Italy, Spain, and Portugal.

Figure 13-3: Educational attainment of the population aged 25–34 years, 1991 and 2005 in selected countries. Upper secondary education includes postsecondary nontertiary education

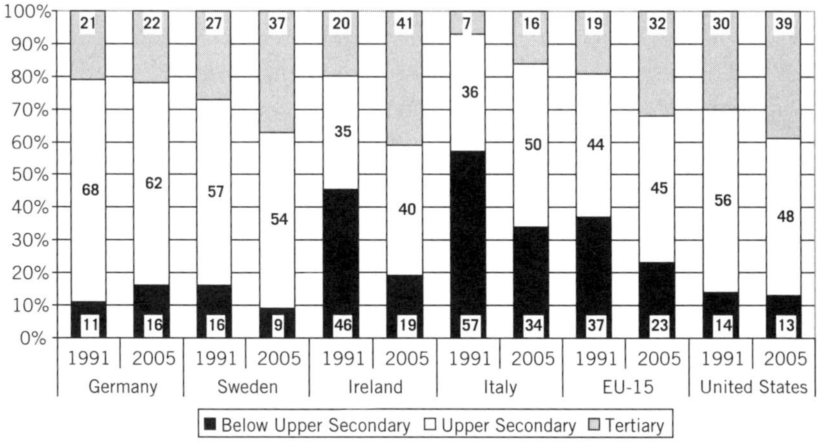

Source: Education at a Glance (2007). Paris: OECD, p. 38ff (and previous editions).

Given the major tasks ahead in education and continuous training, it is important that the EU continues to give special importance to this area. In its Lisbon resolution, the EU has formulated objectives that are intended as a "coherent long-term policy framework" (Pépin 2006: 205) "to improve the quality and effectiveness of EU education and training systems, to ensure that they are accessible to all, [and] to open up education and training to the wider world" (Commission of the European Communities 2006: 4). But what does "better" education mean in actual practice? This question is dealt with in the following section.

MEASURING EDUCATIONAL PERFORMANCE

Education has conventionally been measured by the duration of a person's school attendance or by the highest degree earned in the education or training system. New types of data have recently become available to educational research: those assessing cognitive competencies. These are gathered by a wide variety of surveys of persons at various age levels. The most well-known is surely the OECD's Programme for International Student Assessment (PISA), which measures the competencies of 15-year-old students around the world on a broad front. Whereas PISA 2000 focused on reading skills, the 2003 study centered primarily on competence in mathematics and the one in 2006 on the natural sciences.

The measurement of actual competencies has moved educational research forward, although the reporting has increased in complexity, as certificates as well as competencies are now taken into account. This has indisputably enhanced the usefulness of international comparisons, because identical tests are administered to children of the same age in the participating countries. This facilitates performance comparisons more than rates of attendance or completed grade level do. Who would have dared make any statements about whether 10 years of schooling in Germany are comparable to 10 years of schooling in the United States, Finland, or the United Kingdom before these tests were administered?

Allowing for much finer gradation measurements of competencies also improve our ability to determine an educational system's impact on the distribution of skills. The traditional use of certificates ties the measurement of educational poverty to the completion of secondary school or training and associates educational wealth with the possession of a university degree. Relative educational poverty in relation to national or international standards or the dispersion of skills was virtually impossible to capture with these traditional measures.

Measures of competence are superior in many respects. Even though international comparisons (including those in the press) frequently rely simply on national averages and concomitant rankings, the new measurement offers many more sophisticated indicators of an educational system's performance. As with any index of absolute poverty, however, the point at which one speaks of deprivation or deficiency must be established more or less arbitrarily. Students who do not achieve competence level II are now conventionally said to be absolutely poor in competence.[4] Those classified above level IV are termed absolutely competence rich. Besides these absolute measures, which apply to all countries, relative measures can be calculated as well. Thus it can be determined where a given country's lower or upper 10% lie in the distribution of competence relative to the "established" absolute level of competence richness or competence poverty. Absolute and relative values may coincide but need not have an interface, as illustrated by the case of Finland, a country with hardly any absolute educational poverty by PISA standards.

Measures of dispersion depict the degree to which competencies are distributed unevenly. At an identical mean in the competence distribution, countries may differ in the sense that one may impart similar competencies to all persons, whereas the other one may have a wide variation around the mean. The inequality of cognitive competencies is an important issue to which we will return below.

A major challenge and opportunity for comparative educational research arises from the fact that the measurement of certificates and the measurement of competencies need not converge. This means that rankings of countries may differ depending on the concrete measure we are using. Countries with a high level of poverty in terms of certificates can in fact be countries with low poverty in terms of competence levels. Before exploring this point further, we present the Lisbon objectives of the European Union in order to then use these yardsticks for a comparison of the state of education in various EU member states.[5]

THE LISBON BENCHMARKS

In March 2000, the EU heads of government agreed to make the EU the world's "most competitive and dynamic knowledge-based economy" by 2010 (Commission of the European Communities 2004: 9). The European Council's Lisbon strategy strengthens the role of general and vocational education within the agenda of economic growth and employment for the EU. For the first time, education is now considered a key factor for economic and social objectives (Pépin 2007: 121) and is one of the core areas in the European employment strategy (Bektchieva 2004: 76).[6] The aim of the guidelines is to motivate the EU member states to enlarge and optimize their investments in human capital and to modernize their general and vocational educational systems in response to the demands of a knowledge-based economy and of mounting socioeconomic and demographic challenges.

Discussing the guidelines at the Stockholm summit in February 2001, the education ministers agreed on three major objectives to achieve by 2010: to improve the quality and efficiency of EU education and training systems, to ensure their accessibility to everyone, and to open up education and training to the wider world (Commission of the European Communities 2006: 4; Dion 2005: 302). In 2002 the education ministers accepted the OMC for the implementation of the Education and Training 2010 Work Programme. This method is promoted as an essential element in the Lisbon strategy. It leaves the EU member states the freedom to decide for themselves how to reach the targets, but the improvements are inspected through the exchange of best practice and through periodic monitoring and reporting (Dion 2005: 299; Pépin 2007: 128).

The three objectives formulated at the Stockholm summit in 2001 were later linked to five benchmarks (see next paragraph) and eleven further targets (Commission of the European Communities 2007: 10)[7] associated with the "Education and Training 2010 Work Programme." The five benchmarks aim at: reducing the percentage of pupils with low reading competencies; reducing the percentage of early school leavers (18- to 24-year-olds who leave school without completing upper secondary education); raising the percentage of the 22-year-olds who have completed at least upper-secondary education; increasing the share of graduates in mathematics, science, and technology (MST); and expanding the participation of the adult working-age population in lifelong learning (Commission of the European Communities 2004: 14).[8] These European benchmarks are not considered fixed targets for individual countries but rather as "reference levels of European average performance" (Commission of the European Communities 2004: 14).[9]

The objectives established in Lisbon are clearly based on widely used yardsticks for measuring educational performance. The measures of competence (benchmark 1) go hand in hand with approaches that measure school attendance (benchmark 2), and schooling certificates (benchmark 3). In addition, indicators relating to specific subject areas are being created to measure the degree to which the educational system is oriented to challenges posed by technological change (benchmark 4). Similarly, the necessity of lifelong learning is stressed (benchmark 5). In addition to these challenges and cutting across them, rather unspecified demands for more effective, fair, and open educational systems are made.

There are many untested assumptions underlying this procedure. First, it is supposed that the individual criteria are compatible, complimentary, and uncontradictory. Accordingly, a country with few young people who have not completed upper secondary education would also have few competence-poor pupils. By the same token, there is the notion that equal opportunity is to be measured by participation rates of the total population. In other words, the higher the participation rates are in the upper-secondary and tertiary echelons of education, the greater the degree of equal opportunity is assumed to be. We will return to this point, but first we describe and comment on the state of European education as measured by these criteria.

MEETING THE LISBON BENCHMARKS

Not all European countries participated in all surveys. Some new countries entered, while others left. This implies that a comparison of means or of positions in country rank orders may be misleading as the comparison is based on varying compositions of the group of participant countries. Hence it is advisable to interpret changes within the nation-specific framework of individual countries. We proceed in this way for the five benchmarks and then offer a summary going beyond the single dimensions and across all countries.

Benchmark 1: By 2010, the percentage of low-achieving 15-year-olds in reading literacy in the European Union shall have decreased by at least 20% compared with 2000.[10]

The objective for reading competencies is modest. The Commission accepts a share of 15.5% of the population below the educational poverty line. As shown in Figure 13-4, however, most countries have a considerably higher percentage of poor readers. Worse yet, several countries have made no progress in reducing that figure over time. In PISA 2000, the share of students below proficiency level II in reading comprehension was generally 18.1% (EU-15, not including the Netherlands). In PISA 2006, it rose to 19.5%. Variation was substantial. The

Figure 13-4: Percentage of students below proficiency level II in reading comprehension (PISA 2000, 2003, and 2006).

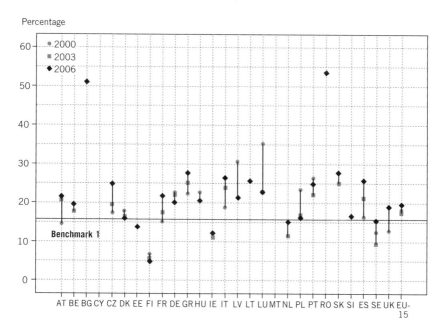

Sources: Knowledge and Skills for Life: First Results from PISA 2000, by OECD, 2001, Paris: OECD; Learning for Tomorrow's World: First results from PISA 2003, by OECD, 2004, Paris: OECD; and PISA 2006. Science Competencies for Tomorrow's World, by OECD, 2007, Paris: OECD. Cyprus and Malta did not participate in any of the three PISA Studies.

member state with the lowest percentage of poor readers in 2006 was Finland with 4.8%. Countries with the highest percentage (above 25%) were Romania, Bulgaria, Slovakia, Greece, Italy, Spain, and Lithuania. The 2006 PISA results also showed that 7.3% of the 15-year-olds in the European countries of the EU-15 did not achieve even the lowest proficiency level (level I). These low achievers have serious difficulties with written information and with any learning process dependent upon written material.

Benchmark 2: By 2010, the average share of early school leavers in the EU shall be reduced to no more than 10%.

The importance of having all member states reduce educational poverty is underscored by the Commission's second measure of educational poverty, the lack of certificates. Early school leavers face a high risk of under- or unemployment on today's labor market, so the share they represent of the EU's 18- to 24-year-olds is to be reduced to an explicit target of 10%. Surprisingly, the criterion of certificates is easier to meet than the one of competencies. In just six years, most countries made progress toward meeting the target of 10% (see Figure 13-5). The share of early school leavers in the total school population of

Figure 13-5: EU share of 18- to 24-year-olds with only lower-secondary education and not in education or training, 2000, 2003, and 2006

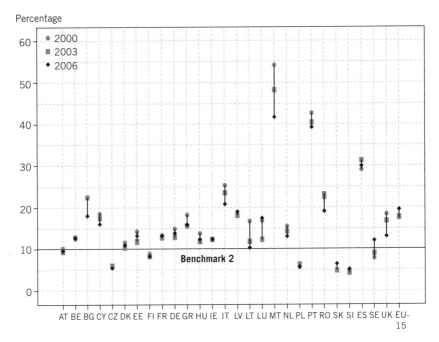

Source: retrieved February 14, 2008, from EUROSTAT Online Database.

the EU is already less than 10% in Finland, Austria, and several of the new EU member states.

Benchmark 3: By 2010, at least 85% of 22-year-olds in the European Union shall have completed upper secondary education.

This benchmark is an *implicit* measure of educational poverty. Although the European Council has not set a benchmark on educational wealth, it does define the share of population it aims to classify as "not poor" (85%). In other words, the share of the EU's 22-year-olds who have not completed upper secondary education should remain below 15%.

Some EU countries have met this criterion (Figure 13-6).[11] New EU member states such as the Czech Republic, Lithuania, Poland, Slovakia, and Slovenia have performed especially well. Austria, Ireland, and Sweden have also achieved the benchmark. Most EU countries, however, have not. Granted, Bulgaria, Cyprus, Denmark, and Italy have obviously increased the percentage of their populations in the category of "not poor" in educational terms since 2000. But the percentage of persons who have completed at least upper secondary school seems to have stagnated in Belgium, France, Romania, and the United Kingdom. The average for the EU-15 has risen to only 75.2% since 2000.

Figure 13-6: Percentage of the EU's 20- to 24-year-olds having completed at least upper-secondary education, 2000, 2003, and 2005

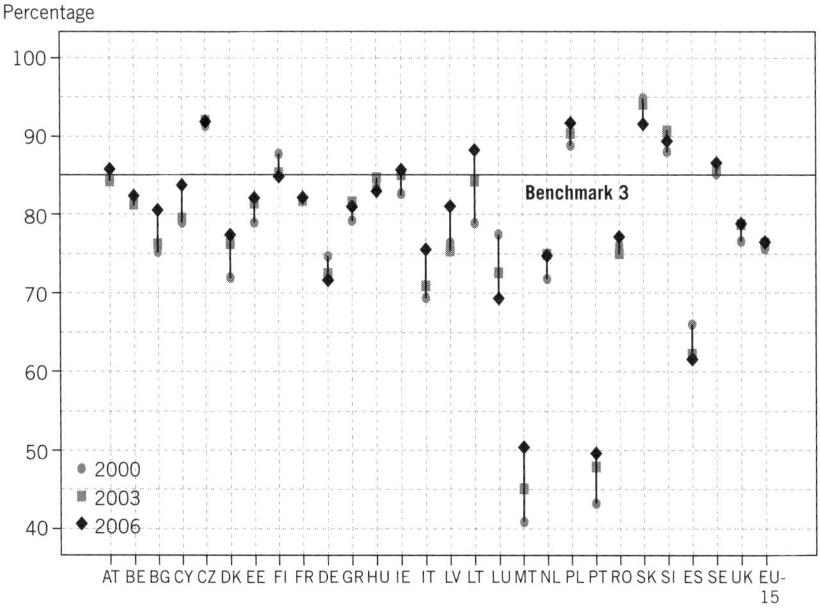

Source: retrieved February 14, 2008, from EUROSTAT Online Database.

Benchmark 4: The total number of graduates in mathematics, science, and technology in the European Union shall increase by at least 15% by 2010.

Changing labor markets have prompted the heads of states and governments to agree to increase the total number of university graduates in MST in the EU by at least 15% by 2010 and to decrease the gender imbalance in those fields. The number of graduates in MST increased in the EU-15 from 576,300 in 2000 to 700,000 in 2005 and thus already exceeds the EU benchmark. The countries with the strongest growth in MST graduates are Portugal (85%), Estonia (85%), and Poland (81%). Little progress has been made toward the second objective—reduction of the gender imbalance among MST graduates. The countries with the highest proportion of female graduates in MST in 2005 were Bulgaria (41%), Estonia (44%), and Greece (41%). The Netherlands (20%), Germany (24%), and Austria (23%) are the countries with the lowest proportion.

Benchmark 5: The participation of the adult working-age population (25- to 64-year-olds) in lifelong learning shall increase to at least 12.5% by 2010.

Europe's aging workforce has moved the European Council to set a target to increase the participation of adults aged 25 to 64 years in lifelong learning[12] and to decide on a modest benchmark of 12.5%. As apparent in Figure 13-7, participation in lifelong learning activities varies considerably from one country to another. High rates are found in Sweden, Denmark, the United Kingdom,

Figure 13-7: Percentage of EU 25- to 64-year-olds participating in life-long education and training four weeks prior to the survey, 2000, 2003, and 2006

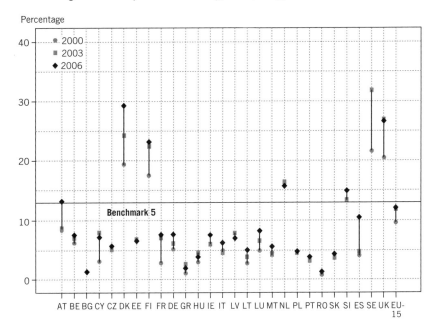

Source: retrieved February 14, 2008, from EUROSTAT Online Database.

Finland, the Netherlands and Slovenia. Most EU countries, however, still have participation rates below 12.5%. The rates of participation heavily depend on educational attainment and age. Adults with a high level of education are involved more than seven times as frequently as low-skilled adults, and older age groups participate much less than younger ones (Commission of the European Communities 2007: 81–82).

In summary, the most crucial targets—reducing educational poverty and increasing lifelong learning—have not been achieved across member states, and more substantial progress is needed in order to face the challenges of the near future (Commission of the European Communities 2007). Granted, some countries already meet most of the criteria. Finland and Sweden, for example, have not only a relatively low percentage of educationally poor people but also high rates of participation in continuous learning. Attendance of courses in technical subjects is climbing too (also among women). Such EU member states are exceptions, however. Most EU countries still have far to go before they achieve the stated objectives. The longest road lies ahead of the most populated EU countries such as Germany, France, the United Kingdom, and Italy, where achievement of the targets by 2010 is improbable. The striking educational shortcomings in those countries sharply contrast with the holistic and convincing orientation that Finland and Sweden have toward tomorrow's knowledge society.

An interesting empirical finding is that a few countries perform well in some dimensions but miserably in others. Slovakia and the Czech Republic, for instance, have very few people who leave school before completing upper secondary education but many competence-poor people and a low share in lifelong learning. This fact raises a host of questions. The first one, of course, concerns the national condition of educational policy. Another issue—and not extraneous one in the present context—is the European Commission's objectives and their usefulness.

PARTICIPATION, CERTIFICATES, AND COMPETENCIES

Taking a closer look at the relation between the single indicators, we confine ourselves to two yardsticks, competencies and educational certificates, which are usually presumed to measure the scope of educational poverty in similar ways. In Figure 13-8, the y-axis shows the percentage of 20- to 24-year-olds who had not completed upper secondary education in 2006. The x-axis refers to the 15-year-olds six years earlier, that is, those tested in the 2000 PISA study. In the absence of panel data, the figure thus serves as an illustration of what certificate level students whose reading skills were tested in 2000 obtained six years later, when they were 21 years old. It is evident that the correlation between the two measures is far from perfect. Applying the benchmarks, one obtains four quadrants. Quadrant 2 shows countries with high poverty in terms of certificates *and* competencies. Most European countries, Portugal and Luxembourg being the most conspicuous examples, appear in this worst-case scenario. Quadrant 3 represents the best possibility: low poverty in terms of both certificates and competencies. Depending on the benchmark applied, one finds few, if any, countries meeting both criteria. Only Sweden and Finland, as well as Austria and Ireland belong to this minority group. Hence for most European countries the Lisbon criteria are challenging indeed. Quadrants 1 and 4 represent cases of crossover. The United Kingdom (quadrant 1) has high poverty rates in terms of certificates but low poverty rates regarding competencies. Quadrant 4 represents countries with low poverty rates with respect to certificates but high poverty rates regarding competencies. Poland and the Czech Republic are illustrations of this mixed scenario.

From the perspective of educational sociology, the weak linkage between these two indicators of educational poverty is intriguing for many reasons. The European comparison shows that they measure anything but the same thing. This conclusion also means that conventional international comparative studies concentrating on one of the two dimensions only tell half of the story.

This also has implications for the matching of educational credentials and labor market positions. For example, it is clear that, on some national labor markets, signaling theory (Spence 1974) focusing on certificates, which are simple to measure, may work well, but on others certificates may prove to be a

Figure 13-8: Correlation between competencies and certificates as measures (in percentages) of educational poverty

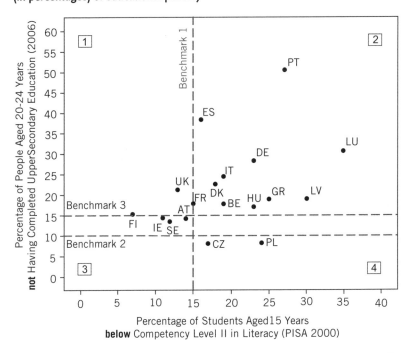

Source: *Knowledge and Skills for Life: First Results from PISA 2000,* by OECD, 2001, Paris: OECD; and EUROSTAT Online Database, retrieved February 14, 2008.

much less reliable signal of skill levels. The reason is that certificates from some countries have no predictable competence rating behind them and are therefore inappropriate guides to the placing of people in the labor market. For instance, employers can hardly depend on what certificates from Poland and the Czech Republic seem to signal. Hence it is necessary to measure actual competencies.

Overall, the relationship between competencies and certificates that appears at the upper end of educational distribution has not undergone much research, yet. Temporal processes of adaptation or deviation are likely to be particularly interesting. In other words, are competencies and certificates converging over time, or are they continuing to diverge? At any rate, these relationships seem to call for increased attention from the OECD and other organizations.

QUALITY OF EDUCATIONAL PERFORMANCE AND EQUALITY OF OPPORTUNITY?

The question of equal opportunity is a major topic in the assessment of educational systems. It is also one of the chief criteria on the EU agenda. So far, however, it has not been translated into a benchmark indicator but is a rather loosely

Table 13-1: Effects of Differentiation and Level in Selected Countries: Reading Competence (PISA 2006)

Level of Competence	Differentiation of Competence	
	Low (Egalitarian)	High (Unequal)
High	1	3
	Finland (265/547)	Belgium (360/501)
	Estonia (279/501)	Germany (359/495)
	Ireland (303/517)	Austria (353/495)
Low	2	4
	Romania (298/396)	Bulgaria (379/402)
	Spain (291/461)	Slovakia (347/466)
	Lithuania (312/470)	Greece (341/460)

Note: The EU mean serves as the basis for classifying the level and differentiation of competence into the categories of "high" and "low." The first figure in the parentheses following each country's name designates the bandwidth of competence between the 95th and the 5th percentile (average for the EU-15: 331). The second figure designates the national mean competence level (average for the EU-15: 472). Data are from *PISA 2006. Science Competencies for Tomorrow's World,* by OECD, 2007, Paris: OECD.

associated, overall guiding objective. Nevertheless, measurements of competence alone make it possible to establish direct links between the benchmarks and equal opportunity without having to resort to microdata.

In this section, we take up the proposal by Allmendinger and Leibfried (2002) to link indicators of quality with measures of the level of dispersion. At a given mean, which can serve as an indicator of quality, the dispersion is used to indicate the inequality of the result. In this way, we can classify and diagnose the individual member states at a given point in time as to whether their manifestations of quality and inequality are changing over time.

Some countries are highly differentiating and students cover the full spectrum of competencies; other countries are rather egalitarian with most students achieving similar competence levels. This dimension of the degree of differentiation should be kept separate from the dimension that designates the level of education. The latter one indicates the extent to which a differentiating or leveling educational system lies at a high or low average level of competence. The typology in Table 13-1 is based on a cross-classification of both dimensions— differentiation *and* level—and yields four types. The case of an egalitarian, high-competence country may be illustrated by Finland (field 1); an unequal, high-competence system is represented by Belgium (field 3); an unequal, low-competence country, by Bulgaria (field 4); and an egalitarian, low-competence country, by Romania (field 2). The dimensions we have formed are closely related to a paramount problem: the fact that educational attainment is determined by a low social background. The countries with an egalitarian and high-competence producing school system tend to be the ones with a comparatively weak link between social origin and scores in competence tests (OECD 2001, 2004, 2007).

The PISA surveys conducted in 2000, 2003, and 2006 permit us to follow the topology of differentiation and level depicted in Table 13-1 across three points in time.[13] Shifts in both the level and divergence of reading competence have occurred since PISA 2000. The changes are particularly manifest in Austria, France, and Italy, where the level of competence has fallen and the divergence has widened. In Latvia, conversely, the level of competence has risen and the divergence has narrowed. Marginal differences are observed in Hungary and Poland. Presumably, these changes are due to educational policy reforms that eventually altered the organizational and governance structure of the educational system, the level of educational spending, or the curricula. Further research on the causes of these observed changes and on the impact that EU educational policy has on national educational policy is yet to be done.

CONCLUSION

Demographic development in Europe and changing demand from tomorrow's labor markets are putting pressure on the educational system and the systems for basic and continuous training. Most European countries know that it is high time to do something. If the individual European countries and Europe as a whole want to remain competitive, then it is essential to improve both the use of educational reserves and the preservation of achieved educational levels through continuous education and training. It is also necessary to grapple with the ever more clearly emerging problems of fairness that are transmitted largely through education and training. If children from low social background and those from migrant backgrounds are not given the opportunity for a good education, they will be excluded from working society for their entire lives and will depend on government welfare.

The OECD and the EU are performing an important mission with their activities in educational policy and are building great momentum that would not be possible at the national level alone. Their focus on educational poverty is to be welcomed, too, and countervails national trends for the funding of elites. Although the EU has no mandate to intervene in the affairs of individual national governments through monitoring or guiding, systematic cross-national comparison will probably not be altogether ineffective.

Nonetheless, this inventory still paints a dark picture. Only Finland and Sweden are meeting the benchmarks satisfactorily. Most of the EU member states have not yet achieved them, and this is unlikely to change dramatically by 2010. The reason is that some of the benchmarks set by the EU do not cluster together. For example, countries with a low percentage of school dropouts are not simultaneously countries with a small percentage of competence-poor persons and vice versa. Our contribution suggests that there is a definite need for research on this topic and it also suggests that processes of finding an occupation are determined by criteria that may differ from one country to the next.

The competence measures supplied by the OECD have great potential for future research on educational systems. Two dimensions—the extent of differentiation between competencies within a country and the average level of competencies—make it possible to delineate four worlds of competence production. Within the European Union, these four worlds are much in line with Castles' notion of distinct families of nations (Castles 1993). In the Scandinavian countries we find little *differentiation* and Sweden is the only case not entirely consistent with this picture. We also discern little differentiation in the Baltic states and in Slovenia. By contrast, differentiation is especially pronounced in the German-speaking countries. With respect to *levels*, competence levels are highest in Scandinavia, especially so in Finland. The Anglo-Saxon countries also have high competence levels. The lowest average values relating to competence are found in the Southeast European countries, followed at some distance by the Southern European countries. The considerable heterogeneity in Europe within both dimensions suggests that in terms of educational policies European countries are far from forming a joint social model but are at varying distances from the benchmarks established by the Lisbon agenda and in this sense even a far cry from convergence.

REFERENCES

Allmendinger, Jutta (1999) Bildungsarmut: Zur Verschränkung von Bildungs- und Sozialpolitik [Educational Poverty: The Relation between Educational and Social Policies], *Soziale Welt*, 50: 35–50.

Allmendinger, Jutta and Leibfried, Stephan (2002) Bildungsarmut im Sozialstaat [Educational Poverty in the Welfare State], in Günther Burkart and Jürgen Wolf (eds) *Lebenszeiten. Erkundungen zur Soziologie der Generationen* [Lifetimes. Exploring the Sociology of Generations], Opladen: Leske and Budrich, pp. 287–315.

Allmendinger, Jutta and Leibfried, Stephan (2003) Education and the Welfare State: The Four Worlds of Competence Production, *European Journal of Social Policy*, 13: 63–81.

Balzer, Carolin and Rusconi, Alessandra (2007) From the European Commission to the Member States and Back—A Comparison of the Bologna and the Copenhagen Processes, in Kerstin Martens, Alessandra Rusconi, and Kathrin Leuze (eds) *New Arenas of Educational Governance*, Houndmills, Basingstoke: Palgrave Macmillan, pp. 57–75.

Bektchieva, Jana (2004) *Die europäische Bildungspolitik nach Maastricht* [*European Educational Policy after Maastricht*], Münster: LIT.

Belitz, Heike, Clemens, Marius, Gehrke, Birgit, Gornig, Martin, Legler, Harald, and Leidmann, Mark (2008) Wirtschaftsstrukturen und Produktivität im internationalen Vergleich [An international comparison of economic structures and productivity], Studien zum deutschen Innovationssystem No. 6–2008, Berlin and Hanover: NIW and DIW.

Boli, John, Ramirez, Francisco, and Meyer, John W. (1985) Explaining the Origins and Expansion of Mass Education, *Comparative Education Review*, 29: 145–170.

Castles, Francis G. (1993) *Families of Nations: Patterns of Public Policy in Western Democracies*, Aldershot: Dartmouth.

Commission of the European Communities (2004) Progress towards the common objectives in education and training, SEC (2004) 73, Brussels.

Commission of the European Communities (2005a) Progress towards the Lisbon objectives in education and training, SEC (2005) 419, Brussels.

Commission of the European Communities (2005b) Proposal for a recommendation of the European Parliament and of the Council on key competences for life-long learning, COM (2005) 548 final, 2005/0221(COD).

Commission of the European Communities (2006) Progress towards the Lisbon objectives in education and training, SEC (2006) 639, Brussels.

Commission of the European Communities (2007) Progress towards the Lisbon objectives in education and training, Indicators and benchmarks, SEC (2007) 1284, Brussels.

Commission of the European Communities (2008) Communication from the Commission to the European Parliament, the Council, the European Economic and Social Committee and the Committee of the Regions, COM (2008) 865, Brussels.

Dion, David-Pascal (2005) The Lisbon Process: A European Odyssey, *European Journal of Education*, 40: 295–313.

Hirschenauer, Franziska (2007) Regionale Arbeitsmarktlage der Älteren: Arbeiten bis 65 längst noch nicht die Regel [Regional labor market situation of older persons: Working until 65 nowhere near the rule yet], IAB-Kurzbericht, 25, Nuremberg.

Kleinert, Corinna (2007) Bildungsanstrengungen [Educational Endeavors], Institut für Arbeitsmarkt- und Berufsforschung: Nürnberg [Institute for Employment Research: Nuremburg]. Online. Available from: http://doku.iab.de/grauepap/2007/Fachkraefte_Material_C7.pdf (accessed 14 February 2008).

Martens, Kerstin and Balzer, Carolin (2007) All Bark and No Bite? The Implementation Styles of the European Union and the Organization for Economic Cooperation and Development in Education Policy, in Jutta Joachim, Bob Reinalda and Bertjan Verbeek (eds) *International Organizations and Implementation. Enforcers, Managers, Authorities?* London and New York: Routledge.

Martens, Kerstin, Rusconi, Alessandra, and Leuze, Kathrin (2007) New Arenas in Education Governance—Introduction, in Kerstin Martens, Alessandra Rusconi, and Kathrin Leuze (eds) *New Arenas of Education Governance—The*

Impact Of International Organizations and Markets on Educational Policymaking, Houndmills, Basingstoke: Palgrave Macmillan, pp. 3–15.

Martens, Kerstin and Wolf, Klaus Dieter (2006) Paradoxien der Neuen Staatsräson. Die Internationalisierung der Bildungspolitik in der EU und der OECD [Paradoxes of the New Raison d'Etat: The internationalization of educational policy in the EU and the OECD], *Zeitschrift für Internationale Beziehungen*, 13: 145–176.

Müller, Walter, Steinmann, Susanne, and Schneider, Reinhart (1997) Bildung in Europa [Education in Europe], in Stefan Hradil and Stefan Immerfall (eds) *Die Westeuropäischen Gesellschaften im Vergleich*, Opladen: Leske and Budrich, pp. 177–246.

OECD (2001) *Knowledge and Skills for Life: First Results from PISA 2000*, Paris: OECD.

OECD (2004) *Learning for Tomorrow's World: First results from PISA 2003*, Paris: OECD.

OECD (2007) *PISA 2006, Science Competencies for Tomorrow's World*, Paris: OECD.

Pépin, Luce (2006) *The History of European Cooperation in Education and Training: Europe in the Making—An Example*, Luxembourg: European Commission.

Pépin, Luce (2007) The History of EU Cooperation in the Field of Education and Training: How Life-Long Learning Became a Strategic Objective, *European Journal of Education*, 42: 121–132.

Ribhegge, Hermann (2007) *Europäische Wirtschafts- und Sozialpolitik* [*European Economic and Social Policy*], Berlin and Heidelberg: Springer.

Spence, A. Michael (1974) *Market Signaling*, Cambridge, MA: Harvard University Press.

United Nations (2007) *World Population Prospects: The 2006 Revision. Population Ageing*. Online. Available from: http://www.un.org/esa/population/publications/wpp2006/wpp2006_ageing.pdf (accessed 14 February2008).

UNESCO (1997) *International Standard Classification of Education - 1997 version*. Online. Available from: http://www.uis.unesco.org/TEMPLATE/pdf/isced/ISCED_A.pdf (accessed 14 August 2007).

Walkenhorst, Heiko (2008) Explaining change in EU education policy, *Journal of European Public Policy*, 15: 567–587.

Weymann, Ansgar and Martens, Kerstin (2007) Bildungspolitik durch internationale Organisationen. Entwicklung, Strategien und Bedeutung der OECD [Educational policy through international organizations: Development, strategies, and impact of the OECD], *Österreichische Zeitschrift für Soziologie*, 30: 68–86.

14

THE U.S. EDUCATIONAL SYSTEM: CAN IT BE A MODEL FOR EUROPE?

PATRICIA MALONEY and KARL ULRICH MAYER

The United States of America historically has been the international front runner in universal secondary education and in the expansion of mass tertiary education (OECD 2006; Fischer and Hout 2006). It is generally considered to have the best research universities in the world and some of the best institutions for undergraduate training: in a recent ranking, 35 out of the top listed 50 institutions in the world and 52 out of the top 100 universities are in the United States[1] (Mayer 2005: 203). The United States is also a front runner in the integration of adult students, primarily through its unique community college system. The United States shares with many European countries an activist policy perspective in which education is seen and used as an instrument to battle both economic and social problems. It has also probably gone furthest in quantifying pupils and teachers' performance through standardized testing. It has attempted to address inequality of educational opportunity across racial, linguistic, and ethnic groups as well as gender: conditional on high school completion and admission test scores, African-Americans achieved equal or even more than equal access to higher education than whites (Roksa et al. 2007; Karabel 2005), although attaining widespread equality in rates of high school completion and test scores among the different races has so far eluded the education system. However, the United States has been successful in aggressively counterbalancing inequities of gender, so much so that there is now increasing talk about the "female advantage" (DiPrete and Buchmann 2006). Its schools of education are considered the best models for training teachers, and it has played a leading role in setting the theoretical and methodological agenda for educational research. The very long period of strong growth of the U.S. economy and the skill bonus enjoyed by the better educated groups over the last decades also suggest that the competencies and skills produced in the American educational system seem to serve the demands of a postindustrialist economy well, although recent research concerning the prevalence of foreign-born doctoral students and instructors in engineering and the sciences has sparked fears about the beginnings of a loss of talented and U.S.-educated immigrants to their home countries (Levy and Murnane 2003). The overall institutional model of the U.S. educational system—a universal 12-year general schooling; short course tertiary education up to the B.A. or B.S. with cumulative credits, graduate and professional schools; a mixture of state and private institutions—has been spreading rapidly across the world.

It, therefore, does seem an obvious thesis that the U.S. educational system either best exemplifies a convergent universal model of education (Meyer 1977) or a model of best practice which the countries of the European Union should emulate (see also Bowen et al. 2005: Chapter 2 and 3). Such a positive external view contrasts, however, sharply with the internal perception that U.S. general schooling and vocational training are dramatically wanting. Low levels of school achievement, widening or persistent achievement gaps between racial and ethnic groups, high rates of high school dropouts, the plight of inner-city urban schools, the crisis of the "No Child Left Behind" federal school policy, the widely varying quality of community colleges and severe doubts about the quality of a four-year college education, the rapidly increasing economic exclusion from good tertiary education due to galloping costs of tuition and fees, the huge imports of foreign students in the areas of engineering and the sciences— all these factors paint a much more dismal picture of U.S. education. Moreover, the United States now lags behind in the proportion of young adults who attain a tertiary education. This picture hardly suggests a model for educational policy-making in Europe or elsewhere.

Allmendinger (1989) has suggested a useful typology for comparing educational systems cross-nationally. She distinguishes two main dimensions—standardization and stratification:

> *standardization* is the degree to which the quality of education meets the same standards nationwide. Variables such as teachers' training, school budgets, curricula, and the uniformity of school-leaving examinations are relevant in measuring the standing of an educational system on this dimension. *Stratification* is the proportion of a cohort that attains the maximum number of school years provided by the educational system, coupled with the degree of differentiation within given educational levels (tracking). This dimension can be measured by examining

the organizational structure of educational systems and/or by data that show the proportion of a cohort that exits at a given educational level. (Allmendinger 1989: 233).

Since Allmendinger's stratification dimension covers only inequality of educational attainment, we should add inequality of opportunity in access as a third dimension.

According to such a typology, the U.S. educational system is highly unstandardized because academic curricula, teachers' salaries and qualifications, and per student expenditure differ significantly among states and localities. A low degree of standardization also makes it difficult to ascertain criteria of success in attaining specific educational levels, although recent policies for testing school achievement have increased standards for performance.

Stratification is formally relatively low at the secondary level. However, this appearance of standardization is undermined by two factors. First, high school dropout rates are significantly higher for disadvantaged groups, which much more frequently receive a lower value G.E.D. (General Educational Development) credential rather than a high school degree. Secondly, the wide range in funding and academic course offerings (or lack thereof) between typical urban and suburban schools affects life chances and admission into higher education, therefore reproducing socioeconomic stratification. The U.S. higher education system is highly and increasingly stratified with its distinction between two-year community colleges and four-year colleges and because of the wide quality differences within these levels and the special role elite colleges play in selecting and placing students. It is generally assumed that high standardization and low stratification favor egalitarian access. Therefore, one would expect a mixed picture for the United States regarding inequality of opportunity. What we are seeing is a model of an unstandardized educational system combined with a middling degree of stratification at the secondary level and a high degree of stratification at the tertiary level. This, then, is the basis of comparison with European alternatives.

We have structured this chapter in the following manner. In the first section, we give a stylized description of the elementary and secondary education systems as they map onto the life course in childhood and early adulthood. In the second section, we describe the persistent achievement gap between the races. In the next section, we discuss some of the varied and widespread public and private responses to that achievement gap. Section four analyzes the present state of higher education in America. Section five examines diversity and inequality in access to that system of higher education, while section six presents issues of skill formation and returns to education. In the seventh section, we return to international comparisons as evidenced in the OECD, Third International Mathematics and Science Study (TIMSS), and Programme for

International Student Assessment (PISA) studies and to the question of the relative quality of U.S. education. In the concluding section, we revisit the question of U.S. education as a model.

INSTITUTIONAL CHARACTERISTICS OF THE ELEMENTARY AND SECONDARY SYSTEMS

Legally, parents are obligated to educate their children from first grade (which enrolls children around the age of 6) until the legally sanctioned dropout age of 15 to 18 (depending on the state of residence). Some parents may increase kindergarten readiness by enrolling their children in private preschools or in the publicly funded Head Start program for economically disadvantaged children, but this is not mandatory. This education may come in the form of sending the children to a formal public or private school, or it may be accomplished through a home-schooling course approved and monitored by the local school district. There is no one set path through the American education system. The flow chart (Figure 14-1) below maps out the traditional path through public schools. Private schools—which service about 12% of elementary and secondary pupils[2]—usually mimic the public school pattern very closely, but may deviate by combining 1st through 12th grade into one school or choosing different years at which to change schools. A small but growing percentage of Americans choose home-schooling for their children (up from 1.7% or 850,000 in 1999 to 2.2% or 1.1 million in 2003), usually due to religious or geographic reasons or dissatisfaction in local schools. Because of the legal obligation to educate children, there is always a requisite second chance built into the system for all children. Children who leave private schools must be accepted into their local public schools. Children who leave public schools (for disciplinary or medical reasons) must either receive home tutoring or free enrollment at a school that can meet their needs.

At or after the legal dropout age, some students leave the traditional schools and attempt to get a G.E.D. credential, or General Educational Development credential. While a G.E.D. is not valued as much as a regular high school diploma, it is accepted as proof of completion of secondary school by employers and institutions of higher learning.

A high school diploma or its equivalent has become extremely common in American society, as seen in Figure 14-2. As of 2005, 86% of American adults above the age of 24 have a high school diploma or G.E.D.[3] There are, on this level, differences between whites and blacks—93% of whites versus 87% of blacks hold a high school diploma or G.E.D. Figure 14-3 shows the gap between those of European and Asian descent and those of African and South/Latin American descent. Of that 86% of American adults, 57% received some additional education in either a higher education setting or a vocational/trade setting. This is a

Figure 14-1: A map of the traditional path through American public schools

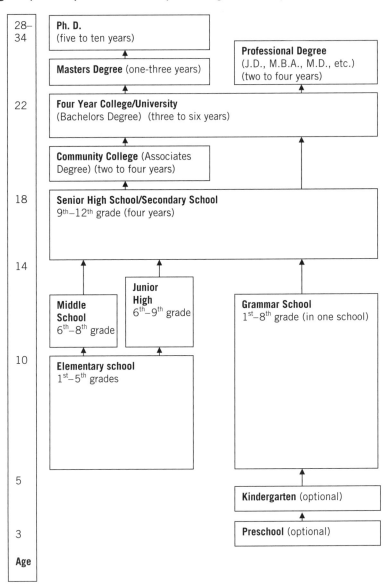

significant increase—in 1971, only 37% of those with a high school diploma or G.E.D. received additional education.[4]

In general, the variety of paths through the American education system reflects the variety of people who travel them. Gender, ethnicity, and socioeconomic status affect both educational opportunity and outcome, but the system itself is universal.

Figure 14-2: High school graduation rates over time

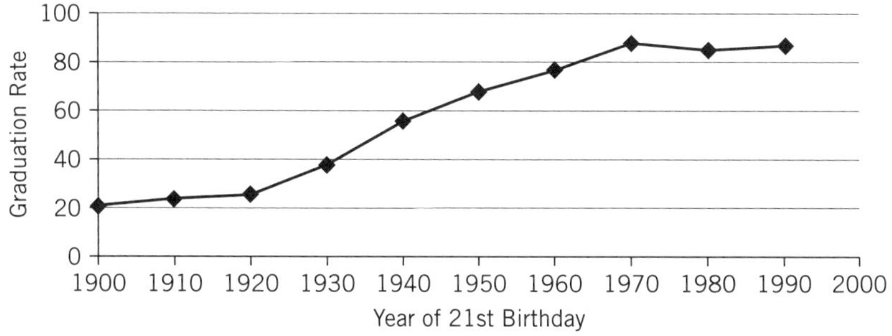

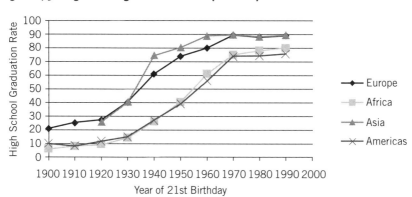

Source: Data taken from Fischer and Hout 2006: 13.

Figure 14-3: High school graduation rates by ancestry

Source: Data taken from Fischer and Hout 2006: 13.

THE ACHIEVEMENT GAP IN AMERICAN SCHOOLS

The phrase "achievement gap" in education and political circles signifies the long-term and steady score gap between white, black, and Hispanic/Latino youth on standardized tests. Using the National Assessment of Educational Progress (NAEP) and SAT scores, researchers have shown that this gap, first recognized in the 1960s, fell by 20% to 40% (depending on the estimate) in the 1970s and 1980s, but then began widening in the late 1990s (Lee 2002; English 2002; Haycock 2001).

While there is likely no single cause for the achievement gap, some posit that this gap is due to socioeconomic circumstances that cause minority children to cluster in urban areas and white children to be in the relatively wealthy suburbs. The local schools then reflect the socioeconomic status of the community

Figure 14-4: Percent Distribution of Total Public Elementary–Secondary School System Revenue 2003–4

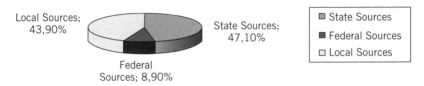

Local Sources; 43,90%

State Sources; 47,10%

Federal Sources; 8,90%

☑ State Sources

■ Federal Sources

☐ Local Sources

Source: U.S. Census, 2003–2004 Report on Public Education Finances.
Note: Total $462.7 billion, percentages do not equal 100 % because of rounding.

because of the particular way America establishes school funding. School funding is mostly determined (with few exceptions) by the local property taxes of the school's surrounding neighborhood. Therefore, a neighborhood with higher property values (and a more wealthy and likely white community) will have a higher-funded school than an area with lower property values and more renters. According to the 2003–2004 Report on Public Education Finances, the U.S. Census reports that the average public school receives 43.9% of its funding from local sources. The distributions of the entire budget can be seen in Figure 14-4.

The federal Department of Education writes on its Web site that "education is primarily a state and local responsibility in the United States."[5] If we looked at only the national average for percent federal funding, this would be true. However, this federal funding is crucial to the survival of the nation's urban districts.

The federal government provides a set amount of money per capita for each district, ranging from $300 to $400 for the wealthy and middle class districts (such as Great Neck School District, about ten miles from New York City) to about $1200 for districts that can receive Title I monies and federal grants for low-income communities (such as New York City itself). This $800 differential may not seem like a large gap, but the federal money makes up a greater percentage of the overall money given to the poorer, urban district. In addition, the urban districts may need more money per capita to pay for remediation and social services for low-income, underprivileged urban students.

This lack of money translates not only into less money for textbooks, supplies, and instructional and administrative staff, but also for the actual physical buildings in which the students are taught. Several researchers have looked at the relationship between the condition of the actual physical plant and student achievement rates—not surprisingly, the better-rated buildings have students whose standardized test scores are higher and dropout rates that are lower than the lesser-rated buildings (Crampton et al. 2004; Branham 2004). This relationship obviously has several confounding variables (students who have lower standardized test scores tend to be of a lower income background, with less money and parental demand for new schools), so causation certainly cannot be established in this case. Since the urban school districts tend to have older physical plants that need more money for maintenance, their budgets have to absorb the cost of ever-increasing immediate repairs on current buildings, leaving little (if any) money to build new buildings for increased student enrollment or to replace outdated or unsafe current buildings. In addition, little open land exists in established urban areas. What land may be available for development or rehabilitation is often prohibitively expensive. Such issues do not exist in comparatively land-rich suburbia and rural areas.

The conditions in urban schools reflect this funding differential. These schools are among the most difficult to staff. Some districts offer special monetary bonuses to teachers willing to teach in hard to staff schools or other financial recompenses—such as student loan forgiveness or New York City's recent housing subsidy for teachers. Experts have long pointed to the lack of experienced teachers in urban schools as a key problem both in closing the achievement gap and attracting new teachers (Lankford et al. 2002). Indeed, the turnover rate is higher in poorer schools than in upper-income areas. The overall teacher turnover rate in America has risen to 8.4% (269,600 teachers), leaving the profession entirely in 2004–05 and 8.1% (261,100), moving from one school to another.[6] Teacher turnover is generally measured as the sum of teachers both moving from school to school and leaving teaching altogether.

Private schools in general have a higher teacher turnover rate than public schools (as of 2001, 21% versus 15%[7]), and if we just looked at the rate of teachers leaving the profession, urban public schools would not fare badly in comparison to private schools or suburban schools. However, when the rate of teachers moving from one school to another joins the analysis, a clear pattern emerges: teachers leave low-income schools in higher rates than higher-income schools (Hanushek and Rivkin 2004). The higher rate of turnover in private schools may be due to the lack of need for time and financial investment in certification—there is less cost in leaving private schools than in leaving public schools. Private school teachers do not need to follow the same certification rules as public school teachers. Figure 14-5 is a graphic representation of these statistics.

This higher turnover rate of experienced teachers necessitates using newer, less experienced teachers in the less desirable, low income schools. And, since recent research has found that the effects of teacher quality greatly outweigh other variables in student achievement, such as effective school leadership or overall school quality (Sanders 2000; Odden and Borman 2004), the need for experienced, expert teachers is paramount.

RESPONSES TO THE ACHIEVEMENT GAP

With the growing concern over America's achievement between white and minority students and America's place on an international educational scale,

Figure 14-5: Reason for teacher turnover by high and low poverty schools

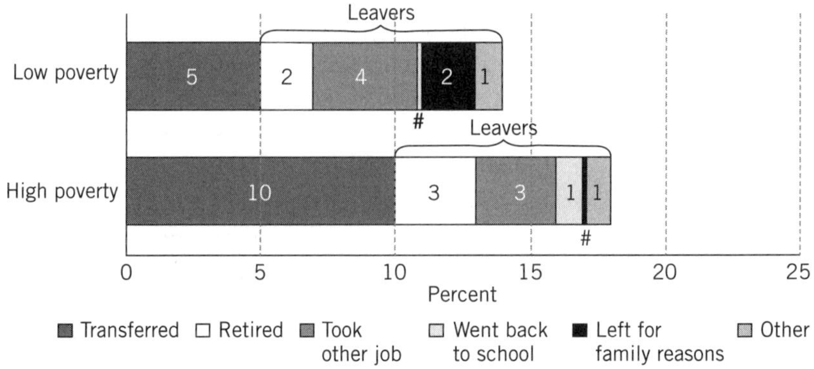

Source: U.S. Department of Education, National Center for Education Statistics, Teacher Follow-up Survey (TFS), "Current Teacher Questionnaire" and "Former Teacher Questionnaire," 2000–01.

the public/governmental sector and private sector have responded with certain interventions. We will first describe the most sweeping of these interventions, 2001's *No Child Left Behind*, then briefly describe three other major policy initiatives: alternative certification for teachers, voucher programs, and charter and magnet schools.

No Child Left Behind

In the past seven years, the face of the American educational system has been changed by the federal mandates of George W. Bush's 2001 *No Child Left Behind*. Students are constantly tested to provide statistics for "data-driven instruction." Federal school funding has become dependent upon those test scores, and public school teachers must now be "highly qualified." To be highly qualified, a teacher must hold a bachelor's degree from an accredited institution of higher learning, must "obtain full state certification or licensure ... [and] demonstrate subject area competence in each of the academic subjects in which the teacher teaches."[8] The law goes on to state that "all teachers teaching core subjects in Title I schools hired after the first day of the 2002–2003 school year must be 'highly qualified'."[9] This means that all incoming teachers must either already have completed the certification requirements or be in the process of attaining a certification or masters degree to be hired by Title I schools. Depending on the state, already hired teachers, no matter their seniority, have between three and five years to attain their certification. Title I schools are those that serve communities with a high proportion of students from low-income families. These schools receive special monies from the federal government for after-school tutoring, free or reduced school breakfast and lunch, and for the educational relocation of students to other, higher performing schools.

Beyond simply achieving a certain benchmark score on the standard-ized tests used to determine student learning, schools must show progressive growth on other state standardized examinations such as the Pennsylvania State Standardized Assessment or the Connecticut Mastery Test. The stan-dards and difficulty of these tests are supposedly correlated with those standards provided by *No Child Left Behind*, but this is often not the case. If schools do not show proper growth or the ability to maintain scores at a certain standard, they face reduced funding or even closure. If the schools do not achieve the benchmark accepted scores for their state each year (called "Adequate Yearly Progress" [AYP]), they are put into "Corrective Action" by the overseeing educational authority (whether that authority is a local board of education or a state department of education depends on the state and school). After five years of not making AYP and being in increasingly puni-tive stages of Corrective Action, the school is shut down, the pupils sent to the nearest well-performing school, and the staff either fired or dispersed to other schools (depending on the need for teachers and the strength of the teachers' union). A school can also take itself out of Corrective Action by achieving what is termed "Safe Harbor," or increasing its test scores by 10% or more each year.

This process would seem to be most aimed at low-performing schools, yet it can also adversely affect high-performing schools with a low to moderate minority or special needs population. Schools with fewer than 20 minority students or fewer than 40 special education or English Language Learner (ELL) students do not have to count those students in the overall AYP test score calculation. Therefore, the schools have an incentive to place (or perhaps misplace) low-performing students into those groups, up until that cut-off point so the school's scores are artificially inflated. However, schools with excellent test scores but whose moderate population (above 40) of special education or ELL students are not testing well will be adversely punished. Essentially, even if the rest of the school tests as the top school in the state, the school can still be put into Corrective Action if it has received a sudden influx of immigrant students who may not test well because they do not speak the language.[10]

However, even schools with the supposed cure-all of "highly quali-fied teachers" are not showing the expected growth in student achievement (Quartz 2003). Some relate this lower achievement to inadequate school fund-ing or community/home issues such as lack of cultural trips or educational resources (Rosigno and Ainsworth-Darnell 1999), intense poverty, and family violence.[11] Others maintain that the tests themselves are biased against minor-ity and/or low-income children (Kohn 2000). Many studies have shown that, in practice, the greatest adverse impacts of standardized testing are inequita-bly borne by African-American and Hispanic students, particularly those of lower socioeconomic status (Madaus and Clarke 2001; Oakes and Lipton 2003;

Walpole and McDonough 2005). These students may be told again and again that they are below grade level, or not gain admission to specialized schools thus disheartening them or causing them to simply drop out. Anecdotally, in Maloney's experience, the vocabulary section of these tests is not geared toward urban children. In 2005, the vocabulary test written for 7th graders in Philadelphia contained the word "coop." When the students were asked, the final word was pronounced by all the children with two syllables as "co-op," referring to the common city usage of cooperative apartments, rather than the test's usage of it as an area for holding chickens. Despite the wide age and reading level range in the classroom (from age 12 to age 16 and from a second grade reading level to a 10th grade reading level), no student knew what a coop was until it was properly contextualized within a sentence—something the test itself failed to do and the teacher was prohibited from doing by test instructions. Even when later contextualized, only about half knew the definition of a coop.

Some states and organizations have sued the federal government to divert the money spent on NCLB testing to other avenues, such as teacher salaries or lower class size (while the federal government does provide financial assistance to the state for the purpose of funding testing, this money may not cover the entire cost of testing and the state must provide the rest). In April 2005, the National Education Association (with the support of several school districts and education officials in different states[12]) sued Margaret Spellings, the Secretary of Education, in a bid to downsize testing and reallocate that money to other purposes, but the lawsuit was dismissed in 2008.

In education, particularly in Title 1 schools, test scores are now paramount under NCLB. They are easily analyzed, easily transportable and communicated, and can be seen as standardizing a curriculum. We do not mean to suggest that standardized tests should be abolished, but rather that they be given their proper place as a tool for instruction within a pantheon of tools such as teacher diagnosis, performance-based assessment, lower class size, etc. The current overemphasis on standardized test scores as the only means for measuring student growth over proportionately negatively effects schools with a moderate minority or special needs student population and may discriminate against minority and urban school children.

No Child Left Behind is not uniformly negative—it has made positive moves toward setting goals for mastery for all children and erasing the racial achievement gap in American public schools. Its focus on setting academic standards is admirable. However, what is admirable on paper is unnecessarily uniform and punitive in practice. Recent steps have been made to reauthorize it as it approaches its five-year deadline, with attempts to remove some of the flaws documented in this section. Hopefully, it will become a means for success for all American children.

Other Interventions—Alternative Certification, Voucher Programs, and Charter Schools

Alternative certification (AC) programs grew out of a need to recruit new teachers into diminishing ranks. Several factors can explain the dwindling number of teachers: educated women's greater access to the job market, low pay, low status, the increasing rate of retirement of graying Baby Boomers—the best explanation may lie in a combination of these factors. Since traditional certification programs that educate and certify teachers through undergraduate majors and perhaps a master's degree are no longer supplying enough teachers, alternative certification programs grew to fill the need.

Generally, alternative certification:

> eases entry requirements, minimizes preparation needed prior to paid teaching, and emphasizes on-the-job training. Such policies have created a variety of state, district, and privately run alternative route programs enabling college graduates to teach in public schools without completing a teacher education program (Zumwalt 1996: 40).

Opinions on alternative certification differ greatly. Proponents maintain that AC attracts diverse teachers (of both race and stage of career development) who are more likely to teach in urban under-resourced schools, that the teachers who enter through AC have higher GPAs than TC (traditional certification) teachers, and that the students of AC teachers actually perform better than the students of TC students (Zumwalt 1996; Bliss 1990; Tatel 1999). Alternative certification programs such as Teach For America or the city-based Teaching Fellows programs provide a temporary corps of approximately 5,000 recent college grads per year for the nation's struggling schools.[13] The opponents of AC argue that it de-professionalizes teaching and does not allow for the accumulation of experience necessary for truly inspired teaching.

Voucher programs are also a controversial subject. In theory, voucher programs give each child a set amount of money to give to whatever school the child's parents wish him or her to attend. The school that attracts the most children attracts the most money. These vouchers would be funded by the local or state school district from the monies gained from both federal and state taxes.

Proponents argue that vouchers provide parents and guardians with greater school choice, allowing the parents to shut down substandard schools by withdrawing their children. Since parents choose the schools for their children, this allows the parent to have more input on their child's education, benefiting both the child and the school. Opponents (notable ones are teachers' unions and public school administrations) believe that those who would take advantage of these programs would leave public schools altogether, thereby stripping more funding from schools that need it the most. There also may be some legal issues involved in voucher programs—since the voucher money comes from governmental sources, if it is used at religious schools, then the government is effectively funding a religious organization, thereby violating the separation of church and state inherent within the American system of government.

Milwaukee, Wisconsin decided to launch a full-scale voucher experiment. Beginning in 1990, children were given public money through vouchers to attend private schools. The students selected for the program came from families whose income was not more than 1.75 times the nationally established poverty line. Surprisingly, the program never reached maximum enrollment, perhaps because the voucher did not cover the entirety of tuition at some local private and religious schools (Witte 1998). After a five- to seven-year period and controlling for race and socioeconomic background, some studies found no difference between children who attended charter schools (see below) and public schools while some studies found that charter schools positively affected children (Witte 1998).

The success of the third policy initiative—charter and magnet schools—varies so much based on the success of the individual school that it is relatively difficult to make blanket statements about their overall success in educating children and closing both the international achievement gap and the national achievement gap based on race and socioeconomic status. Charter and magnet schools are public schools in that they receive government money through their "charter"—a legal agreement between the school and the state. Magnet schools attract the most intelligent and highest-performing children in the district because they have better resources, more experienced and gifted teachers, the attraction of like-minded peers, and have more difficult course work. These schools are usually very difficult to gain admission to (sometimes their admitted-to-applied ratio rivals the Ivy League), and higher education admission is usually almost universal for the graduates. These schools draw criticism from surrounding public schools because they pull the highest performing students—who would increase other schools' test scores—away from their normal zoned public high school.

Charter schools are similar to magnet schools in that parents must opt their children into the school, but dissimilar in that the previous academic performance of the children is almost never considered as a factor in admission. Attendance and behavior is sometimes considered. The parents must choose the charter school for their children, so the children are already self-selected: their families value education and have the time and money to wade through the red tape necessary to transfer the child out of the default public school. Spots in charter schools are highly desirable and usually are won through a lottery of all children who apply.

Charter schools usually require longer school days, more parental involvement, Saturday school, and stricter behavioral standards. If the children or parents do not comply with the rules, then the child is removed to a normal zoned public school. The teachers at charter schools are no longer part of the public school teacher union, so their hours and pay are negotiated individually with the school. Charter schools, while liked by parents, children, teachers, and especially politicians, have achieved mixed success (as measured by the NCLB tests). Some charter school students score well below the public school average and some score well above the average. On average, charter schools and public schools achieve much the same results on the NCLB tests, especially when analyses control for race and socioeconomic status.[14]

No solution to the achievement gap can work in isolation. The multiplicity of interventions has undoubtedly helped some students and certainly changed the face of the public school system. Their results are sometimes positive and sometimes mixed, leaving us with much the same questions and problems with which we began.

HIGHER EDUCATION IN AMERICA

The American system of higher education relies on a different model than its international counterparts. A large portion of Americans enrolled in some form of higher or continuing education either begin or receive all their schooling from community colleges (sometimes referred to as junior colleges). The American Association of Community Colleges reports that, as of January 2007, there were more than 11.6 million students enrolled in 1,202 community colleges across the country, with the average age of student as 29 years old.[15] However, "enrolled" does not necessarily mean that the student is taking for-credit courses or is in pursuit of a degree. This number could be inflated by persons enrolling in noncredit "lifestyle" or elective courses, for example, flower-arranging or personal financial management. The National Center for Education Statistics refines this number of 11.6 million and reports that, of the nearly 17.9 million persons enrolled in any kind of undergraduate education in the United States in fall 2005, over 6.6 million were enrolled in community colleges. This means that community colleges accounted for 36.9% of all undergraduate enrollment.[16] These programs can only confer Associates of Arts (AA) degrees, which are usually referred to as two-year degrees (even though it may take the student longer than two years to complete such a degree). These AAs may then be transferred to four-year senior colleges where the student can (dependent on admission standards) continue with his or her education to receive a Bachelor of Arts degree. The number of community college students entering the most competitive institutions has declined from 10.5% in 1984 to 5.7% in 2002 at private colleges and from 22.2% to 18.8% at public ones (*New York Times*, "Education Life: The Two Year Attraction," April 22, 2007: 22). Researchers differ on the effects of beginning one's education in community colleges. Some evidence suggests that those who come from community colleges are less likely to achieve success in later four-year institutions and later careers possibly because those who begin their higher education at community colleges are usually from lower socioeconomic backgrounds (Monk-Turner 1990; Dougherty 1987). Other evidence suggests that there are no statistically significant earnings differences or differences in the rate of bachelor degree completion between those who begin their higher education at community colleges and those who begin it at a university (Gill and Leigh 2003; Lee et al. 1993).

The advantage to starting one's education at a community college is primarily financial (their enrollment fees are much lower than those at a university[17]) and also educational (Kane and Rouse 1999). Because of their open enrollment policy, students who are not ready to enroll in higher-level courses (perhaps because of insufficient preparation in secondary school) take remedial courses in a smaller, more intimate environment that has a great deal of academic guidance (because there are a great many of them, community colleges are usually geographically closer and numerically smaller than universities) that may be more conducive to learning for struggling students than a larger, more anonymous university. Instructors at community colleges may be very similar to those at local elementary or secondary schools—both elementary/secondary schools and community colleges now require the same credential, a master's degree—in order to be an instructor.

In terms of college degree attainment, the percentage of 25- to 29-year-olds who had completed college jumped from 17% to 29% from 1971 to 2005.[18] When broken down by gender, women earned approximately 58% of all degrees given by institutes of higher education in 2003.[19] Figure 14-6 shows that women's rates of college graduation gained parity with men's in 1980 and exceeded men's in 1990. Rates of enrollment in graduate level programs are also up, from 1.3 million individuals in 1976 to 2.2 million individuals in 2004.[20] This figure corresponds to approximately 40% of those who have completed a college degree.

As seen in Figure 14-7, Asian rates of college graduation mirrored the rates of those of European descent until 1950, when they began to greatly outpace every other major American ethnicity. The rates of those of African and South/Latin American descent remain much the same, much like the pattern of high-school graduation rates seen in Figure 14-2.

Overall, 70% of all bachelor's degrees were awarded to non-Hispanic whites in 2003.[21] This is a much different proportion than in previous years—in 1976, 88% of all bachelor's degrees conferred were to non-Hispanic whites.[22] Table 14-1 illustrates enrollment rates in higher education by race. In all cases, white non-Hispanics are around or above the national average while blacks and Hispanics (U.S. citizens and non-U.S. citizens) are below the national average.

The data on foreign-born students, particularly those entering the American system at the graduate level, show that the higher education system is increasingly relying on foreign-born faculty to teach and research, particularly in the fields of mathematics and in the sciences. Also, as of 2005, the

Figure 14-6: College graduation rates by gender

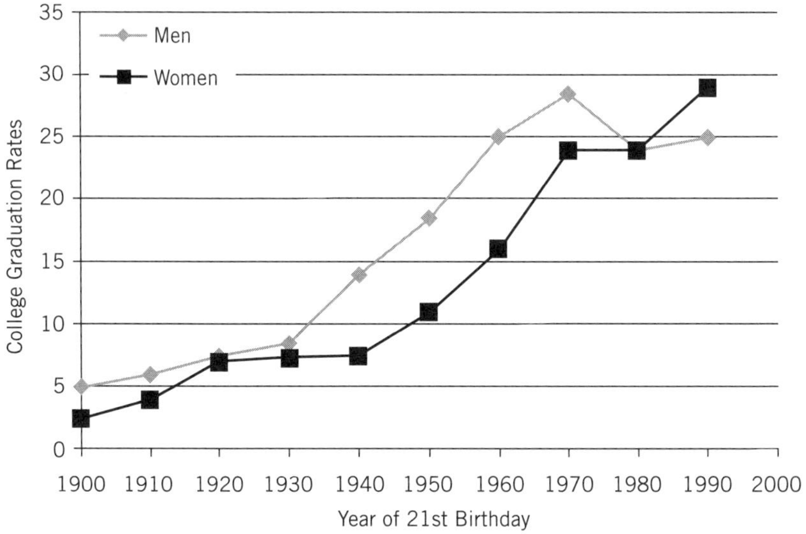

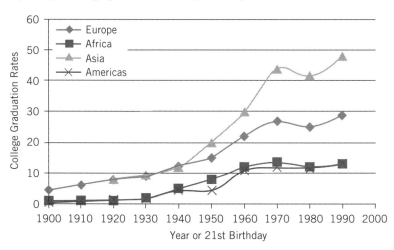

Source: Data taken from Fischer and Hout 2006: 15.

Figure 14-7: College graduation rates by ethnicity

Source: Data taken from Fischer and Hout 2006: 15.

foreign student population earned 34.7% of the doctorates in the sciences and 63.1% of the doctorates in engineering (Matthews 2007), with clear patterns as to the country of origin for the students: India contributed 13.5% of the foreign-born student population, China contributed 11.1%, and Korea contributed 10.4%. Countries that are predominantly Asian, such as Japan, Taiwan,

Table 14-1: Enrollment Rates in Higher Education By Race

| | Enrollment as a percent of all 18- to 24-year-olds | | | | | Enrollment as a percent of all 18- to 24- year-old high school completers | | | | |
| | | | | Hispanic | | | | | Hispanic | |
Year	Total	White, non-Hispanic	Black, non-Hispanic	Total	U.S. Citizens	Total	White, non-Hispanic	Black, non-Hispanic	Total	U.S. Citizens
1980	26	27	9	16	~	32	32	28	30	~
1985	28	30	20	17	~	34	35	26	27	~
1990	32	35	25	16	~	39	40	33	29	~
1995	34	38	27	21	26	42	44	35	35	36
1996	36	39	27	20	26	43	41	36	34	38
1997	37	41	30	22	28	45	47	39	36	40
1998	37	41	30	20	26	45	47	40	34	36
1999	36	39	30	19	24	44	45	39	32	34
2000	36	39	31	22	31	43	44	39	36	43

Source: U.S. Department of Education, National Center for Education Statistics, *Digest of Education Statistics, 2001.*

and Thailand, made up six of the top ten contributors, with Germany (1.6%) as the only European country represented in the top ten (Matthews 2007). With 6% of all doctoral degrees in science and engineering, the United States ranks very low among advanced countries (but about as high as Germany and Japan) (Bowen et al. 2005: 44 f.). Recent immigration reform currently under consideration by Congress would greatly increase the number of visas available for foreign-born students, enlarging the pool of available visas from 65,000 to 115,000 annually.

Some note that this willingness to accept foreign-born students could be seen as disadvantaging the academic acceptance rate of domestic-born minority students and as having a negative effect on the quality of undergraduate teaching (primarily because of language difficulties) (Matthews 2007; Borjas 2000). Others maintain that this large pool of foreign-born students not only adds to the knowledge production occurring within the United States both during and after their stays (approximately 13% of them stay within the United States after receiving their doctorates) (Matthews 2007), but also because the increase in international knowledge and skills can only benefit scientific progress (Stephan and Levin 2001). Whatever the case, the trend of foreign and U.S. interdependence in the realm of higher education is strong and shows no apparent sign of reversal in the near future.

DIVERSITY AND INEQUALITIES IN ACCESS TO HIGHER EDUCATION

A college degree is the entry ticket to practically all well-qualified and well-paid jobs in the United States. "Rags-to-riches" stories without a college degree have become almost unthinkable. But very often, it is more than just a college degree that is required. To a considerable extent, elite positions are reserved for graduates from the best colleges and universities, not only because of the skills the graduates have gained, but also because of the social networks formed within these schools and their alumni associations. Access to such institutions is extremely intense and influences the choice of high schools. Therefore, in this section, we will look at inequalities of opportunities both in regard to access to a college education in general and to elite colleges and universities in particular.

The U.S. expansion of tertiary education has fostered the impression of widely open opportunities to attain a college degree. The best recent analysis of changes in such opportunities over time has been carried out by a group of U.S. researchers (Josipa Roksa, Eric Grodsky, Richard Arum, Adam Gomoran) connected to an international comparative study on the relationships between expansion of tertiary education, the differentiation of the tertiary sector, and inequalities of access (Shavit et al. 2007; Mayer et al. 2007).

According to Roksa et al., some kind of "post-secondary education became open to virtually all high school graduates by the end of the twentieth century, [but] solidification of an educational hierarchy and a split between elite and mass education constrained student opportunities" (Roksa et al. 2007: 168). Parental education and social class had a strong influence on access to higher education, for example, "conditional on high school graduation and other covariates, students with college educated parents were 5–6 times more likely to enter post-secondary education as students whose parents only graduated from high school" (Roksa et al. 2007: 180). Inequality of access to B.A.-granting institutions has even increased over time in comparison to the 1980s and the 1990s. Father's background does not appear to play a (net) significant role in access to two-year institutions, but has a moderate effect on access to four-year institutions. These effects seem to be fairly persistent and stable over time. In contrast, class background has become dramatically more important in the 1990s as compared to the 1980s for access to elite baccalaureate education. These effects vanish once one controls for previous academic achievement. Of course, as seen in the section "Institutional Characteristics of the Elementary and Secondary Systems" on the achievement gap, previous academic achievement is linked with the type of school the student attends and the familial environment that student grows up in—in the real world, previous academic achievement is inextricably linked with class, socioeconomic status, and environment.

Conditional upon entering higher education, blacks have equal access to B.A.-granting universities as whites (Roksa et al. 2007: 186). In regard to access to elite institutions, there has been a significant decrease in the opportunities of African-Americans. Since the 1980s, they were significantly less likely to enter elite colleges than whites. These changes seem to mirror the changes in affirmative action policies. While they were pronounced and aggressive in the 1960s and 1970s, they have been undercut by the Reagan administration and by Supreme Court rulings in the 1980s and 1990s. In fact, top institutions bolster their "diversity" record by recruiting a significant number of immigrant black students. A recent study by Massey et al. (2007) found that 27% of all first-year black students came from the Caribbean and other foreign countries.

Thus, while the pool of highly talented and well-schooled immigrant blacks has been aggressively tapped by admissions offices, the same does not apply to low income whites. As a consequence, the debate in recent years has increasingly shifted to one about the high costs of higher education and the blatant discrimination of low-income white students (Delbanco, 2007: Bowen et al. 2005; Karabel 2005: 538). It is also clear that the advantages of having a significant private share in institutions of higher education come at a cost: the bonuses in admissions going to "athletes" and "legacies" and sometimes children of celebrities enhance the financial viability of private colleges and universities, but undermine the ideal of meritocratic selection (Golden 2006).

Roksa et al. conclude: "The benefits of access to higher education associated with privileged family background have remained stable over time...extensive educational expansion and public policy interventions regarding financial aid have not reduced the advantages with high economic status. The findings regarding race and gender are strikingly different...By the end of the twentieth century, women and African-Americans had made important inroads in access to higher education, and in particular baccalaureate granting institutions" (Roksa et al. 2007: 189–190). Hopefully, these inroads will begin to erase the achievement gap that is so prevalent in the elementary and secondary school systems.

What is astounding from a European perspective is that the ideal of a pure meritocracy was never the norm in the United States for access to higher education. While in the first half of the last century, some vague notion of leadership quality ensured easy access of the sons of well-to-do White Anglo-Saxon Protestants (WASPS), excluding Blacks, Jews, and also mostly women, in the second half, a combination of merit-selection and the above-mentioned bonuses to "legacies," athletes, and minorities operated as an expression of a "diversity" ideal. In the twenty-first century, giving extra merit bonuses in application decisions to males in order to prevent too high proportions of women and to discriminate against Asian-Americans is the latest twist in this game (Golden 2006). While the Supreme Court (*Grutter v. Bollinger* 539 U.S. 306 [2003]; *Gratz v. Bollinger* 539 U.S. 244 [2003]) now denies privileged access solely on the basis of race, it allows consideration of diversity representation. In recent years, some universities have used this allowance of diversity representation to "correct" for the high rates of college graduation by Asians (as seen in Figure 14-7) by disadvantaging them in the college application pool. Even so, graduation rates by first generation Asians have continued to rise, perhaps due to their higher average SAT scores. A rare exception of an institution following meritocratic criteria is California Technical Institute. The result in 2004 was that only one African-American was admitted to the class of 2008, only 30% women and a high proportion of Asians (Golden 2006: 262).

Overall, the American system of higher education privileges those who achieved success in secondary school and on standardized tests like the SAT. Since success in these forums is linked with characteristics such as race, socioeconomic status, and gender, access to higher education is unequal.

SKILL FORMATION AND RETURNS TO EDUCATION

An evaluation of the U.S. educational system centers in the final analysis on its ability to provide the U.S. economy with the human capital it needs for continuing economic innovation and growth. Surprisingly, little is known about the roughly 40% of a cohort entering the labor force directly after high school

(Buechtemann et al. 1993). They encounter a trajectory of inferior "stop-gap" jobs (Oppenheimer et al. 1997), or continue the marginal but intensive work positions they held during high school, like managers at McDonald's (Newman 2000). About a quarter of young black males will spend a considerable time in prison (Western and Petite 2005) and, as of 2000, more than 15% of black females aged 15–19 will experience premarital pregnancy.[23]

It is a fair assumption that most of the associate degrees from community colleges and even a good share of baccalaureate degrees at four-year colleges do not match the qualification levels of, for example, German apprenticeships. Therefore, simply comparing proportions of access, enrollment, and attainment of tertiary education might actually be overestimating the qualification pool produced by the U.S. educational system. Such qualification gaps seem, on the one hand, to be borne out by the high proportion of foreign students and instructors in mathematics, engineering, and the sciences. On the other hand, as Rosenbaum (2001) has argued, it is doubtful whether U.S. employers are at all interested in higher qualifications of the lower half of the workforce. Rosenbaum has shown on the basis of detailed surveys that employers are often not interested in grades or other information from schools as a basis for selection for low-skill jobs, but only in minimal standards of behavior and discipline. This is logical because the organization of work in the U.S. service economy appears to be strongly tailored to low-discretion and high-control jobs, even up to middle ranks. Only those with higher-discretion jobs—those with college or advanced degrees—have experienced a real increase in their income. Those with the lower-discretion jobs—those with high school diplomas or less—have experienced a net loss in income, as seen in Figure 14-8.

Earning wage differentials reflect the very strong demand for highly skilled manpower. Earnings for tertiary graduates in the 25–64 age range were, in 2004, 72% higher on average than those for people with only secondary education. This marks an increase from 68% in 1998. Among the OECD countries, this differential is only higher in Hungary and Chechnya (OECD 2006: 3). Conversely, the penalties for not completing high school are more severe in the United States than in almost any other OECD country. The earnings of the 25- to 64-year-olds without high school completion are 65% of those with high school. And the likelihood of only poverty level wages (half of the median) is (with 44%) particularly high among those without high school. Similar penalties apply also for the employment rate in this group (68% for men and 47% for women [OECD 2006: 6]).

In one aspect, the U.S. educational system appears better than many competitors: the training in "computer literacy." Among the OECD countries, the United States has the highest level of provision with computers in schools attended by 15-year-olds. Based on school principals' reports in PISA 2003, there is, on average, one computer for three pupils in the United States. Ironically,

Figure 14-8: Real hourly wage by education levels

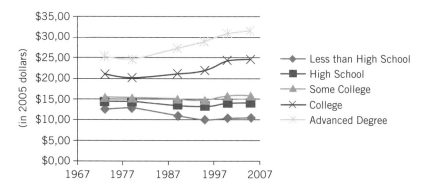

Source: Data taken from Economic Policy Institute, *The State of Working America 2006/2007*.

when seen in context with the OECD countries, the United States actually has a relatively low share of employment in IT-related occupations.[24]

COGNITIVE INEQUALITIES

Articles in American national and local newspapers and trade journals constantly compare American educational statistics with their international counterparts. American students are usually portrayed as "slipping behind" their international peers in all subjects, particularly in mathematics and science. Recent international comparison studies, such as the TIMSS in 1994 (and its follow-up in 1999, TIMSS-99) and the PISA in 2000, 2003, and 2006, provide concrete data on education in more than forty countries. TIMSS sampled from forty-one countries from all regions of the world, surveying thousands of students in hundreds of schools. PISA studied the member countries of the OECD. The mean scores of selected countries in mathematics and reading can be seen in Figures 14-9 and 14-10.

The United States is below the OECD average in mathematics and close to average in reading. The difference in the mean reading scores between the upper and lower quartiles of social structure is high in the United States, but not as high as in some European countries, such as Germany, Belgium, Switzerland, and the United Kingdom. Thus, the inequality in the American education system due to socioeconomic status may not be as great as that in other countries. Figure 14-11 illustrates this fact. The difference in the mean mathematics scores shows much the same pattern.

Since the United States is not only the largest and most heterogeneous country compared here, but also has a disproportionate share of native minorities and immigrants, this finding is surprising. It suggests that the U.S. educational

Figure 14-9: Mean and distribution of student achievement in mathematics, 2003

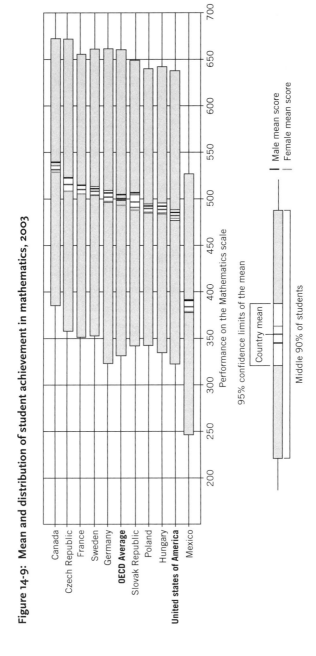

Source: PISA 2003 Database.

Figure 14-10: Mean and distribution of student achievement in reading, 2003

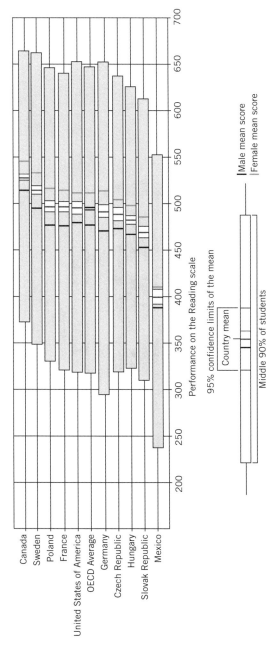

Source: PISA 2003 Database.

Figure 14-11: Difference in the mean reading scores by the upper and lower quartiles of social structure

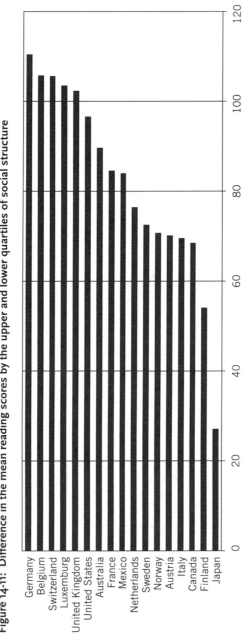

Source: Knowledge and Skills for Life: Results from the PISA Study.

system is not actually doing the worst job in equalizing basic cognitive skills in schools despite the heavy dependence of its schools on local revenues.

CONCLUSIONS: CAN THE U.S. EDUCATIONAL SYSTEM BE A MODEL FOR EUROPE (AND ESPECIALLY THE NEW MEMBER STATES)?

Can the United States provide a social model for Europe and especially for the new member states? Several nontrivial issues reside in this question. First of all, do we have comparable units? The United States is a society with more than 300 million inhabitants heavily concentrated in the urban belts at the East and West Coast with massive migration shifts to the South. It is also a society with strong population growth due to immigration and comparatively high fertility (Lesthaege and Neidert 2006). Both levels of living standards and regulations vary widely among states.

It is, therefore, unclear what the *tertium comparationis* should be for Europe. Clearly not the European Union as a whole, since (except for the Bologna agreement) there is no common educational policy. And single European countries might also be difficult units for comparison due to vastly different population size and, in most cases, a much lower degree of heterogeneity.

With these caveats, let us review and assess the major elements of the U.S. educational system:

1. Although the U.S. educational system is a very costly one (OECD 2006), the system of local financing introduces large inequities in investments per school and per pupil. While partly counteracted by state and federal grants, this cannot counterbalance a massively uneven playing field.
2. The quality of prehigh-school education is about OECD average in reading competency and toward the bottom in mathematics and science proficiency. However, given the heterogeneity of the U.S. population and the inequities of financing, school performance variances are actually surprisingly low.
3. Research has increasingly demonstrated strong early determinants of later cognitive and educational achievements (Reynolds et al. 2001; Heckman et al. 2006). Preschool in the United States is not universal, with low-income children receiving some access through governmental programs such as Head Start and higher income children accessing private preschools.
4. There is almost universal attainment of K-12 secondary level attainment, but this standard is incomplete due to higher dropout rates of blacks and Hispanics and the lower value of supplementary G.E.D. high school degrees.

5. Both positive and negative lessons can be learned from U.S. school educational policy. Monitoring both pupils' learning progress and teacher quality and tying it to test performance has clearly improved some measurements of educational quality. However, the use of market mechanisms through charter schools, the introduction of self-selective magnet schools, and the provision of vouchers have not shown the expected improvements. Moreover, the sole concentration on test results might severely impose a dreadfully restrictive and racially biased ideal of education.

6. The United States has a very poor system of vocational training and does very little to help school-to-work transitions for the more than 70% without a college degree.

7. Judged by the high proportion of foreign students and doctorates in mathematics, science, and engineering, the U.S. educational system cannot produce the skills in demand.

8. Participation rates in tertiary education are high, but are now lower than in many other advanced countries, since expansion has slowed down considerably over the last decades and has concentrated more on two-year colleges.

9. Retention rates between college entrance and college completion are very low at less than 60% within 6 years (Carey 2004). However, the United States has a very flexible system that allows students to earn credits toward a degree, transfer credit between institutions, and finish a degree in much later adult years.

10. The colleges and universities in the United States are enormously stratified with high transaction competition costs (e.g., SAT tutoring) and skyrocketing tuition and fees. The top 50 to 100 institutions of higher learning in America are probably the best or among the best in the world, at least in the quality of undergraduate training and university-based science research. However, the mean and variance of university training are arguably better in many European countries with mostly public institutions and more centralized regulation (Mayer 2005).

11. Based on an aggressive affirmative action policy in the 1960s and the 1970s, the United States has made large improvements in regard to the gender inequalities in educational opportunities (which are now reversed) and in regard to African-Americans (conditional on high-school completion and grades). But it still shows considerable and growing inequalities of opportunity according to socioeconomic background. Moreover, the racial achievement gap is persistent over the recent decades and might even be increasing.

12. Returns to education are large and have increased strongly over the last decades. As shown in Figure 14-8, the hourly wage of holders of advanced degrees in 2005 are three-and-a-half times higher than for somebody without a high school degree and more than double those of a high school graduate.

Thus, the lessons to be drawn from the exemplar of the United States are very mixed ones. The most positive elements are a very pragmatic orientation toward educational attainment, its uses and, consequentially, a strong interventionist policy on empiricist grounds as well as a highly competitive system producing some outstanding outcomes in college education and beyond. The most negative characteristic is the cumulative and often life-long exclusion and marginalization of children starting at the bottom. We would consider it an open issue how effective test-based interventions are for improving both mean levels of cognitive performance and the variances. All in all, the United States has lost its previously unquestioned international frontrunner status in educational development, but the picture is not as bleak as is usually depicted by popular media. Both the United States and Europe have their own endemic issues and challenges—while a comparison of the two is certainly valid and helpful, a ranking of the two is not.

REFERENCES

Allmendinger, Jutta (1989) Educational Systems and Labor Market Outcomes, *European Sociological Review*, 5(3): 231–250.

Bliss, Traci (1990) Alternate Certification in Connecticut: Reshaping the Profession, *Peabody Journal of Education*, 67(3): 35–54.

Borjas, George (2000) Foreign-Born Teaching Assistants and the Academic Performance of Undergraduates, *The American Economic Review*, 90(2): 355–359.

Bowen, William G., Kurzweil, Martin A., and Tobin, Eugene M. (2005) *Equity and Excellence in American Higher Education*, Charlottesville: University of Virginia Press.

Branham, David (2004) The Wise Man Builds His House Upon the Rock: The Effects of Inadequate School Building Infrastructure on Student Attendance, *Social Science Quarterly*, 85, 5: 1112–1128.

Buechtemann, Christoph F., Schupp, Jürgen and Soloff, Dana (1993) Roads to Work: School-To-Work Transition Patterns in Germany and the United States, *Industrial Relations Journal*, 24, 2: 97–111.

Carey, Kevin (2004) A Matter of Degrees, A Report by the Education Trust. Online. Available from: http://www2.edtrust.org/NR/rdonlyres/11B4283F-104E-4511-B0CA-1D3023231157/0/highered.pdf (accessed July 7, 2008).

Crampton, Faith, Thompson, David, and Veseley, Randall (2004) The Forgotten Side of School Finance Equity: The Role of Infrastructure Funding in Student Success, *National Association of Secondary School Principals Bulletin*, 88, 640: 29–52.

Delbanco, Andrew (2007) Scandals of Higher Education, *New York Review of Books*, 29 March: 42–47.

DiPrete, Thomas and Buchmann, Claudia (2006) Gender Specific Trends in the Value of Education and the Emerging Gender Gap in College Completion, *Demography*, 43(1): 1–24.

Dougherty, Kevin (1987) The Effects of Community Colleges: Aid or Hindrance to Socioeconomic Attainment? *Sociology of Education*, 60(2): 86–103.

English, Fenwick (2002) 'On the Intractability of the Achievement Gap in Urban Schools and the Discursive Practice of Continuing Racial Discrimination', *Education and Urban Society*, 34, 3: 298–311.

Fischer, Claude and Hout, Michael (2006) *A Century of Difference: How America Changed in the Last Hundred Years*, New York: Russell Sage.

Gill, Andrew and Leigh, Duane (2003) Do the Returns to Community Colleges Differ Between Academic and Vocational Programs?, *Journal of Human Resources*, 38(1): 134–155.

Golden, Daniel (2006) *The Price of Admission. How America's Ruling Class Buys Its Way Into Elite Colleges—And Who Gets Left Outside the Gates*, New York: Crown.

Greene, Jay P. (2006) *Education Myths: What Special Interest Groups Want You to Believe About Our Schools—and Why It Isn't So*, New York: Rowman & Littlefield Publishers.

Greene, Jay P. and Forster, Greg (2003) Public High School Graduation and College Readiness Rates in the United States, Manhattan Institute for Policy Research: Working Paper No. 3.

Hanushek, Eric and Rivkin, Steven (2004) How to Improve the Supply of High Quality Teachers, Brookings Papers on Education Policy.

Haycock, Kati (2001) Closing the Achievement Gap, *Educational Leadership*, 58(6): 6–11.

Heckman, James, Stixrud, Jora and Urzua, Sergio (2006) The Effects of Cognitive and Noncognitive Abilities on Labor Market Outcomes and Social Behavior, *Journal of Labor Economics*, 24: 411–482.

Kane, Thomas and Rouse, Cecilia (1999) 'The Community College: Educating Students at the Margin Between College and Work', *Journal of Economic Perspectives,* 13(1): 63–84.

Karabel, Jerome (2005) *The Chosen*, Boston, MA: Houghton Mifflin.

Kohn, Alfie (2000) *The Case Against Standardized Testing: Raising the Scores, Ruining the Schools*, Portsmouth, NH: Heinemann.

Lankford, Hamilton, Loeb, Susanna, and Wyckoff, James (2002) Teacher Sorting and the Plight of Urban Schools: A Descriptive Analysis, *Educational Evaluation and Policy Analysis*, 24(1): 37–62.

Lee, Jaekyung (2002) Racial and Ethnic Gap Trends: Reversing the Progress Towards Equity, *Educational Researcher,* 31(1): 3–12.

Lee, Valerie, Mackie-Lewis, Christopher, and Marks, Helen M. (1993) Persistence to the Baccalaureate Degree for Students Who Transfer from Community Colleges, *American Journal of Education*, 102(1): 80–114.

Lesthaeghe, Ron J. and Neidert, Lisa (2006) The Second Demographic Transition in the United States: Exception or Textbook Example? *Population and Development Review*, 32(4): 669–698.

Levy, Frank and Murnane, Richard (2003) *The New Division of Labor*, Princeton at the University Press, New York: Russell Sage Foundation.

Madaus, George and Clarke, Marguerite (2001) The Adverse Impact of High-Stakes Testing on Minority Students: Evidence from One Hundred Years of

Test Data, in Gary Orfield and Mindy Kornhaber (eds) *Raising Standards or Raising Barriers? Inequality and High Stakes Testing in Education,* New York: Century Fund, pp. 85–106.

Massey, Douglas, Mooney, Margarita, Torres, Kimberly, Charles, Camille Z. and Black, Charles (2007) Immigrants and Black Natives Attending Selective Colleges and Universities in the United States, *American Journal of Education,* 113: 243–271.

Matthews, Christine (2007) Foreign Science and Engineering Presence in U.S. Institutions and the Labor Force, Congressional Research Service Report for Congress.

Mayer, Karl Ulrich (2005), 'Yale, Harvard & Co: Mythos oder Modell für Deutschland?', in Hermann Strasser and Gerd Nollmann (eds) *Endstation Amerika? Sozialwissenschaftliche Innen- und Außenansichten,* Wiesbaden: VS Verlag für Sozialwissenschaften, pp. 202–215.

Mayer, Karl Ulrich, Walter Müller, and Reinhard Pollak (2007) Institutional Change and Inequalities of Access in German Higher Education, in: Yossi Shavit, Richard Arum, Adam Gamoran, and Gila Menahim (eds) *Expansion, Differentiation and Stratification in Higher Education,* Stanford at the University Press, pp. 240–265.

Meyer, John (1977) The Effects of Education as an Institution, *American Journal of Sociology,* 83(1): 55–77.

Mishel, Lawrence and Joydeep, Roy (2006) *Rethinking High School Graduation Rates and Trends,* Washington, DC: Economic Policy Institute.

Monk-Turner, Elizabeth (1990) The Occupational Achievements of Community and Four Year College Entrants, *American Sociological Review,* 55(5): 719–725.

National Center for Education Statistics (1989) *Digest of Education Statistics.*

Newman, Katherine (2000) *No Shame in the Game: The Working Poor in the Inner City,* New York: First Vintage Books/Russell Sage Foundation.

Oakes, Jeannie and Lipton, Martin (1999) *Teaching To Change the World,* Boston, MA: McGraw Hill College.

OECD (2006) *Education at Glance. OECD Briefing Note for the United States.*

Odden, Allan and Borman, Godfrey (2004) Assessing Teacher, Classroom, and School Effects, Including Fiscal Effects, *Peabody Journal of Education,* 79(4): 4–32.

Oppenheimer, Valerie K., Kalmijn, Matthijs, and Lin, Nelson (1997) Men's Career Development and Marriage Timing During a Period of Rising Inequality, *Demography,* 34(3): 311–330.

Quartz, Karen Hunter (2003) Too Angry to Leave: Supporting New Teacher's Commitment To Transform Urban Schools, *Journal of Teacher Education,* 54(2): 99–111.

Reynolds, Arthur J., Temple, Judy A., Robertson, Dylan L., and Mann, Emily A. (2001) Long-term Effects of an Early Childhood Intervention on Educational Achievement and Juvenile Arrest, *Journal of the American Medical Association,* 285(18): 2339–2346.

Roksa, Josipa, Grodsky, Eric, Arum, Richard, and Gamoran, Adam (2007) 'Changes in Higher Education and Social Stratification in the United States', in: Yossi Shavit, Richard Arum, Adam Gamoran, and Gila Menahem (eds)

Expansion, Differentiation and Stratification in Higher Education, Stanford: Stanford University Press.

Rosenbaum, James (2001) *Beyond College For All: Career Paths for the Forgotten Half*, New York: Russell Sage.

Rosigno, Vincent and Ainsworth-Darnell, James (1999) Race, Cultural Capital, and Education Resources: Persistent Inequalities and Achievement Returns, *Sociology of Education*, 72(3): 158–178.

Sanders, William (2000) Value-Added Assessment from Student Achievement Data: Opportunities and Hurdles, *Journal of Personnel Evaluation in Education*, 14(4): 329–339.

Shavit, Yossi, Arum, Richard, Gamoran, Adam, and Menahem, Gila (eds) (2007) *Expansion, Differentiation and Stratification in Higher Education*, Stanford: Stanford University Press.

Stephan, Paula and Levin, Sharon (2001) Exceptional Contributions to U.S. Science by the Foreign-born and Foreign-educated, *Population Research and Policy Review*, 20: 59–79.

Tatel, Edith (1999) 'Teaching in Under-Resourced Schools: The Teach for America Example', *Theory into Practice*, 38(1): 37–45.

Walpole, Marybeth and McDonough, Patricia (2005) This Test is Unfair: Urban African-American and Latino Students' Perception of Standardized College Admissions Tests, *Urban Education*, 40(3): 321–349.

Western, Bruce and Petite, Becky (2005) Black-White Wage Inequality, Employment Rates, and Incarceration, *American Journal of Sociology*, 111(2): 553–578.

Witte, John (1998) The Milwaukee Voucher Experiment, *Educational Evaluation and Policy Analysis*, 20(4): 229–251.

Zumwalt, Karen (1996) Simple Answers: Alternative Teacher Certification, *Educational Researcher*, 25(8): 40–42.

SECTION VIII

IMMIGRANT INTEGRATION

15

DIFFERENT COUNTRIES, DIFFERENT GROUPS, SAME MECHANISMS? THE STRUCTURAL ASSIMILATION OF THE SECOND GENERATION IN EUROPE (D, F, GB) AND THE UNITED STATES

FRANK KALTER AND NADIA GRANATO

BACKGROUND AND AIMS

Immigration has become an important phenomenon in virtually every member state of the European Union. While many countries experienced either notable labor migration or postcolonial migration already in the 1960s and 1970s, in the meantime even countries that traditionally were viewed almost purely as sources of emigration—like for example Italy, Spain, and Ireland—have been showing a considerable positive migration balance for a fairly long

Table 15-1: Rate of Labor Force Participation and Unemployment (Men, Age 15–64)

	Labor Force Participation		Unemployment Rate		
	Native-born	Foreign-born	Native-born	Foreign-born	Ratio
Australia	78.7	74.1	6.0	6.5	1.1
Denmark	81.4	63.4	4.4	14.4	3.3
Germany	71.0	64.4	10.3	18.3	1.8
France	69.1	67.0	8.0	13.6	1.7
Canada	78.6	77.7	5.5	6.6	1.2
Netherlands	81.9	68.4	3.6	10.3	2.9
Austria	73.4	70.2	4.3	11.2	2.6
Sweden	75.7	64.2	6.2	13.9	2.3
USA	74.0	80.2	6.9	5.8	0.8
United Kingdom	78.1	72.8	4.7	7.3	1.5

Source: OECD (2005).

time. Similar trends can now be observed for most of the new member states. Almost everywhere in the European Union (EU), the stock of the foreign-born population has grown to nonnegligible amounts.

All over Europe, rising shares of the immigrant populations are accompanied by growing concerns about the consequences of failing integration. Especially in countries with a longer immigration history, evidence now is overwhelming that the incorporation of immigrants proceeds far from smoothly and seems to be more problematic than the experience of classic immigration countries overseas has shown. For example, a recent OECD study (OECD 2005) examines the labor market, which is widely seen as the most important aspect of immigrants' integration (Esser 2000: 304ff; Kalter and Granato 2002). The study reveals that in Europe labor force participation of the foreign-born population is much lower than that of the native born, whereas differences are very small in Australia, Canada, and the United States (see Table 15-1). Furthermore, ratios of unemployment rates of the foreign-born and native-born population also point to the fact that immigrants are better integrated into the labor markets of the classical immigration countries than into the European ones.

Do classical immigration countries like the United States indeed provide better background conditions for assimilation? Is their institutional setting more promising and do they provide more attractive social models in terms of immigrants' integration? Drawing these conclusions appears rather precipitate as inferences about the integrative power of different societies or different institutional arrangements might be misleading when exclusively based on such condensed statistics. One important reason for this being that these highly aggregated figures do not reflect the enormous heterogeneity of the immigrant population between and within countries. Immigrant groups, however, differ considerably in characteristics that are known to be important for being successful in the receiving society, most importantly the human capital they possess or the cultural distance involved. The variation in aggregate outcomes could thus simply reflect different mixtures and different processes of selection with respect to these traits while the basic mechanisms accounting for economic integration do not necessarily differ.

Second, comparing the foreign-born to the native-born population can at most tell part of the story. In the classical immigration countries as well as in many European countries, a notable share of the adult population descends from former immigrants but has no direct migration experience itself. While the success of the direct immigrants might be explained by relatively "obvious" factors as composition or selectivity, it is the fate of their offspring, the so-called second generation, which is widely seen as the true litmus test for the integrative power of a society.

Now, more and more evidence suggests that this test fails in many European immigration countries and this is what causes most societal concern. Interestingly, the integration of the second generation is also at the centre of current scientific and political disputes in the United States. For example, within the prominent concept of "segmented assimilation" (Portes 1995; Portes and Zhou 1993; Zhou 1997), it is argued that the situation of the "new" second generation, representing the children of more recent immigrants into the United States, deviates strongly from the successful historical incorporation pattern. Rather than assimilating smoothly to the mainstream, like the descendents of the former European immigrants, the new second generation would face a serious risk of permanent poverty and assimilation to the underclass. This view, in turn, has been contradicted by others (e.g., Alba and Nee 1997, 2003; Waters and Jiménez 2005) who argue that the model of mainstream assimilation has not lost its importance even with respect to the more recent immigrant groups.

These discussions show that it does not make sense to think of a general and stable "social model" of successful and enduring integration, which could simply be adapted to different contexts. Rather the process seems to depend on a set of structural conditions that might vary between countries but also between groups and over time within a given country. In order to understand country differences properly, one of the major tasks for integration research is to detect the more precise mechanisms that might account for either assimilation or ethnic inequality, and to disentangle and compare them.

Distentangling and comparing mechanisms is what we try to do in the following, concentrating on labor market integration as the most important subdimension of assimilation. Doing this, we will focus on the second generation and compare ethnic groups within countries. Obviously, we cannot do this for every second generation group in all European member states and classical immigration countries. Being pragmatic, we selected Germany, France, and Great Britain which represent the three largest EU countries with considerable shares of the population belonging to the second generation. We compare these three countries to the United States as the allegory for a classic immigration country. The structure of the analysis is given by a rough scheme of mechanisms that is outlined in the next section.

STRUCTURE AND BASIS OF THE ANALYSES

When thinking about the mechanisms which might be important in explaining ethnic inequality, there is a "natural" starting point: mechanisms of general social inequality. It is well known that countries differ in their social fluidity (Erikson and Goldthorpe 1992; Breen and Luijkx 2004). Basically, the core interest of stratification research is on how strong and why one's class destination (D) is influenced by one's class origin (O), and to what degree, and again why, this is mediated by education (E). The analytical scheme is known as the OED triangle (see Figure 15-1) and it has been shown in many comparative projects that the strength of the OE- and ED-link is high almost everywhere but nevertheless shows interesting variance between countries due to different institutional settings (Blossfeld and Shavit 1993; Shavit and Müller 1998; Breen and Luijkx 2004).

Now, immigrants often differ considerably from the autochthonous population of the receiving society with respect to origin or, related, human capital. In many cases they are negatively selected as compared to the indigenous population; in some cases they are positively selected (Borjas 1994, 1999). Given the general stratification processes in a country, this will have an immediate impact on the destination class, in other words, the occupational attainment of their children, the second generation. The strength of the impact will vary between countries according to the strength of the origin–destination link (both directly and via education). This can be captured in the analytical scheme in Figure 15-1 by adding a further nod (M) and a further link (MO). The bold arrows in Figure 15-1 illustrate this "standard path," which is due to selectivity and mechanisms

Figure 15-1: The analytical scheme

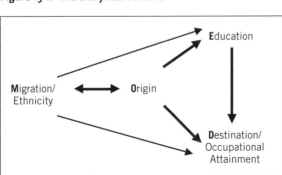

of general social inequality. However, ethnic minority children may face disadvantages (or advantages) either in the labor market or in the educational system that are not mediated by these mechanisms. Traditionally, that is where most emphasis in migration research is put on. These specific ethnic parts of explaining the second generation's occupational attainment are sketched by the additional thin lines (MD and ME) in Figure 15-1.

Given this scheme, the leading research problem of this chapter can be condensed to the question to what degree the patterns of the second generations' structural integration in the three selected European countries and the United States are due to selectivity and the "standard mechanisms" of social inequality or to the more genuine "ethnic" paths. We briefly sketch the main mechanisms the arrows in Figure 15-1 represent and discuss whether and why country differences are to be expected theoretically. We will then try to assess the strength of these mechanisms for selected groups in the four countries empirically.

In doing this, we will heavily rely on the results of a recent comparative project (Heath and Cheung 2007). The idea of this undertaking was to analyse occupational attainment of immigrant groups in several Western countries using comparable data and identical methods of analysis. Although from a methodological point of view, there are still some flaws that call for caution when making strict comparisons,[1] it surely represents one of the attempts that come closest to a cross-cultural comparison of the mechanisms sketched above. The contributions for Germany (Kalter and Granato 2007), France (Silberman and Fournier 2007), Great Britain (Cheung and Heath 2007), and the United States (Model and Fisher 2007) provide us with rich material and will allow us to assess the strength of the MD and the ED path in Figure 15-1. They will also shed some light on the MO link. As the data used in these contributions on most countries do not contain direct measures of social origin, however, we are not able to disentangle the mechanisms leading to ethnic differences in educational attainment. We limit ourselves here to a discussion of the most important findings available in the literature.

The chapter is structured as follows: In the next section, we will sketch the situation of selected second generation groups in the labor markets of the four countries. For the ease of convenience, we will concentrate on results for males only. Then we will disentangle the mechanisms in each country according to Figure 15-1. We will have a brief look at the strength of the ED-link and the educational inequality, before we analyse how much of the ethnic occupational inequalities we observe are due to education or to "genuine ethnic" mechanisms. Then we will review some country-specific contributions on the question to what degree ethnic educational inequality is due to social origin or whether specific ethnic mechanisms are at work here. The last section will discuss the different patterns of second generation (dis-)advantage we observe when we combine all analytical parts.

LABOR MARKET INTEGRATION OF SELECTED SECOND GENERATION GROUPS IN EUROPE AND THE UNITED STATES

This section will sketch the disadvantages or advantages that the male second generation faces in the labor markets of the four countries. As stated above, our principal sources are the specific country chapters in the comparative volume edited by Anthony Heath and Sin Yi Cheung (2007). In the analyses, the second generation as a rule is defined as being born in the host country or having arrived not later than age six. The definition of ethnicity varies between countries due to data limitations. In order to keep the picture transparent, we restrict the discussion to three groups in each country.

The analysis for Germany (Kalter and Granato 2007) uses data from the German Microcensus of 1993 and 1996. Notable case numbers in the second generation can only be found with respect to the traditional labor migrant groups from which we select the three largest, meaning Turks, ex-Yugoslavs, and Italians. In the German data, the definition of ethnicity has to rely on citizenship. For France (Silberman and Fournier 2007), we find information on three major groups defined by parents' country of birth. The group of Maghrebians covers ex-French Algeria, Morocco, and Tunisia. From mostly the same countries came the parents of the Repatriates, who are Europeans and can be distinguished by parental citizenship at birth. The third group are Southern Europeans covering Italy, Spain, and above all Portugal. The French analysis uses data from the INSEE "Formation Qualification Professionnelle" survey 2003. Ethnicity can also be defined by parents' country of birth in the data for Great Britain (Cheung and Heath 2007), which stems from the General Household Surveys available between 1999 and 2001. Here, we consider the second generation groups of Caribbean (Barbados, Belize, Guyana, Jamaica, Trinidad and Tobago = Caribbean Commonwealth), Indian, and Pakistani or Bangladeshi origin. Our colleagues from the United States (Model and Fisher 2007) took data from four waves of the U.S. March Current Population Survey (CPS) and are able to distinguish between various second generation groups, again defined by parents' country of birth. Here, our choice is deliberate: we want to include (a) one of the classic European immigrant groups, as well as two of the "new" groups, (b) one of them known to do very well in the labor market, and (c) one of them doing very badly. Taking the number of cases into account, we end up with (a) Italians, (b) East Asians, and (c) Mexicans.

How well are these second generation groups doing in the respective labor markets? From many possible indicators, we choose class position and rely on a shortened version of the Erikson-Goldthorpe-classification of occupational class that has been widely used in comparative research (Erikson and Goldthorpe 1992, Breen and Luijkx 2004). Five main classes are distinguished: the salariat (professionals, managers and administrators), the routine nonmanual class

Table 15-2: Relative Advantages and Disadvantages of Selected Second Generation Groups in Four Selected Countries Compared to the Indigenous Population (Odds Ratios; Males Only)

		Employed	Salariat	Routine Nonmanual	Petty Bourgeoisie	Skilled Manual
		(Ref.: unempl.)	(Reference: Semi- and Unskilled)			
D	Italian	0.50	0.19	0.46	0.39	0.54
	Ex-Yugoslav	0.53	0.16	0.83	0.24	0.97
	Turkish	0.35	0.05	0.24	0.20	0.54
F	Maghrebian	0.27	0.28	0.50	0.56	0.66
	Repatriate	0.54	1.57	1.16	0.60	0.93
	South European	0.89	0.78	0.76	0.87	0.96
GB	Caribbean	0.31	0.60	0.84	0.59	0.84
	Indian	0.67	2.10	2.73	1.46	0.87
	Pakistani/ Bangladeshi	0.23	0.46	1.50	0.82	0.44
USA	Italian	0.97	1.39	0.98	1.62	1.06
	East Asian	1.42	1.38	1.70	0.61	0.12
	Mexican	0.35	0.27	0.72	0.20	0.59

Source: Calculation based on country chapters in Heath and Cheung (2007).

(clerical and other routine nonmanual employees in administration and commerce), the petty bourgeoisie (small proprietors and artisans with or without employees, and self-employed farmers), the skilled manual class (skilled workers, technicians, and supervisors of manual workers), and the semi- and unskilled class (less-skilled workers in manual, service, and agricultural work). Those who are currently economically active, but not employed are captured in an additional category.

Table 15-2 shows the labor market positions of the second generation groups relative to the indigenous reference population in each country. In the first column odds ratios are given that represent the chances of being employed to being unemployed relative to the respective chances of the reference population. In other words, the cell figure gives the factor with which one would have to multiply the chances of the reference population in order to get the chances of the group at interest. The next four columns show the respective odds ratios when contrasting the four remaining categories of the shortened Erikson-Goldthorpe occupational class scheme against the reference category of semi or unskilled labor.

One clearly sees that in Germany, all three groups suffer severe disadvantages. The chances of being employed for Italians and ex-Yugoslavs are half of the reference group's chances, and for the Turks only about one-third. If employed, all three groups are considerably disadvantaged with respect to social class as they show lower chances of being in higher categories than the semi- and unskilled sector. Among the three groups, Turks are the most disadvantaged, which is a common finding for Germany (Granato and Kalter 2001; Granato 2003; Seibert and Solga 2005).

Also in France, all selected ethnic groups are less successful in entering the labor market than the native-born French. Above all, males of Maghrebian ancestry have a considerably higher risk of unemployment, followed by the Repatriate, and the South Europeans. If employed, Maghrebians are clearly overrepresented in the reference group of semi- and unskilled occupations. The same holds true for the South Europeans, even though the relative differences to the native-born French are less pronounced. In contrast to that, the children of the Repatriate are more successful in gaining access to the salariat than the charter population. Apart from that, they have similar shares in almost all the other occupational categories.

In Great Britain, the picture is similar in some respects, but different in others. When examining the chances of being employed, all groups face disadvantages. For Caribbeans and Pakistanis/Bangladeshis, the odds ratios are even lower than for Turks in Germany. If employed, both groups face disadvantages with respect to almost all class positions, however, on a more modest level as compared to the labor migrant groups in Germany. Most importantly, the Indians outperform the indigenous population in nearly all respects. They have much higher chances to be in the salariat, in the routine nonmanual sector, and in the petty bourgeoisie.

Next, we will compare this to the situation of the selected groups in the United States. We find that the Italians are structurally assimilated with minor differences to the reference population—odds ratios are around 1 and even tend to be higher. East Asians, on the other hand, have higher chances to be employed and to end up in the higher class positions, the routine nonmanual jobs, and the salariat. When it comes to contrasting the semi- and unskilled positions with skilled manual jobs, however, they show disadvantages, meaning that their pattern of labor market integration is U-shaped in a certain sense. Finally, Mexicans do clearly worst. The pattern here is comparable to the labor migrants in Germany or the Maghrebians in France with high relative disadvantages in all respects.

All in all, Table 15-2 reveals that the patterns of structural integration are indeed much more complex than suggested by the highly aggregated statistics shown in Table 15-1. There is not only variation between countries, but also within countries between different groups. Furthermore, the judgement whether there is ethnic disadvantage or not seems to depend also on the specific indicator of labor market integration examined. In the following sections, we will try to analyse what may account for all this variation by disentangling the gross ratios in Table 15-2 according to the analytical scheme in Figure 15-1.

THE IMPACT OF EDUCATION ON OCCUPATIONAL ATTAINMENT

Obviously, the most important explanation of ethnic disadvantage in the labor market is that immigrants or their children lack the resources that are necessary to succeed, above all educational qualifications. How helpful education may be—how strong, in other terms, the ED-relation in Figure 15-1 turns out to be—varies, however, between countries. In order to account for potential country differences in the strength of the relationship over time, it is helpful to recall the basic mechanism behind the ED-relation: According to micro-economic theory, employees will try to maximize their labor market outcomes given their productivity, and employers will try to maximize the productivity of an employee in their hiring decisions given a job vacancy. So, in a perfect market, the best jobs will match with the most productive employees. However, information is incomplete and employers are not able to observe productivity directly. Rather they have to rely on available indicators that can be used as signals of productivity and formal qualifications serve as the best among them (Arrow 1973a; Spence 1973).

The strength of the signalling power is determined, above all, by institutional arrangements, which vary between countries. It is argued that the signalling power is stronger the higher the degree of standardization of educational credentials and the more stratified the educational opportunity is organized (Allmendinger 1989; Müller and Shavit 1998). For example, there is no doubt that Germany is ranking high on both dimensions, thus making the common finding of a relatively strong link between the educational system and the labor market plausible (Müller et al. 1998: 144–151).

In the comparative study where the results we discuss were generated (Heath and Cheung 2007), educational qualifications are measured by a reduced version of the CASMIN scheme (Müller and Shavit 1998) distinguishing five categories (full tertiary qualifications, lower tertiary qualifications, full secondary qualifications, lower secondary qualifications, and none or primary qualifications).

Table 15-3 illustrates the strength of the ED link in the four selected countries with a very rough measure. It shows the odds ratios of being employed and of attaining a certain class position (again using semi- and unskilled occupations as reference) when contrasting the medium educational category (higher secondary) versus the lowest (primary or none).[2]

Confirming many results of comparative social stratification research, we find that in Germany, the impact of education on labor market positions is especially pronounced. In all five columns, the odds ratios for Germany are the largest. The United States ranks second, followed by Great Britain and France.

Apart from all differences between countries, however, Table 15-3 clearly shows that education is a decisive factor in all four countries. Therefore, the next

Table 15-3: The Impact of Education in the Four Selected Countries (Odds Ratios for Higher Secondary Education Versus None or Primary; Males Only)

	Employed	Salariat	Routine Nonmanual	Petty bourgeoisie	Skilled Manual
	(Ref.: Unempl.)	(Reference: Semi- and Unskilled)			
Germany	2.46	65.37	20.70	6.82	3.29
France	1.42	15.18	1.26	2.69	1.08
Great Britain	1.46	13.60	2.69	1.46	0.57
United States	1.73	33.78	7.77	5.26	1.17

Source: Calculation based on country chapters in Heath and Cheung (2007).

Table 15-4: Relative Educational Attainment of the Second Generation in Four Selected Countries Compared to the Indigenous Population (Odds Ratios; Reference Category: Higher Secondary; Males Only)

		Higher Tertiary	Lower Tertiary	Lower Secondary	Primary or None
D	Italian	0.14	0.57	1.29	5.14
	Ex-Yugoslav	0.00	0.33	1.67	5.67
	Turkish	0.13	0.00	1.00	6.13
F	Maghrebian	0.78	0.44	1.11	1.56
	Repatriate	1.08	0.69	0.69	0.69
	South European	0.67	0.78	1.22	1.44
GB	Caribbean	0.54	0.54	1.00	0.69
	Indian	1.54	0.77	0.62	0.38
	Pakistani /Bangladeshi	0.69	0.19	0.75	0.50
USA	Italian	1.20	1.00	0.50	0.50
	East Asian	5.33	4.67	3.00	0.00
	Mexican	0.20	0.90	2.80	4.20

Source: Calculation based on country chapters in Heath and Cheung (2007).

step is to examine the educational situation of the second generation. Table 15-4 shows odds ratios of being in one of the educational categories for the second generation groups relative to the indigenous population. The reference category chosen is higher secondary qualifications, meaning that the odds ratios for this category are set to one.

In Germany, we find a very clear pattern of distinct educational disadvantages. All three second generation groups are clearly overrepresented in the lowest category of primary or no education, and this is most pronounced for Turks. By the same token, all groups are clearly underrepresented in the upper categories. In France, two distinct patterns arise: Compared to the charter population, South Europeans and Maghrebians are slightly overrepresented at the lowest levels of educational achievement, whereas their odds to have higher tertiary education are slightly lower. In contrast, the second generation Repatriate tend to be better educated than the native-born French. In Great Britain, the second generation does quite well in the educational system. Above all, Indians have lower odds of having only primary (or no) qualifications and higher odds to be found in the higher educational categories than people of British ancestry. For second generation Caribbeans and the Pakistanis/Bangladeshis, the pattern is not linear but inversely U-shaped. Here, the odds of primary qualifications are lower relative to those with British ancestry, but the same holds with respect to higher and lower tertiary education. In the United States, second generation Mexicans face likewise severe disadvantages in the educational system as do labor migrants in Germany. In contrast, the remaining two groups outperform the reference group of native born whites with lower odds for lower educational categories and higher odds for higher educational categories. This trend is even more pronounced for East Asians than for Italians.

In sum, the results indicate substantial differences in educational attainment between ethnic groups and between countries.

ETHNIC OCCUPATIONAL INEQUALITY: EDUCATION OR "ETHNIC PENALTIES"?

In this section, we analyse to what extent the observed ethnic labor market inequalities can be explained by education, that is, via the ED path. The reported results stem from regression models that include education as an independent variable and a set of additional controls (age, age squared, and marital status). Table 15-5 shows the effect (odds ratios) of group membership that remains when these variables are controlled for. It captures the degree of ethnic inequality that cannot be explained by educational qualifications. Heath and Ridge (1983) suggested the term "ethnic penalties" to refer to these residual effects of ethnic group membership.

In Germany, educational attainment alone almost perfectly explains the labor market situation of ex-Yugoslavs and Italians. Table 15-5 shows that the odds ratios net of education rise considerably as compared to the gross ratios in Table 15-2. Most odds ratios are not significantly different from equal chances (odds ratio = 1.0) anymore. This reflects the strong impact of education on labor market positions in Germany. The picture is different, however, for second generation Turks. Although here, the odds ratios in Table 15-5 are also clearly higher than in Table 15-2, indicating that education is again able to explain a major part of the group's disadvantage—for Turks, notable and significant ethnic penalties remain, both in terms of employment and class position.

In France, the situation of the second generation Maghrebians is comparable to that of Turks in Germany in as far as significant ethnic penalties remain with respect to employment and positions in all labor market sectors. The difference, however is, that controlling for education reduces these disadvantages only

Table 15-5: 'Ethnic Penalties'—Relative Advantages and Disadvantages of the Selected Second Generation Groups Compared to the Indigenous Population Net of Educational Qualifications and Other Controls (Odds Ratios; Males Only)

		Employed	Salariat	Routine Nonmanual	Petty Bourgeoisie	Skilled Manual
		(Ref.: Unempl.)	(Reference: Semi- and Unskilled)			
D	Italian	0.74	0.73	0.65	1.04	**0.63**
	Ex-Yugoslav	0.79	0.89	1.00	0.90	0.88
	Turkish	**0.50**	**0.29**	**0.33**	**0.77**	**0.57**
F	Maghrebian	**0.19**	**0.30**	**0.50**	**0.42**	**0.63**
	Repatriate	**0.42**	1.38	1.02	**0.49**	0.83
	South European	0.88	1.07	0.75	0.91	1.03
GB	Caribbean	**0.45**	0.90	0.79	1.02	1.07
	Indian	0.68	**1.95**	**2.39**	1.77	0.87
	Pakistani/ Bangladeshi	**0.33**	0.84	1.20	1.67	0.54
USA	Italian	0.99	1.20	0.88	1.31	1.09
	East Asian	1.48	0.94	1.09	0.67	**0.87**
	Mexican	**0.68**	**0.72**	1.03	**0.42**	**0.76**

Values in bold: $p < .05$.
Source: Calculation based on country chapters in Heath and Cheung (2007).

with respect to the salariat. Otherwise, the odds are even smaller than without considering qualifications. The group of Repatriates shows also reduced odds, but significant ethnic penalties are only found with respect to unemployment and access to the petty bourgeoisie. South Europeans do not experience ethnic penalties and their odds tend to rise when controlling for qualifications.

Second generation Caribbeans and Pakistanis/Bangladeshis in Great Britain have similar patterns of ethnic penalties. First of all, the chances to secure a job are significantly smaller for both groups than for people with British ancestry, although controlling for education reduces the disadvantages they experience. Second, their chances of attaining a higher position rise when controlling for education (the only exception being the routine nonmanual sector) and most important, compared to people of British ancestry, no significant differences remain accessing higher labor market positions. In contrast to that, the odds ratios for Indians are somewhat reduced with respect to the salariat and the routine nonmanual sector when controlling for qualifications. However, even the reduced odds ratios net of education are still significantly higher than 1, indicating an additional ethnic advantage. Apart from these two categories, second generation Indians do not experience significant ethnic differences with respect to class position or to being employed.

The labor market chances of second generation Italians in the United States are—as with South Europeans in France—not different from those of the charter population, but in contrast to the French group, their chances are somewhat reduced when education is considered. For East Asians, controlling for education reduces the relative chances considerably with respect to the salariat and the routine nonmanual sector, although only to a level of equal chances compared to the charter population. Only when accessing the skilled manual sector, this group experiences a significant ethnic penalty. For Mexicans, the picture is less favorable. They show the same pattern of ethnic penalties as Turks in Germany. Although the odds ratios net of education are higher than without considering qualifications, significant ethnic penalties remain, the only exception being the routine nonmanual sector.

So by and large, in all countries educational qualifications already tell most of the story of ethnic disadvantages or advantages for most of the groups. Nevertheless, some groups face notable ethnic penalties. Turks in Germany, Maghrebians in France, and Mexicans in the United States are disadvantaged even controlling for education. Indians in Great Britain are still doing considerably better than the reference group when accounting for qualifications.

How can residual ethnic effects net of education be explained? First of all, occupational attainment might depend on material or immaterial parental resources, which may not only or not at all work via education. In the analytical scheme above (Figure 15-1), this is captured by the indirect MO-OD path.

To explain the impact of ethnicity via the direct MD-path, one can in principle find two different starting points. The first would be some form of discrimination, which in a narrower sense of the word means differential treatment that is directly related to an ascribed characteristic (Arrow 1973b), in this case ethnicity. A second branch of explanations relates direct ethnic effects to the lack of skills and resources besides those captured by formal qualifications. A positive residual might be due to a positive selection of migrants on these unmeasured traits (e.g., motivation). In most cases, however, the selection in these traits will be negative. This holds true especially as some of the unmeasured aspects are specific for the receiving society, like language proficiency or other cultural knowledge (Chiswick 1991; Friedberg 2000).

Social capital might be a further, very important resource for occupational attainment. It is well known in the economic literature that social networks play an important role in the labor market (Granovetter 1995; Montgomery 1991: 1408f; Lin 1999). As social networks of immigrants are often confined to their own ethnic groups, it is argued that they might be less valuable with respect to occupational attainment than those of the indigenous population (Portes and Rumbaut 2001: 48; Petersen et al. 2000). However, in the concept of segmented assimilation, it is argued that ethnically homogenous networks under certain conditions might also have positive effects as they might prevent their members from "downward assimilation" (Portes 1995; Portes and Zhou 1993; Zhou 1997). This line of reasoning is used in the context of the relative advantages of Asian groups in the United States.

Unfortunately, we are not able to further disentangle the reported ethnic penalties according to the different branches of explanations, as variables that are related to the sketched mechanisms are not contained in the data sets underlying the comparative study. This holds true for most available data sets with only some rare exceptions. For example, in a recent study based on data from the German Socio-Economic Panel, it could be shown that the penalties for Turks in Germany are mainly due to lacking language proficiency and ethnic composition of friendship networks rather than to discrimination (Kalter 2006). The impact of ethnicity via social origin (the MO-OD path) turned out to be of minor, albeit significant importance.

ETHNIC EDUCATIONAL INEQUALITY: SOCIAL ORIGIN OR "ETHNIC PENALTIES"?

Having seen that educational qualifications are a powerful explanation for the comparatively poor labor market performance of the selected migrant groups, we now turn to examine educational ethnic inequality. Following the paths in Figure 15-1 backwards, the main question is now whether and to what degree the advantages and disadvantages that appear are due to social origin, and thus to mechanisms of general social inequality (OE), or whether additional specific ethnic mechanisms are at work (ME). As in the case of the labor market, we use the term "ethnic penalties" to refer to residual effects of ethnicity here, now with education being the dependent variable and social origin being the crucial explaining variable. In the literature, several explanations for the existence of ethnic penalties can be found: genetic factors (Herrnstein and Murray 1994), cultural factors like differences in orientation toward schooling (Ogbu 1974; Kao and Tienda 1995), differential learning conditions (Portes and Hao 2004), lack of host country–specific capital (Kalter et al. 2007), and discrimination.

In this section, we briefly review the most important findings on the relevance of either social origin or ethnic penalties in explaining the patterns of ethnic educational inequality. Unlike in the sections above, doing so we can not rely on synchronized comparative analyses. While there are a lot of studies and literature reviews for the United States, the state of affairs is less developed with respect to Europe, mostly because adequate data with a reasonable number of immigrants' children and, at the same time, information on parental socioeconomic background is still relatively rare.

In comparative social stratification research, Germany is well-known as a country where the impact of parental socio-economic background on the school success of children is especially pronounced (Erikson and Goldthorpe 1992; Müller et al. 1989). Although some studies report a slightly declining strength of the OE link (Müller and Haun 1994; Kalter et al. 2007), the outstanding role of Germany in this respect has recently been confirmed once again by the results of the international PISA study (Allmendinger and Nikolai 2006). Therefore, it does not come as a surprise that social origin explains most of the ethnic educational inequalities in Germany. Early studies already indicate that only minor disadvantages remain once controlling for socio-economic background, especially for parental education (Esser 1990; Alba et al. 1994). Recent analyses relying on the German Microcensus (Kristen and Granato 2007; Kalter et al. 2007) confirm this finding. Ethnic penalties now even vanish completely, a finding which might somewhat depend on the specific measure of educational success used.[3] So by and large, in Germany, the picture seems very clear: the lack of parental resources and the general process of intergenerational reproduction of social inequalities are the main reasons why the second generation performs poorly in the educational system.

In France, a recent study (Brinbaum and Cebolla-Boado 2007) reports results on the impact of social origin on educational attainment for second generation Maghrebians and Portuguese. As the category of South Europeans in the above analyses of occupational attainment is mainly composed of migrants with Portuguese origin, using the results for the Portuguese group as a proxy for South Europeans in France seems appropriate. Compared to pupils with French ancestry, Portuguese and Maghrebian children achieve lower educational outcomes (Birnbaum and Cebolla-Boado 2007).[4] When parental education as an indicator for social origin is included, the negative impact of ethnicity on educational outcomes disappears for pupils of Maghrebian and Portuguese ancestry.

Several studies have shown that educational attainment of children is connected to their parents' occupational class also in Britain (e.g., Savage and Egerton 1997), although to a lesser extent than in Germany. With respect to the second generation groups selected in this chapter, a recent study (Rothon 2007) documents that pupils with Indian ancestry outperform children of the charter population, whereas the Pakistanis/Bangladeshis and Caribbeans[5] have lower levels of educational attainment. Concerning the crucial question, whether social origin already accounts for these ethnic inequalities in educational attainment, the results suggest that particularly for Caribbeans and to a lesser extent for the Pakistanis/Bangladeshis, residual ethnic disadvantages remain that are not explained by social origin.

When judging the situation in the United States, one can refer to the excellent review by Kao and Thompson (2003). They check available evidence for ethnic inequalities for a series of indicators, such as test scores, grades, track placement, and educational attainment. Roughly, they report that in most of the studies social origin accounts for most of the differences: For example, the fact that Asians outperform the reference group of native-born whites in test scores vanishes once controlling for social background, while a residual disadvantage for Hispanics can still be observed in a study of Kao et al. (1996). The reverse is found for grades, where the disadvantage of Hispanics disappears once including controls for parental education and other familial background variables. Thus the early finding of Mare and Winship (1988) that family background explains more than half of the ethnic differences found in educational attainment can in general be confirmed. The largest negative penalties to be observed are as a rule suffered by blacks, and even if ethnic penalties remain for Hispanics occasionally, they do not reach a similar level by far.

THE SELECTIVITY OF IMMIGRATION

So far, we have seen that, on the one hand, in all four countries, labor market disadvantages and advantages are primarily a matter of education, and that, on the other hand, ethnic educational inequality is for most groups largely explained by social origin. This means that the socio-economic status of the parental generation, in other words the selectivity of immigration, is one of the most crucial background factors to account for the situation of the second generation. In most of the studies cited in the section on ethnic educational inequality among all factors that capture social origin, parents' education seems to be the most telling one. Therefore, Table 15-6 looks at the relative standing of the first generation with respect to education to illustrate the selectivity of immigration. Like Table 15-4, it shows the odds ratios for educational attainment, but now for the first generation.

One can clearly see that all three labor migrant groups in Germany are strongly negatively selected with respect to education. Above all, they have considerably higher odds than Germans to be in the lowest educational group. Moreover their odds for lower and higher tertiary education are much lower than for Germans. Considering the immigration history of Germany, the strong negative selection of the first generation labor migrants is not surprising. The recruitment of labor in the 1960s and early 1970s was specifically aimed at filling gaps at the lower end of the domestic labor market.

In France, the first generation Maghrebians show a U-shaped type of selectivity, as their odds of belonging to the category of higher tertiary education, on the one hand, and of having only primary or no educational qualifications, on the other hand, are both somewhat higher than for people of French ancestry. Maghrebian immigration, mostly from Algeria and Morocco, comprised above all low skilled labor, although later inflows included also a notable number of students coming for secondary or tertiary education. For the South Europeans, we find a pattern of moderate negative selectivity with high odds of having primary or no educational qualifications. As Table 15-6 indicates, the first generation of Repatriates shows also a U-shape pattern.

In Great Britain, all first generation groups show higher odds to end up in the lowest educational category, however their odds-ratios are by far smaller as

Table 15-6: Relative Educational Attainment of First Generation Immigrants in Four Selected Countries Compared to the Indigenous Population (Odds Ratios; Reference Category: Higher Secondary; Males Only)

		Higher Tertiary	Lower Tertiary	Lower Secondary	Primary or None
D	Italian	1.00	0.50	3.00	31.00
	Ex-Yugoslav	0.60	0.60	1.80	7.20
	Turkish	0.50	0.50	1.25	17.25
F	Maghrebian	1.80	0.60	0.80	5.20
	Repatriate	1.88	0.38	0.75	2.00
	South European	1.00	0.50	2.00	16.00
GB	Caribbean	1.25	1.50	2.25	4.50
	Indian	2.40	0.80	2.60	2.40
	Pakistani / Bangladeshi	0.80	0.80	2.60	3.40
USA	Italian	0.67	0.50	0.42	4.33
	East Asian	3.17	1.00	1.00	3.17
	Mexican	0.17	0.50	2.67	30.50

Source: Calculation based on country chapters in Heath and Cheung (2007).

compared to those of the labor migrants in Germany. The patterns of the individual groups are not as uniform as in Germany however. While Pakistanis/Bangladeshis are negatively selected in general, showing higher odds to have primary or no education and lower odds to have higher tertiary education, the Caribbeans have, besides their overrepresentation in lower categories, somewhat higher odds to be in the highest category. The pattern for Indians is also U-shaped, as they are clearly overrepresented at both ends of the educational scale. This reflects the composition of Indian immigration after the Second World War: While many Indian labor migrants were entering unskilled work, there was also a considerable number of highly skilled migrants, for example, Indian doctors.

The first generation Mexicans in the United States are clearly negatively selected with respect to education. When one looks at the highest educational category, the selection bias is even stronger than for the labor migrants in Germany (see Table 15-6). In contrast to that, Asian immigration was more high-skilled from the beginning (Hirschman and Perez in this volume). This is reflected by a U-shaped distribution when looking at the relative educational attainment of the current first generation. The European comparison group of Italians is, if at all, only slightly negatively selected in the first generation with somewhat higher odds for the lowest educational categories and somewhat lower odds for the higher ones.

CONCLUDING REMARKS

Disentangling the mechanisms involved in the integration processes of different second generation groups in various countries shows that the idea of distinct "social models," for example, a European and an American one, which work better or worse with respect to integration is misleading. This becomes clear already by the fact that even within countries, there are huge differences between ethnic groups with respect to relevant characteristics. Further to that, the process of integration is not a monolithic system but rather decomposes into several submechanisms. Thus, for a given group within a country, one mechanism may, relative to other countries, work in favor of integration, while another mechanism makes integration relatively harder.

What is important to note, however, is that in spite of all gradual differences in their strength, many mechanisms work very similarly in all countries. This holds true especially for the processes of general social inequality, which provide a standard trajectory (the OED-triangle in Figure 15-1) for the persistence of ethnic disadvantage or advantage: Labor market integration of the second generation, the key to enduring integration in general, depends, in every country, mainly on educational attainment, which depends, in every country, mainly on parental socio-economic status. Thus existing structures of ethnic inequality are heavily predetermined by the selectivity of immigration (the strength of the OM-link in Figure 15-1). The results of selective migration, that is, the composition of immigrants with respect to resources relevant for integration is what seems to account for most of the variation between groups within countries and for differences between countries.

What is often implied in the discussion about different "models of integration" are institutional settings that affect the additional, genuine "ethnic" mechanisms (the direct ME- and MD-paths in Figure 15-1). And, indeed, we have observed notable country differences in these settings in the sections above. But—apart from the fact that for the general story of the reproduction of ethnic inequality, they turn out to be much less important than the standard path—one finds, again, that these residuals show considerable between-group variance within countries. This suggests that, the effects of institutional settings on the integration processes are not necessarily the same for all ethnic groups. As a consequence, it is also hard to detect clear and distinct "social models" even in this more limited sense. The task would be once more to disentangle these ethnic paths in order to find the relevant mechanisms. Only then would it be possible to decide which precise institutional setting or structural background condition might be responsible for the relative advantage of group A in country X (and thus worth copying) or for relative disadvantage of group B in country Y (and thus worth avoiding).

While theory delivers many rivalling explanations empirical research is still short of studies with convincing evidence. So instead of drawing premature conclusions about the "attractiveness of social models" for the integration of immigrants, bringing about reliable evidence about these more detailed mechanisms will be the most urgent and most promising task for migration research in the next years.

REFERENCES

Alba, Richard D. and Nee, Victor (1997) Rethinking Assimilation Theory for a New Era of Immigration, *International Migration Review,* 31(4): 826–874.

Alba, Richard D. and Nee, Victor (2003) *Remaking the American Mainstream. Assimilation and Contemporary Immigration,* Cambridge, MA and London: Harvard University Press.

Alba, Richard D., Handl, Johann, and Müller, Walter (1994) Ethnische Ungleichheit im deutschen Bildungssystem, *Kölner Zeitschrift für Soziologie und Sozialpsychologie,* 46(2): 209–237.

Allmendinger, Jutta (1989) Educational Systems and Labour Market Outcomes, *European Sociological Review,* 5(3): 231–250.

Allmendinger, Jutta, and Nikolai, Rita (2006) Bildung und Herkunft, *Aus Politik und Zeitgeschichte,* 44–45: 32–38.

Arrow, Kenneth J. (1973a) The Theory of Discrimination, in Orley Ashenfelter and Albert Rees (eds) *Discrimination in Labor Markets,* Princeton, NJ: Princeton University Press, pp. 3–33.

Arrow, Kenneth J. (1973b) 'Higher education as a filter', *Journal of Public Economics,* 2(3): 193–216.

Blossfeld, Hans-Peter and Shavit, Yossi, (eds) (1993) *Persistent Inequality, Changing Educational Attainment in Thirteen Countries,* Boulder, CO: Westview Press.

Borjas, George J. (1994) The Economics of Immigration, *Journal of Economic Literature,* 32, December: 1667–1717.

Borjas, George J. (1999) *Heaven's Door. Immigration Policy and the American Economy,* Princeton, NJ: Princeton University Press.

Breen, Richard and Luijkx, Ruud (2004) Conclusions, in Richard Breen (ed.) *Social Mobility in Europe,* Oxford: Oxford University Press, pp. 383–410.

Brinbaum, Yael and Cebolla-Boado, Hector (2007) The school careers of ethnic minority youth in France: Success or disillusion?, *Ethnicities,* 7(3): 445–474.

Cheung, Sin Yi and Heath, Anthony F. (2007) Nice Work If You Can Get It: Ethnic Penalties in Great Britain, in Anthony F. Heath and Sin Yi Cheung (eds) *Unequal Chances. Ethnic Minorities in Western Labour Markets,* Proceedings of the British Academy 137: Oxford University Press, pp. 507–550.

Chiswick, Barry R. (1991) Speaking, Reading, and Earnings among Low-skilled Immigrants, *Journal of Labor Economics,* 9(2): 149–170.

Erikson, Robert, and Goldthorpe, John H. (1992) *The Constant Flux: A Study of Class Mobility in Industrial Countries,* Oxford: Clarendon Press.

Esser, Hartmut (1990) 'Interethnische Freundschaften', in Hartmut Esser and Jürgen Friedrichs (eds) *Generation und Identität*, Opladen: Westdeutscher Verlag, pp. 185–205.

Esser, Hartmut (2000) *Soziologie. Spezielle Grundlagen. Band 2: Die Konstruktion der Gesellschaft*, Frankfurt a. M.: Campus.

Friedberg, Rachel M. (2000) You Can't Take It with You? Immigrant Assimilation and the Portability of Human Capital, *Journal of Labor Economics*, 18(2): 221–251.

Granato, Nadia (2003) *Ethnische Ungleichheit auf dem deutschen Arbeitsmarkt*, Schriftenreihe des Bundesinstituts für Bevölkerungsforschung Bd. 33, Opladen: Leske & Budrich.

Granato, Nadia and Kalter, Frank (2001) Die Persistenz ethnischer Ungleichheit auf dem deutschen Arbeitsmarkt. Diskriminierung oder Unterinvestition in Humankapital? *Kölner Zeitschrift für Soziologie und Sozialpsychologie*, 53(3): 497–520.

Granovetter, Mark (1995) *Getting a Job. A Study of Contacts and Careers*, 2nd ed., Chicago and London: University of Chicago Press.

Heath, Anthony F. and Cheung, Sin Yi (eds) (2007) *Unequal Chances. Ethnic Minorities in Western Labour Markets*, Proceedings of the British Academy 137: Oxford University Press.

Heath, Anthony F. and Ridge, John M. (1983) Social Mobility of Ethnic Minorities, *Journal of Biosocial Science Supplement*, 8: 169–184.

Herrnstein, Charles and Murray, Richard (1994) *The Bell Curve: Intelligence and Class Structure in American Life*, New York: Free Press.

Kalter, Frank (2006) Auf der Suche nach einer Erklärung für die spezifischen Arbeitsmarktnachteile von Jugendlichen türkischer Herkunft. Zugleich eine Replik auf den Beitrag von Holger Seibert und Heike Solga: "Gleiche Chancen dank einer abgeschlossenen Ausbildung?", (ZfS 5/2005), *Zeitschrift für Soziologie*, 35(6): 144–160.

Kalter, Frank and Granato, Nadia (2002) Demographic Change, Educational Expansion, and Structural Assimilation of Immigrants: The Case of Germany, *European Sociological Review*, 18(2): 199–226.

Kalter, Frank and Granato, Nadia (2007) Educational Hurdles on the Way to Structural Assimilation in Germany, in Anthony F. Heath and Sin Yi Cheung (eds) *Unequal Chances. Ethnic Minorities in Western Labour Markets*, Proceedings of the British Academy 137: Oxford University Press, pp. 271–319.

Kalter, Frank, Granato, Nadia, and Kristen, Cornelia (2007) Disentangling recent trends of the second generation's structural assimilation in Germany, in Stefani Scherer, Reinhard Pollak, Gunnar Otte, and Markus Gangl (eds) *From Origin to Destination. Trends and Mechanisms in Social Stratification Research*, Frankfurt a. M.: Campus, pp. 220–251.

Kristen, Cornelia and Granato, Nadia (2007) The Educational Attainment of the Second Generation in Germany: Social Origins and Ethnic Inequality, *Ethnicities*, 7, 3: 343–366.

Kao, Grace and Tienda, Marta (1995) Optimism and Achievement: The Educational Performance of Immigrant Youth, *Social Science Quarterly*, 76, March: 1–19.

Kao, Grace, Tienda, Marta and Schneider, Barbara (1996) Racial and Ethnic Variation in Educational Achievement, *Research in Sociology of Education and Socialization*, 11: 263–297.

Kao, Grace and Thompson, Jennifer S. (2003) Racial and Ethnic Stratification in Educational Achievement and Attainment, *Annual Review of Sociology*, 29(1): 417–442.

Lin, Nan (1999) Social Networks and Status Attainment, *Annual Review of Sociology*, 25: 467–487.

Mare, Robert D. and Winship, Christopher (1988) Ethnic and racial patterns of educational attainment and school enrolment, in Gary D. Sandefur and Marta Tienda (eds) *Divided Opportunities: Minorities, Poverty, and Social Policy*, New York: Plenum, pp. 173–203.

Model, Suzanne and Fisher, Gene A. (2007) The New Second Generation at the Turn of the New Century: Europeans and non-Europeans in the US Labour Market, in Anthony F. Heath and Sin Yi Cheung (eds) *Unequal Chances. Ethnic Minorities in Western Labour Markets*, Proceedings of the British Academy 137: Oxford University Press, pp. 591–638.

Montgomery, James D. (1991) Social Networks and Labor-Market Outcomes: Toward an Economic Analysis, *The American Economic Review*, 81(5): 1408–1418.

Müller, Walter and Haun, Dietmar (1994) Bildungsungleichheit im sozialen Wandel', *Kölner Zeitschrift für Soziologie und Sozialpsychologie*, 46(1): 1–42.

Müller, Walter and Shavit, Yossi (1998) The Institutional Embeddedness of the Stratification Process. A Comparative Study of Qualifications and Occupations in Thirteen Countries, in Yossi Shavit and Walter Müller (eds) *From School to Work. A Comparative Study of Educational Qualification and Occupational Destinations,* Oxford: Clarendon Press, pp. 1–48.

Müller, Walter, Lüttinger, Paul, König, Wolfgang, and Karle, Wolfgang (1989) Class and Education in Industrial Nations, *International Journal of Sociology*, 19(3): 3–39.

Müller, Walter, Steinmann, Susanne, and Ell, Renate (1998) Education and Labour-Market Entry in Germany, in Walter Müller and Yossi Shavit (eds) *From School to Work. A Comparative Study of Educational Qualification and Occupational Destinations*, Oxford: Clarendon Press, pp. 143–187.

OECD (2005) OECD-Studie über die Arbeitsmarktintegration von Zuwanderern in Deutschland: Zusammenfassung der Ergebnisse, Paper presented at a joint conference of the Federal Ministry of Labour and Social Affairs and the OECD, December 2, in Berlin, Germany.

Ogbu, John U. (1974) *The Next Generation. An Ethnography of Education in an Urban Neighborhood,* New York: Academic Press.

Petersen, Trond, Saporta, Ishak, and Seidel, Marc-David L. (2000) 'Offering a Job: Meritocracy and Social Networks', *American Journal of Sociology*, 106(3): 763–816.

Portes, Alejandro (1995) Children of Immigrants: Segmented Assimilation and Its Determinants, in Alejandro Portes (ed.) *The Economic Sociology of Immigration. Essays on Networks, Ethnicity, and Entrepreneurship*, New York: Russell Sage Foundation, pp. 248–279.

Portes, Alejandro, and Hao, Lingxin (2004) The Schooling of Children of Immigrants. Contextual Effects on the Educational Attainment of the

Second Generation, *Proceedings of the National Academy of Sciences,* 101, 33: 11920–11927.

Portes, Alexandro and Rumbaut, Ruben G. (2001) *Legacies. The Story of the Immigrant Second Generation,* New York: Russell Sage Foundation.

Portes, Alejandro and Zhou, Min (1993) The New Second Generation: Segmented Assimilation and Its Variants, *The Annals of the American Academy of Political and Social Science,* 530, November: 74–96.

Rothon, Catherine (2007) Can Achievement Differentials Be Explained by Social Class Alone? An Examination of Minority Ethnic Educational Performance in England and Wales at the End of Compulsory Schooling, *Ethnicities,* 7(3): 306–322.

Savage, Mike and Egerton, Muriel (1997) Social mobility, individual ability and the inheritance of class inequality', *Sociology,* 31(4): 645–672.

Seibert, Holger and Solga, Heike (2005) Gleiche Chancen dank einer abgeschlossenen Ausbildung? Zum Signalwert von Ausbildungsabschlüssen bei ausländischen und deutschen jungen Erwachsenen, *Zeitschrift für Soziologie,* 34(5): 364–382.

Shavit, Yossi and Müller, Walter (1998) *From School to Work. A Comparative Study of Educational Qualification and Occupational Destinations,* Oxford: Clarendon Press.

Silberman, Roxane and Fournier, Irene (2007) Is French Society Truly Assimilative? Immigrant parents and offspring on the French Labour Market, in Anthony F. Heath and Sin Yi Cheung (eds) *Unequal Chances. Ethnic Minorities in Western Labour Markets,* Proceedings of the British Academy 137: Oxford University Press, pp. 221–269.

Spence, Michael (1973) Job Market Signaling, *The Quarterly Journal of Economics,* 87(3): 355–374.

Waters, Mary C. and Jiménez, Tomás R. (2005) Assessing Immigrant Assimilation: New Empirical and Theoretical Challenges', *Annual Review of Sociology,* 31: 105–125.

Zhou, Min (1997) Segmented Assimilation: Issues, Controversies, and Recent Research on the New Second Generation, *International Migration Review,* 31(4): 975–1008.

16

IMMIGRATION AND NATIVISM IN THE UNITED STATES AND EUROPE: DEMOGRAPHY AND GLOBALIZATION VERSUS THE NATION-STATE

CHARLES HIRSCHMAN AND ANTHONY DANIEL PEREZ

I n this chapter, we review the immigration history of the United States as an illustration of the tensions between national identity and international migration. At various points throughout American history, there have been efforts to limit immigration in order to retain the historical national identity of the country. But the volume and diversity of this effort eventually led to an assimilationist and subsequently to a pluralist definition of American identity.

The ideal of the nation-state, with every people (nation) having a homeland, is a modern concept that only began to take root in Europe in the late nineteenth and early twentieth centuries. Moreover, the highly regulated borders between countries and the routine inspection of passports for international migration are modern phenomena (Torpey 2000: 7). Although nation-states create strong popular bonds of attachment and have almost unquestioned legitimacy in the modern world, the distribution of peoples is only imperfectly aligned with state boundaries. This creates an inevitable division between insiders—those to whom the state belongs—and outsiders—minorities who do not belong to the nation. Some minorities are indigenous with ancestral ties to the national territory, but their political and social status is typically marginalized by the official nationalist ideology. Other minorities are recent immigrants and the descendants of immigrants. In some nation-states, immigrants and their descendents are considered to be permanent outsiders or sojourners regardless of generations of residence. In other societies, the descendents of immigrants can become insiders, but only through acculturation and assimilation to the dominant nation. A third alternative is pluralism, which allows for cultural diversity within a framework of common citizenship and equal rights.

After a brief historical review of the political, economic, and demographic forces that have shaped long distance migration to empires and nation-states, we consider the evolution of national identity and immigration policies in the United Sates. Although the contemporary United States is seen as a "nation of immigrants," the eighteenth century founders identified the nation as primarily those of English descent, or secondarily the peoples of Northwestern European descent who adopted the English language and culture as their own and professed a Protestant faith. Over the course of the last two centuries, there has been a continuing struggle between the forces of inclusion and nativism to define the American nation (Massey 2007). In spite of restrictive immigration laws of the 1920s and the continuing nativist reaction against undocumented migrants, there has been considerable progress in broadening the definition of the American nation to be inclusive of peoples and cultures from many other lands, as well as the descendants of indigenous Americans and Spanish America and, most importantly, Americans of African origin. This struggle is far from complete, but the American experience may be of interest to other countries that are experiencing the conflicts between the need for increasing numbers of immigrants and the historical identity of a nation-state.

HISTORICAL PERSPECTIVE

Nation-states are generally the successors of empires or other premodern polities that were composed of multiethnic populations and migrants from distant lands. Empires were defined by their centers—the city from where the monarch ruled. The boundaries of empires were, however, ill-defined and probably oscillated with the power of the center to extract taxes and conscript labor from the periphery. The cities of empires were invariably multiethnic and drew peoples from a variety of distant locations.

The first imperative for the openness of cities to migrants was simply survival or continuity. All premodern cities (with the exception of those in Japan) were extremely unhealthy and demographic sinkholes—mortality exceeded fertility by a wide margin (Wrigley 1969; McNeill 1976; Hanley 1987). Cities required a continuous influx of labor from rural areas just to maintain their population.

The second imperative that encouraged migration to premodern cites was economic. Migrants from nearby rural areas may have been able to supply unskilled labor for construction, service, and defense, but skilled artisans and merchants were often drawn from distant and culturally distinct peoples.

Knowledge of special skills (e.g., metal workers) and the talents to communicate/trade with distant empires and peoples made outsiders a valued resource (Thomaz 1993: 77–82; Hoerder 2002: Chapter 2). Multiethnic cities were not necessarily harmonious or even tolerant in premodern times, but social and cultural antagonisms were usually held in check because of common interests and political force. The outbreak of violence and war was ruinous for fragile urban institutions as well as for urban peoples (Hawley 1971: 65–66).

During the nineteenth and twentieth centuries, demographic, economic, and political change transformed the world (Massey 2005). The demographic transition (declining mortality followed after a lag by declining fertility) created unprecedented population growth, especially in Europe. Population pressure stimulated waves of long-distance migration, primarily to the New World, but also to other distant lands (Davis 1974).

The era of industrialization was accompanied by the dissolution of empires, the rise and fall of imperialism, and the emergence of many new states. In many cases, state formation was based on the claim of nationalism, which usually implied an ethnic homeland for people with a putative claim of common descent. Nationalism has proven to be an extremely potent ideology of state building in the modern era. Indeed, the boundaries of Europe were redrawn after World War I to give many nations their own state, a policy legitimated by the ideology of national self-determination.

The high rates of domestic population growth in Europe meant that rural to urban migration within most nation states was sufficient for the manpower needs of industrialization. Continued high levels of long-distance immigration were not a necessity for demographic survival or economic prosperity of most European states. The emergence of a system of fixed national borders, strict regulation of migrants, and defining "others" as outside of the political community of belonging seemed perfectly normal and reinforced the prejudices of nationalism and the nation state.

Surveying these developments, historian William H. McNeill (1984: 17) observed that the "barbarian ideal of an ethnically homogeneous nation is incompatible with the normal population dynamics of civilization." According to McNeill, the European nineteenth century ideology of nation building (based on a single people in one country) was only realized by the coincidence of rapid population growth and the incorporation of regional peoples into a national myth of a common language and culture. The logic of nationalism was expressed by Hobsbawm (1992: 134) as "[t]he homogeneous territorial nation could now be seen as a programme that could only be realized by barbarians, or at least by barbarian means." The problems identified by McNeill and Hobsbawm, is the uncertain political status of domestic minorities who do not share membership in the dominant nation of a state and the dysfunctionality of closed borders in a world characterized by interdependence.

An inevitable by-product of nation-states is nationalism, which privileges a population defined by shared ancestry, language, or culture (including religion) as the preferred citizens of any state. The creation of nation states, however, conflicts with the reality that different cultural groups often share the same geography, especially in cities, and that state boundaries often ignore cultural divisions. This has led to new problems of national integration, second class citizenship, and contested national boundaries in many parts of the modern world. Those who do not belong to the nation in a nation-state have the limited options of voice, exit, or loyalty (Hirschman 1970). Loyalty means acceptance of second class status as a minority or perhaps giving up one's identity through assimilation to the dominant population. Exit may mean an exodus to the frontier or to another state where their ancestry matters less. A third possibility, "voice," indicates political discontent at a minimum and perhaps the threat of a rebellion or a secessionist struggle to create a new nation-state.

Just as nationalism was taking hold in Europe in the nineteenth century and beginning to spread around the globe, there were other forces that were expanding the numbers of the potential migrants and the feasibility of large scale long-distance population movements. The most important factors were the acceleration of population growth in many parts of the globe after 1750, opportunities for settlement in frontier societies, and the demand for labor in the emerging industrial economies. Population pressures, with growing numbers of people living at the margins of subsistence, were exacerbated with the commercialization of the agricultural economy and displacement of peasants from the land. In different countries, famines, persecution, and pogroms added to the reasons for exodus in the nineteenth century.

These pressures combined with the cheapening costs of long-distance travel increased the attractions of sparsely settled frontier areas, especially in the New World. All of these conditions led to massive waves of migrants crossing the Atlantic (and the Pacific) from the sixteenth to the nineteenth century (Hoerder 2002). With the depopulation of the indigenous peoples through conquest and the spread of Old World diseases, the New World became the demographic and economic frontier that attracted long-distance migrants from around the world, especially from Europe. The migration to the New World was monumental, both in its demographic size and the diversity of its origins. For the 75-year period from the mid-nineteenth century to the end of the first quarter of the twentieth century, almost 50 million Europeans came to the United States alone (Massey 1988). In spite of some frictions, immigrants were generally welcomed in the New World. Labor was scarce and the endless frontier needed to be settled. Land grants, subsidized passage, and labor recruitment were among the strategies used to induce migrants at various times during the eighteenth and nineteenth centuries (Zolberg 2006).

IMMIGRATION AND NATIONAL IDENTITY IN THE UNITED STATES

The Changing Scope and Structure of Immigration

All Americans with the exception of American Indians are the descendents of immigrants. But some Americans, particularly those of English origin whose ancestors arrived prior to the American Revolution, have considered themselves to be the "native stock" of the American population (Baltzell 1964). The American population has, however, always been much more diverse than the "Anglo-centric" image of the eighteenth century. The first American census in 1790, shortly after the formation of the United States, counted a bit less than 4 million people, of whom at least 20% were of African descent (Gibson and Jung 2002). The estimates of the non-English-origin population in 1790 range from 20% to 40% (Akenson 1984; McDonald and McDonald 1980; Purvis 1984). There are no official figures on the numbers of American Indians prior to the late nineteeth century, but they were the dominant population of the eighteenth century in most of the territories that eventually became the United States.

Almost all African Americans are the descendants of seventeenth or eighteenth century settlers while the majority of white Americans are descendants of immigrants who arrived in the nineteenth or twentieth centuries (Gibson 1992: 165; Edmonston and Passell 1994: 61). Most Americans have acquired a sense of historical continuity from America's founding, but this is primarily the result of socialization and education, not descent.

Each new wave of immigration to the United States has met with some degree of hostility. Old stock Americans generally fear that immigrants will not conform to the prevailing "American way of life" and lessen social cohesion. In 1751, Benjamin Franklin complained that the "Palatine Boors" were trying to Germanize the province of Pennsylvania and refused to learn English (Archdeacon 1983: 20).

Almost 70 million immigrants have arrived since the federal government began counting in 1820 (U.S. Department of Homeland Security, 2006: 8). Although some level of immigration has been continuous throughout American history, there have been two epochal periods: the 1880 to 1924 Age of Mass Migration, primarily from Southern and Eastern Europe, and the Post-1965 Wave of Immigration, primarily from Latin America and Asia (Min 2002; Portes and Rumbaut 1996). Each of these eras added more than 25 million immigrants, and the current wave is far from finished.

These historical trends and patterns are illustrated in Table 16-1, which shows the per cent foreign-born of the total population for each decennial census from 1850 and 1930 and from 1960 to 2000. For the same periods, Table 16-1 also shows the composition of immigrants by region of birth. These dates are selected to show the two major epochs of immigration, but also reflect the availability of data. Data on place of birth were first collected in 1850.

In 1860, on the eve of the Civil War, and after two decades of mass migration from Ireland and Germany, over 13% of the 31 million Americans were of foreign birth. Throughout the nineteenth century, Irish and German Americans, especially Catholics, were not considered to be fully American in terms of culture or status by old stock Americans. In May 1844, there were three days of rioting in Kensington, an Irish suburb of Philadelphia, which culminated in the burning of two Catholic churches and other property (Archdeacon 1983: 81). This case was one incident of many during the 1840s and 1850s when Catholic churches and convents were destroyed and priests were attacked by Protestant mobs (Daniels 1991: 267–268).

These antipathies crystallized in the "Know Nothing Party" (the internal name was the "American" party), which in 1855 elected six governors and sent a number of representatives to Congress (Jones 1992: 134). Their expressed philosophy was simply that of "Americanism," which implicitly communicated the fear of the un-Americaness of immigrants (Higham 1988: 4). Popular support for the Know Nothing Party collapsed in the 1860s when immigrants played a disproportionate role as soldiers for the Union Army.

Immigration increased during the last half of the nineteenth century. During some of the peak years of immigration in the early 1900s, about 1 million immigrants arrived annually, which was more than 1% of the total U.S. population at the time. As a percentage of the total population, the percent foreign-born fluctuated from 13% to 14% during the Age of Mass Migration. If the children of immigrants were counted, more than a quarter of the American population was part of the immigrant community. Since immigrants were disproportionately drawn to jobs in urban areas, the majority of the population in most American cities, especially industrial cities in the Northeast and Midwest, were composed of immigrants and their children during the nineteenth and early twentieth centuries.

With cutoff of immigration in the 1920s, the proportion foreign-born and even the absolute numbers of immigrants declined precipitously in subsequent decades. The 1960 and 1970 censuses counted less than 10 million immigrants— less than one in twenty Americans. With a loosening of immigration restrictions in the 1960s, there was a renewal of mass immigration in the last few decades of the twentieth century. By the 2000 census, there were over 30 million foreign-born persons in the United States—the highest level ever recorded. But with a total U.S. population of almost 300 million, the relative impact is much lower than in earlier times. The per cent foreign-born in 2000 was only a little over 11%. The numbers of immigrants in the late twentieth century is only high relative to the early post–World War II era when immigration was at its nadir. In comparison to most of the nineteenth century, and the early decades of the twentieth century, however, contemporary immigration appears to be "normal"—very

Table 16-1: Percent Foreign-born of the U.S. Population and Region of Birth of the Foreign-born Population: 1850 to 1930 and 1960 to 2000

Year	Foreign-born	Total Population	Percent Foreign-born	Percent Distribution by Region of Birth (for those Reporting Region of Birth)						
				Total	Europe	Asia	Africa	Oceania	Latin America	Northern America
2000	31,107,889	281,421,906	11.1%	100.0%	15.8	26.4	2.8	0.5	51.7	2.7
1990	19,767,316	248,709,873	7.9%	100.0%	22.9	26.3	1.9	0.5	44.3	4.0
1980	14,079,906	226,545,805	6.2%	100.0%	39.0	19.3	1.5	0.6	33.1	6.5
1970	9,619,302	203,210,158	4.7%	100.0%	61.7	8.9	0.9	0.4	19.4	8.7
1960	9,738,091	179,325,671	5.4%	100.0%	75.0	5.1	0.4	0.4	9.4	9.8
				100.0%						
1930	14,204,149	122,775,046	11.6%	100.0%	83.0	1.9	0.1	0.1	5.6	9.2
1920	13,920,692	105,710,620	13.2%	100.0%	85.7	1.7	0.1	0.1	4.2	8.2
1910	13,515,886	91,972,266	14.7%	100.0%	87.4	1.4	—	0.1	2.1	9.0
1900	10,341,276	75,994,575	13.6%	100.0%	86.0	1.2	—	0.1	1.3	11.4
1890	9,249,547	62,622,250	14.8%	100.0%	86.9	1.2	—	0.1	1.2	10.6
1880	6,679,943	50,155,783	13.3%	100.0%	86.2	1.6	—	0.1	1.3	10.7
1870	5,567,229	38,558,371	14.4%	100.0%	88.8	1.2	—	0.1	1.0	8.9
1860	4,138,697	31,443,321	13.2%	100.0%	92.1	0.9	—	0.1	0.9	6.0
1850	2,244,602	23,191,876	9.7%	100.0%	92.2	0.1	—	—	0.9	6.7

Source: Gibson and Jung. 2006. Tables 1 and 2.

similar to the generally high level of immigration throughout most of American history.

Table 16-1 shows that there has been a major change in the sources of immigrants in recent decades. Throughout the nineteenth and early twentieth centuries, upwards of 80% of immigrants came from Europe and most of the rest were from Canada (Northern America). In recent decades, however, the European and Canadian share has dropped below 20%. About half of recent immigrants come from Latin America (broadly defined to include the Caribbean, Mexico, Central and South America, and about one-fourth from Asia). This historical comparison, however, is somewhat misleading.

There was considerable heterogeneity in the national origins of European immigrants during the Age of Mass Migration. Many immigrants from Southern and Eastern Europe were considered "nonwhite" according to the widely accepted racial theories of the day (Higham 1988). For American nativists, the national identity of the United States was still rooted in "old stock" Americans of English Protestant descent. There has always been considerable ambivalence about the magnitude and character of immigration to the United States. There has been general recognition that more people were necessary to settle the frontier, work in the factories, and play other necessary roles, but there were also fears that immigrants might change the composition and character of American society.

The Changing Regulation of Immigration

Some of the major landmarks of U.S. immigration legislation are listed in Table 16-2. This list includes only a few of the major changes in laws and agreements that have shaped American immigration policies. More comprehensive accounts of immigration policies are presented in Bernard (1981) and Hutchinson (1981) and most recently in the comprehensive account and analysis by Zolberg (2006).

In the early years of the republic, Congress passed the 1790 Naturalization Act that established the terms of eligibility of citizenship for "free white persons of good moral character." Although race had not been directly mentioned in the founding documents of the Declaration of Independence and the Constitution, the limitation of naturalized citizenship to whites reveals a narrow definition of national identity that excludes American Indians as well as persons of African and Asian origin. In the following decade, there were several revisions to the terms of the naturalization procedures, including the infamous "Alien and Sedition Act" of 1798 that (among other things) raised the residency requirement for naturalization to 14 years. A few years later, the residency for naturalization was reduced to 5 years.

Generally, the period prior to 1882 is considered to be an "open door era" for immigration (Bernard 1981: 488) but in his magnum opus, Zolberg (2006) reveals a more nuanced interpretation. The 14th Amendment to the Constitution, one of

Table 16-2: Major Landmarks in U.S. Immigration Legislation

1790	Naturalization Act of 1790	Restricted naturalization to "free white persons" of "good moral character"
1865	14th Amendment	All persons born .....in the United States.....are citizens of the United States" interpreted as "jus soli"
1882	Chinese Exclusion Act	Excluded Chinese laborers, renewed in 892 and made permanent in 1902
1907	Gentlemen's Agreement	Agreement with Japan to restrict Japanese immigration to the United States
1917	Immigration Act of 1917	Literacy requirement
1921	Emergency Quota Act	Enacted national origin quotas based on 1910 census
1924	Johnson-Reed Act	Substituted 1890 census as reference for quotas; established numerical limits
1952	McCarran-Walter Act	Reaffirmed national origin quotas; established quota for needed skills
1965	Hart-Cellar Act	Repealed national origin quotas; established visa preferences for family reunification and skills
1980	Refugee Act	Established systematic procedures for refugees using the UN definition of refugees
1986	Immigration Reform and Control Act	Employer sanctions, amnesty for some illegal immigrants, increased border enforcement

Source: Smith and Edmonston. 1997: 22–30 Zolberg 2006.

three post–Civil War Amendments, contained a broad definition of American citizenship that included the former slaves and all persons born in the United States—"jus soli." This right, which is uncommon in most European and Asian countries, has been of paramount importance in allowing the descendants of immigrants to have equal rights with old stock Americans.

The first American effort to close the door to immigration was directed against Chinese on the West Coast in the 1870s (Saxton 1971). By 1882, the anti-Chinese coalition had become so strong that Congress passed, and then President Chester A. Arthur signed, a bill that was popularly known as the "Chinese Exclusion Act" (Hutchinson 1981: 77–84). Although the facts of immigration restriction are clear, the motivations for it are still debated. There is no doubt that the anti-Chinese sentiments were thoroughly infused with racial ideology. Popular prejudices against Asians were openly expressed in newspapers and by most political leaders (Saxton 1971; Daniels 1977). The fact that a similar prohibition was enacted against Japanese immigrants (the so-called "Gentleman's Agreement" of 1907) reveals that race was a primary concern.

The question is whether racism was the primary reason or just a convenient ideology for those who had genuine fears of economic competition with the new immigrants. In her theory of the "split labor market," Edna Bonacich (1972, 1984) argued that much of the antagonism and discrimination against Asian immigrants by working class whites, who led the movement for immigration bars, was based on fears that Asian immigrants' willingness to work for very low wages undercut the incomes of white workers.

The movement to exclude Chinese (and other Asian) immigration to the United States was not a singular event. In his book, *The Great White Walls are Built*, Charles Price (1974) describes how similar restrictive immigration laws were passed in Australia and Canada. Moreover, the restrictions on Asian immigration foreshadowed the movement to exclude immigration from Southern and Eastern Europe to the United States, which culminated with the "national origins" quotas in the 1920s.

The movement to restrict European migration to the United States was a complex phenomenon that played out over decades with a bewildering array of political, economic, and ethnic alliances. The standard economic account posits capital and labor as the main protagonists with business and employer groups advocating free immigration and workers arguing the opposite. There were, however, many other sides to the debate. Immigrant communities, particularly in big cities, were a strong political force against immigration restriction, while Congressional representatives from rural areas were generally opposed to open immigration.

Perhaps the most important force moving the United States toward limits on immigration was the rising tide of nativism—the fear of foreigners, which gradually became intertwined with racial ideology in the first two decades of the twentieth century. American nativism had deep roots in anti-Catholicism and a fear of foreign radicals, but the belief in the inherent superiority of the Anglo-Saxon "race" became the dominant element of the ideology in the late nineteenth century (Higham 1988: Chapter 1). These beliefs and the link to immigration restriction had widespread support among many well-educated elites. The Immigration Restriction League, founded by young Harvard-educated Boston Brahmins in 1894, advocated a literacy test to slow the tide of immigration (Bernard 1980: 492). It was thought that a literacy test would reduce immigration from Southern and Eastern Europe, which was sending an "alarming number of illiterates, paupers, criminals, and madman who endangered American character and citizenship" (Higham 1988: 103).

For three decades, the battle over immigration restriction was waged in the courts of public opinion and in Congress. In 1910, the Dillingham Commission (a congressionally appointed commission named after Senator William P. Dillingham of Vermont) issued a 42-volume report, which assumed the racial inferiority of the new immigrants from Eastern and Southern Europe relative to the old stock immigrants from Northwestern Europe (Bernard 1980: 492). Social Darwinism and scientific racism were in full flower with many leading scholars warning against allowing further immigration of "beaten members of beaten breeds" (Jones 1992: 228–230).

When the passage of a literacy test in 1917 did not have the intended impact of slowing immigration from Southern and Eastern Europe, Congress passed the Emergency Quota Act in 1921 to limit the number of annual immigrants from each country to 3% of the foreign-born of that nationality in the 1910 Census (Bernard 1980: 492–493). These provisions were not strong enough for some restrictionists, who passed another immigration law in 1924 (the Johnson Reed Act) that pushed the quotas back to 2% of each nationality counted in the 1890 census, a date before the bulk of the new immigrants had arrived. The eventual policy was based on infamous "national origins quotas" (Higham 1988: 316–324; Anderson 1988: 140–149). There were no quotas allocated for Asian countries and no mention of any possible immigration from Africa.

Timmer and Williamson (1998) argue that the immigration restrictions that took hold in the United States and many other countries about the same time in the early decades of the twentieth century were primarily motivated by economic considerations and not by xenophobia or racism. There is some evidence that immigration from poorer areas might have slowed the economic gains of domestic workers (Hatton and Williamson 1998; however, see Carter and Sutch 1998), and that the political alliances that did finally lead to immigration restriction were shaped, at least in part, by fears of competition with immigrant workers (Goldin 1994). Although restrictive policies were clearly formulated to address the fears of wage competition of American workers, the conclusion that this was the *only* causal variable ignores the highly charged ideological climate of the era of immigration restriction.

Nationalism and racism were the reigning ideologies of the late nineteenth and early twentieth centuries. Although not every political outcome was determined by these ideologies, they shaped the immigration policy agenda in fundamental ways. In the United States, racial arguments were used by politicians, scholars, and the mass media to convince the American public and the government that the historically open door of immigration should be closed (Higham 1988). This was not an easy case to make in a country whose identity was that of a "nation of immigrants." It took several decades of overt anti-immigrant rhetoric and a broad political coalition before the U.S. Congress was able to pass restrictive immigration legislation that closed the door to mass immigration.

For most of the nineteenth century, immigration had been a necessity because of the high mortality in cities and a general shortage of labor to settle the frontier and to work in the factories of the new industrial age. With declining levels of mortality in the early twentieth century, most countries, including the United States, were generally able to meet their labor needs from natural increase. In such circumstances, the nationalist and racial impulses were, perhaps, given a freer hand to regulate immigration policies over the middle decades of the twentieth century.

THE IMMIGRATION DOOR BEGINS TO OPEN

The imposition of the national origins quotas in the 1920s, followed by the Great Depression and World War II, lowered immigration to its lowest levels since the early decades of the nineteenth century. The "racial" character of the national origins quotas was exemplified by the very limited numbers of Jewish refugees fleeing Nazi Germany who were allowed to enter the United States while the quotas for Great Britain were not utilized. After World War II, U.S. immigration policies came into conflict with America's new leadership role in the international system. If American political ideals were to influence other countries, the discriminatory character of the national origins quotas could be held up as an example of hypocrisy. In vetoing the McCarran–Walter Immigration Act of 1952 (which reaffirmed the national origins quota system), President Truman stated:

> The quota system—always based upon assumptions at variance with our American ideals—is long since out of date. ... The greatest vice of the present system, however, is it discriminates, deliberately and intentionally, against many of the peoples of the world. ..... It is incredible to me that, in this year of 1952, we should be enacting into law such a slur on the patriotism, the capacity, and the decency of a large part of our citizenry (quoted in Keely 1979: 17–18).

Congress overrode Truman's veto, and the national origins quota remained the law of the land for another thirteen years. The domestic and international pressures for immigration reform continued to grow with each passing year. The dam finally broke with the landslide 1964 election, which brought a reform-minded Congress into office. Among the major pieces of Great Society legislation passed was the 1965 Immigration Act, which was championed by a number of senior members of Congress who were the children of immigrants from Southern and Eastern Europe.

The 1965 Hart–Cellar Immigration Act replaced the national origins quota system with a new preference system based on the principles of family reunification and skills. In the decades following the 1965 Immigration Act, there have been a series of new laws that have modified the numerical limits and procedures of immigration and the admission of refugees (Smith and Edmondston 1997: 22–30). In general, these reforms have liberalized immigration to expand the numbers and to create more possibilities for admission.

The sponsors of the 1965 Immigration Act were primarily interested in allowing a freer flow of immigration from Southern and Eastern Europe, the countries hit hardest by the national origins quotas. The primary response, however, has been a major immigration flow from Asia. The first wave of Asian immigrants in the late 1960s and early 1970s were able to utilize the provisions allowing for those in skilled occupations of high demand (nurses, engineers, doctors, etc.) to enter. These early arrivals were then able to use the family reunification criterion to sponsor their relatives. At about the same time, there was a major new wave of immigration from Latin America, especially from Mexico and Cuba.

There have been a series of further changes in immigration laws and policies in the 1980s and 1990s in response to new developments and controversies. One of the most important was the Refugee Act of 1980 that created a regular avenue for refugee arrivals. Prior to 1980, there were ad hoc responses to refugee crises. The 1980 legislation also adopted the United Nations definition of a refugee as a person with a well-founded fear of persecution.

After many years of debate, Congress passed the 1986 Immigration and Control Act (IRCA) that attempted to balance several of the major immigration controversies. Illegal immigrants who had been in the United States for a long time were allowed to stay and were given a path toward citizenship. The other provisions of IRCA were to stop further illegal immigration by hardening the border (walls, fences, more guards) and by imposing sanctions against employers who knowingly employ illegal immigrants. In spite of the well-meaning intentions expressed in the IRCA legislation, the policy has been a colossal failure (Massey et al. 2002).

The movement to a less restrictive policy of immigration to the United States has been paralleled by comparable reforms in other countries. In the early 1970s, Australia ended its "White Australia" policy and allowed significant numbers of Asians to immigrate. In the early 1990s, the countries of the European Common Market loosened restrictions on interstate migration. Citizens of any country in the European Common Market can move to any other country and are free to seek employment or attend schooling on equal terms with natives of the country. The appearance of these common patterns in a number of countries and regions suggests that the nationalist impulse, which sought to limit and control international migration, was waning during the last few decades of the twentieth century.

Underlying the change in immigration policies were broad economic and demographic forces in advanced industrial countries. Population growth has slowed, and there is a shortage of native-born persons who are willing to work in lowly paid positions in the economy, including seasonal agricultural labor. Population aging, the other major demographic trend, has also contributed a slowing rate of growth (an absolute decline in some countries) of population in the working ages. These domestic trends have been complemented with a virtually unlimited supply of potential immigrant labor, sometimes skilled and always highly motivated from developing countries.

The net result has been an increase in immigration in most industrial countries over the last few decades of the twentieth century. Distinctly different patterns emerged in Europe and the United States. Many European countries adopted "guest worker" programs, which were intended to be temporary stays by workers from the labor surplus countries of Southern Europe and North Africa. Guest workers were generally not eligible for citizenship and were expected to return home when their contracts were completed. The United States maintained a formal immigration framework, whereby legal immigrants could apply for citizenship after five years, but also tolerated a parallel system of "illegal immigration."

Both policies reflect an unwillingness to acknowledge the realities of international migration. Most temporary workers did not return home, and they often brought their families and became permanent residents of the host society. The relative openness of the U.S. society to illegal or "undocumented immigration" has led to the conclusion that efforts to regulate immigration are primarily symbolic. Understanding the "failure" of immigration policies requires looking beyond mistaken assumptions and inadequate enforcement to see how deeply embedded international migration has become in the modern world economy.

The magnitude of immigrants in the American economy is shown in Table 16-3, which presents recent (2004) figures on the labor force of persons age 16 and over, subdivided into employed and unemployed by immigrant generation and sex. The first generation includes the foreign-born, the second generation includes the children of immigrants, and the balance of the population is included as part of the third and higher generations.

There are about 137 million jobs in the American economy—as measured by the total number of employed persons. Almost 20 million or roughly 15% of these jobs are held by immigrants (or 29 million corresponding to 21% of all jobs if the children of immigrants are included). If immigrants were competing with native-born workers, this huge number of immigrants would adversely affect the employment prospects of native-born workers. However, the unemployment rate of the third and higher generation workers is only 6%—a very low rate in historical perspective. It seems that the economic role of immigrants is additive and does not subtract from the opportunities of native-born workers (Card 2005; Carter and Sutch 2006).

The unemployment rates of immigrants are comparable to those of the native-born population. These aggregate figures are not completely comparable because of differences in age composition, but there do not appear to be significant differences.

Popular attitudes toward immigration remain ambivalent. The prejudices against immigrants and nativist fears have not disappeared, but their open expression has been sharply reduced. These changes in economics, demography, labor demand, and ideology have contributed to a much freer flow of international labor migration in the late twentieth century (Castles and Miller 1998; Massey et al. 1998).

Table 16-3: Employment Status of the Civilian Population 16 Years and Over by Sex and Generation: 2004 (Numbers in thousands[a])

			Generation[b]					
	Total		First		Second		Third-and-Higher	
Sex and Employment Status	Number	Percent	Number	Percent	Number	Percent	Number	Percent
Total Civilian Labor Force	146,062	100.0	21,168	100.0	9,719	100.0	115,175	100.0
Employed	137,151	93.9	19,857	93.8	9,083	93.5	108,211	94.0
Unemployed	8,910	6.1	1,310	6.2	636	6.5	6,964	6.0
Total Male Civilian Labor Force	77,860	100.0	12,736	100.0	5,131	100.0	59,993	100.0
Employed	72,739	93.4	12,001	94.2	4,744	92.5	55,995	93.3
Unemployed	5,121	6.6	735	5.8	387	7.5	3,998	6.7
Total Female Civilian Labor Force	68,202	100.0	8,432	100.0	4,588	100.0	55,182	100.0
Employed	64,412	94.4	7,857	93.2	4,339	94.6	52,216	94.6
Unemployed	3,789	5.6	575	6.8	249	5.4	2,966	5.4

a Employment status refers to reference week of the survey.

b The foreign-born are considered first generation. Natives with either parent born in a foreign country are considered second generation. Natives with neither parent born in a foreign country are considered third-and-higher generation.

Source: U.S. Census Bureau (2004).

INTERNATIONAL MIGRATION IN THE TWENTY-FIRST CENTURY

The contradictions between tightly regulated international borders and the modern world economy are becoming increasingly clear. Most immigration policies, of whatever type, are residues of the first half of the twentieth century, when regulated borders were a hallmark of modern statecraft. If the role of a state was to promote the welfare of the national population (a group defined by descent or membership), than a clear objective was to keep others (nonmembers of the nation) out, or to keep the numbers of immigrants to very modest levels. Policies of tightly regulated borders developed in nineteenth century nation-building states, initially in Europe and then spread around the globe in the twentieth century, including the traditional immigrant receiving societies in the New World and Oceania.

These policies "worked" because domestic population growth in most countries was sufficient to meet labor demand. Indeed, population growth reached record levels everywhere in the twentieth century. Although rapid population growth created immense pressures in many labor surplus countries, there were few places that needed additional labor or allowed open migration. Passport controls were expensive and irksome to many, but they became accepted as normal features of modern states. Over the last few decades of the twentieth century, however, strains in the system of tight immigration policies were beginning to show.

The first sign was "labor demand" in industrial countries that could not be met by domestic supply, at least not at the wages offered. Employers found it more desirable to import labor from abroad than to raise wages or to mechanize production. If this pattern were found in only one country or in only a few sectors, then it might be possible to consider a fairly narrow explanation in terms of political cultures or market rigidities. The demand for "cheaper immigrant labor," however, spans many sectors (agriculture, manufacturing, construction, repair services, restaurants, and child care) in most industrial countries, including a growing number of rapidly developing countries. The increasingly global international economy seems to create recurrent needs for labor greater than that available from domestic population growth.

The demand for immigrant labor is not restricted to unskilled manual labor. The United States and other industrial countries have encountered a shortage of scientific and engineering workers, particularly in the high-tech sector. This demand has been met, in part, by allowing many talented foreign students in American universities to convert their student visas to immigrant status. There has also been a gradual shift over the last few decades to more open immigration policies for a variety of reasons—refugees, agricultural workers, "illegal" immigrants with long residences in the country, peoples in countries that have too few American citizen relatives to sponsor them, and workers in high demand by U.S. employers.

These moves toward more liberal immigration policies in the United States are part of a broader international context with comparable patterns emerging in other countries. The policy of free movement of citizens in the European Common Market is the most striking example, but there are trends toward generous policies of admitting refugees and temporary workers in many parts of the world. There are even a few examples of more generous citizenship policies, but these are halting, often facing a domestic backlash from nationalist sentiments that have been weakened, but not disappeared (Lucassen 2005).

More liberal immigration policies appear to be highly functional in modern industrial and postindustrial societies. Standard economic theory posits that domestic migration is a functional response to wage differentials between areas. Migration allows for workers to benefit from higher wages in growing areas and stimulates the economy to operate more efficiently by creating larger and more porous labor and consumer markets. Indeed, the logic for lessening barriers to migration is similar to that of international free trade. Economic theory suggests that all countries benefit from the free flows of capital, goods, and technology across international borders. International migration is often excluded from discussions about expanding international trade (such as in the NAFTA debate), largely because of political considerations rather than economic theory (Massey et al. 2002).

Globalization is the most powerful trend in the world today. There are few places on Earth that are not exposed to the presence of the international forces of the mass media, multinational corporations, and Hollywood images. Every commodity from fresh food to electronic products moves around the globe in such profusion that most persons are unaware of the nationality of the producers of the goods (and services) they consume. Although international trade has always created competition between businesses and workers in different countries, the current era with instantaneous communication and cheap transportation has created a qualitatively new international community. In this setting, barriers to international labor mobility are an anachronism of the earlier era. Just as most countries, regardless of political ideology, have striven to make passport lines more efficient in recent times to encourage the very profitable tourist sector, it seems that most twenty-first century societies will ease immigration barriers in order to profit from the increasingly globalized world economy.

REFERENCES

Akenson, Donald H. (1984) Why the Accepted Estimates of the American People, 1790, Are Unacceptable, *William and Mary Quarterly*, 41(1): 102–119.

Anderson, Margo (1988) *The American Census: A Social History*, New Haven, CT: Yale University Press.

Archdeacon, Thomas J. (1983) *Becoming American: An Ethnic History, New York:* The Free Press.

Baltzell, Edward Digby (1964) *The Protestant Establishment: Aristocracy and Caste in America*, New York: Vintage Books.

Bernard, William S. (1980) Immigration: History of U.S. Policy, in Stephan Thernstrom (ed.) *Harvard Encyclopedia of American Ethnic Groups*, Cambridge, MA: Harvard University Press, pp. 486–495.

Bonacich, Edna (1972) A Theory of Ethnic Antagonism: The Split Labor Market, *American Sociological Review*, 37(5): 547–559.

Bonacich, Edna (1984) Asian Labor in the Development of California and Hawaii, in Lucie Cheng and Edna Bonacich (eds) *Labor Immigration Under Capitalism*, Berkeley: University of California Press, pp. 130–185.

Card, David (2005) 'Is the New Immigration Really So Bad?' *The Economic Journal*, 115, 507: F300–F323.

Carter, Susan and Sutch, Richard (1998) Historical Background to Current Immigration Issues, in James P. Smith and Barry Edmonston (eds) *The Immigration Debate: Studies on the Economic, Demographic, and Fiscal Effects of Immigration*, Washington, D.C., National Research Council, pp. 289–366.

Carter, Susan and Sutch, Richard (2006) The Economic Consequences of Immigration for Resident Workers: Perspectives from America's Age of Mass Migration, unpublished paper August 7, Department of Economics, University of California-Riverside.

Castles, Stephen and Miller, Mark J. (1998) *The Age of Migration: International Population Movements in the Modern World*, second edition, New York: The Guilford Press.

Daniels, Roger (1977) *The Politics of Prejudice: The Anti-Japanese Movement in California and the Struggle for Japanese Exclusion*, New York: Atheneum.

Daniels, Roger (1991) *Coming to America: A History of Immigration and Ethnicity in American Life*, New York: Harper Perennial.

Davis, Kingsley (1974) 'The migrations of human populations', in *The Human Population, A Scientific American Book*, San Francisco: W.H. Freeman, pp. 53–65.

Edmonston, Barry and Passel, Jeffrey (eds) (1994) *Immigration and Ethnicity: The Integration of America's Newest Arrivals*, Washington, DC: Urban Institute Press.

Gibson, Campbell and Jung, Kay (2006) 'Historical Census Statistics on the Foreign Born of the United States, 1850-2000', *Population Division Working Paper 81*, Washington, DC: U.S. Census Bureau. Online. Available from http://www.census.gov/population/www/documentation/twps0081/twps0081.pdf (accessed 4 July 2008).

Goldin, Claudia (1994) 'The Political Economy of Immigration Restriction in the U.S., 1890 to 1921', in Claudia Goldin and Gary Libecap (eds) *The Regulated Economy: A Historical Approach to Political Economy,*. Chicago, IL: University of Chicago Press.

Hanley, Susan (1987) Urban Sanitation in Preindustrial Japan, *Journal of Interdisciplinary History*, 18, Summer: 1–26.

Hatton, Timothy J. and Williamson, Jeffrey G. (1998) *The Age of Mass Migration: Causes and Economic Impact*, New York: Oxford University Press.

Hawley, Amos H. (1971) *Urban Society: An Ecological Approach*, New York: Ronald Press.

Higham, John (1988) *Strangers in the Land: Patterns of American Nativism 1860–1925*, 2nd ed., New Brunswick: Rutgers University Press.

Hirschman, Albert O. (1970) *Exit, Voice, and Loyalty: Responses to Decline in Firms, Organizations, and States*, Cambridge: Harvard University Press.

Hobsbawm, Eric J. (1992) *Nations and Nationalism Since 1780: Programme, Myth and Reality*, second edition, Cambridge: Cambridge University Press.

Hoerder, Dirk (2002) *Cultures in Contact: World Migrations in the Second Millennium*, Durham: Duke University Press.

Hutchinson, Edward P. (1981) *Legislative History of American Immigration Policy: 1798–1965*, Philadelphia: University of Pennsylvania Press.

Jones, Maldwyn, A. (1992) *American Immigration*, second edition, Chicago: The University of Chicago Press.

Keely, Charles (1979) *U.S. Immigration: A Policy Analysis*, New York: The Population Council.

Lucassen, Leo (2005) *The Immigrant Threat: The Integration of Old and New Migrants in Western Europe Since 1850*, Urbana: University of Illinois Press.

Massey, Douglas S. (1988) Economic Development and International Migration in Comparative Perspective, *Population and Development Review*, 14(3): 383–413.

Massey, Douglas S. (2005) *Strangers in a Strange Land: Humans in an Urbanizing World*, New York: W.W. Norton.

Massey, Douglas S. (2007) *Categorically Unequal: The American Stratification System*, New York: Russell Sage.

Massey, Douglas S., Arnago, Joaquin, Hugo, Graeme, Kouaouci, Ali, Pellegrino, Adela, and Taylor, J. Edward (1998) *Worlds in Motion: Understanding International Migration at the End of the Millennium*, Oxford: Clarendon Press.

Massey, Douglas S,. Durand, Jorge, and Malone, Noland J. (2002) *Beyond Smoke and Mirrors: Mexican Immigration in an Era of Economic Integration*, New York: Russell Sage.

McDonald, Forrest and Shapiro McDonald, Ellen (1980) 'The Ethnic Origins of the American People, 1790', *William and Mary Quarterly*, 37(2): 179–199.

McNeill, William H. (1976) *Plagues and Peoples*, Garden City: Anchor Books.

McNeill, William H. (1984) Human Migration in Historical Perspective, *Population and Development Review*, 10(1): 1–18.

Min, Pyong Gap (ed.) (2002) *Mass Migration to the United States: Classical and Contemporary Periods*, Walnut Creek, CA: Altmira Press.

Price, Charles A. (1974) *The Great White Walls Are Built: Restrictive Immigration to North America and Australasia 1836–1888*, Canberra: Australian National University Press.

Portes, Alejandro and Rumbaut, Ruben (1996) *Immigrant America: A Portrait*, *second edition*, Berkeley, CA: University of California Press.

Purvis, Thomas L. (1984) The European Ancestry of the United States Population, 1790, *William and Mary Quarterly*, 41(1): 85–101.

Saxton, Alexander (1971) *The Indispensable Enemy: Labor and the Anti-Chinese Movement in California*, Berkeley, CA: University of California Press.

Smith, James P. and Edmonston, Barry (eds) (1997) *The New Americans: Economic, Demographic, and Fiscal Effects of Immigration*, Washington, DC: National Academy Press.

Thomaz, Luis Filipe Ferreira Reis (1993) The Malay Sultanate of Melaka, in Anthony Reid (ed.) *Southeast Asia in the Early Modern World*, Ithaca: Cornell University Press, pp. 69–90.

Timmer, Ashley S. and Williamson, Jeffrey G. (1998) Immigration Policy Prior to the 1930s: Labor Markets, Policy Interactions, and Globalization Backlash, *Population and Development Review*, 24(4): 739–771.

Torpey, John (2000) *The Invention of the Passport: Surveillance, Citizenship, and the State*, Cambridge: Cambridge University Press.

U.S. Census Bureau (2007) *United States Foreign Born Population. Data Tables.* Online. Available from: http://www.census.gov/population/www/socdemo/foreign/ppl-176.html (accessed 11 December 2007).

U.S. Department of Homeland Security (2006) *Yearbook of Immigration Statistics: 2004*, Washington, DC: U.S. Department of Homeland Security, Office of Immigration Statistics.

Wrigley, Edward A. (1969) *Population and History*, New York: McGraw Hill.

Zolberg, Aristide R. (2006) *A Nation by Design: Immigration Policy in the Fashioning of America,* Cambridge, MA: Harvard University Press and the Russell Sage Foundation.

SECTION IX

CONCLUSION

17

THE EPISTEMOLOGY OF COMPARATIVE ANALYSES: WHAT DO WE KNOW?

JENS ALBER AND NEIL GILBERT

The introduction to this volume ended with a quote from de Tocqueville, promising a high standard of objectivity, which strived to link ideas to facts rather than molding facts to fit ideas. In drawing to the close of this volume, we should note that although the many empirical data presented throughout the chapters lend a degree of objectivity to the discussion, subjective judgments based on assumptions and values (rational and well-reasoned as they may be) enter both the selection of the facts that are observed and their interpretation. "Value premises," as Myrdal (1958: 254–55) explained, "are required not only to draw practical inferences from observations and economic analysis but... to direct our observations and carry out our analysis." Not only do subjective judgments enter the selection of operational measures and the facts to be observed, but they also allow different ideas and interpretations to be molded to the same set of facts—as also the two editors coming from different sides of the Atlantic experienced when preparing this volume. In comparing social spending, for example, one often finds countries with a higher level of welfare expenditure depicted as representing a more generous society and having a stronger social safety net than those with lower levels of spending–when the selection of facts is limited to the percentage of GDP allocated for social welfare. But if it is found that the countries with higher levels of spending also have higher levels of unemployment and disability, then, is their level of spending to be interpreted as representing greater generosity and social solidarity or a weaker economy and less healthy labor force? It is possible, of course, that both interpretations capture empirical truths.

WHAT TO COUNT AND WHAT IT MEANS

Empirical assessments of European and American social models depend heavily upon how one views what is knowable—the nature of knowledge, its scope and validity. The issue is complex. Take an apparently straightforward question, such as, are there differences in unemployment rates between Europe and the United States? First, one must agree on what constitutes work and who is counted as unemployed. A woman paid by government to work in a day care center is counted as employed. How do we count the same woman if she is paid a home-care allowance by government to care for her own children at home and also given work credit for that time on her social security account? Should unemployment rates be compared on a cross-sectional basis for a given year or are they based on an average over the period of some business cycle? Does the average length of unemployment spells inform our understanding of differences in unemployment rates between the United States and Europe? How is unemployment counted when a government pays workers to take a sabbatical leave from their jobs, if those jobs are filled by people currently unemployed?

In grappling with the social, political, and economic dimensions of societal well-being in Europe and the United States, the chapters in this volume yield many useful insights into what counts, how to count it, and how to interpret the results. At the same time, these empirical forays into comparative analysis raise many questions about how to fully describe the similarities and differences among the dimensions being measured and what they ultimately signify. Here are some of the findings, interpretations, and methodological twists and turns, which deepen our appreciation of the epistemology of comparative analysis.

TAKING THE MEASURE OF DEMOCRACY

What counts as a good democracy? And to what extent do the U.S. and European models vary according to these measures? Ringen (Chapter 1) and Samples (Chapter 2) come at these questions from different angles, arrive at different answers, and in the process generate new issues about what values, methods, and assumptions inform our understanding of a good democracy. Ringen rejects the conventional approach to comparative assessments of democracies, which measures how democratic they are in light of characteristics, such as the extent to which there is an open, competitive, functioning polity with institutional procedures for the transfer of executive power. Instead of these measures, which show little difference in the degree of democracy among the advanced democratic countries, Ringen seeks to judge the quality of a democracy by what it does for its citizens in giving them the freedom to act as masters of their own lives and by producing outcomes, such as trust and security. To that end, he develops an index of democratic quality based on eight indicators, which are designed to measure not only system properties but also system performance and are used to rank eleven countries. According to this index, the United States ranks toward the bottom of the list, just above Italy and Poland, tied with Spain, and just below France, the United Kingdom, and the Czech Republic. Some of the outcome indicators in the index, particularly the rate of child poverty, are open to different interpretations. For example, on the relative measure of child income poverty, the Czech Republic is scored as having a lower level of poverty than much wealthier countries such as the United States, United Kingdom, Italy, and Germany. However, as Saraceno (Chapter 7) points out, the interpretation of a relative poverty measure is clouded by substantial differences in standards of living and the poverty rate of a country like the Czech Republic would rise well above that of Italy, Germany, and many other countries if a common EU standard was employed. In addition, Ringen's index ranks spending on public health in the United States—based on the UN Human Development Report—as low relative to the other countries in 2002, whereas Castles' (Chapter 5) data for that year based on the Organization for Economic Cooperation and Development (OECD) show the U.S. level of public expenditure on health well above the level indicated in Ringen's index and higher than the average for the EU-12 and EU-14. While Ringen finds no evidence for a joint European social model, as European countries have widely discrepant index values ranging from 0 to 6, the relatively low U.S. index score of 2 is well within the range of the European countries.

Sample's analysis (Chapter 2) draws a much sharper distinction between democracy in Europe and the United States. His criteria of a good democracy include the promotion of individual liberty, seen as the absence of coercive government activities. From this perspective, the less the government takes from citizens in taxes, the less it spends, and the less it regulates, the more individual liberty is allowed to flourish. He recognizes that the idea of liberty as negative freedom from coercion has often been contrasted with the positive freedom to master one's own life, the exercise of which requires a certain level of resources. The positive ideal of liberty requires government to transfer resources from rich citizens to those who have little—and is reflected in Ringen's index by the level of child poverty and government spending on health. Samples perceives Ringen's measures of democracy as reflecting the normative perspective of European social democrats in contrast to his definition, which reflects a liberal U.S. model. Although Samples' perspective portrays Europe with a degree of social democratic uniformity that does not entirely square with the orientation of many conservative governments (and almost disallows more than a decade of Margaret Thatcher's reign over British society), it is not entirely different from the focus of the European Commission, the European Council, and the European Court of Justice on the essential four freedoms of the free movement of goods, persons, services, and capital.

TALLYING VOTER PARTICIPATION

Differences between European and American concepts of democracy are further explored in the chapters on electoral participation by Alber and Kohler (Chapter 3) and by McDonald (Chapter 4). Alber and Kohler's contribution shows that electoral turnout is not only higher in Europe than in the United States, but also much less socially skewed. In terms of levels of turnout, the new member states of the enlarged EU have recently approximated the low American levels, but in terms of the equality of turnout across poor and rich groups or groups with high or little formal education, they are more similar to the Western European nations. Depending on the exact measure—income or education—the turnout gap between those at the top and at the bottom is three to five times higher in the United States than in Europe where the difference is usually limited to below 10 percentage points.

Looking at potential determinants of the discrepant turnout patterns, the authors examine the impact of the procedural rules governing elections, and of the inclusiveness of state institutions. They find that differences in the levels of turnout can partly but not entirely be related to differences in election procedures, because even European countries with similar institutional rules have higher and less socially skewed turnout than the United States. Following Seymour Martin Lipset's notion that in cohesive democracies all groups react similarly to major stimuli, the authors argue that procedural rules provide similar (dis)incentives to all social groups and therefore do not travel far in explaining the much higher inequality of electoral participation in America. According to their analysis, European states are more politically inclusive, because, on the input side, the access to political office is less limited to wealthy citizens who can afford the high costs of media access and of electoral campaigns, whereas on the output side European welfare states are more universal and less categorically selective, thus fostering political integration. In line with this notion, they show differences between Europe and the United States to diminish considerably when the analysis is confined to the pensioner generation whose integration into welfare state schemes is largely similar on both sides of the Atlantic, because American pensioners have Medicare as well as universal pensions.

Sustaining the notion that high turnout is an indication of successful political integration, Alber and Kohler furthermore show that politically satisfied people go more frequently to the polls than dissatisfied citizens. They also find that voting and participation in other forms of political activity are highly correlated and that alternative forms of political engagement—some of which are more frequently found in the United States—are distributed at least as unequally as the act of voting.

The chapter by Michael McDonald shows that national aggregate data for the United States conceal very wide-ranging heterogeneity within the country, because the constitution gives the states the legal rights to regulate and administer elections. In general, the U.S. electoral system invites low turnout, because participation is not only voluntary, but also costly, as voting requires prior registration and most states require their voters to register four weeks or even longer before the election. Following his analysis, registration procedures and the competitive nature of elections are the two major determinants of state-specific turnout, which tends to be higher in states with easy or no registration and in contexts where elections are embattled contests between rival candidates.

With his more fine-grained state-specific data for the United States, McDonald's analyses sustain Alber and Kohler's finding of a huge participation gap between rich and poor voters in America. Turnout in low and high income quartiles tends to be correlated with the overall turnout rate in states, and the gap in turnout is somewhat smaller in states with easy registration procedures. In an attempt to understand what factors structure the size of the turnout gap, McDonald introduces the concept of the "stimulating effect" of elections. When elections are only moderately stimulating, he expects the gap between the poor and the wealthy to widen. When they are very uninteresting, only core voters go to the polls independent of their socioeconomic background, whereas in highly contested and stimulating elections the gap narrows, because the participation of the rich reaches a ceiling and the poor can catch up.

Arguing that the procedural costs of participation affect different groups differently, as individuals of higher socioeconomic status are better equipped with cognitive skills to navigate voting procedures and to process campaign messages, while having also more leisure time, McDonald proposes two major ways to bolster turnout and reduce the inequality of participation: to make voting widely accessible by easing registration, and to make elections competitive so that the act of voting becomes meaningful.

PATTERNS OF SPENDING AND WHAT THEY REPRESENT

Taking an empirical descriptive approach, Castles (Chapter 5) examines cross-national data to map similarities and differences in public spending.

Numerous comparisons are made among several groupings of countries employing standard statistical measures of dispersion—coefficients of variation and standard deviations—to assess differences in the percentage of their GDPs allotted to defense, internal security, social welfare benefits, and other categories of public spending. The descriptive findings yield a number of similarities and differences among the groupings of countries and between the United States and Europe. According to the OECD measure of gross public social expenditure, the United States is shown to have the lowest level of spending on social protection in the OECD countries; it also has next to the highest level of expenditure on defense and public order. Public expenditures on these "night watchman" functions of government amount to about 40% of social security spending in the United States. This figure is two standard deviations higher than the ratio for the next highest countries, which makes the United States exceptional in a statistical sense. The differences among social expenditures as a percentage of GDP wash out when these expenditures are calculated using the more inclusive OECD measure of net total social expenditures (which modifies gross public spending by factoring in taxes, tax expenditures, regulatory transfers, and private voluntary social welfare spending). On this scale, the United States ranks slightly higher than the averages of the EU-14 and OECD countries.

Examining how rates of social expenditures for the United States compare to those of European and other OECD countries, Gilbert (Chapter 6) finds that the empirical answer varies considerably depending upon the metric employed. When the comparative measure changes from gross public social expenditure to net total social outlays as a percentage of GDP, the U.S. rank on social expenditures rises from the bottom third to the top third of twenty-three OECD countries. However, the U.S. rank climbs even higher from the middle to the very top of the list when the metric shifts to comparing the gross or net social expenditure on a per capita basis adjusted for purchasing power parity. Whatever measure is employed, Gilbert suggests that it is extremely difficult to know the substantive meaning of comparative ranks on social expenditure for several reasons. In the absence of any controls for need, for instance, how can anyone interpret if a higher rate (per capita or percentage of GDP) of social spending represents greater social generosity, a stronger net of social protection or just a response to relatively higher levels of unemployment, disability, and aging in a country?

Instead of focusing on its magnitude, another way to analyze social spending is to compare how countries do it. This perspective draws attention to questions such as how much social spending do different countries channel through public and private sources. On this issue, both Gilbert and Castles agree that the U.S. pattern of social expenditure is distinguished by the heightened use of private channels, which, as argued most forcefully by Hacker (2002), have distinct distributional effects.

DEFINING AND RESPONDING TO POVERTY

Europe and the United States tend to emphasize different empirical definitions of poverty, which complicates comparative analyses along this dimension. The official federal definition of poverty in the United States is based on an absolute measure of income, which was adopted by the Social Security Administration in 1969. From the start, this measure was widely debated and continues to be (Orshansky, Watts, Schiller, and Korbel, 1978). The absolute measure or poverty line is calculated by multiplying the cost of the Department of Agriculture's Thrifty Food Plan by three and adjusting the results for household size and annual changes in the consumer price index. As Blank (Chapter 8) notes, according to this index, 13.3% of the U.S. population was classified as poor. In contrast to the absolute poverty measure of the United States, the EU employs a relative measure—percentage of people with income below 60% of their country's median income—to monitor progress toward reducing the "at-risk-of-poverty rate." As Saraceno explains in Chapter 7, this definition is delicately phrased to conceal the fact that none of the EU countries uses the 60% of median income threshold to determine eligibility for income support benefits. Just as in the United States—where the federal poverty line is drawn at a value that roughly corresponds to 40% of the national median income in relative terms—the poverty line in European official statistics is not employed to define eligibility for means-tested welfare benefits.

A review of the at-risk-of-poverty rates after transfers in the EU-25 reveals considerable variation among the countries ranging from 10% to over 20%. These data, however, bear cautious interpretation. Saraceno notes that using a relative national measure to estimate the size of the problem tends to generate lower at-risk-of-poverty rates in many of the Eastern European countries than in Western European countries, despite the empirical reality that the latter are much wealthier than the former. Looking at a more inclusive index for the entire EU, she notes that Brandolini's calculation using weighted averages would put the at-risk rate of poverty at 23% for the entire EU-25 population in 2000, which is just about the same as in the United States.

Examining the major thrust of social policies in response to the poor, which have emerged over the last two decades in Europe and the United States, both Saraceno and Blank point to the increasing emphasis on work-conditioned transfers. In the United States, the 1996 welfare reform replaced the long-standing Aid to Families with Dependent Children (AFDC) program with the more restrictive and work-oriented Temporary Assistance to Needy Families (TANF) program. TANF was a historical reversal of AFDC's entitlement to cash assistance. As such, it breached the clause of the social contract under which the state provided a safety net for families struggling to survive outside the labor force. Under the six decades of the AFDC program, poor families could rely on public aid that provided a modest cash benefit as a social right to which they were entitled for as long as it was needed without the requirement to work or behave in any particular manner. All that changed with the passage of the TANF legislation, which cut four core strands of the safety net by making benefits conditional on work, time-limited, linked to responsible personal behavior, and by ending the federal guarantee of support.

The TANF legislation stipulated that welfare recipients must be engaged in some kind of work-related activity to continue to receive benefits under TANF after their first two years of support. The most stringent federal regulation involves the sixty-month limit on assistance, which bars states from providing federally funded cash benefits to families for more than a total of five years during their lifetime, though states could exempt 20% of their caseloads from these time limits and continue to provide benefits with state dollars. The local discretion and flexibility allowed under federal rules have allowed states to respond in diverse ways—some have implemented requirements that are more stringent than those suggested by the federal regulations and others have adopted more lenient rules, as for example in New York and Vermont, which guarantee ongoing support with state funds (Gilbert, 2008).

Since the late 1980s, a wide range of activation and welfare to work reforms has been implemented throughout Europe. These measures are marked by diverse requirements, opportunities, and incentives. In some countries, social assistance beneficiaries must engage in various activation measures, such as job training, rehabilitation, flex jobs, and light jobs. Some countries require beneficiaries to sign activation contracts, which specify the efforts and activities they will undertake in pursuit of employment. Unlike the United States, the EU countries do not limit the entitlement to poor relief to specific categories of citizens, such as families, and their more general schemes do not impose lifetime limits on the duration of social assistance. But some of the EU countries place similar emphasis on training, work-related opportunities, and voluntary participation as many of the state administered TANF programs in the United States. Despite some persistent differences, Saraceno finds the welfare to work policies in Europe becoming similar to those of the United States.

In addition to the convergence on work-conditioned transfers, policies in support of the poor in Europe and the United States share an increasing focus on measures designed to "make work pay"—a living wage. In the United States, over a dozen states currently permit recipients to make up to $1,000 in earning before losing TANF payments. Similar income disregards for public assistance recipients are found in several European countries, for example, Cyprus, Germany, the Netherlands, Belgium, and Latvia. Income supports for the working poor, such as the Earned Income Tax Credit in the United States, have been developed in the United Kingdom and France, and minimum wage reforms also advance efforts to make work pay. These measures may be a harbinger of a revised social contract concerning the right to public assistance, which shifts the balance between entitlements and conditionality. The erosion of unconditional social rights to public assistance creates fertile soil for expanding social entitlements to employment opportunities and a living wage in both Europe and the United States.

PROMOTING EMPLOYMENT: WHAT WORKS?

In Chapter 9, Eichhorst and Hemerijck show that Europe has successfully moved from managing unemployment to promoting employment. Even though the employment goals set at the Lisbon European Council's 2000 summit have not yet been met fully everywhere, EU countries have recently boosted employment closer to the Lisbon goal of an employment rate of 70%, and in some cases even succeeded in moving ahead of the United States. Displaying convergence to higher employment, European welfare states can no longer be described as inactivity traps nor as impossible to reform. The authors describe a highly dynamic process of self-transformation with more emphasis not only on activation, but also on child care and social investment strategies that enable citizens to combine work and family life.

The authors link this convergence to the successful agenda setting by the European Commission that produced above all what they call cognitive convergence in the sense of a common understanding of problems. The more consensual approach of the EU—linked to soft law and the subsidiarity principle as opposed to the "one size fits all" approach earlier displayed in the OECD Jobs Strategy—has led to an effective narrowing of divergence, and in this sense the soft methods of regulation have proved remarkably successful.

Despite these common trends, the authors also note a persistently large degree of diversity within Europe, which questions the usefulness of the concept of a European social model. Even between nations usually grouped within the same cluster of families of nations or welfare state regimes, they find notable variation. Eichhorst and Hemerijck also show that there are two successful models of employment development in Europe, i.e., the liberal British–Irish approach and the Scandinavian approach. As both succeeded in boosting employment growth to similar degrees despite their widely discrepant welfare state arrangements, the authors conclude that there are alternative routes to success, and that different institutional arrangements continue to be viable. Stressing that the continental welfare states have gone particularly far in the process of self-transformation toward an enabling state, they underscore the importance of political action and the leeway, which policy makers have despite pressures from globalization and despite the constraints from their policy legacies.

In Chapter 10, Richard Freeman gives a balanced and multifaceted account of the strengths and weaknesses of the U.S. economic model. He shows that the U.S. labor market tops European societies in several respects including higher employment rates, lower unemployment with comparatively short spells of unemployment, and comparatively high productivity. The bright side of the American

economy furthermore includes high mobility out of unemployment, rapid productivity growth based on a comparatively high ratio of business-funded expenditure on research and development, and an effective coordination of private and
public research including heavy public investment in basic science and research.
Besides being flexible in the sense of having high annual rates of mobility in and
out of employment and from job to job, the American labor market recurrently
proved very open to new groups including immigrants and women. Even though
American women work more frequently full time than their European counterparts, fertility rates are higher than in Europe, suggesting that the growing
supply of low-wage immigrants has helped to provide domestic services at low
cost. Finally, American workers have repeatedly proved very flexible in adapting to new modes of production, such as computer technology to which even
Americans with noncomputer backgrounds quickly trained themselves, or in
responding to new incentives, such as profit sharing forms of compensation in
which nearly half of the American workforce now participates.

On the dark side, the rapid productivity growth after 1990 did not translate
into commensurate increases in earnings, as real earnings stagnated for many
U.S. workers and earnings inequality increased. If family incomes kept growing nevertheless, this was due to the fact that the number of earners in families
as well as the number of hours worked increased. Declining unionism led to
increasing inequality in earnings and to a shrinking proportion of workers with
health care benefits. Without the labor institutions that let workers participate
in the gains from globalization, Freeman perceives a risk of protectionist sentiments spreading.

Arguing that the great variation in outcomes among countries with similar institutions and even within countries makes it difficult to reach any valid
generalizations about the linkage between institutions and economic outcomes,
Freeman reiterates Eichhorst's and Hemerijck's finding of the viability of different institutional arrangements. Showing that seemingly identical indicators
may conceal considerable differences, his nuanced account also demonstrates
some of the pitfalls of international comparisons. Thus, several EU countries
have similar employment rates as the United States, but their employment is
associated with fewer hours worked, whereas the quality of jobs may not be
comparable. Seemingly similar unemployment rates conceal sizable differences
in the duration and stickiness of unemployment, which tends to be much lower
in the United States where laid-off workers frequently move to new jobs within
a month.

WHERE IS THE LAND OF OPPORTUNITY?

In measuring income inequality and mobility in Europe and the United States,
the works of both Gangl (Chapter 11) and Burkhauser and Couch (Chapter 12)

illustrate how these social facts can be measured in different ways and how they draw attention to the importance of the concrete indicators chosen and to the exact periods selected for analysis. Gangl shows that when the distribution of both market and postgovernment (taxes and transfers) incomes is averaged over six years the results yield a markedly more egalitarian distribution than the distribution of incomes measured at a single point in time. The reduction of inequality using the six-year average is taken as an indicator of mobility, on which there is little difference between the United States and Europe. Using Gini coefficients to compare levels of inequality among eleven European countries and the United States, his findings indicate that on market incomes averaged over six years the United States ranked just slightly below the middle of the group; on postgovernment incomes averaged over the same period, the United States dropped to the bottom (tied with Portugal) of the group. Gangl concludes that there is remarkably little cross-national variation in the extent to which mobility affects the distribution of incomes and that his findings do not support the idea that European welfare states stifle individual initiatives or market dynamics.

Analyzing levels of inequality in the United States, Great Britain, and Germany, Burkhauser and Couch note the importance of controlling for fluctuations in the business cycle in calculating long-term trends in changing distributions of income. Thus, their comparisons focus on the peak years over the business cycle in the three countries. Their analysis highlights how sensitive assessments of income inequality levels and trends are to data sources and even slight variations in methods, particularly the technical procedures in accounting for incomes at the very top of the distribution. Consistently disregarding or "top-coding" the same identical parts of top incomes for all U.S. data sets from the Current Population Surveys, the authors show that the growth in the 1990s was much more evenly spread than the growth in the 1980s and that most of the increase in inequality actually occurred in the 1980s. In this sense, they question and qualify accounts based on other methods or data sets, which draw attention to a massive increase in inequality in the most recent period (Piketty and Saez 2003; Smeeding 2005).

In addition to Gini coefficients and 90/10 ratios as summary indicators of income distributions and their change over time, Burkhauser and Couch employ a refined technique—kernel density estimation—that visually depicts the distribution of incomes according to the percentages of people whose household size-adjusted income are at different levels in the population. Using this technique to describe and compare changes in the distributions of income in the United States, Germany, and Great Britain in the peak years of their respective business cycles, some interesting results concerning economic growth, inequality, and well-being have been revealed. In the United States, for example, between the peak business cycle years of 1979 and 1989 the distribution of income became flatter as the proportion of people (7.8% of the entire distribution) around the mode declined. How did those who moved away from the modal income fare?

The majority of that group (about 82%) shifted toward the higher end of the income distribution. While they got richer, a minority of the group (about 18%) became poorer, sliding toward the lower end of the income distribution. During the peak years (1989 and 2000) of the 1990s' business cycle the modal group continued to decline, but over this period the shape of the entire income distribution shifted toward the higher end so that the level of after-tax income was higher for people in every percentile in 2000 than in 1989. Although changes in the after tax distribution of income for Great Britain during the 1990s' business cycle were similar to those of the United States, the shift that occurred in Germany over this period resulted in a distribution that looked more like the United States in 1989—most people became richer, whereas a smaller group became poorer. This illustrates that inequality may increase (accompanied, perhaps, by a heightened sense of relative deprivation), at the same time as the absolute level of most people's material well-being rises. Overall, both chapters show little differences in mobility rates between the United States and Europe, along with much variation among European countries in levels of inequality.

GRADING EDUCATIONAL ACHIEVEMENT AND OPPORTUNITY

Seeking to advance the EU's educational capacity to generate an unparalleled knowledge-based economy, five benchmarks of educational performance were established at the European Council's 2000 meeting in Lisbon. These benchmarks designated specific objectives aimed for by 2010 in relation to reading literacy, school attendance, completion of secondary school, math, science, and technology graduates, and lifelong learning. Allmendinger, Ebner, and Nikolai (Chapter 13) review the measures employed to chart performance in these areas, the assumptions underlying the relationship between them, and the progress made to date.

Their findings show a weak correlation between the level of reading skills as measured by the OECD's Program for International Student Assessment (PISA) and the achievement of educational certificates among countries, which raises questions about the extent to which educational certifications provide valid signals of skill levels and hence reliable guides for placing people in the labor market. In assessing the movement toward the educational benchmarks established by the Lisbon agenda, the EU's performance to date is marked by limited progress toward meeting the criteria, and in some cases no progress at all. The percentage of students below proficiency level II in reading comprehension actually increased between 2000 and 2006. Overall only Finland and Sweden were meeting all the benchmarks. In addition, there was a high degree of variance in the levels of performance among the EU countries without any clear evidence of convergence, which would justify speaking of a joint European social model in this dimension.

Similar to the appraisal of educational systems in the EU, Maloney and Mayer's (Chapter 14) assessment of educational performance in the United States finds much room for improvement. The United States has a very high proportion of the top-ranked research universities and undergraduate training institutions in the world, is a front-runner in training in computer literacy and has closed (some might say reversed) the gender gap in higher education, with women earning 58% of all the degrees awarded by institutes of higher education in 2003. However, as Maloney and Mayer point out, there is a growing concern about the shortcomings of the U.S. educational system, which include a very poor system of vocational training, a failure to close the persistent achievement gap between white and minority students, an unacceptable rate of high school dropouts, inequities in educational financing, climbing costs of higher education, and unimpressive achievement scores in international comparisons under which American students do not fare as well as the OECD average. According to the PISA data, the U.S. student achievement scores in reading are just about equal to the OECD average, but performance in mathematics is notably below the OECD mean. A word of caution is offered in interpreting comparative scores and levels of educational achievements. The United States has a disproportionate share of immigrants and wide variations in standards of living and educational spending among the states. Surprisingly, however, the authors note that differences in reading scores between the upper and lower quartiles of the social structure in the United States are lower than in some EU countries such as Belgium, Germany, Luxembourg, and the United Kingdom. Thus, despite concerns about the achievement gaps between different groups in the United States, the U.S. educational system may be performing well within the EU range when it comes to equalizing cognitive skill among students from various socioeconomic levels.

IMMIGRATION AND ASSIMILATION

The relatively high proportion of immigrants in the United States and their participation in the labor force is documented by Hirschman and Perez (Chapter 16). Their data reveal that in 2004, first generation immigrants (those who are foreign born) accounted for more than 14% of the total civilian labor force. About 7% of the total civilian labor force was composed of second generation immigrants (those with at least parent born in a foreign land). Thus, altogether in 2004, more than one in five jobs in the United States was held by people who are immigrants or the children of immigrants. Where these immigrants were coming from has changed over time. Between 1850 and 1970, the vast majority of foreign-born immigrants to the United States came from Europe. However, the proportion of European immigrants declined substantially during that period. By 2000, the composition of first generation immigrants had undergone a dramatic shift as the European born became a distinct minority representing only 16% of the foreign born compared to 52% from Latin-America and 26% from Asia. The increase in non-European immigrants did not appear to have had adverse effects on integration into the labor market as 94% of the 2004 immigrants were employed, which was virtually the same rate of employment as that of third- and higher-generation native-born Americans.

Differences in the structural integration of immigrants as measured by the odds to be employed or to occupy selected positions are analyzed by Kalter and Granato (Chapter 15) who compare the labor market experiences of second-generation groups in Germany, Great Britain, France, and the United States. Their findings indicate that in all four countries different groups of immigrants have widely discrepant success in the labor market, while similar mechanisms are at work in all settings to explain the differences—mostly the social background in the parental home and the selectivity of immigration. Taken as a whole, the three immigrant groups (Italian, East Asian, and Mexican) in the U.S. sample have better odds of being employed than comparable groups of immigrants in the other three countries. When the comparative chances of employment are controlled for education and other relevant variables, the employment rates of the U.S. groups remain relatively high. However, when the measure of employment is refined to capture differences classified according to occupational classes, the results are more varied by country and by specific groups. Thus, for example, the odds of being employed in the professional/managerial class for Italians and East Asian immigrants in the United States are somewhat better than those of the indigenous reference population, whereas the reverse is found for the group of Mexican immigrants, who fare, however, better than Turks in Germany. The highest odds of working in professional/managerial positions are found for Indians in Great Britain, followed by the repatriates in France—both groups whose members were raised in households where the language of the host country—English or French—was spoken. In general, the findings suggest that similar mechanisms of the transmission of inequality are at work everywhere so that there are no signs of distinct social models. Whether counted according to rates of employment, occupational class of employment or occupational class controlled for education the U.S. experience is well within the general range of the three European countries in this analysis.

WHAT ABOUT THE SOCIAL MODELS?

Probing various subdimensions of social, economic, and political aspects of transatlantic similarities and differences, the authors in this volume do not always agree about the strengths and weaknesses regarding these various aspects of the functioning of societies. Even their measures and operational definitions of these dimensions vary occasionally as much as their substantive interpretations. In an effort to portray these complex and competing facets of the comparative landscape, we have extracted some of the principal similarities and differences in the social, economic, and political realms of the United States and Europe, which are suggested by the analyses in this volume.

Beyond all details, three implicit general insights of the analyses collected here should be made explicit. First, Europe's outstanding characteristic is its diversity. In every dimension researched in this volume, the margin of variation between EU member states is stunning. Looking at the data displayed here—without squinting—it is difficult to see how the European countries form part of a common social model. This suggests that the frequent references to this model are less rooted in objective facts than in a perceived need to forge a common European identity. This need grew in line with the various EU enlargements from the original EU six to a community of nine, ten, twelve, fifteen, twenty-five to now twenty-seven members. After the arrival of Bulgaria and Romania, the EU now includes about half a billion citizens who enjoy or suffer widely discrepant standards of living. A historical look backward suggests that references to the European social model proliferated in tandem with the successive enlargements, which made the common identity of Europeans more precarious and thus created a need for forging symbolic integration. In a somewhat paradoxical way, this greater need for symbolic integration to which the Commission responded with the emphasis on a joint social model is also related to the very policies of the Commission itself. So far, the focus of the European integration process was on "negative integration" in the sense of breaking down impediments to free trade and pure market relations and of guaranteeing the four freedoms of movement (Scharpf 1996; Crouch 1999). Given that European citizens increasingly voiced their skepticism to this notion of integration when given a chance to express their opinion in a referendum, the Commission was under growing pressure to add some visible aspects of positive integration to the integration process, and the emphasis on the European social model in EU documents serves this function—especially after the attempt to define "united in diversity" as the official motto of the EU was scrapped once the citizens of France and the Netherlands had rejected the proposed treaty establishing a constitution for Europe.

Secondly, the analyses in this chapter also highlight important similarities between Europe and the United States, which have even come more to the fore in recent years when the Commission launched the Lisbon strategy with its emphasis on activation. If the old goal of European social democracy was to limit the sphere of the market and to "decommodify" citizens by granting them access to means of livelihood outside the market, the new goal is to empower as many people as possible to participate in markets, and this new emphasis on work makes European countries in some respects more similar to the United States with whom they already share such important features as being free democracies, market economies, and postindustrial societies. To be sure, the analyses collected here have shown differences of degree between Europe and the United States on many empirical indicators. Whether they add up to enough dissimilarity to qualify as a difference in kind is left to the readers' discretion.

Finally, this volume has shown that much depends on the exact nature of measurement and on the precise definition of the unit of comparison. Several authors have expressed a conviction that comparing frequently small and homogenous European nations to the comparatively huge and heterogeneous United States makes only limited sense and that either comparing the EU as a whole to the United States or single European countries to specific states in the United States would be the more meaningful strategy. If the EU as a whole is treated as the comparable unit, the degree of inequality in Europe matches or even surpasses the degree of inequality found within the United States. At any rate, a penetrating effort to interpret the existence or strength of European and U.S. social models must lend credence to both the similarities and differences—and then come to grips with the differences within Europe. There are also substantial variations within the United States, which are occasionally mentioned, but rarely probed in depth.

In de Tocqueville's time, differences in language, political culture, social class and remnants of feudalism no doubt weighed more heavily in the balance than today. Even though differences of degree between Europe and the United States persist on many empirical indicators, our impression is that Europe and the United States form part of a common Western heritage and are similarly united in diversity as the set of countries that currently make up the EU. Recent developments that we could not foresee when planning this volume furthermore underscore this conclusion. The challenge of the global financial crisis made the distinction between unfettered market economies and social market economies partly obsolete, as governments on both sides of the Atlantic are now pursuing pragmatic solutions, which include higher degrees of regulation and state intervention. The emerging consensus is that in order to be well-functioning, markets need to be embedded in a social and political order, which sets limits to what is acceptable in the pursuit of profits. But not only circumstances, also the actors have changed. Under the new presidency, the United States will presumably pursue a new course in which international coordination and consensus-building with European allies will play a much bigger role. Hence, the unity between Europe and the United States is likely to persist, whereas the diversity may diminish.

REFERENCES

Crouch, Colin (1999) *Social Change in Western Europe*, Oxford: Oxford University Press.

Gilbert, Neil (2008) "Recent Welfare Reforms and Future Directions: Political Issues," paper presented at the Conference on Social Policies in Canada and the U.S., organized by the French Directorate of Research, Evaluation Studies, and Statistics of the Social Ministries, Paris, February 7–88.

Hacker, Jacob S. (2002) *The Divided Welfare State*, Cambridge, MA: Cambridge University Press.

Myrdal, Gunnar (1958) *Value in Social Theory*, Paul Streeten (ed.) London: Routledge & Kegan Paul.

Orshansky, Mollie, Harold Watts, Bradley Schiller, and John Korbel (1978) "Measuring Poverty: A Debate," *Public Welfare* (Spring).

Piketty, Thomas and Emmanuel Saez (2003) "Income Inequality in the United States 1913–1998," *The Quarterly Journal of Economics*, 118, 1: 1–39.

Scharpf, Fritz (1996) Negative and Positive Integration in the Political Economy of European Welfare States, in Gary Marks, F.W. Scharpf, P.C: Schmitter, and W. Streeck (eds) *Governance in the European Union*, London: Sage.

Smeeding, Timothy M. (2005) "Public Policy, Economic Inequality, and Poverty: The United States in Comparative Perspective," *Social Science Quarterly Supplement*, 86, 955–983.

NOTES

Chapter 1 Democratic Quality in America and Europe

1 On confidence, see e.g. Susan J. Parr et al. (2003) and Marta Lagos (2003). On participation see e.g. Hans-Dieter Klingemann and Dieter Fuchs (1995) and Alan Siaroff and John W. A. Merer (2000). On specific cases, see, for example, on Norway, Øyvind Østerud et al. (2003), on Germany, Claus Offe (2003), on Costa Rica, G. O'Donnell et al. (2004), and on Latin America, Daniel Altman and Anibal Perez-Liñán (2002).

2 The concept of 'transgression' is from Arthur M. Okun (1975).

3 The early standard reference is Alex Inkeles (1991). For a later overview, see symposium articles in *Comparative Political Studies* 35 (2002), in particular G.L. Munck and J. Verkuilen. See also, for example, Kenneth Bollen and Robert W. Jackman (1989), Kenneth Bollen and Pamela Paxton (2000), Gretchen Casper and Claudiu Tufis (2002). For a summary of evidence, see UNDP (2002).

4 http://www.systemicpeace.org/polity/polity4.htm

5 www.economist.com/media/pdf/DEMOCRACY_INDEX_2007_v3.pdf

6 Some countries have a higher ranking in human development than in economic development, in recent reports, for example, Sweden, Australia, Greece and Costa Rice, while others have a lower ranking, for example, the United States, Switzerland, Ireland and Denmark, see UNDP 2002.

7 An illustration is in a symposium on the quality of democracy in the October 2004 issue of *The Journal of Democracy* and in Larry Diamond and Leonardo Morlino (2005). In these works, leading experts on democracy bring together a mass of knowledge on the state of democracy across

the world but find no way of answering the question of how to evaluate quality. That is not for lack of information, rather the authors bring to bear on their task too much rather than too little information. It is for want of a methodological apparatus to put the information into and generate analytic results.

8 All the eleven democracies included in this comparison have the same top score for civil liberties and political rights in Freedom House: *Freedom in the World* (annual).

9 For a more detailed discussion of the methodology, see Stein Ringen (2007: Chapter 1).

10 Ideally, I would here have wanted to have a direct measure of democratic consolidation but I have not found relevant data. The best source is the Bertelsmann Transformation Index, which ranks 116 countries in the world by their progress towards market-based democracy, but the democracies that are already "consolidated" are not included. See www.bertelsmann-transformation-index.de. The Bertelsmann Stiftung is presently developing an index of reform capacity in the established democracies (the OECD countries), which may possibly do the job when it is available. My proxy in my judgement works well enough to distinguish between degrees of consolidation at the beginning of the twenty-first century but is obviously not a durable indicator for this purpose. Poland is allocated a score of 0 although universal suffrage was introduced in 1918, because of weak democratic credentials pre-1989. In the case of the Czech Republic, a sore of 1 is allocated on the basis of the 1920 introduction of universal suffrage and the 1918–38 strength of democratic credentials. Spain is allocated a score of 0 in spite of the introduction of universal suffrage in 1931 because of the weakness of historical democratic credentials.

11 Freedom House measures press freedom on a scale from 0 to 100 and designates countries with a score between 0 and 30 to have a free press. All eleven democracies in my comparison are in that category, except Italy, which is classified as partly free. Using 20 as the highest score for a robustly free press, France and Italy are consistently below this threshold, France just below, wherefore I allocate them the 0 score, while the Czech Republic, Poland and Spain oscillate around this cut-off score from year to year, wherefore I by the benefit of doubt allocate them the positive score. See Freedom House: *Press Freedom*.

12 The World Bank index ranges from –2.5 to +2.5. All the democracies in my sample are on about 1.5 or higher, except Italy which is on .68. See http://www.worldbank.org/wbi/governance/pubs/govmatters4.html.

13 On economic versus political power, see Stein Ringen (2004).

14 I discuss in detail both the underlying concept of freedom and the conceptualisation of resources in terms of physical and human capital in Ringen (2007).

15 The score of 1 is allocated to countries with more than 6.6% of GDP in public health expenditure in 2002, the highest level being 8.6%, in Germany. (See UNDP 2005.) Public health expenditures have been on a rising trend in

most of these countries but their ranking and relative positioning is robust for the choice of year around the end of the twentieth century and the beginning of the twenty-first century.

16 Using here the average in the original comparison of twenty-five democracies. The data are from Ronald Inglehart et al. (2004).

Chapter 2 Liberalism and Democracy in America Today

1 This view of government carries over into public opinion more generally. See Hibbing and Theiss-Morse 2002.

2 North, 5.

3 James Madison so described the framers and their opponents, the Anti-Federalists, when addressing the new Congress of the United States in 1789. See Kurland and Lerner (2000): Volume 5, Document 11.

4 See Madison's comments in the U.S. House of Representatives, June 8, 1789, in *The Founders' Constitution*, Volume 5, Document 11. The committee that drafted the preamble apparently believed it was not the proper place for a declaration of the natural rights of individuals since government already existed, Levy 2001: 15.

5 James Madison gave this reason when introducing to Congress the amendments later known as the Bill of Rights. See *The Founders' Constitution*, Volume 5, Bill of Rights, Document 11.

6 Library of Congress, Congressional Research Service 2001. My estimate includes increases since 2000.

7 For the original Reagan economic plan which focused exclusively on the welfare effects of policy changes, see Anderson 1990: 11–121. See also the comparison of the rhetoric of Barry Goldwater and Ronald Reagan in Smith 2007: Chapter 5.

8 http://www.federalreserve.gov/generalinfo/faq/faqbog.htm#1

9 The law was invalidated by the Supreme Court. See Farrier 2004: Chapter 6.

10 Gwartney and Lawson, ibid. Alesina indicates the need for liberalization of overregulated labor, product, and service markets in Europe (Alesina and Giavazzi 2006: 169–170). Alesina and Glaeser (2006: 43) conclude that "the U.S. economy is much less regulated than European economies, both in the labor and in the goods markets."

11 Piketty and Saez 2007: 3–24. See also Alesina and Glaeser 2006: 37 for a similar conclusion.

12 http://www.independentsector.org/programs/research/volunteer_time.html#volunteers

13 "A good will is not good because of what it effects or accomplishes, because of its fitness to attain some proposed end, but only because of its volition, that is, it is good in itself and, regarded for itself, is to be valued incomparably higher than all that could merely be brought about by it in favor of some inclination and indeed, if you will, of the sum of all inclinations." (Immanuel Kant in Gregor 1997: 8)

14 *United States v. Carolene Products Company*, 304 U.S. 144 (1938), fn. 4.

15 The American National Election Studies (ANES) (www.electionstudies. org). The ANES Guide to Public Opinion and Electoral Behavior. Ann Arbor, MI: University of Michigan, Center for Political Studies Table 3.1.1.

16 The National Election Studies (NES), Center for Political Studies, University of Michigan. *The NES Guide to Public Opinion and Electoral Behavior* (http://www.electionstudies.org). Ann Arbor, MI: University of Michigan, Center for Political Studies [producer and distributor], 1995–2000, Tables 6.A.2.2 and 1.A.9]

17 For the 2002 income data, see U.S. Census Bureau 2005: Table no. 669; for educational attainment in 2000 see ibid., Table no. 214.

18 The National Election Studies (NES), Center for Political Studies, University of Michigan. *The NES Guide to Public Opinion and Electoral Behavior* (http://www.electionstudies.org). Ann Arbor, MI: University of Michigan, Center for Political Studies [producer and distributor], 1995–2000, Table 3.1.3, see also file "Ideology by Income." The medians from the years 1990–2000: 26% of the rich are liberals, 23% are moderates and 49% are conservatives. The data show significant variation during this era. The percentage of the richest identifying as liberals varied by 17% (high of 32%, low of 15%), while conservatives had range of 11% (high of 53%, low of 42%). The averages for each group (liberals 25%, moderates 21%, and conservatives 47%) do not depart all that much from the medians.

19 Ibid., Table 3.1.3, see also file "Ideology by Income."

20 Ibid., Table 2.A.2 Party Identification Breakdown by Demographic Groups.

21 The NES offers two different surveys of partisan identification, one three-point scale and one seven-point scale. The latter includes both "independent Democrats" and "independent Republicans." The three-point scale does not. Unfortunately, the NES offers demographic breakdowns only on the three-point scale. As a result, we do not know what proportion of the rich identified themselves as "pure independents" and "partisan independents." That number must be higher than the 10% of pure independents among the rich.

22 See The Center for Responsive Politics, "527 Committee Activity Top 50 Federally Focused Organizations," www.opensecrets.org (accessed February 14 and February 19, 2003).

23 See The Center for Responsive Politics, "Top Individual Contributors to 527 Committees 2004 Election Cycle," www.opensecrets.org (accessed January 14, 2005).

24 Ibid., 92 and 96, Table 4.4: Wawro utilizes a two-stage least squares regression analysis to deal with the typical problems of simultaneous determination found in most campaign finance topics. He concludes: "The coefficient on the entrepreneurship instrument is not statistically distinguishable from zero for either Democrats or Republicans [i.e. members of Congress]. We cannot say with much confidence that entrepreneurship has any effect on investor PAC contributions. From these results, it does not appear that

members will engage in legislative entrepreneurship in order to attract contributions from investor PAC's."

25 Smith 2000: 140. The same conclusion emerged from a detailed study of policymaking during the Reagan era, see White and Wildavsky 1989: 551.

26 On the media, see Groseclose and Milyo 2005. On the universities, see Klein and Stern 2005.

27 Alesina, *Reform* passim.

Chapter 3 The Inequality of Electoral Participation in Europe and America and the Politically Integrative Functions of the Welfare State

1 For more recent synthetic literature building and reflecting upon Lipset's pioneering work, see Lijphart (1997); Wilensky (2002: Chapters 11 and 18); Verba (2003).

2 Condensing various arguments found in Lipset's work (especially Lipset 1960 and Lipset 1997), the following account gives a stylized summary of the "American exceptionalism" school of thinking, which basically started with Sombart's (1906) book on *Why Is There No Socialism in the United States* and Wells' book on *The Future in America* (1906) of the same year. Lipset himself would not have necessarily subscribed to our stylized account of his position as he usually weighed arguments and counterarguments in a complex and differentiated fashion frequently referring to alternative hypotheses.

3 Another factor worth noting is that in America, some 2 million citizens over 18 years of age who are in prisons or who are ex-convicts are disqualified from voting (Shipler 2004: 287). The American prison population in federal or state prisons increased from 0.3 million in 1980 to 1.4 million in 2004. This number does not include prisoners in local jails whose number increased from 182,000 to 714,000. The size of the total population in prison, jail, on probation, or on parole increased from 1.8 million to 7 million by 2004 (U.S. Census Bureau 2007: 209).

4 As far as we know, there is no publication that explicitly relates the idea of a European social model to particular features of electoral turnout. Rather we have "constructed" this interpretation here quasi as the incarnation of "the European dream" (Rifkin 2004), which has perhaps found its most explicit expression in an indirect form in the negative mirror image that Piven and Cloward (1988; 2000) described with reference to the American political system.

5 For empirically based qualifications of this view comparing the policy orientations of voters and nonvoters, see Shaffer (1982) and Bennett and Resnick (1990). Both studies found the differences to be not very big even though the latter research showed nonvoters to be more in favor of spending on welfare programs; see also Leighly and Nagler (2007) for the rather limited effects of deunionization on voter turnout decline.

6 Comparative data on the social structure of European parliaments in historical perspective are given in Best and Cotta (2000) and Best (2007). Neither of these sources reports the income of parliamentarians, while both highlight the growing overrepresentation of university graduates in the postwar period. In the American Congress at least one-third of all Senate members were millionaires in 1997, whereas the number of millionaires in the House amounted to over sixty (Davidson and Oleszek 1998: 210). An Internet source gives the percentages of millionaires for 2003 as 40% for the Senate and 28% for the House (http://www.cnn.com/2003/ALLPOLITICS/06/13/senators.finances/); this compared to a stated proportion of millionaires in the population of 1% (http://www.commondreams.org/headlines04/0630-05.htm). This high overrepresentation of affluent groups in the American Congress is related to the very high cost of election campaigns. In the election cycle 2003–04, the average cost of winning a seat in the Senate was reported as $2.6 million, while the average for a seat in the House was $531,000 (Davidson and Oleszek 2006: 67).

7 For an elaboration, see Alber (2000), McDonald and Popkin (2001).

8 We have used the most recent "first-order" election of each country for which IDEA provides data, that is, the election that is perceived as the key nation-wide election by the voters.

9 Basing international comparisons of electoral statistics on the number of votes expressed as a percentage of the *eligible population* does not completely eliminate all pitfalls in comparisons, because countries may differ in their liberalism with respect to granting the rights of citizenship. Thus countries which restrict citizenship rights—for example by barring prisoners, ex-convicts or the resident alien population from voting—make the denominator of the fraction smaller than countries which grant rights more generously.

10 Country group averages were calculated by summing up the voter turnout rates of each country of the country group and dividing by the number of countries without weighting for population size.

11 Following the convention of ISO 3188, we use the abbreviation "GB" for the United Kingdom in our tables and graphs.

12 While Table 3.1 reports average national voter turnout during the last three elections, the following discussion of the impact of institutional factors refers to the specific setting characterizing each respective election.

13 The extent to which weekday elections actually increase the cost of voting hinges very much upon the opening hours of the polling stations.

14 A number of countries, primarily in Eastern Europe, hold their elections on two consecutive days. These elections were classified as weekend elections, if one of these days was a Saturday or a Sunday.

15 In these countries voter turnout was higher in the presidential elections than in elections to the parliament, which sustains our notion that the former constitute first-order elections.

16 Austria, which has compulsory voting in only two of its states (Vorarlberg and Tirol), was classified as a country without compulsory voting.

17 For countries without compulsory registration, it is not entirely clear if voter turnout rates are based on all eligible voters in the denominator or only on those who actually registered.

18 Detailed descriptions of these various electoral systems may be found on the IDEA web site under http://www.idea.int/esd/glossary.cfm.

19 Based on an analysis of 147 elections, this result has also been demonstrated by the International IDEA (http://www.idea.int/vt/survey/voter_turnout8. cfm).

20 This value results if the average American competitiveness score of 3.47 is entered into the regression equation for Western European countries.

21 Differences in competitiveness and the number of parties were weighted so that the highest observed difference amounted to one, while smaller observed differences were expressed as fractions of this maximum difference.

22 This refers to the results of the ISSP 2004 (23 percentage points). The values of the other surveys are: 19 (EQLS), 16 (ISSP 2002), 15 (ESS 2002) and 12 (ESS 2004) percentage points.

23 This refers to the average gap in both dimensions of social inequality resulting from all considered surveys.

24 http://www.aceproject.org/epic-en/pc.

25 For the European OECD countries, the data listed in the table report the average value of the gross social expenditure ratio from two sources (Adema and Ladaique 2005 for 2001; http://epp.eurostat.ec.europa.eu/ for 2004). For the United States, we have only data for 2001 and for the European non-OECD members we rely on the source for 2004.

26 The 1974 amendment to the Federal Election Campaign Act (FECA) introduced the option of full public financing for presidential general election campaigns in return for an acceptance of certain regulations including spending caps, but this option proved to be increasingly unattractive to the candidates. In the 2004 campaign, financial activities of presidential candidates totaled more than $1 billion, whereas federal matching funds amounted to $28 million, thus covering merely 4% of the total cost of primaries. The two major party nominees received $74.6 million each in public funds to conduct their general election, while the two parties received $14.9 million each from the U.S. treasury for their nominating conventions (see the section on campaign finance statistics in Federal Election Commission 2005b: 63). Historical accounts of the decreasing role of public funding in the financing of presidential campaigns are given in Corrado (2005a,b). In the 2008 election, all major candidates refused federal matching funds for the primaries, while Senator Barack Obama became the first candidate to refuse government funds for the general election.

27 Nonparametric regression can be used to explore the relationship between two variables without making assumptions on the functional form of the relationship. Several techniques for nonparametric regression analysis exist. The technique we have used is Cleveland's (1979) "locally weighted scatterplot smoother" (LOWESS).

28 This is in line with recent research by Andrea Louise Campbell (2002, 2003) investigating the mobilizing effects of social security and showing that those who are more dependent upon public programs are more active.

29 The wording of the question varies between surveys. The ESS and CSES surveys asked how *satisfied* the respondents were *with the way democracy works in their country,* while the 2004 ISSP asked how the respondents *think democracy works in their country.* In Figure 3.6, we have therefore separated the results of the ISSP from the two other surveys.

30 These figures are sensitive to the different wordings of the respective questions in the various surveys.

Chapter 4 Income Inequality and Participation in Elections in the United States

1 Article I Section IV of the United States constitution states, "The times, places, and manner of holding elections for senators and representatives shall be prescribed in each State by the legislature thereof; but the Congress may, at any time, by law, make or alter such regulations, except as to the places of choosing senators." Article I Section II states, "The House of Representatives shall be composed of Members chosen every second Year by the People of the several States, and the Electors in each State shall have the Qualifications requisite for Electors of the most numerous Branch of the State Legislature."

2 The Gini income inequality coefficient is a common income inequality measure, named after Corrado Gini (1912). The Gini coefficient generally describes inequality of any given mathematical distribution and ranges on a [0, 1] interval. In the context of income inequality, a zero indicates everyone has the same wealth and a one indicates that a single person holds all the wealth. Measured another way, the top 5% of Alaska's households had 17.6% of the wealth while in New York these households had 25.3% of the wealth.

3 Voter eligibility for primaries varies among the states. Some states require that voters be registered with a political party in order to participate in a party's primary election while others open primaries to any eligible voter, though they may or may not be required to vote for only one party's primary candidates.

4 These data are available at, http://www.census.gov/cps/

5 The lowest category is less than $25,000which encompasses 23.8% of the citizen voting-age population (CVAP), the next highest is $25,000–$49,999 which encompasses 27.9% of CVAP, the next highest is $50,000–$74,999 which encompasses 20.7% of CVAP, and the highest category is higher than $75,000 which encompasses 27.6% of CVAP.

6 Most states also require registrants to vote at least once every four years to maintain their registration status.

7 In the on-line scholarly journal *The Forum* I discuss the relationship between competition and turnout for the 2004 and 2006 elections, "Up,

Up, and Away! Turnout in the 2004 Presidential Election." (*The Forum* 2(4): 2004) and "Rocking the House: Competition and Turnout in the 2006 Midterm Election." (*The Forum* 4, 3: 2006).

8 According to Shaw (2006), the Bush and Kerry 2004 presidential campaigns both considered Florida, Iowa, New Hampshire, New Mexico, Ohio, Pennsylvania, and Wisconsin as battleground states.

9 States that require registration at least 28 days to 30 days prior to an election include: Alaska, Arkansas, Arizona, Colorado, District of Columbia, Florida, Georgia, Hawaii, Illinois, Indiana, Kentucky, Louisiana, Michigan, Missouri, Mississippi, Montana, New Jersey, New Mexico, Nevada, Ohio, Pennsylvania, Rhode Island, South Carolina, Tennessee, Texas, Virginia, and West Virginia.

10 Conventional wisdom holds that those of lower socioeconomic status favor the Democratic Party because they are generally more supportive than the Republican Party of policy positions that favor the poor. While it may be true that those of lower socioeconomic status favor policies that would increase the money in their pocketbook, it is also true that those of lower socioeconomic status tend to be more conservative on social issues and more in line with the Republican Party (e.g., Erikson and Tedin 2005: 177–186).

11 Census Bureau statistics from the 2000 census show that Mississippi and Louisiana have the greatest percentage of people living in poverty. The median income cut point for the lowest 20th percentile is $7,200 in Mississippi and $7,800 Louisiana, compared with $19,000 in the wealthiest states of Alaska and Connecticut.

Chapter 6 Comparative Analyses of Stateness and State Action: What Can We Learn From Patterns of Expenditure?

1 Vision of Humanity: Global Peace Index, http://www.visionofhumanity. com./index.php (accessed September 19, 2007); and http://www.economist. com/markets/rankings/displaystory.cfm?story_id=9425707.

2 See for example Rich 1989; Moroney 1991; Wilensky 1975; Goodin et al. 1999: 260; and Swank 2001; Hicks and Swank 1992. Based on the OECD data, a 2007 editorial in the New York Times, for example, notes that where social spending is concerned the United States is "almost the stingiest among industrial nations" ("The less-than-generous State," *New York Times*, August 16, 2007).

3 The application of statistical analysis lends an aura of scientific authority to the numbers, but again does not ameliorate their underlying frailty.

4 These indirect taxes vary by country. Average indirect tax rates in the United States are in the 5.3%–7.5% range, compared to indirect rates of 13.5%–20.5% in most European countries (Adema 1999)

5 The proposition that there is a break in the relationship between increased economic growth and higher levels of social expenditure was put forth by Donald McGranahan (1970: 40–54); also see Rys (1946: 15–16).

6 For example, among households living at 50% of their countries' median income, those in the United States have more than twice the equivalized net household income of those in Greece and are 50% higher than those in Sweden.

7 It is not that the Netherlands is an unhealthy place. On the contrary, despite their higher disability claims the Dutch live longer, consume less alcohol, have fewer traffic accidents, and visit a doctor less often than their neighbors in Belgium and Germany. For a discussion of what was then termed the "Dutch Disease," see, for example, Gilbert (1995).

8 An OECD report on the Netherlands suggests that high replacement rates created disincentives to work, along with a permissive cultural climate that made it acceptable to stay away from work for "vague physical and psychological complaints" (OECD 1991: 95).

9 Measures of unemployment in different countries, for example, include the number of claimants who register for unemployment benefits or the number of people in a representative population survey who respond that they are out of work and looking for a job. The meaning of unemployment is socially constructed in that if two mothers stay home each to care for their three preschool-aged children, they are counted as out of the labor force; but if they switched children and paid each other $6.00 per hour to perform the same activity for the other parents' children, they would both be counted as employed (and at $6.00 per hour in the United States, would probably qualify for a federal subsidy via the Earned Income Tax Credit).

10 The OECD (2007: 34) notes that tax expenditure data for subnational units are not counted in the social expenditure index.

11 See Tax Credit Resources. Org (2002–2008); the levels of benefit in these programs vary from 10% to 43% of the Federal Earned Income Tax Credit (Johnson and Lazere 1999: 23–25).

12 Governor Schwarzenegger's proposal for health insurance reform in California would require employers to provide employee's health insurance or to contribute to a state fund for employee health insurance, doctors to pay a 2% fee (otherwise known as tax), and hospitals to pay a 4% fee to the state insurance fund.

13 Credit subsidies, which derive from the difference between interest rates charged by government and market rates for similar loans and the costs of public loan defaults are amorphous and hard to measure, in part because the government subsidized loans can distort the market rates for private loans. For a discussion, see Neil Gilbert and Barbara Gilbert (1989).

14 The assumption of proportionality is muted by focusing on the dynamics of spending rather than the overall magnitude, since differences in the magnitude of GDPs will have no arithmetic impact on the process measures of the percentage of direct/indirect or the percentage of public/ private spending. Examining the processes of spending makes no assumptions about levels of need that are being met. Regarding the issue of incomplete coverage, since the data are mostly of the national level, the analysis is confined to dynamics of social expenditure at that level; while

we might expect that subnational dynamics of spending would mirror the national emphasis, even if it did not there is little reason to assume an interaction effect between national and subnational dynamics would show results that distort national comparisons—for example, that an emphasis on direct methods at the subnational level would induce greater emphasis on indirect methods at the national level. And in regard to the activities of the "other hand" since the comparison is not on magnitude of spending, the question of whether to modify interpretation of that magnitude to the extent that spending is based on creating future debt is not relevant to the analysis of spending dynamics.

15 For an insightful analysis of mandated transfers, see Pietro Nivola (1998).

16 Of course, these measures allow us to make empirical comparisons among the countries. But this is a case of blind empiricism, since we do not know what the measures mean beyond the empirical fact that some numbers are higher than others.

Chapter 7 Concepts and Practices of Social Citizenship in Europe: The Case of Poverty and Income Support for the Poor

1 Brandolini's study also offers a very detailed analysis of the methodological issues involved in the measurement of poverty, particularly at the comparative level.

2 The important overview by Heikkilä et al. (2006) also had to deal with this imprecision.

3 In a study of six "old" EU countries (Bonny and Bosco 2002), eight dimensions were identified as being relevant in shaping the configuration of an income-support measure for the poor: bureaucratic vs. discretionary; family vs. collective solidarity; universal versus categorical; selectivity; recipient duties; generosity; duration; and presence of activation measures.

4 The most decentralized and differentiated system is found in Italy, where municipalities may or may not have a minimum income for the poor and where the target population, income thresholds, and amounts given may vary greatly even within the same region. Since neither Greece nor Italy has a general minimum income provision, they are not taken into consideration here. It should be noted that both countries, together with Spain and Portugal, also do not have universal child allowances, thus lacking this form of minimum income for children (and for families with children), which plays such an important role in other countries in keeping children above the poverty level and in reducing the poverty gap.

5 The Open Method of Coordination (OMC) is a mode of governance developed under the European Employment Strategy at the 1997 Luxembourg Summit, which is based on soft regulatory measures ("soft laws") and mutual learning to improve convergence in areas (such as long-term unemployment, demographic aging, and social protection) that remain the responsibility of the national governments, but that concern the whole of the EU.

6 These fundamental rights are summarized in six chapters: Dignity, Liberty, Equality, Solidarity, Citizenship, and Justice.

Chapter 8 The New American Model of Work-Conditioned Public Support

1 Data from Section 7, Table 9, Committee on Ways and Means (1990).

2 Further discussion of these issues can also be found in Lipset (1996).

3 Esping-Andersen (1990) provides a discussion of the different choices made in the United States and other industrialized countries between the mix of market/government goods.

4 I use the term "recipient" and "woman" interchangeably in this discussion since more than 90% of the adult welfare recipients were single mothers. Welfare funds were available also to low-income married adults with children, but under more restrictive requirements. Relatively few low-income married couples receive cash public assistance, and those who do tend to receive it for only short periods of time.

5 For instance, see Moffitt (1992) or the discussion of cash assistance programs in Blank (1997).

6 The most well-known public criticism was by Murray (1984).

7 See the review of this literature in Moffitt (1998).

8 For a discussion of the political history behind welfare reform, see Weaver (2000) or Haskins (2006).

9 A summary of the key results from some of these experiments is in Bloom and Michalopoulos (2001).

10 For more detailed discussion of the programmatic changes that occurred with welfare reform, see Blank and Haskins (2001).

11 For a more thorough discussion of the EITC, see Hoffman and Seidman (2003).

12 For a summary of the operations and changes in the Medicaid program, see Gruber (2003).

13 These numbers and the numbers in the next paragraph are based on calculations by the author from the March Current Population Survey.

14 See Blank (2002) or Grogger and Karoly (2005). For a recent update, see Blank (forthcoming 2009).

15 Blank (2007) and Blank and Kovak (2009) summarize the evidence about this population and provides citations to the literature on barriers to work among nonworking single mothers who have left welfare.

Chapter 10 Fulfilling the Ballyhoo of a Peak Economy? The U.S. Economic Model

1 OECD 2006b, OECD in Figures 2006–2007, Science and Technology, Research and Development, 2004: 40–41.

2 These economies are Australia, Austria, Canada, Denmark, France, Germany (West), Great Britain, Japan, New Zealand, Northern Ireland, Norway, Spain. Sweden, which is included in the 1999 ISSP but is omitted

from the aggregate of other economies, has very similar attitudes to the rest of the countries.

3 The ISSP is a cross-national collaboration on surveys covering topics important for social science research, which has the virtue that it asks the same questions of persons in different countries, facilitating cross-country analyses.

4 http://www.maxwell.syr.edu/news/releases/041025_inequality.asp

5 These figures are from a CBS April 2008 poll, but polls by other organizations tell a similar story. http://www.cbsnews.com/stories/2008/04/03/opinion/polls/main3992628.shtml; http://www.pollingreport.com/right.htm

6 Calculated from data in US Statistical Abstract, 2008, table 574.

7 http://www.urban.org/uploadedpdf/311373_nonprofit_sector.pdf

Chapter 12 Are the Inequality and Mobility Trends of the United States in the European Union's Future?

1 Most U.S. government statistics focus on before tax income. And the longest continuous yearly source of such information is the CPS (see DeNavas-Walt et al. 2007). Most of the literature focusing on inequality and mobility in the United States is discussed in these terms. (See Danziger and Gottschalk 1993, 1995 for reviews of this literature and Gottschalk and Danziger 2005 for a more recent example.)

Before tax income based on data from the CPS includes: wages and salaries, self-employment income, property income (such as interest, dividends, and net rental income). It excludes capital gains, imputed rent, or in-kind government or private benefits. It does not subtract taxes paid or tax credits received.

2 The starting and ending years of a business cycle are somewhat arbitrary. Rather than define them directly by changes in macroeconomic growth, we use peaks in median income, which will, in general, lag macroeconomic growth. This rule is straightforward in the United States and Great Britain where there are distinguishable peak years in median income. For Germany, income years 1991 and 1992 are similar. We chose 1991; though its median income was slightly lower than 1992, since it was closer to the peak year as defined using standard macroeconomic growth data. Our findings are not sensitive to reasonable changes to the peak years we choose to compare.

3 Household composition, which can change over time, also requires panel studies to use the individual as their unit of analysis (See Gottschalk and Smeeding 1997 for a review of the cross-national comparative literature on income inequality and mobility and Goodin et al. 1999; Gottschalk and Danziger 2005; and Brandolini and Smeeding, 2008 for more recent examples).

4 Burkhauser et al. (2008a) use data for Germany and Great Britain from the Cross-National Equivalent Files (CNEF), prepared at Cornell University. Their data for the United States come from the public use CPS. Following the international literature, they divide total household income

by the square root of the number of persons in the household to control for household size. For the United States, they use the TAXSIM Module, provided by the NBER, to estimate income tax payments in the CPS for the years 1979 through 2000. After tax income is calculated in CNEF data for Germany and Great Britain. (See the Data Appendix of Burkhauser et al. 2008a for more details.)

5 Since most measures of income inequality are sensitive to outliers, Burkhauser et al. (2008a) exclude observations in the top and bottom two per cent of the household size-adjusted income distribution in the German and British data. They use a somewhat different method to control for both outliers and differences in top coding procedures in the U.S. data. To protect the confidentiality of its respondents the public use CPS contains top codes for the high values for each of the various sources of income it collects. Inconsistent changes in these top-code levels and in the assignment of cell mean values to them by the U.S. Census Bureau distort both the levels and trends in measured income and income inequality. Rather than trimming the top 2% of the total household income as is done with the German and British data, Burkhauser et al. (2008a) use a "consistent top coding procedure." That is, for each income source, they find the year where the top-code cuts the distribution of reported income for that income source at its lowest point. They then adjust the top-code values for all other years so that income is cut from that source at the same low point in the distribution of income for that source in all years. This procedure assures that income from each income source is consistently topcoded at the same point in the distribution across all years. Burkhauser et al. (2004b) show that a rule-of-thumb trimming of the top 2% of the public-use version of the CPS yields population samples whose levels and trends in income inequality are similar to those using the consistently top coded method. Later in the chapter, we more fully discuss the sensitivity of measured levels and trends in U.S. income inequality to top-coding and censoring issues.

6 For those familiar with after tax income 90/10 and Gini inequality values provided from the LIS version of the public use CPS for the United States, the values in Table 1 may be surprising. Later in the chapter, we will argue that the failure of those using the LIS data to control for top-coding in the CPS is the major reason for the differences.

7 The mean values reported here are smaller than those reported in Figure 4.1 not only because they are in 2000 rather than 2006 dollars but because they divide total before tax household income by the square root of the number of persons in the household as a method of estimating the amount of purchasing power controlled by each individual in the household.

8 Conclusions about the impact of the tax system on inequality drawn from comparisons of before tax income and after tax income of this type assume no behavioral change in response to government behavior.

9 First-order stochastic dominance is defined as follows: Consider two income distributions y_1 and y_2 with cumulative distribution functions

(CDFs) $F(y_1)$ and $F(y_2)$. If $F(y_1)$ lies nowhere above and at least somewhere below $F(y_2)$, then distribution y_1 displays first-order stochastic dominance over distribution y_2: $F(y_1) \leq F(y_2)$ for all y. Hence in distribution y_1, there are no more individuals with income less than a given income level than in distribution y_2, for all levels of income. Alternatively this can be expressed using the inverse function $y = F-1(p)$ where p is the share of the population with income less than a given income level as: first-order dominance is attained if $F_1-1(p) \geq F_2-1(p)$ for all p. The inverse function $F-1(p)$ is known as a Pen's Parade (Pen 1971), which simply plots incomes against cumulative population, usually using ranked income quantiles. The dominant distribution is one whose Parade lies nowhere below and at least somewhere above the other. First-order stochastic dominance of distribution y_1 over y_2 implies that any social welfare function that is increasing in income, will record higher levels of welfare in distribution y_1 than in distribution y_2 (Saposnik 1983).

10 This is a major change in outcomes from previous results that reported increases in both before and after tax income inequality for the United States and small increases in before tax and no change in after tax income inequality for the western states of Germany in the 1980s (Gottschalk and Smeeding 1997; Burkhauser and Poupore 1997, and Hauser and Becker 1993).

11 While the discussion of top coding issues in this section is in the context of before tax income inequality using the public use CPS data, it equally applies to after tax income inequality since those calculations are based on before tax income information from the public-use CPS.

12 Contrary to the results we present using the CPS data, Piketty and Saez (2003) using U.S. personal federal income tax records data to capture the share of adjusted gross income (the amount of income that is taxable under federal tax law in place each year) by the top 10% of tax units, argue that increases at the very top of the income distribution have significantly increased inequality in the United States. The strength of the Piketty and Saez work is that they can capture the top tail of the adjusted gross income distribution of U.S. tax units. But this is not the same as U.S. before tax household-size adjusted income for all individuals on which the vast amount of research on U.S. income inequality has focused. And it is certainly not the same as after tax income inequality on which most research on income inequality across countries has focused. It is closest in concept to pretax pretransfer income since in the United States, most government transfers (AFCC/TANF, social security benefits) are not taxed.

Piketty and Saez (2003) focus on trends in U.S. adjusted gross income inequality for 1913–1999. But only do so for the top 10% of tax unit filers. They then estimated the share of total adjusted gross income held by this population. While these data have great strengths, they also have some weaknesses in trying to capture trends in household size-adjusted income since adjusted gross income is sensitive to changes in the tax system itself.

This is best seen in their work by the enormous increase in the share of adjusted gross income held by the top 5% and top 10% of the distribution they report after 1986. The beginning of this enormous cliff coincides with the Federal Income Tax Reforms of 1986 that dramatically reduced the tax on personal income and lead very high income tax units to shift their taxable income from corporate sources and tax-free bonds to personal income that was now taxable at a much lower rate.

The vast majority of the increase in the share of adjusted gross income held by the top of the distribution in the Piketty and Saez (2003) data occurs between 1986 and 1988 and is more likely to be due to changes in tax laws than real changes in access to income by very high tax income households. For a detailed criticism of Piketty and Saez (2003), and their subsequent work see Reynolds (2006: Chapter 5). Also see the Web-based *Cato Unbounded* magazine (http://www.cato-unbound.org/) of February 2007 for a spirited debate on whether or not before-tax income inequality has risen since 1989 because of a growth in the share of income going to the very top of the income distribution. See especially the exchanges between Alan Reynolds and Gary Burtless.

Income tax data is now become available for other countries. Bach et al. (2007) find that, like the CPS in the United States, the GSOEP does not capture the very top of the German income distribution. Using German income tax data together with GSOEP data, they find levels and trends in German income inequality over the period 1992–2001 are greater than those found using the GSOEP data alone.

13 On its Web site (http://www.lisproject.org/keyfigure/ineqtable.htm), LIS provides among its income inequality measures for its member countries' after-tax Gini coefficients for the United States that do not adjust for the top coding issues discussed here. As we showed in Figure 4.3, there is an implausible cliff in the Gini value derived from public-use CPS unadjusted income data beginning in 1995, which is also found between 1994 and 1997, the next reported year of public-use CPS data provided in this LIS table. This jump up from 0.355 to 0.372 in after-tax income is to some degree a function of uncontrolled changes in top coding.

Chapter 13 Education in Europe and the Lisbon Benchmarks

1 Articles 149–150 of the EC Treaty state that educational policy is the sole prerogative of the member states. The EU has no authority whatsoever to control, monitor, or evaluate in the area of education (Martens and Wolf 2006).

2 The OMC is used in employment policy and, more recently, in policy on providing for old age (Ribhegge 2007).

3 On the expansion of mass education, see also Boli et al. (1985).

4 The PISA consortium itself uses the term "functionally illiterate" to mean persons found to be below level I and speaks of a "risk group" when referring to those found to be below level II (OECD 2001: 47f.). The terminology

pertaining to educational poverty is spelled out in Allmendinger (1999) and Allmendinger and Leibfried (2003).

5 Another challenge (whose discussion would exceed the bounds of this chapter) is that no one yet knows whether and under what conditions educational certificates have greater explanatory value than competencies (and vice versa) for occupational trajectory and the allocation of opportunities. Initial results on this question are likely to emanate from a relevant study by the German Institute for Employment Research (Kleinert 2007).

6 For a detailed overview of the evolution, expansion and dynamics of EU education policy, see Walkenhorst (2008).

7 The eleven targets are (1) participation in preschool education, (2) special needs education, (3) language skills, (4) ICT skills, (5) civic skills, (6) learning to learn skills, (7) professional development of teachers and trainers, (8) cross-national mobility of students in higher education, (9) adult skills, (10) educational attainment of the population, and (11) investment in education and training (Commission of the European Communities 2007: 10).

8 The European Commission (Commission of the European Communities 2008) proposes to review these benchmarks and to consider new benchmarks in further key areas such as tertiary education attainment, employability and student mobility.

9 In order to monitor the performance and progress of education and training systems in 31 countries (EU, accession countries, candidate countries, and countries of the European Economic Area), the Commission developed 29 indicators (Commission of the European Communities 2006: 3). Since the Lisbon conference in 2000, it has published four progress reports on these objectives (Commission of the European Communities 2004, 2005a, 2006, 2007).

10 In the 16 EU countries for which comparable data were available for 2000, the share of 15-year-olds at level I or below was 19.4%. This would imply a benchmark of 15.5% for 2010.

11 To include enough cases to make a sufficiently representative sample, the EU has based its analyses on an age group consisting of 20- to 24-year-olds rather than of 22-year-olds only.

12 The Commission proposed eight key competencies of life-long learning in 2005: communication in the mother tongue; communication in foreign languages; mathematical competence and basic competencies in science and technology; digital competence; learning to learn; interpersonal, intercultural, social, and civic competence; entrepreneurship; and cultural expression (Commission of the European Communities 2005b).

13 18 EU member states took part at least in the 2000 and 2006 surveys: Austria, Belgium, the Czech Republic, Denmark, Finland, France, Germany, Great Britain, Greece, Hungary, Ireland, Italy, Latvia, Luxembourg, Poland, Portugal, Spain, and Sweden.

Chapter 14 The U.S. Educational System: Can It be a Model for Europe?

1 http://ed.sjtu.edu.cn/rank/2004/top500(1–100).htm

2 National Center for Education Statistics. http://nces.ed.gov/programs/digest/d05/tables/dt05_063.asp?referer=list (Accessed February 5, 2007.)

3 U.S. Department of Education, National Center for Education Statistics (2006). The Condition of Education 2006 (NCES 2006–071).

4 High school graduation rates, especially those that differentiate by race, are not without controversy. While it is beyond the scope of this paper to determine which method of data reporting is most accurate, we chose to use the rates reported by Hout and Fischer and the National Council for Education Statistics (NCES) because they are the most comprehensive and transparent of all the data reporting agencies. Other sources of data include the Current Population Survey and National Education Longitudinal Study. In general, we believe that the most accurate analyses of the data report similar patterns of data, if not precisely the same numbers (Mishel and Roy 2006). Others (e.g., Greene and Foster 2003, 2006) criticize the NCES and CPS as inaccurate and categorize pursuing a G.E.D. as "dropping out," thereby discounting that population from the percentage of those who are counted as graduating high school. This lowers the graduation rate of minorities substantially and may account for widely diverging percentages.

5 http://www.ed.gov/about/overview/fed/role.html (Accessed February 12, 2007.)

6 U.S. Department of Education, National Center for Education Statistics, Teacher Follow-up Survey (TFS), Current and Former Teacher National Center for Education Statistics (NCES 2004–301).
Number Percent Data Files, 2004–05; Teacher Attrition and Mobility: Results from the Teacher Follow-up Survey, 2000–01, U.S. Department of Education.

7 National Center for Education Statistics. http://nces.ed.gov/programs/coe/2005/analysis/sa07.asp (Accessed February 12, 2007).

8 http://www.ed.gov/admins/tchrqual/learn/hqt/edlite-slide008.html (Accessed June 16, 2006).

9 http://www.ed.gov/admins/tchrqual/learn/hqt/edlite-slide011.html (Accessed June 16, 2006).

10 Granted, a student has to be in the country for two years before he or she can be tested for NCLB requirements, but two years language instruction may not produce fluency for all children.

11 http://www.nytimes.com/2006/10/12/nyregion/12math.html?ref=education (Accessed October 13, 2006).

12 Michigan, Vermont, Texas, Pennsylvania, Connecticut, Illinois, Indiana, New Hampshire, Ohio, California, and Utah.

13 http://www.teachforamerica.org, www.teachingfellows.org (Accessed February 13, 2006).

14 U.S. Department of Education. Institute of Education Sciences. National Center for Education Statistics. *America's Charter Schools: Results From the NAEP 2003 Pilot Study,* NCES 2005–456, by National Center for Education Statistics. Washington, DC: 2004.

15 http://www.aacc.nche.edu (Accessed April 11, 2007).

16 U.S. Department of Education, National Center for Education Statistics (2007). Enrollment in Postsecondary Institutions, Fall 2005; Graduation Rates 1999 & 2002 Cohorts; and Financial Statistics, Fiscal Year 2005. NCES 2007–154.

17 As of 2006–7, the tuition and fees at a four-year public school averaged $5,836. The tuition and fees at a four-year private school averaged $22,218. The tuition and fees at a two-year public school averaged $2,272 (College Board 2006: 4).

18 U.S. Department of Education, National Center for Education Statistics (2006). The Condition of Education 2006 (NCES 2006–071).

19 U.S. Department of Education, National Center for Education Statistics (2005). Postsecondary Institutions in the United States: Fall 2003 and Degrees and Other Awards Conferred: 2002–03 (NCES 2005–154).

20 U.S. Department of Education, National Center for Education Statistics (2006) The Condition of Education 2006 (NCES 2006–071).

21 U.S. Department of Education, National Center for Education Statistics (2005) Postsecondary Institutions in the United States: Fall 2003 and Degrees and Other Awards Conferred: 2002–03 (NCES 2005–154).

22 U.S. Department of Education, National Center for Education Statistics. (2005) Postsecondary Institutions in the United States: Fall 2003 and Degrees and Other Awards Conferred: 2002–03 (NCES 2005–154).

23 National Center for Health Statistics. 2004. "NCHS Data on Teenage Pregnancy." http://o-www.cdc.gov.mill1.sjlibrary.org/nchs/data/factsheets/teenpreg.pdf (Accessed May 30, 2007).

24 OECD, Online: http://www.oecd.org/dataoecd/37/13/34963969.xls (Download January 14, 2007).

Chapter 15 Different Countries, Different Groups, Same Mechanisms? The Structural Assimilation of the Second Generation in Europe (D, F, GB) and the United States

1 For example due to the individual peculiarities of the data in each of the countries the definition of ethnicity had to rely on different indicators.

2 The models comprise the total adult male population (age 17 to 59) in the data sets for the countries, that is, it includes the charter population, all immigrant groups and all generations. In the underlying multinomial logit and binary logit models age, age squared, marital status, and ethnic group membership were also controlled for.

3 Kristen and Granato (2007) look at the odds of attaining the "Abitur" (i.e. the graduation from the upper secondary level in Germany) or being in the respective track versus not attaining this level.

4 The analysis uses data of the National Longitudinal Study of the French Ministry of Education. Educational attainment is measured by the grades achieved in mathematics at the end of lower secondary schooling.

5 Caribbeans are comprised in a group that pools pupils with Afro-Caribbean, black African, and other black origins.

INDEX